BUSINESS, GOVERNMENT, AND SOCIETY

Fifth Edition

BUSINESS, GOVERNMENT, AND SOCIETY

A MANAGERIAL PERSPECTIVE

TEXT AND CASES

Originally published as **Business and Society**

GEORGE A. STEINER

Harry and Elsa Kunin Professor of Business and Society and Professor of Management, Emeritus, UCLA

JOHN F. STEINER

Professor of Management and Director of the Center for the Study of Business in Society, California State University, Los Angeles

 Random House Business Division   New York

PERMISSIONS ACKNOWLEDGMENTS

Exhibit 1–5 (p. 13) Reprinted with permission of The Free Press, a Division of Macmillan, Inc., from *Corporate Power and Social Responsibility* by Neil H. Jacoby. Copyright © 1973 by The Trustees of Columbia University in the City of New York.

Exhibit 1–6 (p. 15) Reprinted with permission of Macmillan Publishing Company from *Management Policy and Strategy*, Third Edition, by George A. Steiner, John B. Miner, and Edmund R. Gray. Copyright © 1986 by Macmillan Publishing Company.

Table 1–1 (p. 16)   Copyright © 1984 by the Regents of the University of California. Reprinted from the *California Management Review*, Vol. 26, No. 3. By permission of The Regents.

Table 4–1 (p. 81) Copyright © 1985 by *National Journal* Inc. All Rights Reserved. Reprinted by permission.

Excerpt (p. 167) From Ronald Berenbeim, *Regulation: Its Impact on Decision Making*. Copyright © 1981 The Conference Board.

List (p. 467) From Patrick E. McGuire, *The Product Safety Function: Organization and Operations*. Copyright © 1979 The Conference Board.

Fifth Edition

24689753

Library of Congress Cataloging-in-Publication Data

Steiner, George Albert
  Business, government, and society.

  Bibliography.
  Includes index.
  1. Industry—Social aspects—United States.
2. Industry and state—United States. I. Steiner,
John F. II. Title.
HD60.5.U5S8   1988   658.4′08   87–28526
ISBN 0–394–37474–6

Manufactured in the United States of America

Text and cover design: Glen M. Edelstein

To Our Students
Past, Present, and Future

PREFACE

This book, as its title explains, is about the interrelationships among business, government, and society—from the point of view of business managers. Today, we are witnessing significant changes in these relationships. The impact on management has altered in a major way the attitudes, perspectives, decision making, and functioning of managers in our corporations, particularly of the larger ones. But business is not a passive agent in this drama. It has influenced the relationship in important ways.

We prepared this book for a broad audience, including university students, business managers, and inquiring observers with an interest in business and how it is managed. For each of these groups we believe the topic is of arresting importance because the forces examined here will in one way or another significantly affect their lives.

Changes in the New Edition

The basic framework, content, and thrust of the preceding edition of this text have been retained. However, significant changes have been made that we believe improve the book substantively and make it more interesting for the reader as well.

New subject matter or expanded treatment of old analyses has been added in practically every chapter. We have added much to the coverage of business practices undertaken in response to new environmental influences. Many chapters have been rewritten almost in their entirety. At the same time, topics that have receded in importance since publication of the last edition have been deleted or abbreviated. We have eliminated four chapters and a chapter-length appendix. But the most important parts of the deleted chapters have been retained and integrated in other chapters. And the sequence of chapters has been revised to improve the flow of the discussion.

We have added two new features that we believe not only will heighten the reader's interest in the book, but also will help to elaborate important issues with actual stories and cases taken from the business world. Every chapter begins with a short sketch of developments in a well-known corporation that highlights a major topic of the chapter. Also scattered throughout the book are features that we call "You Be the Judge." These are, for the most part, significant U.S. Supreme Court cases. With this feature the reader is given a chance to test his or her conclusions about each case against the decisions of a majority of the Court.

Cases

As in the last edition, the reader will find one or two case studies at the end of each chapter. Most of them deal with real companies or current situations. In all, there are 23 cases, most of a moderate length. We regard these cases as an important part of the text material. They may be used to provoke class discussion or, in some cases, as illustrative readings that elaborate on the subject matter of the chapters.

Philosophy

Our philosophy of writing text material for this edition has been to present a broad, current survey of business-government-society topics while at the same time achieving some depth of treatment. We aim for precise, detailed, accurate, and well-documented exposition rather than simplification. We believe this book will be challenging to readers, including both undergraduate and graduate students. We hope this proves to be the case for two fundamental reasons—not only as an appropriate challenge, but also because a rich scholarly treatment is ultimately more compelling to readers at all levels than bland oversimplification.

Acknowledgments

This book would not have been possible without the research and writings of many people. We have tried to recognize authors who have been most helpful by citing, where appropriate, their works. We are deeply indebted to them.

Many people have made comments and suggestions concerning the preparation of this fifth edition, too many to name here. We do want to express our appreciation however, to a number of our colleagues in academic life, as follows:

A. Janell Anderson, California State University, Sacramento; Keith R. Blunt, California State University, Los Angeles; James D. Boulgarides, California State University, Los Angeles; Daylin J. Butler, Kansas State University; Dharma DeSilva, Wichita State University; James R. Glenn, Jr., San Francisco State University; Robert Hogner, Florida International University; Jeanne M. Logsdon, Santa Clara University; Daniel J. B. Mitchell, University of California, Los Angeles; Harvey Nussbaum, Wayne State University; Harold Sackman, California State University, Los Angeles; George E. Stevens, University of Central Florida; Donald J. Watson, University of South Florida; Jonathan P. West, University of Miami; J. Fred Weston, University of California, Los Angeles; Erika Wilson, California State University, Los Angeles.

At the John F. Kennedy Library at California State University, Los Angeles, Murray J. Ross, George Rolling, and Alan Stein gave valuable advice on the research process.

Many people in the business community and other organizations were helpful to us and we wish to acknowledge their aid. Among them are: Rev. Willie Barrows, Operation PUSH; R. Clifford Black, IV, National Railroad Passenger Corporation; Earl Brount, Rockwell International Corporation; Robert Charleton, Dow Chemical Co.; Mark Cohen, Mobil Oil Corporation; Brian Daly, Rockwell International Corporation; Kent Dreyvestyn, General Dynamics Corporation; Joan Gilbert, Texaco, Inc.; Jane Gootie, Dow Chemical Co.; William Henry, Jr., Lockheed Corporation; Rich Long, Dow Chemical Company; John Lonnquist, Manville Corporation; Sister Mary Ann McGivern, Loretto Literary and Benevolent Association; John McGuire, General Dynamics Corporation; Austin Marks, Hewlett-Packard Company; J. Duncan Muir, J. C. Penney Company, Inc.; David A. Osterland, Ohio Edison Company; Eleanor Paradowsky, Merck & Co., Inc.; William Smith, Exxon Corporation; Kenneth O. Sniffen, Union Carbide Corporation; Sue

Thompson, Levi Strauss & Company; George Trainer, Ford Motor Company; Arthur Weise, American Petroleum Institute; Judith P. Wilkenfeld, Federal Trade Commission.

We are grateful for help and encouragement from the staff of the Business Division of Random House, Inc., particularly June Smith, Executive Editor; Susan Badger, Acquisitions Editor; Sheila Friedling, Project Editor; and Dan Alpert, Developmental Editor.

We give special thanks for their help to Deborah Luedy and Jean W. Steiner.

George A. Steiner

John F. Steiner

CONTENTS

DETAILED CONTENTS

CHAPTER 4 The Critics of Business 76

PART II BUSINESS AND GOVERNMENT 115

CHAPTER 5 The Government-Business Relationship: An Overview 117

CHAPTER 6   New Patterns in Government Regulation of Business   147

CHAPTER 14 Pollution Policy Issues 426

CHAPTER 15 Consumerism 449

CHAPTER 16   The Changing Internal Face of Organizational Life   488

CHAPTER 17   Minorities, Women, and Antidiscrimination Law in the Workplace   526

BUSINESS, GOVERNMENT, AND SOCIETY

INTRODUCTION

CHAPTER **1** _____

THE STUDY OF BUSINESS, GOVERNMENT, AND SOCIETY

 Every large corporation in the United States and many smaller ones are concerned with a wide range of forces in the business-government-society (BGS) interrelationship. Exxon provides a good example of its complexity.

Exxon was the second largest industrial company in the United States in 1986 as measured by assets. (General Motors was first.) In 1986 its assets were $69.5 billion, its revenues were $69.9 billion, and its net profits were $5.4 billion. It is the world's largest integrated oil company. It engages in virtually every major type of basic energy production, from exploration of oil and gas, to mining coal, nuclear fuels, and other minerals. It is engaged in petrochemical production and until 1987 also manufactured electric motors. It owns and operates fleets of ships, airplanes, and helicopters.

Exxon operates in more than 80 countries of the world and derives 50 percent of its earnings from abroad. It has business in every one of the fifty states, and it employs 135,000 people and has 740,000 stockholders.

The above numbers give some indication of the complex role that a corporation the size of Exxon plays in society. There is no way, however, to picture briefly the extraordinary array of important BGS forces that flow to and emanate from a corporation such as this. The following thumbnail sketch, however, may help to focus on some of their dominant impacts.

The business environment is naturally of exceptional concern to Exxon. For one thing, it is in a highly competitive and volatile industry. In 1982, for example, when the oil price bubble burst, Exxon found its profits declining by

$1.4 billion during the year. It had to close nine refineries, slashed tanker capacity 25 percent, closed 10,000 service stations, and dropped 24,000 people from its payrolls of 180,000 (Kirkland, 1984). Aside from carefully watching world oil price movements, Exxon is concerned with such changing current and future business conditions as foreign exchange rates, interest rates, the demand for gasoline and fuel oil, general economic levels throughout the world, and what its domestic competitors are doing.

The company is deeply intertwined with governments here and abroad. The federal government of the United States has roughly 300 primary agencies, and Exxon's operations are affected by all of them with but a very few exceptions. Aside from the more obvious agencies with which it is engaged (such as the Department of Energy and the Department of Interior), we note the Federal Communications Commission's (FCC) regulations of Exxon's offshore telecommunications, the Bureau of Indian Affairs in relationship to drilling activities, the Maritime Administration and the use of Exxon's ships, the Interstate Commerce Commission (ICC) and pipelines, the Federal Aviation Administration (FAA) and jet engine fuel regulations, and the Securities and Exchange Commission (SEC) and security financing.

With such a wide range of government agencies having some influence on Exxon's activities, one would expect to find a large lobbying force. Exxon, however, has a reputation of not being strident in its lobbying activities but of letting the American Petroleum Institute do much of this work. Exxon has but six professionals in its Washington, D. C., office.

Like many other large companies in the public eye, Exxon has institutionalized the social point of view in its decision making, from top policies through the divisions. The company has a reputation for being attentive to its social responsibilities. A prominent feature of this posture, of course, is its philanthropy. For example, the Exxon Education Foundation is the largest corporate donor to higher education in the United States, with total expenditures in 1985 of $43 million. In addition, each division of the company has an annual contributions budget for cultural and social giving.

In this introductory chapter we present conceptual models for the interrelationships among business, government, and the rest of society. We conclude the chapter with a discussion of the principal characteristics of the BGS found in the remainder of the book, and we present our views concerning what within the BGS field should be covered in a text such as this.

THE NATURE AND SPECTRUM OF BGS RELATIONSHIPS

In the BGS relationship, society is the all-encompassing concept. Both business and government are institutions operating within society. Individual components in society are constantly in motion and interacting to produce changes. Business and government, of course, are in constant interaction. Both, however, influence and are continuously influenced by other aspects of society, such as changing social values, pressure groups, technology, intellectuals, workers, educational institutions, lawyers, consumers, prices, and so on. The mix of these interrelationships varies greatly from time to time.

Exhibit 1-1 conceptualizes one set of interrelationships between business and society. The ellipses include those areas of primary interest in this book. Additional areas of importance to business would include weather, natural resources, military events, language, medicine, geography, and agriculture. The illustration shows that history has an impact on the current mix of relationships in society. The mix and its direction of change are also influenced by current world events and by what is going on in this society at the present time. The changes are influenced as well by future expectations.

In examining the many interrelationships between business and society, one must distinguish among businesses. The business system is not a unified structure. There are giant firms that are larger, at least in terms of cash flows, than most governments of the world. There are also millions of small enterprises. (Most of the economic activity of the nation is conducted through several

EXHIBIT 1–1   BUSINESS AND ITS MAJOR SOCIETAL AREAS OF INTERRELA-TIONSHIP

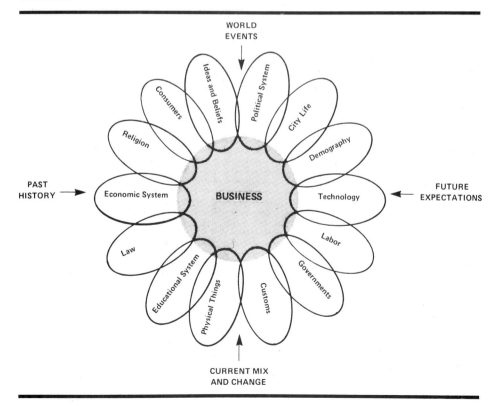

BUSINESS

The term *business* encompasses a broad range of action, from individual pursuits to the work of giant corporations. In this book, the term covers manufacturing, commercial, trade, and other economic activities of both individuals and institutions; for the most part, however, the discussion relates to business organizations and principally to larger corporations. A business institution is not wholly an economic organization, for it has social as well as political characteristics. The discussion therefore considers all three of these aspects of business activity.

GOVERNMENT

Government encompasses a wide range of activities and institutions throughout our country, including school districts; local, county, state, and interstate governments; and the federal government. Government may be defined as the structures and processes through which public policies, programs, and rules are authoritatively made for society. In this book, we are most interested in the economic and regulatory powers of government, especially those of the federal government, and their impact on business.

SOCIETY

As used in this book, the term society means essentially what generally is meant when one speaks of this nation, or the American civilization. Inherent in this concept are three fundamental, interrelated parts that make up the abstraction of society. They are (1) ideas or beliefs, (2) institutions, and (3) material things.

Ideas include such things as attitudes, ideologies, and beliefs. They establish the broad goals of life expressed in terms of what is considered to be good, true, right, beautiful, and acceptable. These ideas and beliefs underlie and dominate the systems of institutional arrangements in society, of which business is one.

Institutions are those more or less formalized ways by which society tries to do something. Examples of institutional systems are the business system, the political system, labor unions, the educational system, the language system, and the legal system.

The third element in society encompasses tangible, material things such as stocks of resources, land, and all manufactured goods. These things help to shape, and are partly products of, our institutions, ideas, and beliefs. Our economic institutions, together with our stock of resources, determine in large part the type and quantity of our material things. As our types and quantities of material things change, so do our ideas and beliefs.

thousand of the largest companies, and for this reason a large part of this book is concerned with these companies.) Some companies do business only in the United States, while others operate in many foreign countries. Some companies are in service trades, and others only mine or manufacture. Some managers have committed their enterprises to improving the quality of life of their employees and people generally, whereas others feel their objective is only to optimize stockholder wealth. Every company is unique. As a consequence, what is a sensible thing to say about the relationship of one business to society may be complete nonsense if applied to another. When discussing the social responsibilities of business, for instance, what is true for a huge, highly profitable corporation may not apply at all to a very small company striving to avoid bankruptcy.

Different elements in society have different impacts on business, and vice versa. The title of this book, *Business, Government, and Society*, highlights the fact that of all institutions in society, the government is the most important influence on business today. Other elements of society, however, also exert strong influences on business either directly, as does new technology, or indirectly through government, as when people want to reduce the pollution of the environment by business.

MODELS OF THE BGS INTERRELATIONSHIPS

Everyone recognizes that the BGS interrelationships are extremely complex. Individuals and groups view these relationships from different perspectives. Depending upon their perspective on business's relationship to its environment, people and/or groups may reach entirely different conclusions about any business-society issue. They may differ radically, for example, about the nature of business's power over society, the motivations of business leaders, the morality of executives, the role of business in society, the social responsibilities of the business community, and any other public issues involving business. Therefore, it is important to know the fundamental model, or conceptual framework, that people use in viewing the BGS relationship.

The following models frequently are used as basic frames of reference for viewing the BGS relationship. We believe that the first two models, despite their popularity, are seriously flawed and lead to irrational interpretations of factual information. Only the later models are sophisticated enough to provide constructive and accurate interpretation of a dynamic business system in a changing society.

The Dominance Model

The dominance model, Exhibit 1-2, is pyramidal and shows society to be hierarchical in nature. To those who subscribe to this model, business and government act in combination to dominate the great mass of ordinary people. Environmental forces are transmitted to the bulk of the population by an elite establishment. Given this mental image of business, government, and society, certain conclusions and interpretations are likely to follow.

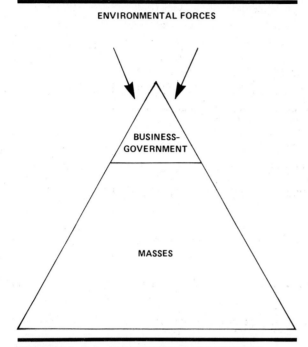

ENVIRONMENTAL FORCES

BUSINESS-
GOVERNMENT

MASSES

EXHIBIT 1–2   THE DOMINANCE MODEL

1. Society is hierarchical, and a small number of influential people and/or institutions dominate it. The business institution is one of these, and business leaders manipulate society from a fulcrum of great power in association with government.

2. Power mainly moves down from the top levels of society. Unlike democratic theory, which postulates that leaders serve the will of the people, the social hierarchy implicit in this model implies dominance by a small group of business managers, politicians, and the wealthy.

3. The policy-making process is dominated by the interests of business and the wealthy and is used as a tool to aggrandize the needs of these groups. Decisions are not widely consultative.

4. The role of business in solving and ministering to societal problems, such as housing, unemployment, pollution, income inequality, urban decay, traffic congestion, and women's rights, is paternalistic at best and exploitative at worst.

5. The political machinery is meshed with economic institutions, rendering any adversary relationship between business and government a fiction. A primary goal of government is to help business.

6. Human nature being what it is, those who dominate this societal hierarchy work to preserve the status quo because existing arrangements are to their

benefit. They have little concern for reforming institutional arrangements to make them more participatory or for changing policies that benefit the rich, such as the tax system.

A number of leading intellectuals have subscribed to theories of the business-government-society relationship based on the assumptions of the dominance model. The "power elite" theory of the confluence of economic and business power popularized by the late sociologist C. Wright Mills (1956), for example, parallels the dominance model. Another version of the dominance model is the idea that business and government have formed a sort of monolithic power that tells people what they must do. This thesis is found in John Kenneth Galbraith's works (1958; 1967; 1973) and is adopted by others (e.g., Reich, 1970; Roszak, 1969). Marxism provides another version of this theory in its central tenet that an elite ruling class that dominates the economy and other institutional forms has been present in every society. Contemporary Marxist thinkers in the United States see such domination by a small capitalist class that controls both government and the economy (Dowd, 1977; Sklar, 1980). To those who subscribe to this symbol of the pyramid, the power of business is too great and the motivations of its leaders are selfish (and perhaps conspiratorial).

We believe that this model is far too simple. It is a gross distortion of reality, and the conclusions derived from it are largely erroneous, as will be demonstrated in the remainder of this book.

The Market Capitalism Model

A second model, Exhibit 1-3, which has been popular with business managers and economists for more than two centuries, is the market capitalism model. This conceptual model visualizes the business system as substantially isolated from social forces in its environment and draws attention to the primacy of market economic forces. It depicts business and industry as existing in a market environment that is influenced and shaped both by business decisions inside the market environment and by impinging social, political, legal, and cultural forces. The market environment in the model acts as a buffer between business units and nonmarket environmental forces.

This conceptual representation of the business-society relationship implies conclusions and interpretations much different from those of the dominance model.

1. Market performance is virtually the only accepted measure of social performance. Because business does not interact directly with the sociopolitical environment, managers concentrate on market goals, not social goals.

2. Market performance justifies or legitimizes the existence of the business unit. Its contribution to society is directly related to the performance of its primary economic function. Noneconomic goals or performance measures are not legitimate guideposts for judging contributions of business.

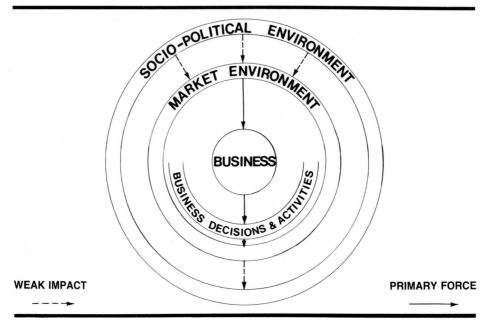

WEAK IMPACT

PRIMARY FORCE

EXHIBIT 1–3   THE MARKET CAPITALISM MODEL

3. Managers should define the interests of their companies narrowly, as profitability and greater efficiency in using scarce resources.

4. Efficiency in economic transactions is the highest good, superseding abstract notions of social justice such as utilitarianism and altruism.

5. Government, not business, has primary responsibility for ministering to social problems. Government institutions are assigned the task of monitoring and adjusting the nonmarket environment of business.

6. Business should respond to market forces of supply and demand and not be subjected to political pressures or government-imposed regulations that cut economic efficiency. Business makes its primary contribution by providing a surplus for society as a result of profitable operations. It can do this best when unhindered by government.

7. Business executives should accept social values as given and do not have a responsibility to work for the resolution of social problems unless these problems register on business firms through market forces or government regulations.

We believe that this model, like the dominance model, has serious drawbacks and does not illuminate fully the role of business in society today. Today, the social responsiveness of business is not as limited as this model would indicate, and many of the assumptions that derive from the model are under attack, as will be seen in later chapters. The model has some acceptability for very small enterprises but not for the larger business organizations that are responsible for the bulk of economic activity in the private sector.

The Business Ecology Model

Ecology is concerned with mutual relations between organisms and their environments. Business ecology, therefore, refers to the relationships of business with various elements in society. The business ecology model, shown in Exhibit 1-4, facilitates the analysis of interactions among business units, the rest of society's institutions, and forces in the business environment. We prefer this model because it promotes understanding of the realistic relationship of business units to other elements in society. (See D. Easton, 1957, for a similar model.)

The business ecology model depicts the business-society relationship as a system of interactions. In this conception, units of business activity are energized by inputs of various kinds. These inputs, which have consequences for both the system and its environment, include economic and sociopolitical demands made by governments, pressure groups, and individuals; and also supports, or attitudes and actions that legitimize the business system. The business system is oriented toward preserving itself, maintaining the integrity of its boundaries, and increasing its control over the environment. On the basis of these inputs, then, the business system creates products and takes actions that affect major areas of society. The impacts of the business system on the

EXHIBIT 1-4   THE BUSINESS ECOLOGY MODEL

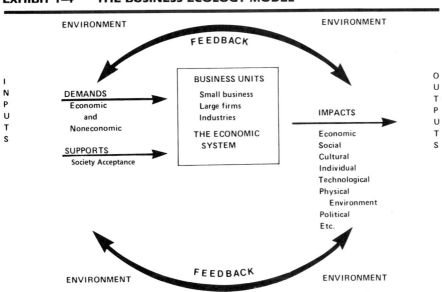

environment result in the creation of a feedback process whereby various groups, individuals, and institutions in society make new demands and increase or decrease their support of business as a result of managers' actions.

What conclusions can be reached with the business ecology model?

1. Unlike models that show business dominating the environment or existing in partial isolation from it, this model clearly implies that business is integrated into the environment and must respond to many forces impinging upon the business system.

2. Society is not basically hierarchical or dominated by a small group but is an interacting network of influences. Any group in the environment may have potential influence on business, and many different forces, social as well as economic, affect executives' decisions.

3. Broad and underlying public support of the business enterprise depends on its adjustment to many different environmental forces. To survive, business must react to a mixture of social and economic forces.

4. The basic function of economic efficiency still can be recognized as essential to the continued survival of the business system, but this basic economic primacy is seen to coexist with continued response to the social environment.

5. The business ecology model shows that the business-government-society relationship will evolve continuously and that business must adjust continuously.

6. The model implies that support for business will be greatest when the impacts of the business system on its environment are more positive than negative, that is, when benefits provided are greater than costs imposed.

This model provides a sound basis for focusing on the two central themes of this book: (1) the way in which the environment is changing the managerial task; and (2) the way in which the role of business in society is changing.

The Dominant Force Model

Exhibit 1-5 is another way of looking at the business ecology model in Exhibit 1–4. It is designed to show the dominant flows of influence in the business-government-society relationship as far as business is concerned. This model shows that the main influence in business comes from changes in societal values, expectations, needs, and demands. These forces influence business through the political processes that affect the private sector. They also influence business directly to the extent that business responds voluntarily to them.

Changes in values, expectations, needs, and demands arise from many forces. One is the changing environment of people, which would include, of course, economic well-being, the physical environment, working conditions, and so on. Business both influences this environment and is influenced by it. Government

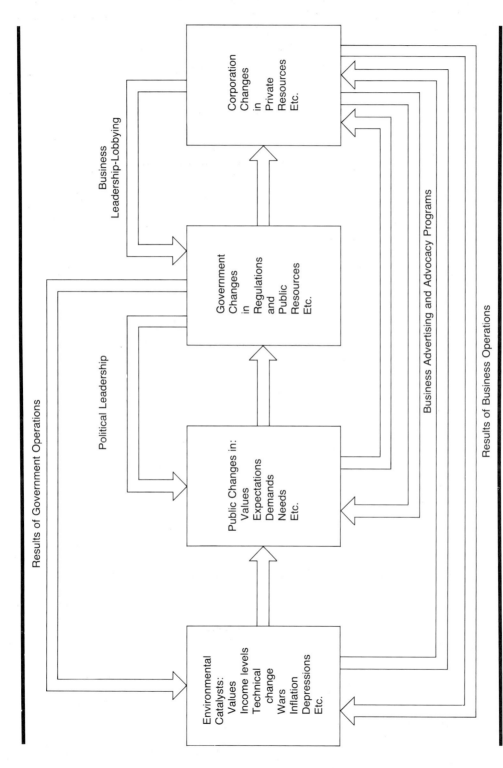

EXHIBIT 1–5   DOMINANT FORCES IN THE BUSINESS-GOVERNMENT-SOCIETY RELATIONSHIP

Source: Based upon a concept of Jacoby (1973). From Neil H. Jacoby, *Corporate Power and Social Responsibility* (New York: Macmillan, 1973).

leadership also influences the environment and social response to the changing environment. Business advocacy advertising may influence public values, expectations, demands, and needs.

This obviously is a dynamic model of influence. The forces operate differently and with varying impact, depending upon a wide range of factors such as the subject or issue under review, the power of competing groups, intensity of public feelings, and effectiveness of government and business leadership.

Over a long period of time, there have been major changes in the dynamics of influence. For example, fifty years ago business paid attention almost solely to stockholder interests and market economic and technical forces. Today such forces are still important but are matched by the influence of government and pressure groups.

What overarching conclusions can be drawn from this model?

1. The BGS relationship is extremely dynamic in its flow of influences.

2. Business responds to its environment.

3. Environmental changes are the most important influences on business.

4. Business is a major initiator of change in its environment, especially through its introduction of new technologies.

The Stakeholder Model

This model is presented to underscore the point that businesses, especially the larger ones in the public eye, are confronted with many constituents who believe they have a stake in the operation of a business; hence the name stakeholder.

Every one of the constituent interests identified in Exhibit 1-6 has multiple parts, and each may present its own set of demands on a company. For example, the circle "governments" covers numerous governments, foreign and domestic.

Influence is not one-way. Stakeholders can be influenced both directly and indirectly by what a company does. A company may affect union workers directly by closing a plant, and it may influence people in a community indirectly by increasing employment. Influence can be both positive and negative. Stakeholder pressures on a company may be direct, as for example, when a bank demands specific actions to protect its loans, or indirect, as when a stakeholder successfully gets government to force a company to act in the interests of the stakeholder (for example, environmentalists get laws passed to reduce pollution by public utilities).

A very small company typically has few constituents of important concern to it (usually stockholders, customers, employees, and the bank). A very large company has many stakeholders, and there will be great variations in the degree to which managers will yield to each of their interests. A pharmaceutical company, for example, will be very receptive to the demands of physicians who use its products. A coal-burning utility will be highly concerned about the expectations of environmentalists.

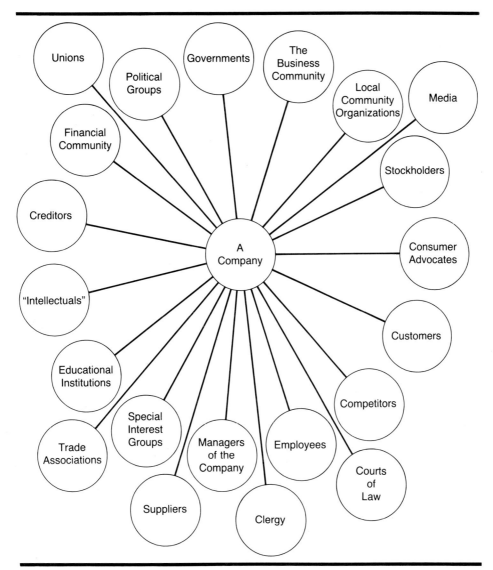

EXHIBIT 1–6   "STAKEHOLDER" GROUPS OF A LARGE CORPORATION

Source: Steiner, Miner, and Gray (1986).

What conclusions can be drawn from this model?

1. Every large corporation has a variety of constituents who have an interest in the way the corporation operates.

2. A large corporation seeks to react appropriately to stakeholders, who are seen as having important actual or potential impact on the operations of the corporation.

3. The corporation will seek to influence its stakeholders in accepting its decisions.

Managerial Attitudes about Stakeholders   The American Management As-Association recently sponsored a study of 6,000 managers. Part of the study concerned the importance with which three different levels of managers viewed a list of business stakeholders, including themselves. Table 1-1 shows that customers came first for top managers but not for supervisory and middle managers. The three levels of managers seemed less than humble, but quite candid, about their own importance. The table is striking with respect to the high status given employees, coworkers, and superiors in the company. The researchers concluded, "The stereotype of managers as running the nation's corporations for the primary benefit of their stockholders does not seem to be borne out by the data" (Posner and Schmidt, 1984: 207). This does not mean, of course, that managers are less concerned with company profit than themselves or their colleagues in the business. Profitable growth is still a dominant objective of managers. What Table 1–1 shows, however, is that it is not the sole objective. It also can be hypothesized that managers understand very well that appropriate concern for major stakeholders will enhance profit potential.

TABLE 1–1   THE IMPORTANCE OF VARIOUS ORGANIZATIONAL STAKEHOLDERS TO MANAGERS*

	Supervisory managers	Middle managers	Executive managers
Customers	5.57	6.10	6.40
Myself	6.28	6.29	6.28
Subordinates	6.06	6.30	6.14
Employees	5.93	6.11	6.01
Boss(es)	5.72	5.92	5.82
Co-Workers	5.87	5.82	5.81
Colleagues	5.66	5.78	5.75
Managers	5.26	5.56	5.75
Owners	4.07	4.51	5.30
General Public	4.38	4.49	4.52
Stockholders	3.35	3.79	4.51
Elected Public Officials	3.81	3.54	3.79
Government Bureaucrats	3.09	2.05	2.90

*Scale of 1 to 7 (1 = lowest; 7 = highest).

Source: Barry Z. Posner and Warren H. Schmidt, "Values and the American Manager: An Update," *California Management Review,* Vol. 26, no. 2 (Spring 1984).

BUSINESS AND THE SOCIAL CONTRACT

Institutions, or systems, in society are not created and accepted as the result of some mystical conception. They exist in order to perform important societal functions. At any time there exists a working relationship between society and its institutions called the social contract. This contract is partly written in legislation but also is found in custom, precedent, and articulated societal approval or disapproval. Whether explicit or implicit, the social contract is the basis for institutional actions.

This fundamental interrelationship between business and society leads to a number of important conclusions. One is that the business institution operates, basically, to serve society's interests as society sees them. Another is that generalizations about the relationship between business and society in the past may not be valid today or tomorrow. The social contract changes continuously. In periods of great change, such as we are witnessing today, there is more pervasive and fundamental rewriting of the contract than in tranquil times. Indeed, today there are many people who feel that the social contract is being rewritten in a fundamental way.

CHARACTERISTICS OF THE ANALYSIS

As you have seen, the interrelationships among business, government, and society are enormous in scope and can be approached in many different ways. The principal characteristics of our analysis in this book are as follows.

Focus on Strategic Management

The central focus of this book is on the many powerful nonmarket forces in the business environment (external and internal) that significantly affect the management of individual firms and on the changing role of the business institution in society. It is widely recognized, especially in the larger corporations, that business firms cannot operate successfully over the long run in conflict with their environments. Managers of successful companies avoid this conflict through effective strategic management of their companies.

Strategic management is a term now in vogue. It describes the formulation and implementation of strategies that adapt a company to its changing environment. By strategies, we refer to the formulation of basic organizational missions, purposes, and objectives; the policies and programs to achieve them; and the methods needed to assure that they are implemented. In the past, strategic management meant essentially adapting to the economic and technical environments. Now, it means adapting also to the socio-political environment. Indeed, these socio-political environmental forces are as dominant influences on corporate strategy as the traditional market forces.

The concept of strategic management does not imply that managements formulate strategies only in response to current events. Quite the contrary, it means that managers try to anticipate future environmental forces so that they can take proactive measures to deal with them.

More specifically, to illustrate, we are concerned with the way sociopolitical forces enter into the formulation and implementation of such strategies as the following:

■ Those that spell out the social responsibilities of the company.

■ Those that react properly to changing social values with respect to such matters as the nature of the company's products or the changing aspirations of the people in the organization.

■ Those that respond appropriately to government regulations concerning such matters as pollution, product safety, and equal opportunity.

■ Those that determine when and how the company will try to influence political processes in matters of concern to the company.

■ Those that change the structure and processes by which the firm responds to environmental forces.

■ Those that affect the ethical standards upon which decisions are made in a company.

This emphasis is based on our conviction that among all the disciplines that must be employed in studying the BGS interrelationships, the managerial (especially its strategic management aspect) is the most appropriate one for BGS courses in schools of business/management/administration. Disciplines other than the managerial may be more appropriate in other academic departments and schools.

Interdisciplinary Approach with a Managerial Focus

A large number of disciplines must be considered in dealing with theory, practice, and policy issues in the business-government-society interface. The more prominent ones are economics, political science, law, philosophy, sociology, science, history, and management. Our approach is an eclectic one in which we attempt to use the most relevant disciplines associated with a particular theory, practice, or policy issue. It is possible to analyze the business-society relationship in an interdisciplinary way but with a dominant disciplinary orientation, such as economics, political science, or law. Our orientation, as we have said, is managerial.

Comprehensive Scope

We have sought to make this book comprehensive in scope. We have tried to cover the large canvas, sketching out all of the most important interrelationships among business, government, and other societal forces. This approach is in contrast to that of selecting and concentrating intensively and exclusively on a few areas such as business social responsibility, pollution, consumerism, equal opportunity, and antitrust. We believe that it is far better for students in a basic course to be exposed to the many dominant interrelationships, even if the exposure is often "light," than for them to dig deeply into only a few areas.

Focus on Theory

We have tried to emphasize theoretical concepts appearing to have some permanence and providing valuable normative guides for understanding environmental forces, the managerial responses to them, and the way in which the business role is changing. We recognize, however, that there is no underlying theory integrating the entire field, nor is there likely to be one in the foreseeable future. The field is extremely diverse, complex, and fluid, and there is no consensus about its precise boundaries.

One can say tentatively, however, that the beginnings of an underlying theory of business and its relationship to society are emerging, but the profile is not clear. There is growing agreement, for example, about the theoretical obligations of corporations to respond to social pressures. In a number of major areas, there are useful theories rooted in relevant disciplines. For example, there are tested political theories concerned with business power, technical theories concerned with pollution issues, legal theories concerned with manufacturer liability, and economic theories concerned with government regulations, to mention a few. We have sought to emphasize such theories where they are relevant to the subject matter of this book.

Issues, Facts, and Conclusions About Policy and Practice

A central focus of this book is to examine and evaluate the more significant issues in the business-society nexus so as to come to conclusions about what appropriate policy and practice should be for business and/or government. One of our goals is to help students to identify the "correct" issues. This means asking the "right" questions and framing the "right" problems. What is "right" often depends upon who is asking the question. Nevertheless, students of this subject must try to get at the basic strategic questions. For instance, there is no question but that technological advance has had serious and unwanted side effects. Is the question how to slow down technological advance to reduce these side effects, as some people advocate, or is it, as others suggest, how to inject into decision-making processes incentives to avoid the unwanted side impacts? Or is it something else? Students of this subject should understand that framing the "right" question is often very difficult and that proposed solutions follow the question once it is asked.

Many times in this book questions will be asked and no answers given. This is because there are no answers. Even if there are no answers, we still are progressing if the right questions are posed.

Once the issues have been identified, what are the facts? Getting the facts may be extremely difficult. For example, what are the facts about the safety of nuclear power plants? What are the facts about the human and economic damage caused by various types of pollution? What are the facts about society's expectations of the social responsibilities of business? We do not have enough facts about these and many other crucial questions.

Once the facts are gathered, it is essential to use them in a proper context. For example, some critics charge that business has not really solved major social problems, and its failure to do so indicates more concern with profits than the social welfare. The first part of the statement is correct but not the second. The facts are correct—business has not solved major social problems—but the perspective of the critics is wrong. It is not business's responsibility to solve major social problems, with a few exceptions to be noted later.

Even with the right issue at hand and all the facts that are available, reasonable people may come to radically different conclusions about preferred policy on issues. The reason, of course, is that people come to the issues and facts with differing ideologies, values, and interests. The Attorney General of the United States looks at the antitrust law somewhat differently from the chief executive of General Motors. At the very least, however, reason is more likely to prevail in society when people can communicate about commonly identified issues and the real facts.

In some instances, but not all, we explain our position on the issue being examined. We do so not to intrude our views on the reader, but rather to help in the analysis, for this book is not designed to "sell" or "explain" one particular point of view. Its purpose is to identify outstanding theories, processes of decision making, and policy issues and to stimulate full, informed, and thoughtful debate about them.

Because judgment is often the final determinant of one's position on a particular issue, it is not an excuse to ignore the facts of a case. A charming story about Michelangelo will illustrate this situation. When Michelangelo had completed his carving of David, the governor of Florence came to look at the finished piece. He was pleased with what he saw, but as he looked at it he mused, "The nose . . . the nose is too large, is it not?" Michelangelo looked carefully at David's nose and quietly answered, "Yes, I think it is a little too large." He picked up his chisel and mallet, and also a handful of marble dust, and mounted the scaffolding. Carefully he hammered, permitting small amounts of dust to fall to the ground with each blow. He finally stopped and asked: "Now look at the nose. Is it not correct?" "Ah," responded the governor, "I like it . . . I like it even better. You have given it life." Michelangelo descended, according to an old chronicle, "with great compassion for those who desire to appear to be good judges of matters whereof they know nothing" (Lerman, 1942: 168–169).

To deplore "shooting from the hip," so to speak, does not suggest as an objective to "know all there is about business and society." We agree with J. Robert Oppenheimer when he observed: "No man should escape our universities without . . . some sense of the fact that not through his fault, but in the nature of things, he is going to be an ignorant man, and so is everyone else." It is an appropriate posture to approach the subject of this book with humility.

BOUNDARIES OF THE BGS FIELD

This book sets forth the BGS field of study as we see it today. Our view, of course, is based on our fundamental focus—the managerial perspective. Others focus on public policy issues, or economics, or political science, areas that are subgroups in our approach.

As noted earlier, the BGS field covers an enormous territory. Exhibit 1-7 shows the frame of reference that we believe is useful in defining the BGS field for a text such as this. On the left is a scale of threats to the legitimacy of business. On the bottom line is a scale concerning the impact of a particular subject on the managerial function of business and/or the business role in society.

A high threat to the legitimacy of business would mean, for example, a force that could sap the vitality of business, weaken the broad acceptance of the business institution, or reduce the efficient functioning of business. A low threat on this scale would mean just the opposite. A high marking on the bottom scale would mean, of course, that management could be powerfully affected by the forces arising in a particular area.

We believe that the field of BGS should fundamentally focus on subjects in the upper right quartile of the matrix. The subject-matter of each of the chapters in this book is in this area, that is, government, social responsibilities of business,

EXHIBIT 1–7   MATRIX TO DEFINE THE BGS FIELD

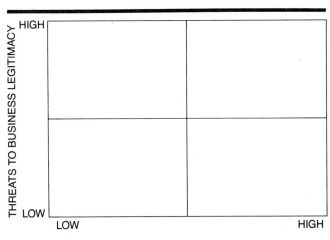

ethics, pollution, consumerism, and so on. Other topics that impact on management of business are excluded because they do not now appear in this area of the matrix. These include, for example, agriculture, national security, demography, and the money and banking system.

The generic topics located in the upper right quartile remain in that position over comparatively long periods of time. They do change, however. Government, of course, is a more or less permanent resident in that area. Twenty-five years ago, pollution and consumerism would not have been found in this area. Thirty-five years ago, the Korean War economy was prominent in the BGS relationship.

Although many of the generic topics remain dominant in the BGS domain, there is constant shifting of emphasis. For example, social audits were of high concern to business in the social responsibility area twenty years ago but are not a significant consideration today. Ten years ago, the basic question in the social responsibility area was whether business has social responsibilities. Now, the argument has been decided in the affirmative, and the focus of attention has shifted to what business is doing to institutionalize the social point of view in decision making. For another example, in the multinational corporate area, the subject of protectionism recently has come to the fore. In the political arena, the issue of political action committees has assumed new prominence. In each of the generic areas that are subjects of chapters in this book will be found those topics which we consider at this time to be the more important ones to include in the BGS relationship and in the intellectual tool kit of students of this subject.

PART I

UNDERLYING FORCES IN TODAY'S INTERRELATIONSHIPS

CHAPTER **2** _____

THE BUSINESS ENVIRONMENT

 Giant Eastman Kodak Company has been jolted in recent years because it did not properly assess its principal environments. In trying to play catch-up with Polaroid in instant photography, Kodak used a process so close to Polaroid's that in 1986 it lost a suit brought by Polaroid for patent infringement. It had to cease production of its camera and recall those it had sold. Now, it is battling legal suits from dissatisfied customers. Kodak failed to appreciate the growing market for videocassette cameras and turned to Matsushita to design and make its cameras. The company made a major diversification into high-volume copiers and lost more than half its market share (from 1978 to 1984) to Xerox and IBM. In 1982 it introduced its Disc Camera and suffered a loss of $300 million, not counting development costs. Diversification into blood analyzers and electronics fizzled. As the premier producer of film in the world, it found Fuji Film eating into its market share and was outbid by Fuji as a film sponsor for the Olympics in Los Angeles. Because 40 percent or more of Kodak's sales have been from foreign markets, the strong dollar hurt the company by foreign currency translation losses. Finally, the loyalty of employees, built up by a long history of job permanence, was shattered by layoffs in early 1986. The company's stockholders were unhappy to see their stock prices drop about 50 percent from 1976 to 1985.

In 1986 "Big K," as it is often called, rebounded strongly with new acquisitions and new products. Indeed, 100 new products—more than ever for this company—were introduced into the company's operations. For example, new automatic 35mm cameras and new film, together with a new easy-to-open container, were marketed. It also introduced new batteries that would last twice as long as existing batteries. Electronic publishing systems, blood-analysis tests, and optical-disk data-storage systems were marketed. Kodak started its drug business almost from scratch. Its development in this area was an outgrowth of its expertise in plastics and chemicals. The company developed a new technology in instant photography and expected to announce a system that thermally prints a color photo on identity cards, such as drivers' licenses. This new technology, believes the management, is a foot in the door of a huge potential market that might one day replace conventional photography. Kodak purchased Verbatim Corporation in 1985, a maker of floppy magnetic disks. This organization was to make and distribute the new optical-storage system. Fuji Film has been feeling the sting of Kodak's aggressive competitive stance. For example, a Kodak blimp is scheduled to plug Kodak film in Seoul, Korea, during the 1988 summer Olympics. Having lost out to Fuji in bidding for sponsorship of the 1986 Olympic games in Los Angeles, Kodak outbid Fuji for the rights to the 1988 Olympics.

Profits and sales hit a peak in 1981 and dropped sharply to a low of $332 million, on sales of $10.6 billion, in 1983. The next year was somewhat better, but analysts projected profits of over $1 billion on sales of about $12.6 billion (the highest ever for the company) in 1987. Part of this turnaround was due to the declining value of the dollar in foreign exchange. Because Kodak depends on foreign operations for approximately 40 percent of its sales, the sharp fall in the value of the dollar in 1986 helped sales and profits substantially.

Colby H. Chandler, chairman and chief executive officer of the company, succinctly stated Kodak's strategy as follows:

> The Kodak goal is straightforward: to use the company's world-class status in the disciplines of chemistry, imaging, optics, and information management with new strengths in electronics and life sciences to maintain leadership in current markets, while establishing strong positions in new areas of opportunity (Chandler, 1986: 5).

To achieve this goal would take more than environmental analysis, of course, but skilled environmental analysis will be fundamental to its achievement.

As the story of Eastman Kodak suggests, for the student of BGS as well as for business managers, there is a continuous need to evaluate forces in the evolving environment of business. For the student, understanding the forces in the business environment provides a solid basis for comprehension of the nature of today's interrelationships among business, government, and society, and it provides insight into possibilities in the future. For business, the environment is the source of opportunities to be exploited as well as threats to be avoided. Those companies that do assess environmental forces on a continuous and more or less formal basis can take proactive measures to adapt to the changing environment. Those that do not are doomed to react to environmental impacts on their operations and will sooner or later falter.

The business environment, in broad terms, is the climate or the surroundings within which a firm operates. The broad concept loses consensus, however, when we move to a description of the environment, the forces operating in it, the perspectives from which it can best be viewed, and a structure that can be used effectively in organizing and facilitating managerial assessment of it (Lenz and Engledow, 1986).

We find it convenient to divide the discussion in this chapter into two parts. The first pertains to the handful of fundamental underlying forces that have evolved over a long period of time and underlie shorter- and medium-range trends in the business environment. Second is the current environment of business. This we divide into two parts, the external and the internal environment.

UNDERLYING HISTORICAL FORCES CHANGING THE BUSINESS ENVIRONMENT

We believe that in a broad sense, order can be found in the swirling patterns of current events; that there is a deep logic in the passing of history; and that the directions of change in the business environment are the product of elemental currents flowing in roughly predictable channels. In brief, change in the business environment is the product of seven deep historical forces.

The Industrial Revolution

The first historical force is the industrial revolution. The break-up of small, local economies and the invention of new machinery and manufacturing techniques in the seventeenth century led to expanded markets and mass-production technology that combined capital, labor, and natural resources in dynamic new ways. The growth of mass consumer societies and a world economy in the twentieth century are but two recent echoes of this industrial "big bang." The ramifications of the industrial revolution ripple out through time to define the strategic business environment in many ways. For example, new and larger factories, massive capital accumulation, management techniques for organizing huge corporations, and the interdependence of world financial markets all articulate its centuries-old premise.

Dominant Ideologies

The second historical force is the impact of dominant ideologies. A small number of powerful, well-developed doctrines define a world view for millions of people. In the United States, we largely adhere to ideologies of capitalism, constitutional democracy, and the great religions such as Catholicism and its offshoot, Protestantism. In the main, these ideologies coexist peacefully. But tensions frequently arise, for example, when the accumulation of great wealth and its translation into societal power may be justified by capitalism but conflict with tenets of constitutional democracy that give mass populations the right to check ruling classes in the exercise of power. These tensions among ideologies have ignited political movements and led to redistribution of power in society. Dominant ideologies also determine the broad cast of public opinion and social values.

Inequality of Human Circumstances

The inequality of human circumstance is the third historical force. From time immemorial, societies have been marked by status distinctions, class structures, and gaps between rich and poor. Inequality is ubiquitous, as are its consequences—jealousy, demands for equality, and doctrines that justify why some people have more than others. Marxism—a dominant ideology in Eastern Europe, Asia, Africa, and Latin America—condemns the capitalist belief that success in the marketplace justifies accumulation of wealth in the hands of one social class. The current emphasis on corporate social responsibility in the business environment is, in a general sense, based upon the need to mitigate the appearance of remote and greatly concentrated wealth.

Scientific Development

The fourth historical force is scientific development. The great scientific developments of civilization since Leonardo da Vinci in fifteenth-century Italy have been fuel for the powerful engine of commerce. From the water wheel to recombinant DNA, business has utilized new discoveries to more efficiently convert basic resources into equity. The development of the computer has brought changes in virtually every facet of the business environment and has had enormous consequences for management theory. Like the automobile in its time, it has changed our society.

Nation-States

The fifth historical force is the nation-state system. The modern nation-state system arose in an unplanned way from the wreckage of the Roman Empire. Today the world is a geographic mosaic of independent countries, each with a separate government to impose social order and economic stability over its territory. Each country asserts its own sovereignty, or right of self-determination. And in each there develop feelings of nationalism, or loyalty to a national identity. The dynamics of this system are a powerful force in the international business environment. Sometimes countries expand territories to encompass new markets or essential raw materials, as did Japan in the late 1930s. The nationalistic feelings of Palestinians deposed from Israeli territory have affected American companies in many ways, from oil companies that have been caught in Middle East conflicts to airlines that lose passengers afraid of terrorism. The international nation-state system is one of the major sources of turbulence in the business environment.

Great Leadership

The sixth historical force is great leadership. The innovations of great leaders change societies. In the third century B.C., Alexander the Great imposed his rule on the Mediterranean world and created new areas of trade for Greek merchants. In our time, Lee Iacocca earned laurels with the less sweeping act of restoring Chrysler Corporation to financial health through the use of a management system. It has always been the case that a small number of individuals in any organization or society are a major force in bringing innovation and change.

Chance

The seventh historical force is chance or accident. Many scholars are reluctant to use the concept of random occurrence as a category of analysis. Yet some changes in the business environment can best be explained as beyond the control of business strategists because they are the product of the unknown and unpredictable. The first Tylenol murders occurred in September 1982, when seven people died from capsules filled with cyanide. This event, perhaps the work of one deranged person, was followed over the years by recurrent cyanide poisonings caused by product-tampering. The result has been an important change in the production and marketing environments of food and over-the-counter drugs. No less perceptive a student of history than Niccolo Machiavelli observed that fortune determined about half of the course of human events and men the other half. We cannot prove or disprove this estimate, but we note it and are not foolish enough to try to improve upon it. The student of the world surrounding business must recognize the role of caprice.

THE CURRENT BUSINESS ENVIRONMENT

The total business environment is composed of many forces, as shown in Exhibit 2-1. The chart suggests that environmental forces influence one another and, potentially, every important functional area in a company. John Muir, the great conservationist, once said, "When we try to pick out anything by itself, we find it hitched to everything else in the universe." So it is in business. Any force that affects it turns out to have roots extending over a wide area. Economic forces, for example, can influence every one of the areas in the outer circle and every one of the areas in the middle circle of Exhibit 2–1.

This chart shows only selected external environmental forces. There are also internal environmental forces. Some of these are, for example, attitudes of people, the ways in which things are done in an organization, the systems and methods employed in a company, the skills of people, and values which managers and employees hold. All of these are called the company culture. Such

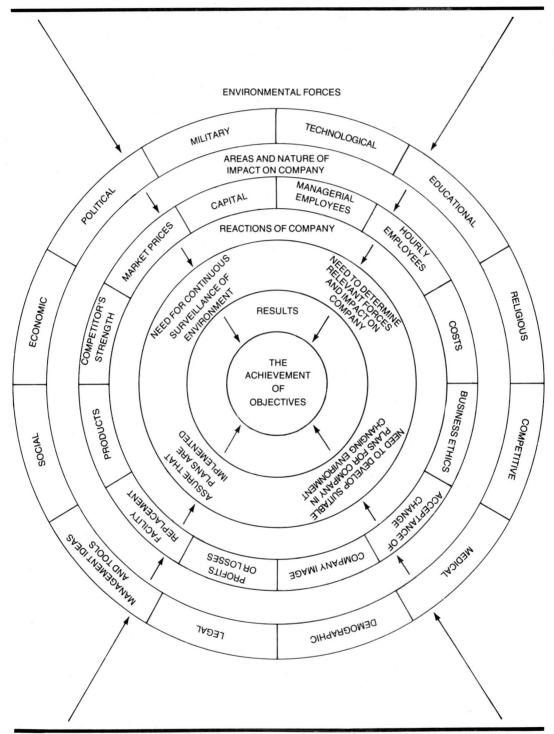

EXHIBIT 2–1   ENVIRONMENTAL IMPACTS ON COMPANY PLANNING

Source: G. A. Steiner, 1969: 204. Reprinted with permission of The Free Press, a Division of Macmillan, Inc., from *Top Management Planning* by George A. Steiner. Copyright © 1969 by The Trustees of Columbia University in the City of New York.

environmental factors are crucial to a company in its operations, including how it formulates strategy and whether the strategy can be implemented properly.

It is worth repeating a point made in Chapter 1, that business is not helpless in the face of environmental forces. Business can influence them, often powerfully. Also, business is an extremely flexible institution and can generally adapt to current and future environmental forces in such a fashion as to maintain its strength and vigor in the face of adverse changes.

Up to this point, we have spoken of environments in general. Our discussion will be simplified if we now narrow the focus to the four major external environments of business and to its internal environment (see Exhibit 2-2). Other environments may, from time to time, affect a business and, for a particular business at some point in time, may be of critical importance. Some of them are shown in Exhibit 2-1, and some will be discussed later. Each of these environments has international as well as domestic dimensions.

Even a very large company cannot make a penetrating assessment of all the current and evolving domestic and international environments that conceivably might affect it. There are simply too many forces involved. But it is not necessary for a company to make such a comprehensive evaluation. What is necessary is for a company to choose those significant forces in the environment that will likely have an important impact on its operations and devote as much energy as possible to understanding and projecting them.

EXHIBIT 2–2　THE MAJOR ENVIRONMENTS OF BUSINESS

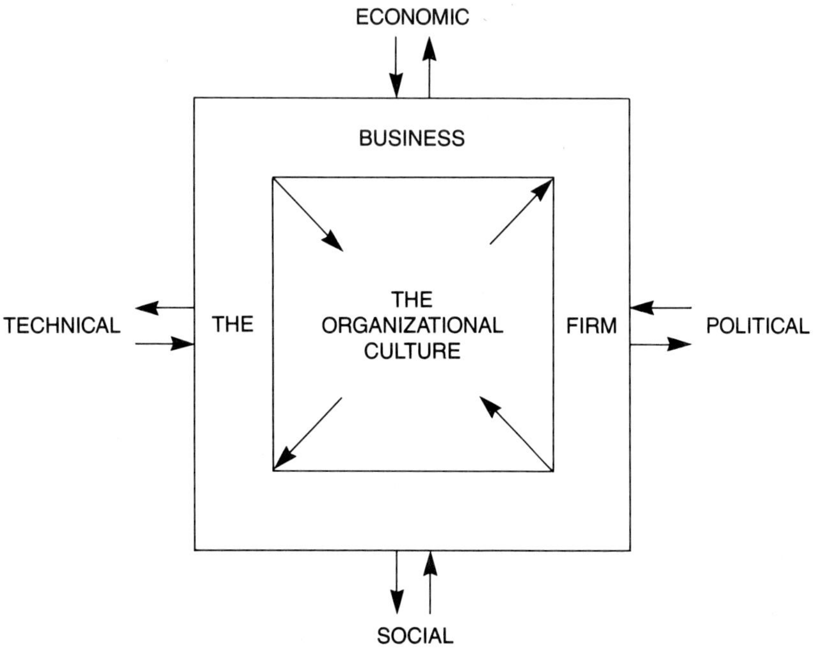

We turn now to a thumbnail sketch of the nature of each of the dominant environments and selected forces operating in them.

THE ECONOMIC ENVIRONMENT

The economic environment covers a vast territory and is, of course, of arresting significance to business. The economic forces of concern to a company range from overall economic activity, as measured by the Gross National Product (GNP), to what a competitor is doing in a local market. We illustrate as follows a few dimensions of the scope, turbulence, complexity, and power of the economic environment of business.

Overall economic activity as measured by GNP has fluctuated widely from the end of World War II to the present. During the past two decades, we have had economic recessions (indicated by a decline or little growth in GNP) about every two to four years. The cycles of recession and prosperity have not been regular nor generally predictable with any accuracy. When GNP is rising robustly, it stimulates business growth and profitability. When it is growing slowly, or declining, business activity is depressed and profits drop or disappear.

The many different components within GNP tend to fluctuate much more than the GNP total. Thus, changes will vary more in such economic forces as consumer and wholesale prices, employment, wage rates, worker productivity, steel production, automobile sales, house construction, and inventories. It is entirely possible, of course, for GNP to be rising, even significantly, but for a business to go bankrupt because of a particular change in one economic force, such as competition, a new foreign tariff, interest rates, technology, a labor strike, consumer disfavor, or a government regulation.

Every important economic force has an impact on a wide range of other economic forces, which in turn affect others. The patterns of change vary with time and in intensity. To illustrate, commodity prices have fluctuated significantly in recent years and will do so again in the future, a matter of concern to business as well as consumers. But when and by how much will prices change? What will be the economic implications? No one really knows. Major changes in the general level of commodity prices will affect interest rates, consumer purchasing, stock and bond prices, basic raw material prices, wage-rate demands, to mention but a few activities. Each of these forces affects other phenomenon. For example, rising commodity prices tend to generate forces that lift interest rates. This, in turn, increases the cost of capital to business and dampens business borrowing for expansion. Rising interest rates also will bring a decline in bond prices. But rising, or lowering, interest rates result not only from commodity price increases. Higher interest rates can result from a too rapid expansion of general economic activity and rising demand for capital, a decline in savings, or rising interest rates in a major foreign country that attracts our limited capital.

Some of our basic industries have been declining in recent years and are likely to continue that trend for some time with spreading adverse impacts on the entire economy. Noteworthy declining industries are steel, agriculture, textiles, and machine tools. Competition from foreign companies has been a special cause of this condition but other factors also operate in each industry. For example, depressed conditions in the agriculture sector, which have resulted in many farm and rural bank bankruptcies, have been due in large measure to shrinking foreign markets for our products. This, in turn, has been caused by an overvalued dollar, expansion of foreign country agricultural output, trade barriers, inept government policies that have raised our agricultural prices above world market prices, and a decline in world agricultural prices.

A significant factor of economic life in the United States is the size of our domestic market. It is by far the largest, most affluent, and growing market in any industrialized country in the world. A single company, therefore, has wide opportunities to exploit it. However, this market also poses great risks. For example, it invites vigorous competition, and competition is probably the single most significant force operating in this market. Despite growing government regulations, which will be discussed in later chapters, our markets are more competitive and freer for individual initiative than in any other industrialized country in the world.

As important as the economic environment is to business, it is matched in significance by the technological, the political, and the social environments, to which we now turn.

THE TECHNOLOGICAL ENVIRONMENT

It is fair to say that virtually every significant problem in modern society is either initiated by or at least strongly affected by technological change. The United States has gone through one technological revolution after another and continues to do so.

For example, in computer science, biotechnology, medicine, robotic factories, and telecommunications, to mention just a few, technology is new. The list of new technologies today is awesome. This phenomenon opens up not only great opportunities for business but also threats. It raises significant problems in the relationships of business to government and society.

A major source of threat to a company in this turbulent technological environment is that many discoveries are made in industries other than those to which they are immediately related. For example, computers were not invented in the office equipment industry, synthetic fibers were not invented in the textile industry, digital watches were not invented in the watch industry, and synthetic diamonds were not invented in the jewelry or abrasives industry. The likelihood is becoming greater that a company may be blindsided by an unexpected discovery outside its industry that makes its product obsolete. It is even more likely that unaware managers will find their products made obsolete by developments in the industry in which they are operating.

Technological threats do not come from domestic sources only. Scientific developments in foreign countries in recent years parallel those in the United States: computer technology in Japan; pharmaceuticals in Switzerland; chemicals and electronics in Germany; electronics and medical sciences in the United Kingdom; and telecommunications, optical fibers, and energy (fusion) in France.

Many technologies that originated in the United States now are used by foreign competitors to outperform our own companies. For instance, Japan imported the first robot from the American Machine and Foundry Company (AMF) in 1967. At that time, this country was fifteen years ahead of all countries in robotics technology. We are still second to none, but Japan has far outstripped the United States in the use of these machines. One result is that Japan has been much more efficient than we in producing automobiles.

Modern technology also has introduced into society some chemicals having potential dangers to the planet and the people on it. Chlorofluorocarbons, for example, are known to eat away the ozone layer in the stratosphere, with very serious consequences. Their use is now partially outlawed. But countless other chemicals produced by industry pose potential dangers whose dimensions are not now known.

New biotechnological inventions and the current revolution in computer science will open up astonishing new opportunities as well as threats to businesses and have deep and fundamental impacts on society. In Chapter 6, we will discuss the new biotechnology and the significant issues which it raises. Here we comment briefly on the new developments in computer science that will have widespread impacts.

Since the 1970s, about every two and one-half to three years we have had a new generation of computers. The trend has been to make them smaller and smaller and cheaper and cheaper. Today, engineers can produce circuit parts for computer chips that are about one-hundredth the diameter of a human hair. Even smaller diameters are promised in the near future. This development will permit the use of extremely small computers in all kinds of equipment, devices, appliances, gadgets, toys, and so on. The new technology also will allow manufacturers to charge much lower prices for their products that use these devices. For instance, the price of a computer that reads to the blind will fall from $23,000 to about $5,000 (Simison, 1986). Imagine the thousands of other valuable uses for very small, cheap computer chips!

In thinking about technological change, it is not enough to consider opportunities and threats to business, or new public policy issues for government, or the immediate impact on the well-being of people. New technology has a deep and lasting influence on those fundamental forces discussed earlier in this chapter. For example, new technology can and often does change the entire way of life, thinking, values, habits, and even the political processes of the nation. The automobile is a classic example of a new technology that enormously affected virtually every aspect of life in this and many other nations of the world. Imagine how the new technologies mentioned above will change this society in the years to come!

THE POLITICAL ENVIRONMENT

This environment covers a range of subjects, from federal government regulations to local party politics. The greatest concern to business in the area is, of course, the actions of governments. But the legal system and our pluralistic society also are of high interest to business. These three aspects of the political environment will now be examined very briefly.

The Governmental Environment

There is today practically no aspect of business that governments cannot and will not regulate if the occasion arises and popular or legislative support exists. In recent years, governments have responded affirmatively to a wide range of public concerns about such matters as product safety, product labeling, advertising, minority employment, honesty, pollution, and worker safety, to mention a few. Accordingly, laws have been passed to deal with these concerns. These, when added to the accumulated volume of laws in the past, have resulted in more government control of business than at any peacetime period in our history. Furthermore, the direction of many of these laws has been to involve government in detailed managerial decision making. Government controls in the automobile industry over emission and safety standards are cases in point.

To the typical businessperson, government regulation is burdensome. Antipollution controls, for example, require vast expenditures of funds by many companies. Equal opportunity regulations influence the ways in which companies employ and treat people. Other laws force managers to act in certain ways with respect to product design, work environment, prices charged, costs of capital, and so on. An often overlooked cost of regulation is the time and energy managers and staff must devote to preparing reports for government.

Business not only is subject to the regulations of the federal government but also must deal with fifty state and hundreds of local governments. In addition, our companies that do business abroad are subject to foreign government regulations.

But governments support business as well. For example, the federal government helps business by making direct cash subsidies to individual companies, it gives business the results of government-funded research, it protects businesses from unfair domestic and foreign competition, and it opens up foreign markets for business by negotiating with foreign governments.

The significance of government in the business environment is profound. Robert Cushman, when CEO of Norton Industries, once observed:

> All of our skills at managing—financial, manufacturing, marketing, research and development and the like—all these put together will not influence our destiny as much as what happens in political and economic arenas. As a consequence, managers of big institutions—whether they be presidents of corporations, universities, foundations, or government agencies—must spend more time trying to

understand and influence external affairs than they spend on the more traditional job of internal management (1980).

The Legal Environment

An executive of a large company remarked that ten years ago his principal legal worries centered on antitrust matters, and everything else was lumped together as a poor second. Today, however, he finds that there are many areas of great urgency, the priorities of which change from month to month, and the number of problems as well as attorney and other legal costs have exploded. Indeed, he said that he has set a goal of having annual earnings five times the legal fees of the company!

Today, in addition to antitrust, other major areas of legal concern to business are securities and stockholder matters; consumer complaints; fair employment practices; product safety; worker safety and health; government contracts; and air, water, and noise pollution. Not only have legal actions against business in all areas increased rapidly, but potential liability for business has also risen explosively. Corporations are exposed considerably more than in the past to legal liabilities for injuries from their products. Also, directors, officers, and other managers of businesses are subject to vastly expanded legal liabilities for their actions and, often, for those of their subordinates. Not only do businesses find their liability insurance rates far higher than in the past, but many who are in exposed positions are unable to get any liability insurance. For example, the BankAmerica board of directors lost their insurance which forced the bank to self-insure the directors.

The newly complex legal environment of business is due in part to increased government regulations, which foster suits against corporations for perceived violations of regulations. Also, courts of law have made it much easier for plaintiffs to get generous awards for injuries for which corporations in the past were not held liable.

Pluralism

Ours is a pluralistic society, which means that it is composed of many semiautonomous and autonomous groups through which power is diffused. These groups exert pressure on governments to act in their interest, and much of the legislation that they influence governments to enact impacts on business. They also exert pressure directly on business to act on their behalf.

In the distant past, business managers could be successful if, working within the rules of the game laid down by government, they tried to satisfy only customers and stockholders. Today the managers of a large corporation must pay attention to a growing number of constituent groups. Dealing with the diverse, often conflicting, and often disruptive pressures of such groups consumes a growing share of managerial time, especially in larger companies. Pluralism will be discussed at some length in the next chapter.

THE SOCIAL ENVIRONMENT

The social environment includes such diverse forces as changing values, education, religion, labor union activities, and the customs and habits of people. Here we will examine only values and criticisms of business.

Changing Values

Values are enduring beliefs that people hold about morals, equality, freedom, democracy, patriotism, and so on.* Values do not change easily, but over time they do. When values change, the impact is felt in the ways in which business, government, and society operate and in how they interrelate. For example, in the 1970s, there was an upsurge in public demand for environmental and consumer protections. These demands grew out of a rise in the values people held for a higher quality of life. There was a significant elevation, for example, in the values of a cleaner environment, higher-quality products, more equality in the workplace, safer products, and safer workplaces. The result was an unprecedented burst of federal legislation.

Over past centuries, some of the fundamental values associated with the BGS relationship have changed significantly, whereas others have changed surprisingly little. For example, public opinion polls clearly confirm that many values supporting the free enterprise system and the role of the business institution in society are still strongly held by most people. In contrast, it is also clear that more people are less willing than in the past to accept the unfettered operation of the free market mechanism and are demanding more and more government protection from its operation.

Following is a review of the current status of some of the underlying values held by people that relate most closely to the business system.

Individualism   Older beliefs associated with individualism centered on the freedom of the individual to pursue interests relatively unimpeded by government. Each individual, in this view, had an opportunity to achieve ends through his or her own efforts. Today, the older view of unrestrained individualism has been modified by concepts of equality, government protection of the individual against market forces, and more participation of individuals in organizations.

---

*There is no simple, generally accepted definition of the term *value*. One scholar of the subject observes that a value is a fundamental, relatively stable, prescriptive or proscriptive belief that a specific behavior or aim of existence is preferred to a different mode of behavior or aim (Rokeach, 1973). This belief is stronger and more stubbornly held than attitudes, fads, or opinions. Values, thus, are general guides that people hold to make decisions and to appraise the results of actions taken by institutions (such as governments or business) and people. They are powerful motivators of people and institutions in society. Unfortunately, there is no consensus about a classification of values (Baier and Rescher, 1969).

Laissez Faire   Throughout our history, a fundamental dogma of people in business, which has been accepted by an overwhelming majority of people, has been minimum government interference in the economic system. The term *laissez faire*, first used by the French, meant literally that government should "leave us alone." This old idea of limited government has been badly bruised in the current massive intrusions of government in the market mechanism. The classical freedom of people in business to operate in conformance with a comparatively unfettered open market mechanism is no longer a reality. The value is still strongly held, however, by many people, as we shall see in Chapter 8.

Property Rights   As a direct result of increased government regulations, but also because of changing legal decisions reflecting new societal values, the rights of property owners have undergone considerable changes. Although entrepreneurs of very small businesses still enjoy considerable autonomy in their use of company assets, managers of the larger companies know full well that they are administrators of private property invested with a heavy public interest. The public is increasingly concerned about how larger companies operate. This concern is reflected not only in government mandate about how property will be used, but also in voluntary allocations of resources by managers, which reflect public as distinct from private interest. For example, managers today are well aware of the necessity to use company property in such a way as to reduce pollution of the atmosphere.

Profit   The old view of profit as the sole end of business is no longer accepted. Profit is still considered necessary by a majority, but attitudes about profit are changing. Society is coming more and more to expect that societal interest be considered as well as business self-interest in pursuing profit objectives. Business managers, especially in larger corporations, take the view today that concern for the interests of the dominant socio-political stakeholders in their companies is the best route to expanding profits for shareholders.

The Protestant Ethic   A central feature of the older concept of individualism was the so-called Protestant Ethic, which placed a high value on hard work, delayed gratification, thrift, loyalty, and obedience to authority. This ethic is being considerably modified by the attitudes of managers and other workers in enterprises. To oversimplify, today's workers place less value on hard work for its own sake. They want, generally, more meaningful jobs, greater satisfaction on the job, and opportunities for advancement. In contrast to the notion of delayed gratification, emphasis today is placed on achieving satisfaction, and this generally means, among other things, going into debt. The questioning of authority has replaced the former blind acceptance of authority. Loyalty to company has eroded in light of a widening acceptance of the view that any employee caught in a conflict between the company and the public interest should resolve it in favor of the latter.

Technology   Traditional values generally accepted the view that technological advancement was in the best interest of society. Today technological assessments are requested of business and government before new developments can be launched. Technological advance is still a high value in society, but restraints are placed upon it that were not accepted in the past.

Materialism   The striving of individuals to increase their possession and use of material goods and services has been a powerful motivator of business. Materialism has been a prime influence in our passion for productivity, efficiency, the spirit of competition, innovation, and growth which, in turn, contributed to the extraordinary rise of Gross National Product that has been recorded since our nation's birth.

The motivation to acquire more material goods and services is still strong but is tempered by the desire for leisure, for a satisfying job even though it may pay a bit less than a stressful job, and for adventures that yield a more satisfying life. This desire does not mean subtraction from material accumulation goals, but addition to them.

Equality   Alexis de Tocqueville, the insightful nineteenth-century French observer of our society, saw equality as the dominant value in American society. Closely related to individualism, equality traditionally meant the elimination of inequalities among people with respect to opportunities for social, political, and economic growth. It meant that conditions should permit individuals, whatever their origins (although in the nineteenth century color was considered to be a question of another order and women were not in reality in the same position as men), to make a life on the basis of ability and character. It was the idea that everyone should have "an equal place at the starting line."

In recent years, the concept of equality has broadened to include rights to receive a wide range of political, economic, and social demands. Professor Daniel Bell of Harvard University has called this the "revolution of rising entitlements" (1975). This has become a concept of equality of results, or an equal outcome for all.

Changing Attitudes and Values Affecting Business

We believe that there is general agreement about the following subtle, but pronounced, shifts in the thinking of people about the functioning of business. Consider how such shifts in attitudes and values change not only the internal functioning of a company but how the firm relates to government and society generally, for example:

From considerations of quantity ("more") toward considerations of quality ("better")

From profligate use of resources to conservation

From the concept of independence toward the concept of interdependence (of nations, institutions, individuals, all species)

From mastery over nature toward living in harmony with it

From the primacy of technical efficiency toward considerations of social justice and equity

From the dictates of organizational convenience toward the aspirations of self-development in an organization's members

From authoritarianism and dogmatism toward participation

From uniformity and centralization toward diversity and pluralism

From the concept of work as hard, unavoidable, and a duty toward the recognition of leisure as valid in its own right

Criticisms of Business

Criticism of business is an important environmental force for business. In the public mind, there is a wide gap between inflated demands it has made on business and the extent to which it perceives that business has or should respond to them. For this and many other reasons, public criticism of business, which rose to strident levels in the 1960s and 1970s, has continued to be a significant factor in the 1980s. Throughout the current decade, most measures of public confidence in business and its performance have remained stable but at low levels where measures of social performance are concerned.

There is nothing wrong with criticism per se. When levied with good reason, it can be effective in improving business performance. Excessive and ill-founded criticism of business, however, can have an adverse impact on the operation of individual businesses because it can lead to excessive government regulation. In this way, it can erode the foundations of the business institution.

Public attitudes toward business are not completely negative. For example, communities throughout the nation are courting business favor through such mechanisms as tax concessions, guaranteeing loans, providing cheap or free land, building access roads to plants, and providing retraining programs for workers. The reason, of course, is to get jobs for unemployed workers in the community.

There is significant ambivalence in society about business. For some reasons, business is roundly criticized; for other reasons, it is applauded and courted. Altogether it is very important for business to understand and respond properly to public attitudes.

OTHER EXTERNAL ENVIRONMENTS

It should be noted that there are many other business environments that can have strong influence on business. For instance, the growth and influence of universities are not only a source of challenge to business values but also a source of new skills. Changing rates of population fertility will have a continuing impact on business. The concentration of unskilled, poor, and uneducated people in urban centers is complicating city governance and, in turn, raising demands for business aid. It also erodes the environment in which business is done. Wars and the threat of wars produce a wide range of impacts on business. As noted in Chapter 1, the future environments of business have an impact on today's business. Alvin Toffler (1970) popularized the term "future shock" to describe the psychological impact of current and accelerating changes on people. He elaborated on this theme in a subsequent book (1980). Naisbitt, in his *Megatrends* (1982), expands on the same subject. All three books set forth in detail how anticipated changes affect today's thinking, decision making, and other aspects of life. The core of effective strategic planning, whether formal or informal, in companies is, of course, perception of relevant forces in future environments.

THE INTERNAL ENVIRONMENT

The internal environment is not as extensive as the external environment, but it plays a cardinal role in the operation of a business. The impact of the internal environment on the management of a business is much different from that of the external environment. Whereas the external environment offers opportunities for and poses threats to the production and distribution functions, and through them, to profits and company vitality, the internal environment has more effect on how resources are organized and managed internally.

The internal environment can be described in several ways. One is to view it as being coterminous with the company culture, the general nature of which was noted previously. Another approach is to identify the main classes of people in an organization. This approach is shown in Exhibit 2-3. Each of the groups in

EXHIBIT 2–3 INTERNAL BUSINESS ENVIRONMENT

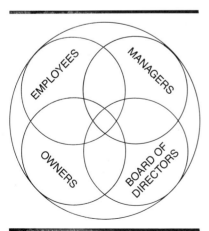

the chart has different goals, beliefs, needs, and so on, which managers must coordinate to achieve overall company goals. The fundamental characteristics of the groups shown in the chart are readily known and need no further elaboration here. Later in the book, we will intensively examine the changing internal life of organizations.

BUSINESS'S IMPACT ON ITS ENVIRONMENTS

We have emphasized that business has both direct and indirect influence over virtually every important facet of this society. Its introduction of technology into society brings in its wake changes in values, which in turn affect what society believes and does. Because of its dominant role in society, there is a tendency for business values to be accepted. Being on time, for instance, is a business value that is also applied in nonwork situations. Rising affluence brings the occasion for changing social priorities. When a company decides to move from one community to another, its influence in these areas can be extraordinary.

The influence of business over its environments can be derivative and indirect or purposeful, as when business seeks to influence directly its environment. The activities of corporate political action committees (PACs), for example, have the avowed purpose in many instances of helping to elect politicians with a conservative, business point of view. The Business Roundtable, a group of chief executive officers of the largest corporations in the United States, has a purpose, among others, to promote legislation in the Congress that helps business. The Allegheny Conference on Community Development is a group of business people that initiated programs to clean up and develop the downtown area of Pittsburgh. These activities represent successful exercises of business power over its environment. But on other occasions, business power has been negligible. For example, when tax reform legislation was passed in 1986, it was passed over the "dead bodies" of legions of business lobbyists. They sought special favors for oil, real estate, mining, textiles, and so on and lost heavily, even though some concessions were gained.

IMPLICATIONS FOR BUSINESS AND THE BUSINESS INSTITUTION

All of these observations have vast and profound implications for the management of business enterprises and the future of the business institution. Currently, the management of business enterprises is significantly different from what it was ten to twenty years ago. Top managers of corporations spend a large part of their time today dealing with environmental problems. These include addressing social concerns of society, complying with new social legislation, communicating with legislators and government executives about proposed laws and regulations, meeting with various interest groups concerning their demands and/or grievances, and administering their organizations in such a way as to respond to the new attitudes of people working there. This agenda is in sharp contrast to that of a top executive of a major corporation twenty years ago, whose decision making was based almost wholly on economic and technical considerations.

One of the questions the senior author put to chief executive officers (CEOs) of our largest companies in a series of interviews a few years ago concerned the amount of time they spent, in the course of performing their management tasks, on external affairs in contrast to the amount of time they devoted to traditional (internal) economic and technical matters relating to the operation of their companies (Steiner, 1983). We recognized, of course, the great difficulty in many instances of disentangling internal from external concerns. With this in mind, we found the range of time spent on external matters was from 25 to 50 percent, on the average, with an occasional high of 80 to 90 percent. For instance, a company that is seeking to locate a plant in a particular place, or is trying to acquire other companies, or is involved in special problems with regulatory agencies may find its CEO spending most of his or her time on these matters over weeks or months.

The CEOs interviewed by the senior author left no doubt about the fact that environmental forces were dramatically changing the managerial task of CEOs of our large corporations. The effects of environmental factors on the CEO, as well as on all other parts of the typical large firm, have brought about significant changes in the organizational structure and decision-making processes of large companies. The changes range from reorganization of the board of directors and decision-making processes at top management levels to all organizational structures in the company and all levels of management.

We conclude this discussion with a quotation from J. D. Ong, chairman of B. F. Goodrich, in an address at Purdue University. He observed:

> Right now, we are seeing the emergence of a number of trends that literally are transforming the industrial world. During such a period it is critical that managers understand more than the technical facets of their businesses. They need to have a vision of the larger world and their role in it.
>
> Simply put, we need people with a broad range of interests and knowledge. We need people who can spot, at an early stage, the economic, political and social trends that will affect their organization. And we need people who can then chart a proactive, rather than a reactive, course of action (1983).

CASE STUDY

ASBESTOS LITIGATION "BANKRUPTS" MANVILLE

It is said that when railways were first opened in Spain, peasants standing on the tracks were not unfrequently run over; and that the blame fell on the engine-drivers for not stopping: rural experiences having yielded no conception of the momentum of a large mass moving at a high velocity.

Herbert Spencer, The Man Versus the State *(1884: 28)*

On August 26, 1982, the Manville Corporation of Denver filed a voluntary petition to reorganize under Chapter 11 of the Bankruptcy Reform Act of 1978. Manville, like the rural peasants on train tracks, was caught dumbfounded by an unprecedented force in its environment—a surge of asbestos-related illness litigation. Manville's bankruptcy declaration is a response that some admired as creative and others criticized as irresponsible. Everyone was surprised. Here is what happened.

The Asbestos Litigation

When Manville filed for reorganization, it was financially sound. In 1981 it earned $60.3 million on sales of $2.2 billion and ranked 181st on the *Fortune* 500 list of industrials. In the first half of 1982, the company reported a loss of $25.1 million, due largely to a recession in the construction industry. Despite this loss, financial analysts were favorably impressed with Manville's low debt-to-equity ratio, and, under ordinary circumstances, the company would have had a sound future. Manville is the only company included in the Dow Jones industrial average ever to declare bankruptcy, and it is perhaps the healthiest ever to do so.

Manville's burden is an avalanche of lawsuits by victims of diseases caused by exposure to airborne asbestos particles. Most of the victims are workers who used asbestos materials supplied by Manville and other asbestos manufacturers.

The company argued that it could not pay future debts from anticipated claims in 16,500 existing asbestos injury lawsuits. These suits were being settled for an average $40,000 a claim; 500 new ones arose each month; and an independent study projected another 36,000 future claims for a total liability by the year 2000 of at least $2 billion and probably many times that amount. In addition, five large claims early in 1982 averaged punitive damage awards of $616,000 each—an unsettling augury. Punitive damages are awarded in excess of due compensation for injury to punish a corporation for flagrant misbehavior. Ordinarily, they are not covered by insurance. It became clear to a special committee of Manville directors, appointed to study the lawsuit problem, that Manville eventually could not pay all the claims against it.

Large awards arose, in part, because of two important changes in legal precedent. First, decisions in state courts in the early 1970s permitted injured asbestos workers to bring tort actions against asbestos suppliers. Earlier, workers could pursue wrongful injury claims only through state worker-compensation systems, where awards were far below the average for tort suits. Second, legal doctrines of product liability changed. Prior to the 1960s, the liability of manufacturers for their products was firmly grounded in the doctrine of negligent conduct. Under this doctrine a manufacturer had to be proven negligent or blameworthy in making or selling a product. The law, however, evolved toward the concept of strict liability, under which manufacturers could be found liable for harm to their consumers even if they were not intentionally or knowingly negligent or irresponsible. According to Section 402A of the "Restatement of the Law of Torts" published in 1965, a manufacturer could be held liable for selling a product "unreasonably dangerous" to a consumer even if no negligence in manufacturing the product was proven. "Unreasonably dangerous" is taken to mean that a product is more dangerous than would be assumed by an average user unless that user were warned otherwise.

As a result of the rise of strict liability as a legal doctrine, it became increasingly difficult for Manville to prevail in litigation. For example, in *Beshada et al. v. Johns-Manville Products Corporation et al.*, the New Jersey Supreme Court accepted the argument that Manville and other asbestos manufacturers could be held liable for asbestos injury even when it could not be proven that years ago they were aware of asbestos dangers. Symptoms of illnesses resulting from exposure to asbestos may not appear until 30 or 40 years after exposure. So in this and other cases, Manville had argued that scientific knowledge about asbestos hazards had not been sufficiently conclusive prior to the 1960s to require manufacturers to warn workers in industries where asbestos products were used. The court rejected this argument, stripping Manville of its primary defense.

These two changes in Manville's legal environment ensured rising settlement costs. In their wake, an entire industry developed to litigate asbestos cases, complete with its own publication, the biweekly *Asbestos Litigation Reporter*, and pressure groups such as the Asbestos Litigation Group (a coalition of 500 lawyers and thousands of plaintiffs suing Manville), the White Lung Association, and Asbestos Victims of America.

The growth curve in the number of lawsuits was astounding. The first against Manville came in 1968, and by 1973 there were only thirteen claims. By 1980, however, there were 5,000, and at the time of bankruptcy filing there were 16,500. In 1983, a total of 24,000 suits faced sixty manufacturers and suppliers; the long-term cost of this litigation was estimated to be $40 to $90 billion. New "rip out and replace" cases by school districts were also a growing concern as educators sued Manville for the cost of replacing asbestos materials in schools.

A Rand Corporation analysis of claims settled at the time of the bankruptcy filing showed that lawyers' fees were larger than awards to plaintiffs. For every dollar received by victims of asbestos illness, $1.71 went to lawyers' fees and legal expenses (*Rand Research Review,* 1983). This arrangement was widely regarded by observers as a flaw in the legal system and unfair to asbestos victims. But the victims' attorneys were securing for them much larger awards than would have been received under worker-compensation systems—even after deduction of lawyers' contingency fees. The charge was also made that the legal system would strain and perhaps topple under the increasing load of asbestos litigation. This might have happened had Manville attorneys milked delay from the system by procedural gambits and multiple appeals of unfavorable verdicts. After Manville's bankruptcy declaration stayed pending lawsuits, however, this problem did not arise. Defenders of U.S. trial courts believed that by consolidating cases and standardizing pretrial procedures the legal system was capable of handling the added caseload.

Adding to Manville's woes was the fact that its insurers refused to pay claims. Manville filed lawsuits against more than thirty insurers. Its current insurers resisted payment with the argument that, because of long latency periods common to asbestos diseases, the damage had been done in past years. Past insurers argued that coverage was invoked only by manifestation of symptoms, not by earlier exposure to injury. Manville countered with a "theory of continuous injury," under which insurers of all periods could be liable because both early exposure and later symptoms produce harm, entitling asbestos victims to compensation. In late 1986 Manville reached an out-of-court settlement with twenty-seven of its insurers for $730 million.

The Bankruptcy Proceedings

When a company files a bankruptcy petition, it asks a bankruptcy court judge for protection from creditors until a future date, when it presents a reorganization plan to pay debts. The reorganization plan must be approved by 50 percent of creditors representing two-thirds of the dollar amount owed. The term "Chapter 11" refers to a section of the Bankruptcy Reform Act of 1978 that consolidates all reorganization sections of prior bankruptcy laws.

In the past, a corporation could declare bankruptcy only if it was insolvent or unable to pay debts as they matured. In 1978, however, the insolvency provision was deleted from voluntary bankruptcy proceedings to relieve the courts of the burden of making financial calculations. Hence, while victimized by changing legal doctrines of product liability, Manville was helped by a change in the bankruptcy laws allowing a company that *may* become bankrupt to petition for reorganization, rather than permitting only companies that *are currently* insolvent to petition.

In a newspaper advertisement the day after Manville's reorganization filing, Manville's chief executive, John A. McKinney, stated:

> To avoid Chapter 11, we would have had to strangle the Company slowly, by deferring maintenance and postponing capital expenditures. We would also have had to cannibalize our good business just to keep going. If recent trends had continued we would have had to mortgage our plants and properties and new credit would be most difficult and expensive to obtain. This is no way to go forward.

The petition for reorganization had the effect of stopping regular payments on interest and principal to large creditors such as Morgan Guaranty Trust, Bank of America, Chemical Bank, Citibank, Republic National Bank, Continental Illinois National Bank, Wells Fargo Bank, and Prudential Insurance Co. It also put the thousands of impending asbestos lawsuits in limbo, as Manville's financial liability was in doubt. "Bold," said *Time* magazine (Kelly, 1982: 18). "Pretty creative," remarked a Harvard Law School bankruptcy professor (Work, 1983: 66). A *Fortune* magazine writer called the move "a particularly daring example of the new uses of bankruptcy" (Cifelli, 1983: 69). Others were less charitable. Manville was accused of "cold-hearted profit motives" and "murder" by a former asbestos worker, testifying at a House subcommittee hearing (Geipel, 1983). "Dubious and unusual at best," cried Senator Robert Dole (R-Kan.) in a next-day statement. "A shoddy effort to escape liability," said Representative George Miller (D-Calif.) (Sherwood, 1982). Both declared an interest in amending federal bankruptcy law to prevent similar abuse in the future.

Shortly after declaring bankruptcy, Manville began an advertising campaign emphasizing its financial health. One ad began: "Today, Manville can operate profitably using only half its productive capacity." Another said: "Manville's assets are a conspicuous strength." But the ads were soon stopped after complaints from the group of creditors and litigants with which Manville was negotiating its reorganization.

Shortly after seeking Chapter 11 protection, Manville also fought off legal challenges to the bankruptcy by asbestos victims. And between 1982 and 1986, a plan of reorganization was hammered out. This plan called for Manville to set up two settlement trusts in 1987 to pay claims and to fund the trusts with a mixture of bonds, cash, stock, and future profits. The first, the asbestos health trust, set up a fund of approximately $2.5 billion for payment of damage claims brought by present and future asbestos victims. Manville is scheduled to pay up to 20 percent of operating profits into this fund over a period of 22 years. The trust will start with 50 percent of the company's stock and could increase that share to as much as 80 percent if needed. The second trust, the property damage trust, is funded by $240 million in cash and insurance proceeds and will pay claims brought by the owners of asbestos-containing buildings. Both trusts are run by trustees who operate independently of Manville management. In addition, Manville set aside over $700 million to pay other creditors and established a $5 million charitable fund for asbestos victims who did not technically qualify for compensation but who were nevertheless deserving of financial help.

During the long bankruptcy period, Manville restructured itself, divesting all asbestos operations and consolidating three operating groups—a fiber glass group, which makes insulation and auto parts; a forest products group, which makes wine cooler cartons, grocery sacks, and folding cartons; and a specialty products group, which includes a variety of businesses from lighting fixtures to palladium mines. The loss of asbestos operations has hurt Manville's earnings, because asbestos was the most profitable of its many businesses. Manville has been continuously profitable throughout the bankruptcy (with the exception of 1982, when it was forced to set aside funds to pay lawsuits). Nevertheless, questions have been raised about its ability to sustain funding for the asbestos health trust fund. It will, however, be years before the consequences of this reorganization and settlement plan are fully evident. If Manville can become modestly profitable, it will continue as an organizational entity. There is now a much lower limit on its payout to asbestos victims than would have been the case under the pre–Chapter 11 torrent of unrestricted litigation. As a condition

THE MANVILLE RECOVERY PLAN

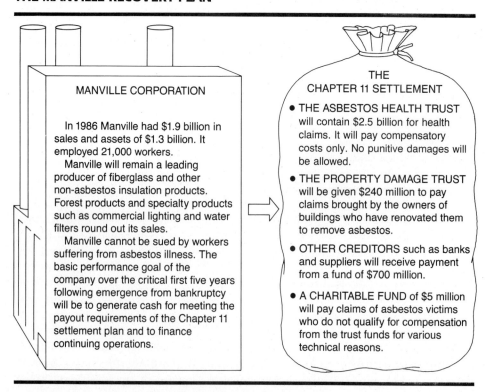

MANVILLE CORPORATION

In 1986 Manville had $1.9 billion in sales and assets of $1.3 billion. It employed 21,000 workers.

Manville will remain a leading producer of fiberglass and other non-asbestos insulation products. Forest products and specialty products such as commercial lighting and water filters round out its sales.

Manville cannot be sued by workers suffering from asbestos illness. The basic performance goal of the company over the critical first five years following emergence from bankruptcy will be to generate cash for meeting the payout requirements of the Chapter 11 settlement plan and to finance continuing operations.

THE CHAPTER 11 SETTLEMENT

• THE ASBESTOS HEALTH TRUST will contain $2.5 billion for health claims. It will pay compensatory costs only. No punitive damages will be allowed.

• THE PROPERTY DAMAGE TRUST will be given $240 million to pay claims brought by the owners of buildings who have renovated them to remove asbestos.

• OTHER CREDITORS such as banks and suppliers will receive payment from a fund of $700 million.

• A CHARITABLE FUND of $5 million will pay claims of asbestos victims who do not qualify for compensation from the trust funds for various technical reasons.

of emerging from the protection of Chapter 11, the company can no longer be sued by injured workers. And the end of lawsuits also brings with it the end of punitive damage awards.

Manville argues that the bankruptcy and reorganization was virtuous. A company publication, *1985 Corporate Profile,* said, "The reorganization plan enables tort claimants to receive equitable compensation; provides early, fair recoveries to other creditors; [and] preserves some equity values" (p. 7). But during the reorganization period, over 2,000 asbestos claimants died, their claims stalled by bickering in bankruptcy courts (C. Mitchell, 1986). A heart-rending letter from a prominent asbestos-illness researcher, Dr. Irving Selikoff, to the New York Times in 1985 underscored the human tragedy behind the Chapter 11 gambit.

Death and disease are not held in abeyance by legal writs. The victims are barred from applying for the financial help needed to ease their difficulties. Men are dying of mesothelioma [cancer of the lining of the chest or abdominal cavity] or lung cancer, unable to seek medical care to ease their last days, and others are not able to afford the medical surveillance that could save their lives. Still others, short of breath, with asbestos lung scarring and no longer able to make a living, can't keep their families together.

It is hard to appreciate the terror of a woman whose husband has been sent home from a hospital with a tracheostomy tube in his throat, unable to afford a nurse, resuscitating him at each emergency, until the final episode. Or widows—of shipyard workers, steam-locomotive repairmen, construction workers, power and utility plant personnel, and other craftsmen—having used slowly accumulated retirement dollars for the illness brought on by asbestos.

Some have written me that they come close to begging in the streets. Others get along by visiting the children in rotation. Often, when I write a widow for scientific information, the reply comes from a trailer park: the house sold. After a lifetime of hard work, to die and to have his widow live in penury is a bitter final reward for a worker (in Brodeur, 1985a: 59).

Asbestos and Worker Health Problems

Asbestos is a generic term for a family of naturally occurring fibrous minerals that have been put to human use for centuries. The first asbestos mine in North America was opened in Québec in 1879 to get at huge Canadian deposits. In 1901, the Johns-Manville Corporation was born of the merger of two independent companies that made asbestos and insulation products. Over the years, the company grew into the world's largest producer of asbestos products. Manville's demise, incidentally, would be an ironic echo of the death from chronic lung disease of Henry W. Johns, the nineteenth-century asbestos entrepreneur, who started one Manville forerunner, the H. W. Johns Manufacturing Company.

World asbestos production increased from 20,000 tons annually in 1916 to 4.3 million tons in 1978 (Epstein, 1979). In its heyday, asbestos had thousands of uses in industry and consumer products, and as an advanced industrial nation close to enormous Canadian deposits, the United States consumed about half of the world's processed asbestos. Asbestos has great value because its fibers are easily woven, do not burn, and conduct heat slowly. This makes it an ideal insulating and fireproofing material. Over the years, asbestos has brought many benefits to society. Many lives have been saved as a result of its fireproofing quality. The use of asbestos on brake linings has increased motor vehicle safety. And the use of asbestos in such products as paint and insulation has added comfort to modern living. No dollar value that can be balanced against the costs of health damage to workers has been placed on these overall benefits.

Harmful worker exposure occurs through inhalation of airborne asbestos particles. Once inhaled, the particles permanently attach themselves to lung tissue. Long-term exposure produces lung scarring, and an irreversible, chronic disease—asbestosis—progressively damages the lungs and makes breathing difficult. Asbestos exposure is also associated with lung cancer, gastrointestinal cancer, and mesothelioma.

Exposure to asbestos is extremely dangerous. Medical studies extending back at least fifty years demonstrate impairment of lung function, scarring of lung tissue, and increased risk of pulmonary neoplasia to be closely associated with heavy, prolonged exposure to asbestos. Indeed, it is a rare worker who survives to a ripe old age unimpaired after working for any length of time at a job where there is heavy exposure to airborne asbestos fiber. So dangerous is the fiber that asbestos illness has occurred repeatedly among family members of asbestos workers whose only exposure was the dust that came into the home on the worker's clothes at the end of the day.

After exposure, asbestos fibers remain in the lungs. They are sharp and tough and continue to produce scarring of the lung tissue that reduces the area available for exchange of gases and makes breathing difficult. Asbestos fibers also irritate bronchial cells, causing them to undergo morphological change and develop into cancerous, invasive cells. Because of the persistent presence of asbestos fibers in lung tissue, latency periods of up to forty years exist in asbestos-lung disease. Even after exposure to asbestos fibers ends, they continue to work their insidious task, until the disease becomes symptomatic years later.

It was not always known that asbestos endangered workers. The first evidence that business realized the dangers came in 1918, when some insurers in the United States and Canada refused to sell life insurance policies to asbestos workers. A number of early studies and accounts in the medical literature addressed a relationship between asbestos and asbestosis and lung cancer. A central issue in the asbestos-illness litigation against Manville and other asbestos manufacturers was whether managers at these companies knew about the dangers of asbestos and failed to warn and protect workers. It has been Manville's position that adequate knowledge of asbestos dangers was not present until 1964, with the publication of a major study of illness among asbestos workers. This assertion, that Manville was ignorant of the dangers until conclusive evidence was available in the 1960s, became known as the "state-of-the-art defense" in asbestos litigation, and all the other companies followed

Manville's lead as co-defendants in numerous suits with Manville. Manville's lawyers were well rehearsed in tactics and testimony buttressing this position, and when Manville declared bankruptcy, the other defendants missed its courtroom presence. Manville adheres to this defense to this day. For example, in Form 10-Q, filed with the Securities and Exchange Commission in September 1986, the company made the following statement.

> During periods of alleged injurious exposure, medical and scientific authorities, government officials and companies supplying products containing asbestos fiber believed that the dust levels for asbestos recommended by the United States Public Health Service did not constitute a hazard to the health of workers handling asbestos-containing insulation products. Accordingly, the Company has maintained that there was no basis for product warnings or special hazard controls until the 1964 publication of results of scientific studies linking pulmonary disease in asbestos insulation workers with asbestos exposure. Thereafter, appropriate warnings were given, including warning labels on packages, instruction booklets and seminars for insulation contractors (p. II–30).

The attorneys for asbestos victims sought to invalidate this "state-of-the-art defense" that was based on alleged ignorance. In taking depositions, information was uncovered that eroded Manville's position. One breakthrough was the testimony of Dr. Kenneth W. Smith, a former company doctor at one of Manville's Canadian asbestos plants. Smith reported, for example, that in the late 1940s, he had information that workers were getting sick and in 1949 sent a report to top officers showing that out of 708 workers whom he had X-rayed, only four had normal, healthy lungs. He further reported that he had withheld information from workers about their condition to avoid upsetting them and shortening their productive days with the company. Dr. Smith was able to document the fact that top company officers—including a future president of Manville—had seen his report, but did not act on it.

In another trial, attorneys for injured workers discovered that Raybestos-Manhattan, the largest U.S. manufacturer of asbestos-containing brake linings, had requested Metropolitan Life Insurance Co. to undertake health surveys of its workers and make recommendations about protecting their health in the 1920s. Metropolitan released a report in 1931 that demonstrated a high incidence of asbestosis among Raybestos-Manhattan workers and issued a strong warning about the health dangers of asbestos exposure. The report was discussed in 1933 at meetings of top officials of Manville and Raybestos-Manhattan, and those officials agreed to keep the information secret to avoid lawsuits. In 1977, an attorney for asbestos victims obtained copies of minutes of this meeting and was able to document for the first time a conspiracy among major asbestos manufacturers to hide evidence of health dangers to workers. The minutes of the 1933 meeting and other documents had been kept in a Raybestos-Manhattan vault for the intervening years, while Manville had destroyed its copies (Brodeur, 1985b). The discovery of this kind of information made it increasingly difficult for Manville to convince juries that its top officers were ignorant of asbestos dangers until 1964, led to record punitive damages, and ultimately forced the Chapter 11 declaration.

In the 1980s the dangers of asbestos are better known, and the demand for asbestos is falling. Canada is the largest producer of asbestos in the noncommunist world and supplies almost all asbestos used in the United States. Between 1979 and 1983, Canadian production declined 45 percent, due partly to recession in construction and partly to increased use of asbestos substitutes (Freeman, 1983). In late 1983 OSHA adopted an emergency health standard that permitted worker exposure only one-quarter as great as that permitted in the past. (The standard is currently being opposed in the courts by industry.) In 1984 the U.S. Environmental Protection Agency (EPA) proposed a ban on asbestos for many nonessential uses. For some uses, however, substitutes are not suitable. As an electrical insulator and component of corrosion-resistant pipe, it has no peer. And although auto manufacturers make more asbestos-free disc brakes now, millions of cars still depend on asbestos-lined drums. Canadian asbestos producers, fighting to save their industry, have undertaken a campaign to promote asbestos. They argue that for many uses, asbestos exposure hazards are low and health risks are minimal. But they have a tough job, and the worldwide market for asbestos has shrunk by two-thirds in the past decade mainly because of fear of health hazards.

The Broader Question: Compensating Victims of Exposure to Toxic Substances

Whatever else may be said of it, the Manville bankruptcy declaration invites society to develop a workable method of compensating victims of environmental exposure to toxic substances. The company believes that a fair compensation system would balance victims' rights to a speedy, appropriate award against the right of Manville's employees, stockholders, suppliers, and management to a continued livelihood.

State worker-compensation systems have been unable to provide victims with the sizable awards they frequently receive when they go to trial. These court awards, which have in the 1980s run into hundreds of thousands of dollars, have been attacked as an injustice by Manville and other companies. They argue that the awards grow out of strict liability trends that permit victories for asbestos victims even where negligence in the making and selling of asbestos cannot be proved. And they also believe that attorneys on both sides of the suits make the cost of compensating victims for their injuries exorbitant. If court awards had continued at the same rate as before bankruptcy declaration, Manville would not have been in existence to pay awards in the 1990s or later. It would have been broke, dismembered by asset liquidation, and unable to continue payouts to victims even at low levels.

Attorneys for the asbestos victims, in contrast, see the huge awards against Manville as a victory for the angels. The contingency fee, they say, allows poor asbestos victims to be represented by good lawyers without having to pay huge legal costs in advance of monetary awards. Lawyers take on the cases in the hope of earning a percentage of the settlement. In addition, they argue that the huge punitive damage awards set a precedent that will make other companies handling other toxic substances especially careful of health hazards. If Manville is allowed to avoid punitive damages, they say, it may become possible for future corporate miscreants to cause cancer in the population and waltz away from harsh penalties by using bankruptcy as a business strategy and paying small claims to the doomed through an administered system.

Since bankruptcy, Manville has advocated innovative strategies for compensating asbestos victims. It has generated and supported at least six bills in Congress designed to set up compensation systems in which asbestos workers' medical claims could be paid at lower cost and with the participation of other parties such as the federal government and the tobacco companies (because asbestos workers who smoke have a much higher risk of pulmonary illness). The company also has supported legislation to limit punitive damage awards in product liability cases and to reverse the trend in the law toward strict liability.

The compensation procedure developed for asbestos victims may establish a precedent for compensating victims of environmental exposure to other toxic substances. Hence, its importance extends beyond the current situation.

Questions

1. Did Manville make responsible use of the bankruptcy laws?
2. Is the Manville reorganization and settlement plan fair to all parties? Which plan is better for compensating asbestos victims: large court awards and settlements or the type of trust fund set up during Manville's reorganization? Should other parties involved in asbestos injury, such as the federal government (as a regulator of worker safety and employer of shipyard workers), labor unions, insurers, tobacco companies, and others, share liability to some degree with asbestos manufacturers?
3. Is current product liability law in need of reform to prevent huge punitive damage awards against the asbestos manufacturers?
4. Does Manville have an ethical right to continued existence? Is there a practical need for the company to stay in business?

CHAPTER 3

CORPORATE POWER AND LEGITIMACY

Michigan, 1921. Gloom settled in the Detroit office suites of General Motors. Its share of the United States car and truck market had dropped from 17 percent in 1920 to 12 percent. At Ford's Dearborn offices, managers were jubilant; the company was running away with a 60 percent and rising market share (Sloan, 1963).

At this time, GM was a producer of middle- and high-priced cars. In its line-up of Chevrolet, Oldsmobile, Oakland, Scripps-Booth, Sheridan, Buick, and Cadillac, only Buick and Cadillac were profitable. Chevrolet was not competitive with Henry Ford's Model T, and General Motors had had to concede the low-price car market.

Then, in April, a special advisory committee was formed at GM under the leadership of Alfred P. Sloan, Jr. The committee recommended a new marketing policy. In simplified form, this policy was that GM would offer a hierarchy of cars, in successively higher price ranges, and that these cars would offer the best value when compared to competitors' models at similar prices.

Few business decisions have had the power of this one. Within five years, the GM line was trimmed to its modern product group of Chevrolet, Pontiac, Oldsmobile, Buick, and Cadillac. Henry Ford's Model T was soon outdated by closed chassis designs and his company reduced to distant second-place finishes for 60 years. GM became preeminent among American car manufacturers, and Alfred P. Sloan became a legendary marketing genius. The real brilliance of the decision, of course, lay in its social consequences. Generations of status-conscious Americans initially purchased cars in the low-price lines and then sought to display their career success by graduating to the higher-priced cars. The Cadillac became a cultural icon for prestige, its market assured.

In the 1970s and 1980s, the validity of GM's 1921 marketing inspiration has eroded due to foreign competition, the reactionary values of postwar generations, and gradual revision of the policy by GM itself. Nevertheless, it will always stand as a landmark in the exercise of corporate social power.

THE NATURE OF POWER

American corporations wield enormous power in many ways and on many occasions. To evaluate corporate power is difficult, because it cannot be precisely measured. In this chapter, we shall discuss corporate power from a variety of perspectives.

Fundamentally, power is the ability of an individual, group, or organization to manipulate the behavior of other individuals, groups, or organizations in intended directions. Power may be actual manipulation or a potential that can be used at will. The exercise of power takes place on a spectrum of force from harsh coercion at one extreme, through strong influence in the middle, to mild persuasion at the other extreme. There are many sources of power. They include wealth, knowledge, arms, religious sanctity, influence over public opinion, and social status.

In our society, there are some strongly held views about the existence and exercise of power. Traditionally, Americans distrust those who hold great power. In a 1985 Harris poll, for example, 56 percent of a nationwide sample agreed that "most people with power try to take advantage of people like yourself" (John, 1985). Power in America is unevenly distributed, as is natural in an industrial society where individual fortunes can freely sort out. But the American social contract philosophy has been that power resides in the ordinary citizen and is delegated to political, economic, and military leaders to act in the common interest. Popular thinking also embraces the concept that power is evil. This is expressed in Lord Acton's celebrated dictum that "power tends to corrupt and absolute power corrupts absolutely." As a result, few Americans profess to seek or admit to having any power. Corporate presidents, for instance, speak of themselves as being "employees" or "agents" of someone or a group having power over them. This self-effacing tendency is exemplified in the words of Henry Ford II:

> Power is never monopolized by a few people at the top. Important changes almost always occur in little steps as the result of the complex interaction of many people at many levels all pulling in somewhat different directions. Everyone who pulls has some influence on the outcome and some share of the power (1970:24).

Spheres of Business Power

There are six major spheres of business power:

Economic power is the ability of the holder to influence events, activities, and people by virtue of control over economic resources, particularly property. It is an ability to influence or determine price, quality, production, and distribution of goods and resources.

Social and cultural power is the ability to influence social activities, values, and systems. It is the ability to influence social institutions, such as the family, and cultural values, mores, customs, life styles, and habits.

Power over the individual affects individuals having direct relationships with a corporation (such as employees, stockholders, suppliers, and community members); affects the general characteristics of individuals; and affects concepts of individualism in society.

Technological power is the influence over the thrust, rate, characteristics, and consequences of technology.

Environmental power is the impact of a company's actions on the physical environment, as in air and water pollution, use of resources, and general community development.

Political power is the ability to influence public policies and laws.

These areas of power obviously are related. For instance, technological developments of corporations influence their own economic power as well as social and cultural values. An affirmative use of political power can, of course, increase a corporation's economic power. A coherent view of corporate power must encompass all six areas of power (Epstein, 1973).

THEORIES OF THE EXERCISE
OF BUSINESS POWER

Theories of the exercise of business power cross a spectrum. At one end is the view typified by Karl Marx, that unrestrained business power results in the exploitation of workers and lower social classes. At the other end of the spectrum are those who hold firmly to the view of Adam Smith, that business power, when unrestrained by government, results in a maximization of the common good. In between, of course, are a wide range of views. In this section, we discuss two views of concentrated business power as abusive: (1) the asset concentration theory, and (2) the power elite theory. Then we discuss the widely held pluralist view that emphasizes restraints on business power.

Concentration of Economic Power Leads to Abuse

The idea that concentration of economic power results in abuse traces its roots back to Populist-Progressive-New Deal attacks on big business. Its basic tenet is that economic power is in fact concentrated in the hands of a few wealthy individuals and the leaders of giant corporations. The insinuation is that this concentrated economic power is translated into influence over the social, cultural, and political life of the nation and that such influence is exercised in a way that is pernicious to the broad public interest.

Corporate critic Tom Hayden, for instance, argues that the imperial corporation has replaced the "economic democracy" that once flourished in American business life. He says:

> Oligopolies control 99 percent of the auto industry, 96 percent of aluminum, 92 percent of light bulbs, 93 percent of steam engines, 90 percent of breakfast foods. While there are two million private firms in America, real power rests in relatively few. The existing competitive sector of genuine entrepreneurs and farmers has little weight alongside the major corporate and financial entities. The early capitalism, in which large numbers of people owned property, in which consumers directly faced sellers, in which there was a kind of economic democracy, was replaced by an impersonal corporatism beyond the structural control of the consumer or voter (1982: 177–178).

Corporate Asset Concentration

The most frequent measure of the degree and extent of corporate economic power is asset concentration. The first creditable compilation of asset concentration data was made by Berle and Means in 1932. They concluded, after an exhaustive study, that the 200 largest nonfinancial corporations in the United States in 1929 (less than .07 percent of all nonfinancial corporations) controlled nearly 50 percent of all corporate wealth and 22 percent of the national wealth. By 1947, the ratio had fallen to 46 percent, and after 1963 it leveled off at 40 percent (Weston, 1981).

Although the concentration of assets in our largest nonfinancial corporations has remained relatively high and constant, their composition has changed dramatically. We have checked the 200 list used by Berle and Means and find that no more than 15 percent of the companies on their list for 1929 remain today. The largest company in 1929 was American Telephone & Telegraph Co. It still is dominant—number 7 on the *Fortune* 1986 listing of large companies—but has been forced to divest its regional telephone systems. The second largest in 1929 was United States Steel Corp. It has now become USX, a company moving away from the steel business.

The same sort of phenomenon exists with respect to concentration in specific industries. (This index is usually calculated by the ratio of sales of the largest companies to total sales in the industry.) Over a long period of time the amount of concentration in the most concentrated industries has remained relatively constant. However, there has been much change in the concentration of different industries as well as particular companies in those industries.

Analysts of asset concentration also point to the existence of "interest groups," or collections of corporations controlled by an entrepreneurial family or a powerful bank. In 1939, for example, Paul Sweezy identified eight such groups in American society as controlling 62 percent of the largest 250 corporations' assets (National Resources Committee, 1939). By the late 1970s, however, only four of these groups were identifiable, and those had shriveled in power—especially the Rockefeller group (Herman, 1981). Other interest groups are identified from time to time, but their significance remains obscure.

Undeniably, assets are highly concentrated in corporations, and the challenging question of who controls them is raised. When Berle and Means wrote *The Modern Corporation and Private Property* in 1932, many of the largest manufacturing and financial institutions were still controlled by the entrepreneurs who had created them or by their descendants. However, a gradual revolution that largely ended widespread family control was already in progress. As big corporations grew, new stock offerings diluted the equity of the founders and their families. Thus, the professional managers who ran the firms—and increasingly were the only ones who understood their complexities—assumed full control in company after company. Although stockholders could formally exercise control over these professional managers, in practice, ownership in giant companies was so fragmented among a multitude of shareholders, each holding a small minority of shares, that concerted action from this quarter to control management was as unlikely as a large oak tree shedding its leaves in a neat stack on the ground. In recent years, large institutional investors such as pension funds and mutual funds have come to own huge blocs of stock in top companies but do not attempt to control management decisions. They prefer instead to follow "the Wall Street rule" and to sell if confidence in management diminishes. Hence, the top management group that leads the largest corporations is in the catbird seat, seldom challenged by an owner or by stockholders. Their use of power is, therefore, closely scrutinized by scholars and social critics who ask: To whom or what are these managers responsible?

Comments on the Theory   Concentration of economic power certainly exists. But it is often difficult to show where and how power derived from asset concentration has been abused. Critics of asset concentration claim that one important manifestation of its *prima facie* evidence of power is that where it exists profits are excessive, prices are higher, and competition is stifled. Our antitrust policy has been based on this so-called *structural theory,* namely, that when the degree of concentration in an industry exceeds some specified number, the conduct, behavior, and performance of those holding this power can be predicted to be undesirable. That is prohibited by our antitrust laws and where present must be eliminated.

This structural theory has been conventional wisdom for almost 100 years, but a new antitrust orthodoxy challenges the structural theory. J. Fred Weston, an advocate of this new theory, concludes, "The empirical evidence is overwhelming that there does not exist valid support of the structural theory of antitrust. It has not been demonstrated that high concentration in an industry is associated with the unfavorable economic performance in any dimension" (Weston and Granfield, 1982: 182–183). This is the so-called *performance theory* which, as Weston notes, has been validated by voluminous empirical data. These two theories are discussed in more detail in Chapter 7.

The conclusions of the performance theory school demonstrate that the fact of possession of power does not prove abuse of power, at least in the economic realm. Certainly there is potential for the abuse of power in the concentration of assets. But the question of the use or restraint of corporate economic power as related to the public interest is complex. Concentrated power is not synonymous with either good or evil intent.

Power Elite Theory

A variant of the abuse-of-power argument is that there exists a small elite of wealthy individuals who, by virtue of their control over economic institutions, constitute a power elite. Those who believe this argue that the concentrated power of wealthy, entrepreneurial families such as the Rockefellers, Mellons, Fords, and du Ponts is combined with the influence of the managers of the largest professionally managed corporations, top politicians, and top leaders in other walks of life to control the nation. The public believes in the existence of an elite. In a nationwide Harris poll conducted in 1984, 74 percent believed that there was "a group of powerful people who really run things in this country" (John, 1984: 38).

The modern impetus for this theory came from the late sociologist C. Wright Mills, who wrote in 1956 of a "power elite" in American society. "Insofar as national events are decided," wrote Mills, "the power elite are those who decide them" (1956: 18). Mills described the American social structure as a single power pyramid. At the top is a small group of the economic-military elite. A second level of power immediately below consists of the lieutenants of the power elite, including politicians and professional corporate managers. The remainder of the pyramid is the large base, which is composed of an undifferentiated mass of powerless citizens.

Shortly after Mills wrote *The Power Elite,* another sociologist, Floyd Hunter, estimated the size of the top elite to be "between one and two hundred men" (1959: 176). More recently, political scientist Thomas R. Dye (1979) studied the exercise of power by a "national institutional elite" of 5,416 individuals in positions to control half of all industrial and financial assets, nearly half of the assets of private foundations and universities, the television networks, news services, leading newspapers, cultural organizations, and the various branches of government.

A perennial student of elites, Professor G. William Domhoff, has written for over twenty years of a dominant managerial class in American society that perpetuates itself in power through social mechanisms, including inheritance of

wealth, attendance at private schools, intermarriage, family offices, and government service. In a recent work, *Who Rules America Now? A View for the 80s,*
Domhoff argues:

> There is a social upper class in the United States that is a ruling class by virtue of its
> dominant role in the economy and government. . . . This ruling class is socially
> cohesive, has its basis in the large corporations and banks, plays a major role in
> shaping the social and political climate, and dominates the federal government
> through a variety of organizations and methods (1983: 1).

Incontrovertibly, America always has had a wealthy upper class. Examination
of tax records shows that in 1771 the richest 1 percent of Bostonians accounted
for 44 percent of personal wealth in the city (MacDougall, 1984). The post–Civil
War years in America were called the Gilded Age in reference to the ostentation
of a small upper class. Its members had great wealth and frequently traced their
backgrounds to the Pilgrims. As a group, they also had a set of unique norms
and customs. On New Year's Day, for example, society families prepared
delicacies such as codfish tongues in black butter and waited for other members
of society to come "calling." The time of day the caller appeared was critical, for
if an important member of rarefied society called very early, it indicated that
other, more important, calls were being saved for the prime midafternoon
hours. When Pierre Lorillard IV, the tobacco magnate, built Tuxedo Park in the
1890s on 600,000 acres north of New York City, the residents of the twenty-two
houses there, in the understated patois of the elite, called their twenty-five-room
palaces on five-acre plots "cottages" (Cable, 1984). The elite separated itself from
the common ruck in many other ways, by favoring sports like polo and yachting,
with vacations in Europe and at exclusive resorts, with the architecture of their
homes, and with elaborate parties where cigarettes were rolled in $100 bills and
ladies found gold bracelets as party favors when they opened their napkins.

Today, there is still a small elite of wealth in America. A recent government
study revealed that in 1983, 0.5 percent of households accounted for 37.1 percent
of the net personal worth of all American households. The study noted that
these "super-rich" had increased their concentration of wealth over the past
twenty years. In 1963, the top 0.5 percent of households controlled only 25.4
percent of net personal wealth (Gordon, 1986). This study has been criticized,
and probably overestimated the increase in concentration of wealth, because it
failed to include assets accruing to the lower and middle classes from pension
funds and Social Security benefits. Nevertheless, a steady stream of scholarly
studies, census reports, and other analyses of income over the years confirm the
existence of a small elite of personal wealth (Lundberg, 1968; Dye, 1986: 57;
Gordon, 1986). As in the past, these "super-rich" often adhere to a distinctive
pattern of living.

Scholars like Domhoff and others locate today's "social upper class" through
the Social Registers published for twelve American cities. Biographical information there reveals that many have attended such prestigious schools as Harvard,
Yale, and Princeton. Many also are members of exclusive private clubs, such as

the Links and Knickerbocker in New York, the California in Los Angeles, the Pacific Union in San Francisco, and the Somerset in Boston.

Members of the elite also attend exclusive private preparatory schools, such as Choate in Wallingford, Connecticut. Domhoff has compiled a list of such schools and considers a person to be a member of the upper class if he or she has attended one.

Those who attend these prep schools are nicknamed "preppies." Most prep schools are in the Northeast and are either secular or Episcopalian, the religious affiliation identified by sociologists as most common in the American upper class. In addition to providing a first-rate education, prep schools are said to inculcate upper-class mores, to begin lifelong upper-class social contacts, and to mix old aristocracy with new money (Gilbert and Kahl, 1982). Graduates of prep schools make their way to elite universities, particularly Ivy League schools and small exclusive private schools, such as Vassar College or Finch College.

One function of the marriage institution, to elite theorists, is to perpetuate upper-class cohesion. Although marriage may be a way for the upper class to infuse its ranks with new ability, members of the elite often intermarry. Prep schools and upper-class social functions such as debutante parties bring adolescents approaching marriage together. Debutante balls follow a centuries-old English tradition in which the upper class of England presented its daughters to the royal court. One study of marriages that were reported on the society pages of the New York *Times* found that 68 percent of brides or grooms were from families listed in the Social Register or had attended an exclusive prep school. Twenty-four percent of the marriages were between two such individuals (Blumberg and Paul, 1975).

Another device for concentrating wealth in the cream of the upper class, the families with great entrepreneurial fortunes, is the family office. The family office is a private organization set up by members of an extended family to manage family assets and financial affairs. Examples are T. Mellon & Sons, Rockefeller Family and Associates, and F. Weyerhaeuser and Company, family offices that manage the fortunes of the descendants of great businessmen. Family members allow the office to work their assets so that, rather than dissipating fortunes through inheritance, the sum is kept intact and leverage is gained. Family offices perform a variety of functions. F. Weyerhaeuser and Company, for example, employs thirty-one people in two offices in St. Paul and Tacoma and provides services that include "paying bills, determining the "best policy" for home, auto, and life insurance, filing tax returns, managing individual portfolios, helping in estate planning, making travel arrangements, and coordinating political and philanthropic giving" (Dunn, 1980:29). The Weyerhaeuser family convenes annually in Tacoma at a family meeting to discuss asset management and make financial decisions.

Finally, the elite of America are said to perpetuate their influence through government service, and there is much evidence that government service attracts wealthy executives and members of the upper class. One study of cabinet officers between 1897 and 1973 showed that 78 percent had been corporate officers or partners in corporate law firms, and 60 percent were listed in the Social Register (Mintz, 1975). A second study of cabinet officers, from the Kennedy cabinet in 1961 through Reagan's inaugural cabinet in 1981, showed that 60 percent came from business and corporate law firms (Gilbert and Kahl, 1982).

Interlocking Directorates   A device for further concentrating both economic power and social contacts among an economic elite is the interlocking directorate, in which directors of one or more corporations sit on the boards of other corporations. Basically, there are two types of director interlock. *Direct* interlock occurs when a director of one company sits on the board of a second company. *Indirect* interlock occurs when two companies that do not share a common director on their boards each have a director on the board of a third company. The fear of elite theorists is that directors who sit on more than one board necessarily have knowledge of the affairs of another company and that this creates a conflict of interest. Allegedly, a small group with multiple ties to giant corporations has inordinate control over commerce because of widespread interlocking.

Within the past twenty years, a number of studies have shown significant director interlock.

■ In 1969 a Federal Trade Commission study showed a total of 1,450 direct and indirect interlocks among the 200 largest industrial corporations (Blumberg, 1975). In the same year, another study, this one of the 250 largest industrials, showed that only seventeen were not significantly interlocked and that this level of interlock was greater than in the 1930s (Dooley, 1969).

■ A 1978 study by the Senate Governmental Affairs Committee of the 130 largest corporations—which controlled $1 trillion in assets, about one-fourth of all corporate holdings—showed 530 direct interlocks and 12,193 indirect interlocks. The study reported that each of the thirteen largest corporations reached an average of 70 percent of the 130 largest "through a total of 240 direct and 5,547 indirect interlocks" (Rowe, 1978).

■ A 1980 study of 797 large corporations showed 1,572 interlocks among 8,623 directors. The analysis showed that larger firms had more interlocks and that interlocking was positively related to several measures of profitability (Pennings, 1980: 66, 189).

Section 8 of the Clayton Act of 1914 prohibits interlocking directorates where two companies by virtue of their location, market, and size compete, and where the elimination of competition by agreement between them would constitute a violation of antitrust laws. These laws are difficult to enforce, but periodically directors resign when questions of conflict of interest are raised. In addition, there is an informal custom that directors should excuse themselves from the room when minor conflicts of interest arise. Regulatory enforcement is inconsistent. The Federal Trade Commission asked Edmund Littlefield, a director of both Chrysler and General Electric, to resign from one board or the other because both corporations manufactured air conditioners. But in *BankAmerica*

Corp. v. *U.S.* (1983), the Supreme Court allowed directors of BankAmerica and Crocker National Bank to remain on the boards of several life insurance companies that were in competition with banks for mortgage and real estate loans.

Is interlocking on company boards and in other leadership positions a method by which a small elite perpetuates its domination of national resources? Two recent studies shed light on this question.

First, Michael Useem (1984) examined the careers, intercorporate affiliations, and political activities of over 5,000 corporate directors and senior executives. He documented the existence of an "inner circle" of business leadership in America that included those who served on the boards of three or more major corporations. This inner circle constituted roughly 10 percent of all corporate directors. Not surprisingly, Useem demonstrated a strong association between membership on several boards and attendance at exclusive boarding schools, high family income, membership in exclusive social clubs, appointment to government advisory committees, and leadership in prestigious business associations, such as the Business Council and the Business Roundtable. Useem believes that this inner circle is exceptionally influential in decisions at high levels of business, government, and civic life.

In a second, broader study Thomas R. Dye (1986) identified 7,314 top institutional positions in 12 different sectors of society. The individuals who occupy these positions, according to him, control half the nation's industrial and bank assets; control nearly half the assets of private foundations; dominate the media and cultural organizations; direct the branches of the federal government; and control the military establishment. The 7,314 positions are held by 5,778 individuals. About 15 percent of the top leaders are "interlockers" who hold one or more positions, and most interlocking occurs in the corporate sector. This means that the remaining 85 percent are "specialists" who occupy only one top institutional position. Like Useem, Dye notes the existence of a tiny inner elite whose members occupy 6 or more important institutional leadership roles. This inner elite is composed of only one-half of 1 percent of the individuals under study. But despite an impressive concentration of power in the hands of this small group, Dye concludes that the fragmentation of power over national resources into many hands is more significant than the concentration of control over some resources in the hands of a small number of "multiple interlockers." He observes:

> There is very little overlap among people at the top of the corporate, governmental, and military sectors of society. To the extent that high government officials are interlocked at all, it is with civic and cultural and educational institutions. It is *within* the corporate sector that interlocking is most prevalent. If there is a "coming together" of corporate, governmental, and military elites as C. Wright Mills contends, it does not appear to be by means of interlocking directorates (1986: 164).

An Evaluation of the Power Elite Model   The thesis that a small ruling class holds power in capitalist societies by virtue of its concentrated ownership of wealth has major weaknesses. First, statistical presentations of the number of corporate directors in the Social Register, director interlocks, concentration of assets, and similar phenomena do not themselves demonstrate either the real exercise of power or the negative public consequences of the condition they portray. It is correct that a small percentage of corporations controls disproportionate assets, but this fact does not, by itself, lead to the conclusion that such a state of affairs is grave. And even if members of an upper social stratum do occupy many positions of institutional power, it cannot be numerically proved that their decisions are bad for the public.

Second, there are many formal and informal restraints on the "power elite" or "governing class." The Constitution, laws, government regulation, and the court system are formal restraints. In addition, informal checks and balances set limits to the exercise of money power; educational and religious institutions train Americans in traditional ideals; pressure groups and public opinion counter wealthy interests; and environmental, civil rights, and consumer interests have forced large corporations to adopt respect for community as a major goal. Unlike in some European, Asian, and African countries, there has never been a tradition of deference toward elites in this country. Much public suspicion of wealth exists.

Competition and technological change have had impacts on the marketplace largely beyond anyone's control. The fates have not respected large size more than small and have bankrupted giants as well as pygmies. For example, out of the 100 largest corporations in 1909, only thirty-six survived on the list until 1948. Between 1948 and 1968, only sixty-five of the top 100 companies continued to hold their rankings (Jacoby, 1973). Today the winnowing continues. The first of the well-known *Fortune* 500 lists was published in 1955, but by 1986 only 187 of the original 500 companies remained on it. Although mergers and acquisitions have deleted some names, most of the disappearances were caused by weak performance (Shanklin, 1986).

In a moment of certitude, Professor Domhoff has written, "Corporate leaders can invest money where and when they choose; expand, close, or move their factories and offices at a moment's notice; and hire, promote, and fire employees as they see fit" (1983: 77). In a large corporation subject to market discipline, labor agreements, and federal antidiscrimination laws, perhaps no statement could be further from reality.

We note also that there is considerable disagreement and infighting in the business community. When the Reagan administration proposed weakening affirmative action laws in 1985, the U.S. Chamber of Commerce supported the move while the National Association of Manufacturers opposed it. When the landmark tax reform legislation of 1986 was being considered, the business community was deeply divided, with industries such as timber, oil and natural gas, banking, and real estate opposing a lower overall corporate tax rate and others, such as wholesalers, retailers, truckers, and grocery manufacturers, in favor. Because of their relative tax positions, General Motors and IBM favored the idea of lower tax rates and a broader corporate tax base, whereas Inland Steel Company, Ford Motor Company, and Goodyear Tire & Rubber Company opposed the idea.

In defense of the elitist model, it has been argued by historians Will and Ariel Durant that throughout recorded history, the concentration of wealth in the hands of a disproportionately small number has been inevitable (1968). In the days when humans were hunter-gatherers, stratification theorists believe that a state of equality existed. When game was hunted and prepared by small bands, the fruits of this labor were widely and equally shared. After the emergence of agricultural civilization, however, material inequality greatly increased, as small elites of wealthy landowners emerged to dominate society. At this stage in the development of human civilization, class inequalities were greatest; the awesome gap between the rich aristocracy and the impoverished bulk of citizenry in the Roman Empire is an example. Mature industrial societies such as the United States are marked by less inequality than agricultural civilizations because the elite that controls productive assets must share rewards with a large class of technically knowledgeable workers, because population growth declines, and because of the development of egalitarian ideologies (Kerbo, 1983).

Human inequality, although inescapable, requires continuous justification. Those at the bottom must somehow be convinced that their lot is fair, natural, or proper. How does the business elite in American society accomplish this? In our society, the palliative is that elites are checked by law and opinion, that high positions are open to the hard-working based on the merit of their achievement, and that much power resides in the common person and is only delegated to ruling institutions. These concepts have proved serviceable in justifying the existence of a privileged, potent upper class. In an influential book, *Wealth and Poverty* (1981) conservative economist George Gilder makes a more subtle rationalization for an economic elite. He asserts that the function of the rich in American society should be to accept risk and invest money in projects that create opportunities for the classes below them. The reward for accepting this risk is greater wealth, from which all classes benefit. Gilder is critical of the welfare state for syphoning off money from the wealthy and big business and using it inefficiently to subsidize the poor when that money instead could be used to create new wealth for society. To Gilder, an elite of wealth and power clearly can play an important, positive role in society.

Pluralist Theory

A counterpoint theory to asset concentration and power elite theory is that pluralism restrains business power. A pluralistic society is one that has many semiautonomous and autonomous groups through which power is diffused. No one group has overwhelming power over all others, and each has direct or indirect impact on all the others. The existence of power in many decentralized groups makes less possible the tyranny of a majority over a minority.

American pluralism is based on several historical factors. The first is the freedom of individuals to join associations, express desires, and seek fulfillment of interests. This freedom has been regarded as essential by Americans, for we are, as Tocqueville observed, "a nation of joiners." This right encourages the growth of new associations to meet new needs of society and individuals.

Second, our Constitution, which diffuses political power through many jurisdictions and branches of government, has given rise to an open system in which groups make their influence felt in many places. Groups shut out from one level or branch of government make their interests known elsewhere. After World War II, for instance, civil rights interests were *personae non gratae* in the legislatures of southern states and in a Congress where elderly southern committee chairmen dominated policy making. Civil rights leaders such as Thurgood Marshall turned, therefore, to the courts and won a series of decisions in state courts favorable to blacks. They also won a number of landmark Supreme Court decisions, including *Shelly v. Kramer* and *McGhee v. Sipes,* the two 1948 cases which struck down restrictive covenants in deeds, and the famous *Brown* school desegregation case in 1952.

Third, the heterogeneity of American peoples and interests has nurtured pluralism. Major native and immigrant groups press for their aspirations. Economic interest groups, including labor, business, agriculture, and consumer groups, are a permanent fixture of politics. And a rainbow of voluntary associations (whose size, permanence, and influence vary) compete in governments at all levels.

Pluralism is not found in all political systems. It was an alien concept in Rome, throughout the medieval world, and under early mercantilism. It was in the medieval world that widespread attacks on authority gave rise to the concept, but it was not until the end of the eighteenth century that the idea was made workable in practice. Pluralism and political democracy are handmaidens. If democracy is to survive, diffusion of power among groups must exist and be guarded.

A pluralistic society imposes immediate, close boundaries on the discretionary exercise of business power. Wise managers anticipate that their power often will be restricted, blunted, challenged, or shared by others. In general, there are four boundaries on managerial power.

1. *Governments* at all levels and in all countries regulate business activity. Although Dow Chemical Co. once considered buying a deserted island, which was not part of any sovereign nation (we are not sure how serious the consideration was), it decided that freedom from taxation, regulations, and political interference ultimately was an illusion.

2. *Social interest groups* form a shifting, kaleidoscopic mirror of power trends in society and restrain business through an array of methods such as picketing, product boycotts, and lobbying for restrictive legislation. Prominent in this century have been labor, environmental, civil rights, religious, consumer, and public interest groups.

3. *Social values* are expressed in civil and criminal law, public opinion, literature, the press, and television. They also are internalized by managers in the education process in schools, churches, training programs, and life experience. Social values include religious, philosophical, and ethical norms, which define imperatives such as duty, justice, taste, manners, and piety.

4. *Economic stakeholders* include stockholders, employees, competitors (represented by market forces), suppliers, and communities where a corporation

has significant presence. A range of actions is open to these groups when corporate power is exercised by management in a way that jeopardizes their economic interests.

Because of the existence of these four boundaries in a pluralistic society, any exercise of business power that affects many interests will elicit countervailing pressures and restrictions from many quarters. Observe that in critical areas such as pollution, minority hiring, and consumer product safety, the discretion of managers is hemmed in by all four of these power boundaries. A decision with little societal impact will, however, create few counterpressures. Chances are good that management can unilaterally decide what color to paint the buildings at a plumbing fixture plant. Exhibit 3-1 illustrates the existence and operation of boundaries on managerial discretion. Just as in the solar system the planets move freely within but cannot escape their gravitational fields, so, too, major corporations in American society remain in orbits determined by the powers of plural interests. The pluralist argument poses a direct challenge to those who decry economic concentration and to elite theorists. If it is correct, no matter how power is concentrated and irrespective of the existence of a plutocracy, corporate power cannot for long abuse the public interest. A pluralistic society simply does not permit sustained irresponsibility.

FIGURE 3–1   BOUNDARIES OF MANAGERIAL POWER

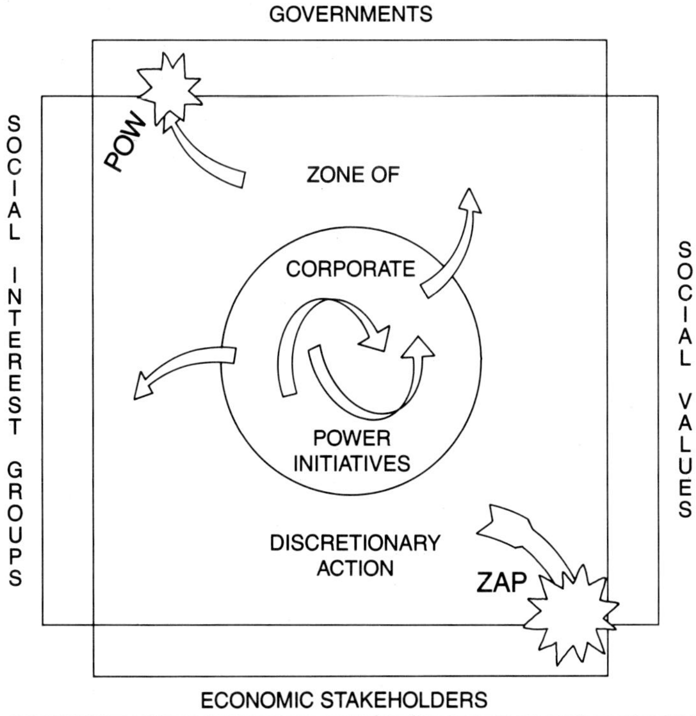

How Pluralism Shapes the Political Process   The pluralist structure of American society has significant implications for the exercise of power in the policy process, implications that contradict the charges of elite theorists. We may best examine the policy process in terms of interest-group theories that view public policy as a result of the exercise of shared power among a number of competing groups.

Early in American history, James Madison gave voice to the theory that there should be checks and balances on interest-group behavior so that a rough and healthy balance would be maintained. Madison, who had attended the Constitutional Convention in Philadelphia in 1787, wrote in *The Federalist* (a series of short articles in the newspapers of New York City beginning in that year) of the evils of "faction." He defined a faction as "a number of citizens, whether amounting to a majority or minority of the whole, who are united and actuated by some common impulse of passion, or of interest, adverse to the rights of other citizens, or to the permanent and aggregate interests of the community" (Rossiter, 1961: 78).

This definition clearly shows Madison's hostility to such groups, but he and the other members of the convention also recognized their inevitability. The Constitution itself reflects the ambivalence of the founders toward factions by, on the one hand, limiting the powers of groups through checks and balances, but, on the other hand, ensuring their formation by the freedoms granted in the Bill of Rights. In that the evils of faction could not be removed, they were to be controlled. The main device for controlling faction and selfish group behavior, however, was not negative restraint in the Constitution, but the creation of a republican government, one in which representatives of the people make policy for them.

This raises an interesting question: Is the United States government a democratic government? Literally, the answer to this question is no. A direct democracy would resemble an old New England town meeting, where all citizens expressed themselves, voted on an equal basis, and decided policy matters by majority vote. A republican government, or indirect democracy such as ours, gives citizens the right to elect a smaller number of delegates who make policy for the rest.

Madison and the other framers felt that direct democracy was not a form of government suitable for maintaining human rights. Sooner or later a majority faction would tyrannize over a minority. "Historically," wrote Madison in the famous Federalist No. 10, "democracies have ever been spectacles of turbulence and contention . . . incompatible with personal security." Our representative government was designed to prevent this unsatisfactory situation by electing some of the wisest citizens to refine public views in the making of policy. Representation also would fragment factions, lower the danger of majority tyranny, and increase the possibility of a rough balance of group pressures. This was so because a stable republic could successfully extend over a larger population than could a chaotic, pure democracy. In a famous passage, Madison eloquently stated the significance of this:

The smaller the society, the fewer probably will be the distinct parties and interests composing it. . . . Extend the sphere and you take in a greater variety of parties and interests; you make it less probable that a majority of the whole will have a common motive to invade the rights of other citizens; or if such a common motive exists, it will be more difficult for all who feel it to discover their own strength and to act in unison with each other (Rossiter, 1961: 83).

The Madisonian *theory of factional balance* is an early theory that postulates a pluralistic political arena of shared powers in which groups compete in rough balance. This philosophy of controlling the excesses of selfish interest while at the same time ensuring free expression is deeply rooted in American political culture. The "public interest" is to be protected by splintering power.

An elaboration of Madison's theory, obscurely dubbed the *rule of concurrent majority*, was suggested by Senator John C. Calhoun of South Carolina shortly before his death in 1850. Calhoun proposed to give each vital sectional or interest group in society veto power over major policies and laws that affected them. Thus, a "concurrent majority," or the unanimous agreement of all major groups, was necessary to implement basic new policies.

Calhoun's theory, contained in *A Disquisition on Government* (1852), is extraconstitutional, but his basic principle of an effective veto over political decisions by major economic, religious, sectional, and ethnic interest blocs is a highly accurate reflection of the working of American government. Indeed, our political institutions—such as Congress and the national nominating conventions—are molded to facilitate compromise among clashing groups. In Congress, for example, the committee system provides a point of access for competing interests away from the limelight of floor debate. It is in committee rooms that group compromises are worked out. The president's cabinet reflects different parties, sections, and religious and ethnic backgrounds. And the two-party system is ideally suited to campaigns with vague platforms that accommodate many interests, because without wide appeal, candidates cannot secure the 51 percent vote needed for election in the common two-candidate race. Calhoun's theory represents an elaboration of Madison's, bringing the latter's closer to current reality (Drucker, 1968).

Early in the twentieth century a new *group process theory* emerged to explain the role of interest groups in politics. Previous theories analyzed laws and government institutions that checked and channeled groups. As first articulated by sociologist Arthur Bentley, the group process theory assumed that groups were the fundamental units of all political activity and that government merely registered demands and reflected group pressures in various compromise policies. According to Bentley, "the balance of the group pressures *is* the existing state of society" (1908: 182). Programs and policies are continuously modified as relations among groups change. Such changes are incremental, and policy solutions are never final. The public interest emerges predominant over the specialized interest, the dynamics of the group process providing their own internalized checks, which prevent the tyranny of one set of interests over another. The difference between this theory and earlier ones is that it deemphasized the role of government institutions and legal structures. This view met with great favor among political scientists, and for years the group process was viewed as beneficial and harmoniously balanced.

Some observers see a profusion of interest groups draining the vitality of the business institution. Mancur Olson, in *The Rise and Decline of Nations* (1982), develops the thesis that the longer societies are politically stable, the more numerous groups become. And the more groups develop and achieve their objectives, the more they promote their members' well-being to the detriment of economic efficiency. Union wage demands and government regulatory programs, for example, increase production costs even as they increase the welfare of particular groups in society. Group success, says Olson, undermines economic success.

The growth of political power among many groups is an uncontested fact. David Vogel writes:

> American politics has become more pluralist in the sense that a far greater number of political interests now have more effective political representation than in the past: consumers, environmentalists, various ethnic and racial minorities, the handicapped, women, the aged, gays—all have seen a significant ability to participate in the political processes (1980: 49).

Business may combat these groups and win temporary victories, but as Joseph W. McGuire suggests, "the history of American business can be traced in terms of the redistribution of organizational satisfactions away from owners and to other groups" (1981: 3).

BUSINESS LEGITIMACY

Legitimacy refers to the rightful possession of power. Over the ages, legitimacy has been conferred by many doctrines. In primitive times, supreme power was often a matter of de facto brute force. In monarchies, the "divine right of kings" legitimated the rule of families presumed to have descended from a deity. Among certain African tribes, as soon as an old king grew ill, his successor clubbed him to death and received his departing soul. The new ruler got legitimacy from this presumed transmigration (Frazier, 1922). In representative democracies such as the United States, the legitimacy of elected officials' exercise of power stems from sanction by the majority and adherence to rules of government, as represented in the Constitution and prevailing popular opinion.

Fundamentally, the source of power conferred upon corporations has been the authority granted by society over the ownership of property. Society has accepted laws, beliefs, and customs associated with the exercise of power over possessed property. Today the grounds of legitimacy for corporate power are shifting. The impact of corporations on their social and physical environments has become too great for the exercise of managerial power to be justified by the legal right of property ownership alone. The conception of the marketplace as a sphere of activity where an impersonal mechanism would hold power accountable is a slim fiction for critics.

Yankelovich has argued that there are three basic types of legitimacy or underlying support for the business system and the exercise of power by corporate managers (Sommers, 1975). An examination of these three areas of support provides a conceptual underpinning upon which a more sophisticated understanding of business's legitimacy can be based. The first area of which Yankelovich speaks is *ideological* legitimacy, or support for the rules of the economic game. He indicates that there is widespread support for basic principles of capitalism, such as private property. The second is *functional* legitimacy, or support for the performance and products of business. Here again, most Americans seem to accept the performance levels of enterprise, although the consumer movement has raised levels of public criticism of business's output, and some ambivalence exists in the public mind. Third is *moral* legitimacy, or public trust and confidence in the motives and morality of managers. It is here that polls show the business community suffering. People have confidence in the fundamentals of the business system, but they lack assurance that these fundamentals are being observed for the public welfare. They support the profit system but perceive "profiteering" to be what is actually taking place.

Do concentration of assets and the existence of a business elite pose threats to business's legitimacy? Inevitably, the concentration of power arouses public suspicion. In the past, public suspicion has led to pressure for reform and government curbs on business power. Repetition of this circuit will be accelerated or slowed by the extent to which managers accommodate their exercise of power to current perceptions of the public welfare. Our pluralistic society will push them in that direction. The extent to which public perception of the use of that power matches societal consensus of what it ought to be will determine the degree of legitimacy supporting corporate operations.

SUMMARY

In this chapter we have examined two basic views about business power. One is that power is concentrated. Economic power is vested disproportionately in a few hundred large corporations, and its exercise is directed by an influential elite. We note the dangers inherent in the aggregation of power, but we conclude that even if such potency exists, it is not proved that it is exercised with evil intent. The theory of a pluralistic society suggests that business is encircled by multiple restraining forces. According to this theory, the antidote to concentrated power is counterbalancing power.

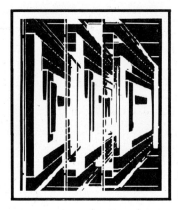

CASE STUDY

CONSTRUCTION OF THE CENTRAL PACIFIC

The term *robber baron* refers to a group of manipulative entrepreneurs who pursued controversial business careers between the Civil War and the early twentieth century. The best-known members of this semipiratical cohort include Andrew Carnegie, Jay Gould, J. P. Morgan, and John D. Rockefeller. These men, prominent in American history books, represent hundreds of others who together constituted a distinct element of unprincipled behavior within the business community of the time.

They began their careers after the outbreak of the Civil War, when political and economic dislocations weakened the settled fabric of national commerce. The war opened the door to unscrupulous promoters, war profiteers, and government war contractors in league with corrupt politicians. The patterns of gaining favoritism by bribing politicians learned at this time were carried over to economic activity after the end of the war. From the 1860s onward, the robber barons also availed themselves of economic opportunities in the developing western territories. Historians believe that the dislocations of the war coupled with a vast increase in the geographic scope of economic activity created a climate in which established norms of business ethics crumbled under the onslaught of ruthless competitors (Destler, 1946).

The robber barons were buttressed in their actions by values of the time, which extolled the virtues of ruthless competition. Particularly popular were the works of Herbert Spencer (1820–1903), an English philosopher who popularized the doctrine called Social Darwinism. Spencer's philosophy provided a moral basis for the accumulation of large fortunes through economic operations which, in the words of historian Henry Demarest Lloyd, made "the Black Flag the emblem of success on the high seas of human interchange." Spencer argued that life was a continuing process of adaptation to a harsh external environment. Businessmen were engaged in a competitive struggle for survival in which the fittest survived. The strongest competitors benefited the human race by their survival and prosperity. This idea enabled the robber barons to justify any effective business tactic, no matter how harsh or cruel, as contributing to a positive end result in the evolutionary process. The widespread acceptance of

Herbert Spencer's doctrines made predatory behavior seem acceptable. Mothers proudly pointed to the actions of Gould, Rockefeller, and their ilk as examples worthy of emulation by their children. In the following quotation, John D. Rockefeller, speaking in a Sunday school address, is a convincing exponent of this brand of competition:

> The growth of a large business is merely a survival of the fittest. . . . The American Beauty rose can be produced in the splendor and fragrance which bring cheer to its beholder only by sacrificing the early buds which grow up around it. This is not an evil tendency in business. It is merely the working out of a law of nature and a law of God (Hofstadter, 1970: 37).

The construction of the Central Pacific Railroad is one of many examples of the infamous commercial activities of the time. Matthew Josephson, a left-wing historian and author of a widely read book entitled *The Robber Barons* (1934), describes the actions of three shop owners in California named Collis Huntington, Mark Hopkins, and Leland Stanford. In 1860 the three combined with a gold miner named Charles Crocker to form a group called the Pacific Associates. The four raised $200,000, which Huntington carried to Washington in a trunk in 1861 and handed out liberally to congressmen and senators in pursuit of a federal charter for a railroad in California. After spending all the money, Huntington came home with the charter and promises of land grants and federal financial support for the fledgling railroad construction project.

In 1863, after Leland Stanford became California's governor, the Central Pacific was able to invoke the power of state government. In May of that year, elections were held in San Francisco for a $3 million bond issue to finance further construction of the railway. Leaving nothing to chance, Leland's brother, Philip Stanford, arrived at the polls in a buggy filled with bags of gold pieces and tossed them liberally into the outstretched hands of the crowd. The bond issue passed.

Later, the Central Pacific raised funds by demanding bond subscriptions from towns through which the roadbed was to pass and by threatening to build elsewhere and cut towns off from "progress." In 1868, for instance, the Pacific Associates extracted 5 percent of the assessed valuation of all of Los Angeles County as the price for connecting the residents there with a rail line to the East. Such a levy was not unusual. In the meantime, Huntington attended to government relations in Washington by spending $200,000 to $500,000 during each legislative session to secure political favors.

Construction of the Central Pacific proceeded, utilizing the backbreaking labor of up to 10,000 Chinese workers who were paid $1 a day. Many did not survive the job. The four Pacific Associates received a total of $79 million in bonds, government subsidies, and investor cash during construction of the railroad. Experts have estimated that almost half this amount was in excess of that needed for legitimate construction costs and made its way into the pockets of the four principals. The railroad, however, was built and in operation.

There existed a substantial number in the society of that time who frowned upon dishonest behavior in business. Among them were clergymen and populist protestors. For this group, the lawbreaking and corner-cutting of the Pacific Associates and other corrupt entrepreneurs were sinful blows to the public interest. Today, the actions of the Pacific Associates would lead to the resignation of public officials, fines by regulatory agencies, possible criminal prosecution of corporate executives, and a public hue and cry. But that is today. We must re-create the social atmosphere of another era to fully understand the Pacific Associates.

The robber barons learned to manipulate the corporate form to their advantage. They committed a hundredfold minor larcenies. They corruptly elicited government subsidy for their activities. And despite their paeans to the beauty of Darwinian competition, they replaced it with monopoly. But these observations do not cement a case against them. In fact, there may be much to be said for them. They burst upon the scene at a time of great ferment, when the economy was expansive and the nation was characterized in part by the raw wildness of the frontier spirit. They were well adapted to this turbulent atmosphere and far removed from the fastidious practices of the pre-Civil War Eastern business establishment. And their accomplishments were enormous. In the words of an economic historian:

> Whatever their amoralities and ruthlessness, they helped to lead American business into the stage of full capitalism, creating gigantic organizations capable of servicing the entire continent or several sections at least. They led in extending the corporation into new and important fields of enterprise, in employing hired executives for routine administration and specialized tasks, and in reserving to themselves exclusively entrepreneurial functions of planning, high strategy, and risk taking (Destler, 1946: 34–35).

Seen this way, the robber barons contributed substantially to the foundations of the robust industrial economy that followed their era. In a utilitarian sense, an argument can be made that the benefits accruing to society from their businesses exceed the damage to the social fabric resulting from their bribes, deceits, and manipulations.

Would more honest business activity have fostered similar economic development? What would have happened if legal and cultural restraints had controlled the predations of the robber barons? These questions cannot be answered definitively. The historical record shows that law and social standards were too weak to force the robber barons into more ethical channels.

Some scholars have argued that an amount of corruption existing during expansive periods in developing societies is desirable. If there exists in such societies a "functional corruption," which departs from ethical ideals but permits fluid, rapid growth by easing barriers that stem from rules, niceties, and rigid laws, then economic development may be faster. One student of social and economic development, Samuel Huntington (1968), has argued that such "functional corruption" serves the public interest at the same time as it promotes selfish gain. He writes:

Corruption may be one way of surmounting traditional laws or bureaucratic regulations which hamper economic expansion. In the United States during the 1870s and 1880s, corruption of state legislatures and city councils by railroad, utility, and industrial corporations undoubtedly speeded the growth of the American economy. . . . A society which is relatively uncorrupt—a traditional society for instance where traditional norms are still powerful—may find a certain amount of corruption a welcome lubricant easing the path to modernization. A developed traditional society may be improved—or at least modernized—by a little corruption (Huntington, 1968: 68–69).

Today we have largely abandoned doctrines of Social Darwinism in favor of new managerial ideologies that redefine the meaning of competition and social responsibility. This changed philosophical backdrop makes today's business environment hostile to wholesale corruption. In addition, generations of scandals and rising public expectations for business behavior have elevated ethical norms far above what they were during the days of the Pacific Associates. Some corruption in business may be inevitable, but it is less likely to be regarded as functional. Today, however, we have the difficult task of looking back more than a century to pass judgment on these robber barons and to clarify their morally ambiguous actions.

Questions

1. Compare the benefits of the robber barons' activities to their costs. From a utilitarian standpoint, can their actions be justified by arguing that benefits exceeded costs?
2. Do you believe that "functional corruption" can be useful in a developing society? In a developed society? Or is honest commercial activity always preferable?
3. What forces in today's pluralistic society would prevent the robber-baron type of exploitation?

CHAPTER **4**

THE CRITICS OF BUSINESS

Sisters of Loretto

The Loretto Literary and Benevolent Institution is an order of Roman Catholic nuns that exemplifies shareholder activism by church groups. The Sisters of Loretto began their activism in 1976 by buying eighty-one shares of Blue Diamond Coal Co. for $19,500. They were intent on pressuring the management of this Kentucky company to improve mine safety, following a highly publicized accident. Since then the Sisters have sponsored numerous shareholder resolutions to make corporations more socially responsible. In 1978, for example, the Sisters' sponsorship of a resolution led Gulf Oil Co. to adopt a policy prohibiting payment of further political contributions in South Korea.

There are about 600 Sisters in the order, 300 of whom are retired. Their primary mission as an order is child and adult education, but they also take active interest in working for social justice in the cities where their houses are located. Even if only one sister feels strongly that she is informed about an issue, perceives an injustice, and is willing to work on it, the others in the order will show solidarity. In the 1980s, the Sisters often have attacked defense contractors and pressured them to reexamine military contracts, end nuclear weapons production, and diversify into civilian products. The Sisters in the St. Louis house, for example, have undertaken activist campaigns against McDonnell Douglas Corp., Monsanto Co., General Dynamics Corporation, and Emerson Electric Co., all of which have headquarters or major facilities in the St. Louis area.

Like other Roman Catholic orders, the Sisters of Loretto have stock holdings. They have set up an eight-member Investment Committee composed of representatives from houses around the country. The committee meets to make decisions about buying and selling stock and voting the shares at annual meetings. Sometimes the Sisters sell the stock of a company from which they do not care to profit. At other times, they buy shares of a company so that they can bring shareholder resolutions against management as part of a campaign of influence. In recent proxy seasons, the Sisters have sponsored or co-sponsored, with other church groups, an average of six to eight socially responsible shareholder resolutions against the managements of defense companies.

A frequent target of the Sisters is General Dynamics Corporation, headquartered in St. Louis. General Dynamics is the nation's largest defense contractor. Its major contracts include the F-16 Falcon jet fighter, the Tomahawk cruise missile, fuselages for KC-10 tanker/cargo aircraft, Stinger and Viper shoulder-fired anti-aircraft missiles, Sparrow air-to-air missiles, Trident missile submarines, vessels for the U.S. Navy and M1 main battle tanks. Each year since 1983, the Sisters have been successful in bringing at least one resolution opposed by management to a vote of the stockholders. In that year, they joined with three other Roman Catholic orders asking the company to withdraw its bid for a contract to manufacture major cruise missile components and asking that workers on cruise missile programs be retrained for other occupations. Together, these groups had 740 shares, or one ten-thousandth of 1 percent of General Dynamics 55.4 million outstanding shares. Only 1 percent of General Dynamics' shareholders voted with the Sisters, but subsequent resolutions in later years have received up to 10 percent of the vote.

The Sisters interpret Catholic theology to hold the production of nuclear weapons and their delivery systems as unethical. They believe that papal teachings and Biblical text condemn the manufacture of such potentially destructive force. They also believe that the money and resources pouring into the arms race could be used more constructively to combat poverty around the world.

At General Dynamics, John McGuire, the corporate secretary, regards the Sisters as well-intentioned but misguided. McGuire is a thoughtful Catholic, with three brothers who are priests. He argues that prevailing Church theology permits production of nuclear weapons for use in deterring a catastrophic event such as a third world war. He believes that the Sisters are errant in their interpretation of Church doctrine and mistaken in trying to impose their anti-weapons views on the corporation. In addition, he believes that it is not proper for them to buy an infinitesimal share of General Dynamics stock and use the shareholder resolution machinery in pursuit of values that are so divergent from those of the company and other shareholders. The company tries to fend off the resolutions if it can. When, in 1986, the Sisters sought to file a resolution requesting that the General Dynamics board have more members with expertise in marketing civilian products, the company filed a detailed, fifty-page report with the Securities and Exchange Commission accusing the Sisters of harassing it and disputing the legitimacy of the filing under SEC rules. As a result, the SEC disallowed the filing.

Throughout recorded history merchants and businesses in many civilizations have been regarded with suspicion. As the story of the Sisters of Loretto illustrates, large corporations today are also the focus of sharp criticism.

In this chapter, we examine criticism of business over a long period of time, discuss underlying causes of antibusiness feeling, illuminate the objectives of various critics, and give examples of specific complaints. Throughout other chapters, of course, we discuss specific demands of critics and management responses.

HISTORICAL TRENDS IN PUBLIC ATTITUDES TOWARD BUSINESS

Current polls show that substantial numbers of Americans have negative opinions about the performance of large corporations.

The Ancient and Medieval Worlds

In early civilizations such as ancient Egypt and Mesopotamia, the Inca and Aztec societies, Confucianist China, and the Hinduized kingdoms of ancient Southeast Asia, the merchant was ranked relatively low on the traditional scale of values (Peacock, 1976). These early societies had a tripartite hierarchy, with rulers at the top, followed by farmers, who made up the great mass of citizens. In the lowest rank were merchants, who were typically regarded as indecent. Perhaps this was because their sharp business practices and temporizing ethics diverged from the more altruistic mores of family and tribal relations developed during generations of recently eclipsed hunter-gatherer society.

Sages of classical civilization were suspicious of greed. In his description of a utopian society in *The Republic*, for example, Plato prohibited the possession of private property to the highest ruling class for fear of corruption and the rise of tyrants. In his *Politics*, Aristotle portrays lending money for interest as a "hated" occupation. Likewise, the Stoic philosophers of ancient Rome, such as Epictetus and Marcus Aurelius, taught that the truly rich person was in possession of inner peace rather than capital or property. These thinkers looked down on the merchants of their day as materialists who, in pursuit of wealth, sacrificed the opportunity to develop higher philosophical and ethical capacities of the mind. Needless to say, this did not deter merchants of that time from accumulating fortunes and neglecting the study of ideals.

During the Middle Ages, the prevailing theological doctrines of the Roman Catholic Church made the populace intolerant of profit making. Merchants were exhorted by religious doctrine to charge a "just price" for their wares or a price that was just adequate to maintain them in the social station to which they were born. Lending money for interest was condemned as sinful. Later, as the Industrial Revolution progressed, the size of the working class grew, and new criticisms of worker exploitation by business arose. With the development of mass consumer economics came criticism of products and marketing techniques.

As this brief historical survey shows, harsh opinions of business have existed in every age.

Attitudinal Trends in United States History

Opinion polls measuring public attitudes toward business were not introduced until the 1930s. But much higher levels of public confidence in business existed during the early years of our nation than exist now. Historians record generally positive feelings toward entrepreneurs, companies, and the business system until the growth of giant trusts in the latter half of the nineteenth century.

The earliest colonies were formed by English trading companies operated by private individuals for profit. It is true that in some instances the motive for colonization was to avoid religious persecution, but the backers of the Pilgrims, for instance, hoped to make a profit. The commercial spirit manifested itself in different ways in colonial America, but it was dominant in most walks of life. The farmer was not a peasant bound to the soil with a pattern of life dictated by custom. Although his way of life was different from that of the retail merchant in the town, they both engaged in buying and selling to make a profit. As the farmer accumulated wealth, he built and ran grain mills and in other ways employed his capital exactly like a merchant. Merchants of great wealth could rise to top status in colonial society in part because there was no tradition of a landed or hereditary aristocracy in the United States, as there was in Europe.

After the Civil War, farmers assailed railroads and grain elevator operators for charging excessive prices and discriminating among customers. This led in many states to the so-called Granger Laws to prevent unjust practices. Still, according to opinion historian Louis Galambos (1975), there existed a great reservoir of respect for and confidence in business until the 1880s, at which time hostility toward large trusts mounted. There was growing hostility in the 1890s, and the image of big business grew increasingly negative. The businessperson was accused of being a greedy, avaricious rascal who robbed investors with worthless stocks, exploited employees in company-owned stores, charged consumers monopoly prices, ran roughshod over weaker competitors, bludgeoned government to act on his behalf, shot striking employees, maintained horrible working conditions, and in other ways evidenced a crude, predatory, and thoroughly unlikable character. The abuses of business during this period were widely publicized by the "muckrakers," who were principally journalists employed by new, rapidly growing magazines and newspapers.

From the Progressive Era at the turn of the century until the Depression years of the 1930s, public confidence in business rose. During these years, corporations continued to grow in size and, instead of associating big businesses with famous founders such as Andrew Carnegie, John D. Rockefeller, Jay Gould, Samuel Huntington, or Cornelius Vanderbilt, the public developed a more impersonal view of the corporation. According to Galambos's study, people began to see corporations as impersonal bureaucracies—a tendency that still exists today.

Between 1915 and 1919 more and more Americans came to judge organized behavior in impersonal terms, stressing collective over individual responsibility. . . . In the 1880s and early 1890s, Jay Gould and the Vanderbilts had been the major symbols of corporate business, and both names bore a heavy legacy of negative connotations. . . . During the First World War, however, most middle-class Americans forgot about the moguls of yesteryear and began to talk about corporate enterprise in largely impersonal terms (pp. 181–183).

In the 1930s, however, big business in general was under sustained attack for the first time in our history because these impersonal entities—corporations—fell into public disfavor. During the 1920s, the idea had been advanced, partly by people in business, that business knew how to achieve a continuing prosperity, and it was widely accepted. The depression of the 1930s proved this view to be wrong and in addition brought to light serious instances of extremely poor judgment, outright criminal negligence, and blatant fraud and theft on the part of prominent and heretofore highly respected people in business. There was a popular feeling that the economic collapse would not have occurred if business managers had been more capable. Criticism of business was accentuated by conservative ideas expressed by a majority of people in business that the role of government in helping to relieve human distress caused by the collapse of the economic system should be very limited.

As a result of the high level of performance of American industry during World War II, business reacquired a good measure of respect. In a poll taken in 1950, for example, only 10 percent of the population believed that where "big business activity" was concerned "the bad effects outweighed the good" (Fisher and Withey, 1951: xiii). This renascence of respect, given largely in recognition of business's ability to advance the economy, continued into the 1960s.

Recent Antibusiness Sentiment

The strong public support business enjoyed following World War II collapsed after the mid-1960s. It was a time of unrest. Strong antiestablishment movements attacked basic institutions for their failure to mitigate serious social problems. Government, labor, the military, organized religion, higher education, medicine, the press, and, of course, business all suffered losses of public confidence. Here are some examples of polls that reflect the extraordinary negative changes in public attitudes toward business.

■ A 1968 poll showed that 70 percent agreed that business tries to strike a fair balance between profits and the public interest. By 1970 the figure had declined to 33 percent, and in 1976 it had plummeted to 15 percent. This was a drop of 55 percentage points in ten years (Lipset and Schneider, 1978).

■ Two ABC News-Harris polls, the first in 1966 and the second in 1979, showed that the percentage of Americans expressing a "great deal of confidence" in the leaders of major companies declined from 55 percent to 19 percent (Shaver, 1980: 46).

■ Between 1965 and 1977, Opinion Research Corporation polls showed that average favorability ratings for eight industries fell from 68 percent to 36 percent. Approval of twenty-two large companies declined from an average rating of 74 percent in 1965 to 48 percent in 1975 (Lipset and Schneider, 1983).

During this period of declining confidence, some population segments were more likely to be supportive of business over a wide range of issues than others. These segments included conservatives, happy people, those whose finances were improving, those satisfied with their jobs, whites, older people, and Republicans. Support for the private enterprise system remained deep and enduring. Only tiny percentages of the public favored government ownership of business.

Table 4-1 shows that early in the 1980s, there was a positive trend in some areas of opinion, whereas negative feelings continued in other areas. The public has become less critical of business. Since the 1960s and 1970s, progress has been made on many of the social problems that aggravated business critics. The

TABLE 4–1   PUBLIC OPINION TRENDS: EARLY 1980s

The Roper Organization Inc. has asked this question every other December since 1978: "Now here's a list of things people have said are or should be responsibilities of business in this country. . . . For each one, tell me whether you think business fulfills its responsibilities fully, fairly well, not too well or not at all well."

| | **Fully/Fairly Well** | | | |
	1978	**1980**	**1982**	**1984**
Developing new products and services	88%	84%	89%	92%
Producing good quality products and services	66	64	73	76
Making products that are safe to use	65	66	76	76
Hiring minorities	74	67	72	70
Providing jobs for people	71	68	53	71
Being good citizens of the communities in which they operate	70	69	75	70
Paying good salaries and benefits to employees	69	70	71	69
Charging reasonable prices for goods and services	33	33	39	48
Keeping profits at reasonable levels	36	36	40	46
Advertising honestly	33	37	38	41
Paying their fair share of taxes	40	42	39	39
Cleaning up their own air and water pollution	40	40	42	38

Source: William Schneider, "Opinion Outlook." *National Journal,* July 13, 1985.

Reagan administration put its imprimatur on pro-business attitudes. There has been a conservative trend in social values, emphasizing patriotism, family, entrepreneurship, the free market economy, and other traditional values. The public has been more supportive of businesses faced with tough foreign competition. Long years of economic recovery and growth have helped, too. In an era of more plentiful, lower-priced oil, the oil industry, one of the most reviled in the 1970s, has benefited from a remarkable reversal of public perception. In 1980, polls showed that 67 percent of the public felt generally negative toward the industry, but by 1986, 52 percent felt generally positive (Byers and Fitzpatrick, 1986).

FACTORS UNDERLYING NEGATIVE ATTITUDES TOWARD AMERICAN BUSINESS

Although the trend today is toward somewhat more positive feelings about business, much criticism still circulates. What causes critical attitudes to persist? Negative attitudes toward business result in part from current events, trends, and values. In addition, public antipathy has complex historical, cultural, and psychological roots. Here we list and explain some significant forces underlying business-directed opprobrium. This list, of course, may be incomplete.

Traditional American Antipathy to Centralized Power

Deeply fixed in the bedrock belief system of American political culture is the fear of concentrated power. Sources of this fear were the experiences of revolutionary America with an imperious England and the acceptance in the United States of the political theories of the English philosopher John Locke, set forth in his *Treatise on Civil Government* (1691). One of the matters Locke was most concerned with was the accountability of power, particularly centralized, governmental power. He elevated the concept of popular sovereignty, or the right of majorities to influence powerful institutions such as legislatures and executives. Hence, with the growth of unprecedentedly large and powerful economic entities that affect the everyday lives of most Americans, the Lockean ideology of anti-bigness and harnessing of central authority has been applied to big business. Americans fear the self-interested motivations of executives and regard large corporations as remote, impersonal entities that cannot be trusted.

Fear of and antipathy to concentrated power has persisted. Concentrated economic power in business has been a constant target of attack. In 1890, Mary Lease, speaking on behalf on the Minnesota Alliance ticket, complained:

> Wall Street owns the country. It is no longer a government of the people, by the people and for the people, but a government of Wall Street and for Wall Street. The

great common people of this country are slaves, and monopoly is the master. The West and South are bound and prostrate before the manufacturing East (Hicks, 1931: 160).

A Gallup poll of 1941 showed 59 percent of a nationwide sample agreeing that "there is too much power in the hands of a few rich men and large corporations in the United States" (Gallup, 1972: vol. I, p. 277). Since 1959, Opinion Research Corporation has asked whether the public agrees that there is "too much power concentrated in the hands of a few large companies for the good of the nation," and the percentage of those affirming rose from 53 percent in 1959 to 76 percent in 1981 (Lipset and Schneider, 1983: 30).

Conspiracy Theories

Over and over in American history it has been alleged that some group (and the tiresome litany includes such diverse groups as city women, European monarchs, immigrants, Jews, blacks, Communists, Masons, Darwinians, munitions manufacturers, international bankers, oil companies, Wall Streeters, and others), acting in secret for its own self-interest, is out to do the public in. This mind-set goes back to the first years of the colonies, when colonists feared papal conspiracies to undermine the Protestant nations of the New World.

The percentage of people in the population who believe in conspiracies is not always small. In February 1974, for instance, a Gallup poll revealed that 25 percent of Americans held oil companies responsible for the creation of the energy crisis existing at that time (*Gallup Opinion Index*, February 1974, no. 104). One month later, Opinion Research discovered that 43 percent of the population believed that the energy shortage was "contrived" by the oil companies to exploit the public (Danhof and Worthy, 1975: 39). As late as January 1985, 67 percent of the public felt that "the oil companies are just waiting for a chance to create another oil shortage so they can increase their prices again like they did in the 1970s" (Byers and Fitzpatrick, 1986: 44).

The persistence of such conspiracy theories makes big business the object of continued cynicism among certain elements of the population. Such theories are difficult to combat, because the circular logic of those who believe them is airtight. Because conspiracies are alleged to be secret and hidden, they cannot be scientifically observed, tested, or disproved. In this way, say conspiracy theorists, the actions of business leaders can be reduced to furtive manipulations that the public should fear.

For a small number of individuals, conspiracy beliefs are a manifestation of paranoid traits. These people overuse the defense mechanism of projection and endow the actions of leaders in business and government with motivations and goals such as greed, prejudice, or a cruel drive for power that would be unacceptable in themselves. For a larger number of conspiracy believers, however, such theories have a more straightforward appeal. They provide simple explanations for complex events and relieve the mind of strenuous thought.

Negative Rumors about Business

Rumors, springing as they do from irrational thoughts, ignorance, fear, and incomplete impressions, are a phenomenon related to conspiracy theories. Some have been very costly to business. In the 1940s, for example, the first king-sized menthol cigarette, called Spud, failed in the market due to a groundless rumor that a leper worked in the factory where it was made (Levy, 1981). In the 1970s, a widespread rumor held that McDonald's hamburgers contained worm meat. This rumor depressed company earnings—particularly in southern outlets —and led to a massive advertising campaign focused on the theme that McDonald's hamburger meat was 100 percent pure beef. Early in the 1980s, Procter & Gamble was hit by two related rumors. In 1980, a tale circulated that the picture of a moon on the Procter & Gamble logo meant that the company had been acquired by the Unification Church of Reverend Sun Myung Moon. In 1981, another story sprang up that the logo, which contains thirteen stars to symbolize the original thirteen American colonies, was a symbol of the Anti-christ and implied that the firm was in thrall to Satan. It was even said that an executive of the corporation appeared on a television talk show admitting corporate contributions to satanic cults. None of this was correct, but the rumors were hurtful. Some fundamentalist Christian groups boycotted Procter & Gamble products. Employees were verbally assaulted by irate store owners and shoppers desiring to repel the satanic horde personally. Procter & Gamble fought back by mailing to ministers around the country testimonials from Rev. Billy Graham, Rev. Jerry Falwell, Cardinal Joseph Bernardin, and others, debunking the rumor personally. It also set up a toll-free line to explain the logo to callers, distributed press releases and booklets, and ultimately brought twelve lawsuits against purveyors of the rumor who could be located. These actions failed to arrest its spread. In 1985, the company dropped the logo from its packaging (while retaining it on corporate stationery and on buildings). Still, the rumor would not die. As late as August 1986, Procter & Gamble brought a $1 million libel suit against a mobile-home park newsletter (circulation 140) in San Jose, California, for reprinting the rumor.

Courtesy of The Procter & Gamble Company.

Rumors are thought to proliferate in periods of social stress, economic hardship, and wartime. According to Frederick Koenig, a rumor expert who serves as a consultant to major corporations fighting them:

Some people see rumors as a way of structuring or understanding reality. A man who is unemployed and just barely scraping by might well be inclined to believe a rumor—even a false one—about a big company's product being contaminated. It somehow makes him feel better to see the corporate giant in trouble. He reasons

THE CRITICS OF BUSINESS

Have You Heard Any of These?

The following are some rumors that in recent years have circulated widely enough to have been mentioned in print. We are not aware of any truth in them.

■ A woman was bitten by a poisonous Asian snake that had hatched from an egg in a pile of coats at a K-Mart store. Her arm had to be amputated.

■ Tobacco companies will redeem cigarette wrappers saved by smokers to purchase seeing-eye dogs for the blind.

■ The oil companies have purchased from an inventor a carburetor that gets 100 miles per gallon. They are hiding it in a warehouse and paying hush money to the inventor.

■ Bubble Yum, a children's chewing gum distributed by Squibb, contains spider eggs.

■ Pop Rocks, a carbonated candy made by General Foods, can explode in children's stomachs when consumed with a carbonated beverage.

■ Flickering Hallmark candles cause lead poisoning.

■ A woman who took out some Kentucky Fried Chicken in a box and ate it in the dark found that it tasted terrible. Later, in the light, she discovered the tail of a rat in the box.

■ A man drinking Coca-Cola from a bottle found a roach inside.

■ Green M&Ms, made by the Mars Company, are an aphrodisiac.

■ The Palestine Liberation Organization covertly presides over a multibillion dollar investment empire.

■ Manufacturers of cosmetics are secretly using material from aborted human fetuses in their products and listing the ingredient as "collagen."

■ Corona Extra, a Mexican beer imported by Barton Beers of Chicago, is contaminated with urine.

---

that his best efforts get him nowhere, so the firm must be cutting corners to be successful. By striking out at a big company and clouding its reputation, he works off some of his aggression (1982: 42).

There is an element of mystery in rumors. It is unclear how they start, and they seem often to die as quickly as they begin. Their function for the American psyche is obscure, and there is little a manager who presides over a powerful and highly visible corporate entity can do to prevent either rumor or conspiracy theories from developing. When they do develop, depending on their nature, some companies choose to fight, and others find it convenient not to comment.

The Dynamics of Group Power

Throughout American history, groups have formed during periods of tension to assert new viewpoints. The 1960s witnessed the rise of four powerful types of groups that saw their grievances rooted in existing arrangements of power and authority. These were environmental, public interest/consumer, civil rights, and anti–Vietnam War groups. Their successful attempts to combat existing arrangements paralleled those of earlier movements such as populism, unionism, and temperance.

The very force and success of demands made by these new, organized elements created a climate in which it became legitimate to criticize big business as representative of the status quo and blame it for some of society's ills. Americans traditionally have placed a high value on a pressure group system that countervails the perceived concentration of power in big business. Elsewhere in this book, particularly in discussions of pluralism and business in the political process, we examine the role of pressure groups more extensively.

The Tension Between Capitalism and Democracy

There is a natural, built-in tension between capitalistic economies and democratic governments because they embody equally legitimate but competing value systems. Capitalistic values include those of economic efficiency, the allocation of resources through an impersonal market mechanism, decentralization of decision making, and self-interest as a major personal motivating force. The democratic political system is marked by popular sovereignty, political equality, and decision making based on majority rule. Society continuously seeks to balance and reconcile these competing value systems and is molded by the ways in which the systems are reconciled.

In the capitalism-democracy processes, business interests are continuously attacked. This attack happens because democracies have leftward centers of gravity and the logic of participation leads to inclusion of more and more have-nots in the electoral and policy processes. Stable democracies have an inherent leftward drive, and left-wing parties win support with measures that increase the relative power and security of the lower strata. In this process, ultimately the mass of people are educated to regard business and corporate interests with suspicion as politicians and political parties can appeal to the masses by attacking wealth and privilege.

Mistrust of Government and Politicians

Conflict between capitalism and democracy produces strains and tensions that must be mitigated by a central authority, and it is for this reason that the government-business relationship largely determines the character of our society. Schattschneider has argued that "the function of democracy has been to provide the public with a second power system, an alternative power system which can be used to counterbalance the economic power" (1960: 121). Between 1964 and 1980, the percentage of people saying that they could "trust the government in Washington to do what is right most of the time" fell from 69 percent to 23 percent, and the percentage saying that "government is pretty much run by a few big interests looking out for themselves" rose from 29 percent to 69 percent (Sommers, 1975). With the advent of the Reagan administration, between 1980 and 1982, a rebound in confidence seemed to occur. The number stating that they could trust government most of the time to do what was right increased to 31 percent, and the number seeing government run by a few big interests fell to 61 percent (Miller, 1983).

There is an enduring fear that power abuse derives from government-business collusion, and so cynicism about big government and big business are related. Also, when the public mistrusts government, it expresses lack of faith in the institution with the most power to control business.

Genuine Abuses in the Business System

The media daily reveal unethical or illegal behavior by people in business. Front-page incidents, such as recent defense procurement and insider trading scandals, do not occur frequently, but other types of wrongdoing such as income tax evasion, fines for pollution, minor price fixing arrangements, illegal campaign contributions, corporate spying, and overcharges for auto repair are epidemic. Thus, when a really heinous corporate crime comes to light, as for instance when the officers of Film Recovery Systems, Inc., in Chicago were found to have knowingly exposed immigrant workers to lethal cyanide fumes resulting in one death, many in the public are willing to regard it as typical business behavior.

The Operation of the Business Cycle

The recurrence of recession and depression in American history has ensured periodic concern about the role of economic institutions and their performance and relationship to government. Panics in the nineteenth century led to a public rage focused on the financial community. The stock market scandals of the 1930s associated with the 1929 market crash tainted business for years. Opinion polls show that people rate economic problems among the most important problems. Polls also show that people may blame business for their economic ills. Lipset and Schneider (1983) correlated surveys of confidence in institutional leadership between 1966 and 1980 with rates of unemployment and inflation and found that as unemployment and inflation rose, confidence in the leadership of major companies and other institutions declined (1983: 62). Historically, economic fluctuation also has been shown to detonate and give expression to underlying trends such as fear of power and belief in business conspiracy (Rostow, 1941).

The Existence of Rising Expectations

The phenomenon of rising expectations is a familiar refrain that implies that there is a gap between expectations and realities in a society accustomed to rapid progress. But affluence has been Janus-faced for business. Americans now are demanding that the very corporations that created the prosperity that led them to unrealistic expectations meet those expectations. When they are not met, business is blamed.

A large proportion of the public believe that they are entitled to many rights. For example, Opinion Research Corporation reported an opinion poll showing that 90 percent of respondents felt entitled to safe products, 88 percent to an improved standard of living, 85 percent to a guaranteed job, 75 percent to as much gasoline as they wanted, 59 percent to free graduate and professional schooling, and 52 percent to a four-day work week (*Public Opinion*, April/May 1981).

The Process of Economic Socialization in Children

Babies are not born with preconceived notions of appropriate economic arrangements. Rather, cultural values, including attitudes toward business, are imparted through a gradual learning process known as *socialization*. This process, as it relates to the learning of economic arrangements, is little studied, but there is evidence that children begin to develop cynical attitudes toward business as early as the third grade (Cooper and Steiner, 1976). Cynicism about business is transmitted through contact with parents, peers, teachers, and media material of all kinds.

Cynicism in children is deeply instilled by recurring historical cycles of scandals involving people in business, such as those during the populist, progressive, 1930s Depression, Watergate, and Contragate periods. These scandals also reinforce and increase adult cynicism.

Public Ignorance of the Business System

A perennial complaint of defenders of business is that critics and the public at large are uninformed about basic business facts. It is argued that if critics better understood the rudiments of the system, there would be less public mistrust. Intuitively, it makes sense to think that perception of fact influences opinion. A 1975 study of American adults by DuPont, designed to measure knowledge and understanding of economic principles and the workings of American business, reported, "The amount people know about economics is correlated with their attitudes toward business. The more information they have, the more likely people are to look with favor on business institutions" (DuPont, 1976). Some telling methodological criticisms have been expressed about this survey, but the existence of a misinformed public remains a tenet of belief for businesspeople.

To change public attitudes, the Advertising Council sponsored a national economic education campaign. Between 1976 and 1978, 9 million copies of a book on business economics were distributed, and magazine and newspaper ads were used to promote knowledge of economics. The result? Follow-up surveys showed no improvement in the public's knowledge of basic facts, and there was no improvement in the respondents' attitudes toward business. The campaign was a failure. Postmortems have speculated that a person's social and employment status are much more significant determinants of positive or negative attitudes toward business than is factual economic knowledge and, therefore, that ignorance of the facts is not primarily responsible for negative attitudes toward business (Fox and Calder, 1985).

The Treatment of Business by Journalists, Novelists, and Scriptwriters

In the United States there are roughly 9,200 newspapers, 10,809 magazines, 9,200 radio stations, and 1,100 television stations (Moore and Kalupa, 1985). The treatment of business in these communication channels has an enormous impact on public attitudes.

A long-standing adversarial relationship exists between business and journalists representing the print and broadcast media. Corporations desire to use the media to convey positive images. The job of editors, reporters, and producers, on the other hand, is to seek out and publish accurate information of interest to audiences. The result of this basic difference of mission is that self-interested companies sometimes accuse the news and entertainment media of distortion, bias, simplification, and omission in reporting about business. Journalists, in turn, argue that business is often uncooperative. Reporters complain of businesspeople "unavailable" for comment, failure to return phone calls, terse news releases, and overprotective public relations offices that shield top executives from the press.

One authority on the business-press relationship, Professor Louis Banks of MIT's Sloan School of Management and a former editor of *Fortune* magazine, believes that press coverage of business has markedly improved in recent years. The attitudes of reporters on social issues typically are more liberal than those of the managers and executives they write about, and this has led to charges of slanting of the news against corporations. Today, however, business reporting has become more sophisticated because the audience for business news is growing and prefers factual reporting to the liberal, muckraking style that cynical audiences relished in past decades. Also, corporations are learning lessons about how to handle media relationships. Although a few firms, such as Amarada-Hess and Winn-Dixie Stores, have a reputation for frustrating reporters with silence, many others have learned to cultivate media relationships for their own benefit. Comments Banks:

> Few editors know, or want to know, that there are thousands of public relations master plans out there that have targeted this or that publication or TV program for a story designed to project the right corporate image to the right audience.
>
> Even if they are vaguely aware that they are targets, editors and producers don't know how often the arrow hits the bull's eye. One vice president for public relations . . . lists his media goals at the beginning of each year and can count on an 80 percent success rate (Banks, 1985: 207).

Some companies strike back at the media when they are victimized by inaccurate reporting. In 1984, for instance, Mobil Oil withdrew its advertising from the *Wall Street Journal* and made employees inaccessible to interviews by its reporters. The immediate occasion for the boycott was an article about construction of Mobil's seventy-story office building in downtown Chicago that the company thought irresponsible because it intimated that there was a conflict of interest when Mobil selected a construction firm that employed the son-in-law of Mobil's chairman of the board. But a long history of allegedly biased reporting about Mobil and oil industry matters was an important factor in the decision.

A frequent target of business's wrath is CBS's "60 Minutes." A number of companies do not, as a matter of policy, cooperate with the program any longer. General Motors is one because, says John McNulty, vice president of public relations, "'Sixty Minutes' is to journalism what 'Charlie's Angels' is to criminology" (Guzzardi, 1985). When the program produced an unflattering segment implying mismanagement at Illinois Power Company, the firm produced a rebuttal videotape, which is not only showed to stockholders and employees, but sent to journalism classes around the country with commentary on reportorial ethics.

The image of business in American literature reflects a mixture of attitudes among novelists but is often negative. In a recent book, *The Businessman in American Literature,* Emily Stipes Watts systematically explores the literary image of business from the colonial period to the post-World War II era and argues that businesspeople and their values have been systematically denigrated throughout. She finds the height of criticism of business in the 1930s, when socialist writers such as Upton Sinclair made powerful, emotional attacks on the capitalist system, but says that "most businessmen depicted in post-1945 serious literature are still characterized as greedy, unethical, and immoral (or amoral)" (1982: 150).

Other analysts present more subtle views. Howard R. Smith (1976), after studying 450 novels with business themes or characters, finds that negative portrayals of businessmen are greatly exaggerated. Rather, novelists have evidenced admiration for virtues such as hard work, achievement, and integrity, which may be distinguished from or even at odds with norms of business life (McWilliams and Plotkin, 1976). The novelist has stood for the individual in the struggle against self, society, and business organizations, and not against commerce per se (Falk, 1958).

It should not be overlooked, of course, that some popular literature has cast business in a favorable light. In the latter half of the nineteenth century, for example, the popular Horatio Alger novels were enormously influential in painting a virtuous picture of business for millions. As one analyst wrote, Alger "was the man who put free and untrammeled competition on the side of the angels, and kept it there until well into the next century" (Holbrook, 1948: 237). Another analyst "remembers the 'success stories' in the *American Magazine* a few decades ago, and characters like Tugboat Annie in the *Saturday Evening Post* who could succeed in business without sacrificing courage, strength, integrity, or compassion" (Sonnichsen, 1983: 277). Still, the main currents of artistic prose have not been friendly waters for business.

The image of business on television and in film is, like that in literature, often negative. In 1981, a conservative watchdog of the media, the Media Institute, studied 200 prime-time television programs on the three major networks and found that two-thirds of the businesspeople were portrayed in a negative light, as greedy or criminals, that roughly half of all business activity depicted was illegal, and that in nine out of ten cases where businesspeople performed positive acts, they were acts of personal do-goodism and had no widespread social impact (Media Institute, 1981).

An additional source of negative stereotypes about the business community is cartoons. The source of humor in the typical business-related cartoon is frequently a not-so-veiled allusion to greed or mistreatment of society for profit. In recent years, the *New Yorker* magazine—a prestigious outlet for the work of some of the nation's leading cartoonists—has printed many such cartoons. That they are a source of laughter for the magazine's readers is perhaps confirmation of the deep public cynicism about the motives of powerful executives and big corporations. The two cartoons reprinted here are representative.

Should we worry that the American populace will develop antibusiness attitudes when they watch the dishonesties of J. R. Ewing on "Dallas" and dozens of other Hollywood-created business villains? Business columnist James Flanigan writes: "To say that enjoying a good villain like J. R. leads to anti-business sentiments is like saying that reading Milton's 'Paradise Lost' leads to devil worship" (1983). But although TV programs may not convert attitudes, they do confirm public cynicism.

"I'll be all right. I was suddenly overcome by a wave of compassion for the poor."

Source: *The New Yorker*, 2/4/85. Drawing by Dana Fradon; © 1985 The New Yorker Magazine, Inc.

"Where there's smoke, there's money."

Source: *The New Yorker*, 4/1/85, p. 45. Drawing by Joe Mirachi; © 1985 The New Yorker Magazine, Inc.

CURRENT CRITICISM OF AMERICAN BUSINESS

The list of criticism of business is virtually endless and growing. The fundamental criticism in every free enterprise economy is that people in business frequently place profit before enduring social values such as truth, justice, virtue, love, and artistic merit. The profit motive is perceived to be less noble than humanitarian motives because it is selfish. Beyond this, other basic criticisms are:

1. Business exploits and dehumanizes workers.

2. Business cheats and harms consumers and promotes extremes of materialism in advertising.

3. Business degrades the physical environment.

4. Business exercises inordinate power to influence government and undermine the public interest.

The multinational corporation is subject to these criticisms plus many others, such as exploitation of underdeveloped host countries, syphoning off profits and depleting capital in host countries, exporting jobs from the United States, and behaving badly with respect to local customs and national plans. This list by no means exhausts the themes in attacks on business.

The nature of attacks and the prescriptions for eliminating perceived ills differ among critics. To oversimplify, there are five basic groups of critics.

Reform-Oriented Activist Critics

This group, which includes well-known personalities such as consumer advocate Ralph Nader and genetic engineering critic Jeremy Rifkin, accepts the basic institutional framework of contemporary society but actively presses for reforms in the way business and other institutions operate. These critics, usually political activists and leaders of groups, set forth specific solutions for the ills they see. Nader, for example, often has suggested specific language to members of Congress who are writing consumer legislation. He maintains a prolific authorship of books and articles critical of business but has slipped in national influence since the 1970s. In annual surveys of leaders in many walks of American life, *U. S. News & World Report* found Nader to be the fourth-most influential American in 1974, but by 1985, he had dropped to twenty-fifth place (April 22, 1974: 30; May 20, 1985: 55). No business executive, by the way, has ever been ranked as high as fourth in national influence; the highest was David Rockefeller, who trailed Nader, in fifth position, in 1974.

Activists may be galvanized by personal situations. Lois Gibbs, a housewife living near the Love Canal dumpsite in Niagara Falls, New York, became the leader of nearby families and later started a nationwide crusade to make business dispose of toxic wastes more safely. Gale Cincotta, a gas station manager's widow, forces banks in Chicago to lend in low-income neighborhoods. She does this by threatening to raise issues that lengthen the regulatory proceedings required when banks seek Federal Reserve Board approval to operate in expanded markets.

Most activism comes not from lone wolves, but from groups that represent the variety of interests in the corporate social environment. There are many examples. INFACT, the Infant Formula Action Coalition, forced Nestlé to alter its infant formula marketing after a seven-year boycott and in 1986 targeted a similar boycott against General Electric to pressure it out of the nuclear weapons business. In 1985, fifty-four Roman Catholic and Protestant church groups combined in a coordinated campaign to pressure twelve leading U.S. corporations to promote the welfare of blacks in South Africa. The campaign included shareholder resolutions, meetings with corporate executives, acts of "public witness," and product boycotts. In fact, every sector of corporate stakeholders in the social environment—consumer, labor, environmental, civil rights, religious —has a warrior class. Throughout this text, we discuss these activist elements at some length.

The demeanor of activists ranges from polite to execrable. Their demands may be reasonable, but often there is a wide gulf between their ideal visions of corporate morality and actual corporate behavior. They may need to attack a caricature of evil business behavior to mobilize a following, but this attack makes dialogue and compromise difficult. Most companies, of course, try to communicate with reasonable critics as part of the job of constituency relations. Individuals in corporate public relations departments may keep in touch with interested groups and potential critics. Stung repeatedly by corporate critics, Texaco in 1980 began a systematic program to reach out and influence constituent groups. A "contituency relations manager" from Texaco visited twenty groups, and by 1983, ten of them were regularly communicating with Texaco in workshops, briefings by corporate executives, refinery tours, and roundtable discussions. Seven of the groups subsequently joined Texaco's lobbying efforts on issues of common interest. To illustrate, in 1982 Texaco and the National Association for the Advancement of Colored People (NAACP) cooperated on legislation involving credit practices in the petroleum industry (Pires, 1983). Although the person who started this program left the company and the systematic series of contacts with groups no longer occurs, Texaco continues a more informal outreach program. It also tries to predict new criticism and work with groups before confrontations develop.

The heavy artillery of corporate activists in recent years has been a provocative campaign of confrontation known as the "corporate campaign." The corporate campaign is the brainchild of labor activist Ray Rogers. Rogers, who finds inspiration in the words and deeds of the abrasive 1960s radical Saul Alinsky, honed the tactics of the corporate campaign in a 17-year-long successful effort to force the J. P. Stevens textile conglomerate to enter into a union contract. Subsequent corporate campaigns have been used mainly by organized labor against recalcitrant managements. They involve a variety of irritating tactics, including:

- Developing coalitions of community and church groups to pressure a corporation's lending institutions, insurers, and other supporters, such as retailers of the firm's products. One church group in Pittsburgh put dead fish in safety deposit boxes at the Mellon National Bank on a Friday afternoon as part of a campaign against USX Corporation for closing steel plants in the area. On Monday morning, the bankers had a malodorous incentive to reexamine their financial ties with USX.

- Directly confronting officers and directors of a company by picketing their homes, demonstrating at their children's schools, and interrupting services at their churches.

- Appearing at shareholder meetings to introduce resolutions, ask questions, and make views known to other shareholders.

- Suing the corporation and individual officers for a variety of trumped up offenses such as racketeering or breach of fiduciary duty.

- Employing more commonplace pressure tactics such as press releases, letter-writing campaigns, public speaking, editorials, picketing, boycotting, and the like.

Nonactivist Liberal-Humanistic Critics

This group includes mainly nonactivist intellectuals who scrutinize business and other institutions and point out blemishes. They see problems of racism, income inequality, sexism, social alienation, abuse of power, environmental degradation, and the like as mistakes or ineptitudes that are separate and distinct from an overall system worth preserving. They seek improvement, not radical change. Included in this group are well-known academicians such as John Kenneth Galbraith, whose peppery books lament the increasing power of private business firms and advocate more public controls of them. Social critics, such as Vance Packard (author, for example, of *The Waste Makers,* 1960), William H. Whyte, Jr. (author of *The Organization Man,* 1956), and Rachael Carson (author of *Silent Spring,* 1962), published books that influenced public opinion to demand business reforms during the period of major social protest in the 1960s and 1970s.

This intellectual tradition is continuously renewed. Orville Schell's 1978 book, *Modern Meat,* raised public awareness of the dangers of antibiotics and hormones used in raising animals. Jim Mason and Peter Singer created a debate about factory farming techniques in their 1980 book, *Animal Factories,* which made an ethical and philosophical case for the existence of farm animals' rights. In 1984, America's Catholic bishops voted to approve a historic draft of a "Pastoral Letter on Catholic Social Teaching and the U.S. Economy." In this letter, the bishops argued that the economic system was not responsive to the needs of the poor. The document presented a series of moral and theological principles for redirecting economic policy to better the lot of the least well off. It further suggested that corporate managers should evaluate their actions based on what these actions do for the poor. The bishops' document led to an important national debate on the morality of the economic system and the effectiveness of government policies.

Marxist and Neo-Marxist Critics

Marxist and Neo-Marxist critics reject current institutional structures and demand replacement with a collectivist state. Unlike liberal-humanist critics, this group finds the faults of capitalism rooted in the free market and private property ownership and demands abolition of these basic institutions.

Marxists remain true to the philosophical and economic theories of their intellectual progenitor (discussed in detail in a later section). Much more common in America, however, are radical neo-Marxists, who represent revisionist schools of Marx's thought. They are well exemplified by a school of "radical economists" that developed in universities around the country in the late 1960s and early 1970s because of radicalization on campuses and the inability of capitalist society to resolve persistent social problems, such as poverty, inflation, and pollution. Marxist scholars have made significant inroads in a number of academic disciplines, including not only economics, but also political science, sociology, and U.S. history. According to one count, there are 12,000 faculty in Marxist-oriented academic organizations and about two dozen Marxist journals (Brock, 1985).

Marxist economists attack traditional economics as a discipline for failing to realize the political aspects of economic arrangements. Orthodox examinations of the market, they argue, fail to demonstrate how capitalist institutions rely for their prosperity on worker exploitation, imperialistic expansion overseas, resource waste, racial and sexual discrimination, income inequality, militarism, and a host of other real and imagined evils.

Marxist and neo-Marxist thinking is ubiquitous in antibusiness organizations. A salient study center for the antibusiness movement is the Institute for Policy Studies in Washington, D.C., which funds anticorporate research and publications that attack business as a villain of class struggle. Marxist thinkers are also influential in other groups, where they condemn monopolistic corporations, pathologies of middle-class culture, and government-business elites. Not many, of course, advocate violent revolution or socialism, and their overall influence is waning.

A recent source of Marxist-influenced, antibusiness rhetoric is the movement of Catholic clergy in Latin American countries known as "liberation theology." Liberation theology combines gospel teachings suggesting that Catholics should act to better the lot of the poor with Marxist dogma explaining poverty as the result of capitalist exploitation. Adherents, mainly priests in Latin America, preach that the private enterprise system is the enemy of the poor and should be changed through class struggle and socialist revolution. The liberation theology movement has met with papal displeasure but worries corporate executives with operations in Latin American countries.

Radical Non-Marxist Critics

Radical non-Marxist critics demand restructuring of the American system but do not agree on what should be done or how. Much antiestablishment criticism is aging now and has an empty, ethereal tone. Charles A. Reich, a professor of law, achieved great notoriety in 1970, for example, with publication of *The Greening of America*. In this book, he condemned the corporate state for stifling individual expression and advocated spontaneous mass conversion to a new life style and liberated mode of thinking called "Consciousness III." He called this new consciousness "the greatest secret in America." It still is.

The last two decades also have seen the appearance of a school of thought that would radically restructure economic goals and institutions by limiting or stopping growth. Critics in this school have emerged with concern for dwindling resources and expanding populations. Schumacher, for example, wrote *Small Is Beautiful* (1973), in which he argumentatively set forth conservationlike ideas from Buddhist economics and urged a new consciousness in which people would live in harmony with nature instead of dominating and destroying it. The method for accomplishing this is rejection of traditional growth ideology.

One variant of radical economic thinking is the notion of "economic conversion," or the idea that defense plants should be switched to consumer goods production. Some labor groups and nuclear freeze proponents believe that the human and material resources that go into weapons could be more productively used in other sectors of the economy. They argue that the massive diversion of capital, labor, and scientific skill since World War II into the relatively poor investment of war material has deprived the U. S. economy of potential growth and productivity. It is, of course, unlikely that defense contractors will respond to these appeals for redirection, but a spirited debate exists (see for example Dumas and Gordon, 1986).

The impact of non-Marxist radicals is usually not great on mainstream opinion. But it is a good guess that their ideas, like the socialists', attain a certain trendy currency and, sometimes in milder guise, become widely recognized gibes at current policy.

Reactionary Critics

Reactionary critics assail the business community for responding to liberal critics, going too far in the direction of nonmarket activities, or undertaking political and moral stands in conflict with conservative ideals. Economist Milton Friedman is a leader of the group that flays business for departing from traditional economic roles in social projects that do not maximize profits and for accepting an enlarged role of government in providing incentives and regulations for business. The laissez-faire orthodoxy of this group is influential with the conservative element of the business community. We feel that it is not fair to call them critics in the ordinary sense, but because their ideas often challenge prevailing practice, these conservative thinkers logically may be included here.

A variety of conservative activists exists. For example, antipornography campaigns attack corporate interests for outrages to decency. A fundamentalist Christian minister from Mississippi, Reverend Donald Wildman, masterminded a campaign against drugstores and convenience markets which virtually forced more than a dozen retail chains to stop newsstand sales of *Playboy* and *Penthouse* in 1985 and 1986. In 1985, a group known as the "Washington wives" formed the Parents' Music Resource Center in Washington, D. C., to combat pornography in rock music. They included Susan Baker, wife of Treasury Secretary James Baker, Nancy Thurmond, wife of Senator Strom Thurmond (R-South Carolina), and Tipper Gore, wife of Senator Albert Gore (D-Tennessee). By appearing on talk shows, writing magazine articles, giving interviews, and mailing literature, the women created widespread debate on sexually explicit, violent song lyrics. Hundreds of radio and TV stations responded to pressure from parents and agreed not to play offensive renditions. Subsequently, record companies started to tag records with labels cautioning parental guidance if lyrics were questionable.

Also in 1985, Senator Jesse Helms (R-North Carolina) made a flamboyant move to topple the management at CBS with a grassroots takeover campaign. He calculated that if 1 million conservatives across the country purchased an average of twenty shares of stock (which would cost about $1,500 at prevailing prices), he would have enough proxies to control management and expunge "liberal bias" at CBS. He sent out over a million letters but dropped the campaign quietly after failing in an effort to replace two directors at the annual meeting in April.

Incidents such as these show that although most critics of big business are liberal or radical, elements of business's behavior aggravate conservatives, too.

MARX AND THE LEFTIST CHALLENGE: A SPECIAL NOTE

The greatest single influence in the ideology of modern international socialism is Karl Marx, a philosopher of genius whose original interpretations of history and economics have transformed the revolutionary countries of the Soviet Union, China, Cuba, and much of the underdeveloped world and posed an incisive critique of modern American and European capitalism.

Marx's Background

Marx (1818–1883) was born in the German Rhineland, the son of a well-educated Jewish lawyer. He was unusually precocious but difficult as a child. When he became a law student at the University of Bonn, his father once showed concern that his son's brilliance was not matched by sensitivity to humanistic ideals and asked in a letter, "Is your heart equal to your head, to your capacities?" After a year at Bonn, Marx transferred to the University of Berlin, dropped his law studies, and plunged deeply into philosophical study and debate. Thus began a period of more than a decade in which he took up radical causes, edited radical newspapers, and was expelled from so many continental countries that he was forced to flee to England. He lived in London from 1849 until his death thirty-four years later.

In England Marx pursued his inquiries in great poverty, spending long hours in the library and smoking cheap cigars while he wrote voluminous notes and manuscripts. He lived with his wife, Jenny, and their children in shocking conditions in Soho, one of the worst slums in London. He hid from dunning creditors in their dirty flat with broken furniture, and some days the family lay in bed with the lights out because all their clothes were in pawn. Of Marx's six children, three died largely as a result of these miserable conditions. Penury injured his pride and health, but he persisted in his work and achieved great fame during his later years.

Marx is best known for *The Communist Manifesto* (1848), a short, biting piece of political propaganda, and *Das Kapital* (1867, with the second and third volumes published posthumously after editing by Friedrich Engels, Marx's lifelong collaborator, in 1885 and 1895), a comprehensive and original treatise of international socialism. The ideas presented in these and other works are worthy of elaboration because of their lasting influence.

Economic Determinism

Unlike previous social analysts, Marx believed that the material conditions or economic arrangements of society determined the course of history. Previous thinkers had emphasized the role of leaders, laws, and political events, but Marx argued that history unfolded according to the laws that govern forces of production and exchange, a doctrine he called *historical materialism*. He argued, for example, that the feudal system gave way to the nation-state system in Europe as a result of economic changes that accompanied the growth of the middle class in townships.

Dialectical Materialism

Marx coupled this doctrine of historical materialism with two other ideas. First, he believed that social change came about through the operation of an all-inclusive process called *dialectical materialism*. In looking at the pages of history, he saw that in ancient and feudal times, economic institutions (like slavery and the feudal land tenure system) gradually came into contradiction with new economic forces, causing epochs of social revolution from which new economic relationships emerged. The dialectic process he saw can be compared to a dialogue in which A states his views, B states contrary views and argues against A's ideas, and then after discussion, A and B agree on a compromise position, C, which retains the truest elements of both arguments. The process does not end there. Because events change and position C becomes untenable, a new argument arises to challenge it, and the process is repeated. Dialectic materialism for Marx was this process painted on the canvas of history, where economic arrangements arise, challenge old ways, and are themselves later challenged. In *Das Kapital* he stated that just as ancient and feudal arrangements had succumbed to material forces that arose to challenge them, so capitalism had reached its hours of destiny because of the socialist challenge. Unlike previous dialectic movements, however, the victory of socialism was to be final, and no new antithesis would arise to challenge the emergence of a classless utopia.

The Theory of Surplus Value

Second, the Marxist *theory of surplus value* was that the capitalist system caused even the most well-meaning capitalist owners to exploit workers. Factory workers, he argued, by adding the only thing that they own to the production process—their labor—create value, and the employer who hires them anticipates that they will create more value than they need to make a living. Capitalist fortunes are then accumulated at the expense of workers. If, for example, a worker is paid $16 a day but produces products that can be sold for $20, the worker has created a surplus value of $4, which can be appropriated by the employer as profit. In this exploitation of workers by capitalism lay its great weakness. When workers realized how they were being exploited, they would revolt and create a socialist system in which private property was outlawed and wealth shared.

The Inevitability of Class War

Marx's *theory of class war* explained how actual changes in property arrangements took place. Every society beyond the most primitive, he said, could be divided into a small ruling class and a larger subject class. The dominant position of the ruling class derived from control over productive processes and the resulting control over the political, legal, military, and intellectual superstructure of society that this bestowed. But because of technological changes in productive forces, the ruling and subject classes come into conflict, and this conflict is most sharply present in capitalist countries because of their tendency to develop extremes of wealth and poverty. The class struggle within capitalist countries would ultimately end in a revolutionary victory of the exploited working class over the property-owning capitalist class. Workers would revolt when they became conscious of their common interest in stopping exploitation and would build a classless society in which the fruits of production would be shared equally.

Concluding Observations

The theory was harsh, unsentimental, and antiliberal. Unlike other philosophies of the period, it emanated from observation and close study of historical fact rather than mental gymnastics by armchair philosophers who disdained a look at the "real world." Moreover, it was all-encompassing, and in the words of Isaiah Berlin, Marx's distinguished biographer:

> The system as it finally emerged was a massive structure, heavily fortified against attack at every strategic point, incapable of being taken by direct assault, containing within its walls elaborate resources to meet every conceivable contingency of war. Its influence has been immense on friend and foe alike, and in particular on social scientists, historians, and critics. It has altered the history of human thought in the sense that after it certain things could never again be plausibly said (Berlin, 1963: 14).

The Marxist critique never really caught on as a political movement in America. The leftist movements in the United States reached a peak in 1912, when Eugene V. Debs, the Socialist candidate for the presidency, polled 6 percent of the popular vote. During the next decade, however, the party was torn asunder by revolt of its left wing, which believed that the success of the Bolsheviks in Russia could be repeated in America and refused to accept moderation.

Although organized radicalism lies dormant, Marx's critique pinpoints troublesome areas of capitalism such as the alienation of factory workers, the dangers of foreign policy based on world power and domination, inequality in income distribution, the difficulties of controlling externalities in the manufacturing process, and additional frustrations. The socialist critique of "monopoly capitalism" is alluring to some intellectuals and malcontents because it embraces new values, incorporates themes of protest popular with social critics and have-nots, and provides a theoretical foundation for their resolution. In addition, the people of socialist and communist countries (whose populations now exceed that of all capitalist countries) provide a living example of an alternative system at work.

Why has Marxist ideology never bloomed in America? The relative affluence of the working and middle classes, the continuous redistribution of wealth through social welfare programs, and the existence of an electoral system of single-member districts, which makes the election of Socialist third-party candidates difficult, are continuous barriers to serious efforts at conversion of political and property arrangements.

ACTIVIST CRITICS WHO ARE CORPORATE SHAREHOLDERS

Two brothers, John and Lewis Gilbert, pioneered the art of shareholder activism in the 1930s. The Gilbert brothers have attended thousands of corporate annual meetings to question officers about such delicate matters as their salaries. In 1942, the Securities and Exchange Commission adopted Rule 14a-8, which required corporations to include on proxy statements resolutions suggested by stockholders about important corporate matters. At the time of the annual meeting, when corporate business is conducted, all stockholders may vote on these resolutions. If they receive a majority of voting shares, they are binding on management. In the 1970s, shareholder resolutions became popular with social activists, especially church groups, as a means of pressing demands for socially responsible corporate action. The Gilberts have filed a large number of them also.

The first use of the proxy mechanism for a socially responsible shareholder resolution occurred in 1970, when a nonprofit public interest group, Campaign GM, qualified two resolutions for a vote in the General Motors Corp. annual meeting. The first, a resolution to expand the GM board of directors by adding public interest representatives, received 2.44 percent of votes cast; the second, a resolution to establish a committee of shareholders on social responsibility, got 2.73 percent of the vote. Although GM management fought with the SEC to keep the resolutions off its proxy statement and opposed them at the annual meeting, within a year GM established a public policy committee on its board of directors and appointed a black minister, the Reverend Leon Sullivan, to the board. Hence, Campaign GM achieved notable impact even though its resolutions got only a tiny fraction of the vote.

Activist critics observed the results of Campaign GM, and soon socially responsible shareholder resolutions were common at annual meetings of large corporations. Resolutions have been sponsored by individuals, universities, labor unions, and pension funds. By 1972, a total of thirty-seven such resolutions were voted on, and the number swelled to 213 in 1976. In the early 1980s, the number of resolutions voted on leveled off at between 100 and 25 annually.

Church investors have set up an organization in New York, the Interfaith Center on Corporate Responsibility (ICCR), to research and coordinate their proxy activities. Its membership includes 200 Roman Catholic orders and dioceses and fourteen Protestant denominations. A second organization, the Investor Responsibility Research Center (IRRC) in Washington, D.C., was established by major universities and foundations to research shareholder resolutions and publish impartial reports for institutional investors who subscribe to its services. More than 170 institutional investors now subscribe.

The movement was spurred on by the publication in 1972 of a book, *The Ethical Investor*, in which the authors developed a rationale for shareholder activism called the Kew Gardens principle (named after the location in New York City of an infamous incident in which a young woman named Kitty Genovese was repeatedly stabbed before onlookers who refused involvement). According to this principle, there are four criteria which, when met, create a moral imperative for shareholder action. First, a *need* for corrective action exists when corporate activity causes injury. Second, *proximity* exists if a person or group becomes a stockholder of an irresponsible corporation. Third, *capability* to help resolve a problem is created when a shareholder has available the proxy mechanism to force discussion of social issues. And fourth, the element of *last resort* arises when social pressure and other methods exclusive of shareholder activism have been tried and failed. When these conditions are met, shareholders have an ethical duty, according to the authors of *The Ethical Investor*, to file resolutions (Simon et al., 1972).

Topics and Tactics of Shareholder Resolutions

Since the mid-1970s, about 20 to 25 percent of each year's crop of shareholder resolutions have been about limiting corporate involvement in South Africa (and other countries with controversial human rights records). Other frequent topics are defense production and nuclear weapons manufacturing, nuclear power, plant closings, marketing of infant formula in the Third World, energy conservation, sales of drugs in the Third World, nuclear power plants, affirmative action programs, environmental pollution, sales of American goods to communist nations, and corporate charitable giving.

Until 1984, shareholders with only a few shares were permitted to file resolutions, and many stockholders with one to ten shares were originators or parties to them. For example, in 1983 the Clergy and Laity Concerned and the Dominican Province of St. Albert the Great proposed to file a resolution with the First Chicago Corporation requiring it to defend its sale of South African krugerrands. The two groups together owned only eleven shares of First Chicago. However, many church groups own hundreds or thousands of shares. And until 1984, shareholder resolutions that achieved a 3 percent vote were eligible for inclusion on the proxy statement for a second year. In 1983, 73 percent of the resolutions received 3 percent or more of the vote. But in January 1984, the SEC changed proxy eligibility rules to require that any shareholder advancing a resolution must have held at least $1,000 worth of stock or 1 percent of outstanding shares for a year. It also required a defeated proposal to achieve 5 percent of the vote to be eligible for balloting the next year, 8 percent in the second year, and 10 percent in the third year. After a legal battle the original resubmission percentages were restored in time for the 1986 proxy season. But in the meantime the number of resolutions voted on dropped from 111 in 1983 to only 48 in 1984 and 52 in 1985. In 1986 the number rose to 85.

The Impact of Shareholder Proposals

How effective are social-responsibility resolutions? In the early years of their use, effectiveness was often limited by poor phraseology, ignorance of corporate operations, and uncompromising attitudes toward management. However, "ethical investors" are becoming more sophisticated and have had growing influences.

Not a single social resolution opposed by management has received a majority vote. Shareholder activists have used the proxy machinery to arouse shareholders and to put corporate management on the defensive. Because large institutional investors are increasingly willing to vote for and even propose such resolutions, the average vote on all of them has risen steadily from 5.2 percent in 1983 to 8.2 percent in 1986. A decade ago it was unheard of for such resolutions to get as much as 10 percent of the vote at an annual meeting. But in 1985 and 1986 two resolutions sponsored by the New York City Employees' Retirement System related to the involvement of Chesebrough-Ponds and Foster-Wheeler Corp. in South Africa set records by receiving votes of 23.1 percent and 28 percent respectively.

Resolutions need not pass, of course, to influence corporate behavior. Each year many are withdrawn after negotiations between management and their sponsors. In 1986, there were twenty-six negotiated settlements out of the 137 resolutions filed. To illustrate, nine church groups filed a resolution asking Burlington Northern to make a report to stockholders on its legal obligations for safe railroad transport of nuclear materials. After negotiations, the company agreed to release information, and the shareholders withdrew the resolution.

CONCLUSION: THE FUNCTION OF CRITICISM

In this chapter we have shown that negative attitudes toward business have been commonplace throughout the history of civilization. Although the business system has had widespread support in America's past, for the last twenty years public opinion polls have shown high levels of criticism.

This criticism is not all bad. The tension and conflict among business, government, and the public that results from ongoing processes of demand and accommodation are vital to societal well-being. Even forces that provoke cynicism are part of a robust and functional dynamic that leads to healthy examination of major social institutions (Chapman, 1969). It is not necessarily a benediction to have an abundance of internal harmony. Machiavelli argued that the quarrels between the senate and the people of Rome resulted in laws that were beneficial to the maintenance of liberty and that greater domestic tranquillity would have enfeebled that great state.

Public antipathy and resistance to the business community are a source of stress that may lead to constructive change of the kind that Thomas Jefferson implied when he argued: "A little rebellion now and then is a good thing, and as necessary in the political world as storms in the physical."

CASE STUDY

OPERATION PUSH NEGOTIATES WITH CORPORATIONS

We are tired of you white folks, you racists and you bigots mistreating us. We are tired of paying you to deny us the right to even exist. . . . We mean business, white folks. We ain't gonna shoot you all, we are going to hit you where it hurts most . . . in the pocketbook.

—*Charles Evers, April 9, 1969, Port Gibson, Mississippi*

Late in 1980, the Coca-Cola Co. was approached by the Reverend Jesse Jackson and other representatives of Operation PUSH (People United to Serve Humanity), a Chicago civil rights organization founded and headed by Jackson. Armed with marketing surveys showing that blacks spent millions annually for Coca-Cola brand soft drinks, the PUSH delegation informed management that the company needed to do more for economic welfare in the black community.

Specifically, Jackson and PUSH demanded that Coca-Cola franchise forty Coca-Cola syrup, wholesale operations to black entrepreneurs in the next ten years; sell five of its 550 bottling companies to blacks within five years; hire a black advertising agency for one soft drink brand; increase deposits and loan activity with black-owned banks; double current levels of advertising in black media; and endow chairs at black colleges.

The official Coca-Cola position has always been that the company was enthusiastic about negotiations to improve its relations with the black community. But insiders say there was resentment. Early in the negotiations, Jackson angered Coke management with a newspaper column that suggested that the company was excluding black participation. Later, Coca-Cola offended Jackson when it dispatched a black vice president to negotiate with him. Jackson angrily demanded a meeting with Donald R. Keough, Coca-Cola's president and chief operating officer, stating that he had "talked to popes and presidents" and wanted the highest authority (Roberts, 1982: 25).

By summer 1981, talks had stalled, and when PUSH held its annual convention in July, Jackson announced a "withdrawal of enthusiasm" from Coca-Cola among black consumers. He accompanied his exhortation with a catchy slogan:

"Don't choke on Coke." Throughout the country, black ministers encouraged their congregations to boycott Coke products, and PUSH activists spread the word. Within three weeks, Coca-Cola agreed to a "moral covenant." Although Coca-Cola states the boycott had no effect, PUSH later pointed to a 14.2 percent rise in fourth-quarter earnings in 1981, which would not have taken place if the "withdrawal of enthusiasm" had still been in force. The Coke-PUSH "trade agreement" was sealed with a handshake between Jackson and Keough. It is not legally enforceable, although Coke is encouraged to honor the agreement by the threat of renewed boycott. Under the final terms of agreement, Coke agreed to do the following:

■ Set up thirty-two new black wholesale distributors of Coca-Cola syrup over the next year and provide special training for them.

■ Set up a venture capital unit to make $1.8 million in low-interest loans to black entrepreneurs in the beverage industry.

■ Establish a pool of black investors qualified to buy Coca-Cola bottling franchises if any became available for sale.

■ Undertake an affirmative action program to boost blacks from 5 percent of management positions to 12.5 percent and to fill 100 blue-collar jobs with blacks.

■ Search for and hire a black to serve on the corporate board.

■ Assign a Coca-Cola brand and an $8 million contract to a black advertising agency.

■ Increase to $5 million deposits and borrowing from black banks.

■ Donate $250,000 in the next year to black charities.

Prior to the agreement, Coca-Cola was generally regarded as progressive with respect to civil rights, but none of its 550 bottlers was black-owned, only two of 4,000 authorized distributors were black, the company spent only $50,000 a year advertising in black media, and it had only about $250,000 in deposit and loan activity with minority banks. The overall PUSH-Coke package was worth an estimated $34 million to the black community.

When the agreement was announced, there was a mild white backlash. Coke's management received many letters criticizing the company for giving in to the pressure. A group called the National Association for the Advancement of White People threatened a reactionary boycott, but it never materialized.

Despite the mild backlash, PUSH reached similar agreements with five other large corporations—with a total value of $1.8 billion in economic benefits to the black community—in the two years following the Coca-Cola agreement. The PUSH message proved so powerful that even when a major corporation —Anheuser-Busch—tried to resist, it was forced into an agreement.

Jesse Jackson Creates Operation PUSH

To understand Operation PUSH, it is essential to understand its creator, the indomitable Jesse Jackson. Jackson was born in Greenville, South Carolina. Some suggest that his intense motivation to acquire power and recognition is a reaction to the humiliation of his having been born illegitimate. Later, Jackson enrolled at the University of Illinois, but he soon left to attend North Carolina Agricultural and Technical State University, stating that the Illinois football coaches would not accept a black quarterback. At North Carolina A & T, Jackson quarterbacked the team, was student body president, and became active in the civil rights movement. After graduation, he entered Chicago Theological Seminary and in 1968 was ordained a Baptist minister.

By this time, Jackson was active in the national civil rights movement and was recognized by Martin Luther King as a potential leader. In 1966 King appointed Jackson head of Operation Breadbasket in Chicago. Operation Breadbasket was a Southern Christian Leadership Conference (SCLC) program started to promote the economic welfare of Chicago's black community. It was as head of Operation Breadbasket that Jackson honed the ideas and practiced on a small scale the tactics that later resulted in multimillion dollar agreements with major corporations. Jackson targeted grocery stores in Chicago's slum areas and pressured them to hire more blacks and reserve shelf space for black products such as Mumbo barbeque sauce and Sparkle floor wax. His confrontational, crusading style met with the approval of the black community in Chicago, but it created friction between Jackson and Reverend Ralph David Abernathy, who had assumed the mantle of leadership of the national civil rights movement after Martin Luther King's assassination in 1968.

Jackson challenged Abernathy's authority as president of the SCLC by operating independently and directing attention toward himself. In 1968, for example, Abernathy organized a Poor People's Campaign and led thousands of the poor to Washington, D. C., where they created a tent city on the Washington Monument Mall. After the protest was well under way, Jackson went to the tent city, declared himself "mayor," and then left shortly thereafter. Questions arose about the sharing of funds between Operation Breadbasket in Chicago and the parent SCLC organization, and ultimately the friction led Abernathy to suspend Jackson from SCLC for sixty days in 1971. Jackson then founded Operation PUSH on Christmas Day 1971, during a rally at the Metropolitan Theater in Chicago's black community.

PUSH Rises to National Prominence

In its early years, Operation PUSH pressured white merchants in Chicago to show greater economic and social responsibility toward the black community. If merchants hired too few blacks or sold shoddy products at high prices, Operation PUSH spread the word through the black community not to patronize their stores. A few modest agreements were reached with such corporations as

General Foods, Schlitz, Avon Products, Millers Brewery, A & P Stores, and regional units of Coca-Cola. For example, after meetings with Jackson in 1975, Burger King Corp. of Miami announced that it would underwrite a $4,000 breakfast at the Seventh Annual PUSH Expo in Chicago, set up a $6,000 scholarship fund for minority college students, and most important, organize a national Burger King/PUSH Day on which Burger King restaurants serving black communities would contribute 10 percent of sales to PUSH (ultimately $19,000 was raised) (Strenski, 1976).

Early in the 1980s, however, Jackson had become the most popular civil rights leader with blacks. A *Jet* magazine poll in 1980 showed him to be number one. And his economic programs came into full bloom. The Coca-Cola trade agreement came first in 1981 and was the model for similar agreements with five other large corporations. The first to follow the Coke agreement was a $61 million trade agreement with Heublein, a large distiller and food products firm with many brand names popular among blacks, including Kentucky Fried Chicken, Smirnoff vodkas, Italian Swiss Colony wine, and A-1 Steak Sauce. Heublein offered to make 122 Kentucky Fried Chicken outlets available to black entrepreneurs and agreed to a multimillion dollar package of expenditures with black-owned banks, insurance companies, advertising agencies, and suppliers. Next came Seven Up, a subsidiary of Philip Morris, which agreed to a similar $51 million package. Burger King USA agreed to a whopping $500 million package. And the Southland Corporation—a large retailer with consumer brands such as Adohr Farms, 7-Eleven, and Chief Auto Parts stores—agreed to a $600 million package.

The next target, however, was resistant. In the summer of 1982, Jackson approached Anheuser-Busch Companies of St. Louis—makers of a number of popular beer brands, including Budweiser, Natural Light, Michelob, and Busch. Unlike some of the other companies approached by PUSH, Anheuser-Busch had an exemplary affirmative action record that was respected in the St. Louis black community. Although black consumers were only 10 percent of Anheuser-Busch's market, 18 percent of its 14,000 employees were black and Hispanic, including 9.6 percent of officers and directors, 7.8 percent of professionals, and 18 percent of technicians. Anheuser-Busch had deposits and loans of $10 million with minority banks, had two blacks on its board of directors, bought $18 million of products a year from minority suppliers, and annually spent $7 million advertising in minority media. True, there were only one black and three Hispanics out of almost 950 distributors, but the company planned to make $5 million in loans to help blacks buy distributorships in the future (Ross, 1982).

Anheuser-Busch's management felt that its level of performance on minority affairs was exemplary and that its accomplishments compared favorably to the negotiated goals of the other five companies with which Jackson had moral covenants. August A. Busch III, the company's chairman, refused to meet with Jackson; therefore, Jackson proclaimed a black consumer boycott of Anheuser-Busch's beer brands. PUSH activists and black leaders publicized the boycott and Jackson's slogan, "Bud's a dud." The boycott was particularly effective in Chicago where, for example, the owner of a liquor store on the South Side brought out cases of Budweiser while a crowd opened the cans and drained them on the sidewalk. A PUSH official wrote:

> So far, of the corporations we have approached, only Anheuser-Busch has shown the disrespect and arrogance to refuse to negotiate an agreement with the Black Community. As a result PUSH has urged all fair-minded people to withdraw their support from Budweiser, Michelob and other products of this company until Anheuser-Busch is prepared to negotiate a "fair share" agreement as other corporations have done. The record of this corporation is insulting to the Black Community. It substitutes their own definition of charity for a relationship of mutual respect and parity. This is unacceptable and we will continue to boycott this company until a change is effected (O'Dell, 1983: 12–13).

There was much support for Anheuser-Busch in the St. Louis black community, and Jackson angered black business leaders there during a speech when he urged black companies to pay $500 each to join Operation PUSH. Jackson implied that those who joined would be the firms that benefited from the economic bonanza when the trade agreement with Anheuser-Busch was signed. Jackson said, "You've got to pay to play." Black leaders rebelled at such arm twisting. The St. Louis *Sentinel*, a black-owned newspaper, ran editorials critical of Jackson and suggested that he was a "charlatan," defrauding the black community. Jackson sued the *Sentinel* for libel but dropped the matter shortly thereafter.

Anheuser-Busch claimed the boycott was not affecting sales, but PUSH received internal company memos showing otherwise. Eventually the company caved in and reached a trade agreement with Jackson. The boycott was hurting the company financially, and management was afraid that a protracted national conflict with PUSH would permanently sour relations with the black community.

PUSH Philosophy and Organization

By 1987, Operation PUSH had a staff of twenty in Chicago and operated in concert with seventy affiliates in large and small cities across the country. During his campaign for the presidential nomination of the Democratic party in 1984, Jesse Jackson resigned as president of PUSH to head the new Rainbow Coalition. But today PUSH remains an important power base for him, and he continues to lead many of its activities. Since the pioneering Coca-Cola agreement, PUSH has reached both formal and informal "fair share" agreements with dozens of white-dominated companies. When all these commitments are added up, they total over $2.8 billion in economic benefits for the black community.

Operation PUSH was founded to achieve material equality for the black community through social activism. It is defined by members as a civil economic organization, not a civil rights organization. Whereas civil rights organizations seek equal rights, Operation PUSH was founded to move a step beyond this and achieve real economic equality for America's 30 million blacks. Instead of civil rights, Jackson frequently speaks of "silver rights."

The organizational philosophy of Operation PUSH is an extension of Jesse Jackson's belief that widespread racism causes economic and social injustice. Jackson believes that American blacks are analogous to an underdeveloped, third world nation within a developed nation and that white corporate leadership is similar to a colonial elite that exploits people in the territory it occupies. Hence, Jackson has explored trade agreements to establish economic relations between black America and the Arab nations, African nations, and Japan. PUSH has accepted controversial donations from Arab interests. A 1979 cash donation of $10,000 led to a four-year investigation by the Justice Department, which uncovered no wrongdoing. PUSH also received $100,000 from the Arab League and $100,000 from the Palestine Liberation Organization.

PUSH has an International Affairs Department, which works to further a new world order in which the rights of the poor and oppressed are recognized. The PUSH foreign policy is often antagonistic to official American foreign policy. For example, PUSH has advocated recognizing the PLO, withdrawal of support for the South African government, cessation of support for the "contras" in Nicaragua, an end to U. S. support of Joseph Savimbi's "freedom fighters" in Angola, and establishing ties between the Cuban people and black Americans. PUSH believes that blacks should not be intimidated by the white establishment into confining their interests to domestic issues, because the struggle for equality and economic rights is worldwide. In addition to the International Affairs Department, PUSH has also organized programs for community services, political action and voter registration, and higher education for blacks. Over the years, PUSH has shown an interest in a wide variety of domestic issues, including police brutality, housing, education, utility company rates, health care, hunger and malnutrition, prison reform, and drug abuse.

Nevertheless, the primary PUSH concern is economic development of the black community. Jackson favors strict enforcement of civil rights laws but feels that blacks are entitled to more than the legal minimum. Instead of receiving larger government doles, they should receive economic benefits from corporations proportional to their investment. To Jackson, investment means consumer spending. Hence, the black investment in a corporation is measured as the proportion of its products they purchase.

To define what trade reciprocity with the black community means to an individual company, Jackson has developed a novel definition of investment. If blacks are 25 percent of a corporation's customers, they should, according to Jackson, be 25 percent of its personnel, drive 25 percent of its trucks, and be 25 percent of its suppliers, contractors, bankers, insurers, and franchisees. Because corporations don't live up to this implicit obligation, economic justice for blacks can be achieved only through explicit trade arrangements. Blacks' fair share of corporate spending is a percentage equal to the percentage of the corporate product or service purchased by blacks, not the spending resulting from adherence to federal affirmative action laws. Federal hiring regulations and incentive programs are only minimums.

"Trade, not aid," is a frequent Jackson battle cry. Blacks spend $200 billion a year as consumers, making them the ninth largest market in the world if compared to national consumer markets. Yet the economic benefits of this spending power primarily benefit the white community. Black businesses remain small. Among the top 100 black-owned businesses, not one is large enough to appear on the *Fortune* 500. Many are auto dealerships. The major consumer product firms in America continue to be white dominated. Although black Americans spend over $2.5 billion each year on tobacco, for example, there are no black-owned tobacco companies; although blacks spend $2.7 billion annually on soft drinks, only five of 640 distributorships are black-owned (Shack, 1986). According to a PUSH policy statement, Jesse Jackson believes that:

> Corporate America must renegotiate its relationship with Black America, changing that relationship from one of economic concubinage to a true marriage in which our convergent interests and legitimate needs are mutually respected and protected. A deliberate shift must be made, through negotiation, from the patently unfair and myopic policy which advocates that Corporate America sell to Black America, but does not in return buy from Black America. In its stead must be institutionalized a system of nonrestrictive trade reciprocity within which corporate America will gain expanded market opportunities and increased profits, and Black America will achieve economic development and trade parity (Operation PUSH, 1986b: 85).

The PUSH philosophy fits into the nonviolent tradition of social protest represented by Thoreau, Gandhi, and Martin Luther King, Jr. It builds on the civil rights campaigns of the 1940s and 1950s which encouraged conformity to the slogan, "Don't buy where you can't work." So rather than calling for violent protest to achieve "silver rights" for black America, Jackson relies on a nonviolent but potent weapon—the black consumer boycott. Boycotts brought Coca-Cola and Anheuser-Busch to their knees, and the threat of a boycott lurks in the background of all Operation PUSH negotiations. Once a "moral convenant" is reached, the same boycott threat ensures that the corporation honors its terms.

The economic boycott has been viewed by blacks as a legitimate weapon since early in the civil rights movement. Until 1982, the boycott had been under a legal cloud because of a long-standing, unresolved case in which white merchants in Claiborne County, Mississippi, sued the NAACP for damages resulting from a boycott in 1966. When Jackson first began negotiations with Coca-Cola in 1980, the legal status of a black boycott was clouded, and Jackson had to use the euphemistic phrase "withdrawal of enthusiasm" when he implemented economic sanctions. But in 1982, in *NAACP et al. v. Claiborne Hardware Co. et al.*, a unanimous Supreme Court ruled that the black boycott in Mississippi was a legitimate exercise of First Amendment rights, including freedom of assembly, freedom of speech, and the right to petition for redress of grievances. Hence, when Jackson warred against Anheuser-Busch in 1982, he was less restrained in directly calling for a boycott.

PUSH boycotts must be taken seriously. There are forty-six PUSH chapters in twenty-six states, and in addition, PUSH has set up a National Selective Patronage Council composed of local black leaders who spread boycott news through PTOs, labor unions, fraternities, and other groups. PUSH also sponsors a weekly rally in Chicago, featuring the PUSH gospel choir and sermons by Jesse Jackson or visiting black evangelists. The rally is carried on radio and is held on Saturday mornings, because Saturday is the biggest shopping day of the week and the best day on which to mobilize action against businesses that have been disrespectful of the black community.

In addition, PUSH has the support of black churches and ministers across the country. The National Baptist Convention U.S.A., in which Jackson was ordained a minister in 1968, is the nation's largest black denomination, with 7 million members in 30,000 churches. Traditionally, social activism has been more deeply rooted in black clergy than white clergy. Many blacks have deep respect for the social and political views of ministers, and ministers are willing to spread boycott news. PUSH claims that it is not a church, but it has an intimate relationship with the black religious community. This relationship is an underlying source of strength and legitimacy. There is a Religious Affairs Department in the PUSH organization that maintains liason with black church leadership across America. And the PUSH negotiation team that tackles large corporations is headed by clergy. The following is an exerpt from the "Position Statement for the PUSH Religious Affairs Department."

> The negotiations led by the ministers represent the means by which we demand accountability of major corporations and industries in America's private sector where Black Americans this year will spend a minimum of $200 billion.
>
> The expenditures, for the most part, constitute an "invisible investment" of $478 million each day: an investment upon which there have been few if any returns. Indeed, when we contemplate the fact that we receive so little in return (less than 6 percent by some authoritative estimates) we recognize the "trade deficit" between Black and Corporate America as one of the most blatant examples of man's violation of his fellow man. It is a sin in its most hideous form (Operation PUSH, 1986a: 121).

PUSH is popular with the black business community. The PUSH International Trade Bureau, described in a PUSH publication as "the nucleus of a black American Common Market," has a board of directors of twenty-five black business executives and 550 member firms and individuals. Membership in the PUSH International Trade Bureau, as stated on an application form, "is open to black-owned corporations and black executives of non-black corporations that would like to be members in order to enhance their corporation's trade relations with black America." Members pay $500 to join and receive certain benefits. PUSH keeps a "match-up file" so that when trade agreements are reached, member black companies can be recommended to participate in the new largesse. Trade Bureau members also receive a newsletter, conference invitations, a membership directory, and a variety of business consulting services.

PUSH's Current Operations and a Look to the Future

Fifteen years after its founding, PUSH is pursuing its goal of black economic equity with undiminished zeal. In 1986, PUSH boycotted CBS-affiliated television stations across the country and got concessions regarding black hiring. That Christmas, a PUSH investigation found that some Cabbage Patch Dolls being sold in toy stores were made in South Africa, and it urged a boycott of those dolls by black consumers. In 1987, Jesse Jackson called for a boycott of cosmetics made by Revlon Inc. because of a statement by a top executive in *Newsweek* that black-owned businesses would begin to disappear because they were being sold to white companies. And after Japanese Prime Minister Yasuhiro Nakasone made a public statement indicating that minorities in the United States lower general levels of education and achievement, Jesse Jackson traveled to Japan, where he visited with executives of Toyota, Matsushita, Sony, and other companies urging them to hire more blacks or face black consumer boycotts in the United States.

In the late 1980s, Operation PUSH is buoyed by historical forces. Jesse Jackson's presidential campaigns, continuing discrimination and black poverty, and a record of successful trade agreements with corporations all give momentum to PUSH. Its message is powerful and antagonistic to corporate America. With the Anheuser-Busch agreement, Jackson demonstrated that PUSH could even conquer corporations with exemplary minority relations records and force them to do more.

PUSH creates a precedent for national consumer boycotts to punish corporations whose social performance falls below the expectations of blacks, environmentalists, Christians, disarmament advocates, or other groups whose members have great purchasing power. If interest group expectations differ from or exceed the corporate performance standards present in law and public policy (as is the case with PUSH), then boycott tactics may force new, extralegal performance standards on corporations. A precedent is set for seeking social goals through economic sanctions against corporations, rather than through political pressures on government. Corporations may be held hostage to interest group demands. This is the PUSH message. Some managers would like to ignore it.

Questions

1. Are the tactics of Operation PUSH, specifically the use of boycotts to divert corporate spending to blacks, unwarranted extortion or a constructive solution to social problems in the black community?
2. Is management correct to make concessions to Jackson, even where corporate equal opportunity programs are in compliance with the law or, as in the case of Anheuser-Busch, exemplary? Or should a brave company try to sit out a boycott and break Jackson's string of successes?
3. Would it be salutary for society if other pressure groups organized consumer boycotts to achieve their social goals? What would happen if the tactic was frequently used? What other groups have large enough memberships to mobilize national consumer boycotts? What factors underly a successful boycott?
4. What companies and industries are likely targets for PUSH now? How should corporations that are potential targets prepare for demands by PUSH and other groups?

PART II

BUSINESS AND GOVERNMENT

CHAPTER 5

THE GOVERNMENT–BUSINESS RELATIONSHIP: AN OVERVIEW

In June 1982, President Ronald Reagan decided to pressure the Soviet Union to relax the martial law that had been imposed on Poland, its satellite state, in December 1981. Reagan banned exports of oil and gas equipment to the Soviet Union both from United States manufacturers and from their foreign subsidiaries. Dresser Industries was among the many United States companies affected by the ban, because Dresser manufactured oil and gas equipment here and in its foreign subsidiaries.

The ban was directed at delaying construction of a gas pipeline from western Siberia to Western Europe. The pipeline was a consequence of the largest East-West business deal in history. This ambitious technical undertaking would extend 2,759 miles and would supply much of western Europe's need for gas. France, for instance, was to get 30 percent of its natural gas from the line by 1990. The French subsidiary of Dresser had a contract to supply twenty-one gas compressors needed to complete the pipeline.

The French government rejected the ban and ordered Dresser of France to honor its contract. The subsidiary ignored this request at first but later abided by it. After weeks of heated exchanges between the United States and its European allies, President Reagan lifted the sanctions against the subsidiaries of U.S. firms (Das, 1985). The Department of Commerce estimated that these sanctions had cost U.S. businesses as much as $2.2 billion and would have tarnished the reputation of U.S. firms for reliability in completing contract agreements for reliability had they not been lifted (Pine and Bennet, 1982).

Dresser never questioned that President Reagan's ban was in the interest of U.S. foreign policy. But it did question whether the ban on shipments from a foreign subsidiary was lawful. However, the Department of Commerce argued that foreign policy is of such paramount importance to the United States that any doubt about whether companies might comply with sanctions would thwart the ability of the President to use export controls to influence foreign countries. George Ball, Undersecretary of State in the Kennedy and Johnson administrations, disagreed with the ban. He said: "If the U.S. government thinks that the pipeline is not a good idea, it should quietly urge that view on its allies and try to persuade them to pursue a different course; that is what alliances are all about" (Ball, 1982).

As the subtleties of the Dresser case suggest, of all the institutions in society, none is more intimately associated with business than is government. The spectrum of relationships varies from Christmastime generosity toward tax-exempt enterprises to virtually complete control over all industry during a major war. For all business, the government is a partner—sometimes silent and sometimes quite vocal. For most businesses, government is one of the greatest influences on activity, and often it is the determining influence on many aspects of the operations of a firm—growth, pricing, production, competition, wages, profits, and investment. No simple treatment of the relationship between business and government can do it justice. A mere listing of points of impact of government on a typically large business would fill page after tedious page.

Several conclusions concerning the business-government relationship today should be stated at the outset.

■ First, during the 1960s and 1970s, the quantity and scope of new government regulations, superimposed on those of the past, have resulted in a new and fundamentally different relationship between business and government. This phenomenon is one of the two or three most significant political facts of our times.

■ Second, the relationship between business and government is basically adversarial. It complicates the managerial task and creates apprehension about the ability to preserve the best of the business institution.

■ Third, many people today believe—conservatives as well as liberals—that government less often solves society's problems than causes many of them. In numerous surveys about both government and business, Americans express a disturbing lack of confidence. Improvement in the business-government relationship has become a matter of the greatest urgency.

■ Fourth, in conformance with his campaign promises, President Reagan, at the very beginning of his administration, took action to reduce and reform the federal regulatory system. He has been only partly successful in this effort. Furthermore, based on past experience, there is high probability that some event or events in the near future will trigger another wave of federal regulation over business.

This chapter describes the basic roles assumed by government that have a major impact on business as well as the legal, economic, and social bases for government involvement with business; and it gives a broad assessment of the current business-government interrelationships. The next two chapters will present the newer patterns of government regulations in some detail.

LEGAL BASES OF GOVERNMENT ACTION TOWARD BUSINESS

The impact of government on business derives from laws applied by individuals in the executive branches of governments or tested in courts of law. These laws and their implementation are, in turn, based upon legal powers given to governments and the administrators of government programs. The fundamental basis for this tower of regulations is the Constitution of the United States.

In the Constitution, most of the economic powers exercised by the federal government are contained in Article 1, Section 8. This section gives Congress the power to levy and collect taxes; to pay debts and provide for common defense and general welfare; to borrow money; to regulate commerce; to establish bankruptcy laws; to coin money and regulate its value; to fix standards of weights and measures; to stop counterfeiting; to establish post offices and post roads; to promote science and useful arts by granting patents and exclusive rights over writings and discoveries; to punish piracies; to exercise exclusive legislation over the geographical seat of government, military establishments, and other lands owned by the government; and "to make all laws which shall be necessary and proper for carrying into execution these foregoing powers, and all other powers vested by this Constitution in the government of the United States, or in any department or officer thereof." A reasonable interpretation of such grants of authority permits the national government in today's economy to do just about anything that is likely to pass through congressional law-making machinery.

The federal government is delegated powers from the states. State governments retain those powers not explicitly or implicitly granted to the federal government or taken by it. States, therefore, may do whatever they choose as long as they are not prevented from doing so by the Constitution or the federal government. Local governments are created by and vested with powers by the states. The more important powers exercised by state and local governments over business enterprises concern powers to incorporate businesses, power to levy and collect taxes, and the police power. The first needs no elaboration. The power to tax has been used not only to raise revenue, but also to regulate and promote business. The policy powers enable states to prevent fraud, ensure adequate service at reasonable rates, protect employees from employer exploita-

Regulating the Hamburger

The ordinary hamburger is the subject of 41,000 federal and state regulations. They spring from 200 laws and 111,000 precedent-setting court cases.

A sampling of the laws governing the hamburger that you buy at the corner sandwich stand or in a fancy restaurant follows:

Bun—enriched bun must contain at least 1.8 milligrams of thiamine, 1.1 milligrams of riboflavin, and at least 8 but not more than 12.5 milligrams of iron.

Content—must be fresh or frozen chopped beef and not contain added water, binders, or extenders.

Growth promoters—use of growth-stimulating drugs must end two weeks before slaughter.

Pickle—slices must be between 1/8 and 3/8 inches thick.

Tomato—must be mature but not overripe or soft.

Cheese—must contain at least 50 percent milk fat and, if made with milk that is not pasteurized, must be cured for 60 or more days at a temperature of at least 35 degrees Fahrenheit.

Inspections—as many as six inspections under Federal Meat Inspection Act can occur as meat is checked before and after slaughter and at boning, grinding, fabrication, and packaging stages.

Mayonnaise—may be seasoned or flavored as long as the substances do not color it to look like egg yolk.

Ketchup—to be considered Grade A fancy, it must flow no more than 9 centimeters in 30 seconds at 69 degrees Fahrenheit.

Lettuce—must be fresh, not soft, overgrown, burst, or "ribby."

Fat—no more than 30 percent fat content.

Pesticides—no more than 5 parts of the pesticide DDT per million parts of fat in the meat.

Source: Adapted from *U.S. News & World Report,* February 11, 1980: 64. Excerpted from *U.S. News & World Report;* Copyright 1980, U.S. News & World Report, Inc.

tion, maintain competition, restrict competition, fix prices of commodities, establish standards for processing food and drugs, establish standards for safety in mines and factories, and in many other ways regulate and promote business.

THE SCOPE OF GOVERNMENT RELATIONS WITH BUSINESS

The federal government, the focus of this chapter, is massively involved with the business community. The following overview illustrates the breadth and depth of the relationship between government and business.

Government prescribes rules of the game. Government prescribes broad rules of business behavior within which individuals are comparatively free to act in conformity with their self-interest. Typical rules of the game concern competitive behavior, labor-management relations, the sale of securities, advertising, business incorporation, and safety regulations concerning automobiles. The regulations vary in the extent to which they restrain an individual business, but they serve to establish the "rules for playing the game."

Government is a major purchaser of the output of business. Out of a prospective GNP in calendar 1987 of $4,526 billion, federal, state, and local governments were expected to purchase $895 billion or 19.8 percent. The federal government was expected to purchase $526 billion of this total. Government purchases range from paper clips to space vehicles. Many companies, and some very large ones, sell their entire output to government. Few companies do not directly or indirectly benefit from government procurement.

The government uses its contracting power to get business to do things the government wants. Businesses that want government contracts must subcontract to minority businesses, pay prevailing minimum wages, comply with safety and sanitary work regulations, refrain from discrimination in hiring, and meet government pollution standards. Government contracting agencies by law must prefer domestic to foreign products (Buy American Act), ship all military and at least one-half of foreign aid goods in United States vessels (Cargo Preference Act), purchase all brooms and similar items from nonprofit agencies for the blind (Blind-Made Goods Act), and purchase only United States-made buses (1969 Defense Authorization Act). It is a case of "no compliance, no contract."

Government promotes and subsidizes business. The government has a complex and powerful network of programs to aid business. Promotion ranges from tariff protections to loans, guarantees of loans, maintenance of high levels of economic activity, and direct subsidies. It is, of course, in the interest of government to ensure growing and vigorous business activity, but the ways in which government promotes business vary enormously and sometimes are highly controversial. For instance, tax incentives to stimulate business to make capital investments are controversial, but training military pilots who subsequently are hired by airlines is not. Both are promotional and worth calculable dollars and cents to the businesses concerned.

Promotion, of course, is not limited to money, but includes favorable legislation and administrative action. For instance, rights given by government to operate a TV station may be extremely valuable. Because the successful promotion of the interests of one group sets a precedent for others, government promotion of business activity steadily expands despite the strong pleading of many business leaders for reduced government expenditures and more limited government.

Government owns vast quantities of productive equipment and wealth. The government is an important producer of goods and services, often in direct competition with private business. It produces goods and services such as rubber, high-octane gasoline, ammunition, guns, ships, atomic energy, postal services, weather-reporting services, and dams. The federal government owns vast stockpiles of raw materials and productive equipment, which it often lends to private industry. It also owns most of the land in many western states.

Government is an architect of economic growth. It has assumed responsibility for achieving an acceptable rate of stable economic growth, as set forth in the Employment Act of 1946. This policy benefits business by reducing economic uncertainty and making long-range planning more feasible. In the past few decades, we have had relative economic stability compared with the unexpected economic crises experienced in the century prior to World War II.

Government finances business. There is no limit to the extent to which the federal government can guarantee loans. Nearly a third of all mortgages written since 1949 have been financed or guaranteed by federal credit agencies. The federal government helps to finance airport construction, harbor improvements, and construction of canals. Direct and guaranteed loans of the federal government to business, farmers, local governments, and individuals amounted to over $1 trillion in 1985.

Government protects interests in society against business exploitation. For instance, many laws protect the interests of investors, customers, employees, and the competitors of a business.

Government directly manages large areas of private business. The word "manage" here means that government dictates a certain amount of decision making. It does not mean that the government is the manager in the way a chief executive of a company manages. In the sense meant here, the government manages important parts of industries through regulation, supervisory surveillance, and joint decision making.

NASA Funds Research for More Efficient Jet Engines

As aviation fuel costs rose along with oil prices in 1973 and 1974, airlines sought more efficient engines for their planes. Fuel costs were almost 50 percent of their total operating costs, and each 1 percent reduction in fuel consumption could save the airlines at least $100 million a year.

The dominant engine manufacturers, General Electric and Pratt & Whitney, a unit of United Technologies Corporation, had some promising proposals for more efficient engines. Both companies, however, were faced with tough competition from Great Britain's government-owned Rolls-Royce and with one another. As a consequence, they were in no position to fund the needed basic research.

The National Aeronautics & Space Administration (NASA) offered a grant of $90 million for the required research. The two companies then added $10 million to the amount of the grant and agreed to share the results of the research.

Based upon this research the two companies went on to produce much more fuel efficient engines. Ultimately, the companies spent approximately $1 billion in developing the engines, which promised at least a 20 percent improvement in fuel consumption over the older engines.

In this case, a small amount of government money, provided when private enterprise could not fund basic research, produced substantial results. The research helped the airlines to lower costs, which, in turn, led to reduced fares.

Was this grant a legitimate use of the taxpayer's money?

Government is the repositor of the social conscience and redistributes resources to meet social ends. Government increasingly redirects resources by transfer payments, research and development expenditures, tax incentives, and subsidies. These traditional means have expanded in recent years. The government also exerts moral pressure on business to act in conformity with generally accepted social goals.

This overview of the many ways in which government affects managerial decision-making in business is only an introduction. It does not convey the massive and complex impact of government regulations on business.

UNDERLYING REASONS FOR GOVERNMENT REGULATION OF THE PRIVATE SECTOR

Federal justifications for regulating the private sector can be divided into two groupings: when flaws appear in the marketplace that produce undesirable consequences; and where adequate social, political, and other reasons for government regulation exist. Regulations until recent years were introduced mostly in response to flaws in the market mechanism; in recent years regulations increasingly have been introduced for broad social reasons (Breyer, 1982).

Flaws in the Market

The competitive market, when functioning properly, yields the "best" answer to the questions of what should be produced, when, and how the product will be distributed. When functioning perfectly, the market mechanism determines how society's resources can be used most efficiently in producing the goods and services that people want (see Appendix B). This competitive model has high appeal in democratic societies because with it social welfare can be advanced without central government control.

Although highly efficient, the free-market competitive model is not flawless. Some of the more important market failures that have justified government action are as follows.

Natural Monopoly   When a firm can supply the entire market for a good or service more cheaply than any combination of smaller firms, it is said to have a natural monopoly. Under such circumstances competition would be wasteful of resources. Typical examples are, of course, public utilities. Unregulated natural monopolies have a tendency to produce insufficient output to meet demand so as to extract a higher price than would exist if competition prevailed. As a result, government traditionally has regulated utilities to determine what they may charge, to establish a minimum quality of service, and to determine the size of profit that is permissible.

Natural Resource Regulation   Exploitation of a natural resource can result in monopolistic practices that should be regulated. For example, the total volume of oil that can be produced in a single field is a function of the number of wells drilled and the rate of pumping. Too many wells and too rapid pumping reduce the field pressure and the quantity of recoverable oil. That should be avoided. Government allocation of limited wavelengths in the electromagnetic spectrum is another example of natural resource regulation.

Destructive Competition   Destructive competition can take many forms, but the classic illustration is an industry with heavy fixed costs, comparatively unable to use fixed capital for multiple purposes, and in which the introduction of new productive capacity is slow in meeting new demands. Railroads are a classic illustration of an industry that, when unregulated, falls into cutthroat competition and rates fall below marginal incremental costs.*

Externalities   Externalities are costs of production that are borne, not by the enterprise that causes them, but by society. A classic illustration is pollution. One steel mill that tries to eliminate air and water pollution will go bankrupt if other mills do not install antipollution equipment. The principle applies to industrial safety practices, health hazards, and jet noise, to give just a few examples.

Inadequate Information   Competitive markets operate more efficiently when everyone associated with them has enough information to make informed choices. To the extent that such information is not available, government finds justification for regulating the knowledge in question. This category covers a very wide range of information, including information for consumers about product quality, warranty, content, and so on; information to workers about work hazards; disclosure of financial information for investors; disclosure of costs of capital to investors; and so on.

Social, Political, and Other Reasons for Regulation

During the past several decades there have been a number of structural and value changes taking place in our society that have resulted in increasing pressure on government to interfere in the market mechanism.

Quality-of-Life Demands   Pressures on government and business to meet new quality-of-life demands are significant causes of new government regulations.

Concern for Individuals   Concern for individuals has always been a cause of federal regulation. The very first Congress of the United States passed legisla-

---

*In recent years, as will be discussed in the next chapter, several industries have been partly deregulated, including railroads.

tion to help poor and indigent sailors. Help to individuals has expanded to include programs for safe working conditions, better and safer products for consumers, eliminating discrimination in employment, and providing better health care.

Business Abuses   Unethical and immoral actions of business are, of course, a subject for regulations that aim to prevent their occurrence.

Equality   New definitions of equality give rise to new entitlements, which in turn result in government regulations to provide them.

Resolution of National Problems   For more than 200 years, the United States has been a nation, and since around the turn of the century, we have been a national economy. But not until recently have we become a national society in the sense that shocks felt in one part of the country are immediately felt in every other part. As our nation became a national economy, the federal government took on increased responsibilities in resolving the problems that accompanied its development, such as the regulation of railroads, of banking, and of aviation. These are still problems of a "national society," but more and more the "national society" evidences quality-of-life problems, such as pollution, which demand national solutions.

Regulation to Benefit Special Groups   It is possible for regulations to be passed, largely as a result of special group pressures on the legislative process to pass measures in their own selfish interests. The justification for such legislation, however, is based not on that objective but on more lofty goals. Nevertheless, a good bit of regulation does protect the interests of special groups, such as manufacturers of steel and producers of peanuts.

Conservation of Resources   Federal regulations seek to conserve our natural resources such as agricultural land, pristine forests, lakes and mountains, clean air, and endangered species.

Other Social and Political Causes of Regulation   Federal regulations also spring from national security requirements, resolving group conflicts, and alleviating risks of groups and individuals. Most government regulations before World War II attempted to reduce risks of groups and individuals from economic hazards. Today much regulation attempts to reduce other risks, such as physical harm from pollution or working conditions.

Why Business Sometimes Seeks Government Regulation

It is true that people in business loudly protest government regulations and yet seek government help on their behalf. Why do business leaders sometimes lobby the government vigorously for regulations?

First, they may fear chaos in their markets without government regulations that set specific standards. For example, companies have asked the Federal Trade Commission (FTC) to step up its regulation of deceptive advertising. The FTC recently had discontinued regulating some types of deceptive advertising practices and left such regulation to individual states. But some companies would rather have one set of federal standards to guide their actions than a welter of different state standards.

Second, regulation can help companies to avoid competitive disadvantages by taking costly unilateral action to meet public expectations. One polluter that installs expensive antipollution equipment finds itself at a competitive disadvantage if other polluters do nothing. Federal standards in such cases permit managers to meet both societal and stockholder interests.

Third, once managers have spent money to comply with a law, they may lobby to keep the law on the books. For example, when Occupational Safety and Health Administration (OSHA) decided to relax cotton-dust regulations for small textile mills, the many operators who had spent substantial sums to comply with OSHA's standards did not want to see the standards relaxed and those who had not spent funds thereby achieve a competitive advantage.

Fourth, and probably most important, companies want protection against competitors. As discussed in Chapter 19, many businesses today are lobbying in Congress for protectionist legislation against foreign competition.

Finally, managers may perceive new opportunities for profit and other tangible benefits in specific legislation. Current pressures by the oil industry to get the Congress to levy an oil import tax is a case in point. Although such a tax does have some merit from a national point of view, it would clearly benefit oil producers.

Because the public tends to perceive business as monolithic, it is cynical when it sees businesspeople seeking, on the one hand, to reduce government regulations and, on the other, lobbying to establish regulations on their own behalf. In fact, those managers who denounce government regulations are not always the same ones who lobby for specific regulations. But sometimes they are one and the same (Worrell and Gray, 1985). In such cases, public cynicism may be justified.

CHANGING HISTORICAL PATTERNS OF GOVERNMENT-BUSINESS RELATIONSHIPS

In our history, there have been four primary peacetime waves of government regulatory action affecting business. There also have been periodic expansions of government economic controls during major wars (see Exhibit 5-1). Government regulatory activity historically has come in sudden bursts, or "waves." It has moved in a ratchet-like pattern. Each wave has been triggered by the rise of popular demand for government to solve particular problems. After each burst of activity, the rate of new regulation has leveled off or declined. Except after

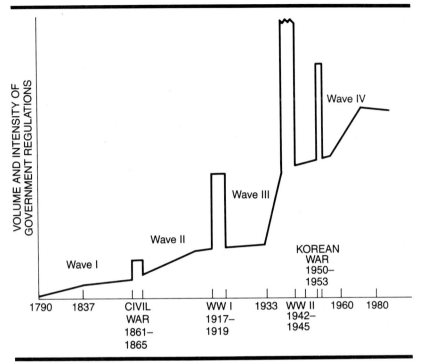

**EXHIBIT 5–1   HISTORICAL WAVES OF GOVERNMENT REGULA-
TION OF BUSINESS**

wartime, the declines have been minimal. Generally each new wave has brought with it more regulatory activities than existed previously; the exception has been the controls imposed during wartime, which were usually lifted following the end of hostilities.

The Myth of Laissez Faire

From the very beginning of our history, government has exerted more power over economic activity than is considered acceptable in classical capitalistic theory. The framers of the Constitution were determined to give the central government more, not less, power than it had under the Articles of Confederation. From that day to this, businesspeople, farmers, and other interest groups have pressured government to act on their behalf. Government has responded, and there has therefore been an increasing divergence of practice from theory. We look with pride on the rugged individualists in our early history who cleared the soil and carried on the business of that small society. But when the record is examined in detail, it becomes clear that they were not at all content with their world and pressured the government for help.

The political process has always been used by individuals and organizations to redress grievances that could not be redressed in the market or in the courts.

Naturally, as society became more complex, problems mounted, so that government was increasingly asked to interfere in the economic processes to help individuals. Until the Depression of the 1930s, government regulation of business was within the tolerable limits of classical laissez faire philosophy. Controls over business have experienced their greatest growth since then.

The First Wave   This wave of government regulation took place from 1790 to 1837. During this period, government predominantly promoted business. The second law passed by the first Congress, for example, gave a 10 percent discount on tariffs to goods brought here in American ships. The government gave vast financial subsidies and huge land grants (to be sold) to private interests for the building of turnpikes, canals, and railroads. Behind this generosity was widespread recognition of the need for better transportation in the colonies after problems in transportation had arisen during the Revolutionary War and the War of 1812. Agrarian interests also lobbied for more efficient means of getting produce to market. So large were state and local government loans that the many defaults of the depression of 1837 forced a number of them into bankruptcy. Limits in state constitutions today on loans to business stem from this period.

During this period, too, several states passed laws making it easier than before for businesses to incorporate. Before, each charter had to be formulated by the legislature. Now incorporation became virtually automatic. This development, together with a Supreme Court decision in the Dartmouth College case of 1819, significantly boosted corporate growth and industrial development. In the Supreme Court case, the New Hampshire legislature amended the charter of Dartmouth College to make it a public institution. The college trustees sued to regain the original charter, by which the college was a private institution. The Supreme Court ruled that state legislatures could not impair a contract, and the charter "is a contract, the obligation of which cannot be impaired without violating the constitution of the United States." The corporate form thereby gained freedom from arbitrary post-facto legislative interference.

The Second Wave   This wave of government regulation took place during the late nineteenth and early twentieth centuries. As a result of overproduction, farm prices fell sharply after 1865, and the farmers turned on the railroads in their disappointment. Accordingly, a number of states enacted laws to control railroad abuses (for example, charging more for a short than a long haul) and instituted reforms (for example, requiring that railroads state maximum rates). Later, in 1887, the federal government created the Interstate Commerce Commission to regulate interstate railroads.

A great wave of industrial consolidation in the 1880s led in 1890 to the Sherman Antitrust Act to control them. Further controls over business activity were provided by the Food and Drug Act and the Meat Inspection Act of 1905 as well as by the Clayton Act of 1914. Basically, this wave, in contrast to the first wave, saw expanding government regulation to curb the abuses of an ebullient, aggressive, and often irresponsible business world.

There were, however, some positive developments for business. The Supreme Court ruled in the Santa Clara case in 1886 that corporations are cloaked in the mantle of the Fourteenth Amendment to the Constitution. This amendment had been passed in 1868 to protect blacks and forbade states to abridge the privileges and immunities of citizens; to deprive any person of life, liberty, or property without due process of law; or to deny to any person within its jurisdiction the equal protection of the laws. The Court ruled that a corporation is a person and that therefore the benefits of the amendment extended to it. In effect, states could regulate corporations, but the regulations had to be developed through accepted legal procedures and be nondiscriminatory as compared with those covering individual citizens. This armor proved to be highly protective to business in the legal jungles of regulation.

Efforts by federal, state, and local governments to introduce social reforms, such as permitting workers to strike and improving working conditions, met with repeated rebuffs by the Supreme Court. For example, the State of New York attempted to reduce the hours of work in bakeries to ten a day. But this attempt, said the court in *Lockner v. New York* in 1905, was an unreasonable, unnecessary, arbitrary, illegal, and "meddlesome interference with the rights of the individual" and contrary to the Fourteenth Amendment.

The Third Wave   This wave of regulation was brought about by the Great Depression of the 1930s, one of the most severe human and economic catastrophes ever to strike the American people. In combating this crisis, the federal government assumed an entirely new role in economic life and in its relationship with business.

The statistics of this depression starkly reveal the extraordinary tragedy. For instance, GNP dropped (in current dollars) from $103.1 billion in 1929 to $58 billion in 1932. Industrial production was almost halved between these two dates. Durable goods production in 1932 was one-third the 1929 level. Steel production in 1932 was at 20 percent of capacity. The unemployment rate rose in 1933 to 25 percent of the labor force. Thousands of businesses and farmers went bankrupt, and millions of investors lost their life savings.

The New Deal of Franklin D. Roosevelt was an attempt at solution that broke new ground. The federal government for the first time assumed responsibility for stimulating business activity out of an economic depression. The federal government undertook to correct a wide range of abuses in the economic machinery of the nation, particularly in business, and amassed more far-reaching laws to this end in a shorter period of time than ever before or since. For the first time it assumed responsibility on a large scale for relieving the distress of businesspeople, farmers, workers, homeowners, consumers, investors, and other groups caused by adverse economic events.

The Fourth Wave   A groundswell of interest in improving the quality of life in the 1960s and early 1970s led to the fourth wave of government regulations. The result was the development of new government controls that involved government ever more deeply in managerial decision making,

You Be the Judge

In the one hundred days following the inauguration of President Franklin D. Roosevelt in 1933, Congress passed some of the most far-reaching peacetime legislation in the nation's history. Among the new laws was the National Industrial Recovery Act (NIRA). The National Recovery Administration (NRA) was created to administer the act and undertook the most ambitious experiment in industrial organization ever attempted in this country.

The heart of NRA activity lay in "codes of fair competition." The codes provided among other things for a minimum scale of weekly wages, maximum hours of work, collective bargaining by labor unions, prohibitions of child labor, prohibitions of raising prices beyond those justified by pay increases, and a refusal to deal with those who did not sign the agreement. Details of the agreements were hammered out by business trade associations and organized labor, and each code pertained to a specific industry. When government officials approved a code, it became law. Several million employers operated under the codes, and the public was encouraged to boycott those employers who did not display an emblem of the "Blue Eagle" that indicated compliance with industry codes.

The Schechter Poultry Corporation, of New York City, fell under the NRA's Live Poultry Code. Schechter slaughtered chickens and resold them to local retailers and butchers. The government charged the company with violating several provisions of the Live Poultry Code, including selling tubercular chickens, not paying the minimum wage, and not honoring the code's provisions for maximum work hours.

The company argued that the NIRA was unconstitutional. A long history of Supreme Court cases, said the company, concluded that the right of the government to regulate interstate commerce under the commerce clause of the Constitution (Article 1, Section 8) did not extend to local manufacturing and processing operations such as Schechter's.

The government argued that 96 percent of the poultry sold in New York City came from out of state and that activities of Schechter substantially affected the stream of interstate commerce and that the firm's plant operation therefore fell within the regulating scope of the government. The government pointed to a history of Supreme Court decisions that stopped state regulation of local activities when they directly affected interstate commerce. How would you have decided this case?

THE COURT'S DECISION

The Supreme Court unanimously declared the NIRA unconstitutional (*Schechter v. U.S.,* 1937). First, said the Court, the act put too few restrictions on the president and granted him "virtually unfettered" power to prescribe codes throughout industry, "an unconstitutional delegation of legislative power."

Second, said the Court, "Neither the slaughtering nor sales by defendant were transactions in interstate commerce. . . . After the (poultry) has arrived and has become comingled" with the mass of property within the State and is there held solely for local disposition and use (the flow of commerce stops). . . . The poultry has come to a permanent rest within the State." Thus, the commerce clause could not apply to the defendant, and the NRA codes were unconstitutional. To conclude otherwise, said the Court, "There would be virtually no limit to the Federal power, and for all practical purposes we should have a completely centralized government." But as usual, the Court left a loophole. It said that the commerce clause could apply to an essentially local or intrastate activity which had "direct" effects on interstate commerce. (See Cortner, 1970, for an excellent discussion of this and the following Jones and Laughlin case.)

Importance of the Decision

The Schechter decision was a devastating blow to the regulatory, relief, and reform program of Franklin Roosevelt. So incensed was President Roosevelt that in 1937, he sent Congress a proposal to reorganize the nation's judicial system. He recommended that the Supreme Court be expanded by six members, something that could be done constitutionally with congressional approval. The idea, of course, was to let Roosevelt pick judges who would more liberally interpret the constitutional powers granted to the federal government. But Roosevelt's "court-packing plan" created a national furor and was never implemented.

You Be the Judge

Under powers granted by Congress in the National Labor Relations Act of 1935, the National Labor Relations Board (NLRB) ordered the Jones and Laughlin Steel Corporation to cease and desist from engaging in unfair labor practices. The corporation said that the board had no powers to make such demands and the issue went to the Supreme Court for resolution in *NLRB v. Jones and Laughlin Steel Corp.*

At the time Jones and Laughlin was the fourth-largest steel company in the country. It employed 22,000 workers, of whom 10,000 were in the Aliquippa plant in Pennsylvania, the target of the NLRB's suit.

Jones and Laughlin had a long history of strife with labor unions, strife that was exacerbated by deep depression in the steel industry and huge financial losses. The NLRB pointed to a long list of unfair labor practices in the Aliquippa plant, including firing union labor leaders on grounds of trivial violation of company rules and the refusal of the company to recognize the rights of workers to organize and bargain collectively.

Jones and Laughlin argued that its Aliquippa plant was engaged entirely in production, a local activity that the Court had said was not interstate commerce. It argued that the NLRB's claim that it had the power to regulate interstate commerce under the commerce clause of the Constitution was, therefore, invalid.

The NLRB argued that the plant was a conduit through which a steady stream of interstate commerce passed. Therefore, a strike in the Aliquippa plant, which was threatening, would have a direct, substantial, and immediate impact upon interstate commerce. Because the federal government could regulate interstate commerce, it clearly had the power, said the NLRB, to prohibit Aliquippa managers from engaging in unfair labor practices. How would you have decided this case?

Continued from page 131

THE COURT'S DECISION

Four days after President Roosevelt submitted his court-packing plan to Congress, the Supreme Court began hearings on this case and four others which tested the constitutionality of the National Labor Relations Act and, of course, the powers of the NLRB. In April 1937, the Court voted 5 to 4 that the NLRB was acting upon legitimate constitutional authority. The Court found that under the commerce clause, obstructing interstate commerce was a suitable matter for congressional attention and that it had the right to delegate that power to the executive branch in the National Labor Relations Act. A strike or work disruption at the Aliquippa plant would produce such an obstruction.

Congress cannot be held powerless to regulate, said the Court, "when industries organize themselves on a national scale, making their relation to interstate commerce the dominant factor in their activities. . . ." In later decisions, the Court applied this doctrine to a cannery that shipped only one-third of its output to other states and to a power company that sold an insignificant part of its current across state lines. Furthermore, said the Court, the right of employees to organize was a "fundamental right" equal to that of employers to organize their businesses.

Significance of This Decision

The complete reversal of the Jones and Laughlin decision from the Schechter case opened wide the door for federal regulation of individual businesses. It was, with other contemporary cases, one of the most important legal foundations supporting the flood of federal regulation that has been enacted since then. It illustrates also that the Supreme Court's interpretation of the Constitution reflects the change in its environment.

---

enormously increased the volume of regulation, and tightened government's control over business—precisely the topics that make up the subject of much of this book.

War Blips   As Exhibit 5–1 shows, wars have brought sudden increases in government controls. During the Civil War, neither the North nor the South exercised much direct control over production or prices. Both governments financed hostilities by printing money. The National Banking System, created in 1863, was designed to help the federal government sell bonds. Although it only marginally helped in financing the war, it was a positive development.

World War I witnessed the introduction of nationwide controls over production, prices, the movement of commodities, and the allocation of commodities to users. The war ended, however, before these controls began to "bite." But they constituted a prototype for the comprehensive nationwide regulations that were instituted during World War II and, to a lesser extent, during the Korean War. After both wars, as we have said, the wartime controls were almost completely abandoned.

A MIXED, FREE ECONOMY

Government regulation of business has evolved to the point today that in principle virtually no aspect of business and overall economic activity is closed to government action. Despite this comparative open door to intervention, the remarkable fact about the American economy is not how much of economic life the government controls but how much it does not. Although the federal government directly controls or indirectly influences economic activity to a significant degree, the economy is in no way centrally administered or controlled.

The great bulk of goods and services are produced by individual business firms whose resources are not owned or managed by government. Millions of individual proprietors, consumers, and workers, corporations, labor unions, and farm cooperatives are relatively free to choose from among alternative courses of action. These groups and individuals determine in large degree how scarce resources are used. Although it is true that some of these decisions are made within a framework of rules laid down by government, people are rather free to pursue their economic interests as they see fit. Ours is a mixed economy in which individuals enjoy much economic freedom, in which the free market mechanism is still a powerful allocator of resources, but in which governments, especially the federal government, exercise pervasive and strong controls. One of the most important questions facing the nation today is whether this blend of government control and individual initiative is in reasonable balance.

AN OVERVIEW OF THE BUSINESS-GOVERNMENT RELATIONSHIP

Generally speaking, older regulations were designed to repair flaws in the market mechanism and, to a lesser extent, to prevent injustices among people by reducing some social and economic risks of life. More recent regulations have been aimed preponderantly at improving the quality of life in the United States.

Government's impact on business is not necessarily negative. It very often is munificently positive. No government action in economic life is wholly negative or wholly positive. Restraint for one person or business may mean freedom for another. One function of government is to implement the wishes of the people about the kind of freedom that shall be restrained in order to advance another.

Government regulations have achieved important benefits. Business could not operate and society could not prosper without certain types of regulations.

Regulations have protected and subsidized business interests as well as consumer and general-public interests. Regulation has helped society achieve economic and social goals. It has helped improve the position of minorities, achieve cleaner air, hold business accountable, prevent abuses of the market mechanism, prevent monopoly, reduce industrial accidents, and so on. The pluses of government regulation are many.

The issue today is not the justification for a particular type of regulation (government finds legal, social, and political justification for virtually any type of regulation it chooses to employ), but the choice of regulatory methods and the sheer volume and cost of the regulation.

In the aggregate, the costs of today's government regulations seem to be greater than the benefits, using costs and benefits in the broadest sense. The market mechanism in many instances has been weakened rather than strengthened by government regulation and in important segments has been supplanted by government fiat. Efficiency in the marketplace has in fact been impeded by political considerations in too many instances.

Over thirty years ago, an examination of the power relationships between business and government concluded that the scale was balanced reasonably well (G. A. Steiner, 1953). Two decades later (1975), the balance still seemed reasonable. Today it is our judgment that the overall balance is significantly upset in favor of government. We are not alone in this assessment. Both Republican and Democratic leaders, including the President of the United States, give regulatory reform a high priority on the political agenda. It certainly is of the highest importance to business leaders. The general population still may favor government regulation, but it is fearful of it.

THE SECOND MANAGERIAL REVOLUTION

The first managerial revolution occurred when the old entrepreneurial class of managers was replaced by corporate professional managers. This change took place, of course, over a long period of time, but gained public attention in the milestone study of Berle and Means, called *The Modern Corporation and Private Property*, in 1932. The second managerial revolution, according to Weidenbaum, is now taking place. It is identified by the massive transfer of power from the managerial class to a new class of public servants in the federal government armed with authority to make decisions heretofore reserved for managers in privately owned and operated businesses.

Every staff office and line operation of a large corporation today must abide by laws pertaining to its specific responsibility. Exhibit 5–2 illustrates the point. It should be kept in mind that the multiplicity of laws and detailed regulations relating to each area shown in Exhibit 5–2 could not be included on this single chart. Not illustrated on the chart is the degree to which government actually makes detailed managerial decisions in an increasing number of business areas.

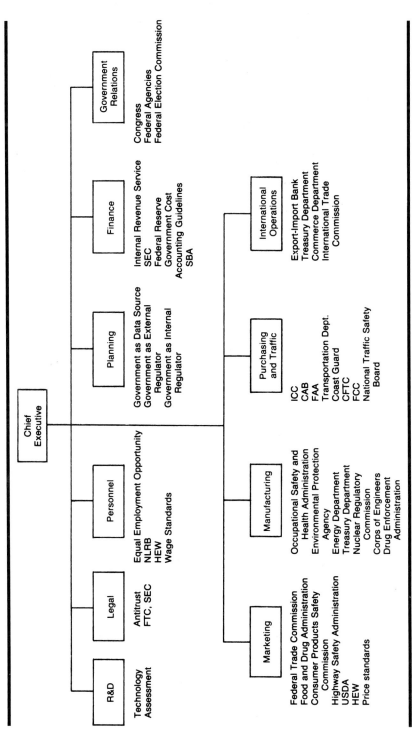

EXHIBIT 5-2   TYPICAL INDUSTRIAL CORPORATION AND FEDERAL GOVERNMENT RELATIONS

Source: Weidenbaum, 1981: 375. Reprinted from Murray L. Weidenbaum, *Business, Government, and the Public,* 2nd ed., © 1981, p. 375. Reprinted by permission of Prentice-Hall, Inc., Englewood Cliffs, N.J.

For example, the chairman of General Motors commented: "Government today has something to say about how we design our products, how we build them, how we test them, how we warrant them, how we repair them, the compensation we pay our employees, and even the prices we may charge our customers" (Orme, 1977: 7).

THE FUTURE OF THE BUSINESS SYSTEM

Will the business institution survive? Growing government participation and often control of the internal decisions of business managers are eroding a traditional managerial prerogative in the business-government relationship. In the past, regulations typically established policies within which individuals could operate. There were exceptions to this practice, but generally, the government did not become involved in making or controlling specific managerial decisions except in industries such as railroads, electric power utilities, and banks. There is no doubt that increasing government regulation is inevitable. It is not inevitable, however, that it weaken or reduce the efficiency of the private sector or create unnecessary problems. An important task for business, government, and society in the years ahead will be to resolve economic, social, and political problems in such a way as to strengthen our democratic institutions and preserve the best of the business institution.

CASE STUDY

AMTRAK

Amtrak is our only national passenger railroad. It has been the subject of controversy since its founding in 1971. The issue, very plainly, is whether the federal government should subsidize this company.

Amtrak is the marketing name for the National Railroad Passenger Corporation, which provides rail passenger transportation to the major intercity markets in the United States. Its controlling stock is in the hands of the United States government. However, Amtrak is not a government agency in the usual sense of that term, but a corporation structured and managed like other large businesses in the private sector. It competes with all other modes of transportation in the marketplace.

Creation of Amtrak

Amtrak was created by the Rail Passenger Service Act of 1970 because intercity rail passenger service had deterioriated to the point where it was no longer profitable for the railroads, equipment was antiquated and constantly breaking down, and service to passengers was steadily worsening. The story can be told in cold statistics. In 1929 the nation's railroads operated about 20,000 passenger trains and carried 77 percent of intercity passenger traffic. By 1950 more than half the trains had disappeared, and the railroads' share of total intercity passenger traffic had dropped to 46 percent. By 1970 railroad passenger trains had only 7 percent of the market, and only 450 trains were in operation. Of these, 100 were in the process of being discontinued and were operating with only one or two cars. Airplanes, buses, and cars were carrying most of the intercity traffic.

Railroad passenger service operated a deficit each year after 1927, except during World War II. In 1957, a record deficit of $723.7 million was recorded (Hilton, 1969). By 1969 the deficits were around $600 million. Not a single railroad operated its passenger trains at a profit.

Throughout the 1960s, Congress was pressured to solve what many considered to be a national calamity. It introduced new legislation that argued that our cities could not rely on massive construction of highways and airports to meet the nation's transportation needs and that a viable national rail passenger system was essential in the event of a future national emergency. In addition, the legislation argued that cities would be choked with smog without rail service to carry passengers and that existing track and right-of-way (while deteriorating) was still a valuable national asset that should be upgraded. With a little help from government, it was asserted, the system could be made to operate profitably.

The Rail Passenger Service Act of 1970

Amtrak's charter states:

> The Corporation shall be a for-profit corporation, the purpose of which shall be to provide intercity rail passenger service, employing innovative operating and marketing concepts so as to fully develop the potential of modern rail operating service in meeting the Nation's intercity passenger transportation requirements.

Excluded from Amtrak's operations were short-haul or commuter services. Subsequent legislation permitted Amtrak to operate commuter services for local agencies so long as the corporation was fully compensated. Today Amtrak also is permitted to operate limited commuter service as a part of its basic system.

Amtrak was to assume operation of the passenger business from various private railroad companies who subscribed to its service. In return, the railroads had to pay Amtrak 50 percent of their passenger service loss for the year ending December 31, 1969. The railroads could pay cash or contribute equipment or services of the same value. They also could elect to receive common stock for the value of these payments rather than taking a tax write-off. As an incentive for railroads to subscribe to the stock, nonsubscribers had to operate their passenger trains until January 1, 1975. Of the twenty-three companies operating passenger trains at the time, only three failed to subscribe. None of these roads now operates passenger trains.

Amtrak is managed by a nine-person board of directors. Most of the board members are appointed by the President of the United States and approved by the Senate.

Amtrak is a quasi-public company. It has some characteristics of a private company, but its decision making is much influenced by public bodies. Its budgets must be approved by the Congress. Congresspeople and state officials often have pressured Amtrak into instituting special routes in their home states or other areas without regard to profitability. The Department of Transportation also exercises much formal and informal control.

Initially Amtrak operated over right-of-way owned by private railroads. Over time, however, the federal government authorized Amtrak a total of $2.5 billion to purchase and operate right-of-way, stations, signaling, and safety devices on the route from Boston to Washington, D.C., a total of 456 miles. Amtrak today owns a total of 650 miles of track, operates about 24,000 miles of track, and employs around 25,000 people. It is the sixth-largest public carrier of passengers. It has substantially modernized its rolling stock and significantly reduced its ratio of cost to revenue.

The act of 1970 committed the federal government to guarantee $100 million in loans, with the possibility of further guarantees. The government granted $9 million for operating and development costs. Subscribing railroads supplied $5.5 million each month in exchange for their stock in the operating company..This will be recognized today as a modest financial support. At the time, however, it was considered enough to get Amtrak on its feet and profitable within two years.

That did not happen. Therefore, the Amtrak Improvement Act of 1975 changed the method of federal funding. Instead of loan guarantees, the act provided for direct grants from Congress for capital improvements and operating expenses. Amtrak's highest deficit financed by the federal government was $896 billion in fiscal 1981. It declined to $656 billion in fiscal 1987.

The Pros and Cons of Federal Support to Amtrak

The Reagan administration was never happy about funding Amtrak's deficit, although in the early years it reluctantly agreed to continue federal financing. But for fiscal 1986, it recommended zero budget for the system, a drastic proposal that raised a storm of controversy. The pros and cons that follow have been compiled principally, although not entirely, from sources in this period. Although the numbers vary a little, the arguments apply as well today as in 1985. The issues are the same, except that the president's 1988 budget recommended that Amtrak be sold to private interests.

Can the United States Afford Amtrak?

CON   David Stockman, as Director of the Office of Management and Budget (OMB), told the Senate that the nation faces "massive threatening baseline deficits. . . . The fiscal problem . . . dwarfs into insignificance the specific and particular dislocations that may attend the termination of a program like Amtrak." Stockman observed that Amtrak ranks well behind other claims on the federal budget. "In a budget that must be pared back drastically," he said, "it ranks near the bottom of the program priority scale because it provides a transportation amenity that the Nation cannot afford and can readily do without" (1985: 15). "There are few programs that I can think of that rank lower than Amtrak in terms of the good they do, the purpose they serve, the national need they respond to" (1985: 36).

Secretary of Transportation Elizabeth M. Dole testified that until 1985, Amtrak had received $11 billion (including $2.5 billion for the Northeast Corridor [NEC], the route from Washington, D.C., to Boston) and would cost taxpayers another $8 billion by 1995. "This is more than we can afford," she said (1985: 160).

Pro   Amtrak responded by saying that a huge deficit is not a sound reason for eliminating a particular program, and although there are some programs that have a higher priority, Amtrak should not be denied support. "Fiscal priority is a basis for establishing the balance between expenditures" (Amtrak, 1985: 3). The company argued that Amtrak's request for fiscal 1986 was a modest 2.6 percent of the federal government's expenditures for all transportation and only .07 percent of the total federal budget. This amount, said Amtrak, was minuscule compared with the support typically given to railways by Western European governments. For example, Belgium allocates 1.46 percent of its GNP and Italy 1.28 percent to railroads whereas Amtrak was requesting only .02 of the GNP.

Is Amtrak a National Necessity?

Con   Stockman argued before the Congress that:

> A system that accounts for only a fraction of the 1 percent of the millions of people who move between intercity destinations each year is not a significant part of the way people move in this country, and to terminate this system could not make a major difference unless somehow you could persuade me or others that one-quarter of 1 percent makes a critical difference (1985: 16).

Stockman argued that the loss of Amtrak would not play havoc with travel in the Northeast Corridor (NEC), as Amtrak claimed. The availability of other means of travel—buses, airplanes, and private automobiles—would minimize any disruption. Others argued that outside the NEC, Amtrak actually provided little service. In many areas, it scheduled a single train a day, which often reached town in the middle of the night. Said the senator, "One would think Congress could recognize a turkey when it saw one" (Armstrong, 1985: 207).

When asked whether Amtrak was necessary in the event of a national emergency, Secretary Dole replied that it was not; air traffic could be utilized for longer hauls and buses and trucks for shorter hauls, she said. Although rail passenger capacity was vital during World War II, it is no longer (1985: 180).

Pro   Amtrak responded as follows:

> Intercity passenger trains are a significant part of the transportation network of all developed countries. Amtrak significantly offsets congestion in the Northeast corridor, provides service to intermediate cities on long distance routes in a way no airline can match, is more energy efficient than anything but a bus, and runs in all kinds of weather when everything else is at a standstill. And Amtrak is a national program because the Constitution of the United States makes interstate commerce a federal responsibility (1985: 2).

Senator Ernest F. Hollings said that he found it hard to believe that a system that carried 20 million passengers a year, served 500 communities, and employed 25,000 workers could be called useless (1985: 2).

According to Amtrak (1985: 6), the system carried 46 percent more passengers in the NEC than all the airlines combined. The company observed that the tunnels and streets of New York already were clogged, and if Amtrak passengers had to find other modes of transportation, the tunnels and airports would be clogged every day except Sunday.

Senator Arlen Specter observed that without Amtrak "the United States would be the only industrial nation without rail passenger service. . . . It is a matter of great national importance" (1985: 214).

Has Federal Support Favored Amtrak over Other Modes of Transportation?

PRO   According to opponents of Amtrak, continued subsidies have permitted the corporation to compete unfairly with other modes of transportation. Stockman calculated that each Amtrak rider was subsidized by $35 (1985: 28). Because Amtrak has been able to cut fares in competition with airlines and buses, intercity bus service has seriously eroded. Senator Philip M. Crane commented that "subsidizing a private, passenger railway is not the responsibility of the federal government, as it decreases market competitiveness and only contributes to our budget deficit" (1985: 38).

Amtrak losses vary among routes. Losses per passenger amounted to $132.60 on the Chicago to New Orleans route, the greatest of any route. Almost that much was lost on the Chicago to Los Angeles line. Lowest losses were $10.16 on the heavily traveled route between New York and Philadelphia (Dole, 1985: 192).

Opponents point out that a large part of the federal subsidy to airlines, buses, and private automobiles is paid from user fees and taxes, while Amtrak's subsidy comes from general funds contributed by all taxpayers. It is not correct, they assert, to compare aggregate subsidies to different modes of transportation.

CON   Amtrak claims that it has benefited less from federal subsidies than competing modes of transportation.

> The airlines and bus lines are the beneficiaries of a massive federal and state investment in interstate highways, a federally operated air traffic control system, and municipally owned airports constructed with tax-free bonds. By contrast, Amtrak constructs, owns and operates its stations, and must fund (or pay contracting railroads for) dispatching costs, signal systems, grade crossing protection, track and tie replacements, and routine maintenance of way (1985: 18–19).

From 1972 to 1985, Amtrak received $11 billion in subsidies, contrasted with $42.7 billion allocated to the Federal Aviation Administration for the airlines. Fifty-one percent of this came from federal general funds and not user charges channeled through the Airport and Airways Trust Fund to the airlines. In addition, Amtrak argued, tax deductions by business for travel by air costs the Treasury far more than Amtrak's direct federal support. It also argued that aviation benefits from the use of tax-free airport-construction bonds, and the training of many pilots is paid for by the federal government. Altogether, W. Graham Claytor, Jr., President and Chairman of the Board of Amtrak, testified before Congress that indirect subsidy to the airlines amounted to $33 per passenger, an amount comparable to the subsidy for Amtrak (1985: 14).

Between 1972 and 1985, the government spent a total of $424.6 billion on highways. The federal government primarily allocated Highway Trust Funds to state and local governments for use in construction and rehabilitation of the highway system. But most highway financing came from state and local governments out of tax revenues. Buses received subsidies from general funds, though in amounts much below other modes of transportation (Amtrak, 1985: 54–56). Said Senator James M. Exon, "I suspect that the bus companies would not very likely be in business today if they were paying their full share (of road construction and maintenance)" (1985: 38).

There is no doubt about the fact that intercity bus service has declined significantly in recent years. But, said proponents of Amtrak, the decline was more from increased automobile ownership and formidable competition by airlines with their discount fares than to lower Amtrak fares. These forces have been particularly noticeable in the NEC.

Does Amtrak Subsidize Higher Income Groups?

Pro   Stockman argued that the income of Amtrak passengers is higher than average for the population as a whole and that the highest-income passengers travel the NEC. Fifty-eight percent of the NEC passengers had incomes in 1985 over $30,000, compared to 37 percent of the population with incomes that high. Systemswide, 51 percent of Amtrak passengers had incomes over $30,000 in 1985. Only 23 percent of NEC passengers and 31 percent of all Amtrak passengers had incomes under $20,000 in 1985, compared with 45 percent for the population as a whole.

Bus passengers had the lowest median incomes and included more younger and older people. Stockman argued that 48 percent of Amtrak passengers were between 25 and 44 years of age, their most productive years, and least in need of subsidy (1985: 49).

Con   Amtrak countered by saying that when Stockman compared income levels of NEC passengers to those of the total population, he was comparing apples and oranges. Amtrak NEC riders tend to be businesspeople with incomes higher than average, and the data for this route merely reflect the demographics of the area.

But data for the entire system show a different picture, Amtrak argued. Forty-seven percent of Amtrak's long distance passengers (including passengers to and from the NEC) had family incomes under $20,000 in 1985, a time when the average family income was $28,000. People over 55 accounted for 36 percent of long-distance passengers. Together, these figures show that Amtrak served the elderly and the lower end of the economic spectrum (Amtrak, 1985: 49–50).

What Happens If Amtrak Subsidies Cease?

In hearings before Congress, the Reagan administration argued that the loss of Amtrak would minimally slow the economy and would reduce federal deficits. It said that private enterprise (alone or with assistance from state governments) would buy Amtrak assets and that any gaps in rail-service would be filled by other modes of transportation. Those opposed to selling Amtrak took the position that costs would far exceed benefits, even if private interests bought Amtrak assets. Here are some details of these positions.

Will Private Enterprise Step in to Operate Amtrak?   If private interests were to buy Amtrak at a price reasonably approaching the asset value of the company, that would resolve basic issues associated with federal subsidies. But will private enterprise step up to the opportunity?

PRO   When pressed on this question, David Stockman said that most of Amtrak's assets were in real property in the NEC (not in rolling stock), which could be sold readily because the short-haul traffic in the NEC was profitable enough to attract a private buyer (1985: 24).

In her testimony, Secretary Dole was more cautious. She agreed with Representative Jim Slattery when he said that a buyer probably would not be interested in trying to run Amtrak. But, she added, "If there is a demand, I believe it will be filled." She offered a number of alternatives that could make Amtrak self-supporting either to present management or to a prospective private buyer.

■ Users of the NEC right of way should make a more equitable contribution to Amtrak. If Amtrak were no longer in operation the additional costs of freight in the NEC would be about $212 million a year. In this light, railroad and commuter lines that jointly use Amtrak right of way might justifiably contribute more to Amtrak.

■ Institute a one-year wage freeze by Amtrak employees.

■ State and local governments might make a modest contribution for services of Amtrak in their areas. There are eight states in the NEC and thirty-six others with Amtrak routes. If states in the NEC contributed about $19 million a year and the others $8.9 million, this and income from other alternatives would largely meet subsidy requirements (1985: 187).

CON   Some people are skeptical about selling Amtrak to a private buyer for anywhere near book value of assets, which was set at $3.6 billion by Stockman (1985: 50) and at $3.1 billion by Amtrak (1985: 53).

Senator Arlen Spector said: "The private sector will not pick up lost Amtrak services. The cost of doing so in competition with publicly subsidized air and highway transportation would be prohibitive" (1985: 218). Senator Alfonse M. D'Amato observed that: "Although the administration has claimed that profitable Amtrak routes could be picked up by combinations of state, local, or private entities, it has not yet met with any parties willing to do so" (1985: 222).

Amtrak's reservations about private interests taking over the system are founded on a number of realities. First, when Amtrak was founded in 1971, no railroad's passenger service was profitable, as we have noted. Second, Amtrak has had inquiries from private interests to operate trains, especially luxury trains or summer resort services. "But upon serious examination of the costs involved, the interest almost inevitably fades" (1985: 47). Third, the American High Speed Rail Corporation proposed to operate frequent, rapid (160 mph) trains between Los Angeles and San Diego. But after years of research, it did not go ahead. Finally, Amtrak said that it doubted whether anyone would buy the NEC property at any price, because the economics simply were against it.

Of course, Amtrak or a private investor might operate profitably if all of the alternatives suggested by Secretary Dole were implemented. A question remains as to whether this is possible.

Impact Of The End Of Federal Subsidy To Amtrak

David Stockman observed that in the absence of a sale or continuation of government subsidy, Amtrak would immediately be taken into bankruptcy court. A bankruptcy judge would weigh the claims of various creditors and allocate liquidation income among them. Although claimants would lose, there would be no out-of-pocket cost to the federal government (1985: 26).

A second alternative would be to reduce slowly the size of the annual federal subsidy. This plan would be unsatisfactory, said Stockman, if for no other reason than it would immediately result in Amtrak's eliminating its most unprofitable routes. Layoffs would follow, and union contracts would require severance payments to employees equal to or above the operating costs that might be saved by shutting down those routes.

Amtrak objected to bankruptcy. It asserted that the liquidation of Amtrak's assets would yield about ten to fifteen cents on the dollar and that the costs of closing down Amtrak would exceed any liquidation income or other benefits.

Amtrak agreed that slowly reducing the size of the federal subsidy would not be satisfactory. It also agreed that the alternatives suggested by Secretary Dole are uncertain and the political and economic problems in implementing them awesome. Among other things, the forty-four senators would have a strong interest in protecting Amtrak in their states.

David Stockman argued that the weakest and most "pitiful" argument to support Amtrak was that "it would cost more to shut Amtrak down than to continue to waste money" on it and urged Congress to "recognize that nothing significant or important is going to happen nationally" with an end to federal subsidies to Amtrak (1985: 23). He also argued that the costs of labor protection negotiated between Amtrak and the unions, estimated to run as high as $2 billion, would be absorbed in any bankruptcy settlement. In any event, he concluded "Clearly there are enough assets on the system . . . to more than satisfy the claims of labor and others." (1985: 23).

Amtrak claimed that the government would be obliged to pay severance to railroad workers because the agreements—requiring the payment of up to six years' wages following discontinuance of Amtrak service—were not entered into by Amtrak. They were included in the enabling legislation and were certified by the Secretary of Labor. Amtrak noted that:

> In mandating these labor arrangements, Congress intended to make Amtrak attractive to experienced railroad employees who might be reluctant to come to work for a fledgling company begun as a two-year experiment. (In a business that had almost always lost money worldwide.) Without such a directive, it is unlikely that Amtrak or any other corporation would have made such agreements (1985: 51).

Meanwhile, the Reagan administration said that Amtrak, not the federal government, would be liable. Secretary Dole said that the enabling legislation set up Amtrak as a corporation, not an agency of the federal government. The Supreme Court upheld that view, as did the General Accounting Office (Dole, 1985: 203–220), and the prestigious law firm of Covington and Burling (Dole, 1985: 75–83).

It also has been argued that if Amtrak were discontinued and all 25,000 employees laid off, the Railroad Retirement Account would be $3.9 billion less by the year 2000 (Dole, 1985: 177), and the Railroad Unemployment Insurance Account, from which sickness benefits as well as unemployment compensation are paid, would face serious cash flow problems in an amount difficult to calculate. Whether Amtrak went into bankruptcy or were taken over by private enterprise, the lives and careers of employees and related organizations would inevitably be seriously harmed.

Shippers in the NEC would be forced to pay higher freight costs because the railroads would be forced to pay a higher share of the operating expenses along the corridor. Travelers in the NEC would have to find other modes of transportation, with inevitable congestion in transportation systems. If Amtrak were taken over by private enterprise, the cost of rail service inevitably would be greater. For example, Amtrak calculated that if the system were dismantled, there would be an extra 986,000 passengers a year at Washington's National Airport. It also calculated that if the 31,000 Amtrak passengers in the NEC and New York State switched to automobiles, gasoline consumption would increase by 35 million gallons a year, and new highway and arterial street construction expenses would consume billions of dollars (Amtrak, 1985: 43).

Amtrak claimed that 132 of the communities it served in 1985 had no certified air carrier within 30 to 50 miles, and seventy-nine had no intercity bus service.

About half of Amtrak's passengers and 75 percent of its passenger miles are outside the NEC. Many people therefore would be stranded because they neither had automobiles nor money for taxis to get to distant cities where they would find intercity transportation. But Stockman countered that for virtually everyone, alternative means of transportation would be available. Secretary Dole testified that the president of the American Bus Association assured her publicly that every community served by Amtrak would have bus service if Amtrak disappeared.

Questions

1. As a member of Congress, you must decide how to vote on whether Amtrak should be given no subsidy by the federal government at the end of next year. How would you vote and why?
2. Should passengers of Amtrak be asked to pay the full costs of service to them?
3. Should Amtrak abandon unprofitable routes, stick with potentially profitable routes, and charge passengers full cost on these routes? If your answer is yes, explain whether this plan would be politically possible.
4. If your answer to question 2 is affirmative, how do you feel about airline and bus passengers?
5. Why should railroads using the NEC for freight and commuter service not be forced to pay their full share of the cost to Amtrak? How easy would it be to calculate such costs of track and equipment and to get agreements about fair shares?
6. If Amtrak were to go into bankruptcy and the bankruptcy judge required Amtrak to continue operations, in the national interest, who do you think should cover any deficit?

CHAPTER **6** _____

NEW PATTERNS IN GOVERNMENT REGULATION OF BUSINESS

Advanced Genetic Sciences, Inc. (AGS), is a small company located in Oakland, California. But it illustrates huge new issues in federal regulation as well as in law, ethics, agronomy, and environment. Founded in 1979, AGS is a high-technology company that applies advanced biological techniques to develop new products for the agricultural and food-processing markets.

AGS came to public attention when the Environmental Protection Agency (EPA) lifted a ban on the company to conduct outdoor tests of a frost-blocking bacteria called Frostban. In November 1985, AGS got approval from the National Institutes of Health (NIH) to be the first company legally authorized to conduct these tests on strawberry plants near Monterey, California. The Monterey County supervisors quickly passed an ordinance banning the experiment for a year. In the meantime, a disgruntled employee of AGS told the EPA that the company had conducted an outdoor experiment with the organism contrary to EPA rules. EPA promptly rescinded the approval granted by NIH and fined the company $20,000.*

Steven Lindow, a scientist at the University of California, Berkeley, whose research was partly supported by grants from AGS, sought and received

_____

*In April 1984, a Cabinet Council Working Group on Biotechnology was formed to coordinate government regulations in this area, because many government agencies were involved. The three principal agencies were the United States Department of Agriculture (USDA), the Food and Drug Administration (FDA), and the EPA. The council allocated for regulatory purposes biotechnology areas among these agencies and gave the EPA authority over AGS testing.

permission from the EPA to conduct an experiment on potatoes in November 1984 that would use the same technology as that of AGS. Roadblocks immediately were placed in his way. The people in Monterey County, where Lindow's experiments were to take place, strongly objected to the tests. They were joined by four activist groups that filed suit in the U. S. District Court of the District of Columbia to block the tests. Judge John Sirica granted the injunction in *Foundation for Economic Trends v. Heckler* (1984). In May 1986, after almost three years of legal struggles, Lindow was granted permission by the EPA to conduct his outdoor experiments. The next month, AGS got permission to test outdoors.

AGS and Lindow are engaged in genetic engineering, a branch of biotechnology. According to the Office of Technology Assessment, biotechnology includes any technique "that uses living organism (or parts of organisms) to make or modify products, to improve plants and animals, or to develop microorganisms for specific uses." Biotechnology is an old science. For example, the fermentation process in making wine uses microorganisms to convert sugar into alcohol. What is new and dramatic in the field today is the ability of scientists to alter the structure of cells to affect the growth characteristics of microorganisms. These alterations promise a new class of products as exciting as those based upon the microelectronic computer chip that ushered in the information revolution. New medicines to cure human and animal diseases, new seeds that will grow disease-resistant and larger plants, new insecticides to kill bugs, new products to produce larger and healthier animals in a shorter period of time, cheaper and more nutritious foods, and new enzymes to absorb toxic wastes are but a few of the possibilities.

The federal government has had a powerful role in funding the biomedical and other fundamental research in biology, biochemistry, and genetics that has formed the basis for the new biotechnology. The NIH, the National Science Foundation, and the Department of Defense have sponsored basic research that lies at the foundation of the new biotechnology.

The first genetics firm founded for commercial purposes was Genentech, Inc., in 1977. Growth of private commercial firms was slow until the Supreme Court ruled in *Diamond v. Chakrabarty* in 1980 that microorganisms could be patented under existing law. General Electric became the first company to get such a patent. After that, the creation of new companies to do research in the field was explosive.

Very simply, AGS has genetically modified a bacterium that ordinarily causes frost to form on plants when the temperature is below 32 degrees Fahrenheit. In greenhouse tests, AGS's product reduced the point at which frost forms to about 23 degrees Fahrenheit. It is estimated that this product, if successful in outdoor testing, will save over $1 billion annually in crop damage.

But, as we have noted, this new technology has generated a storm of controversy. Jeremy Rifkin, the head of Washington-based Foundation for Economic Trends, is representative of those who are opposed to its use. He says that this new technology will introduce "thousands of genetically engineered microbes, plants, and animal strains . . . to our ecosystem, every year, all over the world." The introduction of genetically modified organisms into the atmosphere, he argues, could well eclipse by an order of magnitude the damage that has been caused by the release of petrochemical products into the world's ecosystems (*Multinational Monitor*, 1986).

The federal government and scientists disagree with this position. Following the initial ban on AGS outdoor testing, the EPA assigned an audit team to evaluate AGS's experiments. The team concluded that AGS was conducting its experiments according to accepted laboratory practices and that it was not likely that outdoor experiments would produce any adverse effects. Upon the basis of this report, EPA granted AGS permission to test, as noted above.

The new biotechnology raises many significant questions:

■ Is there enough oversight of biotechnology experiments?

■ Are federal, state, and local laws adequate to deal with this burgeoning field?

■ How should agencies involved in regulation coordinate their actions so that they avoid unnecessary gaps in regulation or impending progress in the field?

■ Is there a need for new congressional legislation?

■ How can environmental and other hazards in testing and use of the new biotechnology products best be assessed?

■ How can risks be evaluated creditably?

■ What will be the benefits of this new technology? To consumers? To agriculture? To the economy? To business?

■ Are there ethical problems in tampering with healthy genes?

■ Are there ethical conflicts when academic researchers team with private businesses to make commercial products?

■ Whose priorities will determine how this powerful new technology will be applied?

■ When the federal government approves a genetically engineered product, what criteria should it use? If it uses cost/benefit analysis, what rules should be established to guide the analysis? If the public interest is a major criterion, who should determine what it is?

These will not be easy questions to answer, but they certainly will be asked as new patterns of regulation in the development of the biotechnology field.

In the last chapter we discussed the underlying reasons for, and the scope and direction of, government's regulation of business. The result of more than 200 years of government regulation of business is a massive mountain of regulations that embody great complexities for business, conflicts to be reconciled, opportunities to be exploited, threats to be avoided, burdens to be borne, and reforms to be initiated. This is an extraordinarily wide territory to cover and not easy to grasp. In this chapter, following a brief résumé of the government regulatory life cycle we explore in depth the many different major dimensions of today's federal regulation of business. This is followed by an analysis of the ways in which regulations are affecting the managerial roles, processes, and structures in business organizations. We note many defects in current regulatory patterns but treat the question of regulatory reform in the next chapter.

THE REGULATORY LIFE CYCLE

The government regulatory life cycle begins with the *emergence of an issue*. A problem such as air pollution may have existed for many years, but until public attention is focused on the problem, government action is nonexistent or negligible. Activists, interest groups, and media attention bring the issue to public attention. Second is the *formulation of a government policy*. In this stage, the issue is debated, hearings before Congress are held, pressure groups are formed to lobby legislators, alternative solutions are proposed, and, finally, a bill is formulated and funding provided for its implementation. The third stage is the *implementation of the legislation*. The agency (or agencies) responsible for implementation develops and enforces specific regulations spelled out in the legislation and/or developed to implement the broad policy directives in the legislation. These regulations are circulated, business's actions are monitored and, when necessary, informal or formal corrective actions are taken. (Details of this step are elaborated in the accompanying box.) The next step is *modification of the regulation*. Following experience with the regulation, it may be appropriate for the regulatory agency or the Congress to amend the basic legislation. Then follows a stage of relaxation when public attention moves to higher priorities

Where Do Regulations Come From?

Like people, regulations have an origin. But the process of producing regulations is not widely known or discussed by the average citizen.

Regulations do not come into being until Congress passes legislation authorizing the establishment of a regulatory agency to enforce public policy in a certain area. The Civil Rights Act of 1964, for instance, set forth broad provisions making discrimination in the workplace illegal and established the Equal Employment Opportunity Commission to enforce compliance.

Once set up, the agency is faced with the continuous problem of making specific rules to implement broad, general legislative mandates. Therefore, federal regulatory agencies go through a process of *rulemaking*. It works like this:

1. The agency publishes a notice in a daily government publication, the *Federal Register,* outlining a proposed rule. All proposed agency rules are published there to notify interested and affected parties.

2. Agency staff research the impact of the proposed rule.

3. Interested and affected parties—such as companies and trade associations—are invited to formal hearings to give oral testimony about the proposed rule. Anyone may submit written comment to the agency.

4. The agency reviews all information and writes a rule. This rule is then printed immediately in the *Federal Register* and later in the *Code of Federal Regulations,* an annual compilation of all current federal regulations.

5. The rule remains in effect until rescinded by the agency, struck down by a federal court, or superseded by new legislation in Congress.

Federal regulatory agencies do more than make rules, however. They also conduct *adjudication proceedings* when companies or individuals are accused of violating regulations. Here is how these proceedings work:

1. The agency notifies a person or company that it is conducting an investigation.

2. Agency personnel or hired investigators gather information through interviews, subpoenaed documents, and preliminary hearings.

3. After the investigation, the lead investigator for the regulatory agency may recommend that the agency issue a consent order. A proposed consent order then is published in the *Federal Register* for comment by interested parties. After receiving comment, the agency may issue a revised consent order. Basically, a consent order stipulates that a company agrees to stop a practice without admitting illegal behavior.

4. If a consent order is not appropriate, an agency conducts a formal adjudicative trial presided over by an administrative law judge. Evidence is introduced, witnesses are called, and the litigating parties are present. The proceedings are conducted according to provisions of the Administrative Procedure Act of 1946, which spells out the rights of all parties and stipulates procedures to be used.

5. At the conclusion of the trial, the judge issues a written decision. It forms the basis for a formal order to remedy the practice or behavior in question. The ruling may be appealed in the federal court system.

Regulatory agencies use similar adjudication procedures, as set forth in the Administrative Procedure Act, to issue permits, grant licenses, and set rates when these activities are part of their mandate.

The rule-making and adjudicative processes used by federal regulatory agencies are very open and systematic. The procedural rights of regulated interests are protected at every juncture by the Administrative Procedure Act, the Freedom of Information Act (1966), and the Privacy Act (1974). But the cost of the protections granted regulated parties is excessively slow agency procedure. It often takes years for agencies to promulgate rules or set rates.

and government surveillance is relaxed. Finally, for a few regulations, the problem originally addressed may be solved, or new circumstances may give rise to different alternatives, as happened with airline deregulation. In either case, *deregulation* is the final stage in the life cycle.

DIMENSIONS OF TODAY'S FEDERAL REGULATION OF BUSINESS

It is not easy to portray the sheer volume of regulations to which business is subject, let alone measure reliably its full impact. The following discussion is designed, however, to illustrate magnitudes.

The Volume of Regulatory Legislation

In 1977, the Senate Governmental Affairs Committee found that the *Code of Federal Regulations,* which contains current general and permanent regulations of federal agencies, filled a 15-foot-long shelf with 60,000 pages of fine print. Another survey counted 9,800 forms sent out by federal departments and agencies with 556 million responses each year (*Congressional Quarterly*, 1982: 1).

The *Federal Register* is a fine-print publication that sets forth proposed and new regulations of federal departments and agencies. Exhibit 6–1 shows that in

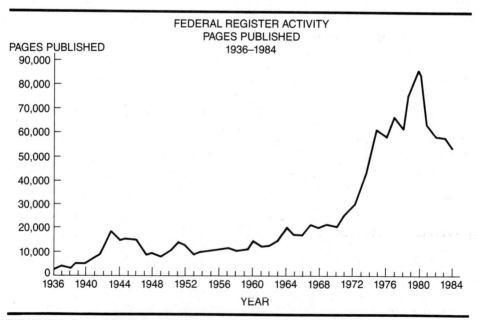

EXHIBIT 6–1   FEDERAL REGISTER ACTIVITY PAGES PUBLISHED 1936–1984

Source: Office of the Federal Register.

recent years there has been a substantial decline from the peak reached in 1980. Especially noteworthy is the steep rise from 1970 to 1980.

As late as the mid-1950s the federal government assumed major regulatory responsibility in ony four areas: antitrust, financial institutions, transportation, and communications. Today some federal agency regulates some part of virtually every business activity. The volume of regulations varies, of course, from industry to industry. The steel industry probably is obliged to be concerned with more regulations than the average industry. One government study revealed that this industry had to comply with 5,600 regulations from twenty-

Independent Commissions

Agency	Year Est.
Interstate Commerce Commission (ICC)	1887
Federal Reserve System (Fed)	1913
Federal Trade Commission (FTC)	1914
Federal Home Loan Bank Board (FHLBB)	1932
Federal Deposit Insurance Corporation (FDIC)	1933
Federal Communications Commission (FCC)	1934
Securities and Exchange Commission (SEC)	1934
National Labor Relations Board (NLRB)	1935
Civil Aeronautics Board (CAB)[1]	1940
Federal Maritime Commission (FMC)[2]	1961
Equal Employment Opportunity Commission (EEOC)	1964
Occupational Safety and Health Review Commission (OSHA)	1971
Consumer Product Safety Commission (CPSC)	1972
Commodity Futures Trading Commission (CFTC)[3]	1974
Nuclear Regulatory Commission (NRC)[4]	1975
International Trade Commission (ITC)[5]	1975
Federal Election Commission (FEC)	1975
Federal Energy Regulatory Commission (FERC)[6]	1977

1. Successor to the Civil Aeronautics Authority, established in 1938.
2. Assumed the regulatory functions of the Department of Commerce's Maritime Administration, established in 1936.
3. Successor to the Agriculture Department's Commodity Exchange Authority, established in 1922.
4. Assumed the regulatory functions of the Atomic Energy Commission, established in 1946.
5. Successor to the Tariff Commission, established in 1916.
6. Assumed functions of the Federal Power Commission, established in 1930.

Source: From *Federal Regulatory Directory,* copyright 1982 Congressional Quarterly.

seven agencies. These regulations ranged from costly EPA standards for coke ovens to detailed OSHA rules prescribing, among other things, that workers must wash their hands and faces before eating lunch (U.S. Council of Wage and Price Stability, 1976). Today, government is intimately involved in every factory, workplace, and home. OSHA, for example, is required to protect millions of workers in millions of workplaces against occupational injury and sickness.

The present volume of government regulations of business is so large that no corporation can faithfully comply with all the laws and regulations to which it is subject. Commenting on this point, Walter Wriston, then CEO of Citibank, said:

> What worries me is that General Motors and Citibank have a fighting chance of obeying all the new regulatory laws because we have the staff and the big-time lawyers to do so. But most small businesspeople do not. They cannot even find out what the law is. There are, for example, 1,200 interpretations by the Federal Reserve staff of the Truth in Lending Act. Now, 90 percent of the more than 14,000 commercial banks in this country have fewer than 100 employees. If you gave every staff member those regulations and started them reading, they wouldn't be finished by next year (*Time*, May 1, 1978: 44).

Costs of Regulation Are Significant

There are no adequate measures of the full cost of federal regulations of business, but a few statistics are illuminating. Administrative costs of federal regulatory activities rose from $1.6 billion in fiscal year 1970 to $6.7 billion in 1980 and were estimated to be $9.4 billion in fiscal year 1987. In 1970, there were 86,160 staff people involved in economic and social regulation.* This level rose to 126,406 in 1980 but was projected to decline to 113,361 in fiscal year 1987 (Chilton, 1986).

Both the executive branch and the Congress have periodically tried to reduce the burden of paperwork. The result has been about the same as that of King Canute sweeping back the waves of the ocean. Each year the cost increases. The Federal Paperwork Commission, formed to study the cost of paperwork, calculated that the cost borne by industry is approximately $25 to $32 billion per year. The ten largest firms in the United States are estimated to have spent between $10 and $12 billion on paperwork, an average of more than $1 billion each, and to have filled out more than 10 billion sheets of paper a year (U.S. Commission on Federal Paperwork, 1977). The great majority of direct reporting costs of larger firms is in the new regulatory areas: safety and health, energy,

---

*Social regulation includes consumer safety and health, job safety and other working conditions, environment and energy. Economic regulation includes such areas as finance and banking as well as general business.

equal opportunity, pension programs, and the environment (Buchholz, 1980). Figures for cost of paperwork prepared by business in meeting government regulatory requirements are comparable today.

A rigorous study was made by Arthur Andersen & Company for the Business Roundtable of incremental costs to forty-eight large companies in complying with six federal agency programs. The study concluded that incremental costs amounted to $2.6 billion. Incremental costs were defined as only those that the companies would not have borne in the absence of regulation. The six programs were those of the EPA, EEO, OSHA, DOE (Department of Energy) ERISA (Employee Retirement Income Security Act), and the FTC. The $2.6 billion incremental cost was equal to 43 percent of what the forty-eight companies spent on research and development and to 16 percent of net income (Arthur Andersen & Co., 1979; Simon, 1980).

A primary and unanswered question arises about the justification for these regulatory costs. There are, of course, offsetting benefits, a point that will be discussed later, but there are also many cases in which costs exceed benefits. To illustrate, Irving Shapiro, when chairman of the board of Du Pont, said that his company spent $1.2 million to reduce particulate emmissions in one plant by 94 percent. He said this was a justified expenditure. However, federal regulations required an additional reduction of particulates by 3 percent. The costs of meeting this standard totaled $1.8 million and, said Shapiro, there was no detectable difference in air quality between the 94 and 97 percent reduction. This was equivalent, he said, to paying 80 cents for a dozen eggs and an additional $1.20 for a piece of eggshell (Shapiro, 1978: 37).

All the above are monetary costs. Other costs may be more significant. Government regulations are changing the cost structure of industries, institutional relationships in the business world, the balance of power between government and business, and the skills needed for successful business management. These changes cannot be measured, of course, but must be considered in any tally of total costs.

Traditional Industry versus Functional Social Regulatory Agencies

There are striking differences between the "old model" and the "new model" of regulation. The new model might be called *functional social* regulation in contrast to the older, *industrial* regulation. All regulation, of course, is "social" in that it is ultimately concerned with social welfare, but there are basic distinctions between the models.

As shown in Exhibit 6–2, the old style of regulation was concerned with one industry, such as railroads, airlines, drugs, and so on. The focus was on such matters as markets, rates, and obligations to serve the public. Some regulations cut across industry lines, but the main focus was on industrial segments. In contrast, the newer, functional regulations cut across industrial lines. They are broader in scope and are concerned with one function within an organization, not the organization as a whole. As a result, of course, the newer regulations

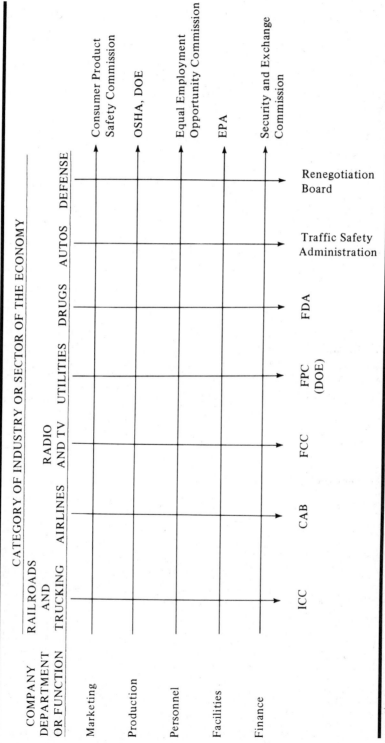

EXHIBIT 6–2   COMPARISON OF THE OLDER AND THE NEWER REGULATORY MODELS

Source: Adapted from Murray L. Weidenbaum, *Business, Government, and the Public*, p. 14. Copyright © 1977. Reprinted by permission of Prentice-Hall, Inc., Englewood Cliffs, New Jersey.

affect far more industries and companies than older regulations and, therefore, more customers.

Newer Regulations Have Different Purposes and Apply Different Policies and Methods

We can illustrate some of these differences between old and new regulations. First, the purposes of the new legislation differ from those of the older regulatory activities. For example, the older independent regulatory agencies, such as the CAB, FCC, FTC, ICC, and so on, were designed to prevent monopoly; to increase competition; to establish uniform standards of safety, security, communications, and financial practice; and to prevent abuses of managerial practices. The newer regulations are the results of pressures to improve the quality of life. As such, their purposes are to clean the environment; to employ minorities; to ensure greater safety and health of workers; to provide more information to consumers; to protect consumers from shoddy products; and so on.

Second, in the achievement of their purposes the newer agencies do not establish policy to guide private industry in its operations but specify in detail what shall be done. In other words, the Consumer Product Safety Commission (CPSC) does not rely on broad policy guidelines of safety but prescribes specifically what can and cannot be done. The National Highway Traffic Safety Administration (NHTSA), which now administers the Motor Vehicle Safety Standards Act of 1966, specifies the safety features that automobiles must have. This is what Charles Schultze calls a "command and control" method of regulation. He points out that once a decision is made to intervene in the market, the current pattern of regulation is not to seek to alter incentives in the marketplace, modify information flows, or change institutional structures. Rather, it is almost always to choose the direct intervention, the command and control technique. Seldom do we try other alternatives, "regardless of whether that mode of response fits the problem" (Schultze, 1977: 13).

Third, legislation also is often lengthy and specific. Traditionally, government regulatory legislation set broad policies, with comparatively little specific policy guidance, and gave the regulatory agency wide powers to set specific regulations in conformance with the public interest and the policy guidelines set by the Congress. The Food and Drug Administration, for example, is directed to permit the marketing of drugs only when the agency has been convinced that the product is "safe and effective." The agency must decide what these words mean. The Federal Reserve Board has wide latitude in managing the nation's money and credit. Such wide latitude is also granted to regulatory agencies administering the newer social legislation. The EPA, for example, has broad policy leeway in establishing national air quality standards, supervising states in the development of clean-air plans, and administering funds to clean up toxic-waste dumps. However, there is a tendency in some newer legislation for the Congress to be specific in setting standards (for example, clean water standards in the Clean Water Act of 1977 and various standards for automobile speed, safety, and gasoline mileage).

The trend away from delegating broad authority to the regulatory agencies toward more specific instructions will undoubtedly accelerate as a result of a Supreme Court decision in June 1983. In *Immigration and Naturalization Service v. Chadha,* a case concerning deportation, the Court by a seven to two ruling dramatically altered the balance of power between Congress and the executive branch. In more than 200 laws, beginning in 1932, Congress permitted a single chamber to veto an executive branch regulation, or required both House and Senate action, or, in some cases, authorized committees of Congress to veto a regulatory action. For example, in 1982 Congress vetoed an FTC rule concerning disclosure of defects in used cars. What Congress has done, of course, is to grant broad authority to the executive branch and then say: "If we do not like the way you develop regulations to achieve the policy, we will veto them." This the Court said was unconstitutional.

According to the Court, the Framers of the Constitution decided that "the legislative power of the federal government [should] be exercised in accord with a single, finely wrought and exhaustively considered procedure." That procedure demands that a measure be approved by both houses of Congress and presented to the President for his signature or veto. When Congress delegates to the executive branch of government the authority to issue regulations, it "must abide by its delegation of authority until the delegation is legislatively altered or revoked," said the Court.

One of the first reactions of the House to the Court decision was to pass a bill imposing new restrictions on the Consumer Product Safety Commission (CPSC). It also may revoke some of the broad authority it has dispensed in the past. Observers of Congress believe that this decision will inevitably lead Congress to narrow its grants of authority and be more specific in delineating what it wants the executive branch to do. This will, of course, significantly restrict the executive branch.

Two significant results follow from these patterns. First, government today is a very active managerial partner with business executives. Government always has been a partner with business but never so directly active in the management of an enterprise as today. It is active all the way from the governance of corporations to the specific ways in which products are produced and distributed. Many business managers today in fact act as agents of the government without being under contract. Second, by putting emphasis on "command and control" regulations, we lose the creativity and incentive of individuals to seek alternative efficient solutions to problems that the regulations address.

Lack of Accountability of Independent Regulatory Commissions

There are about a dozen powerful independent regulatory commissions, such as the FTC, CAB, SEC, and FRB, and about forty smaller ones that operate very differently from the newer agencies such as the EPA and OSHA. The latter operate much like a typical government department or bureau within a department in that they are subject to executive as well as judicial control. The independent regulatory commission is not.

These agencies have been established by Congress and are quasi-arms of that body, but they are lodged administratively in the executive branch to carry out regulatory responsibilities approved by the legislature. They report to the President, but he can remove commissioners only for good cause, such as malfeasance in office. Although they are not completely removed from controls, the authority over them is not direct and unequivocal. They are in fact microgovernments embodying the tripartite powers of the government —legislative, judicial, and administrative.

The commissions enjoy legislative powers in the sense that they are delegated responsibilities by Congress to administer laws that give them a good bit of discretion. The commissions have administrative powers in the sense that they perform an executive function. They have powers to administer laws by enforcing their rules and regulations. They have subpoena powers. Some of them conduct business operations. The board of governors of the Federal Reserve System, for example, participates directly in certain banking functions. They have broad planning functions, such as the ability of the ICC to allocate resource use of transportation systems through regulations, rates, and investigations. The powers and functions of commissions, however, differ a great deal. Commissions also enjoy judicial power. They can determine what the rules will be in the future and enforce them. They act as a judicial tribunal in hearing cases and adjudicating claims within the commission law. The Supreme Court insists that commissions act according to the law, follow rules in coming to decisions, and make decisions on the basis of fact. If these principles are not followed, or if there is an issue of constitutional law involved, the Court reviews commission decisions. Otherwise, the Court takes the position that the decisions are matters of fact and not of law and will not interfere. In other words, the Court will not review a decision of the commissions to determine whether it is a wise one, even though the Court might come to a different conclusion on the basis of the same facts. The Court intends to review decisions only when they may be contrary to constitutional law. Thus, commission decisions tend to be final.

Conflicts among Regulations

There always have been conflicts among government regulations, but the number, intensity, and incidence have been mounting. Cases have arisen in which the EPA demanded that a plant convert to oil from coal, to reduce atmospheric pollution at the same time as plants were ordered to convert from oil to coal by the Department of Energy (DOE) to reduce oil consumption. Antipollution requirements have forced some companies to abandon marginal plants, a policy that conflicts with federal goals of reduced unemployment. Economists have for a long time pointed out that minimum wage legislation increases teenage unemployment, although national policy clearly seeks to reduce unemployment, which is far too high among teenagers.

Flapdoodle Standards and Specifications

One significant dimension of federal regulations is the growth of so-called nonsense regulations. Classic examples are found in early OSHA regulations, many of which now have been expunged. For example, "Exit access is that portion of a means of egress which leads to the entrance to an exit." "When ascending or descending [a ladder], the user should face the ladder," "Jacks which are out of order shall be tagged accordingly, and shall not be used until repairs are made." Such trivia have little to do with the really important causes of industrial accidents and worker illness, which are supposed to occupy the attention of OSHA. Nonsense regulations are not, of course, confined to OSHA. Other regulatory agencies are just as guilty of this shortcoming. For instance, the Charles Hanson Company in Georgia had manufactured Red Fox denims for twenty-eight years. Several years ago, the FTC said that the company could no longer use the name. Why? The denims did not have any red fox fur in them, said the FTC! The Pentagon has drafted eighteen pages of specifications for the

---

A Fishy Story

A heavy run of steelhead trout, back to spawn, overcrowded the National Fish Hatchery in Lewiston, Idaho. Someone suggested that the excess trout be given to the Valley Food Bank, a local, private, nonprofit agency that would distribute the fish to needy people. The Interior Department, which operated the hatchery, agreed with this solution.

Unfortunately, someone discovered that Interior had no authority to do this. Therefore, it was proposed that the fish be transferred to the Department of Agriculture. Agriculture was to declare the fish surplus government food and give them to the needy. Unfortunately, existing law said that Agriculture had to deal only with state agencies in distributing surplus foods. Meanwhile, the trout began to die. The food bank offered to buy the fish and dispose of them some other way. The only other way was to declare the fish scrap. Unfortunately, the law said that surplus government foodstuffs classified as scrap had to be identified as "unfit for human consumption."

To untangle this knot, an interested Lewiston resident called a friend in the White House. The State of Idaho was asked to act as middleman in solving the problem. Agriculture lawyers worked with the state in preparing necessary papers to release the fish to the food bank through the state of Idaho. But to distribute the fish, the food bank needed federal approval in declaring that all federal health and safety requirements had been met. Unfortunately, the Department of Commerce, not Agriculture, had to make an inspection to give this approval. This inspection was supposed to cost $3,000, but the White House obtained a waiver for this fee. Red tape was finally cut, and the fish were transferred.

Source: Adapted from *U. S. News & World Report,* April 4, 1983. Copyright 1983, U. S. News and World Report.

traditional holiday fruitcake. For example, candied orange peel must be "thoroughly deragged and processed with sugar and corn syrup to not less than 72 percent soluble solids." Flavoring "shall be pure or artificial vanilla in such quantities that its presence shall be organoleptically detected." Diced candied pineapple must be in quarter-inch chunks, and shortening must have the "stability of not less than 100 hours." Senator Sam Nunn of Georgia has called this the "cost-is-no-object fruitcake." (Weisskopf, 1986). Although many silly rules have been eliminated or modified, many remain.

New Technological Issues

The new policy regulations raise significant and controversial technological issues, as illustrated by the AGS example at the beginning of the chapter. We all want clean air, clean water, a reduction of noise, and protection of workers from carcinogens. But no one knows how much of a particular chemical particulate or gas in the atmosphere may cause what type of illness, in which individuals, and when. Yet new regulations create difficult and costly problems of compliance. Unfortunately, there are wide differences of opinion about the need for and the results of much of this regulation. For instance, what is the acceptable air quality in each region, city and town, and industrial establishment? What are acceptable levels of cotton dust, benzene fumes, dioxin? When is a drug safe to be sold? As we have become much more sophisticated in identifying and measuring carcinogens, we need modifications in the law to provide for weak concentrations, especially in instances where the exposure is voluntary. There must be some balance in evaluating regulations in terms of risk. As it is, regulations prohibit use of some materials that have far less risk to life than everyday practices, such as driving an automobile.

We have always known that the world is complex, but with growing scientific knowledge more and more hazards to life are becoming apparent. Decisions about technical matters, such as whether to put fluorocarbons or other substances in spray-propelled fluids, are no longer being left to private industry. No one knows in all cases what a "rational" decision is or how it should be made. Scientific findings are continuously raising such difficult technical questions. They reflect, of course, a growing awareness of hazards to human life and a national policy to reduce them. The policy is not in question here, but the fact is that new regulations do become embroiled in controversial technical issues undreamed of in the past.

Delays in Administrative Decision Making

As we have noted, the process of decision making in regulatory agencies is slow. Businesspeople have complained for years about excessive delays in decisions concerning matters vital to them. A few recent cases illustrate the point. In 1982, the federal government settled antitrust suits against AT&T and IBM that had been in process for over a decade. The Dow Chemical Company had plans to build a multimillion-dollar petrochemical complex in northern California, but after two years of effort to gain the required approval for sixty-five permits, it abandoned the effort. A public utility in California today must get clearances from thirty agencies to build a plant, and any one of the agencies can deny the permit. To introduce a new drug in the United States and meet all FDA requirements may take as much as ten years and cost from $50 to $60 million.

Accelerated Pace of Regulatory Reform

A very important new pattern of federal regulation is the accelerated pace of reform. Begun in the Carter administration, the pace of reform picked up considerably in the Reagan administration. So important has this trend been that we devote much of the next chapter to it.

REGULATORY IMPACTS ON MANAGERIAL ROLES, PROCESSES, AND STRUCTURES

CEO Involvement in Political Affairs

Traditionally, the strategy of the majority of top business executives in the United States has been to maintain a low profile in the public forum and an intractable position against government initiatives that affect the business institution. The mountain of government regulations and the low level of credibility with which business must contend today provide convincing evidence of the disastrous consequences of that strategy. To be sure, the lack of involvement of business leaders in the legislative and administrative processes of government has not been responsible for the growth of government regulation. But the lack of business involvement has resulted in the enactment of legislation that might not have been passed or that might have been considerably modified in favor of business, had business leaders become more involved. Business leaders did get involved in the political processes in the past. But the strategy of business leaders today is to get even more involved and their involvement today is much more sophisticated than in the past.

In the survey of CEOs and their top managers made by the senior author and referred to in Chapter 2, there was a consensus among CEOs of larger corporations that they must be able to swim in political waters as easily as in the traditional economic and technical environments of the corporations. Reginald H. Jones, former CEO of General Electric, made this point in an interview with the author and in a number of speeches:

You Be the Judge

The California Public Utilities Commission (PUC) permitted an anti-utility consumer group to seek members and contributions by placing inserts in bills to consumers from the San Diego Gas & Electric Company (SDG&E). This ruling was instigated by TURN (Toward Utility Rate Normalization), an activist group that advocated onerous state regulation of utilities. The members attended PUC meetings dressed as lightbulbs to attract media attention. TURN argued that SDG&E included political commentary about events affecting the utility in its mailings to consumers, a right granted by the U. S. Supreme Court. So, TURN demanded that the PUC either halt this practice by SDG&E or permit TURN to include its literature in SDG&E mailings. SDG&E argued that it had a right to turn down such requests. The PUC ruled that because utility bills often do not weigh the full ounce paid for by a first-class postage stamp, TURN could use the leftover space for its material. How would you have decided this case?

THE DECISION OF THE U.S. SUPREME COURT

The California Supreme Court upheld the PUC but the U.S. Supreme Court reversed the ruling. In a five to three decision, the Court held that states may not force privately owned utilities to include with customers' bills information from consumer activists and other self-appointed public interest groups. Justice Lewis F. Powell, writing the majority opinion, said that forcing companies to include such material in their billings to customers violated their constitutionally protected right not to speak.

Managers of the future will of necessity have much greater political sophistication. Like it or not, government is becoming an ever more pervasive factor in economic life. It is no exaggeration to say that for most managers, the main problems—the main obstacles to achieving their business objectives—are made in Washington. . . . This is why we say that the main problem of business these days can only be solved in the arena of public policy. Therefore business managers are obliged to become students of public affairs. They must learn how to hold their own in public debate, and know their way around Washington (Jones, 1978).

Political involvement can cover a wide spectrum, from the halls of Congress to local regulatory agencies. It can range from concentrated work on major pieces of legislation to encouraging employees to vote. It can include working with trade associations that seek to influence legislation or administrative decisions, or performing services for politicians, or taking public positions on public issues. A number of these activities will be considered in other parts of this book. At this point, we wish to deal with what managers see as the necessary talents for success in Washington, D.C.

Requisite Talents for Success in Washington, D.C.*

To be effective in Washington, D.C., requires skills considerably different from those needed to run a business successfully. In the survey of CEOs noted above, the talents needed to be effective in legislative halls and administrative offices of Washington, D.C. (as well as in state and local governments) were described as follows:

■ *A good understanding of the political and decision-making processes in Washington, D.C.* To be effective in the political processes of the nation's capital, executives and their staffs need a basic understanding of how the government operates. Among other things, they must understand the relationships that influence decision making by the Congress, the President, and the regulatory agencies; the political considerations in decision making; the levers of power; and the composition and operations of the Congress.

■ *An understanding of how politicians think and are motivated to act.* Businesspeople must understand the way elected politicians think. The typical politician is very sensitive to the interests of people, particularly those of his or her constituents. Politicians entertain the ideas of others even though they themselves may have diametrically opposed personal views, and they can freely and with good humor discuss issues with those who hold opposing points of view and philosophies. They understand and are skilled at identifying and weighing trade-offs, making compromises, and negotiating consensual agreements. They have great skill in sensing trends. They do not take political disagreements personally. And above all, they are extremely sensitive to making decisions that are most likely to assure them of winning the next election.

■ *An understanding of how regulators think and are motivated to act.* Regulators generally think and act differently from politicians. However, they too are generally very sensitive to the many forces impinging on their decision making. Some have biases toward business and others do not. Most of them are persuaded by thoughtful and well-presented cases. Most take seriously the mandates of their statutory legislation.

■ *The need for diligent homework on each case.* The "good old buddy" network no longer works in Washington. "Table thumping" is not effective either. Effectiveness in Washington requires that an executive skillfully present a well thought-out, sensible case. A case must be reasonable, contain all the relevant facts, and be presented persuasively. The homework includes thorough knowledge of the bill or regulation in question.

---

*Reprinted with permission of The Free Press, a Division of Macmillan, Inc., from *The New CEO* by George A. Steiner, Copyright © 1983 by The Trustees of Columbia University in the City of New York.

The presentation of a case is more persuasive if both the pros and cons are forthrightly presented. The case must be presented with candor and should never deliberately mislead. The attempt to mislead often brings a quick loss of credibility. A case is the more persuasive the more the business executive understands the issues that are beyond the immediate interests of his or her company and the more the executive shows understanding of the political issues in the case. As George P. Shultz, the former CEO of the Bechtel Corporation and the current Secretary of State, put it:

> While in the government, I tried to see all comers insofar as time allowed, and I found great variety among those who visited me from business. An important dimension of variability involved the homework done by the visiting businessmen. Many came in very poorly prepared, with only a bitch and a groan and without real substance to back up their points or practical suggestions for dealing with them. Diplomatic and polite though I am by nature, many of these petitioners went away feeling that I was unresponsive and unsympathetic.
>
> Increasingly, however, it seemed to me that businessmen were learning that homework pays off. This is not simply a matter of being factually informed and reasonably objective in presentation. It also means looking beyond the very narrow interests of the individual company or industry and offering some connection between what the businessman wants and the broader public interest (Shultz, 1979: 93).

■ *An ability to establish and use organizations at home and in Washington to help influence public-policy decision making.* In today's world of complex public policy issues, the CEO needs plenty of help in preparing a good case and making sure that it is presented persuasively. CEOs, for instance, need to know when, where, and with what information political activity will be most effective. They need to know who should be seen and when, the precise nature and position of the forces seeking to influence a particular legislator or regulator, and how to build grass-roots constituent support, if appropriate, for their position. Influencing public policy is an extraordinarily complex, difficult, and demanding task, and CEOs need help if they are to be effective at it.

■ *A sensitivity to and an understanding of public opinion and how to influence it.* Abraham Lincoln, more than a century ago, showed keen appreciation for public opinion when, as a candidate for the U.S. Senate, he said in a campaign speech in Ottawa, Illinois:

> In this and like communities, public sentiment is everything. With public sentiment, nothing can fail; without it nothing can succeed. Consequently he who moulds public sentiment goes deeper than he who enacts statutes or pronounces decisions. He makes statutes and decisions possible or impossible to be executed.

■ *A recognition of dangers in becoming involved in political processes.* CEOs generally recognize the many risks associated with involvement in the processes of government, but those in this sample believed that the advantages of involvement well outweighed the risks. To illustrate some of the risks, an executive may be misquoted, or quoted out of context, with adverse effects on him or her personally or on the company. He or she may be treated rudely in testifying before Congress. Those on the opposite side of an issue may accuse the CEO of all sorts of postures, interests, and activities that are alleged to be contrary to the public interest. Even associates, shareholders, and customers may not agree with the CEO's position and say so in strong language. Still, the advantages are worth the risks, in the opinion of the sample (G. A. Steiner, 1983: 59–63).

The Washington Office

Many larger corporations (about 500 today) have offices in Washington, D.C. These offices perform many functions, such as the following:

First, the Washington office provides information to the company's officers and staff about developments in Washington that are of relevance to the company. High on the list, of course, would be legislation and proposed regulations. It is important for a Washington office to establish contacts with people in government to provide a continuous flow of useful information.

Second, the office provides services for visiting personnel from the company. It might, for example, advise the CEO about whom he or she should see, when, and the level of conversation most appropriate. It might mean helping the CEO prepare the proper briefs and responses to legislative and agency proposals.

Third, the company's office represents the company among various agencies in the executive branch and among members of Congress. This is, of course, a lobbying function.

Fourth, the office provides analysis and research on subjects dealt with in Washington and of concern to the company. The subject matter can range from a recommendation that the company alter its strategy in dealing with a particular person or issue to an analysis of the technical consequences of a proposed new regulation.

Fifth, the office must coordinate its activities with those of other organizations in Washington that deal with business affairs, such as the Chamber of Commerce.

Sixth, the office personnel must thoroughly understand what is going on in the company if they are to perform adequately the other functions noted here.

Finally, the office functions better if its people understand the people with whom they must deal. This means, of course, a good bit of socializing.

Organizational Structures and Management Processes

Regulations, together with other environmental impacts on companies, have brought about significant change in organizational structures and internal decision-making processes. Let us here examine how regulations have centralized decision making and how that process has changed management. In setting the company's policy for responding to regulations, top managers can be guided by one of four models.

> 1. At a minimum, the message that comes through is: "It is desirable to comply with regulations in this area"; or a more pragmatic: "We will operate in a manner that keeps us out of trouble with the regulatory bodies."
>
> 2. A more restrictive stance would go beyond a generalized "policy" to include more specific guidelines or procedures. In this approach, top management's position may be: "It is desirable to comply with regulation, and this is how we believe we ought to do it."
>
> 3. Still more restrictive is the use of monitoring after the fact. It adds up to: "It is desirable to comply, this is how it ought to be done, and the staff will be checking to see how effectively the policy of compliance is implemented."
>
> 4. And most restrictive of all is a system that states: "Compliance is a corporate objective. This is how we will do it. Consult with and check all major decisions with appropriate functional heads to make sure that they are consistent with this policy, and staff will be checking to see how effectively this policy is implemented" (Berenbeim, 1981: 9–10).

A survey of 401 companies in many different industries that responded to nine types of regulation showed that most companies followed the third model. Most managers interviewed expected movement to the fourth model and tighter controls by central headquarters in companies (Berenbeim, 1981).

In following the third model, many companies, especially the larger corporations, centralize direction over regulatory matters (for example, equal opportunity, pollution, work safety, insurance and pensions, consumer affairs, product liability, and so on) in one or more departments located at central headquarters. In the early development of these regulations, in the mid-1960s, for instance, many companies relied on their individual operating units to do what was required. Most companies did not need much corporate-level supervision. But the number of regulations mounted; became more difficult to understand; involved more complex legal, technical, economic, and administrative problems in implementation; and required new and massive reporting. The need for centralization of policy, implementation, surveillance, and reporting to government agencies became apparent in more companies. The result, of course, was a withdrawal of managerial authority that had been lodged in operating divisions.

The degree of centralized control varies greatly, depending upon the regulation in question, the nature of the industry, and the size of the company. Decisions and actions having high-risk consequences tend to move up the managerial ladder of decision making. Thus, decisions associated with regulations of the EEOC, EPA, and CPSC move rapidly to higher levels in most companies. Compliance decisions for OSHA regulations tend to be centralized much more quickly in a mining company than in a bank.

There is great variation among companies, of course, in the degree of authority given managers to operate within company policies. Generally speaking, centralization does reduce the authority of managers at lower levels. Managerial authority is reduced by the need to follow old policies, to consult about new policies and procedures, to ask for staff advice in interpreting government policy and regulatory details, and by the imposition of audits by central headquarters. This process also slows down the decision-making process and frequently raises problems of communication and coordination.

CONCLUDING OBSERVATIONS

John Maurice Clark, a distinguished economist and a perceptive observer of the changing business-government relationship, observed over fifty years ago:

> The frontiers of control [government by business] are expanding. They are expanding geographically, increasing the importance of national functions as compared with those of local governments and compelling the beginnings of international regulation. And they are expanding in the range of things covered and the minuteness of regulation. . . . Whether one believes government control to be desirable or undesirable, it appears fairly obvious that the increasing interdependence of all parts of the economic system . . . will force more control in the future than has been attempted in normal times in the past (Clark, 1932: 129).

We add to this projection, which we accept for today, that public demands for a better quality of life for everyone in this society will expand the volume and scope of government regulations. As we have said, it is not regulation per se that is at issue but the fact that costs exceed benefits in far too many specific cases and so far as the aggregate regulatory apparatus of government is concerned. We simply must introduce appropriate reforms in the system if we are to avoid even greater economic, social, and political problems.

But in reforming the regulatory system, we must always bear in mind the benefits of that system. We must not throw out the baby with the dirty bath water. As the Tolchins remind us:

> Regulation is the connective tissue, the price we pay for an industrialized society. It is our major protection against the excesses of technology, whose rapid advances threaten man's genes, privacy, air, water, bloodstream, lifestyle, and virtual existence. It is a guard against the callous entrepreneur, who would have his workers breathe coal dust and cotton dust, who would send children into the mines and factories, who would offer jobs in exchange for health and safety, and leave the victims as public charges in hospitals and on welfare lines. . . . Regulations provide protection against the avarice of the marketplace, against shoddy products and unscrupulous marketing practices from Wall Street to Main Street. They protect legitimate businessmen from being driven out of business by unscrupulous competitors, and consumers from being victimized by unscrupulous businessmen (Tolchin and Tolchin, 1983: 22–23).

As our society becomes more complex, we shall get more regulations. We must seek a realistic and appropriate balance between the real need for regulation and their negative side effects. We turn to regulatory relief and reform in the next chapter.

CASE STUDY

CONTROLLING ACID RAIN

Acid rain has been a major issue since the early 1980s. Simply put, it is an environmental problem that has turned into a complex political, scientific, engineering, and economic dilemma. Since 1982, at least twenty bills to establish acid-rain control programs have been introduced in Congress, but none has passed because major regulatory alternatives are both seriously flawed and highly controversial.

The Problem

Acid deposition, popularly called acid rain, occurs when acidic compounds in the atmosphere fall on the earth in rain, snow, fog, hail, or dew. Acids may also be deposited in dry form, as airborne acidic particles settle to the ground.

Acid deposition originates in the emission of sulfur dioxide (SO_2) and nitrogen oxides (NO_x). Most SO_2 comes from the fuel combustion process in power plants, factories, and smelters; most NO_x from those same sources and from mobile sources (autos, trucks, planes, ships, and rockets). In coal-burning power plants, for example, SO_2 is created during coal combustion from pyritic and organic sulfur that fuse into fly ash and oxidize. NO_x is created when nitrogen and oxygen in the air inside a boiler combine during the high temperatures of coal combustion. Utilities emit 68 percent of the annual 21.4 million tons of sulfur dioxide in the United States. Utilities and mobile sources account for 78 percent of NO_x.

In the atmosphere SO_2 and NO_x are carried by the winds to far places. While airborne, they mix with reactive hydrocarbons. In the presence of sunlight, water vapor, and other chemicals, acids such as sulfuric acid and nitric acid are produced. When these acids reach the ground, they may change the natural balance of soils, alter water quality in lakes and rivers, stunt forest growth, damage man-made structures, and harm human health.

Rain in the United States is becoming more acidic. The acidity of rain is measured on the pH (potential of hydrogen) scale from 0 to 14. Rain is considered acidic if the pH drops below 5.6. In the early 1980s, the average acidity of rainfall in the Northeast, the area with the greatest problem, was about 4.4.

It has been estimated that acid deposition causes $5 billion damage annually in the United States, most of it in the Northeast. In the Adirondack Mountains in New York, 212 of 2,200 lakes and ponds are now dead, unable to support fish because of excessive acidity. In Maine, the acidity of rainfall has increased forty times since the turn of the century. Soil acidity stunts tree growth by limiting the trees' ability to absorb nutrients and has slowed growth in New England forests. If anything, the situation is worse in Canada, where at least 1,600 Ontario lakes are dead, thirteen rivers in Nova Scotia have lost salmon-bearing capacity, and another 1 million lakes are thought to be vulnerable to acid rain damage (McMillan, 1986: 9). Acidity dissolves toxic metals, such as cadmium and uranium, in lake beds and leaches lead and copper from pipes to create hazardous drinking water. Sulfide-stress corrosion may on occasion cause catastrophic failure of metals. Corrosion from acid rain has been implicated in military jet accidents and fatal bridge failures (Scholle, 1983: 30). Sulfur dioxide in airborne particulate form is a known cause of respiratory disease, but acid rain droplets are not inhalable and so do not pose a direct health hazard.

Acid deposition is only one environmental impact of extensive, world-wide coal combustion. Coal burning contributes to carbon dioxide buildup in the atmosphere—the "greenhouse effect"—a global problem that scientists now suspect may alter the climate in the next century. In addition, it releases toxic trace elements such as arsenic, cadmium, lead, mercury, and nickel into the atmosphere. Coal burning increases background radiation slightly by freeing naturally occurring radionuclides in coal ash. And because coal mining is a relatively hazardous occupation, hundreds of miners are killed at it each year.

Scientific Controversy

There is nothing mysterious about acid rain. It is an air pollution problem caused by fossil fuel combustion. Yet although there have been over 3,000 studies of the problem, considerable controversy exists about how serious it is. Some believe that acid rain is causing irreversible, cumulative damage. For instance, David R. Brower (1985), chairman of Friends of the Earth, calls acid rain "a global disaster, a silent and virulent assault on our air, water, forests, wildlife . . . and on human health." Others believe that acid rain may seem to be a problem in media stories that play on public anxiety but has not been proven to cause the environmental damage attributed to it. In a recent speech, Carle E. Bagge, president of the National Coal Association, compared acid rain stories in the press to UFO sightings and argued that "little damage can be documented" (Bagge, 1986: 701). Who is correct? The answer, like the polluted skies over the Ohio River Valley, is not clear.

In the summer of 1983, two substantial, government-sponsored reports were released that showed a convergence of scientific opinion. Reports by the White House Office of Science and Technology and the National Academy of Sciences stated that there was no longer any doubt that acid rain was a serious environmental problem. The reports also said that stack emissions from about fifty big coal-fired utility plants in the Ohio River Valley were the primary cause of detrimental acidity in the Northeast. They concluded that existing data, though incomplete, showed a one-to-one relationship between SO_2 and NO_x emissions from these plants and the levels of acidity in downwind areas. In March 1986 another major report was released by the National Academy of Sciences. The report was an exhaustive review of three more years of research, and it again concluded that a "causal relationship" exists between SO_2 emissions, acidic rain, and increased acidity in water bodies. The report cautioned, however, that because of the complexity and delicacy of atmospheric reactions and ecological changes, it was difficult to prove the cause of acidification in a rigorous, scientific sense. The report named acid rain the culprit in lake acidification and declining fish populations but said that there was not yet enough evidence to prove that it harmed forests.

The weak confirmation of problems caused by acid rain stems from the exacting nature of scientific proof. Although scientists can establish with certainty that emissions rise into the atmosphere and create acidic rain and can establish that ecological damage is occurring, they cannot establish the exact mechanism by which acid rain causes this ecological damage. Therefore, scientists are reluctant to state that emissions from utilities are the primary cause of acid rain until other explanations such as natural sources of acidity, climatic change, biotic stress, and competition among plant and animal species are fully understood. This task may take many years. And the slowness with which scientific proof is forthcoming has led some to reject the acid rain hypothesis altogether (Bagge, 1986). One critic, who argues that observable acidification is a natural process, writes that:

> The amount of acid generated by nature is now known to be far greater than that contributed by industrially generated acid rain. Take bird droppings, which are a relatively minor contributor to the problem. A calculation based on Audubon Society data shows that the droppings hit the U.S. at a rate of about one million per second, and the 150 million tons of droppings per year outweigh sulfur dioxide emissions by something like six to one (W. Brown, 1986: 126).

Control Strategies

A variety of methods for controlling acid rain exist. All, unfortunately, have serious drawbacks. They include the following:

1. *Liming.* Liming is the process of spreading substances such as soda ash, potash, dolomite, or powdered limestone to increase alkalinity in soil or water. Liming has been used for years to combat acidification from fertilizers, and since the 1950s it has been used with success in some water bodies. Liming is effective, but its use over broad areas would be experimental. Because liming does not treat the cause of acid rain, its benefits are temporary, and reapplication is necessary. Although the costs of liming are considerable, they would be far lower than strict controls on electrical utility boiler emissions. One study estimates that the cost of liming several hundred of the most acidified lakes in

upper New York would be only $2 to $4 million a year (Office of Technology Assessment, 1984: 112). By comparison, strict emission controls on industrial facilities could cost up to $5 billion a year.

2. *Coal Switching.* Currently, Ohio River Valley utilities burn high-sulfur coal mined in Ohio and the East. But vast reserves of low-sulfur coal exist in western states. Switching to western coal would substantially reduce sulfur emissions, but problems exist. The energy content of western coal is lower, so plants would burn more. Utilities currently have twenty- to thirty-year contracts for eastern coal that would have to be broken at some penalty cost. If massive western coal purchases began, prices and transportation costs might change unpredictably due to new supply and demand forces. In addition, some utility boilers are designed for high-sulfur coal. Coal switching would not reduce NO_x emissions produced during combustion. Massive strip mining, with all its environmental damage, would be necessary to get 60 to 80 million tons of western coal annually. And because low-sulfur coal has a lower iron content than high-sulfur coal, the electrostatic precipitators commonly used in scrubbers would not be as efficient in removing fly ash.

3. *Precombustion Coal Cleaning.* Coal can be washed to reduce its sulfur content. It is crushed to ⅜-inch particles and bathed in water. Sulfur-containing impurities, such as iron pyrite, fall to the bottom of the tank, while organic matter remains on the top. At best, up to 40 percent of sulfur content can be removed. If all utilities used this process, annual SO_2 emissions could be reduced by three to five million tons. But the largest SO_2 reduction is achieved with high-sulfur, eastern coals. Western coals are naturally high in moisture content, and when the washing process increases their moisture, their heating value is further lowered. A compensating benefit, however, is that coal washing lowers ash content. This decreases slagging in boiler pipes, increases heat transfer, and reduces boiler maintenance costs. Coal washing has increased generating capacity at some plants and has paid for itself (Green, 1983: 47). It is the least costly engineering control, but it does not remove NO_x emissions.

4. *Flue Gas Desulfurization.* This is the most expensive and the most efficient option. FGD requires construction of 60- to 100-foot-tall towers and the attachment of chemical processing plants to boilers. Exhaust gases from boilers are showered with aerosol mixtures of electrically charged ground lime and water. Sulfur dioxide reacts with this mixture, and when the resulting sulfurous combinations are drained away, tons of sludge have to be trucked to landfills at great cost. Massive amounts of lime are consumed. FGD is expensive. Capital costs are about one-third the cost of a generating plant, and with maintenance and operating costs added, it is ten times as expensive as coal washing. When operating, FGD systems also eat up about 6 percent of the power being generated. Extensive use of stack gas scrubbers would increase utility bills in the Midwest 10 to 50 percent. FGD systems remove 90 to 99 percent of SO_2, but they are not effective in controlling NO_x emissions. Under the provisions of the Clean Air Act of 1970, flue gas desulfurization can be required only in plants constructed after 1970. If Congress passed additional acid-rain control requirements mandating this technology for older plants, they probably could not be retrofitted easily.

5. *Experimental Control Technologies.* There are a number of innovative techniques for reducing SO_2 and NO_x emissions in power plants. They include systems for injecting limestone into boilers along with coal to absorb SO_2 emissions and burning coal and oil at lower temperatures to reduce production of NO_x. Such systems are promising but are not ready for full-scale application. They are being used in pilot plants and limited experiments at operating plants. As a general rule, they require either new boilers or extensive retrofitting of old boilers. The new technologies will not become attractive until they have been proved serviceable. In the future, however, it seems likely they will control emissions at lower cost than flue gas desulfurization and with equal efficiency.

The Politics of Acid-Rain Control

One consequence of weak scientific evidence for acid-rain damage has been a lack of incentive to set up a regulatory program mandating expensive remedial measures. Until 1985, the Reagan administration supported only a modest investment in research. Then, at the urging of the Canadian government, the President appointed a special envoy, Drew Lewis, to discuss with Canada mutual actions for solving the problem of acid rain. The resulting negotiations led to the publication of a special report in January 1986 stating that acid rain was a serious problem and calling for the United States to spend $5 billion to develop the newer, clean-burning coal technologies. President Reagan endorsed this report, but neither he nor Lewis endorsed a strict emission-control requirement for industry.

In the spring of 1986, the Acid Deposition Control Act was introduced in the House of Representatives. The bill failed to reach the House floor for a vote, but it had 160 cosponsors among House members. The bill established strict emission limits and reduction timetables for SO_2 and NO_x emissions, mandated the toughest NO_x emission controls ever engineered for autos and trucks, and imposed a nationwide tax on electricity generation to be used to help industry buy emission-control equipment. This bill would have imposed enormous costs on industry and utility ratepayers. It would also have significantly lowered precursor emissions of acid rain.

Powerful political forces collide over national policy on acid rain control. The Acid Deposition Control Act ultimately failed in 1986 because critical actors in this policy debate opposed it. Following is a brief exposition of the major interests.

Environmentalists advocate high-cost regulatory programs involving a mixture of control options, including FGD. In Washington, environmental groups support legislation calling for expenditures of up to $50 billion between now and the turn of the century to control SO_2 and NO_x emissions. In their view, the pollutants that cause acid rain should be controlled now. Waiting for strict evidence of the causal link to ecological damage risks irreparable damage to fragile aquatic environments, forests, and animal populations. The costs are large but affordable; the benefits are difficult to quantify but surely equal or greater. If, as was estimated by the Office of Technology Assessment, the cost of the Acid Deposition Control Act had been $3.4 to $4.3 billion a year, this is roughly the cost of one new nuclear aircraft carrier and is less than the nation spends on video games.

But the *utility industry* is frightened by the prospect of an expensive new emissions-control program. Its lobbyists point out that in the past decade, the nation has spent $160 billion to control air pollution to meet the requirements of the Clean Air Act. Because of existing controls SO_2 emissions from utilities fell 26 percent between 1973 and 1982, while at the same time the amount of coal burned increased by 68 percent (National Coal Association, 1986). Radically increased expenditures are not warranted now, because there is no firm evidence that reducing emissions will control acidity problems. (Knowledgeable observers say, however, that many utility executives privately believe that the environment is being harmed but cannot speak out without encouraging the grandiose abatement schemes of environmental lobbies [Super, 1986].) If utilities are forced to spend billions on stack gas-scrubbers, they will not be able to move along the new clean-burning technologies as fast. Right now these technologies probably are five to ten years away; but they are even further away from development if borrowing capacity is strained to pay for scrubbers in the late 1980s.

Industrial users of electrical energy side with the utilities. In hearings pertaining to the Acid Deposition Control Act of 1986, representatives of auto, steel, and aluminum companies testified that if utilities had to meet the strict emission controls in the bill, their electricity costs would increase 10 to 12 percent at a time when they were locked in a competitive struggle with foreign producers whose costs would not be raised in this way (Haymaker, 1986). Because of international competition, companies in these and other industries would be unable to raise prices and would suffer accordingly.

Sectional interests are divergent. *Governors of midwestern states* fear the economic dislocations of high control costs. Ohio, for example, has been one of the most sluggish states in controlling air pollution. Ohio politics are dominated by a powerful web of utility, manufacturing, and labor interests, which has long opposed strict environmental standards. In Ohio, environmentalists are politically weak, and pollution control is widely equated with lost jobs. The fears of the Ohio industrial establishment have some basis in reality. Rising electrical costs could make some plants in Ohio's ailing smokestack industries noncompetitive and force layoffs. Switching to low-sulfur, western coal could cost the jobs of up to 38,000 coal miners in Ohio and eastern states. The unemployment rate for coal miners is already high—65,000 jobs have disappeared since 1980—so powerful miners' unions are against coal switching. Incidentally, an amendment to the Clean Air Act gives governors the power to prohibit utilities in their states from buying out-of-state coal—a concession to special interests that could prove costly in the acid-rain wars. *Governors of eastern states* are whipsawed between popular demands to control pollution damage to lakes and forests and the threat of unemployment to coal miners. *Governors of western and Sun Belt states* are opposed to strict national emissions limits because these "emission caps" make it more difficult to add new industry. Industrial growth in Texas, Arizona, Florida, and Alabama, for instance, might be constrained if nationwide emission limits for SO_2 and NO_x were set at levels proposed in the 1986 legislation.

The *Canadian government* wants strong, immediate remedial measures. Acid rain has been a source of strain in recent United States–Canadian relations. Emissions from the United States are implicated in about 70 percent of acidic deposition in Canada because of prevailing air currents from the Ohio River Valley. In addition, the majority of Canada's population lives near the Great Lakes, where acidification is pronounced. Largely for these reasons, acid rain is a more prominent political issue in Canada than here. For years the Canadian government has agitated for stricter United States controls, even hiring former presidential aide and lobbyist Michael Deaver to press its case with the Reagan administration. Largely because Deaver acted as a lobbyist less than a year after being involved in acid-rain decisions within the Reagan administration, conflict of interest charges were brought against him.

Lee Thomas, head of the *Environmental Protection Agency,* has advocated only continued enforcement of existing emission control requirements coupled with patience until the results of further scientific research become available over the next few years. Under pressure from the Canadians, *President Reagan* agreed to the proposal of the special envoy to spend $5 billion, split equally between the federal government and industry, to develop clean coal technologies. His approach to the issue was conservative, in keeping with his philosophy of not imposing expensive regulations on business until their benefits are determined to be greater than their costs.

In *Congress,* no strong consensus on acid rain exists. The Senate Environmental Committee is composed mainly of senators from northeastern and western states. It has considered bills that impose most of the cost of pollution control on midwestern utilities and their customers. In contrast, the House Committee on Energy and Commerce is dominated by midwesterners and has favored bills, like the 1986 bill, that would spread control costs through a tax on all utility customers in the United States.

The *public* is concerned about acid rain. An Opinion Research Corp. poll taken in August 1986 showed that 34 percent of those interviewed believed that acid rain was a "very serious" problem, 41 percent a "somewhat serious" problem. But only 40 percent believed that coal-burning electric power plants caused acid rain (60 percent blamed nuclear power plants), and only 9 percent believed that electric power consumers should pay clean-up costs (National Wildlife Federation, 1986).

Major Alternatives

The country is faced with a choice among alternative courses of action. The first invites the least political resistance; the ones that follow are increasingly conflict prone.

1. Wait for further research. Enforce existing emissions standards, and encourage utilities to make additional, voluntary reductions. Require utilities to

do some relatively inexpensive coal washing to remove 3 to 4 million tons of SO_2 from annual emissions of 27 million tons. This step would be a token concession to the Canadian government and to U.S. environmentalists. But take no chance of damaging a fragile economy locked in combat with foreign industries. Hope for early development of fluidized bed combustion furnaces, now predicted to advance the technology of emission control but still a decade away.

2. Require strict emission controls—including extensive FGD—to reduce SO_2 emissions from utilities by 10 to 12 million tons annually. Pay the $40 to $50 billion bill between 1985 and 2000 by: (a) taxing utility customers in the forty-eight continental states one-thousandth of a cent per kilowatt hour of electricity used; (b) making midwestern utility customers foot the bill, perhaps along with customers in eastern states with acidity problems; and/or (c) strengthening NO_x emission controls on motor vehicles to standards required only in California, thereby adding approximately $200 to their purchase price; (d) taxing motor vehicles for NO_x emissions that contribute to acid rain.

3. Place a nationwide cap on SO_2 emissions. Require all new sources, such as generating plants, to offset an amount of SO_2 equivalent to new emissions by reducing an equivalent emission elsewhere in the region or nation. Thus, overall emissions of SO_2 would not be allowed to increase, and in the meantime consensus could develop about reduction measures and their financing. Offsets, of course, are expensive and could slow industrial development in the Sun Belt, where growing demands for electricity are forecast. New generating capacity would be more expensive with an emission cap in place.

4. Generate more electricity with nuclear energy. As more nuclear power plants come on line, the need for coal-fired plants will lessen. Nuclear plants do not emit SO_2 and NO_x. If the languishing nuclear-power industry cannot increase nuclear generating capacity due to high costs and poor public image, then the nation can consider greater use of solar energy. But photovoltaic solar power systems cannot yet produce the massive amounts of electricity needed to offset the shut-down of large coal-fired facilities.

5. Lower public expectations and require decreased energy use. Develop and implement conservation programs. Tell people to accept the radically changed life styles inevitable in the wake of halving energy consumption west of the Mississippi.

Questions

1. Tons of industrial emissions enter the atmosphere each year. Environmental acidification is taking place. Should the government wait for rigorous scientific proof of a cause-effect relationship between these two processes, or should it take vigorous action now?
2. Which of the alternatives listed at the end of the case is best for the country? Why? What other options exist?
3. What kind of acid rain program is possible, given the existing constellation of political interests in acid rain control programs? What are the different values and ethical concerns of the major parties in the acid rain control debates?

CHAPTER 7

REGULATORY RELIEF AND REFORM

 On February 14, 1983, General Motors Corporation announced that it had reached an agreement with Toyota Motor Company of Japan to coproduce a small, front-wheel-drive automobile in a GM plant in Fremont, California. Despite strong opposition by Chrysler Corporation and Ford Motor Company, the Federal Trade Commission (by a vote of three to two) provisionally approved the joint venture in December 1983.

GM and Toyota together planned to invest $300 million in the project, including the $130 million plant that GM owns. The joint venture is to manufacture automobiles derived from a Toyota model currently sold in Japan. The cars will be sold to GM for distribution through its dealers. Production is limited to a single manufacturing facility producing no more than 250,000 cars per year. The joint venture is limited to the manufacture of vehicles for twelve years from the date of the first car that is manufactured, or from December 31, 1997—whichever comes first. The agreement provides that exchanges of competitively sensitive information between GM and Toyota will be limited to information necessary to achieve the legitimate purposes of the joint venture.

GM and Toyota will each hold a 50 percent equity interest in the new company. The company will be managed by its own board of directors, half of whom will be appointed by each company. Toyota will provide management expertise and will appoint the president and chief executive officer. GM will provide financial expertise.

The United Auto Workers and the people of the city of Fremont support the project. The major critics are Chrysler and Ford, who claim that the project is contrary to our antitrust laws. These two automobile manufacturers are supported in this contention by FTC commissioners Michael Pertschuk and Patricia P. Bailey.

On January 12, 1984, Chrysler Corporation brought suit in the United States District Court for the District of Columbia to stop the joint venture. The Department of Justice urged the court to dismiss the suit on the grounds that the joint venture is not contrary to the antitrust laws.

In testifying before Congress, L. A. Iacocca, chairman of the board of Chrysler, said:

> What, really, is the issue here? *Size*. And Power. GM's sales are bigger than the GNP of all but 25 countries in the world; add Toyota, and their combined sales are bigger than the GNP of all but *20* countries. In the U.S. Market, which is the one at stake, they are bigger than all the other automotive companies in the world . . . *put together* (February 8, 1984).

In Chrysler's suit, it was also pointed out that GM and Toyota make over 50 percent of all cars sold in the United States and that one of every two automobile dealers in the United States sells GM or Toyota products. The joint venture will have sales of $1.5 billion a year, equaling the sales of the company ranked 232 on the *Fortune* 500 list.

Both commissioners Michael Pertschuk and Patricia Bailey agreed with Iacocca that concentration of economic power is in violation of the antitrust laws. Commissioner Pertschuk summarized the argument this way:

> The American automobile industry, until the 1970's, was a complacent oligopoly. Product innovation was too sluggish, prices were too high, promotional expenses became bloated, and management and labor inefficiencies became entrenched. The development that undercut this oligopoly and started us on the painful, but ultimately beneficial, road toward competitiveness has been the imports of foreign, particularly Japanese, cars. The Voluntary Restraint Agreement began a reversal of this trend by creating a wall against further Japanese imports. This trade barrier has inevitably been a step back toward the historic American oligopoly and one that increases the power of GM to set prices for the industry. Under these circumstances, it is a fundamentally misguided decision to sanction this type of cooperative arrangement between the dominant domestic manufacturer and the leading importer. To justify such risks to competition we should require a substantial showing of true procompetitive benefits. These are not present (Pertschuk, 1983).

FTC Commissioners George W. Douglas and Terry Calvani were joined by FTC Chairman James C. Miller III in rebuttal:

> Because the structure and the small size of the venture does not appear to pose any significant structural problems, traditional concentration analysis . . . will be of limited value. As a result, the Commission's analysis has sought to identify the potential efficiency benefits and antitrust concerns associated with the venture and to balance these factors. . . . The Commission has provisionally determined that the proposed Fremont venture . . . creates a substantial likelihood of producing significant procompetitive benefits to the American public. The Commission has concluded that these procompetitive benefits to the American consumer would

outweigh any anticompetitive risks, *provided* that the scope of the venture is restricted. Accordingly the Commission has provisionally accepted a consent agreement that provides the appropriate safeguards (Miller, Douglas, and Calvani, 1983).

Traditionally, concentration in an industry has been considered to be in violation of the antitrust laws. In recent years, however, there has been a tendency to consider performance rather than structure in dealing with monopoly issues. This case illustrates that important shift.

As the decade of the 1970s drew to a close, general dissatisfaction with government regulations increased. Demands for reform also intensified. Even those who had in the past strongly favored expanding government regulations have expressed belief in the need for reform. Senator Edward M. Kennedy, for instance, criticized the government mentality that "sees regulation as the natural order of the universe, that equates the *Federal Register* with holy writ, and that believes anything the marketplace can do the government can do better."

Ronald Reagan was elected to the presidency in 1980 partly because of his promise to bring relief from federal regulations. Like presidents before him, he found that this was not an easy thing to do. Why? One reason is that whenever the government intervenes in the economy it typically confers benefits on some groups of people and, directly or indirectly, burdens on others. In so doing it inevitably creates vested private interests in a continuation of that particular activity. This fact applies not only to direct budgetary decisions but to government regulation of economic activity. Irrespective of the merits of the case those groups that are favored exert powerful pressure on the legislature and executive branch to maintain the status quo.

Although in this chapter we focus on government regulation by the federal government, state and local governments also have followed the federal model of expanding regulation of business. In commenting on this point *Business Week* observed the following:

> Two years ago the Reagan revolution started to put regulatory federalism into practice—with the ardent approval of the business community. But today many corporate officials believe the states are spewing out too many regulations, at significant risk and cost to the country. A growing chorus of corporate executives is calling for renewed federal intervention to set uniform national rules in a number of specific areas. The Administration's "New Federalism" has "resulted in a state regulatory nightmare," moans Anthony E. Anzalone, director of government affairs for Sterling Drug Inc. "You think you're serving one master well, and suddenly you're serving a 50-headed hydra" (September 19, 1983).

This chapter begins with a summary of the Reagan administration's efforts to reform federal regulation as well as an assessment of its accomplishments. Then we focus on the most important proposals that have been advanced to bring about more reform.

REGULATORY RELIEF, REFORM POLICIES, AND PROGRAMS OF THE REAGAN ADMINISTRATION

Ronald Reagan campaigned for office on a platform that was committed to cutting federal regulations. He promised mainly to reduce the burdens of the legislation that had grown rapidly during the 1960s and 1970s, but he also favored deregulation of older legislation. His program was labeled more relief than reform, and it was a centerpiece in his promise to revitalize the American economy.

Early Regulatory Directives of the Administration

On January 22, 1981, almost immediately after taking office, President Reagan announced the creation of his Task Force on Regulatory Relief. Vice President George Bush was named chairman, and other members were cabinet officers.

The basic duties of the task force were to review major new regulatory proposals, assess existing rules that appeared to be costly to the national economy or burdensome to a particular industry, and oversee the development of legislative proposals. Vice President Bush said that the task force would be governed by three general principles:

■ Federal regulations should be initiated only when there is a compelling need.

■ Alternative approaches to regulation (including no regulation) should be considered and the approach selected that imposes the least possible burden on society consistent with achieving the overall statutory and policy objectives.

■ Regulatory priorities should be set according to assessed benefits and costs of proposed regulations.

The President also created in the Office of Management and Budget (OMB) a new regulatory watchdog—the Office of Information and Regulatory Affairs (OIRA). OIRA was given substantial powers not only over new regulations (as noted below in Executive Order 12291), but also over reporting forms to be completed by business for federal agencies. Congress set forth this authority in the Paper Reduction Act of 1980. The head of OIRA served on the Bush committee, and the two organizations worked closely to coordinate their activities.

Executive Order 12291, issued on February 17, 1981, gave review authority over regulations to the director of OMB. The director of OMB, however, was made "subject to the direction of the Task Force." Executive Order 12291 required that agencies prepare regulatory analyses (RAs); it stated this requirement as follows:

SEC. 2. *General Requirements.* In promulgating new regulations, reviewing existing regulations, and developing legislative proposals concerning regulation, all agencies, to the extent permitted by law, shall adhere to the following requirements:

(a) Administrative decisions shall be based on adequate information concerning the need for and consequences of proposed government action;

(b) Regulatory action shall not be undertaken unless the potential benefits to society from the regulation outweigh the potential costs to society;

(c) Regulatory objectives shall be chosen to maximize the net benefits to society;

(d) Among alternative approaches to any given regulatory objective, the alternative involving the least net cost to society shall be chosen; and

(e) Agencies shall set regulatory priorities with the aim of maximizing the aggregate net benefits to society, taking into account the condition of the particular industries affected by regulations, the condition of the national economy, and other regulatory actions contemplated for the future.

Regulatory proposals with few economic consequences and involving only a few people were exempt from formal analysis. But those with prospective major economic impacts and involving many people were obliged to make a very elaborate and expensive analysis, called a Regulatory Impact Analysis (RIA). Regulations that might have an impact on the economy of $100 million or more each year; significantly increase costs to consumers, industries, or governments; or have a significant adverse impact on competition, investment, or employment required an RIA. (The requirement for such an analysis was not new, however. It was first required by President Nixon under Executive Order 11821 in November 1974. President Carter, in March 1978, required analysis of costs and benefits under Executive Order 12044.)

President Reagan buttressed these policies and programs with the appointment to cabinet and subcabinet level posts of like-minded individuals—those who were dedicated as he was to reducing the burden of government regulations, including the deregulation of some industries. A number of the new appointees were drawn from regulated industries and could hardly have been expected to deal harshly with their own industries.

Accomplishments Claimed for Regulatory Relief and Reform

The Presidential Task Force on Regulatory Relief issued a final report on August 11, 1983, and then turned over its business to other agencies. The task force report claimed that, since 1981, its efforts had produced administrative and legislative changes that would save more than $150 billion in private sector and state and local funds over the next decade. According to the report, $110 billion of the total savings would come from modification or rescission of unnecessary existing regulations. The additional $40 billion would be in the form of increased income to consumers, generated by the removal, during the Reagan administration, of interest rate ceilings, particularly as a result of passage of the Garn-St Germain Depository Institution Act of 1982, which provided for the partial deregulation of financial institutions.

Hundreds of old regulations were modified, and many proposed regulations were never issued. For example, regulations such as the following affecting the automobile industry were modified and abandoned. The speed at which bumpers must resist damage was cut from 5 to 2.5 miles per hour. The requirement that after 1982 automobiles had to be equipped with passive restraints was delayed and then revoked (the Supreme Court in June 1983 overturned the revocation). For example, the administration decided not to stiffen fuel economy standards to replace those expiring in 1985. Proposals to set standards for seat-belt comfort and convenience and to set safety standards for tire rims were abandoned. The number of new proposed regulations was cut substantially, as shown by a decline of some 20 percent in the pages of the *Federal Register*.

There were some notable deregulations of industries. Building on the initiatives of the Ford and Carter administrations, the Reagan administration deregulated railroads and trucking. Airline deregulation, accomplished in the Carter administration, was continued with the abolition of the Civilian Aeronautics Board, in December 1984. The administration deregulated natural gas, financial institutions, parts of the communications industry, oil pipelines and intercity buses. Not in all instances, of course, was the deregulation total. There is still, for example, much federal regulation of these industries. The report of the Presidential Task Force pointed with pride to the fact that the Reagan administration had institutionalized regulatory reform. It said that there was in place, for the first time, a "credible, effective, and even-handed Executive oversight mechanism, centered in OMB, for the review and coordination of new regulations." (Bush, 1983).

Also on the plus side, from a business viewpoint, have been the new attitudes at the top of the regulatory agencies. The adversarial relationship that prevailed between business and the executive branch during the Carter administration was partly replaced with a more cooperative stance. This change was typified in OSHA. In the agency's annual report for 1981, the administrator said:

> During 1981 OSHA undertook a major campaign to change the focus of the Agency from one of adversarial enforcement to one of cooperative assistance. . . . The Agency is working hard in order to change the prior adversarial relationship that existed between employers and employees into a coalition in which everyone works together to achieve the common goal of a safe and healthful workplace.

The first budgets of the Reagan administration sharply reduced expenditures of the regulatory agencies. Since then, however, budgets have increased total expenditures of the regulatory agencies. Indeed, after inflation adjustments, the total dollar value of these budgets remained virtually unchanged between fiscal 1980 and fiscal 1987. However, regulatory staff dropped by about 14 percent between these years. Drastic reductions were made in some agencies, such as the Interstate Commerce Commission, the Federal Railroad Administration, the National Highway Traffic Safety Administration, and the Employment Standards Administration. Increases were made in some agencies, such as the Farm

Credit Administration, the Federal Reserve Banks, and in the Environmental Protection Agency (following the resignation of the administrator in 1983 and the appointment of a new administrator after congressional hearings on mismanagement in the agency).

The administration also changed antitrust policy, as we will discuss later in this chapter. The administration sought to reprivatize substantial parts of federal business activity, but without much success, as is also discussed later in this chapter. Perhaps the most important long-term accomplishment of the Reagan administration is the substantial number of conservative judges which it appointed to our highest courts of law.

An Assessment: Revolution or Blip?

There is no doubt that significant change has taken place in regulatory policy and programs. These changes include White House review of regulations; the development of regulatory guidelines, especially cost-benefit analyses; a slower pace in launching new regulations; a shift from confrontation to cooperation; a reduced cycle of regulatory decision making; appointment of relief- and reform-minded regulatory agency leaders; and a decline in regulatory staffs.

But critics of the Reagan administration's policies and programs point to a number of important deficiencies. One was the failure of the administration to get Congress to change statutes that would make regulation more efficient and effective. For example, the strict provisions of some regulations (such as the unattainable goals specified by the Clean Water Act of eliminating the discharge of all pollutants and making all lakes and streams fishable and swimmable) need modification. On the other hand, broad grants of authority that permit agency regulators to establish law contrary to the wishes of legislators (for example, the congressional veto of FTC rules concerning disclosures for used automobiles) also need to be clarified. The administration in its first two years spent most of its political capital in pushing social expenditure reductions, tax reductions, and defense expenditure increases through Congress. If there is to be any permanent improvement in regulations, there must be changes in basic legislation.

The administration ran into serious roadblocks in applying its cost-benefit principle. For example, the Toxic Substances Control Act *requires* the EPA to consider cost-benefit factors in applying the law. The Clean Air Act *permits* the EPA to consider cost-benefit analysis. The Delaney Amendments to basic FDA legislation implicitly *forbid* cost-benefit analysis. The same is true with the Endangered Species Act.

In a milestone case on June 17, 1981, the U.S. Supreme Court dealt a critical blow to cost-benefit analysis where the enabling legislation casts doubt about its applicability. OSHA decided to use cost-benefit analysis in setting cotton-dust standards for worker health. Justice William J. Brennan, Jr., writing for the majority in a five-to-three decision, said that economic and technical feasibility constitute the only limits on OSHA's power to lay down worker health and safety standards. He said:

Congress itself defined the basic relationship between costs and benefits, by placing the "benefit" of worker health above all other considerations save those making attainment of this "benefit" unachievable (*American Textile Manufacturers Institute* v. *Donovan* and *National Cotton Council* v. *Donovan*).

Justice Brennan noted that some regulations required cost-benefit analysis, but not those promulgated by OSHA. He also said that only Congress could amend the law to require OSHA to conduct cost-benefit analyses of its health standards. Subsequent court decisions have reaffirmed this principle: that whatever the consideration given to costs and benefits, an agency cannot substitute its judgment for rules laid down by the Congress in legislation.

Some critics have observed that the Reagan administration, rather than breaking new ground, followed a trend toward deregulation and regulatory relief begun under the Carter administration. This is not entirely accurate because regulatory budgets and personnel grew rapidly until the last year of the Carter administration, when the pace slowed. The Reagan administration did more than slow down the pace. It substantially reduced regulatory personnel.

The administration's deemphasis of regulations has drawn congressional fire. One storm centered, for example, on the EPA. EPA was accused of misusing funds for toxic waste cleanup and of abuse of the public trust by its officials, who made "sweetheart deals" with industrial polluters and then destroyed incriminating evidence. Other agencies have been also criticized by Congress for various misdeeds in administering the law. OMB, for instance, has been criticized constantly for "sitting on" regulations, weakening them, pressuring regulatory agencies into not proposing regulations, undermining the implementation of existing regulations, holding private meetings with industry, and operating in secret. OMB denies these charges. In 1985, OMB said that 71 percent of the rules submitted to it for review were approved without change. About 23 percent had to be changed "to make them consistent with the president's regulatory principles," said the agency (Havemann, 1986). Some criticism naturally follows when OMB acts against a pet project of a member of Congress. Since 1980, Congress also has prohibited the Federal Trade Commission from monitoring agricultural marketing orders, and each year since November 1983 it has prohibited OMB from spending any money to review marketing orders. These actions, of course, reflect the power of vested agricultural interests.

Finally, as we suggested earlier, there is a growing chorus of demands for the federal government to allow business to march to the beat of one drummer rather than fifty. As the federal government has deemphasized regulation, states have stepped in to fill gaps in implementation and have initiated new regulations in the absence of federal actions to meet new problems.

If our regulatory apparatus is really to be as effective and efficient as it should be, basic reform is imperative. Without a full range of reforms it is likely that the efforts of the Reagan administration will amount not to a revolution but only to a pause in the continued expansion of federal regulations and their defects.

© Chicago Sun-Times: cartoon by John Fischetti. Reprinted with permission.

REVISING THE ANTITRUST LAWS

The distaste of the American people for monopolistic practices in business has been deep and has resulted in a massive set of regulations and laws governing business practices. Today the antitrust laws are a prominent feature of every manager's environment, especially those in large corporations. These laws cover a wide range of actions concerning the acceptable size of companies, the market shares they enjoy, and the behavior that can lessen competition. Here we discuss how the application of our antitrust laws has changed substantially in theory and practice in recent years.

The Sherman and Clayton Acts

Our basic antitrust laws are the Sherman Act (passed in 1890) and the Clayton Act (passed in 1914). There have been few amendments to these fundamental laws. But judgments about the legality of various business practices today differ greatly from those of ninety, fifty, or even twenty-five years ago. These changes are partly attributable to changes in the law, but mainly to shifts in Supreme Court decisions.

Background of the Sherman Act   The immediate grounds for the passage of the Sherman Act lay in the rapid development of monopolistic practices following the Civil War. The Standard Oil Trust and its many imitators in the 1880s provoked formidable opposition among small-business owners, farmers, and the general population. This was a period of concentration of economic powers, price fixing, market sharing, and other monopolistic agreements among formerly competing companies. So widespread was the opposition to the monopoly movement that the Sherman Act passed the Senate with but one dissenting vote and passed the House without opposition.

Basic Provisions of the Act   The two most significant sections of the Sherman Act are 1 and 2. Section 1 reads: *"Every contract, combination* in the form of trust or otherwise, or *conspiracy, in restraint of trade* or commerce among the several States, or with foreign nations, *is hereby declared to be illegal"* (italics added). Section 2 says: *"Every person who shall monopolize,* or attempt to monopolize, or combine or conspire with any person or persons, to monopolize any part of the *trade* or commerce among the several States, or with foreign nations, *shall be deemed guilty* of a misdemeanor, and, on conviction thereof, shall be punished by fine"* (italics added).

Much has been written about the purpose of the Sherman Act, but one of the best statements was given in a Supreme Court opinion:

> The Sherman Act was designed to be a comprehensive charter of economic liberty aimed at preserving free and unfettered competition as the rule of trade. It rests on the premise that the unrestrained interaction of competitive forces will yield the best allocation of our economic resources, the lowest prices, the highest quality, and the greatest material progress, while at the same time providing an environment conducive to the preservation of our democratic political and social institutions. But even were that premise open to question, the policy unequivocally laid down by the Act is competition (*U.S. v. Northern Pacific R. R. Co.,* 1958).

This legislation did not provide anything new legally, because monopolistic agreements had been held unenforceable under common-law prohibitions of agreements that unreasonably restrained trade. But many states had experienced problems in applying these laws to giant companies doing business in many states. With the Sherman Act, however, these conspiracies now were offenses against the federal government.

Early Supreme Court Decisions   The first decisions of the Supreme Court to interpret antitrust law met with disbelief and dissatisfaction. In the first case brought to the Court, *U.S. v. Knight* (1895), the Court decided that a gigantic sugar refining company, which controlled 98 percent of the market, had not violated the act. This ruling naturally encouraged merger and concentration. The decision was reversed in several celebrated cases, such as *U.S. v. Standard Oil* (1909) and *U.S. v. American Tobacco* (1911). Both of these companies enjoyed about 95 percent of their respective markets and the court declared this percentage contrary to the law. However, the Court also said in passing judgment that there were reasonable and unreasonable restraints of trade and that if other large companies were to use their powers reasonably, they would not run afoul of the law. The Court did not define the meaning of these words, which became known as the "rule of reason."

The Clayton and Federal Trade Commission Acts

Dissatisfaction with these decisions and the legal uncertainties they posed to business led to the passage of the Clayton Act and the Federal Trade Commission Acts of 1914. The Clayton Act sought to identify those monopolistic practices which were prohibited by law. The FTC Acts created an agency to continuously supervise and administer the antitrust laws and to stop "unfair methods of competition in commerce, and unfair or deceptive acts or practices in commerce . . ." (Section 5 (a) as modified by the Wheeler-Lea Act of 1938).*

The Clayton and FTC acts are long and their language often fuzzy. Section 7 of the Clayton Act, the most important section for the present analysis, is comparatively simple:

> *no corporation* engaged in commerce *shall acquire,* directly or indirectly, the whole or any part of *the stock* or other share capital of another corporation engaged also in commerce *where the effect of such acquisition may be to substantially lessen competition* between the corporation whose stock is so acquired and the corporation making the acquisition *or to restrain such commerce in any section or community or tend to create a monopoly of any line of commerce.* (Italics added.)

Other sections of the Clayton Act spelled out in some detail price discrimination and exclusive dealings that "may . . . substantially . . . lessen competition or tend to create a monopoly in any line of commerce. . . ."

SUPREME COURT DECISIONS CONCERNING FIRM SIZE, PRICE FIXING, AND MERGERS

A thumbnail sketch of the history of Supreme Court decisions about firm size, prices, and mergers is useful in understanding present law and the controversies associated with it. It is also a fascinating account of the many ways in which the relationship between business and government has changed.

---

*The Department of Justice has the authority to enforce the Sherman Act and shares jurisdiction with the FTC in Clayton Act cases. The FTC can issue orders to business enforcing provisions of both acts, but only the Department of Justice can prosecute for criminal violations of the antitrust laws. The Supreme Court, of course, has the final word in interpreting the application of both laws.

Shifts in the Legality of Size and Price Fixing

For decades after the Clayton Act, the Supreme Court continued to apply the "rule of reason" in deciding the legality of companies with high market shares. In 1916, for example, the Court said that it would not destroy a company even though it produced 90 percent of the nation's cans. The reason for this position, said the Court, was that the company "had done nothing of which any competitor or any consumer of cans complains, or anything which strikes a disinterested outsider as unfair or unethical" (*U.S. v. American Can Co.*). In 1920, a steel company that controlled over two-thirds of many steel products was not broken up because "the law does not make mere size an offense or the existence of unexerted power an offense" (*U.S. v. United States Steel Corporation*). In 1927 a company that controlled 64 percent of its market was not held to be in violation of the law (*U.S. v. International Harvester Co.*).

In contrast, in a series of cases going back to 1899, the Court held price fixing to be a per se violation, meaning that no extenuating circumstances could make price fixing legal. For example, in 1927 the Court held, "The power to fix prices, whether reasonably exercised or not, involves power to control the market and to fix arbitrary and unreasonable prices. The reasonable price fixed today may through economic and business changes become the unreasonable price of tomorrow." It did not make any difference, said the Court, whether the agreement to fix price was loose or formal (*U.S. v. Trenton Potteries Co.*, 1927).

These two lines of thought encouraged the very thing that the Sherman Act was designed to stop. Because price fixing was illegal but large size was not, firms merged to form huge companies with enough power to monopolize markets. In later cases the Court recognized the irony of this result and extended the rule of reason to price fixing as well as to company size. In 1933, for example, price fixing was held to be legal because the price agreements in question were designed to end injurious competition and to promote a "fair market" (*U.S. v. Appalachian Coals, Inc.*). In 1945 the Court held that a company with 90 percent of the primary aluminum market in this country was a monopoly contrary to the law. The power to fix prices by such a company, said the Court, was inherent in its size (*U.S. v. Aluminum Co. of America*). This doctrine was upheld in 1946 in *U.S. v. American Tobacco Company*, and again in 1948 in *U.S. v. Paramount Pictures*. But also in 1948, in *U.S. v. Columbia Steel* the Court seemed to slip back into its more permissive attitude. In this case, a steel company had 51 percent of the rolled-steel or ingot capacity on the Pacific Coast. This share was held not to be unlawful. Size is significant, the Court said, but the steel industry itself is big.

Conglomerates and Threats to Competition

Most of these cases involved mergers (both horizontal and vertical) and the behavior of one or a few companies with large shares of a market. In the late

1950s and 1960s there was a wave of mergers consummated by conglomerates.*
This activity receded in the 1970s but picked up again in the 1980s. The legality
of the size and behavior of these firms had to be decided by the courts.

In a milestone case, *U.S. v. Brown Shoe Company* (1956), the Supreme Court
said that one must look not only at total concentration but concentration in
particular markets. Furthermore, combinations were illegal if they posed a
potential threat to competition. In this case, Brown Shoe, a producer, acquired
the G. R. Kinney Company, an independent chain of shoe stores. Together they
controlled 2.3 percent of total retail shoe outlets and 1.5 percent of the nation's
shoe output. But in some local areas, sales of women's shoes ran as high as 57.7
percent of the local market. In forty-seven cities, the combined share of
children's, men's, and women's shoes was a little over 5 percent. The Court said
that if it approved this merger, competitors would do the same thing, and this
move would encourage the oligopoly Congress sought to avoid. It was therefore
important to nip in the bud incipient threats to competition.

In subsequent conglomerate cases, the Court widened the antitrust net. It
rejected a merger of a small with a larger company even though the two did not
compete. The reason: the larger company could be a "deep pocket," a "rich
parent" that could open up all sorts of possibilities for the small company to
undersell or otherwise "ravage the less affluent competition" (*FTC v. Reynolds
Metal Company*, 1962). In another case, the Court rejected the merger of a small
and a large company because there would exist a clear probability of reciprocal
buying that would weaken competition in the industry (*FTC v. Consolidated Foods
Corporation*, 1965). Two years later the Court agreed with the argument that even
though two companies that wanted to merge were not competitors, the
possibility that potential competition in an industry might be inhibited was
enough for it to deny the petition to merge (*FTC v. Procter & Gamble*, 1967).

It is true that such theories as incipient threats to competition, "deep pocket,"
probable reciprocal buying, and potential threats to competition would, if
companies acted as the Court said they might, result in injury to competition.
These theories seem to be based on the idea that it is better for consumers to
forego the efficiencies that could accrue to a merger in order to avoid a
hypothetical future injury to competition.

---

*A *horizontal merger* is one that combines the activities of companies within the same industry,
such as two steel mills. A *vertical merger* takes place when a company acquires other firms, either
back in the production chain, toward raw materials, or forward, toward consumers of final
products and services. For example, a merger of a company producing fabricated steel shapes
and forms with one mining iron ore and one building steel bridges is a vertical merger. A
conglomerate merger is neither horizontal nor vertical and involves two firms that are engaged in
unrelated lines of business. A simple illustration would be the merger of a producer of wooden
office furniture with a company owning and mining coal.

Conglomerate mergers can, of course, be of different varieties. For example, the acquired may
be completely unrelated, or they may associate with a basic company purpose. Conglomerates
may merge with firms that are not directly competitive, such as those with common production
or distribution characteristics, or companies in the same general product line but making sales in
different geographic regions.

Schumpeter on Competition

". . . [The] kind of competition which counts . . . [is] the competition from the new commodity, the new technology, the new source of supply, the new type of organization (the largest-scale unit of control, for instance)—competition which commands a decisive cost or quality advantage and which strikes not at the margins of the profits and the outputs of the existing firms but at their foundations and their very lives. This kind of competition is as much more effective than the other [i.e., competition between makers of identical products—e.g., between fountain pen makers, who were put out of the fountain pen business with introduction of ball-point and felt-tip pens] as a bombardment is in comparison with forcing a door, and so much more important that it becomes a matter of comparative indifference whether competition in the ordinary sense functions more or less promptly; the powerful lever that in the long run expands output and brings down prices is in any case made of other stuff."

Former Professor Joseph A. Schumpeter of Harvard University

At about the same time, the Court reaffirmed its prohibition of price fixing, excessive domination of a market by large corporations, and any behavior that seemed likely to weaken competition. For example, the Court ruled that no corporation should seek or exercise the power to control the prices in or to exclude others from a market (*U.S. v. Grinnell Corp.*, 1966). It ruled that a dominant company must not engage in any monopolistic restraint, such as cutting off rivals from essential sources of supply (*Zenith Radio Corp. v. Hazeltine Research, Inc.*, 1969). The allocation of exclusive territories to distributors or dealers to exclude competitors was forbidden (*U.S. v. Arnold, Schwinn & Co.*, 1967).

In the 1970s, as the Court took economic performance and efficiency more into account its decisions changed once again. The Court held, for instance, that a merger could take place when the acquired company was of little competitive significance (*U.S. v. General Dynamics*, 1974). It indicated in other cases that it was ready to consider the impact of mergers and price fixing on markets rather than to decide cases solely on the basis of corporate size, market shares, or industry concentration. For example, in *Cargill, Inc. and Excell Corporation v. Montfort of Colorado, Inc.* (1986) the Court said that it would not prevent a merger simply because a competitor believed the combination would, after the merger, result in loss of profits when the merged companies reduced price. The plaintiff had to show the Court that it actually suffered from such predatory pricing. Of course, it could not do so.

Structure versus Performance

Until recently the Supreme Court, as well as government regulators and academic economists, leaned toward the structure theory in deciding antitrust cases, as supported by most of the scholarly studies on concentration and merger. In the late 1960s, however, an increasing body of impressive evidence emerged that contradicted this view in support of the performance theory.

In 1949 Professor Edward S. Mason argued in a landmark article that public policy toward industrial organizations ought to aim at promoting sound market structures as well as efficient business performance. The market structure and performance tests, he observed, "must be used to complement rather than exclude each other" (E. Mason, 1949: 1280). By *performance* he meant product and process innovation, reductions in costs by various managerial and technical methods that were passed on to consumers in lower prices, suitable capacity in relationship to output, profits not out of line with other industries, and emphasis on product and service rather than excessive advertising expenditures. Since Mason wrote his article, there has been sharp controversy between those who argue for a structural public policy and those who support a policy based on performance.

The conventional economic wisdom up to recent years and still held by many was that the structure of the marketplace is a reliable index of monopoly power. More precisely, the theory argues that the more concentrated the sales and assets of a few firms in an industry, the greater the monopoly power of those firms. Not only is there substantial concentration today of sales and assets in individual industries but there is high concentration of all corporate assets in the largest companies in the United States. In that everyone is opposed to monopoly, the proper public policy is one that slows down and reverses this trend. If not, in three or four decades we will be dominated by concentrations of economic power in our large corporations.

Excessive concentration of market power, it is argued, gives corporate managers discretionary power to fix market prices, determine which products come to market and in what volume, and make excessive profits. Furthermore, monopoly power has produced price inflation, inefficiencies in production and, of course, a decline in competition.

Structuralists argue that if competitive markets can be created by breaking up concentrations of economic power or by preventing mergers of large firms, individual companies will behave competitively, with economically desirable performance. Therefore, they argue, large concentrations of economic power should be broken up. Antitrust policy will be clearer and more effective if there is some fixed rule based on structure.

This market-concentration doctrine is rebutted by others. Some argue that concentrations of economic power in large companies are due to market forces and not to motivations to monopolize. Large size is a necessary concomitant to a large economy. In certain industries, large companies and concentration are essential because of the heavy capital investment needed to do business. Industries do not become concentrated unless there is a basic economic reason for large-scale operations. Business structure is therefore the result of underlying economic forces.

Many observers see competition rising rather than declining. They see there are many forms of nonprice competition which take place. Smaller firms can specialize and take advantage of any excessive pricing of large companies. High profits of large firms may be associated more with efficiency than the exercise of monopoly power. Product innovation is a major source of competition by large firms because they can afford heavy research and development expenditures that small firms cannot.

In sum, it is the performance and behavior of large firms that should be examined and not simply structure. An atomistic market structure would be quite out of tune with the demands of modern society and would, in addition, bring about economic distortions and inefficiencies.*

A few other issues between the market structurists and the business performists may be presented in capsule form. The structurists reject performance because they say there are no clear and acceptable standards for measuring performance. Those who emphasize performance do so because they say there are no suitable standards to measure acceptable structure. Structure is favored because when it is suitable, there will be many competitors, the market will regulate economic activity, and government interference in the market mechanism will be unnecessary. Those who hold to performance point out the extraordinary change that would be required to bring about anything approaching pure competition. Furthermore, if cost advantages of size are prevented, will not the cost to consumers be excessively high? Structurists say it is not performance which is sought, but competition. There is an implicit assumption that if structure is acceptable, there will be better products, improved service, and lower prices. But it is said that mergers and company expansions are necessary to ensure efficiency, which benefits society. It is pointed out that structure can be perfect, as in atomistic competition, and performance terrible because market conditions lead to cutthroat competition. And so the arguments, like a shuttlecock, move back and forth from one position to another. To many observers, both sides make good points.

Research Supporting the Performance and Structure Theory   A typical measure of concentration of market power is the ratio of sales of the largest companies to total sales in an industry. These data, of course, vary greatly from industry to industry. It is true that in some industries (mainframe computers, automobiles, and jet engines, for example), the four largest companies account for well over 70 percent of the value of total domestic shipments. In most industries, however, the concentration ratio for the four large companies is under 50 percent. Longitudinal studies show that the concentration ratios for most industries have remained remarkably stable (Weston, 1978). When world markets are considered, the concentration, however, drops substantially for virtually all major industries.

Earlier studies suggested that high concentration led to excessive profits (Blair, 1973). However, later studies have shown a lack of correlation between conventional measures of concentration and excessive profits (Weston, 1978). Contrary to structure theory, new research shows that substantial price flexibil-

---

*See Appendix B for a full explanation of atomistic markets and competition.

ity exists in concentrated industries and that price increases during inflationary periods were lower in industries dominated by "super concentrations" than in those less concentrated. Productivity also has risen faster in concentrated than in other industries. Structuralists allege that innovation in concentrated industries is less than in nonconcentrated industries, a fact which is difficult to prove but which is challenged by some studies.

Such research findings do not reject completely every assertion by structural theorists. Some concentrations at some time and place may result in excessive profits, price inflexibility, inhibitions to innovation, and so forth. They do conclusively show, however, that for most cases of concentration, structure theory describes the opposite of reality.

Significance of Corporate Divisionalization   One of the very important recent developments partly explains the wide difference between structural and performance theories. It is that major corporations have transformed themselves from one-product to multi-product firms. Between 1949 and 1969, the number of firms with multiple product divisions among our largest 200 companies jumped from 20 to 76 percent of the total (Rumelt, 1974). This trend has continued, and now very few of our largest companies have only one product line and one centralized management.

This change is of cardinal significance in antitrust theory. The assumption that our large corporations are huge monolithic enterprises leads to very different conclusions about behavior than the assumption that they are multi-product, decentralized organizations. Huge corporations that are centrally controlled and have one or a few products do tend to suffer from all the classical managerial deficiencies of massive bureaucracies. They may very well behave economically as the structure theorists claim. However, what goes on in the typical divisionalized corporation with many products, even though the corporation is very large, is much different.

A decentralized corporation with major divisions like General Electric, for instance, is divided into so-called strategic business units (SBUs). These units, with only moderate control from company headquarters, have considerable authority to operate as independent businesses. They enter into a competitive market populated heavily by divisions of other conglomerates. This market typically is highly dynamic and volatile. The SBU faces serious competitive threats, such as new products developed by other firms both in and outside the industry; technical advances in products developed by competitors; new substitute products that may render the SBU's products obsolete; and foreign competition. The result, of course, is strong pressure on the SBU to maintain its competitive position.

To stay competitive, the SBU may try to protect itself in many ways. The SBU may differentiate products; expand research to improve the quality and consumer acceptance of present products; invest in new equipment to increase productivity; cut costs by speeding inventory turnover; increase advertising expenditures; lift market share by cutting prices and costs per unit; develop more efficient distribution methods; stimulate worker participation in the decision-making processes to advance product quality, worker productivity, morale, and so on. All these forces and many others inevitably improve efficiency and benefit consumers. Companies and SBUs that depend upon nothing but the presumed power of their high market share are doomed to lose share and eventually go bankrupt.

Basic in structural theory is the assumption that managers form mergers with other companies to increase their power in the marketplace. Some mergers have been engineered by entrepreneurs molded after the industrial buccaneers of the late nineteenth century. Their motivations range across a wide spectrum —power, the fun of the game, money, and the like. Some have acquired underpriced companies with the hope of selling assets piecemeal for a total financial gain. Some apparently have forced a reluctant takeover target to buy back the acquirer's stock at a premium to end the takeover attempt. Some have acquired companies with large tax write-off carryovers that would help the acquiring company to shelter future profits. Some few may have been motivated solely by an effort to acquire economic power in the marketplace.

But in most recent mergers, the overwhelming drive has been economic efficiency. More specifically, the underlying purposes have included: growth of sales and profits, avoidance of dependence on one product line, stability of sales and earnings over the business cycle, acquisition of needed technology and fuller employment of technological capabilities, reduction of costs by using an underemployed distribution system, entry into foreign markets, acquisition of raw materials, use of excess productive capacity, completion of a product line, taking advantage of tax laws, and a combination of these objectives. Unquestionably, many mergers have been prompted by the fact that it has been less costly (because of comparatively low share prices in the stock market) for one company to acquire another through the purchase of stock than to achieve these objectives through internal growth.

On the other side of the coin, in many instances the acquired company has sought the merger. An aging owner of a company, for example, may wish to retire by selling the firm to another company, a firm may be in financial trouble and need access to cash, or it may be apparent to both companies that joint efforts will more readily achieve mutual economic objectives.

A veritable revolution in management techniques has facilitated the growth of large and prosperous corporations with virtually independent subsidiaries (SBUs). For example, we have learned much about how managers must deal with people in organizations to get the best results. Techniques have been perfected concerning how to identify opportunities in the environment; how to appraise current and future competitive threats; how to manage a portfolio of SBUs with many different products, resource needs, problems, and opportunities; how to develop better communications and information systems; how to automate production lines for greater efficiency; how to minimize manufacturing and distribution costs; and how to optimize the results of research.

The central reality is that most mergers, as well as the increase in size of companies through internal growth, have resulted because managers have had to make sure that their companies, and each SBU or division, are strong in highly competitive markets. Operating efficiency is the key to achieving this result. But our antitrust laws and the thinking of jurists have not changed enough to reflect these realities.

Reagan Administration Proposals for Reform

In February 1986 the Attorney General and the Secretary of Commerce introduced five legislative proposals to the Congress on behalf of the White House to change substantially antitrust legislation.

One proposal concerning mergers was incorporated in the Merger Modernization Act of 1986. Central to the bill were proposals to change the wording of Section 7 of the Clayton Act so that it would look at concentration and mergers through the lens of economic efficiency rather than merely structure. The new legislation would require, for example, that efficiencies deriving from a merger be considered in any question of legality and that there be a significant probability that a merger will be harmful before it is prohibited. The bill proposes that vague language like "lessen competition" be clarified such that anticompetitive mergers are only those that "substantially increase the ability to exercise market power." Finally, the bill proposes to broaden the definition of the market when the degree of concentration of firms in the market is considered. For example, the new definition would include firms currently in the market as well as those that might enter the market in the future. Concentration would also be considered in terms of the world market and not only the domestic market.

A second bill, the Antitrust Remedies Improvement Act of 1986, would eliminate triple damages, which can now be awarded in antitrust suits. Many problems have arisen with the current law. For example, threats by competitors to initiate a complaint may tend to coerce rivals into abandoning or restricting actions that might actually enhance efficiency and lower prices to consumers. The new legislation would allow courts to award only actual damages plus other costs deemed appropriate by the court.

The Foreign Trade Antitrust Improvements Act of 1986 would amend the Sherman and Clayton acts to clarify those factors which courts take into consideration in cases involving the application of antitrust laws to commerce with foreign nations.

The Interlocking Directorate Act of 1986 would amend the Clayton Act to permit interlocking directors where the overlap of competition is a very small part of each firm's business. It is argued, and properly, that there is little if any risk of conflict of interest in such instances.

Finally, the Promoting Competition in Distressed Industries Act of 1986 would amend the Trade Act of 1974. It would permit the President to grant limited antitrust exemptions to mergers and acquisitions among members of an industry injured by foreign competition.

Concluding Comment

The performance theory of antitrust is likely to continue competing with the structure theory for some time to come. Although antitrust decision-making leans to the performance viewpoint the older structure theory still is strongly held. For example, in June 1986, the FTC commissioners unanimously agreed to go to court to block Pepsico's purchase of the Seven-Up Company from Philip Morris Company as well as Coca-Cola's previous acquisition of Dr. Pepper. The reason given was that the two mergers would place 80 percent of all United States soft-drink sales in the hands of the two industry giants. Competitors complained, and the FTC agreed, that the merger would unfairly limit competition in the $25 billion soft-drink industry. However, in 1983, the FTC had to decide between the structure and efficiency theories. It chose the latter in the General Motors–Toyota Motor Company joint venture case discussed at the beginning of this chapter.

We conclude with this critical question: Will the Congress, the executive branch of government, and the courts lean more to the performance or the structure theory? The answer will be of the highest importance to business, to the character of the economy of the United States, and to our relations with global competitors.

PROPOSALS FOR FEDERAL REGULATORY RELIEF AND REFORM

Federal regulatory relief and reform has been a dominant issue in national life since Franklin Roosevelt ran for the presidency in 1932. Succeeding administrations dealt with the issue but none more assiduously than the Reagan administration. This administration has indeed accomplished much in relieving business of many regulatory burdens. It has not been as successful, however, in achieving basic regulatory reforms. With respect to both relief and reform much remains to be done.

We reiterate that federal regulatory action deeply involves the political processes. The more significant the regulation, the more intense becomes the controversy surrounding it, and the more difficult it becomes to make even marginal changes. So, all of the proposals suggested below if initiated would become embroiled in the politics of regulation.

Rely More on the Free Market

Economists, as well as the general public, are strongly in favor of relying more on the free market mechanism. This means not only an inhibition against unnecessary controls, but also more reliance on market incentives in meeting regulatory goals. When the market is functioning ideally, there is no superior mechanism for using scarce resources efficiently to produce the goods and services that society needs at prices people are willing to pay. As noted in Chapter 5, a major responsibility of government is to prevent abuses in the operation of the free market mechanism and to facilitate its operation in the most effective and efficient manner.

Government's functioning with respect to the free market has been a mixed bag. It has stimulated competition by deregulating a number of industries. On the other hand, protectionist legislation for many products, from peanuts to automobiles, has reduced free competition. The desirable condition, of course is for the government, as in an old song by Johnny Mercer, "to accentuate the positive, decentuate the negative." In our complex society, striking this balance is not easy, but it is a goal toward which we must constantly strive. Some major policies that might be used to achieve this end follow.

Reduce Command Controls and Substitute with Incentive Controls

Command controls require firms and individuals to meet specific standards or behavior patterns and are enforced by civil and, in some cases, criminal penalties or loss of government contracts. Some controls achieve the regulatory objective directly. For example, automobile manufacturers have had to improve the fuel efficiency of their cars to meet specific standards and thereby have conserved gasoline. Other standards are employed because it is believed that complying with the standard will result in meeting the control objective. OSHA's standards, for instance, are presumed to bring about conditions that will reduce job-related injuries to workers.

Command standards have many weaknesses. For example, they are generally difficult to enforce because they are applied so widely that it is impossible to monitor compliance completely. For example, OSHA cannot inspect all the plants within its authority. Federal and state inspection programs together cover no more than 4 percent of firms to which regulations apply. Since standards are static and the world is dynamic, they must constantly be updated. Such rule making is time-consuming and frequently confusing to those regulated. Standards also can be counterproductive if they deflect efforts from the ultimate objective to compliance with the standards. For example, management may feel that all obligations to patients who use a new drug are fulfilled if the FDA approves the drug's introduction. Or, resources for job safety may be exclusively devoted to meeting OSHA standards without giving careful attention to specific hazards.

The use of fixed standards is justified as a regulatory tool when there is a strong causal relationship between the standard and the objective of control *and* when there are no alternatives. Certain health hazards, such as unallowable levels of carcinogenic pollutants in the work environment or nuclear power plant safety standards, are best dealt with by fixed standards.

But for many command controls, alternatives do exist that allow for more individual freedom. Market incentives are alternatives to most command controls. Market incentives impose prices and/or costs upon unwanted outcomes. Companies faced with such costs seek to reduce them in order to remain competitive and thereby move toward achievement of the regulatory objective. Achievement of the objective is, therefore, decentralized. Economic incentives can take many forms, such as taxes, fees, fines, and penalties. The most effective are those that set the cost in relation to the size of the offense and those in which inspection is frequent enough to ensure that companies comply before the inspector arrives.

The present penalty structure generally does not meet these requirements. Penalties for pollution violations, for example, are generally low compared with costs to society. Despite the army of regulators, inspections are usually not frequent enough to ensure general compliance. In too many cases, business is willing to face a potential fine of, say, $1,000 in order to avoid spending far more to be in compliance. OSHA launched a program to exempt construction companies from routine inspections as inducements to the companies to develop their own tough inspection programs. In three years only 66 companies asked for limited relief, and only 19 requests were granted. In companies that have developed their own systems, as approved by OSHA, safety records have improved dramatically. Why have so few companies asked for exemption? It is because chances of OSHA inspection are minimal and fines for violations are small compared to the costs of setting up private inspection systems (Rohlich, 1986). However, Terrence Scanlon, chairman of the Consumer Product Safety Commission, claimed that the voluntary-agreements program of the agency was working well in more than fifty product areas and that it was saving CPSC a great deal of time and money.

At this stage in our regulatory history it would not be possible to replace command controls with incentive regulations even if there were a consensus to do so. We have built a mountain of detailed regulations, interpretations, court cases, administrative processes, and expectations of command controls, so that only gradual conversion is possible.

Proposals for Deregulation

Strong recommendations for complete or partial deregulation are frequently made because it is believed that resources will thereby be used more efficiently in the public interest. Deregulation is a shorthand word that means two different things. First, it can mean the removal of regulations so that reliance is placed on the free market mechanism. Second, it can mean relaxation or reform of regulations to make the regulations more efficient and effective by reducing costs, increasing the benefits, eliminating nonsense rules, and so on. The first applies to many regulations in the economic area, as noted above. The second applies more to social regulations, such as relaxation of pollution controls. Although much has been accomplished in recent years in both areas, most people believe that much more can be done. For example, further deregulation of natural gas, agriculture marketing orders, and tariff protections would expand free markets and competition.

Harness the Power of Self-Interest

The core advantage of free markets in achieving social purposes is basically self-interest, which, fortunately, has been broadened today by the acceptance of voluntary social responsibilities by more and more managers. Schultze has evaluated this force as follows: "Harnessing the 'base' motive of material self-interest to promote the common good is perhaps the most important social invention mankind has yet achieved" (1977: 18) This is a bit of an exaggeration, yet it does make a valid point. It seems strange, says Schultze, that

> For a society that traditionally has boasted about the economic and social advantages of Adam Smith's invisible hand, ours has been strangely loath to employ the same techniques for collective intervention. Instead of creating incentives so that public goals become private interests, private interests are left unchanged and obedience to the public goals is commanded (Schultze, 1977: 6).

Stress the Comparative Advantage of Government and Business

An effort should always be made to determine whether business or government can best perform an activity that is needed by society. Each has strengths and weaknesses. There clearly are certain activities that government can perform more efficiently than individuals in the private sector. For example, in dealing with the energy crisis, Mobil Corp. recognized that only government can perform significant functions:

Only government can set forth national goals and work out the necessary compromises to reconcile conflicting regional and other interests and to recognize the priorities among various energy sources.

Only government can develop the ground rules under which private industry must work.

Only government can formulate a national policy on environmental trade-offs that will strike a sensible and workable balance between unacceptable environmental risks and unacceptable economic risks.

Only government can hammer out the sort of balanced policy that does not permit extremist approaches to environmental protection to delay for years programs toward achievement of national goals on energy (Mobil, 1978).

Government is the superior institution to express common social goals, to establish policies, and to tax for social purposes. But government has grave deficiencies compared with other institutions in performing certain other functions. As we have noted, government action stimulates interest groups.

Costs of government management of productive facilities are likely to be higher than those of the private sector because of a requirement for accounting for "the last penny," because equal attention must be given to unimportant and important elements of the activity, because in government personnel loyalty is often more valued than efficiency, and because any activity assumed by government becomes part of a huge bureaucracy with inherent inefficiencies resulting from its size.

Business can avoid these problems more readily than governments can. Even the largest businesses are smaller than governments and therefore enjoy an advantage in flexibility and adaptability. For these reasons, it seems sensible to assign to governments and businesses the production of those goods and services that clearly are their responsibility and that each can produce at the lowest cost, using that word broadly.

Reprivatize

Selling government-owned production and service facilities to the private sector is called reprivatization. Reprivatization jokingly has been called "a little yard sale" of excess government assets. The Reagan administration strongly advocated this policy because Reagan long was hostile to big government and believed that the private sector can do a better job at less cost than federal agencies can. Furthermore, the sale of assets, it is argued, will reduce the huge budget deficit of the government.

People have proposed reprivatizing the Federal Housing Administration, Amtrak, the Naval Petroleum Reserve, federal grazing and timberlands, hydropower and irrigation water systems, airports, the postal service, and weather satellites. Almost all of these proposals have run into congressional fire storms, and very little has been sold. Despite efforts to sell assets, the federal government is actually increasing them. For instance, at the end of 1985, the government became the effective owner of seventeen troubled savings and loan institutions with nearly $15 billion in assets. This arises because the Federal Savings and Loan Insurance Corporation, which insures deposits in most S&Ls, must by law take over companies in financial difficulty.

Some of the federal impetus toward reprivatization also arises from the widespread policy of state and municipal governments to contract out public services to private firms. They contract out vehicle towing, legal services, streetlight operations, solid waste disposal, street repair, hospital operation, ambulance service, data processing, and other services. The claim has been made and substantiated that private enterprise can do these things more cheaply and efficiently than local governments.

But municipal transfers of such activities to the private sector are not without their critics. For instance, it is claimed that reprivatization costs jobs and opens up only lower-paying jobs for those affected. Critics also fear corruption, since it is alleged that ethics in government are higher than in some private businesses.

Each major proposal for reprivatization of federal assets draws its own set of supporters and critics. For the post office, it is said that the federal government could operate as efficiently as private enterprise and with comparable costs were it not for legal requirements to subsidize certain types of mail and congressional authorization of higher wages and benefits for postal workers than for private mail services.

REFORMING THE
REGULATORY PROCESS

There are still other recommendations for reforming the government's regulatory processes affecting business.

Structural versus Strategic Reform

In the past thirty-five years we have had five major comprehensive studies of our regulatory commissions. They all were headed by prestigious, responsible, and knowledgeable people such as former President Herbert Hoover. They all failed to remedy the basic problems of the regulatory agencies largely because they focused primarily on structure and not on functional strategy. Organizational structure certainly is important, but even more necessary is a reformulation of regulatory strategy. In mind is a systematic examination of objectives to be achieved by a specific regulation and then specific strategies to achieve the objectives in the most efficient and effective manner. To implement the strategies, it is necessary, for example, to decide upon the preferred combination of powers granted to the executive branch, the incentives to be used, the foremost processes and techniques to be employed, and the resources required. Any significant change in basic regulatory legislation will need strong political leadership. This means that important political personalities must be persuaded to lead. They must make the issues politically visible to the public, and they must marshal sufficient political force to assure the enactment of needed legislation. Airline deregulation is a classic illustration of the successful achievement of this approach to regulatory reform (Breyer, 1982; see case study at the end of this chapter).

Even a cursory review of the history of airline deregulation shows how time-consuming and difficult it can be. The lesson, of course, is to choose carefully the priorities for initiating this process.

Regulatory Administration

In addition to problems created for regulatory agencies by basic statutory legislation and court decisions, deficiencies in government regulation spring from poor management. While some laws are well managed, the administration of others is nothing short of scandalous. The following recommended reforms are not presented in any order of priority:

To begin with, there should be stronger top-management supervision of regulatory agencies. President Reagan greatly improved regulatory control by establishing a cabinet committee and by giving the director of OMB strong authority. This centralization of control needs to be further strengthened by a much more powerful assertion of the authority already granted by executive orders.

The authority of the President to review agency regulations should be extended to include the regulations of the independent regulatory agencies. In March 1982, the Senate passed the Regulatory Reform Act, which does this, but the House has not acted on the measure. This is a delicate issue because there are very legitimate reasons why Congress established the independence of many agencies. However, there also are compelling reasons for improving the administration of our regulatory apparatus, and much can be accomplished by giving the President limited authority to approve or disapprove many of the regulations of independent agencies.

Despite inhibitions in legislation and court decisions, more attention should be paid throughout the government to cost-benefit analysis.

Uncertainties and unnecessary burdens on industry would be eliminated if the governmental decision-making processes were accelerated and if trivial regulations were eliminated.

There are many other administrative improvements that might be noted. One suggestion, for instance, is to transfer control of public hearings on proposed regulations from the administrative agency concerned to a neutral authority better able to make unbiased decisions. Criteria for appointment and promotion should be tightened to ensure that highly qualified and competent administrators move into key decision-making posts. Means should be found to make it easier for top managers to discharge incompetent managers and staff.

INNOVATIVE POLITICAL AND JUDICIARY PROPOSALS FOR REFORM

The above regulatory reform proposals follow conventional lines. There are other proposals that are less conventional for reforming the political processes which could improve our regulatory posture. Several of these are presented here.

Pass Sunset Legislation

There is no orderly procedure for reviewing federal regulatory agencies to determine whether or not important changes should be made in their mandates and operations. During the past few years "sunset" bills have been put before Congress, but to date none has been passed. Sunset legislation is urgently needed. Sunset legislation would require the President to make recommendations to the Congress for changes in specific regulatory agencies. In a given number of years, say eight or ten, the President would be obliged to report on all major regulatory agencies. If Congress failed to act upon the President's recommendations for a particular agency, the agency's powers would be curtailed or eliminated. In this way, Congress would be forced to act to continue the agency as is, to alter its powers, or to bring about its demise.

Sunset laws have been advocated for years. In 1978, the Senate overwhelmingly passed a sunset bill that set a ten-year reauthorization cycle for most federal programs. But the House did not act on the bill and it died. Since then, enthusiasm for the idea has faded. One important reason is that committee members in both chambers of Congress have become increasingly concerned about the work load they bear and the additional burden that sunset laws would create.

Reform Congress

Observers of the political scene take the position that a serious recent phenomenon in Congress is the decline of party leadership power and the rise in power of autonomous committee and subcommittee chairpersons. Members of these committees are biased against remedies that harm their constituents, and they have the power to block such initiatives in the Congress.

> Those with the incentive to advocate and pursue remedial courses of action—the President and major party leaders—lack the institutional power to effect these changes. The problem, then, is not one of uncontrollable policies. It is one of mismatched capabilities and incentives—those who can change policies, will not; those who want to, cannot (Hardin, Shepsle and Weingast, 1982: 5–6).

What is needed is reform in Congress. Specifically, more power needs to be put in the hands of the budget committee, the appropriations committee, the rules committee, and chairpersons of full committees. Also needed is tighter coordination between the President with the legislative process (Hardin, Shepsle, and Weingast, 1982: 23).

Prepare Congressional Cost-Benefit Analysis before Legislation Is Passed

Although provisions have been made for economic analysis of proposed regulations in the executive branch, there is no program in Congress for making a systematic cost-benefit analysis of new legislation. One of the shortcomings in the development of regulatory legislation is the tendency for Congress to take prompt action in dealing with an urgent problem without considering the costs involved. It is difficult to prepare a convincing cost-benefit analysis of new legislation in a new field, but the thought involved in making it might well prevent ill-conceived regulations.

Create a Technical Supreme Council

Technical problems in regulation are escalating dramatically, and our mechanisms for dealing with them are antiquated. Certainly the public should be protected from hazards to health, for example. But how far should government go? Reputable technical experts come to different conclusions about such important issues as the dangers of nuclear power plants, the desirability of protecting a particular endangered species, acceptable water quality in a given area, or how much of a particular carcinogen is to be permitted in a specified area and under particular circumstances. At present, too many of these decisions are made by people in government and in courts of law who do not have deep technical knowledge about the subjects to be decided.

We suggest that a Supreme Council for Technical Policy be established to decide, or to help government officials decide, difficult questions such as these. Such a council should be composed of exceptionally well-qualified men and women from different disciplines and backgrounds. Its stature should be comparable to that of the Supreme Court of the United States.

IMPROVE BUSINESS BEHAVIOR

Progress in reforming government regulation of business will depend somewhat on business behavior. It is important that business, especially the larger companies, assume social responsibilities beyond producing goods and services efficiently. As noted in Chapter 4, business is not held in high esteem in this society, and there are deep antipathies to business, especially the large corporation. History is clear on the point that this attitude makes it much easier to legislate new regulations and rigorously enforce old rules. Better business behavior will modify these patterns in favor of business.

Individual businesses and groups of business people also must act responsibly in lobbying and dealing with regulatory agencies. Lobbies and pressure groups can and do perform many valuable services, but if their selfish interests are pursued at the expense of the public interest, the welfare of the nation is not served. There is no implication in this statement that there is always a conflict between selfish business interests and the public interest. Both can be advanced at the same time. For instance, a tax incentive to industry to buy capital equipment during low economic activity can help individual businesses and advance the general welfare.

ON BALANCING THE PUBLIC INTEREST AND INDIVIDUAL ECONOMIC FREEDOM

Emphasis in this discussion has been on regulatory reforms that expand individual economic freedom. Now we discuss principles that may be applied that limit economic freedom.

Individual economic freedom should be limited only to fill a need that is clearly demonstrated to be in the public interest. Complicated and interdependent social and economic relationships demand some limitations on the exercise of individual economic freedom. Each encroachment on individual economic freedom, however, ought to be roughly measured against the gains to society as a whole sought in the control measure. Individual freedoms should not be restricted unless there results a correspondingly greater increase in benefits to the community as a whole, desired by the community, and achievable in no other way. This is not an easy test to apply or meet. It is difficult at times to determine when the principle is followed. Broadly, for example, it means that bankers are not free to use resources at their disposal as they see fit. Their economic freedom is restrained to protect their depositors. Probably a central issue in increased taxation is the fact that individual rights over income are restricted with every increase in taxes. Presumably, the restriction is justified because the rights of others as well as the individual taxpayer may be advanced by the expenditures of government. If business profits are taxed for funds to subsidize the income of farmers, an effort should be made to determine whether the public advantage is great enough to justify the tax.

Economic goods may be divided into two types: individual goods and social goods. The two types differ essentially in terms of demand and, from the point of view of government, in the likelihood of private production in socially sufficient quantities. Individual goods are usually divisible, their costs of production can be allocated to the purchaser, and the amount produced can be adjusted to individual demand. In this category are such things as apples, nuts and bolts, tractors, locomotives, and pencils. Social goods are usually not divisible, are associated with collective demand, and may not be produced at all, or may be produced in very limited quantities, by individual enterprises. Such goods benefit the entire community, and the costs are not and cannot be directly borne by individual consumers on the basis of their consumption. Such goods are education, flood control, conservation of resources, and national security. How far should the government go in producing them? The maxim is that the government should increase the production of social goods (assuming community demand) no further than the point at which the marginal social benefit is the same from all government expenditures, per dollar of the expenditures, and is equal to marginal social cost.

Marginal social benefit is the total net gain in satisfaction to the community over time from the production of an incremental unit of a social good. Thus, the marginal social benefit of an expenditure is equal to the total net benefit to the community of the incremental dollar that government spends on a social good. Marginal social benefit therefore would be, in soil conservation, for instance, the net satisfaction to the community from the last dollar spent by the government for this purpose. Total benefits are measured by the benefits to persons getting funds from soil conservation, together with benefits to society in many different directions, such as flood control when it is tied into conservation, reforestation, the curtailment of soil depletion, and so on.

Marginal social cost, in contrast, is what society gives up in using resources for producing the social good. It is the cost to society measured by the alternative use of the resources spent on the last unit of the social good.

Additional expenditures for a social good run into a law of diminishing returns. After a certain point, the benefits to society of additional social goods decline, and the marginal cost mounts. At some point, theoretically, the production by government of social goods balances with the social cost of producing those goods. At that point, the community is getting the maximum advantage out of the production. Expenditures beyond that point result in a social cost greater than the social benefit. Below that point the spread between benefit and cost might make additional expenditures worthwhile to society.

Now, quite obviously, it is not possible to apply this measure with any degree of precision. And even if it were possible to apply it with mathematical accuracy, it might not be desirable to do so. For example, the community calculation of social benefit might lag far behind the realities of the need for substantial expenditures, say, for national security. Government leadership in the face of a threat to national security might push the expenditures for national security beyond the point where there is an equation between marginal social benefit and marginal social cost, as the community at the moment might see it. The community might gradually shift its concept of costs and benefits over time, but government as the protector of the social and economic systems may have to act promptly at any one point in time. The whole principle is extremely rough—so rough, in fact, that it remains a general principle rather than a precise yardstick. But it is a principle that is significant in focusing attention on alternative costs of action. It emphasizes the need for government to weigh social and individual advantage against individual and social disadvantage.

OUTLOOK FOR REGULATORY REFORM

No matter how "obvious" may be the need for a reform in our regulatory system, powerful forces operate to resist change. Among them certainly is the sheer inertia in bureaucracy. In addition, despite all of the clamor for reform, it has a weak political base. One reason for this is that the general population is not excited about reform. Aside from business, the ultimate beneficiaries are generally unaware of their stake in reform. Because the benefits of reform to one person are very small in relation to the costs involved in bringing it about, there is a lack of initiative by individuals except those in business. But those who are likely to lose by reforms, including those in business, are strongly opposed to reform and pursue their case in government agencies. Furthermore, politicians find it expedient to yield to these conditions. The result is a coalition of congressional committees, bureaucrats who administer the laws, and interest groups—constituting a political power that resists quick and substantial regulatory reform. There is no comparable opposing political power (J. Wilson, 1980).

In this light, one should not expect any massive regulatory reform. However, it is not too much to hope that with patience and slow but steady progress in building on the initiatives already taken (for example, civilian aviation deregulation, gradual oil and gas deregulation, pressure for sunset legislation, and so on), the proposals made in this chapter may gradually be accepted in part or in whole.

CASE STUDY

AIRLINE DEREGULATION*

After forty years of federal regulation of the commercial airline passenger industry, President Jimmy Carter, as an important part of his administration's economic agenda, launched the Airline Deregulation Act (ADA) in October 1978. The act effectively eliminated most federal regulations governing passenger airlines. It was expected to benefit consumers through increased marketplace competition. The ADA permitted air carriers to enter or exit routes freely and to compete on fares. Other provisions concerned service to small communities, job protection, and so on. Although economists and businesspeople in general welcomed the measure, some airlines opposed deregulation of the industry. Airline labor unions were also against the legislation, because they feared that the smaller carriers would be eased out by the industry giants. Smaller communities were worried that airlines would neglect them in favor of more profitable metropolitan centers.

In a lecture delivered in the autumn of 1977, Alfred Kahn, as chairman of the Civil Aeronautics Board (CAB) and an enthusiastic proponent of airline deregulation, spoke on the prospects of "a fascinating venture in applied economics":

> During the next several years . . . I look to a more variegated airline industry structure, in which the traditional rigid geographic and functional boundaries between different carriers and categories become blurred and governmentally protected spheres of influence less distinct, a structure that offers the maximum possible assurance of continuation of the competitive spur and that offers exciting new opportunities for managerial enterprise. And I look for a corresponding and increasingly variegated set of price and service options, competitively offered to passengers and shippers (Kahn, 1978: 59).

Although it has been several years since the airlines were deregulated, the industry remains in a state of transition. Deregulation has stimulated competition on prices and services. Passenger fares have generally come down, but on certain routes have gone up significantly. New routes have been introduced, while others have been eliminated. There has been a spurt in airline mergers,

---

*By T. K. Das, Baruch College, City University of New York.

acquisitions, and bankruptcies. According to some analysts, this transition is likely to lead to an oligopolistic situation in which six to nine major carriers and some twenty to thirty regional airlines will dominate the field. There is some apprehension that this may result in steep fare increases in the future. Although the industry has still to settle down in the deregulated environment, some legislators have expressed their reservations about the emerging conditions. Senator Robert Byrd (D - West Virginia) stated that he regretted only two votes that he has cast during his long career in the U.S. Senate. One was against the Civil Rights Bill of 1964, the other in favor of airline deregulation in 1978. Representative Gene Taylor (R - Missouri) also regretted his vote for deregulation, predicting the oligopolistic consolidation of the industry. As he put it: "Once it falls into the hands of about six carriers, we'll be paying $1,000 to travel from St. Louis to Los Angeles" (Dallos, 1986: 20).

Transition to Deregulation

The Air Commerce Act of 1926 was the first piece of federal legislation concerning the regulation of the airline industry and was confined primarily to safety requirements. There were no economic restrictions on people who operated airlines. Successful air carriers generally were those that had airmail contracts with the U.S. Post Office Department. The various airmail statutes and the bidding for the airmail contracts were the principal factors governing the growth of the airline industry for over a decade, until the Civil Aeronautics Act of 1938 was passed.

The 1938 act was wide-ranging in scope. It not only superseded the Air Commerce Act of 1926 and various airmail legislation, but, most important, introduced regulations designed to promote economic growth of the airline industry. It also provided for more comprehensive safety regulations. The economic regulations were similar to those regulating public utilities.

The Civil Aeronautics Board (CAB) was set up under the 1938 act to regulate air fares and route entry and exit. Safety control was mostly in the hands of the Federal Aviation Administration. The broad thrust of federal regulation of the airline industry remained unchanged up to 1978, although some restructuring of the laws was carried out in the Federal Aviation Act of 1958.

Automatic Market Entry

To enhance marketplace competition, the ADA permitted air carriers to choose airline routes freely. It removed all restrictions on the choice of origin and destination cities. The CAB no longer had the authority to control the number of carriers in specific markets.

This automatic market entry program was to be phased in to minimize the possibility of unhealthy competition during the transition to a deregulated market. For three years, until the end of 1981, a carrier needed no prior CAB approval to introduce one route per year. At the same time, a carrier was given the option of identifying one existing route per year which would be protected from the automatic entry of other carriers. The authority of the CAB over control of domestic routes ended in December 1981.

However, the CAB continued to have the authority to grant operating rights to air carriers that wished to introduce new services. This authority was clearly delineated to ensure that new routes were "consistent with the public convenience and necessity." Thus, if an airline failed to provide a specified minimum level of service, the CAB had the authority to revoke the operating rights. But the CAB was no longer required to determine whether a service was needed by the public. So long as a route was not inconsistent with the interest of the public, the operating certificate would be available to any carrier. The CAB also continued to be responsible for ensuring that anticompetitive and monopolistic industry practices did not develop.

Airport Access

With the growth of airline traffic over the years, authorities are finding it increasingly difficult to resolve problems of safety and congestion at airport terminals. Limited capacity at airports has effectively negated the notion of unrestricted market entry in many cases.

Certain contractual obligations have remained from the days of regulation. For example, majority-in-interest provisions allow the majority of airlines at an airport to veto capital improvements and airport expansion projects. These arrangements may restrict market entry. Given the escalating demand at the busiest airports for gates and ground facilities, it is no surprise that airlines face considerable problems in acquiring slots or the rights to land and take off.

Price Competition

A special report on airline marketing published in the August 1983 issue of *Air Transport World* noted:

> The new freedom made possible by deregulation has given U.S. airlines a chance to do many new things with their marketing departments. It has also given the industry an equal opportunity to make mistakes, and it has. Some observers feel that the industry is currently going through another transition period with its marketing effort. The past two years have been a severe test for marketing and how airlines go about chasing their customers. The recession and the resulting overcapacity have caused a lot of problems, especially the urge by some airlines to chase passengers with price—any price (*Air Transport World*, 1983: 31).

Indeed, the report quoted top marketing executives in the industry as saying that price formed the major tool for competitive marketing.

> Carriers used it for many things: to woo passengers away from competitors, to gain recognition when entering a new market, to develop feed traffic, etc. The discount

fare became the norm, the fare structure disintegrated, and few people knew what fares applied anymore, there were so many and they were all so complex.

One of the results of all this was a profit-margin decline that became so bad people were beginning to wonder if there was a future for the airline industry. In the fourth quarter of 1982, 80 percent of the passengers in the U.S. were traveling on some sort of discount. This swelled to 89 percent during the first quarter of this year. Yields declined to the point where the major carriers were getting 10 cents or less per revenue passenger mile (*Air Transport World*, 1983: 26).

In the years since deregulation, price competition from the lower-fare airlines has led to significant changes in the traditional fare structures. This development has been blamed for an estimated 120 airline bankruptcies since deregulation. The drastic price cuts by regulatory authorities could prove unfair if a large airline were to use them to drive a smaller rival out of its market with the aim of raising fares again later.

Service in Small Communities

The fear that deregulation could result in the loss of service to small and isolated communities prompted the provision in the ADA to guarantee "essential air transportation service" for ten years. The CAB was to do this by subsidizing the airlines serving the routes in question. The CAB was also empowered to order any existing airline to retain essential air service routes to such communities. Despite these provisions, there have been reports that many small cities have had to suffer in terms of the quality of air service after deregulation. William Leonard reported that in the first eighteen months of deregulation, seventy-five smaller cities being served by major airlines found that this service was replaced by local and commuter airlines with smaller planes (Leonard, 1983: 454). An added inconvenience to the passenger from small communities is that the commuter and regional carriers mean a loss of nonstop flights to the bigger cities. As of early 1982, commuter airlines provided the only airline services to 58 percent of all U.S. cities that had scheduled service.

Congress had recognized the need to ensure continued service to communities that might otherwise be abandoned or receive unacceptably poor service after the ADA. The subsidy program for sustaining local service carriers operating among small communities was phased out at the end of 1985. However, the Essential Air Service Subsidy Program assures service to eligible communities through 1988.

According to Matthew V. Scocozza, Assistant Secretary of Transportation, the federal government paid airline subsidies of $26 million in 1986. This compares with the CAB subsidy of commuter airlines in sixty-five cities in 1982 at a cost of $16 million (Wines, 1982: 408), which worked out to an average of about $35 per passenger. For certain towns, this figure was more than $100 per passenger.

Although some communities have benefited from improved service since deregulation, many others have experienced a reduction in service.

According to Avmark Inc., an aviation management and marketing service, commercial air service was available at the time of deregulation at 523 non-hub cities. Since then, 108 of the cities have been given improved service; 19 have more seats but fewer flights; 96 have more flights but with smaller planes and fewer total seats; and 150 have lost all service (Dallos, 1986:21).

Employment Protection

The ADA provided for compensation of up to six months for employees with at least four years of service with an air carrier if they lost their jobs, had their wages cut, or were forced to relocate due to increased competition in consequence of deregulation. Very little seems to have been done to implement the employee protection provisions in terms of either federal subsidies for workers laid off as a result of deregulation or to ensure that such workers have the right of first hire as required under the statute. According to one analysis, 30,000 airline workers lost their jobs between 1978 and 1982, but none had received any benefits, because the necessary rules had yet to be drawn up (Wines, 1982: 409). The requisite rules were published after considerable delay by the Carter administration in 1980, and their adoption is believed by many union leaders and others to have been blocked by the Reagan administration (Glines, 1983: 18). Related statistics about the employment situation among airline pilots show that of the 35,000 members of the Airline Pilots Association, 5,000 were laid off (*National Journal,* October 8, 1983, p. 2076). Also, the pilots are said to have given the airline industry wage and benefit concessions amounting to $1 billion in 1983.

Although there has been no problem in defining a protected employee, an employee must be deemed eligible to collect benefits. However, owing to administrative delays, legal entanglements, and disagreements over employee eligibility, financial benefits have yet to be paid under the employment protection program.

The Consumer

According to Senator Edward Kennedy (D - Massachusetts) the air deregulation bill, "while preserving the government's authority to regulate health and safety, frees airlines to do what business is supposed to do—serve customers better for less" (Leonard, 1983: 454). This rationale was one of the prime considerations behind the ADA. But whether the consumer has actually gained from the ADA is open to debate. In analyzing this question, Leonard makes the following observations:

> There has been a great deal of new competition, sharp discounts, wars among trunks in long-haul markets. For the economy-minded traveler willing to take the time to shop around, the situation is probably better, as there is a wider choice of

discounted fares, of carriers, and aircraft than ever before. For the business traveler, however, frills are gone, flights have been reduced in number from the major airports, and on many flights no first-class service is available. The business and professional traveler has undoubtedly experienced a decline in service. Service to many small cities also has declined following the substitution of local and regional carriers for departing trunks, which flew more modern planes with greater frequency of service and offered a higher proportion of nonstop flights to major metropolitan areas. For the average economy-minded traveler—and he or she now represents a majority of passengers—there is no doubt that choice is greater and fares are cheaper (Leonard, 1983: 457).

Deregulation has helped bring airline travel within the reach of millions of travelers. The number of passengers in the United States rose from 292 million, on 14.7 million commercial flights, in 1980 to an estimated 392 million passengers, on 19.2 million flights, in 1986. The FAA foresees over 650 million passengers and 26.4 million flights in 1997 (Main, 1986: 50).

The increase in passengers has been accompanied by an increase in the number of written and telephone complaints to the Department of Transportation about the quality of airline service. A major factor contributing to the deteriorating standard of service is the overburdened system of airports and airways. In a story published in *U.S. News & World Report*, the spokesman for the Dallas-Fort Worth Airport is quoted as saying: "I remember when you were going to fly, you put on a coat and tie and the planes were not crowded—you could travel in class and style. Today, it's like taking a bus" (1984: 66). Although it notes that air fares on the competitive routes were kept in check after deregulation, the report observes that "a bewildering jumble of airline connections, dozens of fares to the same destination, sudden airline bankruptcies, congestion, and circuitous routings are just a few of the rough spots passengers must negotiate even before they leave the ground" (p. 66).

Passengers may be further inconvenienced by the increasing trend among most airlines to rely on the "hub and spoke" system, whereby a number of flights interconnect at "hub" airports. The main advantage of a highly developed hub-and-spoke operation is that it multiplies the pairs of cities that an airline can service with a given amount of mileage. The percentage of flight departures at hubs has increased considerably since deregulation. "Since a large proportion of city-pair markets cannot support convenient nonstop service, hub-and-spoke operations have proved to be the dominant networking strategy of air carriers since deregulation" (Bailey, Graham, and Kaplan, 1985: 196). Congestion and delays are inevitable with this type of operation, and delays "snowball" during bad weather. In July 1984, the *New York Times* reported:

> The frequency of delays at the nation's airports is mounting, and federal officials say no quick solution is in sight. Delays for the first four months of the year were up 55 percent over the same period in 1983 . . . and because the situation grew worse in May and June, delays were up 75 percent over the same period last year. Top FAA officials attribute the situation to deregulation of the airlines, a resurgent economy, and a lack of restraint by airlines and charter and private operations. . . .

Agency officials say the operators are trying to put too many planes into the air at peak periods, and the system cannot accommodate the demand. There are isolated cases in certain periods at particular airports, the agency says, when many more take-offs and landings are scheduled than could possibly be handled by the most experienced force (Brenner, Leet, and Scott, 1985: 82–83).

This trend toward hub-and-spoke systems can be traced to the airlines' efforts to service their passengers to their destinations without any interline transfers. Usually, the system is justified for markets that do not warrant nonstop service. As one airline executive put it; "It's not part of the hub-and-spoke concept to inconvenience passengers who could go nonstop. But with deregulation, the incentive is there to market hubs in order to hold onto passengers" (*Air Transport World*, 1983: 27).

Safety

The responsibility for ensuring that the safety regulations in the airline industry are carried out remains with the Federal Aviation Administration. Questions have been raised about whether intensified competitive pressures and the entry of a number of new carriers into the airline industry have diluted safety standards. Deregulation did not seem to make a difference in the accident rate. This fact has been explained by some as a natural consequence of the reduction in peak-hour flights after the strike of 12,000 air traffic controllers in August 1981.

However, the number of operational errors since deregulation has seemed to increase. Near misses increased steadily between 1981 and 1985. Each aircraft is supposed to fly in a safe "envelope" of empty airspace measuring 1,000 feet vertically from the plane and five miles horizontally. The FAA defines a near miss as two planes coming within 500 feet of one another or a pilot reporting danger of a collision. Reported near misses jumped from 311 in 1982 to 776 in 1985. For the first five months of 1986, 305 near misses were reported, more incidents than reported in the same period of 1985 (Main, 1986: 52).

"In its early budget-cutting days," reports Main (1985: 23), "the Reagan administration reduced FAA inspectors from 1,748 to 1,494. The inspectors available to check out the major airlines fell from 674 to 500." The number of carriers more than doubled during this period. The FAA planned to hire 1,000 flight controllers.

Yet another aspect of airline safety has to do with improvements in airports and traffic control. According to one analyst:

A $12 billion federal plan to modernize airports and air traffic control is far behind schedule. The reason: the Reagan administration will not spend the money accumulating by the billions in a government trust fund financed by airport taxes levied on passengers and freight. Some $4 billion is uncommitted in the trust fund, helping the Office of Management and Budget make the federal deficit appear smaller, but not helping the airlines and passengers at all (Main, 1986: 52).

The Passing of CAB

The CAB was destined under provisions of ADA to cease operating on December 31, 1984. Various essential functions of CAB were handed over to other federal agencies. Accordingly, the CAB's regulation of the airline industry was gradually relaxed. Full rate and route authority was phased out over a four-year period. The CAB's authority over domestic airline mergers, intercarrier agreements, and interlocking directorates was transferred to the Justice Department on January 1, 1983. Most other functions of the CAB shifted to the Department of Transportation, which established a new consumer affairs office to attend to airline passenger complaints. International negotiation and small community air service were transferred to the Postal Service. The CAB ceased all operations on January 1, 1985.

The subsidy program for maintaining service to small communities was phased out at the end of 1985. However, a new subsidy program to guarantee essential air service to specific communities continued until 1988.

Re-regulation?

Some people are having second thoughts about whether all of the ADA provisions were beneficial to the airline industry, consumers, and labor. A study completed in late 1984 concluded: "After six years of deregulation, it is still not possible to render a final verdict on whether on net balance, deregulation is producing a domestic air transportation system better or worse than what previously existed" (Brenner, Leet, and Scott, 1985: xi). The all-out price war among the airlines and the massive business losses that followed cast doubts about the wisdom of unregulated competition in the industry.

At the end of 1985, the top six carriers controlled a little less than 70 percent of the market. In one year, that market share had risen to nearly 80 percent. Industry analysts predict that when the current shake-out is over, only eight or nine carriers will remain from a total of twelve, with about 30 smaller feeder operations. Many people, including regulators, believe this concentration will ultimately lead to higher fares for passengers because of reduced competitive pressures in the industry.

Several airlines have developed expensive automated systems that combine travel agents' ticketing, reservation, and accounting systems. The two predominant systems are the Sabre (American Airlines) and the Apollo (United Airlines). These computerized reservation systems have become a major source of airline profits. However, these carrier-controlled reservation systems may have anticompetitive effects on small carriers. Some have charged that several of the airlines have designed their systems so that travel agents are more apt to ticket passengers on their particular airlines' flights. Travel agents consider these systems necessary for keeping track of the many available fares which change on very short notice.

A critic of deregulation has observed:

Whether substantive corrections will be made in the Airline Deregulation Act of 1978 remains to be seen. One thing seems certain: unless changes are made, the world's most efficient and safest mode of transportation will continue to deteriorate daily. Cut-throat fares, excess capacity, and free entry and exit have dealt chaos to an industry that was formerly noted for its stability, safety, and dependability" (Glines, 1983: 17).

Senator Mark Andrews (R - North Dakota), chairman of the Senate Subcommittee on Transportation, went to the extent of drafting legislation for re-regulating the fare structure, in order to negate the harmful effects of cut-throat price competition. As Andrews explained: "You'd have to be deaf, blind, and dumb not to notice that something has gone wrong since deregulation came in. The airline industry is something we have to consider, at least a little bit, as a public utility. . . . Do we help the public by letting these ruinous bankruptcies go on?" (*National Journal*, October 8, 1983, p. 2047). Even Alfred Kahn publicly expressed his view, in July 1987, that deregulation had gone too far. Some reregulation of airlines was needed, he said.

Questions

1. The ADA of 1978 was designed to improve competition in the industry and thereby benefit the consumer. In your judgment, has the public interest been advanced since the act was passed? Explain what you mean by "the public interest," and defend your position.
2. Undoubtedly many employees, stockholders, cities and towns served, and customers of airlines have been adversely affected by deregulation. Are such hardships sufficient to warrant reregulation? If you advocate modification of the ADA, specifically what would you recommend?
3. Are the airlines like a typical public utility and, therefore, subject to the same type of regulations as public utilities, or are they similar to a typical service industry, and therefore, do they merit no more or less government regulation than a service industry?
4. What do you think the airline industry will look like in 1995?

BUSINESS IDEOLOGIES AND SOCIAL RESPONSIBILITIES

CHAPTER **8**

CHANGING MANAGERIAL IDEOLOGIES

 Following a career in the U.S. Army, and five years with Montgomery Ward, General Robert E. Wood joined Sears, Roebuck and Company. From 1924 to 1954 he led Sears to become a major economic enterprise and a socially responsible one as well. He believed that a large corporation was more than an economic institution; it was a social and political one as well.

In the Sears *Annual Report* for 1936, General Wood wrote:

> In these days of changing social, economic, and political values, it seems worthwhile . . . to render an account of your management's stewardship, not merely from the viewpoint of financial reports but also along the lines of those general broad social responsibilities which cannot be presented mathematically and yet are of prime importance.

He outlined the ways in which Sears was discharging its responsibilities to what he said were the chief constituencies of the company—customers, the public, employees, sources of merchandise supply, and stockholders (Worthy, 1984: 173). In speaking about constituents, General Wood repeatedly put the stockholder last "not because he is least important," he said, "but because, in the larger sense, he cannot obtain his full measure of reward unless he has satisfied customers and satisfied employees" (Worthy, 1984: 63). He also asserted and acted on the belief, said Worthy, who served as a vice president at Sears for many years under General Wood, that "the management of every business should preserve the balance of the interests of each [constituent]" (Worthy, 1984: 64).

General Wood repeatedly lectured his managers on the need to be good citizens in the communities in which they operated. To him, good citizenship meant much more than participating in community affairs and contributing to local charities. He believed that Sears should strengthen the economic base of the areas it served by helping to revive declining industries, reducing unemployment, bringing new industries into the community, and strengthening those that were there.

General Wood was building on a tradition begun by Julius Rosenwald, one of the founders of Sears. In 1912 he offered to contribute $1,000 to any county that would employ an agricultural expert to advise farmers on how to be more efficient. In two years he made grants to 110 counties. These grants led to the Smith-Lever Act of 1914, which set up the county-agent system that has become such an important part of national agricultural policy.

General Wood repeatedly stressed the need for maintaining high ethical standards in the conduct of business. While still at Montgomery Ward, he lectured his buyers as follows:

> I want merchants who are truthful; who are square; who are incapable of dishonorable or petty tricks; who have the respect of the seller; who are gentlemen in the broadest sense of the term. . . . I want no man in this organization who does not measure up, in his personal and business conduct, to the standards I have outlined (Worthy, 1984: 235)

General Wood can be said to have embraced a new managerial ideology, described in this chapter.

For two hundred years the classical business ideology had dominated the thinking of people in business about the responsibilities and role of business in society. While still widely accepted, especially in smaller organizations, this ideology is more and more being modified by a more modern managerial ideology. Following a brief discussion of the meaning of ideology, we describe in this chapter the essential ideas of the classical business ideology and the newer managerial philosophy. We comment on inconsistencies in the ideologies, obvious gaps, and ideologies that compete with them. It is not our purpose here to argue with or evaluate any particular aspect of these ideologies; that will be done in some detail in subsequent chapters.

WHAT IS A BUSINESS IDEOLOGY?

A business ideology is the patterns of thought characteristic of the business classes. It is the system of beliefs, values, and objectives that concern, defend, and justify business behavior. In this respect, ideology is synonymous with business creed and philosophy. An ideology has several important characteristics. It is selective in subject matter in that it does not seek to cover every facet of business interest. It is based on intuitive views, education, logical argument, and subjective values. More often than not, it is a reflection of self-interest. Business ideology, like other ideologies, often is expressed in language designed to appeal to the emotions of the listeners. Usually the language is simple, if not oversimplified.

Not all managers subscribe to what we call a business ideology, and some take exception to the view that there is a prevailing ideology. Many managers hold a mixture of ideologies. Also, it should be noted, managers change their ideologies over time.

PURPOSES OF THE BUSINESS IDEOLOGY

Some of the more important purposes attributed to business ideology are as follows:

■ An ideology justifies and rationalizes actions of people in business. Operating a business is an extremely complex activity. Not everyone views the results of the operation of a business in the same way. What may be rational to one person is irrational to another. An ideology establishes a framework of logic and rationality that, one hopes, will be accepted by others.

■ An ideology describes an ideal. Events in this world constantly exert changes in the ways in which business operates. An ideology establishes reference points within which events that might be contrary to the ideology can be contained.

■ Closely associated with this purpose is that of slowing down institutional changes and reforms. Most people recognize that the status quo cannot be maintained. An ideology, when creditable, can slow down change and give the business time to find ways to adapt to new modifications. The ideology promotes stability in environment but permits change.

■ An ideology establishes standards for judging or appraising business organizations, their policies, and their leaders. An ideology sets forth values, aims, or methods of operation and in so doing establishes standards against which people in business may be judged.

■ An ideology explains causal factors that may lead to failure or success. The ideology asserts that when it is followed, the results will be successful in terms of the ideals set forth explicitly or inferred in the ideology. If there is interference, especially by government, but also by other institutions in society, this may foretell and explain failure.

■ An ideology is articulated to gain adherents. The ideology that is clearly expressed is more likely to be accepted than one that is fuzzy, unwritten, and ambiguous. A clearly articulated ideology that makes sense to a particular group is likely to solidify commitment to the ideology.

■ The business ideology serves to help people in business to meet the strains of their occupation. This is called the "strain" theory. People in business play many roles, and often they find conflicts among the values associated with different roles. They are managers, owners, voters, members of society, competitors, husbands or wives, parents, church members, and so on. For example, economic life demands that managers be competitive, but this may conflict with their role as good neighbors to the competitor whom their action forces out of business. Business executives are faced with uncertainties of environment, and they are responsible for the outcomes of decisions over which they have limited control. Some of their roles place on them a responsibility—for community welfare, for instance—that they may think conflicts with other roles—protector of stockholder interests, for instance. Ideology helps people in business to alleviate anxieties arising from role conflicts and to maintain the psychological ability to meet the demands of their occupation in light of such conflicts. It thus has an important function in relieving the strain of business activity.

■ Finally, typical managers think of themselves and of business in general as being important to the progress of society. They believe that threats to the business system are threats to society in general and to their important roles in particular. Their ideology, therefore, is a shield against the erosion of their own group's role.

In sum, a business ideology is supposed to protect the interests of people in business as they see their interests. In the classical business ideology those interests were essentially short-run. In current modifications of the classical ideology the interests are both short and long-run. The difference, as we shall see, results in significant modification of the ideological content.

THE CLASSICAL IDEOLOGY

The classical business ideology finds its taproots in the exposition of capitalism by Adam Smith and his followers (summarized in Appendix B). Here are highlights of this ideology. (For a fuller exposition the reader is referred to Friedman, 1962; Monsen, 1963; Sutton et al., 1956.)

Government

The classical view of government is hostile and distrustful. Government is considered to be inherently evil, powerless to create, and negative in its relations to industry. There are many reasonable explanations of why managers hold this view. Government may be a scapegoat for those obscure forces that cause the outcomes of business decisions to differ from expectations. Business denigrates government because its administrators are not held to the same types of accountability imposed on people in business. Government is a regulator of business and is resented. The hostile attitudes reflected in the American revolt against the tyranny of a central government have probably carried over to this day. Above all, government should not interfere in the operation of the free-market mechanism.

The Free-Market Mechanism

In the classical view, the unfettered operation of the free market is the greatest institution created to advance the well-being of individuals in society. No other mechanism is as efficient in utilizing scarce resources, in maintaining individual freedom, and in raising material standards of living. The free-market mechanism must be maintained and perfected in the interests of everyone.

Competition

Competition is the touchstone of the economic system and, when allowed to operate without interference by government or by monopoly, will produce an overall harmony with many benefits to society. The ideology is filled with warnings of the evils attendant upon government and labor interference in the competitive processes. People in business holding the classical ideology still talk as though they are always faced with a cold, impersonal market mechanism over which they have no control.

Consumers and Service

Consumers and service to them hold a supreme position in classical ideology. The consumer is pictured as having great and ultimate power over the fate of business managers. If managers meet consumer demands, they will succeed; if not, they will fail. Consumers are considered to be independent and fickle. Aggressive advertising is necessary and justified because it stimulates consumers and business activity. Similarly, service is seen as being in the interests both of consumers and society for "bringing a better life to all."

Government Finance

The ideology demands the reduction of taxes. The rationale is that taxes divert resources from business and consumers to unnecessary government expenditures. Taxes furthermore stifle individual initiative and risk taking.

Government debt is considered like the debt of an individual or a company. The mounting federal debt, in the classical creed, is a clear sign of impending bankruptcy. Budgets must be balanced at all times, and when surpluses are generated debt should be paid off. The general business view is that expenditures are nearly always higher than they should be.

The issuance of currency must match the needs of society so that price inflation is avoided. A stable currency is indispensable to sound economic activity and the growth both of business and the nation.

Profit

Prominent in the traditional philosophy, of course, is the importance of profit. Managers should seek to maximize profits for the benefit of the common stockholders. High profits indicate that managers are doing a good job and performing their proper role in society.

Property Rights

People should be able to own property and to use it as they see fit. This not only is a guarantee of individual rights, but also is essential for efficient operation of the free-market mechanism.

Labor

Bargaining between employee and employer should be on an individual basis, free of compulsion or coercion by government or unions. This idea is captured by the slogan "right to work," which stands in opposition to the closed shop and other union security rules, including strikes. Large numbers of managers, however, today accept the right of employees to join unions, to bargain collectively, and to maintain job security irrespective of union membership. On the other hand, the creed insists that other rights must also be protected. This means, for instance, that violence, boycotts, organized picketing, and other such kinds of union activity should be prohibited. Furthermore, unions are considered to be monopolies and should therefore be subject to the antitrust laws. The traditionalist sees industrywide bargaining as a monopoly power and resists it.

Management, according to the creed, has a right to administer its property as it sees fit without union interference. Encroachment on what are considered to be managerial prerogatives by contract work rules is resisted. The ideology says that wage-rate increases should be correlated with rises in productivity. Union restrictions of output are deplored. Indeed, the ideology asserts that the true road to prosperity for all is increased productivity.

International Trade

Not unexpectedly, one finds a schism in attitudes toward trade. Classical theory, of course, as all for free trade; but when free trade conflicts with self-interest, as it often does, protectionism is advocated. Industries threatened by cheaper foreign imports want to be protected. Others not so threatened and benefiting from foreign trade want reductions in trade barriers throughout the world.

Economic Growth

Classical ideology places faith in the natural operation of the competitive system to recover from cyclical downswings and to ensure higher levels of economic output over time. Given freedom from interference by government and labor unions, the system is held to be self-correcting.

Importance of the Businessperson

One of the dominant themes in the classical ideology is praise for the achievements of the business system such as rising output, higher standards of living, and "the conversion of the luxuries of yesterday's rich to the necessities of today's masses." Nonmaterial benefits are also praised, such as business's spirit of service, the ability of those with talent to find personal achievement in the business world, and the great possibilities to find a type of freedom that this system alone makes possible. The importance of people in business and the justification for their relatively high salaries are not neglected.

Variations in the Ideology

Not all business people who accept the classical ideology accept all of its aspects. For example, many small business persons unashamedly seek and accept government aid for their class. Some larger companies seek government aid for themselves or their industry but generally not for large companies as a class. However, over a long period of our history, there has been remarkable consensus in business on this above ideology. Nevertheless, over time, more and more managers have accepted an ideology with more deviations from the classical until in recent years there can be identified a new managerial ideology.

CHANGING ENVIRONMENTS MODIFY THE BUSINESS IDEOLOGY

Over the past two centuries environmental forces have brought major changes to the business ideology. As illustrated in Exhibit 8–1, the modern ideology held by many managers, especially in the larger corporations, is a mixture of some anachronistic debris from the past, enlightened adaptation to the needs of contemporary society, and many classical principles. Among smaller companies, as the exhibit also shows, most managers generally cling to the classical ideology.

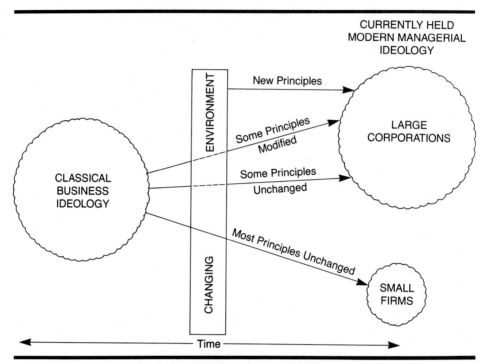

EXHIBIT 8–1   CHANGING MANAGERIAL IDEOLOGIES

The significant foundations of the new managerial ideology are shown in Exhibit 8–2. The chart illustrates that significant environmental forces have affected the basic values and attitudes of society generally about the operation of individual businesses and the business institution in general. The composite of these changes has produced the new managerial ideology. As these forces change in the future, so also will the ideology. The new ideology is not likely to remain as unchanging as the classical ideology; it is more of a pragmatic operational code responding to reality than an ideal.

THE MODERN MANAGERIAL IDEOLOGY

The modern managerial ideology is less complete and specific than the classical ideology. It is still evolving. And there is certainly less consensus about its content. Nevertheless it seems much more widely accepted today than even a decade ago and is likely to grow in general acceptance in the years ahead.

Many ideas in the modern managerial ideology have been expressed by business leaders over the past 100 or more years. Only during the past three decades in the United States, however, has the ideology begun to take a

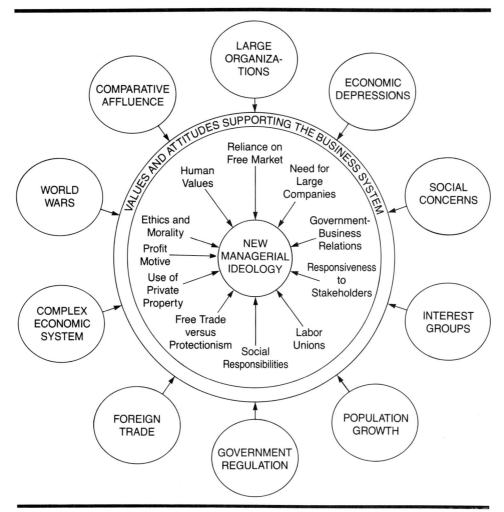

EXHIBIT 8–2   FOUNDATIONS OF THE NEW MANAGERIAL IDEOLOGY

reasonably comprehensive form and acquire growing acceptance among business leaders. The main themes were articulated fairly cohesively and comprehensively in the 1950s and 1960s by executives who participated in the McKinsey Lectures at Columbia University and business leaders associated with the Committee for Economic Development (CED).

The Committee for Economic Development

The CED is a group of some 300 business executives and educators, most from large organizations, who speak principally from business's point of view and only for themselves. It was organized in 1942 because its originators believed the old ideology was deficient in dealing with the economic problems that were anticipated to follow World War II, particularly the need for government to exercise more power in reducing the disastrous effects of an expected economic depression. The depression did not take place, but government's role in economic life increased. The CED has published several hundred research monographs covering issues of concern to business and the nation.

The McKinsey Lectures

These lectures, sponsored by the Graduate School of Business of Columbia University and the management consulting firm of McKinsey & Company, were given by chief executives of the largest corporations in the United States during the 1950s and 1960s. They were published in book form.* The lectures were neither an individual nor a collective effort to present a complete new ideology; each speaker presented his own views about the subject he chose to address. In the aggregate, however, they and the CED policy papers established a creditable foundation for the new managerial ideology.

Compared with the flamboyant and often arrogant business speeches of the late 1800s and early 1900s, the tone of these speeches was calm, thoughtful, cautious, and perhaps at times a bit apologetic. The statements were not meant to replace the classical ideology, only to modify some of its basic propositions and to add a few others. We turn now to the tenets of this new ideology.

Managers Must Balance Constituent Interests

The new ideology sees the responsibilities of managers as being more than the maximization of stockholder interests. It accepts the idea that managers have responsibilities to many interests focused on their organizations. David Rockefeller expressed this view as follows:

> The old concept that the owner of a business had a right to use his property as he pleased to maximize profits has evolved into the belief that ownership carries certain binding social obligations. Today's manager serves as trustee not only for the owners but for the workers and indeed for our entire society. . . . Corporations have developed a sensitive awareness of their responsibility for maintaining an equitable balance among the claims of stockholders, employees, customers, and the public at large (Rockefeller, 1964: 22–23).

---

*Each lecture was on a broad topic selected by the speaker. See Cordiner, 1956, when President, General Electric Company; Houser, 1957, when Chairman of the Board, Sears, Roebuck and Company; Blough, 1959, when Chairman of the Board, United States Steel Corporation; Greenewalt, 1959, when President, E. I. du Pont de Nemours & Co., Inc.; Kappel, 1960, when President, American Telephone and Telegraph Company; Folsom, 1962, when Director and Management Adviser, Eastman Kodak Company; Watson, 1963, when Chairman of the Board, International Business Machines Corporation; Rockefeller, 1964, when President, The Chase Manhattan Bank; Donner, 1967, when Chairman of the Board and Chief Executive Officer, General Motors Corporation; and Wright, 1967, when Chairman of the Board, Humble Oil & Refining Company.

Business Social Responsibilities

The idea that business firms, especially the larger ones, have social responsibilities is found throughout the McKinsey Lectures and in CED policy statements. The executives treated this prickly question in a number of different ways, and from a variety of points of view. But they always concluded that they had social responsibilities in managing their enterprises.

The CED, in a milestone statement called the *Social Responsibilities of Business Corporations* (1971), strongly accepted the idea that "business functions by public consent, and its basic purpose is to serve constructively the needs of society—to the satisfaction of society" (p. 11). Society today, said the report, has broadened its expectations of business into what may be described as "three concentric circles of responsibilities."

> The *inner circle* includes the clear-cut basic responsibilities for the efficient execution of the economic function—products, jobs, and economic growth.
>
> The *intermediate circle* encompasses responsibility to exercise this economic function with a sensitive awareness of changing social values and priorities: for example, with respect to environmental conservation; hiring and relations with employees; and more rigorous expectations of customers for information, fair treatment, and protection from injury.
>
> The *outer circle* outlines newly emerging and still amorphous responsibilities that business should assume to become more broadly involved in actively improving the social environment (15).

Classical ideology focused solely on the first circle. The new view, of course, is that managerial responsibilities go much beyond this point. But this does not mean diminished profits. On the contrary, say top executives in larger corporations, it is in the self-interest of corporations to assume social responsibilities.

The drafting committee of the CED had great difficulty in getting the report accepted by the CED Policy Committee, but eventually it succeeded. At the time, the average manager did not accept the concepts in the report fully or enthusiastically. In the years that followed, however, more and more managers, particularly of larger corporations, embraced the basic ideas in the report.

In a *Statement on Corporate Responsibility* (1981), the Business Roundtable, an organization of approximately 200 chief executives of the largest corporations in the United States, said that the pursuit of profit and assumption of social responsibilities were compatible:

> Economic responsibility is by no means incompatible with other corporate responsibilities in society. In contemporary society all corporate responsibilities are so interrelated that they should not and cannot be separated. . . .
>
> A corporation's responsibilities include how the whole business is conducted every day. It must be a thoughtful institution which rises above the bottom line to consider the impact of its actions on all, from shareholders to the society at large. Its business activities must make social sense just as its social activities must make business sense (*Statement on Corporate Responsibility*, 1981: 12, 14).

In commenting on the policy debates in the Committee for Economic Development, Alfred C. Neal, long-time president of the CED and an economist, summarized how top executives of large corporations saw their primary goal:

If maximizing profit is not the be-all and end-all of corporate behavior, and if an intricate and complicated set of socially responsible actions is not only desirable in terms of the welfare of the corporation but also in terms of stockholders in general, what goal is the large corporation seeking? For operating companies, as opposed to investment companies, the answer from both executives and academics was unequivocal: The primary goal is perpetuation of the institution, keeping the company growing and a viable part of the country. This goal the behavioral scientists translated into ecological terms: the prime essence of ecology is to ensure viability and growth. But in taking that view, corporations must be in business to make a profit because profits are indispensable to remaining viable, to remaining alive. Beyond remaining alive, the executives stressed the need for growth, as has been noted earlier. A company must have growth because that is the only way it can perpetuate itself as an institution. It must attract outstanding young people to have a strong management organization. To do that it must be able to provide increased opportunities for individual growth and development through growth of the company. . . .

To avoid any misinterpretation of the foregoing discussion, I will summarize it in my own way. The profit-maximizing, almost mindless concept of the firm used by economists and the widely divergent view of many executives of large companies result mainly from a difference in perspectives. Economists think of firms as being so numerous and small that they need not take the external consequences of their actions into account; hence, they use a profit-maximizing rule. Executives of large companies know that what they do affects constituencies outside the firm and even outside the country. They must take such constituencies into account. Their primary goals must be survival and growth, both of which would be jeopardized by mindless profit maximizing. If, as will be demonstrated later, large companies dominate the economy, the second view must be the working basis for policy making (Neal, 1981: 91).

Source: *Business Power and Public Policy Findings of the Committee for Economic Development* by Alfred C. Neal. Copyright © 1981 Praeger Publishers. Reprinted by permission of Praeger Publishers.

Cooperation with and Acceptance of Government Power

Unlike the classical ideology, the modern ideology accepts a certain partnership with government in society. James Roche, when chairman of the board and CEO of General Motors Corporation, expressed it this way:

Business and government can ill afford to be adversaries. So mutual are our interests, so formidable are our challenges, that our times demand our strengthened alliance. The success of each largely depends upon the other. Today, business and government are each becoming more involved in the affairs of the other (Roche; 1969: 6).

Although executives find this to be a prickly subject, they do accept the principle. This does not mean, of course, that they accept the idea of full partnership with government, or coordination of private and public activities in a central planning system, or that they accept all government regulations. Not at all. They fear government. Today's attitudes, however, are different from those of the classical ideology. That was an implacable antipathy (except when wanting something from government, such as subsidy). Today's view recognizes the need for more government regulation of business, but also for more mutual understanding and support. Today's executives believe that government regulation has gone too far. They would accept the appraisals of this matter in preceding chapters. They believe that there is nothing incompatible in their seeking relief from and reform of government regulation and blocking regulation they consider to be contrary to their interests, while at the same time accepting the need for cooperation and coordination in dealing with a number of tough socioeconomic problems (CED, 1982).

Irving S. Shapiro, former DuPont chairman, in *America's Third Revolution: Public Interest and the Private Role* (1984), urged more companies to get involved with governments in dealing with social problems. He claimed that more and more executives see their companies not only as "machines cranking out profits" but also as organizations well equipped—and well advised for their own survival—to work with public organizations on social problems. To be a more constructive force in this cooperative effort, however, he urged that business:

> shed its Number One myth, which is that government is just a business being run badly. In truth, government is a different sort of enterprise from private commerce. . . . It hears a different drummer. . . . Business deals in the hard coin of efficiency, government revolves around such softer notions as equity, fairness, and consent (Shapiro, 1984: 71).

Reliance on the Free-Market Mechanism

A thawing of the businessperson's traditional antipathy to government does not mean abandonment of the principle of the free-market mechanism. In the speeches, writing, and actions of business executives today, one finds a strong reaffirmation of the importance to society of maintaining an efficient free-market mechanism. Any erosion of that system is viewed with alarm. Precisely what this means is not easy to define. It clearly does not mean that they believe we should strive to return to a classical atomistic competitive model described by Adam Smith. They clearly reject any sort of central comprehensive planning. They do believe that a proper blend of appropriate government regulation and free initiative in the marketplace will produce a healthy, free-market mechanism. The emphasis is on maximizing individual economic freedom and restraining excessive exercise of government power.

Need for Big Organizations

Large organizations are not well justified in traditional ideology, a shortcoming that the managerial ideology seeks to correct. In the McKinsey Lectures, as one might expect, the emphasis is on large businesses, and the writers point with pride to the accomplishments of and the need for large organizations. Cordiner, for example, said: "Without . . . large-scale economic enterprises, a nation is today a second-rate power and its people suffer both lower standards of living and greater vulnerability to attack by aggressive nations" (Cordiner, 1956: 3). The McKinsey lecturers also took pains to point out that competition among large companies was much different from that among small companies, but equally rigorous and demanding.

Stress on Human Values

Every one of the McKinsey lecturers dwelt at some length on the treatment of people in organizations. Indeed, it is the dominant theme in this series. The views of the managerial ideology are in stark contrast to the one-sided doctrine of self-interest in the classical creed.

Houser felt that the most important tasks of managers concern people:

> It can no longer be taken for granted that ability will find its own level. In this age of the corporation, management must take specific steps to make sure that people have an opportunity to grow and develop; otherwise too many of them are likely to be lost in the labyrinthine processes of the organization. This is one of the major responsibilities of management today, a responsibility not only to its own people but to our free society (Houser, 1957: 4).

Kappel asked the question "What makes a vital business?" and answered it: "Vital people make it" (Kappel, 1960: 5). He then elaborated on why and how. Watson said he believed IBM's most important philosophy was "our respect for the individual" (Watson, 1963: 13; italics omitted). Several writers (Kappel, Blough, and Greenewalt) also pointed out that some conformity is necessary but that a large organization can stimulate innovation and creativity in people, can provide satisfying jobs, and can facilitate individual growth.

Labor

Despite the great importance of labor power, which business managers see as a formidable competitor, very few CED reports have been published on the subject; and, except for a discussion by Blough, the matter was almost completely ignored by the McKinsey lecturers. For many managers, the classical ideology regarding labor is still fundamental. More and more of them, however, accept the legitimacy of labor unions with relative equanimity.

International Trade

The CED takes a more liberal view of free trade than the classical ideology, which, although equivocal, leans to protectionism. In one statement (1959) the CED acknowledged advantages in some protection from free world markets. But in later statements it put itself in the ranks of those seeking to reduce tariff barriers. For example, in 1964 the CED said: "Our principal recommendation is that the United States should seek in free world trade negotiations to obtain tariff reductions from its trade partners in return for reciprocal United States concessions, coming as close as possible to cutting free world tariffs by 50 percent, across the board" (CED, 1964: 8). Subsequently, the United States did orchestrate broad international tariff-reduction agreements. Today, except for executives in a few hard-pressed industries such as steel and automobiles, most executives are in the free trade camp.

Ethics and Morality

Although the classical ideology was silent about a businessperson's ethics, some men and women in business honored the highest moral and ethical dealings in business. General Wood, discussed at the beginning of this chapter, is a case in point. Another is J. Frank Grimes, founder of the Independent Grocers Alliance. He claimed that his religious beliefs were the foundation of the great success of his organization. However, most business people in the late nineteenth and early twentieth centuries were not perceived as having high ethical standards.

In 1924, the United States Chamber of Commerce Committee on Business Ethics prepared a sort of national code of business ethics with fifteen commandments (Parker, 1924). Although this statement of principles was officially accepted by a large number of business people and organizations, it actually received mixed reviews. Some saw it as a new morality for business, others dismissed the statement as mere platitude.

Very little was said about morality in the McKinsey Lectures or CED policy statements. But the importance of ethical principles in business was implicit in a number of the documents. Individual businesspeople, such as Chester Barnard (1958), and academic leaders, such as Harvard University's Benjamin Selekman (1959), also underscored the importance of business people adhering to high ethical and moral standards. These developments reflected the interests and pressures of society in general and raised the level of moral concerns in business. One result was the widespread publication of codes of ethical principles, which corporations prepared for their employees. In some instances, the codes were mere public relations documents; in others they were taken seriously and implemented. These developments received new impetus in the early 1970s as a result of the Watergate scandal in the Nixon administration and the revelations that bribes were being paid by multinational corporations abroad.

Ethical behavior today is a key element in the newer managerial ideology. Most managers in our corporations, especially the larger ones, are emphatic about its importance. They accept the views expressed by Reginald Jones when he was chairman of General Electric Company:

> The people rightfully expect something more than technical competence in the managers of our large corporations. They look for a moral center—some evidence that we are operating from higher principles than expediency or narrow self interest.
>
> These are entirely reasonable expectations, and if they are ignored they quickly become a matter of law. So if the manager of the future wants to hold the respect of his peers and keep his company out of the coils of the law, he will be absolutely scrupulous in matters of law and ethics, and make sure that these same standards are upheld at all levels of the organization (Jones, 1980).

GAPS AND SHORTCOMINGS IN THE IDEOLOGIES

Even in their fullest exposition the classical and the new ideologies cover only part of the landscape and generally ignore things not easily explained or not pleasant to consider. Let us consider some of these major blanks or inadequately covered issues.

The Classical Ideology

This ideology says little about business bearing any of the social costs of progress, such as unemployment, water pollution, or urbanization problems. In their evaluation of the creed, Sutton and his colleagues point out that it "rarely makes any claim on the esthetic quality of modern life, the superiority of the moral standards of our present society over those of earlier societies or of other countries, or the piety of life under the system. . . . Nowhere in the creed is there any suggestion that conflict exists between religion and capitalism, humanitarianism and money seeking" (Sutton et al., 1956: 49). The ideology is glorified for its record and strength in raising the material well-being of society. Strangely enough, however, little space is given to the great improvements brought about by the capitalist system in noneconomic values such as health, span of life, and equal opportunity. The creed fails to point out that there are many reasons for the success of this society in improving well-being of its members aside from business, as important as business is.

The New Managerial Ideology

The new ideology fills a number of gaps in the classical ideology but also has shortcomings. For instance, until the Watergate and payoff scandals of 1976–1977, very little was said about morality and ethical standards. The ideology still clings to the myth of stockholder control of large corporations.

As pointed out earlier there is much less unanimity among business leaders on the substance of the new managerial ideology than there was, say 100 years ago, about the classical ideology. This has given rise to an image of ambiguity among business managers on many subjects. The new ideology, like the classical one, for instance, treats relationships with government ambiguously, if not a little hypocritically. Today, as in the past, businesspeople denounce government intervention in the economy in general terms but accept it, and often demand it, when their own interests are threatened. However, there is a much better understanding and acceptance of government intervention in economic and social matters by business leaders today than in the past. The public also sees ambivalence in other areas of the new ideology, such as dedication to protecting and improving the physical environment, acceptance of labor unions as bargaining agents for workers, extolling free competition yet failing to remain competitive in foreign markets, as well as discrepancies often seen between rhetoric and the actual performance of social responsibilities.

AN ESTIMATE OF WHICH MANAGERS HOLD WHICH IDEOLOGY

To view the changes in business ideology in some perspective, we estimate the percentages of managers who hold predominantly to either the classical or newer ideology to be as follows:

	Largest Companies	Medium-Size Companies	Smallest Companies
Classical Ideology	20	60	95
New Managerial Ideology	80	40	5

This is our estimate. Others may, of course, differ. There can be little difference, however, over the fact that ideas fundamental to the new ideology are spreading throughout the business community. As these new views become more generally accepted by business managers and replace traditional views with which they conflict, the business ideology will be more in tune with the changing expectations of society.

The large modern corporation has yet to win completely the prize of legitimacy. It is not likely to do so with an ideology that fails to respond appropriately to the aspirations of the American people. Many business leaders today understand and accept this idea.

COMPETING IDEOLOGIES

The business ideology has never gone unchallenged, but the strength of opposing views is greater today than ever before. A major competitor is, of course, the federal government, whose exercise of power is based upon its own ideology. The ideology of government is a strong challenger because it is a determinant of ultimate aims to which the business system moves as well as of the means employed to get there. Much government activity is based upon pressures from various groups in the community, including business, with ideologies that contradict the business creed. The civil bureaucracy itself follows its own ideology. So does the military bureaucracy within the executive branch and political parties in the legislative branch. Other groups with competing ideologies of importance to business are labor, agriculture, public school teachers, and intellectuals. Their collective strength is a major neutralizing force for business ideology.

INDIVIDUAL COMPANY VALUE SYSTEMS

Every business firm has its own fundamental beliefs, convictions, attitudes, and ideas, explicit or implicit. These are not so much ideologies, although they draw from ideologies and complement them, as value systems. Because individuals differ in every company, these value systems are unique to each company. These values constitute the fundamental driving force in each business and may be more important in its success than its material assets. Thomas Watson, when chairman of the board of IBM, emphasized this view:

> This then is my thesis: I firmly believe that any organization, in order to survive and achieve success, must have a sound set of beliefs on which it premises all its policies and actions. Next, I believe that the most important single factor in corporate success is faithful adherence to those beliefs. . . . In other words, the basic philosophy, spirit, and drive of an organization have far more to do with its relative achievements than do technological or economic resources, organizational structure, innovation and timing. All these things weigh heavily on success. But they are, I think, transcended by how strongly the people in the organization believe in its basic precepts and how faithfully they carry them out (Watson, 1963: 3).

There is no doubt that the value systems held by top managers of a company are reflected in the entire network of aims of the enterprise. Whether written or not, these values have the profoundest impact on the direction in which the company moves and the way in which it operates. This assertion, while obvious to us, has not often been tested by rigorous research.

CONCLUDING COMMENT

James O'Toole, Professor of Management at the University of Southern California, has pointed out that the American corporate system has no clearly elucidated ideology. This is both a strength and weakness of the modern corporation, he says. Our corporate system "is flexible, pragmatic, and compatible with the democratic processes of change and control; but its ability to justify itself with a single coherent argument leaves it vulnerable to attack" (O'Toole, 1979: 98). In the absence of a broadly based and accepted rationale for the structure and behavior of business, critics often go unchallenged. Not only can critics say almost anything about the large corporation, but they can often find some corporate executive to support the accusation. Perfecting the new modern ideology and broadening its acceptance in business and the community will reduce this weakness over time.

But the newer ideology never will be completely accepted. As O'Toole concludes, "The fact that business leaders do not think or behave in a monolithic fashion is perhaps the strongest case for the continued existence of autonomous corporations in a free society" (O'Toole, 1979: 98).

CASE STUDY

CHRYSLER CORPORATION BAILOUT

In his autobiography *Iacocca*, Lee A. Iacocca, chairman and CEO of the Chrysler Corporation, detailed his version of the historic government "bailout" of his company in 1979. Commenting on that experience, he said that he and his staff had done everything possible to save the company from bankruptcy, but it was not enough. The only recourse was government help. To seek this help, he had to change his ideology radically. But he rationalized the shift in this way:

> Believe me, the last thing in the world I wanted to do was turn to the government. But once I made the decision, I went at it with all flags flying.
>
> Ideologically, I've always been a free-enterpriser, a believer in survival of the fittest. When I was president of Ford, I spent almost as much time in Washington as in Dearborn. Then I went to the capital for only one reason—to try to get the government off our backs. So naturally, when I was back in Washington as chairman of Chrysler to make the case for government help, everybody said: "How can you? How dare you?"
>
> "What choice do I have?" I answered. "It's the only game in town" (Iacocca, 1984: 192).

This case explores conditions leading to the Chrysler federal loan guarantee and the principal arguments advanced for and against it. The debate split into strongly opposed camps the business community, politicians, and special interest groups in the general population. The controversy continues to this day—and will recur in the future.

Background

In early August 1979 Chrysler Corporation orally petitioned the United States government, through the Treasury Department, for $1 billion immediate cash aid. The top management of Chrysler said that it had a cash flow crisis and that if it were not corrected, the company would be forced into bankruptcy. Although it was generally known in financial circles that Chrysler was in trouble, this proposal of the nation's third largest automobile producer (sales in 1978 were $13.6 billion) came as a surprise to both the public and the government.

During the preceding eighteen months, the company had lost $466 million. In the second quarter of 1979, the loss was $207 million, the largest in automotive history, and the company anticipated that total losses for 1979 would be from $600 to $700 million.

Chrysler was loaded with a huge inventory of large automobiles, which were not selling on the market. Its share of the market fell from 12 percent in 1977 to 10.7 percent in the summer of 1979, and total sales in the second quarter of 1979 were down 28 percent from the same period in 1978. During the 1979–80 period, Chrysler calculated that it had to spend $1 billion in addition to normal outlays to meet federal automobile regulations. The company had hoped to be able to satisfy this capital need, but because of its cash projections, it saw no way short of federal aid.

Chrysler chairman John J. Riccardo said, "We are not talking about bailout, we are not talking about handout, we are not talking welfare. We are talking about money we intend to repay." He asked the government to give the company an "accelerated tax credit" of $500 million in 1979 and another $500 million in 1980. Under tax law at the time, the losses of a company could offset profits for up to five years, which meant, of course, reduced income taxes. Chrysler's proposal was to give up future loss offsets in return for $1 billion in 1979 and 1980. The company made no promise that the government would eventually break even on this arrangement, but it did say that it expected to make a profit in 1981.

Treasury Secretary G. William Miller rejected the Chrysler proposal because he said that it would amount to an interest-free, unsecured cash advance from taxpayers' funds and that would be contrary to "the principle of free enterprise." However, he said that the administration "recognizes that there is a public interest in sustaining [its] jobs and maintaining a strong and competitive national automotive industry." Therefore, he proposed, and President Carter accepted, a loan guarantee of $500 to $700 million, providing the company prepared a plan to ensure the continued viability of its operations. The plan, said the secretary, was to include substantial contributions and concessions from all who had an interest in Chrysler's future—namely, management, employees, stockholders, creditors, suppliers, other business associates, and government units.

Chrysler's Actions to Improve Cash Position   Chrysler's management took many significant actions to improve its cash position. For example, it agreed to sell its receivables—the right to collect payments from car buyers—for $730 million. It sought to reduce its exceptionally large inventory of $700 million in 435,000 unsold cars and trucks by offering rebates amounting to $400 per car. It sold a number of subsidiaries. For example, it sold its wholly-owned Chrysler

Realty Corporation for $200 million in cash. It sold its operations in South Africa. The company laid off about 25,000 hourly workers and began discussions with the United Auto Workers (UAW) for wage and fringe benefit concessions. A wide range of other cost-reduction measures were undertaken. Discussions were begun with banks to refinance loans. The company obtained a $370 million investment from the British government for its subsidiary there. But these measures were not enough, and the company exerted continued pressure on the federal government for help.

In late 1978 the Chrysler board of directors named Iacocca president to bring new leadership to a company facing bankruptcy. He and John Riccardo, the company chairman, proceeded to try to save the firm. They asked the government for tax concessions, a request frequently made by business interests and often granted. This time, however, it was denied, and the debate about what to do proceeded heatedly in and out of government for many months. In September 1979, Riccardo resigned and Iacocca became chairman and the leader of Chrysler's plans to save the company.

He skillfully orchestrated a coalition which ultimately resulted in the government's bailout through a loan guarantee. This coalition included conflicting special interests, such as labor, management, banks, the government, suppliers, and the communities likely to be adversely affected by a bankruptcy. (The story of how this coalition operated is told in fascinating detail in *New Deals: The Chrysler Revival and the American System* by Reich and Donahue [1985].)

Chrysler Corporation Loan Guarantee Act of 1979

This act was signed by President Carter in December 1979. It created a Chrysler Corporation Loan Guarantee Board with authority to commit to guarantee loans up to $1.5 billion, if the company submitted a plan that included an aggregate amount of nonfederally guaranteed assistance of at least $1.43 billion. In mind, of course, were concessions from lenders, suppliers, dealers, state and local governments, sale of equity securities, sale of assets, and wage and salary reductions. The company satisfied this requirement, and eventually a total of $1.2 billion in federal loan guarantees was committed by the board.

Should the Government Have Helped Chrysler?

The critical issue in this case is whether or not the federal government should have stepped in to help Chrysler. A storm of controversy surrounded this case. To oversimplify, there were those who strongly opposed government help because it was said it would challenge the tradition of competition and the survival of the free-enterprise system. Then there were those who approved government help in recognition of the need, they said, of government's involvement in the private sector to advance the public interest. Although there have been few cases like that of Chrysler, the issues raised in the case are of fundamental importance in the business-government relationship. The following arguments were advanced for and against government help in this case.

Arguments Against Federal Aid   Thomas A. Murphy, chairman of General Motors, voiced the core argument of those opposed to the proposal. He said that such action "presents a basic challenge to the philosophy of America, the free enterprise system." He went on to say that if government bails out businesses that fail in the competitive race, "It removes and compromises that discipline in the marketplace." No company should be insulated from competition, he said. "Competition is inherent in our American system, and competition is what got us where we are today," he added (Stuart, 1979).

An editorial in the *Wall Street Journal* of August 3, 1979, made the same point: "To maintain a healthy economy, government must simply let companies adapt to their changing fortune, cutting losses before they become unmanageable."

It was argued by others that management problems lay at the root of Chrysler's difficulties and that the government should not be asked to rescue inefficient managers from the consequences of their ineptitude. For instance, it was pointed out that Chrysler had acquired failing companies in Europe that created severe cash drains, that the company had stuck too long with large "gas guzzlers," and that the company delayed too long in launching a subcompact car to compete with GM's Vega and Ford's Pinto (*Business Week*, August 20, 1979; Moritz and Seaman, 1981).

There were those who said that the government bailout would build inefficiency, waste, and mismanagement into corporate boardrooms if adopted as a matter of policy. It was argued that removal of the danger of bankruptcy from the economic system would lead to a decline of profit-oriented decisions, to lazy management, shoddy products, an erosion of creativity in the introduction of new products, and a general decline in national economic growth (*Business Week*, March 24, 1980).

It was argued also that government-subsidized companies could get loans at lower rates of interest than could companies without such guarantees. This advantage would be an incentive for federally supported companies to borrow more and reduce the available pool of capital for the healthy companies, which would result in further increases in interest rates and a widening of the cost advantage to government-supported companies.

Also, it was argued, the nation's bankruptcy laws provide a proven mechanism for companies to exit from the economic system, if they are no longer useful and wanted. Or, if there is vitality in a failing company, the bankruptcy laws also provide a proven process, known as reorganization, which gives a company an opportunity to rehabilitate itself.

Altogether, the basic case against government aid to Chrysler was an ideological one. Dean Phil C. Neal, of the University of Chicago Law School, put it succinctly in his testimony concerning the L-1011 loan guarantee (see below for details):

The whole objective of the competitive system is to maximize economic productivity by channeling resources into the most efficient hands. The failure of a firm, assuming that it cannot be made profitable through the structuring of ownership and management that will flow from reorganization proceedings, is a signal that it represents an inefficient or wasteful combination of resources (U.S. Congress, 1971: 385).

Arguments for Government Help   It was argued with considerable justification that bankruptcy of Chrysler would result in an immediate loss of about 360,000 jobs with rippling effects throughout the economy and a final unemployment tally of 500,000. It would, of course, result in millions, if not billions, of dollars of losses among thousands of businesses and accelerate a national economic recession, which was just beginning in the summer of 1979.

Some help from the government was justified, it was said, because bankruptcy of Chrysler could leave the federal Pension Benefit Guaranty Corporation with a responsibility of about $800 million in insured but unfunded pension obligations to Chrysler's employees. Help now, it was said, which might be virtually costless to the government, might save the government many millions of dollars in the event of Chrysler's bankruptcy.

It was also pointed out that Chrysler's bankruptcy would leave only two strong United States automobile companies—Ford and General Motors. In the absence of Chrysler, these two companies could have three-quarters of the domestic automotive market, a dangerous concentration of power. This argument is countered with the observation that today there is plenty of foreign competition in the American automobile market, which is likely to continue. Furthermore, if Ford and General Motors did monopolize the market, there are many things the government could do to restore competition.

It was argued that when the federal government gave a loan guarantee of $250 million to the Lockheed Aircraft Corporation in 1971, because of the financial difficulties of that company stemming from the L-1011 program, a precedent was set for distressed companies like Chrysler. Others pointed out, however, that circumstances surrounding this arrangement were very different from those facing Chrysler, not the least of which was the fact that the British government asked for the guarantee since it was financing Rolls Royce, the producer of the engines for the Lockheed L-1011, and it wanted to make sure its support would not be wasted with a bankrupt Lockheed. (The loan, made by banks but guaranteed by the government, was paid off in 1977, and the government pocketed a fee of $31 million.)

If the L-1011 loan guarantee was not a precedent, it was said, then guaranteed loans to the steel companies at the time were. For instance, the Economic Development Administration in the Department of Commerce was authorized to make loan guarantees of $550 million to the steel industry. In August 1979, Wheeling-Pittsburgh Steel Corporation got a $100 million loan guarantee. This, it was said, illustrated but one of billions of dollars of loan guarantees made by the federal government to agriculture, small businesses, urban housing development, and students.

Ezra Solomon, professor of finance at Stanford University, summarized such arguments for government support in these words of testimony given in connection with the L-1011 debates:

> The case for approving a loan guaranty seems very clear to me; by so doing, we avoid potentially large losses in employment, output, and exports, which society would suffer as a result of [the company] going into bankruptcy. Given existing employment conditions in the manufacturing sector of the economy and in the capital markets here and abroad, the adverse effects of such a business failure could be serious indeed. Certainly the cost to the government of offsetting such adverse effects, after the fact, would be many dozen times larger than the likely cost of extending a loan guaranty now. Indeed, given the various safeguards incorporated in the terms of the loan guaranty, the likely cost of positive action is close to zero (U.S. Congress, 1971: 1189).

One observer commented that the old profit test of survival works beautifully in a simple society composed of small and perfectly competing companies. In today's extremely complex world, that simple formula should, on occasion, be replaced by something in the nature of a societal cost-benefit analysis. Public opinion, this observer went on to say, tends to be pragmatic rather than ideological. That is, people are more worried about jobs and income than the purity of competition. So, political processes have resulted in government protection from the rigors of competition in many areas—sugar beet growers, cattle ranchers, steel makers, textile producers, and so on. We are developing a two-tier competition. The classical type still exists among very small businesses. It also exists among product divisions of large corporations. For the largest corporations, however, there is a drift toward protecting them from competitive forces, for a while at least, if their failure may do great damage in the economy. That is a fact of life. Is it in the long-run interests of the nation? That I do not know, he said.

Other Considerations

Although Thomas Murphy strongly objected to the government guaranteeing loans for Chrysler, he and others taking his position blamed unnecessary, costly, and sometimes arbitrary government controls for a large part of Chrysler's trouble. He said, "I think something should be done about the government standards. I think we should address the whole problem of regulation, sort it out and make sure it gives all Americans, all of the competitors, a fair shake" (Murphy, 1978).

William Randolph Hearst, Jr., likewise opposed the loan guarantee on ideological grounds but insisted in strong language that we should ask such questions as these:

> Shouldn't we be concerned whether [Chrysler] . . . workers have, through their unions, priced themselves out of the market?

Shouldn't we be concerned that our politicians, responding to the wishes (sometimes whims) of the environmentalists, have turned the automobile into an impractical machine, too costly from a consumer's standpoint? Shouldn't we be concerned that our corporate tax laws which take away 50 percent of the profits of a large outfit like Chrysler, have stifled the ability of many companies, particularly those bordering nonprofitability, to reinvest in new plants and equipment? Shouldn't we be concerned that we have triple taxation on American-made cars—the corporate tax, plus the tax on dividends, plus the sales tax—to such a degree that new investment is discouraged (Hearst, 1979)?

Herbert Stein, a former member of the Council of Economic Advisers under Presidents Nixon and Ford, raised questions of ambiguous government philosophy:

The plight of Chrysler Corp. has revealed to some commentators the merits of the free enterprise system. They have discovered that the system implies losses as well as profits and that it would be wrong—unfair, inefficient and inconsistent with the system—to "bail out" a corporation that makes losses.

Fine. But where were these commentators when the profits of the oil companies were reported? How many explained to their audiences that the system implies profits as well as losses, and that it would be unfair, inefficient and inconsistent with the system to tax away the oil company profits? None.

But, I can hear them say, the oil company profits were windfall profits, Yes, and Chrysler losses are windfall losses. If the price of gasoline were still 50 cents a gallon, people would still be buying Plymouth Furys and Chrysler would still be making money.

A philosophy in which the government says to the private sector that your losses are your own but your profits are ours could not survive if consistently followed to its logical conclusion. Fortunately, we follow nothing consistently to its logical conclusion (Stein, 1979).

The UAW was reported to want the government to buy $1 billion of Chrysler's stock to help the company and to gain a voice in management. John Kenneth Galbraith made a similar recommendation and added a few other comments about government aid:

It does seem reasonable, especially as one reflects on the impressive sum involved, that those providing this largesse seek some small concessions. Thus, if, as taxpayers, we are to invest one billion dollars in Chrysler, could we not be accorded an appropriate equity or ownership position? This is thought a reasonable claim by people who are putting up capital. Also, as Chrysler becomes a publicly funded business, may we not properly ask that its executives confine their compensation to [say] the general range of pay thought acceptable for the President of the United States. Compensation is now rather higher, although not, one judges, as a reward for good profit performance. And most important of all, in this high noon of the great conservative revolt, could we not ask that all corporations and all corporate executives that approve, or acquiesce by their silence in this expansive new public activity, refrain most scrupulously from any more of this criticism of big government (1979)?

One final consideration concerns the political processes by means of which the loan guarantee was approved by the federal government:

> Chrysler . . . could perhaps be rationalized by a special variant on the infant industry argument. But anyone who observed the actual process by which the loan program was developed would be bound to conclude that the decision to approve the loan program was made on an *ad hoc* basis, without regard for any articulated policy. The model of public action that best fits the events surrounding the Chrysler loan program can be found in the enduring work of E. E. Schattschneider (1975). He submits that in a policy debate the side that takes the initiative and succeeds in defining the situation in a way favorable to its interests has gone a long way toward winning. The supporters of the Chrysler loan program evaluated various alternative assistance programs and then chose the preferred one. They promoted their proposal by preempting a number of key arguments in support of their position, including cost to the government, social welfare, economic efficiency, and international economic considerations. The comprehensive case supporting the proposal, irrespective of the validity of the individual arguments, defined the issue to the advantage of the loan program's proponents. Opponents were forced to turn their energies to rebutting the case for the program's many alleged benefits. In the process, neither side paid much attention to the question of defining a general policy that might serve the national interest. That still remains a task for the future (Freeman and Mendelowitz, 1983: 452–453).*

What Happened to Chrysler after the Guarantee?

Chrysler survived and prospered. The company lost $1.097 billion in 1979; $1.71 billion in 1980; $476 million in 1981; and $69 million in 1982. Profits rose to $1.635 billion in 1985. Estimated net profits for 1986 were $1.2 billion. In August 1983, Chrysler paid off the last of its $1.2 billion in government-backed loans, seven years ahead of schedule.

The company pursued a comprehensive set of plans and programs to achieve these ends. Costs were cut drastically. For example, salary expenses were reduced dramatically, and the work force was cut from about 160,000 to 80,000. Union and nonunion workers made wage and benefit sacrifices of about $1.2 billion. Production was made much more efficient, and productivity increased substantially. Quality of product rose impressively. The break-even point in 1983 was one-half that of 1980. A $6.6 billion product improvement program was put in operation (Iacocca, 1983; *Time*, March 21, 1983).

In an unwritten trade-off for financial concessions from the UAW, Douglas A. Fraser, the union president, was named to the board of directors of Chrysler. He became the first union leader to sit on the board of a major U.S. corporation.

At the time the loan guarantee was being discussed, the federal government decided to trade the guarantee for stock warrants with a right to buy shares in

---

*Reprinted from Brian M. Freeman and Alan I. Mendelowitz, "Program in Search of a Policy: The Chrysler Loan Guarantee," *Journal of Policy Analysis and Management* (Summer 1982), pp. 452–453. Copyright © 1983, Association for Public Policy Analysis and Management.

the future at $13. At that time the stock sold for around $5 per share. In mid-1983, Chrysler asked the government either to do nothing about the rights or to sell them to Chrysler for about $17. The government rejected both offers. Finally, in September 1983 Chrysler bought back the warrants in open bidding for $21.602 per share. The government made $311 million on the transaction. There were many who said the government was extracting the last ounce of blood.

Questions

1. What are the major issues raised in this case for managers, government, and society?
2. What is your position on whether the federal government should or should not have given the guarantee? Explain your position in detail and defend it.
3. Are the loan guarantees for steel companies, students, and so on the same as the type of guarantee given to Chrysler? How do they differ? Do such loans justify, as a matter of precedent, the Chrysler-type loan?
4. Research the Lockheed L-1011 loan guarantee. Did it set a precedent for the Chrysler loan? Do the two cases provide a precedent for government bailing out large companies when they fail?
5. Do you agree or disagree with the statements made by Thomas Murphy, William Randolph Hearst, Herbert Stein, and John Kenneth Galbraith?
6. What is the significance of the statement made by Freeman and Mendelowitz?
7. Do you think the federal government was morally justified in getting stock purchase rights from Chrysler? Was the government on solid moral grounds in exercising the rights at full value?
8. Do you think it is a good or bad idea for heads of labor unions, such as Douglas Fraser, to represent unions on boards of directors?
9. Should the federal government take an equity position in an ailing company to help it, as do the British?

CHAPTER 9

THE SOCIAL RESPONSIBILITIES OF BUSINESS

 Medical history records that the first organ transplant, that of a kidney, was performed in a Boston hospital in 1954. Today organ transplantation is commonplace. But medical technology has outstripped public awareness. In 1987, there were approximately 50,000 transplant operations, yet only 15 percent of potential donors gave organs, and thousands who might have been helped had to wait. So Dow Chemical Company started a major program to encourage donation of organs.

Dow began a multimillion-dollar, national, public education program on organ donation and contributed $1 million to the American Council on Transplantation. In each of Dow's sixty-five domestic locations, a chairperson was selected to spearhead a variety of activities designed to make employees and the public more aware of the shortage of transplantable organs. All 25,000 Dow employees were given literature and asked to discuss the subject with their families. (Family discussion is extremely important, because even when a person carries an organ-donor card, doctors will not remove organs without permission from the next of kin.) Because many are reluctant to discuss the subject of death, Dow included guidelines for these discussions in a brochure. It was suggested, for example, that everyone listen thoughtfully, that decisions not to donate organs be respected, and not subject to pressure, and that the family together make a pact to carry out the wishes of each member. The company later produced a video tape, "Ordinary Heroes," for use at community meetings.

In 1986, the program expanded. Dow commissioned a nationwide Gallup poll on public attitudes toward organ transplantation and donation. It found that 50 percent of Americans who had heard of transplants were willing to donate their organs after death, but only 20 percent had completed a donor card, and only 26 percent had talked with their families. It showed that blacks were only half as likely to donate organs as whites. And another finding was that 63 percent of the respondents felt it appropriate for a doctor or nurse to initiate discussion of organ donation with family members upon the death of a loved one (Gallup, 1986: iii-iv).

Based on these findings, Dow took several actions. First, it expanded its efforts to educate the public by, for example, having millions of Boy Scouts distribute literature and posters across the country. Second, because kidney failure is more frequent among blacks than any other racial group, and because more people wait for kidneys than for any other organ, Dow developed a program to educate blacks about the need for organ donation. Clive O. Callender, a black physician at Howard University in Washington, D.C., undertook interviews to discover why blacks were less likely to donate and found a variety of reasons, including lack of information, religious fears and superstition, distrust of medicine, and a preference for donating organs only to other blacks (Dow, 1986). Dow sponsored trips by Callender to Detroit, Chicago, Los Angeles, Philadelphia, and New York, all cities with large black populations, where he made speeches and had media interviews.

And third, because many people were willing to be approached about donation at the time of a loved one's death, and because 60 to 80 percent of those approached agreed to donations, Dow used its lobbying force to promote required request legislation, which makes it mandatory for hospitals to approach relatives of accident victims to ask for organ donations. By 1987, thirty states had passed such laws, and behind-the-scenes prodding from Dow lobbyists was important in gaining political support for the measures in many states.

In 1985 President Reagan awarded Dow a Presidential Citation, and in 1986 Dow chairman, Paul F. Oreffice, accepted a special award from the Department of Health and Human Services on behalf of the program. The program continued in 1987. Its distinctive graphics in green, orange, and gray and its slogan, "Transplant a Miracle!," tie together with millions of posters, T-shirts, buttons, pamphlets, and press releases.

A notable aspect of the program is that it is unrelated to any of Dow's commercial interests. In the words of Robert Charlton, the Dow employee directing the program, "We wanted to insure that the program could not be dismissed because there was a commercial gain for the company involved" (Charlton, 1986).

The Dow program is a stellar example of corporate responsibility, but it is only one of thousands of such programs, some big, some small, some expensive, some not. In this chapter, we describe other examples of corporate social programs and explore the conceptual and theoretical nature of corporate social responsibility. No one has "the answers" about what should be done, when, how, or by whom. This is, therefore, an exploratory examination of the theory and concepts of social responsibility, what managers are thinking about the issue, and a few guidelines for action.

WHAT IS MEANT BY THE SOCIAL RESPONSIBILITY OF BUSINESS?

There is no consensus in or out of business about the meaning of business social responsibilities. In the classical view of business responsibility, a business is acting in a socially responsible fashion if it strives to utilize the resources at its disposal as efficiently as possible in producing the goods and services that society wants at prices consumers are willing to pay. If this is done well, say classical economic theorists, profits are maximized more or less continuously and firms carry out their major responsibilities to society.

It has never been accurate, of course, to say that business failed to display charitable impulses. Even business leaders known for their predation in the marketplace have made notable social contributions. For instance, during his lifetime John D. Rockefeller gave away $550 million and endowed the Rockefeller Foundation. Andrew Carnegie, author of a famous article entitled "The Disgrace of Dying Rich," gave away $350 million during his lifetime to social causes, built 2,509 public libraries, and gave thousands of organs to American churches. However, in business history, as in economic theory, the main thrust of endeavor has been the pursuit of strictly economic goals.

While this primal responsibility of business is recognized today, there has developed a view among managers and scholars that total social responsibilities are broader than profit maximization.

Many efforts to encapsulate this new, expanded definition of social responsibility in a few words have been made; almost every author in this field has tried. Here are a few examples:

■ The businessman's decisions and actions taken for reasons at least partially beyond the firm's direct economic or technical interest (Davis, 1960: 70).

■ Obligations to pursue those policies, to make those decisions, or to follow those lines of action which are desirable in terms of the objectives and values of our society (H. Bowen, 1953: 6).

■ The intelligent and objective concern for the welfare of society that restrains individual and corporate behavior from ultimately destructive activities, no matter how immediately profitable, and leads in the direction of positive contributions to human betterment, variously as the latter may be defined (Andrews, 1971: 120).

Fundamentally, these definitions say that actions taken by a business that in some degree help society to achieve one or more of its objectives are socially responsible. Most managers, by the way, prefer terms other than "social responsibility" because to them these words connote a fixed obligation with unclear commitments. They prefer synonyms like "social concern," "social programs," "social challenge," "social commitment," or "concern with public programs."

Corporate Social Program Areas

The first comprehensive list of social program areas was prepared by the CED in 1971. It included about sixty specific programs in ten major categories, such as economic growth and efficiency, education, employment and training, civil rights and equal opportunity, urban renewal, pollution abatement, conservation, recreation, and so on. Specific programs in the CED list, to pick a few, are installing modern pollution-abatement equipment, providing day-care centers for children of working mothers, augmenting the supply of replenishable resources, improving management at all levels of government, and building or improving low-income housing. Thousands of such detailed programs can, of course, be identified as possible areas for business social programs. A more recent CED statement on *Public-Private Partnership* (1982) underscores the responsibility of corporations to work with government and civic groups to ameliorate urban problems. Table 9-1 sets forth an illustrative list of major social program areas for corporations today.

In thinking about social programs, it is useful to distinguish between those that may be classified as internal or external to a business. Internal social

TABLE 9–1   SOME AREAS OF CORPORATE RESPONSIBILITY TO SOCIETY

Product safety
Economic growth
Education and training
Urban renewal
Low-income housing
Minority enterprise
Improving government efficiency
Elderly and handicapped care and training
Environmental protection
Preservation of historic sites
Support for the arts
Community health programs
Hunger/poverty abatement
Recreational facilities
Consumer education
Day-care centers
Impact of plant closings
Quality of work life
Due process for employees

responsiblities, for instance, can be concerned with ensuring due process, justice, equity, and morality in employee selection, training, promotion, and firing. Or they may relate to such things as increasing employee productivity or improving the worker's physical environment. External social responsibilities refer to such actions as stimulating minority entrepreneurship, improving the balance of payments, or training and hiring the hardcore unemployed.

Responsibility to Stakeholders

Many different groups, institutions, and individuals are stakeholders in the corporation because they are affected by its operation. As a result, the corporation has responsibilities to them. At the very least, the corporation should not knowingly do harm to important stakeholders. At most, there is an emerging ethic that the corporation should seek to enhance their welfare. But whose? A large corporation affects so many elements of society it does well just to discover and classify its stakeholders, let alone help them all. As Elmer W. Johnson, a group vice president of General Motors, wrote:

> The theoretical range of GM's accountability is almost infinite. The consequences of its activities fall not only on persons but also on institutions, future generations, and even nature itself. GM cannot assume the same degree of accountability for all the possible consequences of its operations. Accordingly, GM must place priorities on its lines of accountability to various groups, and it must determine where it can have the greatest impact and use its resources most effectively (1986: 175).

Corporations that carefully consider their obligations generally agree on a short list of stakeholders to which they owe primary obligations. Four stakeholder groups dominate, usually in the following order.

1. *Customers* are courted because their satisfaction is essential to the continued existence of the business. Progressive corporations feel responsible for customer health, safety, and well-being. Without satisfying customers, there are not enough sales and profits to sustain even basic corporate social performance.

2. *Employees* give their time, energy, and loyalty to an employer. Over the course of many years they devote their lives to pursuing company goals. In return, socially responsible corporations feel an obligation to provide a high quality of life for workers. Many firms, such as Control Data Corporation, make it policy that their obligation is to protect employees from layoff. For years, Control Data used part-time workers and subcontractors to cushion its employees against commercial downswings. When it had to close plants in the mid-1980s, it took extraordinary measures to ease the pain for workers and communities.

3. In *communities* where a company has a prominent presence with a plant, retail operation, or other facilities, it has pronounced impact. Corporations that

emphasize social responsibility therefore try to improve local communities. Levi Strauss & Company has, for example, set up Community Involvement Teams in every locality around the world where it has facilities. On these teams are employees who identify urgent community needs, develop plans to meet them, and take action. They get funds and help with grantsmanship from corporate headquarters in San Francisco.

4. *Stockholders* are the owners of a publicly-held corporation. They risk their money and are owed a fair return on that investment. Management must earn a profit and exercise wise stewardship of corporate resources in order to protect shareholder interests. It is believed, however, that in order to fully discharge its duty to the shareholders, the responsible corporation must fulfill its social obligations to other stakeholders as well.

Although a corporation is accountable to many stakeholders, the four noted above are typically prominent in large companies and many smaller ones. Is this new? Not at all, as we pointed out in the last chapter. Many executives in the past believed that they were responsible for balancing the interests of these stakeholders in their corporate decision making.

THE CASE FOR BUSINESS ASSUMPTION OF SOCIAL RESPONSIBILITIES

There is no one core idea in the argument that business has social responsibilities. Fundamentally, there seem to be three major core ideas, not mutually exclusive: Corporations are creatures of society and should respond to societal demands; the long-run self-interests of business are best served when business assumes social responsibilities; and it is one means to reduce or avoid government regulation and public criticism.

Society Expects Business to Assume Social Responsibilities

The argument is that corporations are creatures sanctioned by society, and when society's expectations about their functioning change, so should the corporation's actions. Many business leaders accept this argument and express it in different ways. David A. Koch, president of Graco, Inc., puts it this way: "The people allowed us to set up corporations. If, as businessmen, we are not responsible to the people, the people won't allow our franchises to exist" (Moskal; 1981: 60). Gerhard Bleichen, when chairman of the board of the John Hancock Mutual Life Insurance Company, said that "it never occurred to me that there was a time when American business was at liberty to operate in conflict with the interests of society" (Bleichen, 1972).

A manager operates within a set of cultural norms and restraints. These are certainly economic but also legal, political, social, and technical. They are powerful, and the manager knows instinctively that as they change, corporate decisions must conform. Sethi argues that there exists a "legitimacy gap" between the response of business to nonmarket social forces and societal expectations of what business should be doing (1979: 65). If this gap grows too large, the corporation will be brought to heel. In truth, many managers accept the idea that because society expects them to assume social responsibilities, they must try to do so. If not, the argument runs, either society will force them to do so through laws, or society may no longer permit them to exist. In either case, it is in the enlightened self-interest of a company to react to society's wishes. History confirms that an institution with power that is not used in conformity to society's desires will lose that power.

Long-run Self-interest of Business

In a milestone policy statement of the CED, a group of prominent managers concluded, "It is in the enlightened self-interest of corporations to promote the public welfare in a positive way" (CED, 1971: 25). The statement continued: "Indeed, the corporate interest broadly defined by management can support involvement in helping to solve virtually any social problem, because people who have a good environment, education, and opportunity make better employees, customers, and neighbors for business than those who are poor, ignorant, and oppressed" (CED, 1971: 26). The continuing belief of business leaders in this notion is affirmed in a *Statement on Corporate Responsibility* by the Business Roundtable. "Business and society have a symbiotic relationship. The long-term viability of the corporation depends upon its responsibility to the society of which it is a part. And the well-being of society depends upon profitable and responsible business enterprises" (*Statement on Corporate Responsibility*, 1981: 12).

It would profit business little to ignore social problems. In the long run, deteriorating cities, consumer dissatisfaction, employee mistrust, harsh government regulations, inflation, rising crime levels, pollution, and poverty are the components of economic stagnation, not corporate welfare. Corporations cannot escape their attachment to and dependence on the social cohesion of American society. The fates of both corporation and society are inextricably linked in the long run.

Avoidance of Government Regulation

Since the 1960s, as the reader is well aware, government regulation of business has expanded greatly. Business leaders, sensitive to this intrusion, feel that voluntary amelioration of social ills through social responsibility programs is preferable to government regulation that makes action mandatory. A survey of 116 CEOs in 1984 showed that 71 percent agreed that "if business is more socially responsible, it will discourage additional regulation of the economic system by government" (Ford and McLaughlin, 1984: 670). If new regulations are inevitable, business may be denied participation in hammering out the rules if it volunteers its services only after its stubborn resistance to change has been overcome by public pressure. If managers avoid government regulation by responding to social demands, they are likely to reduce their costs, since regulation in general is more expensive than social programs likely to be pursued by business. They also will retain their flexibility and freedom in making decisions and in meeting competition. They restrain concentration of power in government and thereby advance their own relative power.

Executives Are Concerned Citizens

Like everyone else, people in business wear a number of hats. As citizens they see the need for social action. As executives they may have the power to do something and accept the challenge. Most of what executives do in the social arena may be in reaction to societal pressures and justified in their minds on the grounds of self-interest. Yet, as concerned citizens, many executives welcome the opportunity, however they justify it, to participate in the development of a better world.

A few top corporate executives are remembered for leading their firms to stellar social performances over the years. For example, Robert Anderson, founder and chairman of ARCO, made ARCO unparalleled in the oil industry in its environmental concern and had the courage to break with other business leaders in the 1970s by advocating stringent auto emission controls. William Norris, founder and CEO of Control Data Corporation, was a visionary in promoting corporate applications of computer technology to the solution of social problems. J. C. Penney, founder of the J. C. Penney Company, wrote a code of ethics in 1913 that still guides the company today; and Robert Wood Johnson, longtime CEO of Johnson & Johnson, developed a formula for balancing stakeholder interests that is credited with inspiring the alacrity of the Tylenol recalls in 1983 and 1986.

These are a few stars (and perhaps there are conspicuous reprobates who should better remain anonymous on these pages). But often, as Andrews points out, "corporate executives of the caliber, integrity, intelligence, and humanity required to run substantial companies cannot be expected to confine themselves to their narrow economic activity and to ignore its social consequences" (Andrews, 1971: 133). They may derive much pleasure from being socially responsible. The feelings of Thornton Bradshaw were revealed, for instance, when, as president of ARCO, he wrote:

> For example, should Atlantic Richfield spend a certain amount of money each year to operate a playground track and field program, the ARCO Jesse Owens Games, because it brings unwonted opportunity and pleasure to thousands of kids, many underprivileged, and perhaps disposes local officials kindly toward our Company?

We think a youngster's joy makes the whole thing worthwhile, though I admit the notion is arguable (ARCO, 1981: 3).

THE CASE AGAINST BUSINESS ASSUMPTION OF SOCIAL RESPONSIBILITIES

No worthy argument can be made that business may act irresponsibly without penalty. But one strongly held view, as we have said, is that business is *most* responsible when it operates efficiently to make profits, not when it goes out on a limb to solve social problems. James Russell Lowell caught the essence of this argument in the following rhyme:

Not a deed would he do
   Not a word would he utter
Till he weighed its relation
   To plain bread and butter.

There are several variations on this theme.

Contrary to the Basic Functions of Business

The core of the strongest arguments against business assumption of any responsibilities other than to produce goods and services efficiently and to make as much money as possible for stockholders is that business is an economic institution and economic values should be the sole determinant of performance. This is called the classical view because it hews closely to the dictates of classical economic theory. A pertinacious exponent of this view is Nobel laureate Milton Friedman, a respected economist who makes this clear statement on the side of the classicists:

There is one and only one social responsibility of business—to use its resources and engage in activities designed to increase its profits so long as it stays within the rules of the game, which is to say, engages in open and free competition, without deception or fraud. . . . Few trends could so thoroughly undermine the very foundations of our free society as the acceptance by corporate officials of a social responsibility other than to make as much money for their stockholders as possible. This is a fundamentally subversive doctrine (Friedman, 1962: 133).

Friedman argues that in a free-enterprise, private-property system, a manager is an employee of the owners of the business and is directly responsible to them. Because stockholders want to make as much profit as possible, the manager's sole objective should be to try to do this. If a manager spends stockholder money in the public interest, he or she is spending it without stockholders' approval and perhaps in ways they would oppose. Similarly, if the cost of social action is passed on to consumers in higher prices, the manager is spending their money. This "taxation without representation," says Friedman (1970), should be rejected. Furthermore, if the price on the market for a product does not truly reflect the relative costs of producing it, but includes costs for social action, the allocative mechanism of the marketplace is distorted. The rigors of the market will endanger the competitive position of any firm that adds to its costs by assuming social responsibilities.

An addendum to Friedman's view comes from management theorist Peter Drucker, who wrote recently that the most urgent social need that business can fulfill is to create capital to finance industrial development. He makes a strong case against using business capital on social problems.

> The greatest need today is for capital formation. Anything else done by business is antisocial activity.
>
> When educational institutions come begging to business for handouts, business should turn them down. Philanthropy of this sort—putting money where the need is greatest rather than where the opportunity is greatest—is an antisocial activity. It destroys social capital.
>
> The proper way to attack social problems is through public providers and private suppliers. Just giving money doesn't solve social problems. Business is a most effective force when trained people and the profit motive are used to attack problems.
>
> When business people are told, "If you don't give us X dollars, we will have to close down the medical school," perhaps the best thing to do is to let it close down (Zemke, 1983: 61).

Social Responsibility Will Weaken Our Freedoms

Milton Friedman believes that management actions to solve social problems, lead to inefficient use of resources and also threaten political freedoms. He argues that the doctrine of social responsibility means acceptance of the socialist view that political mechanisms rather than market mechanisms are the appropriate way to allocate scarce resources to alternative uses. A manager undertaking activities in the public realm is performing social and political functions and becomes, in effect, a civil servant. The result is that managers will come under growing public scrutiny and eventually may be elected or appointed to reflect public attitudes. This would constitute a dangerous fusion of political and economic power, which ought properly to be kept separate.

Capitalism, with its market mechanism, fragments economic power and separates it from central government control. This system preserves political liberties by keeping power out of the hands of those who would violate human rights to enforce their vision of betterment. Friedman believes that history vindicates this view: "I know of no example in time or place of a society that has been marked by a large measure of political freedom, and that has not also used something comparable to a free market to organize the bulk of economic activity" (Friedman, 1962: 9; see also Hayek, 1944).

The conclusion, for those who subscribe to this view, is that economic and political freedom are linked, and we should not threaten economic freedom by encouraging diversion of capital to social programs run by business. Once again, efficiency is equated with responsibility.

We Do Not Want Business Values to Dominate Us

Theodore Levitt supports the classical view because he fears domination of business values.

> But at the rate we are going, there is more than a contingent probability that, with all its resounding good intentions, business statesmanship may create the corporate equivalent of the unitary state. Its proliferating employee welfare programs, its serpentine involvement in community, government, charitable, and educational affairs, its prodigious currying of political and public favor through hundreds of peripheral preoccupations, all these well-intended but insidious contrivances are greasing the rails for our collective descent into a social order that would be as repugnant to the corporations themselves as to their critics. The danger is that all these things will turn the corporation into a twentieth-century equivalent of the medieval Church. The corporation would eventually invest itself with all-embracing duties, obligations, and finally powers—ministering to the whole man and molding him and society in the image of the corporation's narrow ambitions and its essentially unsocial needs (Levitt, 1958: 44).

Levitt's fear is that the values of the more prominent business managers will dominate the values of society. He does not want social values determined in this way. In the past, societies suffered in which values were determined by one major institution, whether it was the church, the military, business, or something else. This concern is echoed by Irving Shapiro, former DuPont executive, who says that, "Unless they are careful, executives can get sucked into controversial areas where they don't have any particular competence, and in extreme cases their efforts to help could amount to unwarranted meddling" (Steckmest, 1982: 152).

Government, Not Business, Should Solve Social Problems

The foregoing are arguments generally advanced by conservatives. However, liberal and radical thinkers too often oppose business's assumption of social responsibilities. For example, the view is advanced that government, not business, should take the lead in solving social problems. What is needed, they assert, is not more socially responsible companies but a more responsive government. More regulation of business is preferable to permitting corporations to decide what is in the public interest. It is also argued that business assumption of social responsibility is a means of lulling a gullible public to sleep, while an exploitive elite preserves its power. Some radical activists, such as Michael Harrington, today chairman of the Democratic Socialist Organizing Committee, conclude that the assumption of social responsibilities by business is merely a Band-Aid for dealing with social problems. What is needed, they say, is a major change in our socioeconomic system. In sum, those opposed to the assumption by business of social responsibilities cover a spectrum from the most conservative to the most radical.

AN ASSESSMENT OF THE ARGUMENTS

Critics of the conservative view point out that the classical thinkers want corporations to do something they cannot do, and that is to ignore societal demands on them. The "rules of the game" really have changed for business. Friedman's position is that managers ought to optimize stockholder wealth so long as they stay within the rules of the game. He explains that the rules of the game refer to economic considerations. This simple market model of business response to its environment is obsolete, especially for larger corporations, if it ever really was an accurate description of reality. A more explanatory model is the business ecology model (see Chapter 1), which shows business responding to an overall societal environment, not simply to its markets, as is the case with the market capitalism model. Because stakeholders are numerous, politically powerful, and organized, corporate managers must consider the social impact of their decisions on these stakeholders. If the words "rules of the game" are modernized, there may not be much difference between the Friedman view and that of those who argue for social responsibilities.

Those who argue that the assumption of social responsibilities will lead to society's being dominated by business values very much overstate the trend. In the aggregate, as noted in Exhibit 9–1, the total is very small. Business is so far from going to extremes that this assumption is equivalent to forecasting that a leaky faucet will bring on the Johnstown flood.

The same can be said for the view that if business pursues social responsibilities, the end will be performance measurement on political rather than economic scales. This would, say the conservatives, lead to economic inefficiency. If business were measured only on political standards, there is little doubt that economic efficiency would suffer, but business is not now and will not likely in the future be so measured.

Some opponents of social responsibility say that profit maximization is essential for achieving economic efficiency in a free market economy. But as Nobel laureate and professor of economics Kenneth Arrow points out:

> There are two types of situations in which the simple rule of maximizing profits is socially inefficient: the case in which costs are not paid for, as in pollution, and the

case in which the seller has considerably more knowledge about his product than the buyer, particularly with regard to safety. In these situations it is clearly desirable to have some idea of social responsibility, that is, to experience an obligation, whether ethical, moral, or legal (Arrow, 1973: 309).

The proponents of social responsibilities are saying that society is not substituting one set of expectations for another. Rather it is broadening the standards by means of which corporate performance is to be judged. But obviously what is meant by this differs from person to person. On the one hand, there are those who seem to believe that a business enterprise really has responsibilities that may require actions that have no direct bearing on profits. On the other hand, some feel that business has a responsibility to find profit opportunities in solving social problems, but no obligation to do more than that.

There are some people who assert that the new views about social responsibilities represent nothing more than a modification of the old profit-maximizing goal of business. In the past the emphasis of business was on maximizing short-run profit, but now a shift has taken place to put a greater emphasis on maximizing long-range profit. The basis for the shift is that managers see many things happening in the environment today that will affect future profits, and they feel they must take action to optimize long-range profits, even though it reduces short-term profits.

In considering this position, it is important to understand the meaning of profit maximization. To the economist, this is a precise concept that can be measured quantitatively. It means that a firm will attempt to increase its output so long as the marginal revenue from the last item produced is greater than the marginal cost of that item. At that point where marginal cost equals marginal revenue, the firm will receive its maximum profit. This concept is found in all elementary economics textbooks; it means literally that a firm that seeks to maximize profits in this sense will not make any decision that will prevent it from getting the highest possible profit for its stockholders.

The economist's strict concept of profit maximization is not an acceptable operational goal for today's larger corporations—assuming they could achieve such a goal, which they rarely can. Much more appropriate is a concept of required and rising profits—or those needed to satisfy the many claims made on the enterprise, including the level necessary to meet the satisfactions of managers from participating in the resolution of social problems, improving the quality of life of employees, and making this a better society. A company that can reach the level of profits required to balance properly the interests focused on its operations is in a position to take social actions. A company not in so favored a position may be unable to assume them.

We conclude with one final argument, that business action in the social realm will distort democratic processes by permitting a small elite of corporate managers to exercise their powers over society and preserve their selfish profit goals. This Marxist specter is completely at odds with reality. Rather than business dictating which actions to undertake, as the Marxists imply, business must respond to strong pressures from all quarters in society and satisfy strongly felt demands. Corporations cannot win with Marxists. If they have no social responsibility programs, they are profit-mongers. If they have social programs, they are conspiring to dominate the situation in their own interests.

ASSESSING MANAGERIAL MOTIVES

What about the motives of corporations and corporate leaders? How should we evaluate statements and actions of social responsibility framed in gradiose terms when clearly corporations and managers may be acting in self-interest? Suspicion of managerial motives is longstanding. In 1909, for example, Coleman du Pont, president of DuPont, made a remarkable offer to build a new 103-mile superhighway from Wilmington to Dover in Delaware, the state where DuPont is headquartered. Political opponents in the state legislature, aware that Coleman du Pont had political ambition, at first rejected the offer, fearing he would gain votes from this grandstand play. Farmers along the planned right-of-way responded to du Pont's generosity by raising the price of their land. The determined du Pont, however, overcame opposition and built the highway, U.S. Highway 13, which became the most modern in the country at the time. In 1924, the highway was given free of charge to the state of Delaware (Mosley, 1980: 227, 262).

Firms may be responsible only under great pressure. In 1984, for example, William K. Coors, the chairman of Adolph Coors Company, was quoted in the *Rocky Mountain News* on a number of remarks widely construed as racist (although he later sued the newspaper for libel saying that the reporter had taken his remarks out of context). These *faux pas*, including the comment that blacks "lack the intellectual capacity to succeed," were quoted nationally and added fire to ongoing boycotts of the company by black, Hispanic, and labor groups. With sales dropping in states like California and Texas, Coors signed pacts with minority groups and agreed to use more minority suppliers, hire more minorities, and spend millions supporting minority causes. Coors has kept the bargain and gone beyond, even sponsoring rodeos in honor of black cowboys in frontier days and publishing salutes to outstanding Hispanic athletes. In 1985, a year after the pacts were signed, Coors sales were up 14 percent, mostly due to the return of minority beer drinkers (Simons, 1986).

Must corporations be entirely altruistic to be truly responsible, or should these examples cause cynicism? In the *Foundations of the Metaphysics of Morals,* philosopher Immanuel Kant developed a perfectionist test of intentions. The test of ethical action was, according to Kant, acting from a "good will" that was good in itself, independent of consequences achieved. Human actions could be divided into "moral" actions that truly proceeded from a good will and "prudential" actions that accorded with truly moral actions but were taken out of self-interest. The sometimes self-interested actions of corporations do not meet the strict Kantian test, but perhaps they are helpful and it is appropriate for a capitalist society that morality and self-interest find felicitous combination.

THE CONCEPT OF VOLUNTARISM

In Exhibit 9-1 we have tried to capture in a simple picture several important concepts. As the exhibit shows, business has economic responsibilities and social responsibilities established by government and expressed in legal requirements. Included here also are responsibilities demanded by outside groups and accepted under pressure by business (for example, union contracts). Voluntary action is undertaken in response to an awareness of changing social values and priorities. Most decisions are made in response to traditional economic forces. Fewer are dictated by government, and even fewer are voluntary social actions.

The magnitude and relationships among these areas in the chart are estimates. Yet they serve in a somewhat elementary fashion to reveal several significant points. First, a comparable drawing of one hundred or even twenty-five years ago would show substantially different magnitudes. Second, the area of voluntarism is not really great in terms of the totality of corporate actions. Yet it is of very great significance to business as well as to society.

Within the voluntary area are zones of action. First are programs that might be called "legal plus." These are actions that go beyond present legislation and are considered to be socially responsible, such as employee safety, antipollution measures, or minority hiring and promotion programs. Second are programs about which there is a national consensus, such as contributing to local charities

EXHIBIT 9–1   VOLUNTARY BUSINESS SOCIAL RESPONSIBILITIES COMPARED WITH TOTAL BUSINESS

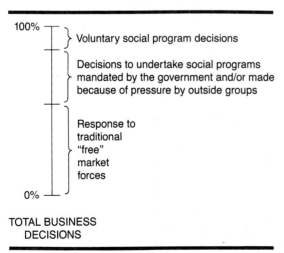

100% — Voluntary social program decisions

Decisions to undertake social programs mandated by the government and/or made because of pressure by outside groups

Response to traditional "free" market forces

0% —

TOTAL BUSINESS
DECISIONS

or to education. Third is an area about which there is no consensus. For instance, many church groups condemn defense contractors for manufacturing nuclear weapons components and suggest that cessation would be socially responsible. Others, however, disagree and would regard voluntary fore-swearing of defense contracts as irresponsible.

SOCIAL AND ECONOMIC PERFORMANCE: ARE THEY RELATED?

Is there a reward for virtue? Are socially responsible companies more profitable than those that are not? Does their stock perform better? Are they better managed? It would be nice to answer yes to these questions. Unfortunately, after more than 100 empirical studies of the relation between social performance and profits, no clear answer is available.

Some studies show that social responsibility and economic performance are, indeed, positively related.

For example, Sturdivant and Ginter (1977) divided sixty-seven firms into high, medium, and low levels of social performance and showed that, by four different measures of profitability, the most socially responsible corporations were also most profitable. They also demonstrated that the managers of the more socially responsible firms had liberal attitudes that favored social intervention by corporations to minister to social problems such as poverty, discrimination, and protection of human rights. Another explanation frequently advanced to explain the association of profits and social responsibility is the enabling factor of higher profits. A profitable firm has more resources for social programs; it is easier to do good when doing well.

Other studies, however, show a negative or unclear relationship between social and economic performance. Bowman and Haire (1975) studied eighty-two companies in the food-processing industry and concluded that those companies with a medium level of social responsiveness were more profitable than either the high- or the low-performance companies. A study of sixty-one firms in many industries by Cochran and Wood (1984), which used more sophisticated statistical analysis than earlier studies, showed only "marginally significant" and "weak" links between corporate social responsibility and financial performance.

A problem for researchers is that it is difficult to measure corporate responsibility. Responsibility varies with factors such as a firm's location, size, profitability, strategy, management philosophy, product, important stakeholders, and so forth. Hence, when researchers divide companies into the more and less virtuous, they are inevitably subjective. Also, many factors aside from social responsibility enter into financial performance—so many, in fact, that it is difficult to control for them. There are also many ways to measure profitability. Researchers have not yet conquered these complexities, and so the jury is still out.

SOCIALLY RESPONSIBLE INVESTING

Although a positive relationship between corporate social responsibility and financial performance has not been substantiated, a growing number of investors in mutual and money-market funds are attracted to portfolios of socially responsible companies. By 1986, at least a dozen such funds existed. For example, the Calvert Social Investment Fund, which is both a money-market fund and a separate stock portfolio, has "social screens" for investments. It rejects firms that pollute heavily, that operate in South Africa, that are associated with nuclear power, that are major weapons producers, or that deal in liquor or alcohol. The fund started in 1982 and had grown from $35 million in 1984 to $103 million in 1986. Its performance was slightly better than overall mutual and money market fund averages each year between 1983 and 1985.

Most of the socially responsible funds have done as well as or better than ordinary investment funds. The amount invested in them is growing. These funds represent a combination of a conservative morality and a liberal ideology that see business as a despoiler of nature and plunderer of society for profit. To date, these funds affect so little equity capital that they exert no pressure on corporations that offend their values. But they offer a needed service for a growing number of "ethical investors" who want to make investments that support their social views.

Pressures on Institutional Investors

The impact of individual ethical investors in social responsibility funds is not significant, but institutional investors who act as trustees of state, city, and union pension funds and of college endowments own almost half of publically traded stock and the majority of shares of large companies such as IBM. Managers of these institutional funds are sometimes pressured by activist groups to use their portfolio purchasing and diverstiture policy to force corporations to be socially responsive. The principal concerns behind these pressures are multitudinous. Institutional managers have been asked to liquidate investments in corporations operating in South Africa, major defense contractors, nuclear weapons, component manufacturers, tobacco companies, chemical companies, drug companies, infant formula manufacturers, companies perceived as antiunion, and other firms that have somehow offended a politically active segment of society.

Usually, large institutional investors resist such pressures and prefer to invest for maximum financial return, arguing that it is a fiduciary duty to institutional clients to do so. But occasionally, enough political pressure is created to force a change in investment policy. Between 1983 and 1986, for instance, a number of states and municipalities passed resolutions requiring disinvestment of holdings in American firms doing business in South Africa.

A number of difficult questions arise when such political pressure is exerted. For example, how can a portfolio manager decide which companies should be favored and which avoided? IBM, for instance, has long been condemned by activist groups for selling computers to the South African government. Yet IBM also ranks high on many lists of the most socially responsible companies. In 1985, it gave more contributions to charities, community projects, the arts, and education than any other company.

Activist disinvestment groups seek to substitute social and political objectives for prevailing policies of maximum return. They attempt to control institutional capital for their own social ends. Of course, once a precedent is established for buying or selling stocks for social reasons, a case can be made for avoiding investment in virtually any company. A political or social disinvestment standard could expose an institutional investor to huge financial losses, including brokerage fees, opportunity costs, or worse. As Derek Bok, president of Harvard University, asks: "What could a university do, for example, if it received an urgent demand to stop doing business with the telephone company or the local electric utility?" (Bok, 1982: 288).

Other problems are created for institutions by political and social disinvestment policies. Institutions do not always have the resources to research the behavior of corporations in which they invest, and on emotional issues information may be unreliable. The dubious practices of a corporation may contribute little if any to corporate profits, as was the case with Dow Chemical Corp. and the napalm contract attacked so vigorously by students in the 1960s and 1970s. Institutional share divestiture may have negligible impact on a corporation because often it attracts no public attention and because most institutional investors own too few shares to influence market price more than trivially. Active shareholder campaigns might accomplish more.

To date, big institutional investors have not screened investments using criteria of social responsibility. But they are becoming more activist in their approaches to management and could, if they choose, exert considerable pressure on stock prices. In the final analysis, there is no reason why managers of investment portfolios ought not exert pressures on companies in which they invest. However, the pressures ought to be in the interests of the constituents of the investment manager, as they see their interests, and not as the manager thinks he or she sees him.

BUSINESS AND MAJOR SOCIAL PROBLEMS

Business Is Not Solely Responsible for Solving Social Problems

Business is a predominant instrumentality in society for dealing with major social problems, but it is not the institution of sole or last responsibility. It is government that has the central role in dealing with such problems. Business has incentives for working on these problems, as noted previously. It has great talents that it can exert, such as the development of new equipment to reduce pollution of various types or the free contribution of managerial knowledge to government agencies. A central issue in dealing with social problems concerns the extent to which government should provide incentives for business to become involved in solving social problems when it does not appear to business to be profitable to do so. It also must be pointed out that other institutions in society, such as universities, labor unions, and religious institutions, and people themselves, individually and in groups, can make valuable contributions to overcoming major social problems.

Social Responsibility and the Costs of Doing Business

Will not the socially responsible company be put at a competitive disadvantage? If it goes too far, the answer is yes. However, a great many social responsibilities can be pursued without substantial costs to an enterprise—for example, improving due process within the company, encouraging managers to lend their knowledge in resolving local community as well as national problems, and locating plants in underprivileged areas. Many social responsibilities are consistent with making profits. Some may be costly, such as not closing a marginal plant in a community dependent upon it, making large capital equipment expenditures to reduce pollution, and giving heavily to the community for beautification.

Business must develop a new concept of costs. The costs of doing business are not solely those concerned with purchasing, producing, and distributing goods and services in the traditional accounting sense. Most managers say that their most precious assets are people. If so, the preservation and use of those assets entail a cost beyond the money wage. All thinking managers know that much of the cost borne by society for many activities (education, for instance) is of enormous benefit to business. Business does pay taxes, but it is questionable that it bears a cost equal to the benefits derived. Finally, many costs are borne by society as a result of business activity that business does not fully defray. For the first two groups of costs, a business may ask itself whether it is doing enough to carry its share and, if not, whether it wishes to assume further responsibilities to do so. In the last case, there are two questions. One concerns the social responsibility a firm may feel for bearing some of these costs, and the other deals with legal liabilities. The boundaries overlap.

How Much Social Cost Should Business Bear?

Social costs are the total costs of business activity, including immediate costs of production plus all other costs. For instance, a factory dumping pollutants into a clear stream incurs two kinds of costs. One is the cost of its operation; the other is the cost that results from changes in the stream's ecology—perhaps human and animal disease, perhaps the destruction of natural beauty. To the extent that business does not bear these external costs, they must be borne by others.

These "other costs" include a spectrum of elements. They may involve direct and indirect losses to third persons, such as reduced real estate values from nearby factory noise. They include human damage in the form of disease, accident, unemployment, disturbance of social relationships, and changes in the life style of groups. They may include defaced landscapes, ugly buildings, or traffic congestion. Some costs are incurred immediately; others may take a long time to be felt. Some costs can be measured in dollars such as the price for cleaning up a polluted stream. Others, such as the impairment of health resulting from air pollution, cannot be gauged in quantitative terms. Indeed, the determination of many social costs depends upon the value society attaches to a particular impact and its relationships to the benefits of social change.

Capitalism has been called "an economy of unpaid costs." This means that a large part of the actual costs of production are not counted as business expenses but are shifted to and borne by third persons or by the community as a whole. As society has become more complex, there has been a rise in the unpaid costs of business. Earlier in our history, these costs generally were considered to be implicit by-products of economic life, and regarded as the short-run price to be paid for the higher economic efficiency and long-run social advantage resulting from the operation of the economic system. Eventually, laws were passed to force business to meet unpaid costs where injury to third parties could be reasonably determined. The political history of the United States increasingly has reflected popular unwillingness to bear the social costs of economic development without help from government. Throughout this history, business pressure groups have sought to avoid the assumption of social costs that had been transferred to others.

In considering business responsibility for social costs, it should be remembered that business also creates social value. Important benefits accrue to society through business's activities. A business, for instance, may introduce an innovation that will cut the costs of making a particular product. Assuming no other significant cost than that of production, the result is a net gain in social value. A company may erect a beautiful building, tastefully landscaped. Or it may contribute to advancing knowledge. Theoretically, a business firm should in the long run cover all costs of production and should profit from the social benefits it creates. This attitude suggests that in the long run, social costs should be borne by those responsible for creating them, or those who bear them should be compensated. It also suggests that a firm should be compensated in accordance with its contribution to social benefit. Unfortunately, in only a comparatively few instances can such cause-and-effect relationships be isolated and measured. More often, the determinants cannot be identified or quantified.

CRITERIA FOR DETERMINING THE
SOCIAL RESPONSIBILITIES OF BUSINESS

There is no magic touchstone or standard for determining social responsibilities. Because the concept is not expressed in concrete, legal, or axiomatic terms, managers of daily corporate operations and strategic planners must be thoughtful about the precise nature of responsible corporate behavior. What might be acceptable overall guides to business's assumption of social responsibilities? We suggest the following.

First, there is no formula for all businesses or any one business. Each firm must decide for itself. Business can take action, but it is not compelled to do so except when law and custom determine otherwise. The first social responsibility of each business is to think carefully before acting about what it thinks its social responsibilities really are. In deciding what to do, the values and interests of top managers are, of course, guiding considerations. The levels and directions of public expectations that top management thinks are focused on the company are also guiding considerations. Companies are expected to be philanthropic in the communities in which they do business. A public utility is expected to take special pains in training and hiring underprivileged local unemployed workers. The public expects an aircraft manufacturer to be especially careful about product safety, as compared with the expectation, for instance, of a manufacturer of lawn mowers.

Second, business must be considered to be predominantly an economic institution with a strong profit motive. Business should not be used to meet noneconomic objectives of society in a major way without financial incentives. As the Business Roundtable says in its *Statement on Corporate Responsibility*, "If a corporation is not profitable in the long run, there is no way that it can fulfill any responsibilities to society. If the bottom line is a minus, there is no plus for society" (1981: 5). It is of paramount importance that no action be taken to erode the profit motive in American business ideology. The fundamental justification for this view is supported by Will and Ariel Durant, who looked over the broad sweep of history they so assiduously chronicled and concluded that "the experience of the past leaves little doubt that every economic system must sooner or later rely upon some form of the profit motive to stir individuals and groups to productivity. Substitutes like slavery, police supervision, or ideological enthusiasm prove too unproductive, too expensive, or too transient" (Durant and Durant, 1968: 54). We must continue to judge business performance primarily on the basis of economic criteria.

Third, business should be expected to take the long view and perform socially responsible actions that might temporarily lessen net profits but that are consistent with profit interests of the company in the long run. Clearly, the long-range self-interest of business lies in correcting such problems as unemployment, civil disorders, environmental pollution, and crime.

Fourth, an individual business has social responsibilities, says Keith Davis (1960), commensurate with its social powers. That power and responsibility go hand in hand is an idea as old as civilization itself. This can be only a rough guide to action, but it can be a useful one. For instance, company A is the major employer in a town, and company B is an employer of only 5 percent of the people in the town. Both companies are planning to move. It would seem that, other things being equal, company A should give more thought to its social responsibilities in moving than should company B. Having said this, however, we still do not know to what extent the formula of co-equal power and responsibility should alter the decision of company A.

Companies also, Davis says, have "socio-human responsibilities." Considering a business as only an economic institution may lead to the conclusion that it has some responsibilities concerned with the economic costs of unemployment, but not with the erosion of human dignity or social disorganization that accompanies unemployment. A business may be concerned with increasing creative capability in individuals to improve productivity, but not with attempting to help workers get more self-fulfillment from their jobs. Davis says that this is wrong because business deals with the whole person in a whole social structure. Furthermore, managers have socio-human power, that is, power over the quality of a person's life. As such, they have socio-human responsibilities commensurate with that power. Again, this equation yields no sure answers in any situation, but it should help.

Fifth, and closely associated with the preceding point, is the matter of company size and type. As a firm grows larger, it influences more and more people. Society then takes a greater interest in what it does, and the company in turn thinks more carefully about its responsibilities. As corporations acquire more power over people, there is pressure for them to install policies, rules, and actions so that individuals are less likely to be treated unjustly or without due process. The social responsibilities of the smallest entrepreneur-owner business are not many, but there are some. For example, a very small business in an urban slum has a social responsibility not to raise prices arbitrarily nor to sell defective goods as first quality.

Social responsibilities differ with respect to types of company. The special position of public utilities was noted above. A company involved in the mass production of a competitively priced product is in a very different position with respect to the feelings and personal interests of employees in leading the good life at work from, say, a technically oriented and highly profitable laboratory staffed by Ph.Ds. A mining company is in a different position with respect to employee safety from, say, a small real estate office.

Sixth, no one should expect a business voluntarily to jeopardize its ability to attract stockholder investment. If a corporation diverts substantial sums of money to social purposes, it will significantly reduces its average return on capital, which in turn will bring reduced growth rates, a lower market evaluation of its securities, or both. This sort of thing cannot, of course, long continue. A company guilty of serious air and water pollution may be forced to clean up its waste even though the impact may have great profit consequences. But a company that has profit levels well above the industry average may find leverage in assuming social responsibilities of greater magnitude than would a company much below the industry average.

Seventh, an effort should be made to determine which agencies in society are best able to deal with social problems, and proper responsibilities should be assigned to them. In some areas, the government is clearly the best agent (for example, in national security). In other areas, business is the best (for example, in producing goods). An individual business should choose only those social responsibilities it can best manage. Traditionally, business does a better job when the task entails a minimum of political involvement, does not get directly into the democratic political processes, deals with a physical problem that can be quantified and measured, and is one in which it has experience. A business that can pass on costs to consumers (for example, a public utility may use less efficient workers and get higher rates because of higher costs) may do more than one faced with a highly elastic and declining demand for its product.

Eighth, business should be obliged to internalize more of its external costs. In the past, businesses were excused from bearing such costs of production as air and water pollution, scarring hillsides in the search for coal, and defacing natural beauty because society held the economic output of business to be of higher priority. Today, priorities are shifting and business is expected to bear more social costs.

Ninth, managers can be guided in calculating the appropriateness of corporate activity by following the law and beyond that by analyzing the intent of public policy in relevant areas where their operations have a social impact. Preston and Post (1975; 1981) suggest that appropriate guidelines for responsibility are found in a public policy "framework." "Public policy includes," they argue, "not only the literal text of the law and regulation, but also the broad pattern of social direction reflected in public opinion, emerging issues, formal legal requirements, and enforcement or implementation practices" (1981: 57). It may not be clear what relevant public policy guidelines are. Much study and research may be required and many policy areas are not characterized by full consensus. Yet public policy is unquestionably a source of norms and standards for helping corporations to determine their social responsibilities.

CONCLUDING OBSERVATIONS

There is a wide diversity of opinion about the nature of corporate social responsibility. But all companies have this responsibility. Its achievement is an art, not a science. It is not a precise activity following clear rules and guidelines. But more companies are systematically and routinely injecting the social viewpoint into their policies and programs on an orderly, rather than an ad hoc, basis. This is called institutionalizing the social point of view. It is the subject of the next chapter.

CASE STUDY

WAR TOYS

The wolf also shall dwell with the lamb, and the leopard shall lie down with the kid; and the calf and the young lion and the fatling together; and a little child shall lead them.

—Isaiah 11:6

"We need reinforcements, folks . . . here's the supply . . . General, you have to realize that you'll be held responsible . . . we need more support . . . General, sir, I have to get in there . . . but I want . . . Fire—over there. . . . The others are coming, hey, you: stay there . . . over there, they are attacking again. . . . Fire . . . it's burning . . . hurry up, another tank . . . God, it's heavy. . . . Quick, away with the jeep . . . alarm, faster, alarm . . . fire, come on. . . . Hey, you, handle the flak. . . . The Americans are running short of men . . . no more men, gee . . ."

—Thomas, an 11-year-old German child, playing with tanks and soldiers in his room
(Buettner, 1981: 104)

Today's toy store is a miniature arsenal. It contains playthings fashioned in the image of every manner of past, present, and future weapon. In a tour of the aisles, a child can see pistols, rifles, artillery, bows and arrows, knives, warships, warplanes, military "action figures," war strategy games, laser weapons, and armed star cruisers.

War toys are not unique to modern America. They are—like balls, blocks, tops, and dolls—ageless and found in all cultures. In primitive societies children pretended that sticks were spears and practiced war games. Archeologists have found toy soldiers in excavations of ancient Greek and Roman dwellings. During the Middle Ages, young princes were trained in the art of generalship by advisers using war toys. A famous 1516 woodcut by Hans Burkmair, entitled "Games of the Young Emperor Maximilian," shows the young boy-ruler and his royal entourage firing a cannon, stringing a longbow, shooting a bird off a branch with a crossbow, and jousting with miniature figures of mounted knights placed on a table.

Toys and Cultural Values

Cultural values are learned during play. Toys and the way they are used reflect the influence of the larger, adult society. They may, for instance, reflect a nation's concept of a hero. In ancient Rome, children played games with toy chariots and emulated great heroes of the races in much the same way American children played with Hasbro Corporation's popular "G.I. Joe" figures after World War II.

Toys and games also may be influenced by the values and events of a historical period. The board game "Monopoly" was a big hit when introduced in 1934 because, as one toy analyst writes, the unemployed "loved playing tycoon, and men who were homeless needed to build dream castles" (Kaye, 1973: 41). One era with a pronounced and lingering impact on toyland is that of the American Wild West. During the 1870s and 1880s the epic adventures of cowboys and Indians thrilled readers around the world. Children in America and Europe played with six-shooters and tomahawks. The fad became a permanent theme in children's games, partly because fascinating Western events occurred just when the toy industry developed the technology to mass produce toys at affordable prices. The allure of the Wild West for children the world over helped give birth to the modern consumer market for toys.

Today, the proliferation and mass advertising of toys of all kinds, including war toys, is a reflection of our society's materialistic, consumption-oriented values. The United States toy market is the world's largest. In 1985 there were roughly 850 toy manufacturers, with 60,000 employees, producing an estimated 150,000 products for sale in 140,000 retail outlets. Five U.S. makers—Hasbro Products, Mattel Toys, Coleco Industries, Kenner Parker Toys, and Fisher-Price Toys—dominate the market, with 45 percent of sales (Owen, 1986: 67). About 50 percent of toy sales occur during the fourth quarter each year. The record year of 1985 produced sales of $12 billion for the industry. Although 1986 sales were flat, the industry's future is bright.

Societal trends outside the toy industry underlie continuing sales growth. The number of children between the ages of 4 and 12 is growing 10 percent annually. Their parents have rising disposable incomes, and the Toy Manufacturers Association reports that the average sum spent on toys for each child rose from $100 a year in 1980 to $175 in 1985. A growing number of remarriages multiply the number of parents and grandparents for some children further increasing spending on toys. And increasing life expectancy promises that grandparents will live longer and have more time to spoil grandchildren.

Other factors pushing up toy sales have come from within the industry. Discount retail chains, such as Toys "R" Us (where one of every six toy dollars in the U.S. is spent), have brought discount merchandising trends to the toy industry and have changed toys from a largely seasonal sales item to a year-round staple. This growth of toy discounters has, for example, forced big department stores that ten years ago set up a toy department only just before Christmas to keep a toy department all year. Otherwise, customers turn away permanently to the discounters. Toy manufacturers have, of course, zealously promoted their products in this fertile demographic and retailing climate. They spend up to $25 million to introduce new products, advertise heavily, and create and sell television cartoon series based on characters in their toy lines. These TV series have provoked enormous criticism because they blur the distinction between programming and advertising.

Finally, of course, the use of war objects as playthings may reflect the martial values of a society. German children learned war games at school until the end of World War I. Later, German parents of the World War II generation tried to deemphasize war toys and inculcate antimilitaristic values in their children. In a study involving European children, children from Austria, which has a strong military tradition, more often chose war toys over such playthings as animals and dolls than did children from Holland, which has a history of antimilitarism (Buettner, 1981: 107). In 1979, Sweden, another country with a strong antimilitarist tradition, banned the sale of war toys. Underlying pacifist values are similarly reflected in Swedish television programming, which has virtually no Westerns or crime/action series and where the use of violence to attract larger audiences is prohibited.

Attacks on Toys

Toy makers have been criticized through the ages—sometimes unfairly. In 1746, Jumping Jacks, the most popular toy in France, were banned because officials believed pregnant women who looked at their spindly limbs would give birth to deformed babies (Kaye, 1973: 167). Toys are geared to cultural values; when those values come under attack, so do toys that reflect them. In the United States many toy product lines have recently come under attack because of underlying changes in social values.

Toys that perpetuate racial and ethnic stereotypes are no longer appropriate, due to pressure from minority critics and widespread acceptance of principles of equality. For years toy manufacturers perpetuated racist images. Most toys mirrored white society. For instance, although a few black dolls were marketed, they were invariably slaves or minstrels, never authority figures. Writing in the *Journal of Black Psychology*, Doris Y. Wilkinson points out, "Creators of stereotyped Black toys have translated and incorporated the ideology, attitudes, and customs of a race-conscious social order," and this has been a "propaganda strategy that supported at the level of play the stigmatization of African-American males" (Wilkinson, 1980: 11). The damage of such stereotypes may be significant. In the mid-1960s a psychiatrist studying black children's self-images placed both black and white dolls in front of black children. The children invariably preferred to play with white dolls (Kaye, 1973: 82). Similarly, Kathleen and James McGinnis, authors of *Parenting for Peace and Justice*, criticize the toy industry for stereotyping Native Americans as warlike. They note that "packages of little plastic cowboys and Indians always have the Indians with rifles or tomahawks" (McGinnis and McGinnis, 1983: 63).

Feminists have accused toy manufacturers of perpetuating harmful sex-role stereotypes. Much criticism has been focused on Mattel's Barbie doll, one of the most successful mass appeal toys in history. In the early 1960s, Barbie and her male companion, a "dream date" named Ken, were marketed along with fashions and accessories. Both were white. Barbie's outfits reinforced traditional feminine roles such as "Friday Night Date," "Career Girl," "Dinner at 8," and "Sophisticated Lady." Ken's outfits reflected masculine roles such as "Dreamboat," "Campus Hero," and "Ski Champion." Feminists complained. Barbie was also accused of fostering the acquisitive instinct in little girls, who learned to manipulate their parents into getting more clothes and accessories for Barbie. Critics alleged this behavior might carry into adult life; women who had played with Barbie might pressure their husbands to buy things for them. Some found Barbie even more sinister. In 1966, Dr. Alan F. Leveton, director of the Pediatrics Mental Health Unit at the University of California Medical Center in San Francisco, said:

> We are seeing children who are excited and disturbed by dolls like Barbie and her friends. . . . Boys are being seen at the clinic who use Barbie for sexual stimulation, a fact which might trouble the same parents who are scandalized by comic books and pinball machines, were it not for the fact that Barbie masquerades as a child's toy. Both boys and girls are introduced to a precocious, joyless sexuality, to fantasies of seduction and to conspicuous consumption. This reflects and perpetuates a disturbing trend in our culture, which has serious mental-health complications (*National Peace Education Bulletin*, 1966: 2).

Barbie survived criticism and celebrated her twenty-ninth anniversary in 1988. Today's Barbie doll is, however, marketed in nonwhite, ethnic forms. There is a Hispanic Barbie and a black Barbie with hair that can be both straightened and curled.

In the 1960s and 1970s, the toy industry, like other industries, was attacked by consumer advocates. Toys were criticized for shoddy construction. Toy ads were said to exploit naive children and subvert parental authority. Toy companies stood accused of creating desires for tasteless merchandise such as bouncing eyeballs and ghoulish monsters. In 1971 a crusading critic named Edward M. Swartz pained toyland with a viciously critical book entitled *Toys That Don't Care*. Swartz meticulously slandered toys with electrical hazards, sharp points, or edges; toys that shot dangerous projectiles; toys that were too loud; toys that glamorized drug use; toys that were toxic if ingested; and toys that were extremely flammable or blew up. The toy industry, in short, shared the avalanche of ill will felt by other industries in the era of consumerism. One overzealous writer, caught up in the mean spirit of the day, even compared the toy industry to the auto industry, saying, "Both have the gall to blame the public for accidents: Detroit's scapegoat is the bad driver, while toy manufacturers say 'kids will be kids'" (Cross, 1971: 765). These criticisms created a market niche for sturdily constructed toys with sensible, educational themes. Companies such as Fisher-Price, a division of Quaker Oats, and Little Tykes now dominate this market segment. Other market niches have been filled by small companies that make toys representing social values important to specific market segments. For instance, a growing number of religious toys, such as Grace the Pro-Life Doll and Heroes of the Kingdom action figures from biblical times, are made by small companies that cater to fundamentalist Christians. Olmec Corp. markets a line of black, Hispanic, and Asian action figures which are advertised in magazines such as *Essence*. As a socially responsible gesture, Mattel markets a line of disabled dolls, Hal's Pals, and donates the proceeds to charities for disabled children.

Psychological Effects of War Toys

A recurrent criticism of toy sellers is that they encourage and glorify violence by selling toy guns and other war equipment. The criticism stems from timeless parental concern that war toys sold to impressionable boys aged three to ten (girls rarely play with them) (1) increase aggressive behavior; (2) embody the idea that conflict resolution through violent physical force is acceptable; (3) encourage development of militaristic attitudes in successive generations; (4) desensitize children to the brutality of killing and destruction; (5) foster the development of black and white, good guy–bad guy perceptions of conflict; and (6) legitimize hunting animals for sport. War toy manufacturers and sellers, say the critics, must bear moral responsibility for psychological damage in children and for the subsequent damage to peoples and nations that results from the predispositions to violence in adults who grew up with war toys.

Lines of action figures such as G.I. Joe, Masters of the Universe, and Marshall BraveStarr have attracted additional criticism. Action figures usually come with elaborate prepackaged legends or stories that tell children about the figures' personalities, backgrounds, and friendly or unfriendly dispositions. This theme-giving reduces the child's role in creating a play fantasy. In addition, the figures representing forces of evil, such as the outlaw Tex Hex in the Marshall BraveStarr line, are often strange and different in appearance. This pronounced dissimilitude teaches children that the enemy looks different and comes from a foreign place, a lesson children do not need at a time when people of dissimilar races, ethnic groups, and backgrounds come together in schools and neighborhoods. Children who are taught to associate evil with unfamiliar appearance may contribute to a growing xenophobia in American society.

But war toys are defended by some developmental psychologists, who argue that children naturally have aggressive instincts and that play warfare is a cathartic outlet. To appreciate this argument, it is necessary to understand the nature of child's play. Play serves important functions. Through play, children increase their knowledge of the world and learn to solve problems. They learn about society—its social roles, sex roles, and values—and experiment with adult behaviors to develop competence. In addition, children release energy and develop strength, coordination, logical reasoning, and abstract reasoning through play. Adherents of psychoanalytic development theories believe that, moreover, play enables children to resolve inner conflicts (Erikson, 1977). Hence, play prepares children for adulthood by allowing them to experiment with the complex social roles they will assume in modern American life.

Two examples of popular action figures. In 1987 the G.I. Joe® line was the best-selling toy in the United States. Random House photo by Stacey Pleasant.

In the 1930s, anthropologists observing a primitive African society, the Tale, concluded that as young boys playfully practiced shooting barbless arrows, they were preparing for adult responsibilities, which included hunting with deadly poisoned arrows (Schell and Hall, 1983). Similarly, children who play at doctoring, parenthood, or warfare may be engaging in important adaptive behavior. Play fighting is a common rehearsal for adult life among the young of animal species and human young may be genetically predisposed as well. Consider the experience of one German mother who tried to instill pacifist values in her children—an experience common in all cultures.

> Our children listened carefully and appeared to have understood what we were trying to teach them. But gradually and evidently independently of our endeavors their armoury in the play-room multiplied. We did not buy the plastic monsters of the Western or war kind for them, but they themselves took care of this "increase of

power" with their spending money and swapping, just to roam the streets and playgrounds in hordes, fully weaponed and wildly gesticulating—being sheriffs, TV detective heroes, cowboys, or gang leaders . . . how little they understand of the non-violence we were trying to explain to them all those years (Buettner, 1981: 104–105).

Nobody knows exactly why children develop a taste for guns and battle toys. Peer group pressure is a frequently cited factor. The appeal of active, adventurous play themes is another. Other explanations offered by psychologists are that the gun holds attraction as a phallic symbol, that young boys wish to multiply their power by using weapons, that war toys are intrinsically interesting gadgets, and that they symbolize problematic issues such as evil and death, which the child must learn to handle emotionally. A less subtle explanation, of course, is that the child is imitating the adult world.

Does play with war toys make children more aggressive? A small body of experimental research on children between the ages of four and eight years uniformly indicates that it does. Four studies have measured aggressive and antisocial behavior in children who have just played with war toys and in children who have played with neutral toys such as farm animals, dolls, or coloring books. The studies all show increased levels of "inappropriate" aggression and antisocial behavior among children who have just played with toys evocative of violence (Feshbach, 1956; Mendoza, 1972; Turner and Goldsmith, 1976; Wolf, 1976). These results are contrary to the so-called "catharsis hypothesis," which is that children playing games with war toys drain their aggression and are less aggressive afterward. The studies do not make clear how long the aggressive aftereffects of war play last. It is, of course, a nightmarish, currently unsolvable research problem to prove that playing with tanks and guns as a child causes the development of violence-prone, criminal, or militaristic attitudes in an adult. No experimental research projects address this topic. Among some who deal with children on a daily basis, however, there is an intuitive feeling that war toys engender aggressive behavior. For this reason, "Most preschools have rules that say children can't bring war toys to school because when they do it escalates fighting, kicking, and biting—behavior that is intended to inflict physical and psychological pain" (Dreyfuss, 1986).

The toy industry defends war toys. Toy manufacturers claim that toys teach lessons about patriotism, forces of good and evil, and the nature of war—all unalterable elements of adult life. Toy makers operate in a very competitive market, and there is perennial demand for war toys. Stiff competition ensures that some manufacturers will fill demand even if others voluntarily give up war-toy revenue. (One critic scoffs at this defense, saying: "No one argues that a drug pusher is a wholly innocent third party providing a neutral service; so also, if the country is addicted to war and violence, we cannot rationally view the toy industry's role as simply one of catering impersonally to this addiction" [Swartz, 1971: 71].) Says Stewart Sims, formerly an Ideal Toys executive, "it is not a toy company's role to create an artificial society, one that doesn't exist. Because if we did that, we would be superimposing our own values on the world" (Shorrock,

1983: 14). Another spokesperson for the toy industry, Penny Richman, says bluntly: "Playthings correspond to what's going on in society" (Kooi, 1986).

Changing Values and War Toys

Attitudes toward war toys have varied in the United States. A few protests were organized during World War I. Despite the level of global carnage in World War II, that conflict did not elicit attacks on toy makers (with the exception of a few angry parents who destroyed toys imported from Germany). A helpful pamphlet on child rearing published during the war even suggested that parents appreciated war play. "Boys have always played games that gave release to their war-like feelings," it said, adding that "a certain amount of such play is needed by most normal young males at any time" (Child Study Association, 1942: 9).

After 1945 demand for war toys grew steadily. Some toy companies, such as Lone Star Products and Parris Manufacturing, specialized in making guns for children. G.I. Joe, a foot-high doll introduced by Hasbro Industries in 1946, is one of the best-selling toys of all time and epitomized the kind of war toy that is popular in a victorious, patriotic nation pursuing an expansionist foreign policy based on military alliances.

There is evidence that attitudes toward war toys were lenient in the early 1960s. A 1963 survey of nursery school classes at Pacific Oaks University in Pasadena, California, indicated that 90 percent of teachers and students, 84 percent of mothers, and 79 percent of fathers agreed that "children should be allowed to use guns." Only eleven mothers and fathers out of 139 surveyed felt that children should "never be allowed to use guns" (Polifroni, 1964: 13).

But later in the decade a confluence of historical forces altered American attitudes toward war toys. The assassinations of John F. Kennedy, Martin Luther King, and Robert Kennedy—combined with widespread crime and racial violence—fostered strongly negative feelings toward guns. Guns, and handguns in particular, were seen as the major culprit behind domestic violence in America. Furthermore, the dismal, prolonged military involvement in Vietnam deprived patriots of a victory to rally around and soured public attitudes toward the military. Unlike the G.I. of World War II, the Vietnam veteran was not a national hero.

Changed public attitudes pulled the rug out from under gun and war toy sales. Toy stores such as F. A. O. Schwarz adopted policies of not carrying such merchandise. Later, chain stores such as Sears, Marshall Field & Co., and K Mart Corp. followed suit. Hasbro furloughed the G.I. Joe product line in 1976 when orders virtually ceased. Toy makers began to emphasize new electronic products and video games.

A parallel movement occurred in Europe. In 1969, Pope Paul VI admonished European toy manufacturers for failing to accept moral responsibility for toys that invited dangerous attitudes and aggressiveness. In Austria, Kinderfreunde, an organization concerned with child rearing, campaigned for a ban on war toys. In West Germany, the minister of justice called on toy manufacturers to reduce the volume of war toys produced. And two international organizations, the International Playground Association and the World Council of Organizations of the Teaching Profession, took up the campaign to stop production of war toys.

But times change. By the late 1970s the market for toy guns had returned in the United States. Experts attributed a sales rise of 32 percent in 1979 to such factors as fading memories of Vietnam, the advent of peaceful times, and the popularity of a few hit Western films. Between 1980 and 1982, sales of guns and other war toys tripled to an estimated $325 million. By 1985, they had tripled again, to over $1 billion (LaFranchi, 1986). Again, events in the larger society explained the changed consumption pattern. The Reagan administration's emphasis on defense preparedness placed weapons in the news. The trials of U.S. Marines in Lebanon and the successful invasion of Grenada kindled new feelings of patriotism. In the spring of 1986 America's patriotic pride was rekindled by an air attack against Libya. Two hit movies starring Sylvester Stallone portrayed a lone heroic figure battling communism and terrorists.

Toy companies were quick to exploit this growing interest. Hasbro, for example, brought back the G.I. Joe product line in 1982 as a "Mobile Strike Force Team," modeled on the rapid deployment force concept that was emergent in the strategic thinking of the U.S. armed services. In its new incarnation the G.I. Joe doll was heavily advertised on television, and late in 1982, it became the beestselling toy advertised on television in the country. The G.I. Joe line conforms to a new emphasis on antiterrorist and commando warfare in war toys. In keeping with the trend, Lionel Corp. has made it possible to have a "Commando Assault" train set under the Christmas tree. Playco Toys manufactures an "Attack Force Green Beret 'A Team' Leader Weapons Set" featuring a "'Battle Sound' Uzi Submachine Gun." The set contains a commando knife, grenade, and the gun. Coleco Industries cashed in on the Rambo craze with a line of toys that included bicycle horns shaped to resemble hand grenades.

Shortly before Christmas 1985, an international war toy boycott was started in Canada. It spread throughout the United States and Europe. At one time, over 100 groups were involved, including antiwar groups such as the New England War Resisters' League, groups against violence such as Action for Children's Television, and a California group led by peace activist Jerry Rubin. The boycott continued into the 1986 Christmas season but had no measurable effect on the booming market for endless permutations of toy guns and action figures. An early boycott publication, *The Mobilizer*, preached, "These toys teach children that war is an acceptable way to settle disputes, and that killing others is a perfectly honorable profession" (*Mobilizer*, 1985). Thomas Radecki, a psychiatrist who heads the National Coalition on Television Violence, estimated that in 1986 the average child saw 800 war-toy advertisements and 250 war-toy programs on television (LaFranchi, 1986).

The boycott and criticism of war toys are signs that the resurgence of the war toy market comes at a time when many parents are deeply concerned about the psychological trauma of the nuclear arms race on children. In addition to conventional weapons, the systematic elves of the toy industry make replicas of doomsday weapons, such as Revell's B1B bomber, Polaris submarine plastic model kits, and Estes Industries' solid fuel-propelled Pershing rocket and cruise missile models. Many parents must make a difficult choice. Should they deny war toys to children, thereby creating the allure of forbidden fruit? Or should they allow their offspring to arm themselves and thereby conform to playground trends, although perhaps diminishing their ability to resolve future conflicts nonviolently? Toy manufacturers are determined to give parents this choice.

Questions

1. Do you favor banning war toys? Given the state of competition in the toy industry, will voluntary restraints serve to make fewer objectionable toys available? What guidelines for industry would you suggest?
2. Visit a toy store. Are there any war toys in it that offend you as a consumer or parent? Which ones?
3. Do toy companies have an ethical responsibility not to sell war toys? What measure of responsibility do parents have if children use them?
4. Do you think that war toys inflict psychological harm on children? Why or why not? Is televised violence an equal or greater cause of violent behavior in children?
5. Should the toy industry have anticipated the charges of critics over the past twenty-five years? How can the industry examine changes in its environment today to anticipate future criticism and prepare for it with socially responsible marketing and strategy?
6. What changing values in society today portend changed attitudes toward either war toys or other kinds of toys tomorrow?

CHAPTER **10**

INSTITUTIONALIZING SOCIAL CONCERNS IN BUSINESS

 The Hewlett-Packard Company (HP) is a major designer and manufacturer of more than 10,000 products and systems in computers, calculators, test equipment, medical equipment, and scientific instrumentation. In 1986 it ranked as the fifty-first largest industrial corporation in the United States, with total orders of $6.4 billion and net earnings of $489 million. Slightly less than half of its business is generated outside the United States. The company employs 84,000 people.

It is corporate policy at HP "to honor our obligations to society by being an economic, intellectual, and social asset to each nation and each community in which we operate." This purpose has been institutionalized through philanthropic and employee-volunteer programs. HP is among the top half-dozen largest philanthropic donors among industrial corporations, with a total of about $50 million in 1987. The largest part of the company's grants program is in equipment.

The company's executive committee and foundation set broad policies for the grants program. The grants are implemented through a network of committees and individual employee initiatives at all levels in the corporation. There are four main categories of programs at HP.

Community grants are made to service agencies (e.g., health, arts, and other services) located in the immediate neighborhoods of the divisions of the company. Each division makes its own decisions about such grants through a Community Contributions Committee, in which employee membership rotates periodically. Both cash and equipment grants are made.

National grants contribute to the development of science, engineering, technology and medicine. Programs include equipment grants to education; engineering and computer-science faculty development and faculty loan programs; science- and engineering-oriented affirmative action contributions; philanthropic underwritings of university high-technology centers; and cash and equipment grants to nationally active, nonacademic organizations in the arts and human service fields when creative bridges between the sciences and the humanities can be built. Various committees at company headquarters and in the divisions share in making decisions about these grants.

A third set of programs matches employees' philanthropic cash donations. HP matches (one to one) employee gifts to such organizations as United Way and universities. It matches three to one employee gifts of equipment to both public and private educational institutions.

Finally, HP makes direct equipment contributions and cash awards in countries in which it does business and where such donations are permitted.

Some of the financing for these programs comes from the HP foundation, and some of it is included in the annual budgets of the divisions of the company as operating expenses, not philanthropy. Most of HP's grants are to education. Indeed, HP ranks in the top three or four companies in the nation in the size of its contributions to education. In addition to equipment and cash donations, the HP programs include many voluntary employee contributions. Employees get involved with schools and colleges after a grant is made. This involvement takes many forms, such as helping teachers in the use of the equipment donated, serving on curriculum committees, and teaching. HP encourages other organizations to become involved in community-support programs. For example, the American Electronics Association recently funded a $6 million program to aid doctoral engineering candidates, following a program started by HP.

Hewlett-Packard is one of many companies to show its social concern actively. In the 1970s, corporations began weaving a bright thread of social concern into the conservative tapestry of existing policy and strategy. In the late 1970s, larger corporations had formalized a variety of programs to inject social concerns in decision making. This trend has continued, and today more and more firms have institutionalized the social point of view. This chapter is concerned with important aspects of this institutionalization.

PATTERNS OF CORPORATE RESPONSE TO SOCIAL DEMANDS

Historically, prevailing philosophical attitudes and patterns of external pressure on corporations have shaped business's social responses. Hay and Gray (1974) have written that the social perspectives of management evolved through three phases—the profit-maximizing phase of the late 1800s, the trusteeship phase of the 1920s and 1930s, and the quality-of-life phase beginning in the 1970s. Murphy (1978), on the other hand, sees four eras of social responsibility: (1) the philanthropic era lasting up to the early 1950s, in which corporate responsibilities were largely met through charitable contributions; (2) the awareness era from 1953 to 1967, in which corporations recognized new obligations and became involved in urban affairs; (3) the issue era from 1968 to 1973, in which corporations focused efforts on alleviating problems in issue areas such as pollution, racism, urban decay, and controversial technology; and (4) the responsiveness era from 1974 on, in which corporations are institutionalizing routines and procedures for responding to social pressures. Carroll argues that over the last century, the relative importance of discretionary, ethical, and legal obligations has dramatically increased across the board in industry (1981). These observations by several authors reinforce an intuitive feeling that despite considerable variation among individual businesses, there were broad similarities in the voluntary responses of industry to social demands during successive historical eras.

When focus shifts to individual corporations, a variety of responses to social pressures is evident. We believe that response patterns can be classified into five dominant categories. First is *rejection.* In this stance, a company denies any obligation whatsoever to engage in any social responsibilities beyond obeying the law and operating economically and efficiently. This is, of course, a negative and unplanned approach.

Second is *reaction.* For example, in the early 1970s, Firestone Tire & Rubber first marketed the ill-starred Firestone 500 steel belted radial tire. Over a six-year period, the excessive failure rate of these tires led to at least thirty-four deaths, sixty injuries, and hundreds of accidents. Firestone resisted early efforts by the National Highway Traffic Safety Administration to force remedial action but ultimately had to conduct two huge recall campaigns.

Third is *defense.* Following the 1982 midterm elections, business was heavily criticized for massive campaign contributions made through political action committees. On December 7, a month after the elections, Mobil Corporation ran an advertisement in newspapers around the country defending political action committees and saying in part that the company was "outraged by the false characterization of business-organized political action committees as spenders of shareholders' money to exert undue pressure on the workings of democratic government."

Fourth is *accommodation.* An experience of Coca-Cola Co. illustrates this response mode. In 1980, Coca-Cola planned a national contest to promote its new soft drink, Mr. PiBB, in which a "Mr. PiBB Girl" would be selected. This woman was to be chosen based on her resemblance to a composite picture of five actresses. She was to have the eyes of Susan Anton, NBC's "Golden Girl"; the mouth of Debby Boone, daughter of singer Pat Boone; the hair of Pam Dawber, star of *Mork and Mindy;* the face shape of Melissa Sue Anderson of *Little House on the Prairie;* and the nose of actress Kristy McNichol. Coca-Cola U.S.A. was forced to withdraw this contest after Atlanta bottlers refused to participate and a black school principal in Chicago raised questions about racial bias. All the women were Caucasian (Carroll, 1981).

Fifth is *proaction,* or the making of an anticipatory response designed to prevent criticism. For example, Monsanto Co. responded to public fear of chemicals and strict new medical and environmental tests used by government agencies by setting up a "devil's chemicals project" to examine existing products for trace contaminants of dangerous chemicals such as dioxin. It is company policy at Monsanto to assess formally possible hazards of a new substance or material at multiple stages of research and development. Included in this category would be participation of the members of the Business Roundtable.

These stages, of course, are artificially isolated instances on a broad continuum of corporate social concern and response. In between complete rejection at one end and utter devotion to exemplary social performance at the other, one finds a wide range of types of reaction and proaction. We believe that in the years to come, the current era will be seen as one in which corporations, especially the larger ones, became increasingly anticipatory in their response to social concerns and sought actively to influence public debates about important matters affecting business.

INSTITUTIONALIZING SOCIAL ACTION IN CORPORATE DECISION MAKING

From a societal view, as well as from the view of top managers who accept the idea of social responsibilities for their firms, it is desirable to have the social point of view institutionalized. This means that once a top social policy has been formulated, its implementation becomes a part of the day-to-day, routine decision-making processes throughout the company. Managers consider it in their decision making without continuous surveillance by higher-level managers. When an activity is not institutionalized, it is likely to be periodic, separate from the critical activities of the business, easily forgotten by busy managers, and perhaps controversial.

It is important to recall from the last chapter three types of social action programs. First are the programs pursued because of legislation, such as equal opportunity or safety. In this category also are programs undertaken because of contractual arrangements with labor unions, such as those concerning equitable hiring, promoting, and firing of employees. The second category includes company social programs that top management decides voluntarily to undertake. Included here would be programs initiated by managers in the organization without pressure from inside or outside. Also included would be programs undertaken as a result of pressures from groups inside or outside. In the third category are social programs undertaken by managers throughout an organization on a voluntary basis and not dictated by higher-level managers.

If a company is to avoid legal penalties for noncompliance, it must, in the case of the first class of actions, establish policies, plans, procedures, control mechanisms, and incentives to ensure that goals are achieved in conformance with law and contract. In this way, the social program is entwined in the decision-making processes of the company, from top to bottom. If this is not done and if top management does not continuously survey activities, lower-level managers may sabotage the program if they find themselves in opposition to it on value, economic, or other grounds.

Similarly, actions of the second type may not be undertaken in organizations even when policy has been announced, in the absence of implementation procedures, rewards, and penalties. The problem here is somewhat different, however, because here the motivating force results from greater top-management interest and not from any legal compulsion. Lower-level managers not in complete sympathy with the program may be more difficult to persuade than when legal sanctions are involved. This is especially true, as noted below, if social goals and manager-financial goals are in conflict.

Finally, it is even more difficult for top managers to get lower-level managers to act in the third category if they are not disposed to do so. There is a world of difference between lofty top management rhetoric at high levels of abstraction —"Olympian megathoughts," as one manager put it—and specific actions on the front lines of lower-level managers.

Because of such considerations, most companies begin the pursuit of voluntary social programs gradually and only slowly develop full-scale programs by means of which they become institutionalized in the decision-making process. Before we examine this transition, it is worthwhile to comment further about why there is resistance to institutionalizing social programs (both government-dictated and voluntarily undertaken) in many companies.

REALITIES OF INJECTING VOLUNTARY SOCIAL ACTION INTO THE DECISION-MAKING PROCESS

Chief executives of companies are thought to have extraordinary power to get things done in their enterprises. When asked about their power, however, they begin talking about how little power they have. President John Kennedy used to comment frequently to visitors: "I agree with you, but I cannot speak for the State Department." What he meant was that even with all the power at his command, he found it difficult to move the State Department to act as he wanted it to act. Much the same problem exists for the chief executive of a large company.

Every organization has a culture. It is composed of the styles and behavior of managers and other personnel; shared values of people in the organization ("the way we do things around here"); the policies and strategies of the organization; the skills and capabilities of personnel from managers to workers; the composition and functioning of staffs; the structure of organizational units, such as divisions and departments; and the systems which bind operations together, such as the accounting, budgeting, and informational systems.

Top executives have an important hand in the design and operation of such a total system, but they also must operate within the culture. The power of chief executives is restrained because they know that if they force a significant change in the culture, the results may not be entirely what they want. There are serious risks in trying to change a culture quickly. This does not mean that chief executives do not have power. They do. It means that wise managers exercise their power very carefully and, if possible, gradually and with the concurrence of others in the company.

If the complex culture of a corporation has not taken social concerns into consideration in decision-making processes, the decision of top management to do so may seriously conflict with traditional ways of doing things in that company. The gap between top management's concept of needed social responsiveness and the traditional managerial processes may be broad and difficult to bridge.

This point was confirmed by an exhaustive study of Robert Ackerman (1975), when he was a professor at the Harvard Business School. He found that the institutionalization processes ran into three major difficulties:

1. The separation of corporate and division responsibilities was threatened.

2. The planning and control systems were inadequate to evaluate and explain social responsiveness.

3. The executive performance, evaluation, and reward processes did not recognize performance in terms of social concern.

These findings are as applicable today as when the study was made.

To these barriers we should add attitudinal resistance. A traditional response of many managers, when faced with pressures to do something new, is to deal with the matter in an ad hoc, fire-fighting mode on the assumption that the issue is temporary and will go away. Another form of resistance is to deal with such new pressures through a typical public-relations effort. If managers hold the classical managerial ideology, as described in previous chapters, they have deep mental resistances that naturally challenge institutionalization of the social view.

A CONCEPTUAL MODEL FOR MANAGING SOCIAL RESPONSIVENESS

The model in Exhibit 10-1 shows that the process of institutionalization moves through a series of phases. The process begins with a growing concern of top management about a social matter that may have potentially significant impact on the company. Top management also may wish to deal with a social issue even though it may not have a direct and important impact on the firm's operations. Top management then makes a commitment to action and formulates a policy that will guide corporate decision making.

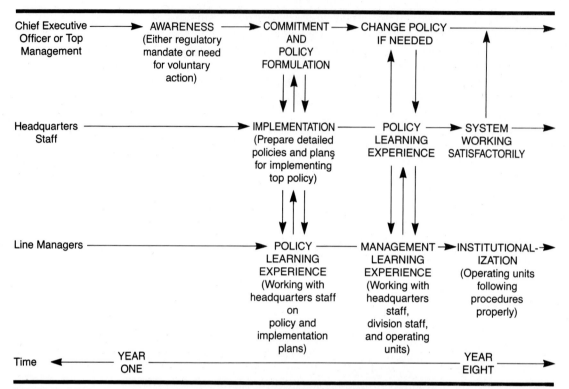

EXHIBIT 10–1   A CONCEPTUAL MODEL OF THE PROCESS OF INSTITUTIONALIZING THE SOCIAL POINT OF VIEW IN A LARGE DIVISIONALIZED CORPORATION

In a second phase, policies and plans are developed by staff personnel with continuous dialogue among top managers and division managers. The objective of this process is to make sure that the policies and plans are appropriate and can be implemented effectively and efficiently. If any important problems surface, the policies and plans are modified.

In a third phase, tactical plans are translated into specific procedures and rules and become part of the daily decision-making routine of operating personnel. This administrative learning experience should serve to eliminate problems and assure smooth implementation of company policy and plans.

In the fourth phase, the system is working satisfactorily and the policy is fully institutionalized.

This is, of course, a highly simplified model of what actually happens in a company. Both Ackerman (1975) and Murray (1976) in their studies of this process concluded that it took eight years to fully institutionalize into the decision-making processes the social programs that they had studied. This seems like an excessive amount of time. It is long, but consider the time it actually takes to overcome the many barriers to institutionalization discussed above. Add to this the problems of managers in trying to determine what they should do, for example, to implement government programs that are not clear, not fully understood, conflicting, and subject to change. This sort of situation is typical with new government regulations. In this light, it is not at all remarkable that institutionalizing new programs takes so long. Considering the experience of the past ten years with social programs, however, the institutionalizing process should not take as long today in the typical company.

MAKING OPERATIONAL THE SOCIAL POINT OF VIEW

As we have pointed out, the institutionalization process involves all important aspects of corporate management. Space does not permit examination of all the programs that a company employs in institutionalizing social programs, and so we focus only on the most significant ones.

Formulating Social Policy and Strategy

The basic philosophy and frame of reference of the top management in a corporation are of basic importance in formulating social policy. This philosophy is generally expressed in the formulation of a company's statement of mission or in its creed. Most of our large corporations include in such statements strong objectives about social concerns. We noted Hewlett-Packard's statement at the beginning of this chapter. Most major corporations have similar policy statements. For instance, General Motors managers carry with them a 3- by 5-inch card entitled "General Motors Guiding Principles." There are eleven principles, and the final one is: "We will participate in all societies in which we do business as a responsible and ethical citizen, dedicated to continuing social and economic progress." Johnson & Johnson's credo states: "We are responsible to the communities in which we live and work and to the world community as well. We must be good citizens—support good works and charities and bear our fair share of taxes. We must encourage civic improvements and better health and education."

Top Management Leadership

When taken seriously, such policies are powerful forces in assuring that decision making will reflect social concerns throughout an organization. If top management does not express and show by action its commitment to such policies, there will be indifferent, or no implementations of them in the organization. This is not an easy responsibility to discharge, for reasons noted previously. It requires constant attention and leadership by top managers, beginning with the chief executive officer. It requires, in addition, attuning the corporate culture to social concerns, making the necessary organizational changes, training and selecting managers for social concerns, relating performance measurement and reward systems to social concerns, and developing informational flows that reflect social concerns in the community and corporate actions.

Changing the Corporate Culture

Institutionalizing social concerns in decision-making processes requires important alterations in the corporate culture. The CEO must take the lead in this effort. It may involve changes in all of the elements of a corporate culture that were identified above. This difficult task can be and has been done very successfully (Kanter, 1983; Schein, 1985).

Donald R. Stephenson, Director of Corporate Communications at Dow Chemical Canada, Inc., describes how he and his staff went about "changing the attitudes of a lot of hard-nosed, profit-oriented management people" (1983: 319). Stephenson believed that top-level Dow managers, such as former chairman Carl Gerstacker, had socially enlightened attitudes but that these attitudes had not yet seized the hearts and minds of middle management. He and his staff put together several hundred copies of a book intriguingly entitled *Dow's Secret Weapons*, which was a collection of elevating quotations from speeches by important Dow executives and prominent scholars on subjects such as profits, relations with external groups, corporate objectives, and people development. The preface stated that the material in the book represented Dow operating philosophy.

Rather than distribute this publication widely, Stephenson planted copies with a few sympathetic managers and let word leak out that copies of the book were available, but only on request. "Lo and behold," said Stephenson, *"Dow's Secret Weapons* became over many months a prized acquisition among hundreds of managers, its contents used in many a presentation, and the philosophies employed in hundreds of ways right down to the grass roots" (Stephenson, 1983: 319). This is an interesting story, and undoubtedly the book had a significant influence in changing attitudes at Dow. However, much more in a company's culture needs to follow changes in attitudes. Changing attitudes is central to making changes throughout the culture, but it is not enough in itself.

Managerial Selection and Rewards

In interviews with top executives, the point was frequently made to the senior author that among other traditional requirements for promotion, managers have to have some sensitivity to sociopolitical forces (G. Steiner, 1983).

The socially sensitive manager must be supported by an appropriate evaluation and reward system. Middle managers in corporations typically are evaluated and rewarded on the basis of short-range financial performance. Under such conditions, it is difficult to convince the middle manager that long-range trends or social concerns are relevant to job success. In addition, middle managers are at a different stage in their life cycle from top managers; they relate differently to family and community responsibilities and are perhaps more concerned than senior managers with personal career goals as opposed to broad organizational goals.

This being the case, compliance with social policy may take a back seat to achievement of quarterly goals. Some companies deal with the short-term performance myopia of middle management by making social performance part of the reward structure. For example, nonfinancial objectives may be set for minority hiring, government relations, and community involvement. Objectives are specific enough that performance can be measured. A proportion of incentive pay (say 50 percent) is given for good performance in meeting these objectives. Nonfinancial objectives differ according to the manager's job, but in the case of a plant manager, they might be heavily weighted toward environmental protection and health and safety goals. If social actions involve out-of-pocket costs, a manager's profit objectives should be adjusted accordingly.

Managerial Training Programs

Companies make available to managers a variety of training programs. Rogene Buchholz (1980) surveyed companies about their educational programs with environmental or public policy content and found many different programs, including: sending managers to university seminars, conferences, and institutes that deal with public-policy matters; sending managers to advanced management programs, in which public-policy material constitutes part of the content; scheduling management retreats and seminars, some of which deal with public-policy issues; involving employees in the creation of social programs for the company; assigning employees to the company's charitable-foundation advisory committee; and inviting university faculty to speak before management groups about public issues.

Organizational Changes

Structural changes are confirmation of the institutionalization of social responsiveness. Structural changes may begin at the very top of the organization, on the board of directors' level.

A company that is seriously concerned with social affairs may add to the board one or more directors with a broad social point of view. This is not a suggestion that such directors "represent" society but that they bring the societal view to the top decision-making level of the company.

Many companies have created board committees to direct social policy. In 1970, General Motors Corporation created the Public Policy Committee composed of five outside members of the GM board. The committee meets once a month and has made recommendations to the GM management, covering a wide range of subject matter. It has no direct power, but the committee has been highly influential in getting social programs under way at GM. Other companies having comparable board committees are Ford Motor Company, IBM, Kimberly

Clark, and Philip Morris. We discuss these committees more extensively in Chapter 20.

More and more companies, particularly large ones, are setting up special staff departments to handle matters related to social issues. A survey of 192 larger companies, in 1977, revealed that 31 percent had established a permanent department (or departments) that was responsible for dealing with recurring social decisions and making policy recommendations (Holmes, 1977: 4). A similar survey, in 1981, showed that of 400 responses, 361 firms had public affairs departments (Public Affairs Research Group, 1981). More than 50 percent of existing public-affairs offices have been created since 1970.

The public-affairs function of a company embraces those activities that it pursues to accommodate the political, social, and economic environment in which it operates. This activity is somewhat different from the traditional public relations function, which is concerned with the evaluation of public attitudes and the execution of programs to enhance image and product acceptance. The public-affairs function may include the public-relations function, but it covers a greater area. In some companies, however, the public-affairs function is placed under the jurisdiction of the public-relations unit; in others, the public-relations unit is under the public-affairs unit; in still others, the two are separated. The well-developed public-affairs function encompasses the following major areas: government relations, community relations, social forecasting and planning activities, corporate communications, and public-issues management. We comment in the next sections on the forecasting and issues-management functions. We discuss the other functions elsewhere in the book.

EVALUATING ENVIRONMENTS

Information provided in what are called *environmental assessments (EAs)* is a strategic element in a corporation's development of social programs. Most companies develop information about the social environment within broad environmental analyses that encompass all areas of importance to a company. Sometimes, however, separate evaluations are made only of the social environment.

It is important to note at the outset that this is a messy area of analysis. There is no uniformity in definitions, purposes of analyses, organizational arrangements for making EAs, techniques of analysis and evaluation, the uses of results in decision making, the scope of evaluations, or the design of evaluations and use systems. We believe that the following discussion captures the essence of theory and practice in the field, but there is no consensus about either.

The Spectrum of Environmental Analyses

Because most social environmental analyses (SEAs) are made in larger, total environmental analyses (TEAs), it is informative to consider the broader frame of reference. TEAs encompass four major areas of analysis—economic, technical, political, and social.

Traditionally, environmental analyses contained mostly economic evaluations of such matters as GNP, prices, markets, interest rates, availability of raw materials, and so on. The most important part of TEAs today is the economic analysis. In recent years, surveillance of the technical environment of a company has received increasing attention. This surveillance involves review of such factors as potential new discoveries in the physical sciences of interest to a company, new engineering improvements in products by competitors, new materials that could improve a product, or new product designs that can cut costs of production and/or improve product performance. The economic and technical areas of environmental surveillance are still dominant in today's TEAs.

With the growth of multinational companies, it became increasingly important for managers to have detailed understanding of the political and social changes taking place in the countries in which they were doing business. As a consequence, political-risk analysis was incorporated in the TEAs and often made independently of but in complement to the economic and technical analysis. Political-risk analysis involves examination of all political and social forces of interest to a company in the geographic areas in which it does business. Such evaluations may include economic, technical, and social forces as well as political forces. We shall return to political-risk analysis in Chapter 19.

Even more recently, corporations have become aware of the great significance of understanding the impact of changing social forces on their companies. SEAs have, therefore, become a part of the TEAs and, as we said above, are also done independently of economic and technical studies. SEAs place emphasis on the early detection of major changes in such forces as social attitudes, laws, life styles, social norms, and so on. They focus particularly on areas of special interest to the company, such as changes in values of consumers; style preferences of consumers; and attitudes of people generally about such matters as day-care centers for working mothers, quality of work life, ethical standards in business, and so on.

In sum, comprehensive environmental analyses made today in more and more companies encompass four major, interrelated areas. They become basic premises in the strategic planning processes of corporations. This means they are fundamental in the development of company policies, strategies, tactical operating plans, and decision making.

An Environmental Analysis Model

To sharpen the focus on the role of SEAs in decision making, we present a simplified model of EA in Exhibit 10-2. Because we have discussed the content of the block on the left of the chart, we move to organizational responsibility for making EAs.

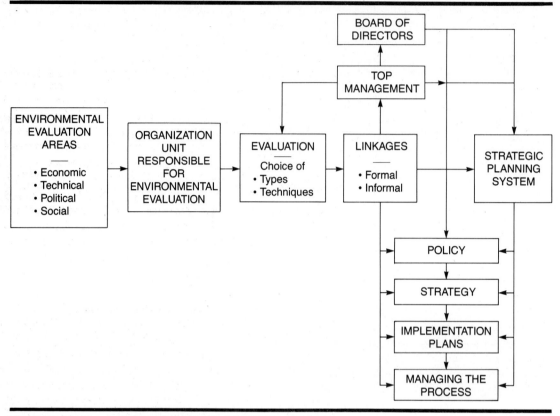

EXHIBIT 10-2   ENVIRONMENTAL ANALYSIS MODEL

Who Makes the Evaluations?   Economic and technical evaluations typically are made in corporate planning units or special staff units, such as the office of the chief economist or the office of the chief scientist. Only the largest corporations have such special staffs. When a corporation evaluates the social and political environment, the public-affairs department often is responsible. A few of our largest corporations have special staffs to make SEAs (Lenz and Engledow, 1986). Even in studies by these staffs, economic and technical trends may be reviewed, although the main focus is on social and political forces.

Social and Political Evaluation Types and Techniques   The social and political evaluation of the environment proceeds, of course, from specifications of the type of evaluation to be made and techniques to be employed. Here we identify two major types: macro focus and functional focus. The latter focuses on a specific current task or future concern about a product or service of an operating unit. For example, the analysis might focus on how changing social attitudes of consumers will affect the sale, design, price, etc., of a particular product. The macro focus is concerned with broader topics, such as emerging issues that may have an impact on company strategy. These issues include the changing attitudes of people in organizations, women's rights, and demands for more federal regulation of advertising.

The Choice of Techniques in SEA   The palette of analytical techniques that can be employed is large. Techniques range from the purely intuitive to the comprehensive, systematic, and interdisciplinary. We shall return shortly to an examination of the methods typically used in business today.

Communicating Results   Next in the model are linkages, the connections between the results of the analysis and managerial thinking and planning. In Exhibit 10–2, we identify two types of linkage, formal and informal. Formal linkages are prescribed procedures for the passage and use of information. They might, for example, be incorporated as a systematic ingredient in a formal strategic planning process, or they might be a specified periodic reporting to top management. The informal linkage, as the name implies, is a more casual, ad hoc, passage of information, such as communications with either top management or the corporate planning staff in informal meetings.

Because the public-affairs staff is frequently involved in making social and political environmental evaluations, we should say more about its activities. The Public Affairs Research Group (1981). School of Management, Boston University, examined comprehensively the functions of the typical public-affairs office and found that it was deeply involved in: 1. identifying public issues for corporate attention; 2. setting priorities for dealing with these issues; 3. providing forecasts of social and political trends to corporate planning staff, divisions, and departments; and 4. reviewing corporate and division plans for sensitivity to emerging social and political trends. For all these activities, the public affairs officers believed that their influence on planning was substantial.

Exhibit 10–2 shows that there is a linkage between top management, including the board of directors, and the strategic planning system. This linkage can take many forms, such as the establishment of policy and strategy for action in the social-political area or discussions that may influence planning in the company. The chart also shows that top management may, in the absence of a well-formulated strategic planning process, directly establish policy and strategy for implementation.

The Strategic Planning System   In most large companies, there is some type of formal strategic planning system. Formal strategic planning is, in essence, the systematic identification of opportunities and threats that lie in the future environment (external and internal) which, in combination with other relevant data (e.g., company strengths and weaknesses), provides a basis for a company's making better current decisions to exploit the perceived opportunities and to avoid the threats. It is an orderly process which, to simplify, sets forth basic objectives to be achieved, strategies and policies needed to reach the objectives, and tactical plans to make sure that strategies are properly implemented. It is a structure of plans. The structure and linkages among plans vary from company to company and from time to time in the same company. Formal strategic planning enables companies to respond in an organized way to increasingly complex market and social forces and to do so in a way that is in keeping with internal resources and managerial philosophy. When social issues are part of strategic thinking in the planning process, social responsiveness tends to be included in corporate strategy, policy, and decision making.

Implementing Social/Political Policies and Strategies We need not dwell on the remainder of our model. Policy and strategy formulated either in the planning process or in an ad hoc manner really are useless without implementation. The entire management process must be addressed to assuring that the policies and strategies are carried out. This means the creation of detailed tactical plans and managerial supervision of these plans.

The Multiple Purposes of Social/Political EAs The fact that social and political evaluations have so many different but important purposes leads to much experimentation in processes employed in making them, organizational arrangements for their evaluation and use, and flows of information about the evaluations. Some of the important uses of these evaluations are as follows:

- They help to clarify the future range of uncertainty in the sociopolitical environment for managerial thinking.

- They make explicit basic assumptions about the future and assure that the assumptions are consistent and creditable.

- They force consideration of alternative futures in place of reliance on a single projection.

- They identify major threats and opportunities so that risks can be contained, crises avoided, and opportunities exploited.

- They provide a context for evaluating strategies.

- They provide mind-stretching exercises for managers and staff. This is an educational purpose but also may help to assure that managers focus on environment continuously rather than sporadically, systematically rather than randomly.

- They train managers and staff to be more sensitive to and to be better able to assess systematically the evolving environment of the company.

- They provide a basis on which managers can set priorities for the company's attention to sociopolitical issues.

- They help managers to understand the general forces in government and society that may affect the company.

The Scope and Methodology of EAs We noted above the difference between the macro and micro, or functional, focus. Scope may also differ in breadth of analysis. Some studies may be made for a comparatively narrow range of subject matter, such as changing consumer preferences or interest rates. Other studies may cover the four main areas in a TEA. The time frame of EAs also ranges from the few years to come to well into the twenty-first century. Both the scope and time frame heavily depend on the purposes of the study.

EAs may be done on an irregular, regular, or continuous basis. Irregular EAs tend to be ad hoc, crisis inititated, reactive, and focused on the near term. Regular EAs are periodically updated studies of selected events, proactive, and near term. Continuous EAs are carefully structured systems, covering a broad range of environments and long periods of time (Fahey, King, and Narayanan, 1981).

The range of methodology used in EAs is very wide. For economic analysis and technical EAs, for example, many qualitative and quantitative computer-based methods may be used. For SEAs, or for EAs in which the major focus is sociopolitical and the range far into the future, the most widely used method by far is the intuitive search. The next most widely employed method is scenario construction. Other widely used techniques are systematic qualitative search, Delphi, trend analysis, cross-impact analysis, and impact/probability matrix. Any two or all of these techniques often are used in the preparation of a comprehensive scenario. Before discussing each of these methods, we should mention that nomenclature in this area varies widely, among both academicians and practitioners. For example, scenarios have been referred to as futures research, futures explorations, alternative futures, survey research, scanning, exploratory planning, and environmental forecast, among others.

Intuitive Search   This technique is used by all managers who concern themselves with the changing environment. It involves a random, unsystematic, qualitative search for information, by means of which the manager comes to conclusions about forces in the environment of concern to him or her and the company. The selection of information and its evaluation are based upon experience, judgment, insight, and "feel." When done by experienced managers who continuously survey the evolving environment, it is more powerful than any other technique.

Scenarios   Scenarios are credible descriptions of the future based upon careful analysis of complex, interacting social, economic, political, and technological forces. They are not predictions of the future but disciplined and structured judgments of future possibilities. They set forth fundamental projections about anticipated trends and their outcomes. They are also designed to fit a particular set of needs of managers.

Scenarios with a social focus include the General Electric Company's formerly ongoing project for evaluating changing social values that might have affected the company in the 1980s and beyond. Another scenario was the result of the EPA commissioning the Stanford Research Institute to prepare alternative futures up to the year 2000 that would be useful in developing environmental policy planning. The Shell Oil Company recently completed a scenario concerning public, worker, and plant community attitudes toward carcinogens and cancer risks. For a number of years, this company has had a sophisticated environmental-analysis program (Zentner, 1981).

Systematic Qualitative Search   Sears, Roebuck & Co. used systematic qualitative searches to provide information for its managers. The staff assigned to make the EA maintained well over 100 categories for classifying information that bore on the company's future. The categories included population changes, income distribution, values and life styles, public attitudes toward corporations, employee privacy, agricultural productivity, and government regulations. The accumulation of information started with printed matter. Added to this were interviews with academic experts and knowledgeable people in business, government, and professional associations. Periodically all this information was analyzed and conclusions drawn about major trends that were of significance to Sears managers in their decision making.

Delphi   The Delphi technique is a way to distill expert opinion into a vision of the future. It works this way. A group of experts is selected, and each person is asked to express individually an opinion about the probability of a future event or events in his or her area of expertise. Each expert then makes a prediction in a second round of statements. After several more rounds, advocates of the technique agree that the likely result is a convergence of expert opinion on the most likely predictions of a future event or situation. Originated by the Rand Corporation in the 1950s, this technique has enjoyed much popularity and success among such corporations as DuPont, Scott Paper, AT&T, Lever Brothers, and Montana Power Company.

Trend Analysis   Trend analysis is a technique to study how events may affect or move one or more trends. For example, if recent trends have shown a steady rise in public demands for removing carcinogens from the atmosphere, a trend analysis will study those forces which may accentuate the trends in the future, reduce the force of public demands, or continue present trends.

Cross-Impact Analysis   Cross-impact analysis is a method to structure the study of how events affect each other. Because events are interelated in time, and some events do not occur unless others do (or do not), a technique such as this is used to study the relationships among events. A matrix is used to facilitate analysis. Events to be studied are listed in the vertical column, and those which will be affected by a particular event are listed horizontally. For example, assume that on the left side of the matrix, the event is "the invention of an automobile engine that will get 100 miles for every gallon of fuel." If the time horizon is 1995, a probability for the happening of this event is calculated at say, 0.8. This calculation then is used to make a probability calculation for items listed horizontally, such as the chance that "the United States will import over 50 percent of its total consumption of oil"; "the price per barrel of crude oil will be over $20"; and "utilities will switch from gas and coal to oil." Sophisticated cross-impact models may have dozens of items for which probabilities are calculated.

Probability/Impact Matrix   With a probability/impact matrix, events foreseen for the future are analyzed in terms of their probability and potential impact on the company. General Electric used this technique in the mid-1970s and concluded, for example, that in the 1980s major issues for the company would concern managing the new work force. The company would be concerned with job enlargement, equality of opportunity, and demands for greater participation in decision making. A matrix used with this technique is shown in Exhibit 10-3.

PUBLIC-ISSUES MANAGEMENT (PIM)

PIM Defined

Like other terms in the area of social issues, there is no consensus about the meaning of public-issues management (PIM). For us, PIM is concerned with identifying public issues of importance to business executives, analyzing their significance to their company, deciding about actions to be taken to influence public attitudes about the issues, and devising methods to implement the actions.

Most managers always have had some concern about public issues and sought to react appropriately to them or to take a proactive stance to influence them. What then is new today? There is more urgency today for executives to take

EXHIBIT 10–3   IMPACT/PROBABILITY MATRIX

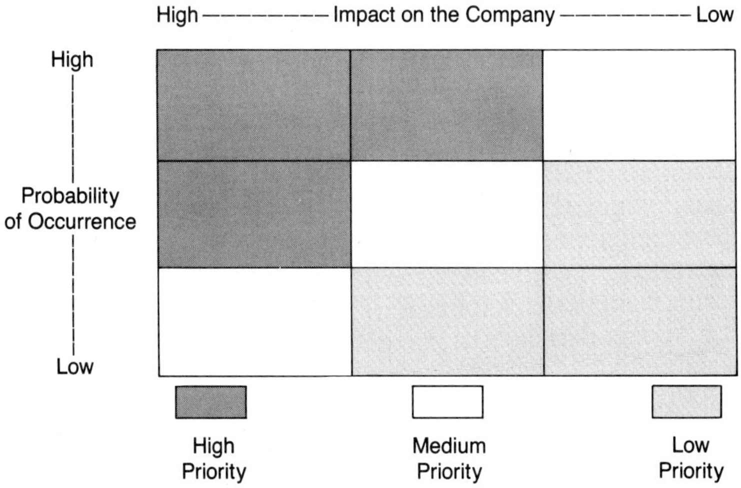

corporate positions in dealing with public issues. The many unpleasant surprises for managers in the recent past—unprecedented public pressure to act on behalf of interest groups, massive increases in government regulations, and changes in the tax laws—have taught managers that they cannot afford to stand idly and not seek to influence, understand, or adapt to important public issues.

PIM has various purposes among various companies, but fundamentally the purposes are to allay tensions between the firm and society, avoid expensive surprises in the environment, cope with social change through proaction instead of isolation and resistance, and engage in meaningful participation in the creation of public policy. It is unlikely that a large, highly visible firm can comfortably exist today without a PIM of some type.

Toyota Motor Sales U.S.A., for instance, was formed in 1957 and concentrated on marketing Toyotas. There was little emphasis on public relations or public affairs throughout the 1970s. But at the end of 1979, American auto makers successfully lobbied for restriction of Japanese imports and an increase in duties for automobile components and truck cab chassis entering the United States. In March 1980, the company finally formed a public affairs department. Phil Broman, government and industry-relations manager for Toyota U.S.A., remarked:

> I think we are the classic case of a company that was reactive in its approach to its public affairs. Basically, we are a group of marketing Boy Scouts who felt that if we did a good product quality job, if we satisfied the consumers, that we probably wouldn't have to worry about any political problems. Well, nothing was further from the truth (in Epstein and Preston, 1982: 84).

Organizing for PIM

Professor Rogene Buchholz (1982) studied the *Fortune* 500 companies and found that 91 percent of them had established issues-management programs. He also found that three-quarters of the companies in his survey said that public-issues management was either extremely or very important.

There are great variations in corporate programs for PIM. Among the largest companies, as noted earlier in the chapter, the structuring begins at the top, with board of director committees concerned with public policy issues. Also, as noted above, the typical public-affairs department is usually the center for developing data upon which a company determines its public-issues strategy and also for preparing plans to implement the objectives decided by management. This process can take many directions. To illustrate, when Reginald Jones was chief executive officer at General Electric, he formulated the company's position on the basis of staff research and then participated in public-policy discussions in Washington, D.C., with the President, the Congress, and the bureaucracy. He also used the material as a basis for his many public speeches. At Union Carbide, public issue papers are prepared by top management and staff and sent to plant managers and corporate-headquarters staff for their information and use. In some companies, such as The Continental Group, Inc., an elaborate network of employees, stockholders, other organizations, and influential citizens is alerted to help disseminate the company's position on important public issues (G. Steiner, 1983).

PHILANTHROPIC PROGRAMS

Philanthropy means the giving of money, time, products, or services to help the needy or to support institutions working to better human welfare; it is a synonym for charity. Corporations engage in philanthropy. A legacy of America's colonial ties was the transplantation from England of the notion that part of the role of an enlightened businessperson was to make charitable contributions. As they grew, large corporations also began giving money to various causes and, over the years, this giving has become more organized and sustained. Hence, one way that social responsiveness is institutionalized in companies is through philanthropic programs.

The Legality of Corporate Philanthropy

During the nineteenth century and into the twentieth, courts of law held that a corporation existed only to provide profits for distribution to stockholders. Corporate giving was identified as an *ultra vires* act and therefore illegal. The first major break in this thesis came in the Revenue Act of 1935, when Congress made it possible for corporations to deduct from taxable earnings their charitable contributions, up to 5 percent of net profits before taxes. This was raised to 10 percent by the Economic Recovery Act of 1981. Most states now also have such legislation. The legal requirements that directors of corporations must exercise sound business judgment and act in a fiduciary capacity to corporate interests are not relaxed, however.

The legality of using corporate funds for purposes other than clearly charitable giving under the Revenue Act, however, continued to be very doubtful. This restraint was removed in 1953 by the A. P. Smith case, in which the Supreme Court refused to review a decision of the highest court in New Jersey. The board of directors of the A. P. Smith Company, manufacturers of machinery and equipment for water and gas industries, gave Princeton University $1,500 as a contribution toward its general maintenance. Questioned by the stockholders, the corporation sought a declatory judgment asking that its action be sustained. The New Jersey Supreme Court, in affirming a lower court decision, said:

> The contribution here in question is toward a cause which is intimately tied into the preservation of American business and the American way of life. Such giving may be called an incidental power, but when it is considered in its essential character, it may well be regarded as a major, though unwritten, corporate power. It is even more than that. In the Court's view of the case, it amounts to a solemn duty *(A.P. Smith Manufacturing Company v. Barlow)*.

Philanthropic Allocations

Overall corporate giving rose from $2.4 billion in 1980 to $4.3 billion in 1985, a large sum. Still, it is far less than the charitable contributions of individuals, who gave $71.3 billion in 1985. In fact, corporate charity is only about 5 percent of all charitable giving in the country each year. Business contributions cannot be expected to offset cuts in social programs stemming from deep federal budget cuts. In 1985, the corporate charitable-contributions pie was divided as follows: education, 38.9 percent; health and human services, 27.7 percent; civic and community activities, 18.8 percent; culture and art, 10.7 percent; and all other, 3.9 percent (Platzer, 1986). In addition, as noted previously, corporations contribute the time of their employees and various products and services.

In most corporations, the process of making charitable contributions is managed by public-affairs or public-relations departments. A small number of companies have established separate foundations to make gifts. Often the contribution process is not very systematic. A single staff person may control the contributions budget. Individuals, groups, and causes may submit proposals for corporate funding to this staff person, who may make donation decisions in conjunction with a contributions committee. There may be few criteria for giving and little follow-up to see how the donation has been used.

In some companies, the contributions process is more systematic. As federal budget cuts have squeezed social programs, corporations have in turn been beset with requests for money. Some, such as Mellon Bank in Pittsburgh, have developed philosophies for contribution decisions. Mellon Bank's Community Affairs Division operates according to a philosophy that one role of bank contributions is to enhance the self-sufficiency of nonprofit, community-service organizations. Instead of just responding to grant proposals from organizations that want money, the bank also stimulates programs that further the self-sufficiency goal. For example, the bank underwrote a book, *Discover Total Resources,* that helps nonprofit organizations understand how to get resources of all kinds from local communities. The bank also trains nonprofit organizations' managers in fund-raising techniques. It publishes several reports that describe and evaluate its contribution activities. Another form of contributions philosophy is that of Mobil Oil, which sets aside 2 percent of the cost of every building and installation for the purchase of art. This long-standing corporate policy traces its origin to the charitable impulses of Mobil's progenitor, John D. Rockefeller. In any case, as demands for contributions increase, more companies are developing systematic guidelines for giving and are monitoring the results of their contributions.

Cause-Related Marketing

There are many ways in which charity may profit a company, but none so direct as when marketing activities are combined with social programs. In the past five years, a small number of firms have experimentally linked charity with product sales, while many others have watched with interest to gauge public reaction.

For example, General Foods tried to attract the attention of mothers by donating 10 cents to Mothers Against Drunk Driving for every Tang coupon redeemed. General Foods also donated 50 cents to the maintenance of national park trails for every Post Natural Raisin Bran boxtop mailed in because it perceived a connection between this cause and the psychological profile of targeted buyers.

A pioneer in cause-related marketing is American Express, which for years has mixed philanthropy with its mainstream credit-card business. In 1983, it began a program of trimonthly donations to the Atlanta Arts Council based on the frequency and type of card used in the Atlanta area. It contributed 5 cents for each card transaction, $2 for each new card issued, and $5 each time travel arrangements exceeding $500 were made with the card. In a similar campaign, the company raised a $1.7 million contribution to the restoration of the Statue of Liberty. Another campaign, called "Project Hometown America," raised money for local organizations throughout the country which had demonstrated an "innovative approach to solving a pressing local human problem."

Marketing campaigns such as these must be carefully presented to the public. People may see them either as a method for carrying out corporate social obligations or as a crass marketing tool. What, for example, would be the public reaction to a brewery that contributed $1 to a rehabilitation center for alcoholic teenagers with each six-pack sold?

If cause-related marketing programs are generally successful, corporations may tend to support social programs that lend themselves to sales campaigns. These programs, picked from an array of contenders, may or may not be the most worthy. Such innovations illustrate that social responsibility can be tied to competitive, profit-oriented behavior. But so far, these programs have not made much money, because the expense of advertising them usually exceeds the revenue they generate. In most American Express campaigns, for instance, the costs of promoting the project have exceeded the amounts raised for charity.

CORPORATE SOCIAL REPORTING AND THE SOCIAL AUDIT

In the early 1970s, considerable pressure was put on corporations to make and publicize social audits. The movement represented an acceptance of the idea that corporations were accountable to the public for their social activities and programs.

The business social audit is a report of social performance, in contrast to the financial audit, which is concerned with economic performance. There are two fundamentally different types of social audits. One is required by the government. A large corporation, for example, must report to the government about many programs, such as tests of flammable textiles (FTC), performance in meeting pollution standards (EPA), and minority employment (EEOC). The second type of audit is for programs voluntarily undertaken by a company. Virtually all audits of voluntary programs are of the inventory type, that is, a general description of what a company has done (Bauer and Fenn, 1972; Corson and Steiner, 1974).

Many corporations add a section to their annual report to stockholders that discusses their social programs. Some publish separate reports. These range from public-relations statements to thoroughly researched, illuminating reports. A good example of the latter is the annual report of the General Motors Corporation, entitled *Report on Progress in Areas of Public Concern.*

A study of 284 corporations (mostly larger companies) in 1973 showed that 76 percent said that they had made a social audit (Corson and Steiner, 1974). Since then, pressure on corporations to make social audits has declined. Part of the reason is that government regulation and reporting requirements have led to increased corporate disclosure of the social actions that concern the public.

Many corporations today continue to prepare and disseminate periodic reports on their voluntarily assumed social programs. But the reports usually are not complete and, with few exceptions, seem to be more cosmetic than accountability reports. The idea, however, is not dead. It has surfaced periodically ever since it was first proposed in the 1940s. It is likely that some time in the future, public pressure will again build for it.

CONCLUDING OBSERVATIONS

The demands that corporations, especially the larger ones, continue to expand their efforts to help society to achieve its economic and social objectives are strong, growing, and not likely to diminish. To meet these demands in an appropriate fashion, corporations will continue to perfect the institutionalization of the social point of view in their decision-making processes.

CASE STUDY

THE UNION CARBIDE CORPORATION AND BHOPAL: A CASE STUDY OF MANAGEMENT RESPONSIBILITY

In 1984, the year of the tragic events in Bhopal, India, Union Carbide Corporation was the nation's thirty-fifth-largest industrial corporation. The giant firm, which was founded in 1886, had grown from a small dry-cell battery company into the nation's third-largest chemical producer, with a net profit of $199 million on $9.5 billion in sales. It employed 98,366 "Carbiders" at 500 facilities in thirty-seven countries, and foreign sales were 31 percent of total sales. The company had a variety of product lines, including petrochemicals, industrial gases, welding equipment, popular consumer products—such as Prestone antifreeze, Eveready batteries, Glad bags, and Simoniz wax—and high-technology products and services for the electronics, aerospace, and chemical industries.

Although the third-largest U.S. chemical producer, Carbide ranked only sixteenth in profitability. Its petrochemical sales were 28 percent of total sales in 1984 but only 23 percent of operating profits; Carbide, a low-cost producer of petrochemicals such as ethylene, had been slow to divert its resources to more profitable business lines. To make matters worse, the entire chemical industry had been in a slump for several years. In addition, new Saudi Arabian petrochemical plants were coming on line in 1985 and 1986. Chemical companies worldwide now faced competition from those Saudi plants, which had access to low-cost raw materials. In anticipation of Saudi production, chemical manufacturers the world over were reducing capacity. Hence, by 1984, Carbide's strategy was to emphasize growth segments in its other operating divisions.

Union Carbide had a reputation as a socially and environmentally concerned company; a 1983 *Fortune* magazine survey ranked Carbide in the upper half of the chemical industry for environmental responsibility. The historical record, however, contains blemishes. In the 1930s, at the Gauley Mountain, West Virginia, tunnel project, 2,000 workers were exposed to unsafe levels of silica dust, and 476 died from pulmonary fibrosis. In the 1970s, an alloy plant in Vienna, West Virginia, became a national symbol of industrial air pollution. Cancer studies showed elevated rates of certain cancers among workers at several Union Carbide plants. The company also had a number of more minor pollution and safety violations. But in 1977, Carbide added Russell E. Train, former head of the EPA, to its board of directors and, shortly thereafter, set up a corporate department of health, safety, and environmental affairs.

Union Carbide's Plant in Bhopal

Union Carbide first incorporated in India in 1934, when it began to make batteries there. It operates through an Indian subsidiary in which it owns a 50.9 percent majority interest and Indian investors, a 49.1 percent minority interest. Among Indian investors, the Indian government predominates. Through a set of investment firms operating under the Public Financial Institutions, it owns roughly half the 49.1 percent minority interest. This jointly owned subsidiary, named Union Carbide India Ltd. (UCIL), trades its shares on the Bombay Stock Exchange and is operated entirely by Indians. In 1984, UCIL had fourteen plants and 9,000 employees, including 120 at the Bhopal plant in central India. Although UCIL contributed less than 2 percent to Carbide's revenues, it was the fifteenth-largest in sales among all Indian companies in 1984. Most of its business was from the sales of Eveready batteries.

Union Carbide elected to build a pesticide plant in Bhopal in 1969. At that time, there was a growing demand in India and throughout Asia for pesticides, due to the burgeoning "green revolution," a type of planned agriculture that requires intensive use of pesticides and fertilizers in the cultivation of special strains of food crops such as wheat, rice, and corn. Although pesticides may be misused and pose some risk, they have great social value as well. Without pesticides, there is no question that damage to crops, losses in food storage, and toxic mold growth in food supplies would mean the loss of many lives from starvation and food poisoning in developing countries like India. It has been estimated that pesticide use increases India's annual crop yield by about 10 percent—enough to feed roughly 70 million people. In India, about half the nation's population of 750 million lives below a minimum caloric intake established as a poverty line by the government. The chances of an Indian dying from starvation are astronomically greater than those of dying from pesticide poisoning or a Bhopal-type disaster.

In the early 1970s, the small Bhopal plant made pesticides from chemicals imported to the site. The plant was supported by the government of the city of Bhopal and the state of Madhya Pradesh, which reduced the plant's taxes as an incentive. In 1975, however, UCIL was pressured by the Indian government to reduce its imports. The company proposed to manufacture methyl isocyanate (MIC) at the plant rather than shipping it in from Carbide facilities outside the country.

MIC is an intermediate chemical used in pesticide manufacture. It is not a final product. Rather, MIC molecules are created and then used to react with other synthetic organic chemicals to produce uniquely shaped molecules that interfere with the natural chemistry of insect nervous systems and thus act as chemical weapons within pests. The two pesticides made by an MIC reaction process at Bhopal, with the trade names Sevin and Temik, are carbamate pesticides that disable a critical enzyme in the nervous systems of pests, leading to convulsions and death.

In 1975, Carbide received a permit from the Ministry of Industry in New Delhi to build a methyl isocyanate unit at the Bhopal plant. Two months prior to approval of this permit, the city of Bhopal had enacted a development plan that required relocation of dangerous industries to an industrial zone 15 miles outside the city. Pursuant to the plan, M. N. Buch, the Bhopal city administrator, tried to relocate the UCIL pesticide plant and convert the site to use for housing and light commercial activity. This effort failed for reasons that are unclear, and Buch was shortly thereafter transferred to forestry duties elsewhere.

Between 1975 and 1980, the MIC unit was constructed from a design package provided by Union Carbide's engineering group in the United States. Detailed design work was done by an Indian subsidiary of a London firm, Humphreys & Glasgow Pvt. Ltd. The unit was built by local labor using Indian equipment and supplies. The reason for such heavy Indian involvement with the plant was an Indian law, the Foreign Exchange Regulation Act of 1973, which requires foreign multinationals to share technology and use Indian resources.

In 1980, the project was finished, and the MIC unit began operation. During construction, large, unplanned slums and shantytowns called *jhuggis* had grown up near the plant, peopled mainly by manual laborers. At the same time, the plant became much more dangerous, for it had begun to manufacture the basic chemical ingredients of pesticides rather than simply to make pesticides from shipped-in ingredients. One step in the manufacture of MIC, for example, involves the production of phosgene, the lethal "mustard gas" used in World War I.

In 1981, a phosgene gas leak at the Bhopal plant killed one worker, and a crusading Indian journalist wrote a series of articles about the plant and its potential dangers to the population. No one heeded these articles. In 1982, a second phosgene leak forced temporary evacuation of some surrounding slum areas. Also in 1982, a safety survey of the plant by three Carbide engineers from the United States cited approximately fifty safety defects, most of them minor. The report stated that there was no imminent danger from the plant, and subsequently all suggested changes in safety systems and procedures were made (except one troublesome valve outside the accident area). It must be added that because of a downturn in the Indian economy and stiff competition from other pesticide producers marketing newly developed, less expensive products, the Bhopal plant had lost money for three years in a row. As revenues fell, the plant's budgets were cut, and it had been necessary to defer some maintenance, lessen the rigor of training programs, and lay off some workers. At the time of the accident, the MIC unit was operating with a reduced crew of six workers per shift rather than the normal twelve—a condition some process-design engineers thought unsafe.

Union Carbide's Relationship with the Bhopal Plant

The Bhopal pesticide plant fit into the Union Carbide management hierarchy as depicted in the organization chart in Exhibit 10-4. Although some Americans had staffed the plant and had conducted safety inspections in the early years, Carbide turned the plant completely over to Indian personnel after 1982. It did so under government pressure to increase the self-sufficiency of Indian industry. Plant safety inspections after 1982 were the responsibility of the Indian subsidiary, UCIL. At the time of the accident, therefore, line responsibility for the day-to-day operations and safety of the plant rested with the plant manager, an Indian employee of UCIL. The plant operated with a great deal of autonomy. But Union Carbide had majority ownership of UCIL and, in addition, was represented by five members on the UCIL board of directors, four from Union Carbide Eastern, Inc., and the fifth from the international headquarters group.

UNION CARBIDE'S ORGANIZATION STRUCTURE AS RELATED TO THE BHOPAL PLANT

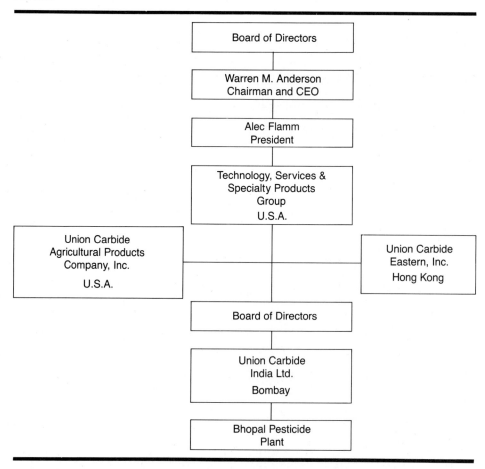

The Bhopal plant was also in close contact with the management of Union Carbide Agricultural Products Company, Inc., which was Carbide's arm for the production and marketing of pesticides.

Top management at Union Carbide's Danbury, Connecticut, headquarters received monthly reports from the Bhopal plant and approved major financial, maintenance, and personnel decisions. Carbide engineers also provided UCIL and the Bhopal plant with the processing manual on MIC that was supposed to guide plant operations.

In the reporting relationship, Union Carbide's top management in Connecticut had ultimate managerial responsibility for the operation of the Bhopal plant. Shortly after the accident, Chairman Warren M. Anderson stated in interviews that Carbide accepted "moral responsibility" for the tragedy. Nevertheless, the Bhopal plant was but one of hundreds of sites worldwide in which the company had an equity interest. For this reason and because of the vast physical distances separating the two sites, Carbide's U.S. management team delegated considerable authority over operations to UCIL's management team on the spot. The exact nature of this shared authority is unclear and may never be fully revealed unless the gas victims' claims come to trial.

The Gas Leak   In the early morning hours on Monday, December 3, 1984, the Bhopal plant became the scene of the worst industrial accident in history. Here is what experts believe happened.

On the evening of December 2, storage Tank 610, one of three storage tanks at the MIC unit, was filled with 11,290 gallons of MIC. The tank, which had a capacity of 15,000 gallons, was a partly buried, stainless steel, pressurized vessel (see Exhibit 10-5).

At about 9:30 P.M., a supervisor ordered a worker to clean out a pipe in the MIC storage complex by washing it out with water. The worker, although knowing that valves in the plant were often leaky, failed to use a slip blind, a simple device that seals lines to prevent water leakage into adjacent pipes. This action violated instructions in the MIC processing manual.

Either because of this careless washing procedure or deliberate sabotage elsewhere, 120 to 240 gallons of water entered Tank 610, initiating a powerful exothermic (heat-building) reaction. Workers were unaware that the reaction was proceeding that night. At 10:30, tank pressure was logged at 2 pounds per square inch. Then, at 10:45, a new shift came on duty. At 11:00 P.M., a new operator in the MIC control room noticed that the pressure in tank 610 was 10 pounds per square inch, but he was unconcerned because this was within tolerable limits, the gauges were often wrong, and he did not read the log to discover that pressure was five times greater than it had been 30 minutes earlier.

As the reaction continued, the temperature in Tank 610 increased. Unfortunately, the refrigeration units that cooled the tanks had been shut down for five months as an economy measure. Had the tanks been refrigerated, as the MIC processing manual required, the heat build-up from the reaction with the water might have taken place over several days instead of several hours.

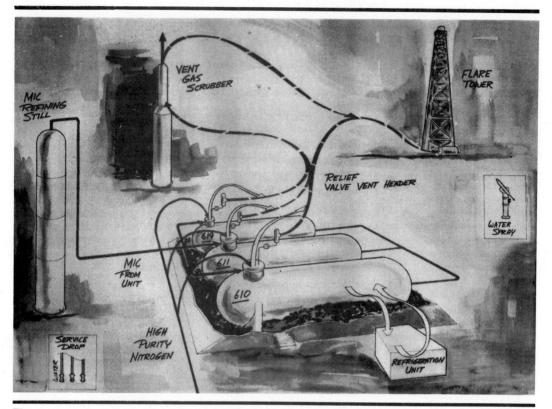

The tank storage area and safety equipment in Bhopal. Unfortunately, the refrigeration unit was off, and the vent gas scrubber, flare tower, and water spray failed to prevent disaster. The service drop in the lower left corner is a likely route of entry for the water that caused the reaction. Courtesy of Union Carbide.

As pressure increased in the tank, a leak developed. At 11:30, workers smelled MIC, and their eyes watered. At 11:45, one worker spotted a small, yellowish drip of MIC from some high piping and informed his supervisor. The supervisor suggested fixing the leak after a tea break scheduled for 12:15 A.M. on December 3.

At 12:40, the tea break ended, and a worker in the MIC control room spotted a gauge showing that the pressure in Tank 610 was 40 pounds per square inch. It rose in a short time to 55 pounds per square inch, the top of the scale. A glance at the tank temperature gauge brought more bad news: the MIC was vaporizing at 77 degrees F, 36 degrees higher than the safety limit specified in the MIC processing manual. After reading the gauges, the worker ran out to look at Tank 610. He felt heat radiating from the tank and heard the concrete over it cracking. Within seconds, a pressure-release valve opened, and a white cloud of deadly MIC vapor shot into the atmosphere with a screech.

The worker ran back into the control room and turned a switch to activate a vent gas scrubber, a safety device designed to neutralize any escaped toxic gases from the MIC unit by circulating them through a caustic soda solution. The scrubber, however, failed to operate because it had been shut down for maintenance. Subsequent investigation established that even if the scrubber had been on-line that night, it was not designed to handle the temperature and pressure reached by the MIC in the tank and would have been quickly overwhelmed. A flare tower designed to burn off toxic gases before they escaped into the atmosphere was also off-line; it had been disassembled for maintenance, and an elbow joint was missing. Another emergency measure, which transferred MIC from Tank 610 to one of two other storage tanks, was impossible as well, because records showed that both of those tanks were full or nearly so. This situation also violated procedure in the MIC processing manual, which called for leaving one tank empty as a safety measure.

At about 1:00 A.M., an operator turned on an alarm to warn workers of danger from toxic gas. The plant superintendent, who had arrived in the control room, directed that a water spray be turned on the escaping MIC vapor to knock it down, but this had little effect. At this time, most workers in the plant ran in panic, ignoring four parked buses, which they were supposed to drive through the surrounding area to begin evacuation of residents. Only two workers stayed in the MIC control room. They shared the only available oxygen mask when the room filled with MIC vapor. Finally, at about 2:30 A.M., the pressure in the tank dropped, the leaking safety valve resealed, and the MIC leak stopped.

Over a two-hour period, about forty-five tons of MIC had leaked out in a white cloud that spread across twenty-five square miles of the sleeping city. That night the wind was calm, the temperature about 60 degrees, and the heavy chemical mist lingered just above the ground. The gas attacked people in the streets and seeped into their homes. Those who panicked and ran into the night air received higher doses of toxic vapor. Unprotected animals suffered the same fate as humans. As word of the gas leak spread, many Bhopal residents fled the city, including many of the relatively affluent suburbanites who owned cars. The poor in the slums and shantytowns near the plant were left to bear the brunt of misfortune.

As the poisonous cloud blanketed its victims, MIC, a very active compound, reacted with water in their eyes and was absorbed in normally transparent corneal cells, rendering them opaque. Residents with cloudy, burning eyes staggered into aid stations, permanently or temporarily blind.

Many victims suffered shortness of breath, coughing fits, asthma-like symptoms, and painful breathing. In the lungs, MIC molecules attached to the pulmonary parenchyma, or lung lining, causing a chemical burn. Fluid oozed from burned lung tissue and built up in the lungs, a condition called pulmonary edema, and many victims literally drowned in their own secretions. When they did not suffocate from edema, chemical burns destroyed sheets of the cells that facilitate the exchange of gases in breathing and the clearing of foreign matter from the lungs. In survivors, the burned tissue eventually healed but was covered with a tough protein substance called fibrin, which created areas of

TABLE 10–1   BHOPAL IN PERSPECTIVE: NOTEWORTHY INDUSTRIAL ACCIDENTS IN RECENT DECADES

DEATHS	LOCATION AND DATE	NATURE OF EVENT
10,000	Worldwide, each year	United Nations estimate of total pesticide-related deaths.
8,000–10,000	United States, each year between 1985 and 2000	Estimated deaths from past occupational exposure to asbestos.
2,347	**Bhopal, India, 1984**	Estimate of deaths from MIC vapor leak at pesticide plant.
561	Oppau, Germany, 1921	Ammonium nitrate explosion in fertilizer warehouse.
561	Texas City, Texas, 1947	Ammonium nitrate explosion on tankers in port.
500	Cubatao, Brazil, 1984	Gasoline explosion from pipeline leak.
476	Gauley Bridge, West Virginia, 1930–1932	Silicosis deaths among miners on a tunneling project of a Union Carbide subsidiary.
452	Mexico City, 1984	Explosions of liquefied natural gas storage tanks.
400 (estimated)	Al Basral, Iraq, 1971	Methylmercury poisoning from improper application of fungicide to barley and wheat cargoes.
215	San Carlos, Spain, 1978	Explosion of propylene gas truck in recreation area.
207	Ludwigshaven, Germany, 1948	Dimethyl ether vapor cloud explosion from improper filling of tank car.
131	Cleveland, Ohio, 1944	Explosion of liquefied natural gas tank.
40	Staten Island, New York, 1973	Vapor ignition during repair of liquefied natural gas tank.
28	Flixborough, England, 1974	Cyclohexane vapor cloud explosion at chemical plant.
28	Sevaso, Italy, 1976	Accidental release of cyclohexane cloud at chemical plant.
20	United States, 1971–1985	Use of Dalkon Shield intrauterine birth-control device.
13	Chernobyl, Russia, 1986	Reactor fire and explosion causing release of radioactive cloud. Long-range cancer deaths from radiation estimated as high as 5,000 to 10,000.
7	Cape Kennedy, Florida, 1986	Explosion of space shuttle *Challenger* due to faulty seal on solid rocket booster.

pulmonary fibrosis that reduced breathing capacity. The injured were also in great danger of respiratory infections as they recovered.

There is no known antidote for MIC exposure. Treatment consisted of administration of oxygen, mechanical ventilation of the lungs, the use of diuretics to maintain fluid balance, and the short-term use of steroids to decrease lung inflammation. Sedatives and painkillers were an adjunct treatment. Often, however, doctors were helpless. Unfortunately, many residents of the slums around the plant were already in poor health from living in poverty and suffered from malnutrition, tuberculosis, and a variety of infections. These chronic conditions exacerbated the effects of MIC injury.

How many died in Bhopal? The Indian government issued 1,450 death certificates, but many families built funeral pyres without consulting local authorities. The local police department estimated 1,900 death. Bhopal's mayor said 3,000. Other Indian officials suggested a toll as high as 7,000 to 10,000. Finally, in November 1986, the Indian government established an official death toll of 2,347. About 200,000 of Bhopal's roughly 700,000 residents were exposed to the gas, and the government estimates that 30,000 to 40,000 were seriously injured. Victims continued to die in hospitals from gas-related injuries long after exposure, and visitors to Bhopal describe sounds of coughing and wheezing wherever people congregate.

Union Carbide Reacts

Few management problems are more severe than those that faced Warren M. Anderson, age 63, chairman and CEO of Union Carbide. Awakened early in the morning on Monday, December 3, Anderson rushed to Carbide's Danbury, Connecticut, headquarters and learned of the rising death toll. In the early morning hours, when the extent of the disaster was evident, an emergency meeting of a senior management committee was held. The committee sent emergency medical supplies, respirators, oxygen (Carbide products), and an American doctor with extensive knowledge of MIC to Bhopal.

The next day, Tuesday, December 4, Carbide dispatched a team of technical experts to examine the plant and find out what had happened. Production of MIC was halted immediately at Carbide's plant in Institute, West Virginia. A press conference was held. Staff members were pulled from other duties to work in corporate communications and return phone calls. On Thursday, Anderson himself departed for India. He went both as a symbol of top-level commitment and as an on-the-scene crisis manager. Only two phone lines into Bhopal were operative, and it was proving difficult to get information in Danbury about events there. Upon arriving in Bhopal, Anderson was arrested, charged with criminal negligence, briefly detained in the guest house at the Bhopal plant, flown to New Delhi, and then asked to leave the country. He may still face legal action in India.

With worldwide attention focused on Bhopal, Carbide held daily press conferences. It released copies of the 1982 safety inspection of the Bhopal plant. Anderson made two videotapes telling employees to bear up, and 500 copies of each were dispatched to plants around the world. Christmas parties were canceled. Flags at Carbide facilities were flown at half-mast. All of Carbide's nearly 100,000 employees observed a moment of silence for the victims. Many employees contributed to a relief fund. Carbide gave $1 million to an emergency relief fund and offered to turn its guest house in Bhopal into an orphanage. Union Carbide India Ltd., partner in the Bhopal plant, gave $840,000 to emergency relief funds. Months later, Carbide offered another $5 million to the state of Madhya Pradesh, but the money was refused because Carbide requested specific accounting of expenditures, and the government found this too demanding. Both companies also contributed to a victims' medical-care research program at Hamidia University Hospital in Bhopal.

In the days following the disaster, Anderson assumed full responsibility for management problems and events related to Bhopal. Alec Flamm, president and chief operating officer of Carbide, assumed full responsibility for normal business operations. A five-member board of directors' committee, chaired by former EPA head Russell E. Train, was set up to oversee the management response to Bhopal-related issues.

Investor confidence in Carbide was shaken. Carbide's stock fell from about $49 at the time of the disaster to a low of $32.75. As lawsuits were filed on behalf of the victims, with a potential payout exceeding Carbide's net worth, Standard & Poor, a rater of securities, lowered Carbide's debt rating, an action that made it more difficult and costly for the company to raise money. Anderson, as spokesperson for Carbide, had to undertake the delicate task of assuring investors that the company would continue to make profits while appearing not to show callous disregard for the human tragedy in Bhopal.

Lawsuits against Union Carbide

No sooner had the MIC vapor cleared than a flock of American lawyers arrived in Bhopal to seek litigants for damage claims against Union Carbide. Attorneys walked the shantytown streets signing up individuals for class-action suits. Names of potential litigants were sold for profit. In the confusion, Bhopal residents signed many papers, and many subsequent damage suits overlapped plaintiffs as a result. These events, said a *Wall Street Journal* editorial, were "a second tragedy."

The American lawyers who rushed to Bhopal defend their actions by making three points. First, if multinational corporations could be tried in U.S. courts, a single global liability standard would exist to promote safety. Second, big awards by juries, such as the recent ones against the Manville Corporation and the A. H. Robins Company, act as effective curbs on corporate irresponsibility. And third, after the disaster, these lawyers kept the victims on center stage so that their plight was not forgotten.

Shortly after the MIC leak, the Indian government paid settlements of about $800 to families of those who died. A program of smaller awards to injury victims was undertaken, but it was not completed due to administrative problems. Union Carbide offered a settlement of $300 million to the Indian government. Acceptance would have meant immediate aid to victims and surviving family members, but the government rejected the offer as inadequate.

American lawyers, who altogether represented an astronomical $50 billion in damage claims against Carbide, sought to have the Bhopal victims' cases tried in U.S. courts. There, they could seek large punitive damages and profit from the American contingency-fee system, under which they could claim a percentage of the ultimate awards to their Indian clients. They are not licensed to practice law in India and cannot try the cases there. The Indian government brought suit against Union Carbide for $17 million and passed a law making itself sole representative of all gas-leak victims. It preferred to have the cases tried in the United States because it felt that awards might be larger. Union Carbide wanted a quick settlement and in May 1986 offered the victims $350 million (which ultimately could exceed $500 million after sitting in an interest-bearing compensation fund). The American lawyers rushed to accept this compensation package, but the Indian government refused it.

Then, later that month, federal judge John F. Keenan of New York ruled that the victims' compensation cases should be tried in India, stipulating that strict United States rules of discovery could be applied by an Indian court and that Union Carbide would be required to pay any judgment against it. This turn of events left the U.S. lawyers with nothing. Union Carbide, its settlement offer rejected, preferred trial in the backlogged and inefficient Indian court system to that of the United States. It felt that because Indian courts rarely give large damage awards and are not jaded by frequent multimillion dollar negligence suits, as are United States courts, an Indian venue probably would mean a lower ultimate payout. Carbide may, of course, be wrong, because the Indian court system is now in the world spotlight and could come under government pressure to lodge a tough settlement against a foreign company.

In the Aftermath

In the weeks following the Bhopal tragedy, there was a strong backlash against Union Carbide, the chemical industry, and multinational corporations. This was perhaps unfair, because the record of safety in the chemical industry is generally excellent. Nonetheless, the world reacted. Townspeople in Livingston, Scotland, rejected plans for a new Union Carbide plant for blending industrial gases. A judge in Brazil banned imports of MIC. Protestors demonstrated at Union Carbide plants worldwide. At home, the American public was cynical about Carbide's actions. A *Business Week*/Louis Harris poll in mid-December reported that only 48 percent of the public gave a rating of "good" to Carbide for "its overall reaction to the disaster"; only 36 percent gave a "good" rating for "telling the truth about what happened in India" (Jackson, 1984: 40).

Early in 1985, a number of safety-oriented bills were introduced in Congress. The National Transportation Safety Board raised federal standards for shipping toxic chemicals. Chemical companies reviewed their safety controls. Insurance companies made their liability policies covering industrial risk more restrictive and more expensive. And a number of cities passed "right to know" laws requiring chemical plants to reveal listings of dangerous chemicals on their premises. For its part, Carbide resumed production of MIC at its Institute, West Virginia, plant but ended shipments of MIC from that plant to its Woodbine, Georgia, pesticide-formulation plant. Instead, it shipped aldicarb, a less volatile chemical produced further down the pesticide-production process stream. The company made costly improvements in the safety systems of the Institute MIC unit and pledged $120 million in new safety and environmental expenditures.

In March 1985, the Bhopal investigation team at Union Carbide released its report at a major press conference. The twenty-four-page report focused primarily on the results of more than 500 experimental chemical reactions undertaken to explain the chemistry of residues left in Tank 610. The investigation team was prevented by Indian police from interviewing the UCIL workers directly involved in the MIC unit. Hence, the report focused on technical factors, including the equipment involved and the chemical reactions that would explain the molecular composition of the tank residues.

The Carbide team concluded that the accident had been caused by entry of water into the tank. This conclusion concurred with the findings of an investigative team of *New York Times* reporters who, several months earlier, had researched the accident with access to plant personnel, documents, and equipment that police denied to Carbide.

How did the water enter the tank? The *Times* reporters concluded that the water probably had entered the tank when the employee (mentioned earlier) washed out the adjacent pipe without using a slip blind, a violation of procedure. The Union Carbide report stated that "the source of the water is unknown" but focused attention on possible entry through misconnection of a water line at a utility station near the tank.

Utility stations (or "service drops," as they are sometimes called) are located throughout chemical plants and provide needed services. Typically, they contain headers for compressed air, water, nitrogen, and steam—all essential for chemical plant operation. At the utility station near Tank 610, the nitrogen and water lines are located together (see Exhibit 10–5). The Carbide investigative team hypothesized that if a worker had deliberately or accidentally connected tubing to Tank 610 with the water line at the service drop, the resulting flow could account for the amount of water necessary to create the reaction that occurred.

It is possible that a worker might have confused the nitrogen and water headers. At one time Carbide claimed that the accident was caused by sabotage. But by 1986, the company claimed in court briefs filed in India that a disgruntled employee deliberately unscrewed a pressure gauge on Tank 610 and connected the water line from the nearby service drop to admit the water that caused the reaction. Carbide no longer called this action sabotage, however, believing that the employee never intended the damage that occurred. Carbide investigators reject the hypothesis developed by *Times* reporters that water was inadvertently introduced in large quantities into the tank when the worker began to wash out the pipe. Although a slip blind was not used, it was improbable that enough water to cause the reaction in Tank 610 would seep into it through a series of reportedly closed valves. More likely, water was directly introduced into the tank through an open line. In its briefs, however, the Indian government has consistently claimed that water entered the tank during the routine washing. Some legal experts feel that the company still could be found guilty of negligence even if a deliberate misdeed or sabotage occurred.

Carbide Faces Difficult Times   Unfortunately for Carbide, disaster soon struck again, neutralizing whatever public relations gains had been made by its careful responses to the Bhopal crisis. On August 11, 1985, a 200-yard wide cloud of yellowish gas escaped from the Institute plant and sent 135 nearby West Virginia residents to the hospital. The next morning, a picture on the front page of the *New York Times* showed paramedics taking small children to the hospital on stretchers. The unlucky 135 received hospital treatment for burning eyes, breathing difficulty, and other pulmonary complications, but the injuries were not serious. The escaped gas was not MIC, but analysis showed it to be composed of other chemicals that could have been fatal in larger doses. Carbide once again suspended production at Institute pending investigation. That investigation related a series of human and procedural errors leading directly to the toxic discharge. Another $88.2 million in lawsuits was filed against Carbide, and in April 1986, OSHA fined the company $1.4 million for "conscious, overt, and willful" safety violations at the Institute plant. This was the largest OSHA fine ever imposed.

In addition to problems caused by gas leaks, Carbide had to fight for its independence when in August 1985—the same month as the Institute, West Virginia, gas leak—GAF Corporation announced that it was accumulating Carbide shares for a possible takeover bid. In December, this takeover effort materialized. In a month-long war of wills, Carbide successfully repelled GAF, but only at the cost of taking on enormous new debt to buy back 55 percent of its outstanding shares.

In order to remain in business, Carbide had to reduce this debt and began to do so by selling its profitable consumer-products divisions in 1986. It sold its battery division to Ralston Purina and its home and auto product divisions to First Boston, Inc. The sales, although lucrative, left Carbide a smaller, weaker company. Its work force was reduced by 25 percent, and its sales declined by 23 percent. It had lost its most profitable business lines, and its survival depended more on its troubled, mainline petrochemicals business.

By early 1987, Carbide and the Indian government were maneuvering in the Indian court system. India claimed that Carbide was wholly responsible for the gas leak because the Bhopal plant was poorly designed and maintained. Carbide argued that responsibility lay with the Indians who ran and designed the plant, the Indian government, which allowed slums to arise on its boundaries, and the employee who put water in the tank. In late 1986, the Indian court forced Carbide to set aside $3 billion in unencumbered assets to pay possible claims. At the time of the Bhopal gas leak, Carbide had about $200 million in insurance. Most observers feel that a settlement in the range of $350 to $500 million could be taken in stride by the company. It has already distributed $6 million to victims through the Indian government and has pledged another $14 million for housing and medical help to be spent through various international relief agencies. This money is to be applied to any future settlement. Speculation in the press has it that the Indian government has its sights set on a settlement of around $700 million. Even if the two sides reach an amicable settlement, it is clear that the incident at Bhopal has tragically altered the shape and behavior of Union Carbide for many years to come.

Questions

1. Who is responsible for the Bhopal accident? How should blame be apportioned among the parties involved, including Union Carbide senior management, UCIL managers, workers at the MIC unit in Bhopal, governments in India that issued permits and provided incentives for the plant, slum dwellers who moved near the plant in illegal settlements, Indian environmental and safety inspectors, and others?

2. What principles of ethics and responsibility are applicable to the actions of the parties in question?

3. Did Union Carbide gain an advantage when damage claims of Bhopal victims were moved from the United States to an Indian court? Do you agree with Judge Keenan's decision to send the cases there?

4. What steps should be taken in American and Indian society now that this disaster has occurred?

5. Did the management of Union Carbide respond to the disaster in the best possible way? What other actions could have been taken? Did Carbide do everything possible to help itself, the chemical industry, and victims of the escaped MIC? What should be done now?

PART IV

ETHICS

CHAPTER **11**

ETHICS IN THE BUSINESS SYSTEM

PENTHOUSE® In September 1984, *Penthouse* magazine ran nine nude photographs of Vanessa Williams, the reigning Miss America and the first black winner of that title, in erotic poses with a white woman. These pictures had been taken two years before by a New York City photographer named Tom Chiapel, for whom Miss Williams had worked. Miss Williams alleged that she had been promised that only she would see the photos and that she and the other model would appear in silhouette. In a press conference she explained further.

> He said I would not be recognized and my posing for this experiment would be completely in confidence. . . . [He] directed both of us to assume different poses. Each pose was set up. At no time was there any spontaneous or ongoing activity between myself and the other model. . . . I never consented to the publication or use of these photographs in any manner (*Jet*, 1984: 60–61).

Despite Miss Williams's expression of innocence and indignation, Bob Guccione, publisher of *Penthouse*, claimed to have a release for publication of the photographs and the authentication of Miss Williams's signature by a handwriting expert. The issue of *Penthouse* that contained the photographs became a hot commodity. Newsstands and stores around the country sold out quickly, and street-corner entrepreneurs scalped copies at exorbitant rates.

A mild public outcry arose. Many people criticized *Penthouse* for mortifying Miss Williams when she had only two months left to reign. But Guccione defended his action. He argued that she had defrauded pageant officials when she signed her Miss America contract because she had not disclosed that past photos might be a source of embarrassment. Miss Williams, he argued, was the source of her own problems. He said that it was no more appropriate for him to wait until the end of her reign as Miss America to publish the photographs than it would have been for the *Washington Post* to wait until the end of Nixon's presidency to publish Watergate revelations. Hugh Hefner, publisher of *Playboy*, claimed that he had turned down the photos because they had not been taken with the intent of publication. He criticized Guccione: "When one is publishing a magazine that has erotic content, if you don't approach the business that you're in with a moral set of values, then we're in a lot of trouble." In retort, Guccione noted that Hefner had stored nude photographs of Suzanne Somers only to publish them years later when she became famous. He added that Hefner was "a moral cripple and a liar" (Smolla, 1986: 162).

Pressure arose for Vanessa Williams to resign her crown. Officials of the Miss America Pageant and corporate sponsors such as Beatrice Foods, Gillette, Nestlé, McDonald's, and American Greetings were concerned lest the "spirit of the pageant" and the "dignity of the crown" be compromised (Ehrenreich and O'Reilly, 1984: 11). Eventually, Miss Williams saw the impossibility of continuing her reign and called a press conference to resign. She was replaced by the first runner-up, Suzette Charles, Miss New Jersey.

In the end, everyone profited but Miss Williams. Photographer Tom Chiapel received an estimated $100,000 for the pictures. *Penthouse* magazine sold a record press run and made, according to one estimate, a "windfall" profit of $4 million (Morgan, 1984). The corporate sponsors of the Miss America Pageant had protected the virginal image of the contestants, an image that has had considerable commercial value for sponsoring companies. Although Miss Williams sued photographer Chiapel, she has yet to receive an award or settlement. (The magazine was protected from legal action by the First Amendment.) The photographs had damaged her reputation and foreclosed profitable opportunities that ordinarily await a former Miss America.

This story raises ethical issues, including the fundamental issue of profit at the expense of other values—in this case the welfare of another person. What *Penthouse* did was legal, but was it ethical?

Mark Twain once said, "To be good is noble. To tell people how to be good is even nobler, and much less trouble." This chapter is not designed to tell people how to be good, but rather to discuss current trends in American business ethics and to explain basic sources of business ethics and approaches to an understanding of the subject. In the next chapter, we discuss more specific, practical guidelines for making ethical business decisions. Throughout, our focus is on the ethical situation of managers of large corporations.

WHAT ARE BUSINESS ETHICS?

Ethics is the study of what is good and bad, right and wrong, and just and unjust. Business ethics, therefore, is the study of good and bad, right and wrong, and just and unjust actions in business. The material used in the study of ethics is a mass of principles, rules, values, and thoughts concerned with what conduct *ought* to be. The application of this material to business activity is an art involving judgment about the motivations behind an act and its consequences. This judgment, based on principles and standards of ethical conduct stemming from religious and philosophical thinking, cultural values, legal codes, and human conscience, determines whether an action is ethical or not.

Discussions of ethical issues in business frequently emphasize refractory and unclear situations, perhaps to show drama and novelty. Although all managers face ethical conflicts and difficult problems, the vast majority of ethical problems in business yield to resolution through the application of clear guidelines. The Eighth Commandment, for example, prohibits stealing from another and clearly makes practices ranging from theft of a competitor's trade secrets to taking a screwdriver home from work unethical. A misleading or lying advertisement violates a general rule of the Western business world that the seller of a product should not purposely deceive the buyer about its price or quality. This general understanding stems from the Mosaic law, the Code of Hammurabi, Roman law, and other sources and is part of a general ethic favoring truth that has remained unchanged for at least 3,000 years (Benson, 1982: xvi). Thousands recently responded to a printed ad in newspapers around the United States offering a roach killer for $2. The ad stated: "No chemicals! No sprays. No dangerous poisons. Safe to use even with small children around. Never misses. Sure-fire!" Respondents got two blocks of wood connected by a short string. An instruction sheet told them to catch a roach, place it on one of the blocks, and crush it with the other. But despite the cleverness of this product, its advertisement in this manner is clearly unethical in the Western tradition.

In general, ethical traditions that apply to business favor truth-telling, honesty, protection of human and animal life and rights, respect for law, and operation in accord with policies adopted by society to achieve justice for citizens. Some of these touchstones go back thousands of years. Other ethical standards, such as the principle that a corporation is responsible for the health and safety of its workers, have emerged quite recently. In keeping with the long ethical heritage of business, most business actions can be clearly shown to be ethical or unethical; it may be difficult to eliminate some unethical behavior, such as the illegal activity of organized criminals, but knowing the rightness or wrongness of actions is not difficult in the majority of cases. This is not to say, of course, that universal clarity exists. Ethical problems may easily arise and persist. The definition of kickbacks, for instance, is blurred in currently popular airline frequent-flyer programs. Managers traveling at corporate expense may earn free trips and reduced fares by repeatedly flying on one airline. Frequent-flyer awards are given to the individuals who fly, not the companies that pay for tickets. Thus, after regularly spending their employer's money with a single supplier, these managers are given a free flight in return. Some companies have asked airlines to report frequent-flyer awards given to their employees, but the airlines have refused.

In addition, major ethical quandaries exist that are neither easily resolved nor trivial in their consequences. These include moral debates over questions such as the corporate presence in South Africa, the production of nuclear weapons, and the payment of bribes to get foreign business. Although numerous ethical standards apply to these situations, there are conflicts among them that prevent easy resolution. The point remains, however, that the novelty or gravity of problematic instances should not obscure the existence of clear ethical guidelines for most business behavior.

TWO THEORIES OF BUSINESS ETHICS

There is an old debate, present both in the business community and in the literature of business ethics, about whether ethics in business may be more permissive than general societal or personal ethics.

One view is that commercial activity is amoral and that actions should be based solely on consideration of economic self-interest. This *theory of amorality* saw its apex of popularity during the nineteenth century, when doctrines of Social Darwinism and laissez-faire economics were popular. Indeed, some blue-chip corporations that developed during the period when "survival of the fittest" was a prevailing business ideology must admit to a checkered past. For example, John D. Rockefeller, founder of the Standard Oil Trust, reportedly spied on competitors by bribing their employees, gave kickbacks to railroads, blew up a widow's oil refinery when she refused to sell out, and lied to a congressional committee (Josephson, 1934). In 1903, Henry Ford started Ford Motor Company with $28,000 from eleven investors. They supplied the money and he the technical expertise. In 1919, Ford appointed his son president of FMC and planted a rumor that he was going into partnership with Harvey Firestone to build a new car to compete with Ford. This new car would allegedly sell for $100 less than the $460 Model T. Another rumor started by Ford was that he was planning to sell his shares of Ford Motor stock to General Motors. The eleven stockholders, alarmed by the false rumors, sold their stock back to Henry Ford at bargain prices, making Ford Motor Company entirely family-owned—the point of this carefully constructed artifice (Dahlinger, 1978: 124).

Throughout a long period of our history, the question of ethics was neglected in business or was not a subject of doubt because of the popular notion that business and personal ethics existed in separate compartments. Dan Drew, a builder of churches and the founder of Drew Theological Seminary, typified the compartmentalization of business decision making in the nineteenth century in these words:

> Sentiment is all right up in the part of the city where your home is. But downtown, no. Down there the dog that snaps the quickest gets the bone. Friendship is very nice for a Sunday afternoon when you're sitting around the dinner table with your relations, talking about the sermon that morning. But nine o'clock Monday morning, notions should be brushed aside like cobwebs from a machine. I never

took any stock in a man who mixed up business with anything else. He can go into other things outside of business hours, but when he's in the office, he ought not to have a relation in the world—and least of all a poor relation (Stone, in Bartels, 1963: 35).

Classical economists often have supported the theory of amorality when arguing that the common good is best achieved by the individual pursuit of self-interest and profits by those in business, rather than by activity based on conscious moral purpose. Morality, they say, will emerge from the overall workings of the market and not from individual do-goodism. This comforting argument may mitigate the guilt of a manager who undertakes ethically questionable actions. Religious codes of ethical behavior do this when they make reference to evil spirits, fate, or original sin, all of which have the effect of absolving individuals from some measure of blame and sheltering them from the full force of guilt. Similarly, the competitive pressures of the market system provide release from the burden of guilt and justification for behavior that would be condemned in private life (Wuthnow, 1982: 81). And so Daniel Haughton, chairman of Lockheed, found it permissible to pay $38 million in bribes in the 1970s to save jobs in the United States and profit stockholders and management. Since foreign competitors were willing to make these questionable payments, the market ethic permitted their payment. As one management scholar has argued, the "core values" of business economic growth, power, the drive for profits, rational calculation of gain, pragmatism, and loyalty to the spirit of capitalist ideology incline business to raw-edged ethics that are "perhaps no part of the intention of the individual businessperson caught in the system's toils" (Frederick, 1983: 147).

A second major ethical orientation is that it is possible to harmonize high levels of personal ethics with the demands of business life. This is the *theory of moral unity*, which holds that business actions can be judged by the general ethical standards of society, not by a special set of more permissive ethical standards. Only one basic ethical standard exists.

Indeed, many in business have been ethically pure. An example is James Cash Penney. Although we now remember Penney for the successful construction of a chain of retail outlets, his first enterprise was a butcher shop. As a young man, Penney went to Denver and, finding notice of a shop for sale, wired his mother

---

Capacity for the nobler feelings is in most natures a very tender plant, easily killed, not only by hostile influences, but by mere want of sustenance; and in the majority of young persons it speedily dies away if the occupations to which their position in life has devoted them, and the society into which it has thrown them, are not favourable to keeping that higher capacity in exercise.

John Stuart Mill, *Utilitarianism* (1863).

for $300 (his life savings) and purchased it. The departing butcher advised that Penney's success would depend heavily on trade from a nearby hotel. "To keep the hotel for a customer," the butcher explained, "all you have to do is buy the chef a bottle of whiskey a week." Penney regularly made the gift, and business was good, but gradually the opinion of his father, who reviled alcohol, preyed more and more on his mind. He resolved not to make profits in such a manner, stopped giving the bribe, and at the age of twenty-three was flat broke when the shop failed. Penney later started the Golden Rule Department Store in Denver and argued that his principles of honesty contributed to his ultimate success. A number of companies, such as J. C. Penney's, have successfully operated on religious principles and high moral standards, and their example counterbalances the gamesmanship ethos.

To those who adhere to the theory of amorality, the market is not an excusing condition for misconduct. Philosopher Armin Konrad dismisses the right of managers to exist in "ethical sanctuaries," arguing that all professionals, including doctors, lawyers, educators, and public administrators, are faced with ethical conflicts. But there are no grounds for avoiding these conflicts and the ethical judgment necessary to resolve them with high standards simply because one is a business manager. People in business are a part of society and must be sensitive to the ethical rights of others and meet human obligations (Konrad, 1982). Nor is business analogous to a game. Rather, it is a vital social institution. People's lives depend on it. To compare business to a poker game with special rules, insulated from generally applicable ethical principles, is to trivialize an essential institution and way of life (Gillespie, 1975).

According to the theory of moral unity, people act in organizations as individuals and citizens, not as cogs in an impersonal machine. The strong precedent set by the military tribunal at Nuremberg, which tried Nazis for war crimes, indicates that Western society expects members of organizations to follow the dictates of their conscience and reject forced implementation of unethical policies. Just as no Nazi war criminal argued successfully that he was forced to follow an order in an impersonal military chain of command, so no business manager may claim to be the helpless prisoner of competitive forces or organizational loyalties that crush free will and justify unethical actions.

We are left with the intriguing question: Do any factors excuse unethical business behavior? The answer is yes. Essentially, the factors that diminish responsibility for ethical behavior in business are the same as those that diminish ethical responsibility in other areas of life. Perhaps no explication of these factors in the last two thousand years has improved much on that given by Aristotle in *The Nicomachean Ethics.*

According to Aristotle, ethical behavior is a state involving voluntary choice, and only unethical actions that are involuntary can be excused. The two factors that may lead to involuntary behavior are *ignorance* and *incapacity* to perform an action. A person may be ignorant of facts or the consequences of an act. For example, a manager may manufacture a product according to a chemical formula unknowingly stolen by subordinates who kept their espionage secret. Later, despite conscientious testing and regulatory oversight, the chemical product proves harmful to consumers. In both these cases, involuntary ignorance diminishes ethical wrongdoing. (Naturally, negligence in getting facts increases culpability, as does failure to have an interest in acquiring knowledge of relevant ethical principles.) Incapacity arises from circumstances that render actions involuntary. Circumstances leading to incapacity arise when: (1) a course of action may impose unrealistically high costs—for example, an automobile manufacturer cannot be expected to prevent all traffic deaths since the costs of a perfectly safe vehicle in materials, design, and production are staggering; (2) there may be no power to influence an outcome—for example, a manager of an oil company doing business in the Middle East cannot end national frictions or religious differences; (3) no alternative exists—for example, the continued use of asbestos is inevitable despite the human health costs; and (4) external force may compel action—for example, a manager may pay excessive and unjust taxes in a foreign country because a corrupt ruler demands them.

Aristotle cautions, however, that "There are some things such that a man cannot be compelled to do them—that he must sooner die than do, though he suffer the most dreadful fate" (Aristotle, 1953: 122). Unlike cases of ignorance, cases of unethical behavior involving circumstantial coercion are never completely involuntary, since a manager can always voluntarily refuse to comply with an external force. Was Cy Osborne, an executive vice president of General Motors in the 1960s whose son suffered irreversible brain damage in a Corvair accident, compelled by GM's ethic of managerial team play to permit sales of an unsafe car? Executives and scholars who argue that the market is a force majeure that overrides individual values give too little credit to the strength of human will.

Ethical Practice in Business

Opinion surveys show that the American public believes that astoundingly high levels of unethical behavior exist in business. For example, a national survey conducted in mid-1985 revealed that 55 percent of the public thought that most corporate executives were dishonest (Clymer, 1985). A 1987 survey indicated that 49 percent felt that white-collar crime was "very common" in business (Jackson and Collingwood, 1987). These opinions are fairly typical of survey findings over the past twenty years. Is public perception accurate?

The level of ethical behavior in the business system is not subject to an accurate, aggregate measure. It varies among individuals, companies, and industries. Conspicuously unethical managers are regularly uncovered, their misdeeds publicized. Yet the unmasking of bad executives probably exaggerates the ethical problem for the public. For every Aldo Gucci (former chairman of Gucci Shops, Inc.) who pleads guilty to evading $7 million in income taxes, thousands of top executives honestly report earnings. For every Sunshine State Bank, the Miami bank taken over by drug smugglers, there are thousands of honest financial institutions. For every corrupt Wall Street investment banker, such as Dennis B. Levine who got $12.6 million in profits from illegal insider trading deals, there are thousands of brokers who trade legally (see box, p. 326). Conspicuous breaches of ethics should not be mistaken as indicative of the level of ethical practice in the business system as a whole.

Insider Trading Scandals

In November 1986 Ivan Boesky pleaded guilty to profiting by trading stock on insider information, that is, knowledge not available to the public. Boesky reportedly was worth hundreds of millions of dollars, was highly respected in financial and philanthropic circles, and, in the eyes of some people, was a genius at detecting incipient mergers before the public knew about them. This ability, it was thought, let him buy securities at low prices and sell them at much higher prices as bidding for the securities by merger contestants pushed up prices.

Boesky's "genius" turned out to be a pipeline to investment bankers who were engineering corporate takeovers. As part of his guilty plea Boesky not only paid a fine of $100 million (and agreed to plead guilty to a criminal charge) but implicated senior executives in some of Wall Street's most prestigious investment banking companies. At this writing (spring 1987) Rudolph Giuliani, the federal prosecutor in the case, has gotten guilty pleas and/or prison terms for over a dozen men involved in profiting from insider trading and says that this is but the tip of the iceberg. For example, Dennis B. Levine of Drexel Burnham Lambert pleaded guilty, paid a fine of $11.6 million and got a two-year jail sentence. Ira B. Sokolow, of Shearson Lehman Brothers, gave up $120,000 in profits, pleaded guilty to passing stolen information, and was sentenced to one year in jail. Robert M. Wilkis, of Lazard Freres, was sentenced to one year in prison. David S. Brown of Goldman, Sachs, agreed to pay $145,790 and was sentenced to 30 days in jail (Bianco and Weiss, 1987). These men violated, among other laws, Section 10B5 of the Securities Act of 1933. This law makes unlawful, because it defrauds the public, the use for private profit of information held by insiders and not available to the public.

Boesky identified Martin A. Siegel, cohead of the merger department of Drexel Burnham Lambert and formerly with Kidder, Peabody & Co., as one of his informants. Siegel first became involved when Martin Marietta Corp. fought to avoid a takeover by Bendix Corp., in 1982. He told Boesky about Martin's retaliatory bid, Boesky bought 52,500 shares of stock, and he made a quick profit of $120,000. Later Siegel leaked information on other impending mergers (he was involved in over 500 of them). On one, involving Carnation Co., he made over $28 million. Boesky's agents paid Siegel $700,000 for his stock tips, sometimes passing to him in public places briefcases stuffed with cash. Siegel agreed to surrender $9 million in illegal profits and faced up to 10 years in prison after pleading guilty to tax evasion and securities fraud violations (Vise, 1987).

Some of those indicted passed information to employees in their own companies in other departments. In investment banking firms, some departments work on mergers and acquisitions and other departments trade in securities. Sometimes the purpose is to make money for their companies and at other times it is to maintain a stable market for securities floated by the investment bankers. Wall Street firms have always maintained that there is a "Chinese Wall" between such departments and have strict policies against the passing of insider information between them. The recent scandal, however, indicates that in some companies the wall is more like Swiss cheese.

Fines and prison sentences for the people involved do not end the story. A number of companies, including Unocal (see case at end of Chapter 20), have sued companies where these men were employed, claiming breach of contract. Litton, for example, is suing Lehman Brothers for $30 million in damages for allegedly letting news of its takeover of Itel Corporation leak into the market. Litton claims that because of these leaks, it was forced to pay millions of dollars more in Itel stock than it otherwise would have done.

In addition, investment bankers are threatened with new government regulations. Senator William Proxmire, chairman of the Senate Banking Committee, promised that he would push for a comprehensive overhaul of our laws regulating insider trading and corporate takeovers.

But far more than the law is involved. Low standards of morality foster and sanction such acts. Investment banking has not always been above reproach, but many in the business clearly reject unethical behavior. "Integrity and honesty are at the heart of our business," says "Business Principles," a guideline to ethical conduct included in the annual report of Goldman, Sachs & Company. "To breach a confidence or to use confidential information improperly or carelessly would be unthinkable." What has happened?

There is no ready answer to this question, but one thing is clear: "They [those involved in the scandals] have their own ethic," writes Myron Magnet, of *Fortune* magazine's Board of Editors, "and it centers on money." (1986: 68). Harold Williams, former administrator of the Securities and Exchange Commission and now Getty Foundation chief, observes: "The concept of 'Let the market govern' relieves one of one's sense of responsibility" (Magnet, 1986: 68).

There are systemic problems in some industries. In 1985 the banking industry was scandalized when a number of banks—including several of the largest —were fined heavily for failing to report large cash transactions. Most of these transactions assisted drug traffickers in laundering money. The defense industry has for years been tarnished by kickbacks to purchasing agents from subcontractors. In the pharmaceutical industry, a disturbing pattern of failure to disclose negative side effects has been revealed. In 1984, for example, SmithKline Beckman Corporation pleaded guilty to thirty-four charges of misconduct brought by the Department of Justice for failing to reveal adverse side effects of a high blood pressure medication, Selacryn. Sixty deaths resulted. In 1985, Eli Lilly & Co. pleaded no contest to similar charges that it hid information about the adverse effects of an arthritis drug, Oraflex. Oraflex killed 100 people. And A. H. Robins Co. sought Chapter 11 protection in 1985 when overwhelming evidence that top executives had failed to act on knowledge that the Dalkon Shield contraceptive device was dangerous led to huge court judgments against the company. Twenty women died from the Dalkon Shield.

What is ethical practice like at mundane operational levels of business where millions of employees toil each day? Although systematic attempts to measure everyday ethical practice are handicapped by conflicting standards of measurement and the difficulty of determining the difference between what people actually believe and what they say they believe, a number of surveys shed light on everyday ethical practice. We emphasize here two important survey findings.

First, significant unethical behavior exists. Surveys have documented it for years. For example, a recent survey reported, among other findings, that 18 percent of business executives polled personally had been approached by suppliers for kickbacks, 10 percent had been asked by their bosses to do something illegal, and 47 percent had fired one or more subordinates for unethical behavior (Ricklefs, 1983). Another survey reported that nationally, 33 percent of employees admitted to calling in sick when they were not, 18 percent padded expense accounts, and 22 percent felt that some circumstances justified stealing from an employer (McBee, 1985: 52).

Second, surveys taken over the past twenty-five years show a trend toward less conflict between business ethics and personal ethics for employees. Two large-scale surveys of readers of the *Harvard Business Review*, the first in 1961 (Baumhart, 1961) and the second, an update of the first in 1976 (Brenner and Molander, 1977), reveal less conflict. When asked whether they had ever had a conflict between their roles as a profit-oriented businessperson and as an ethical person, 76 percent in 1961 said they had. In 1976, however only 57 percent reported such conflicts—a decrease of 19 percent. A third major survey of managers, in 1982, found still lower levels of ethical conflict. When managers were asked whether they agreed that "I find that sometimes I must compromise my personal principles to conform to my organization's expectations," 41 percent of supervisory managers agreed, along with 26 percent of middle managers and only 20 percent of executives (Schmidt and Posner, 1983: 31).

There have been a number of additional findings in surveys of ethical behavior over the years. A few that have been consistent stand out. The general public thinks that business ethics are lower than do business managers. The behavior and example of one's superiors is listed by managers as the most important single influence on ethical or unethical behavior in an organization. People in business are cynical, as suggested by survey findings that executives see their companies as more ethical than the competition, and other employees as less ethical than themselves. Younger managers are less ethical than older managers —apparently age and the socialization process increase ethical sensitivity. Older managers state more often than younger ones that the ethical climate of the company is more important for job satisfaction. And finally, for years surveys have reported that the general public sees falling business ethics, while business people tend to see rising ethics.

Individual versus Corporate Ethical Responsibility

The ethical behavior of the corporation is also a subject of inquiry. In 1982, for example, *U.S. News & World Report* reported that 115 of the 500 largest corporations had been convicted of a major crime or had paid a civil penalty for "serious misbehavior" between 1972 and 1982—a rate of 23 percent (1982: 25). But can a corporation be held ethically, in addition to legally, responsible for antisocial actions, or is ethical responsibility always vested in the human beings who are its employees? A vigorous debate exists on this question (see, for instance, French, 1984; Velasquez, 1983).

One view is that corporations are moral entities and may be held responsible for their behavior. Some corporate decisions are not attributable solely to individuals because the internal decision-making process focuses collective efforts and gives groups a purpose and force greater than that of the component individual wills. Company strategies, policies, controls, and norms harness employees and may create an organization climate in which unethical behavior is tolerated. Agreeing with this idea, John Z. DeLorean, former vice president of General Motors, writes that "the system of American business often produces wrong, immoral, and irresponsible decisions, even though the personal morality of the people running the business is often above reproach" (Wright, 1979: 61). Executives at GM acceded to production of the rear-engined Corvair automobile, knowing that it was dangerously unstable in high-speed turns. "There wasn't a man in top GM management who had anything to do with the Corvair," says DeLorean, "who would purposely build a car that he knew would hurt or kill people" (Wright, 1979: 67). But as good team players, the executives first failed to speak out when its safety was questioned and later sought to suppress information showing the car's deficiencies. A perversely intriguing part of DeLorean's story is the list of relatives of top executives at GM who were killed or injured in Corvair accidents. The human cost of corporate loyalty in this instance was high.

A second view is that ethical responsibility attaches only to individual corporate employees. In this view, two factors are required to establish ethical responsibility. First, an action must cause harm. Second, the action must be accompanied by an intent to act. But there are no corporate actions not attributable to individual members and their intentions. Furthermore, if a corporation were to be held responsible for social crimes, it follows that it could be punished and then all its members—including those who were not involved in the mischief—would suffer. It is not possible to punish organization charts, decision structures, or corporate cultures—only human employees.

We conclude that this is a debate between extreme positions. Ethical responsibility for corporate behavior clearly rests with individual managers. It can never be delegated by top executives, who must establish strong information and control systems. But there is no question that an organizational climate of low ethics gathers momentum and undermines the integrity of some employees. Indeed, a number of corporations recognize the power of company culture to reinforce the ethical climate and attempt through management training to create cultures in which profit pressures are not allowed to create ethical conflicts. Allied Chemical Corporation, which holds ethics training seminars for its managers five times a year, is one example.

SOURCES OF THE BUSINESS ETHOS

Every executive is at the center of a web of values connecting interrelated value systems. Six repositories of values influence people in business: genetic inheritance, religion, philosophy, cultural experience, the legal system, and professional codes. These systems have varying degrees of authority over individuals and in the same individual over time. Common bonds such as the principle of reciprocity are threaded through these sources of ethics and bind together the majority of individuals in society.

Genetic Inheritance

Embedded deeply in our value systems is the accumulation of genetic inheritance. Sociobiology provides a basis for arguing that evolutionary forces operating to promote the survival of groups have an important influence on the development of such traits as cooperation, organizational loyalty, mercy, and even extreme altruism that leads to self-sacrifice for the common good. Such traits, of course, have a fundamental impact on the development of ethical systems.

According to theoretical models of gene frequency in populations, a genetically based trait of altruism will evolve when the average fitness of all individuals within groups displaying it is greater than the average fitness of all individuals in otherwise comparable groups that do not display it (Boorman and Levitt, 1973). Sociobiologists point out that altruistic traits have evolved in many lower species, and it is unrealistic to assume that natural selection has not played a part in their development in humans. For example, workers of ant species leave the nest when sick or dying to avoid contaminating it. Honeybees die protecting their hives because their barbed stingers tear apart their viscera when they sting. The soldiers of some termite and ant species place themselves in the most dangerous positions to defend the nest, while workers run inward to avoid harm (Wilson, 1971: 321).

Theoretically, humans have developed similar altruistic behaviors. Major components of the social ethics of business organizations, such as the sanctity of contracts, organizational loyalty, generosity toward coworkers, and the formation of alliances, may be genetically predisposed behaviors that confer advantage in the evolutionary struggle. Individuals who exhibit such behavior are more likely to accrue a biological advantage over rivals because, according to sociobiologist Edward O. Wilson, "The behavior of individual members in particular cultural settings determines their survivorship and reproduction, hence their genetic fitness and the rate at which the gene ensembles spread or decline within the population" (Lumsden and Wilson, 1981). The implication for business is that managerial responses to moral challenges will be shaped and limited by the genetic predispositions of individuals. "The genes," Wilson remarks, "hold culture on a leash" (Wilson, 1978: 176).

Religion

One of the oldest sources of inspiration for ethical conduct is religion. More than 100,000 different religions exist today and pose a confusing welter of ethical creeds and belief systems to a seeker. But despite doctrinal differences, the major religions, and particularly the Judeo-Christian tradition that is dominant in American life, converge in the belief that ethics are an expression of divine will that reveals to the faithful the nature of right and wrong in business and other areas of life. The great religions are also in agreement on fundamental principles, similar to the building blocks of secular ethical doctrine. The principle of reciprocity toward one's fellow humans is found, encapsuled in variations of the Golden Rule, in major religions such as Buddhism, Christianity, Judaism, Confucianism, and Hinduism. The great religions preach the necessity for a well-ordered social system and emphasize in their tenets the social responsibility of people to act in such a way as to contribute to the general welfare, or at least not to harm it. Built upon such verities are many other rules of conduct.

The value of precepts such as the Ten Commandments, the Golden Rule, and the Sermon on the Mount in the Judeo-Christian heritage have often been extolled as guides for business activity. Donald V. Seibert, former chairman of J. C. Penney Company, Inc., advocates daily Bible reading for executives and says that two books are particularly relevant to business. "Proverbs," he has written, "is replete with references to the proper approach to business transactions, such as "A wicked man earns deceptive wages, but one who sows righteousness gets a sure reward" [11:18]. And Jesus's teachings and parables in Matthew have enough practical wisdom in them to provide a blueprint for almost an entire working experience" (1984: 119–20).

In fact, a survey of executives by Daniel Harris shows that 86 percent agreed that the use of Christian resources such as prayer, scripture reading, meditation, and church worship sharpen their judgment and give an increased sense of moral imagination and obligation (Harris, 1981: 8–9).

There is, of course, no scientific proof for the validity of religious ethics; acceptance and belief are acts of faith. For this reason religious ethics are not accepted by all; many in business are doubters who question the existence of a Divine Will. Chester Barnard, for instance, a management scholar and former president of New Jersey Bell, has, along with others, questioned the applicability of spiritual guides to business conduct. To him they "seemed to have . . . little application or relevance to the moral problems of the world of affairs" (1958: 3). Barnard argued that biblical injunctions were the product of simple rural and agrarian societies characterized by the nomadic life of lambs and shepherds described in the Bible. In this society simple personal relations dominated and the Judeo-Christian ethic that developed to regulate these situations could hardly furnish complete rules for activities such as international trade, where people were too numerous and remote to have reality as individuals. He also lamented that Christian ethics were too perfectionist since they set up ideals that could not be attained in concrete business situations in which failure to live up to an abstract ideal did not necessarily mean immorality. Thus, although many in business find strong guidance and great comfort in religious teachings, others, like Barnard, find them substantially irrelevant.

Other management scholars, however, have shown the relevance of the Judeo-Christian tradition. Williams and Houck write that although the Bible has few, if any, ethical prescriptions directly applicable to modern corporate life, it is an inspirational wellspring of models, analogues, and stories that can increase ethical sensitivity and teach important lessons (Williams and Houck, 1978, 1982). The story of the rich man and Lazarus (Luke 16:19–31), for instance, teaches concern for the poor and challenges the Christian business manager to improve the living conditions of the less privileged. The parable of the prodigal son (Luke 15:11–32) sets out an image of an unconditionally merciful father—a model applicable to ethical conflicts in the superior-subordinate relationships in large corporations.

While some in business doubt the efficacy of religious values, they are a source of inspiration to most and, in any case, they are a repository of some of the most enduring and humane values in Western civilization, along with, if we agree with Bertrand Russell, some of the harshest. Writes Russell: "I do not myself feel that any person who is really profoundly humane can believe in everlasting punishment" (Russell, 1957: 17).

Philosophical Systems

The Western manager looks back on over two thousand years of philosophical inquiry into ethics. This rich, complex, classical tradition is the source of a variety of widely embraced notions about what is ethical in business. Every age has added new ideas to this tradition, but it would be a mistake to regard the history of ethical philosophy as a single debate which, over the centuries, has matured to bear the fruit of growing ethical wisdom and clear, precise standards of conduct. Even after two millennia, there remains considerable dispute among ethical thinkers about the nature of right action. If anything, standards of ethical behavior were arguably clearer for ancient Greek civilization than for twentieth-century Americans.

In a brief circumambulation of milestones in ethical thinking, we turn first to the Greek philosophers. Greek ethics, from Homeric times onward, were embodied in the discharge of duties related to social roles such as shepherd, warrior, merchant, citizen, or king. Expectations of the occupants of these roles were clearer than in contemporary America, where social roles such as those of business manager or employee are more vague, overlapping, and marked by conflict (MacIntyre, 1981: 115). Socrates (469–399 B.C.) asserted that virtue and ethical behavior were associated with wisdom and taught that insight into life would naturally lead to right conduct. He also initiated the idea that men should respond to a moral law higher than man's law, an idea that protestors have used to demand supralegal behavior from modern corporations. Plato (428–348 B.C.), the gifted student of Socrates, carried his doctrine of virtue as knowledge further by elaborating the theory that absolute justice exists independently of individuals and that its nature can be discovered by intellectual effort. In *The Republic*, Plato set up a fifty-year program to train rulers to rule in harmony with the ideal of Justice. Plato's most apt pupil, Aristotle, spelled out virtues of character in *The Nicomachean Ethics* and advocated the study to develop knowledge of ethical behavior. A lasting contribution of Aristotle is the Doctrine of the Mean (or Golden Mean), which is that people can achieve the good life and happiness by developing virtues of moderation. To illustrate, courage was the mean between cowardice and rashness, modesty the mean between shyness and shamelessness.

The Stoic school of ethics, which spans four centuries from the death of Alexander to the rise of Christianity, glorified the trend toward character development in Greek ethics. Epictetus (A.D. 50–100), for instance, taught that virtue was found solely within and should be valued for its own sake, arguing that virtue was a greater reward than external riches or outward success.

In business, the ethical legacy of the Greeks remains as a conviction that virtues such as truth telling, charity, obedience to the law, good citizenship, justice, courage, friendship, and the correct use of power are important. An unethical manager may still try to trade integrity for profit, of course, and sacrifice character for business success. We condemn this, in part, due to the teachings of the Greeks.

Moral philosophy after the rise of Christianity was dominated by the influence of the great Catholic theologians St. Augustine (354–430) and St. Thomas Aquinas (1226–1274). Both extolled the need for right relations between man and God and asserted the primacy of religion over philosophy. The function of worldly activity was to prepare the soul for the kingdom of heaven. The Christian religion was the source of ethical expectations based on faith in God and the wisdom of God, as revealed in specific rules such as the Ten Commandments and other injunctions found in the Old Testament—for example, those for the ethical treatment of the poor in Psalms 9 and 12 (Benson, 1982: 51).

With the Enlightenment came a decline in the religious domination of ethical thinking. Secular philosophers such as Baruch Spinoza (1634–1677) tried to demonstrate ethical principles logically rather than ordain them by reference to God's will. Immanuel Kant (1724–1804) tried to find universal and objective ethical rules in logic.

Another milestone came when Jeremy Bentham (1748–1832) developed a utilitarian system as a guide to ethics. Bentham observed that "nature has placed mankind under the governance of two sovereign masters, pain and pleasure," and that the ethical worth of an act was the extent to which it produced the greatest increment of pleasure over pain. The legitimacy of majority rule in the United States rests in part on Bentham's theory of utility as refined later by J. S. Mill (1808–1873). Utilitarianism also has sanctified industrial development by legitimizing the notion that economic development brings benefit to the overwhelming majority; thus the pain and dislocation it brings to a few may be ethically permitted.

Other philosophers of the era such as John Locke (1632–1704) developed and refined doctrines of human rights, leaving an ethical legacy supporting belief in the inalienable rights of human beings, including the right to pursue life, liberty, and happiness, and the right to freedom from tyranny. Our leaders, including business leaders, continue to be restrained by these beliefs.

A "realistic" school of ethics also developed alongside the "idealistic" thinking of Spinoza, Kant, and the Utilitarians. The "realists" believed that nature was dominated by a mixture of good and evil and, therefore, that human relations were naturally marked by the same. Machiavelli (1467–1526) argued that important ends justified expedient means. Herbert Spencer (1820–1903) wrote prolifically of a harsh ethic based on the evolutionary process where the good is that which survives, and the bad that which fails. Friedrich Nietzsche (1844–1900) rejected the ideals of earlier ethics, saying they were prescriptions of the timid, designed to fetter the actions of great men whose irresistible power and will was regarded as dangerous by the common herd of ordinary mortals.

Nietzsche believed in the existence of a "master morality" in which great men made their own moral rules according to their convenience and without respect for the general good of the average person. In reaction to this "master morality" the mass of ordinary people developed a "slave morality" that shackled the great men. For example, according to Nietzsche the great mass of ordinary men celebrated the Christian virtue of turning the other cheek because they did not have the power to revenge themselves on great men. He felt that prominent theories of the day were recipes for timidity and once said of utilitarianism that it made him want to vomit.

At the turn of the century, G. E. Moore founded a new school of ethics (the emotivist school) by espousing the doctrine that all ethical judgments are nothing but expressions of personal preference and cannot be objectively proven right or wrong or shown as contrary to divine will. This rejection of both religion and principle has not, however, stopped the philosophical debate about ethics in our century. Managers continue to seek religious guidance for their actions and philosophers seek to build new ethical principles appropriate to the age.

The legacy of more than 2,000 years of recorded ethical debate is such that no single approach or principle is proven superior to others as a guide to right conduct in business. The wise student of business ethics will examine managerial behavior from a number of perspectives and make judgments only with humility that is born of the knowledge that there is centuries-old disagreement about moral standards.

Cultural Experience

Culture may be defined as a set of traditional values, rules, or standards transmitted between generations and acted upon to produce behavior that falls within acceptable limits. These rules and standards always play an important part in determining values because individuals stabilize beliefs by anchoring their conduct in the culture of the group. Civilization itself is a cumulative cultural experience in which people have passed through three distinct stages of moral codification (Durant, 1968). These stages correspond to changing economic and social arrangements in human history.

For millions of generations in the *hunting stage* of human development, ethics were adapted to conditions in which our ancestors had to be ready to fight, face brutal foes, and suffer hostile forces of nature. Under such circumstances a premium was placed on pugnacity, appetite, greed, and sexual readiness, since it was often the strongest who survived. Trade ethics in early civilizations were probably deceitful and dishonest by our standards, and economic transactions were frequently conducted by brute force and violence.

Civilization passed into an *agricultural stage* approximately 10,000 years ago, beginning a time when industriousness was more important than ferocity, thrift paid greater dividends than violence, monogamy became the prevailing sexual custom because of the relatively equal numbers of the sexes, and peace came to be valued over wars, which destroyed crops and animals. During the early agricultural period, forms of barter and exchange developed, and later the church worked its way upon commerce with teachings of ethics and a reward for ethical behavior—salvation and everlasting peace.

Two centuries ago, society entered an *industrial stage* of cultural experience, and moral values once again reflected the changed environment, institutions, and ideas. The rise of factories, management expertise, international trade, technology, capitalist economic doctrines, and materialistic philosophies, for example, brought changes in ethical standards. More recently, the family has declined as a source of moral teaching. Institutions such as the church, which traditionally inculcated ethics in new generations, have been weakened by social change. Fewer than 40 percent of Americans attend religious ceremonies today, compared with 85 percent in colonial times. Because of Supreme Court decisions and sectarian controversies, public schools do not teach moral principles through religious doctrine. Owing to the widespread impact of value-neutral theories in the behavioral sciences, colleges in recent years have downgraded the teaching of ethics.

Many of the most difficult ethical problems that business managers face arise from changing cultural experience. Corporate social responsibilities, for example, are occasioned by growing affluence and rising public expectations. The consumer movement has posed new ethical issues for business related to such diverse matters as auto safety and carcinogenic agents in food. The presence of computers has raised new issues of privacy rights unlike those debated in agricultural days when biblical injunctions were first phrased. Accumulating scientific evidence showing environmental and human damage from industrial products and manufacturing processes is new in this century and creates the need for consensual ethical guidelines for environmental protection. Because business must face these portentous ethical problems, it is on the cutting edge of cultural experience. Yet, at the same time, it has never been less clear what adequate ethical standards are. A cartoon in the *New Yorker* once depicted a cluster of managers sitting around a conference table. They all looked perplexed and confused, and the boss talked into the intercom to his secretary. "Miss Jones," he said, "will you please send someone in here who can tell right from wrong!" The boss had a point. Our business system is more morally complex than ever in our history.

The Legal System

The law is a codification of customs, ideas, beliefs, and ethical standards that society wishes to preserve and enforce. As social views about what is right and wrong change and crystallize, they are reflected in new laws or the abandonment and neglect of old ones. A major cause of higher ethical standards in business is the addition of laws to prevent violations of what society considers to be proper. Of course, the law does not establish all standards of ethics for society. Law simply cannot blanket all areas of conduct, and this is even more true today than in the past. Law is a reactive institution, and the enactment of new statutes always lags behind the opportunity for business to take advantage of emerging situations.

Nevertheless, over the past twenty years, a "legal explosion" of new government regulations, product liability doctrines, consumer and stockholder lawsuits, changes in tort law, and new criminal statutes have forced corporations to comply with rising standards of ethical behavior. More of the corporation's activities are subject to legal control, and there has been an expansion of the civil and criminal liability of executives for violations of the law.

There are a number of administrative and legal weapons for getting corporate compliance with the law. There are two main methods for sanctioning illegal corporate behavior: fines and prosecution of individual managers. Neither is unflawed as a device for controlling corporate crime.

Fines may be levied to take away ill-gotten gains. Often, they include punitive payments designed to punish wrongful behavior. For example, in 1985 General Electric pleaded guilty to defrauding the federal government of $800,000 on a Minuteman missile contract. A manager in a Minuteman plant and his subordinates falsified worker time cards (without the worker's knowledge) under the mistaken assumption that the complexity of government contracts made cost-sharing between projects legitimate. After pleading guilty, General Electric agreed to reimburse the government for the $800,000 and was fined an additional $1,040,000. Fines such as this create adverse publicity and damage managerial careers, but they often are financially insignificant. (The GE fine was the equivalent of a $25 fine for a person with a $50,000 annual income.) Courts hesitate to impose truly damaging fines because their burden would fall partly on innocent bystanders—shareholders, workers, suppliers, and others who had no knowledge of or control over the corporation's deviant behavior, but whose livelihood depended on its benefactions. In 1985 the Treasury Department fined Crocker National Bank $2,250,000 for thousands of unreported cash transactions in violation of the Bank Secrecy Act of 1970, an act designed to prevent money laundering by the underworld. The fine could have been as high as $7.9 million, but Crocker executives talked Treasury officials into the lower amount because the bank's financial position was weak.

Fines that are fixed in dollar amounts in civil and criminal statutes often do not hurt large corporations. Fines could be assessed in proportion to a firm's assets or revenues—as is sometimes done under European Economic Community rules—but it might not be equitable to fine one firm twenty times more than another for the same transgression. Fines are also ineffective in changing the weak organizational controls or corrupt corporate cultures that sometimes lead to illegal behavior.

The second legal weapon for sanctioning corporate crime is the prosecution of individual managers. In the past, judges have been reluctant to sentence managers to jail terms for fraud, embezzlement, polluting the environment, or breaking health and safety laws. Managers ordinarily do not violently endanger society, may not have the motive or opportunity to repeat a crime, and would further crowd prisons. Investigating corporate crimes also is difficult for prosecuting attorneys, who are faced with a mass of highly technical corporate documents to review, a network of complex organizational relationships to sort out, and the conflicting priority of violent street crime to compete for their resources. Corporations ordinarily are defended by highly competent defense lawyers; the states' case ordinarily is championed by underfunded, less experienced attorneys. For these reasons, U.S. and state attorneys with limited resources for prosecution find it easier to justify simple indictments for street criminals and shy away from the complex corporation cases.

Nevertheless, some highly publicized cases against executives who have violated criminal statutes have led to prison terms. In a landmark 1985 conviction, three managers of Film Recovery Systems, a Chicago firm that recovered silver from used photographic film, were sentenced to 25 years in prison when an employee died after exposure to uncontrolled cyanide fumes from a vat used in the extraction process. The three were convicted after an investigation revealed that they had known of the dangers but had failed to inform employees or install air filtering in the plant. The same year, Jacob F. Butcher, a Tennessee banker, was sentenced to twenty years in prison after pleading guilty to charges that he fraudulently used funds and precipitated the failure of eight banks that he controlled. In 1986 an even harsher sentence was meted out by a Maryland court to Jeffrey Levitt, owner of two savings and loan institutions, which failed due to his fraudulent real estate schemes. Their failure precipitated widespread turmoil in Maryland's banks. Levitt was fined $12,000, forefeited $10 million of personal property, and was sentenced to 30 years in state prison. These sentences are atypical; but they serve notice on managers that criminal behavior may result in more than a company fine or a slap on the wrist.

Other methods for punishing corporate crime exist. Combinations of fines and prison terms have been meted out. Courts have appointed directors to preside over organizational changes designed to enforce better behavior. Some corporations have paid their fines to community service projects, and executives have been ordered to spend long hours working for charity. Sometimes courts require advertisements and speeches to publicize wrongdoing. In 1982 the Japanese Health Ministry shut the plants and warehouses of Nippon Chemiphar, a drug company, for eighty days when it was found guilty of illegal marketing practices. This action caused a serious decline in the firm's stock prices (Kennedy, 1985: 446). Whatever sanctioning devices are tested and adopted by the courts, they should not cripple or render inefficient legitimate corporate activity.

Codes of Conduct

Conduct codes are a common source of ethical norms for business. Three types deserve mention. First are company codes. More companies have ethics codes today than ever before. Opinion Research Corporation in 1980 found that 73 percent of the corporations it surveyed had a code, and half of those codes had been written between 1976 and 1980 (Doughty et al., 1980: 11). By 1984 a similar survey found that 93 percent of the *Fortune* 1,000 industrial and service companies responding to a survey had written codes of ethics (Center for Business Ethics, 1986).

Transportation and utility companies have fewer codes than companies in other industries, perhaps because they are already heavily regulated by government and do less foreign business. Foreign transactions in a world of variable ethics are a major source of conflicts. The so-called "antibribery law," the Foreign Corrupt Practices Act of 1977, has inspired many corporations to institute ethics codes encouraging compliance with that law. Indeed, 86 percent of the companies in the Opinion Research Corporation survey stated that encouraging employee compliance with the law was the most important reason for initiating a code, making this the most frequently given reason. A content analysis of 281 ethics codes reveals, furthermore, that the most frequently prohibited behaviors are extortion, inappropriate gifts, and kickbacks, followed closely by conflict of interest problems and illegal political payments (Chatov, 1980).

There is no standard format for codes of ethics. Many are written at high levels of abstraction and contain the injunctions of religion, philosophy, or traditional practice. The short two-and-one-half-page statement of ethics of the Koppers Company, for example, states that management accepts the teachings of the great religions in regard to moral and ethical conduct and cannot improve upon them. The Golden Rule is found in many such codes. Employees of Denver's Samsonite Company, for example, carry small marbles with the Golden Rule printed on them. Longer codes often begin with a short general statement. The "Cummins Practice on Ethical Standards," for example, states:

> For Cummins, ethics rests on a fundamental belief in people's dignity and decency. Our most basic ethical standard is to show respect for those whose lives we affect and to treat them as we would expect them to treat us if our positions were reversed (Williams, 1982: 20).

Some codes are lengthy and detailed. IBM's *Business Conduct Guidelines* is a thirty-two-page booklet with seven sections and sophisticated, color-coded graphics identifying each part.

Corporations institutionalize ethics in varying degrees. In the Center for Business Ethics survey mentioned earlier, 44 percent of the firms responding had ethics training programs for managers, 18 percent had ethics committees, and 3 percent had judiciary boards to resolve conflicts (Center for Business Ethics, 1986). These efforts sometimes are expedient. In the wake of a series of procurement fraud charges, General Dynamics Corp. instituted a corporate ethics program, and it became a critical factor in getting subsequent defense contracts.

In May 1985, Navy Secretary John Lehman suspended Navy contracts with General Dynamics worth over $1 billion, citing as one reason a "pervasive corporate attitude" inappropriate to the public trust. The company had been caught in a series of unethical and illegal acts. Managers were shifting expenses from fixed-price contracts to contracts that permitted cost overruns. The company had given numerous, expensive gifts to Admiral Hyman Rickover and his wife. Executives charged country club dues to military contracts, and Chairman David Lewis billed the government for his flights from company headquarters in St. Louis to his farm in Georgia. The condition for lifting the suspension of General Dynamics from Pentagon contracts was a fine of $676,000 for the gifts, cancellation of $22 million in overcharges, and the installation of a strict ethics code. The company responded to the latter condition with a 20-page booklet on business ethics and a series of detailed policies on a variety of issues. An ethics committee was set up on the board of directors composed entirely of outside directors, and a professor from the University of Chicago was hired to direct the ethics program. In 1986 ethics hotlines were established over which employees could report questionable behavior, anonymously if they wished. The telephones have devices to prevent tracing, and recording machines attached to them are kept in locked places. The company has new, stringent requirements for filling out workers' time cards and for billing government contracts. A draconian policy on giving and accepting gifts or entertainment prohibits employees from accepting even trivia like calendars or pens from subcontractors. When military personnel visit General Dynamics facilities, they must pay 25 cents for each cup of coffee they drink (Worthy, 1986: 74).

Other companies, such as the Norton Company, the world's largest abrasives manufacturer, have institutionalized ethics to a high degree without being prodded by scandal. Norton has established an ethics code and updated it frequently, publishing it in eight languages for foreign employees. A board-level Corporate Ethics Committee issues bulletins after discussions of gray areas in the code, monitors and investigates compliance, and recommends changes to the Norton board of directors. Recently, for instance, the committee deliberated reimbursing managers for dues to clubs that discriminate in membership on the basis of race, religion, or sex and decided that although Norton managers could join such clubs, the company would not reimburse them for their dues, as with nondiscriminatory clubs (Purcell, 1985).

A second type of code is found in company operational policies that set up rules and procedures that have an ethical content. Included here, for instance, are specific policy statements concerning such matters as hiring, promoting, firing, dealing with suppliers, and handling customer complaints. General Motors, for example, has a detailed gift code describing proper relations with company suppliers and dealers. These stipulations, like more general codes of ethics, protect employees from unethical advances by those outside the company.

Third, many in business are members of professional and industry associations that have codes of ethics of varying elaboration. The "Affirmative Ethical Principles" of the American Institute of Certified Public Accountants is less than one page long. The Santa Clara County Auto Recyclers Association prints its "Code of Ethics" on a matchbook which states that "Customers are urged to send accounts of positive or negative treatment to: S.C.C.A.R.A. Ethics Committee," and gives an address. The "Television Code of Ethics" of the National Association of Broadcasters, on the other hand, is lengthy and enforced by a nine-member review board with approximately three dozen full-time staff members. However, trade association statements, though older than most corporate ethics codes, are usually limited in specificity and effectiveness because of fear of antitrust violations and feeble enforcement powers.

Codes of ethics may make positive contributions beyond their public relations value. Developing a code is an occasion for members of a firm to think through ethical conflicts and duties. Existing codes may clarify proper actions and employees pressured toward ethical compromise may be able to protect themselves by invoking specific provisions. Although codes are an upgrading force, one should not exaggerate their efficacy. Many contain highly principled statements but are neither specific nor helpful in developing principled ethical reasoning skills in employees. Not all companies with codes make a concerted effort to institutionalize ethical behavior. Codes are more effective when they are combined with measures such as ethics committees, judicial enforcement boards, and training programs.

THE ROLE OF INDIVIDUAL PSYCHODYNAMICS

Some managers are unethical and others scrupulously honest. Ethical values are displayed through the prism of individual personality, so the process of personality development explains in part why ethical propensities differ.

Sigmund Freud (1856–1939) explained human personality as consisting of three parts. The *id* is the source of primitive, aggressive impulses. The *ego* shapes and directs these impulses in conformity with the realities of the outer world. And the *superego* both provides an ideal image of the self and incorporates a conscience to police behavior (Freud, 1933). The conscience part of the superego incorporates parental discipline about the rightness and wrongness of particular actions. According to developmental psychologists, the child, being in a helpless and dependent state, must satisfy parental authority. On an elemental level, pleasing the parents is a matter of survival to the child and so the child is receptive to parental moral teaching and begins to incorporate ethics at an early age.

The conscience is largely formed in childhood and in adulthood is an internal reservoir of parental authority with the power to mete out psychological reward and punishment. The power of the conscience to do this is believed to be derived from an internal diversion of part of the primitive destructive effect of the id. Incidentally, a vivid proof of the presence of the conscience is the polygraph, or lie detector. Changes in respiration, pulse rate, and skin chemistry are the measurable effects of the action of the conscience when a person violates the built-in parental prohibition against lying.

The tremendous force of the conscience in ethical affairs may be illustrated in the fate of Eli M. Black, chairman of United Brands Co., who leaped to his death from the forty-fourth floor of the Pan American building in Manhattan in 1975, shortly before *Wall Street Journal* reporters discovered that United Brands had paid a number of overseas bribes. Black was the son of a rabbi and was shaken, according to friends, when a director of the company, who was not supposed to know about the payments, raised a question about them. We may speculate that the seeds of Black's destruction were planted in his conscience and that, in making foreign payoffs, Black turned his internal police state against himself as an implacable foe. On a more mundane level, work itself is a powerful source of appeasement for the pressures of the conscience. Through work an individual may achieve worthy goals of the conscience through punctuality, productivity, and honesty (Levinson, 1981). The need of some workers to do high-quality work represents the desire to meet the stern dictates of the conscience.

The way in which a manager perceives and utilizes ethical principles available in society is also a function of the dynamics of personality development. Various abnormal developments in personality are associated with the pathological application of ethics. For example, demands for moral perfection may be neurotic if they are based on the need to be superior to others rather than on a healthy desire to improve oneself. Emphasis on justice may be a camouflage for vindictiveness and sadistic tendencies based on the neurotic need to redress childhood humiliations and assert neurotic superiority (Horney, 1950). The tyranny of the superego in obsessive-compulsive personalities often leads to the development of a harsh and unyielding moral judgment, which the person directs against both self and others. The obsessive-compulsive neurotic may spend a lifetime trying to live up to impossibly high moral ideals rather than unleash the anxiety that would come from failure to be perfect (Shapiro, 1965: 41). Psychopathic insincerity and lying are common traits in impulsive personality types and stem from flawed development of the conscience. The psychopath is typically an "operator" who is ethical when necessary or in self-interest, but who does not feel pangs of conscience for behaving unethically. A person with paranoid tendencies may erroneously perceive conspiracies among colleagues or company management and employ rigorous ethical standards to condemn these allegedly harmful, though entirely fictitious, schemes. Many "wheeler-dealers" in the business community may in reality be among the 3 to 10 percent of the population suffering from mood disorders, such as manic depression (Fieve, 1975: 27). At the height of elation, a manic may be so euphoric as to feel immune from ethical considerations. Psychotic individuals are out of touch with reality and may engage in violent and unethical behavior because they are unable to understand the consequences of their actions.

Research suggests that the ability to use moral reasoning may also develop in stages and differ among individuals. Lawrence Kohlberg, an educational psychologist, demonstrated through twenty years of following the lives of seventy-five American boys (now men) that there are six sequential stages of moral development. The child moves from complete reliance on external rules and standards to states of increasing reliance on internal controls as follows: (1) avoidance of breaking rules in order to avert punishment, (2) obedience to ethical standards to satisfy self-centered needs and to elicit reciprocity from others, (3) subordination of self-interest to group interest to please others and gain their approval, (4) respect for the law and authority as necessary to preserve the social system, (5) flexible interpretation of legal authority as balanced with the rights of individuals, and (6) principled reasoning with ethical concepts of personal choice. Most individuals in Kohlberg's study attained stages four and five by adulthood, but only a few progressed to stage six (Kohlberg, 1969). If Kohlberg's theory is correct, business managers respond differently to common problems of business ethics depending on their level of moral development.

In conclusion, the ethical implications of personality are a significant part of corporate life. Ethical behavior is an integral part of all human behavior, and, to the extent that personality development imposes burdens of abnormality, anger, anxiety, fear, self-doubt, and neurotic needs, individual ethics may be altered to facilitate the personality integration activities of the ego. Some managers are therefore unethical and others scrupulously honest because of internal impulses as well as external constraints.

CASE STUDY

A. H. ROBINS CO. AND THE DALKON SHIELD

This is the story of a venerable and proud company brought to its knees by a dime-sized contraceptive device. The company, A. H. Robins, grew from an apothecary shop started in 1866 by a pharmacist named Albert Hartley Robins into a prosperous multinational with $700 million in sales and 6,100 employees in 1985. Were it not for the firm's persistence in selling the Dalkon Shield intrauterine device in the face of clear evidence of its dangers, Robins might today be flourishing. But during the 1970s, Robins' management lost its way. Oblivious to signals of danger, it opened itself to lawsuits, government restrictions, public criticism, and hostile investigative reporters. In 1985 it was forced to seek protection under Chapter 11 of the bankruptcy laws to escape costly lawsuits.

Today, the company limps toward reorganization. Despite record earnings every year after 1980 (except 1984, when money was set aside to help pay for lawsuits), its stock trades at a fraction of its former price, avoided by institutions and sensitive mainly to developments in the bankruptcy proceedings. Business analysts note its strong product lines—Chapstick lip balm, Robitussin cold medications, Sergeant's flea and tick collars, and a variety of prescription drugs—and believe that reorganization will be successful. If it survives Robins will avoid the fate of at least 20 women who died of Shield-related complications.

Intrauterine Devices

An intrauterine device (IUD) is simply a foreign object placed in the uterus to lower fertility. No one is sure exactly how it works. In their heyday they came in a variety of shapes and sizes. There were rings, spirals, loops, bows, T-shapes, and contorted forms that defy description. Some released copper or progesterone slowly into the body to enhance contraceptive effect. All these permutations were attempts at greater contraceptive effectiveness in a process not yet fully understood. Much study of how IUDs work has been undertaken. It is thought that they function by stimulating cellular actions which cause fertilized eggs to be rejected by the endometrium or womb lining so that embryos cannot implant and receive nourishment from the mother's body. The question remains as to whether IUDs are contraceptives or abortifacients.

One of the earliest uses of IUD technology was by ancient desert nomads, who placed stones in the uteri of their camels to prevent pregnancy from occurring during prolonged marches (Edelman et al., 1979). IUDs were not much used in humans until the late nineteenth century and the first real medical experimentation came in the 1920s. They continued to languish until the 1960s when, simultaneously, new designs incorporating flexible plastics became available and women, aware of the drawbacks of birth-control pills, sought alternatives.

For women who could not tolerate the pill, remember to take it, or feel comfortable with its risks, IUDs were an attractive alternative. Once inserted in the uterus in a minor procedure done at the doctor's office, the IUD generally requires no further attention. Its contraceptive effects end promptly with removal. Adverse side effects risked in IUD use include abdominal pain, cramps, bleeding, and heavy menstruation. IUDs also pose a risk of pelvic inflammatory disease, a dangerous infection by bacteria associated with the foreign object in the uterus that spreads throughout the reproductive system and body. IUDs occasionally perforate the uterine wall as well.

Development of the Dalkon Shield

The Dalkon Shield was invented in the late 1960s by Hugh J. Davis, M.D., an assistant professor of obstetrics and gynecology at the Johns Hopkins University School of Medicine. To sell the new IUD, he and two partners, an electrical engineer named Irwin Lerner and an attorney named Robert Cohn, formed the Dalkon Corporation. The word Dalkon was derived from combinations of the three partners' names. The device was called a shield because its shape was similar to a policeman's badge.

Although Davis originally patented the IUD in 1967, Lerner tinkered with it and added ten fin-like projections around the sides so that it would stay more firmly in the uterus. In 1968 this altered design was patented, and Lerner the electrical engineer, rather than Davis the physician, was listed on the patent application as sole inventor. In Davis' mind this renunciation of patent right apparently freed him to use medical research facilities at Johns Hopkins University to study the Shield's efficacy, even though he owned 35 percent of the Dalkon Corporation, which sold the Shield—a clear conflict of interest (Mintz, 1985).

Davis conducted a clinical study to show that the Shield was safe and effective. In February 1970 he published an article in the *American Journal of Obstetrics and Gynecology* containing data on 640 users. It showed a pregnancy rate of only 1.1 percent, lower than the 1.4 percent rate typical for birth-control pills. Davis noted no serious side effects from the shield, and, of course, failed to note his financial interest in the product.

In 1971 Davis also published a book, *Intrauterine Devices for Contraception*, in which he compared the Dalkon Shield to other IUDs and concluded that it was

The Dalkon Shield was made of plastic. Side projections anchored the device in the uterus; the tail string extended into the vagina, and women and their doctors could check the position of the device. Courtesy of Planned Parenthood of New York City, Inc. Random House photo by Stacey Pleasant.

superior. Later, both this book and the article were criticized as highly misleading by other medical researchers. For example, in his study of women fitted with Shields, Davis had followed his subjects for only five and one-half months. This was insufficient time to show the typical pregnancy rate among shield wearers of over 5 percent or to observe the predictable development of pelvic infections. Moreover, he failed to follow up on women who dropped out of the study, the very women most likely to have become pregnant or to have had complications.

The Dalkon Shield began to sell based on this foundation of trumped-up medical evidence. It came on the market at a time when sexual mores were loosening and when many women were having second thoughts about birth control pills because of recent congressional hearings regarding their adverse side effects and risks. To increase sales, Davis and his partners tried to find a major pharmaceutical firm that would market the device nationally. This is how A. H. Robins entered the picture.

A. H. Robins Co. Buys Rights to Sell the Shield

Early in 1970 Robins, which was looking for an entry into the booming market for birth-control devices, purchased rights to the Dalkon Shield. In those days the Food and Drug Administration (FDA) required no premarket testing of medical devices such as IUDs, and so Robins could enter the market immediately. It did so without conducting any research on the device to confirm its safety or effectiveness.

Robins began an aggressive campaign to market the Shield to doctors around the country through a sales force of several hundred that had been trained in a special sales pitch about the device. The sales force was pressured to meet quotas, as the following 1971 telegram from one division sales manager to his sales force shows:

> Northern Division will not be humiliated by a lack of Dalkon sales. If you have not sold at least 25 packages of eight, then you are instructed to call me. Be prepared to give me your call-back figures. No excuses or hedging will be tolerated, or look for another occupation (in Mintz, 1985: 67).

Ads in medical journals were another part of the marketing campaign. They emphasized that the Shield had been "anatomically engineered" to fit the uterus. They billed the Shield as a logical choice for women who were not good candidates for the pill, including young women inexperienced with birth control, those with adverse reactions to the pill, those in mass programs at birth-control clinics, and those too disorganized women who couldn't follow the daily regimen. Some of the ads in 1971 and 1972 featured a chart showing low pregnancy rates in four studies—two of which, including the earlier study by Davis, had been done by physicians with a financial interest in sales of the Shield and the other two poorly designed.

By 1971, the Shield—which cost $.25 to make but was sold to doctors for $4.35—was outselling all other IUDs. Eventually it grabbed a 40 percent market share; 2.9 million were sold in the United States. Part of the reason for the Shield's success was that the company took the unusual step of marketing the IUD to general practitioners (GPs) as well as to obstetricians and gynecologists. The latter were the usual market for IUDs because of their specialized knowledge, but Robins chose to market the Shield to GPs in order to reach the majority of women who consulted only their family doctors about birth control. Some members of the Robins Medical Advisory Board cautioned against this move, but to little effect (Mintz, 1985: 71).

Storm Clouds Gather

For several years the Shield was the hottest selling device in an expansive IUD market. Each year between 1970 and 1974, over 1 million new women chose to be fitted with an IUD. But as customers multiplied, problems arose. Doctors reported large numbers of pregnancies among Shield users, including a higher than normal number of ectopic (extrauterine) pregnancies requiring surgery. Other women required surgery to remove IUDs that had penetrated the uterine lining. Many suffered infections of the reproductive system and abdominal area triggered by bacterial contamination of the womb related to IUD use. These women required X-rays, antibiotics, blood transfusions, and at times major surgery to remove diseased organs. Women who became pregnant with IUDs in place frequently miscarried in the second trimester or lost their babies when bacterial infections required septic abortions. Many surgeries and miscarriages left women sterile, turning the allegedly carefree method of birth control into an involuntary nightmare.

Although these complications were associated with all IUDs, the Dalkon Shield ultimately proved to be far more risky than its competitors. One reason was the design of its tail string. The Shield, like other IUDs, had a short string dropping from it into the vagina so that women and their doctors could check the position of the IUD and make sure it was properly sited. This was an important safety measure, since a lost IUD might perforate the uterus and enter the abdomen. But the tail string on the Shield, unlike those of competing devices, was made of interwoven fibers and acted like a wick that drew bacteria from the vagina up the microscopic paths between the fibers into the womb; this "wicking" was the cause of an unusually high rate of pelvic inflammatory disease among women wearing the Shield. Studies by Robins employees demonstrated the dangers inherent in this tail-string design, and several employees in the factory where Robins manufactured the Shield suggested switching to a monofilament tail string to obviate the problem. An alternative string was sought and found, but it cost 6.1 cents per device compared to the older string's cost of .63 cents per unit. No change was ever made. And the Robins employees never pursued the matter outside the company.

In 1973 a subcommittee of the House Government Operations Committee held hearings on the need to give the FDA authority to regulate intrauterine devices. At these hearings, doctors and FDA officials testified about problems caused by the Shield. But at this time, the problems beginning to appear had not been documented systematically, and Jack Freund, vice president for research and development at Robins, rebutted the critics with information from company studies. Here is an excerpt from his extensive testimony.

> We have sponsored ten prospective clinical studies of the product totaling 1,703 insertions, designed for individual patient exposure periods of at least twenty-four months. At a sixteen months data cutoff date, involving 11,728 women-months of use, statistical analysis—life table method—of data from these studies reveals the following rates per 100 women: pregnancy, 1.6; expulsion, 2.9; medical removal, 13.2; and continuation, 76.9. There was one uterine perforation reported in this group of patients. . . .
>
> Since we acquired the Dalkon Shield, and after an estimated 1.8 million insertions, we have received approximately 400 voluntary reports of problems associated with use of the shield. In general, these have been of the nature associated with other IUDs (Freund, 1973: 304–305).

But by early 1974, studies had appeared showing pregnancy rates among Shield wearers as high as 10 percent. Stories of Shield complications appeared in medical journals. Robins reacted to accumulating criticism by calling a one-day conference in February to bring together experts on IUDs to discuss the situation. As a result of this conference, Robins sent letters to approximately 120,000 physicians advising them of the reported septic abortions and deaths and recommending removal of the Shield in patients who became pregnant or termination of pregnancy if the Shield could not be removed.

Still, evidence mounted that the Shield was more dangerous than other IUDs. In May, the Center for Disease Control in Atlanta released a study linking the Shield to 73 percent of IUD hospitalizations among women who had never borne children and showing that the overall risk of IUD-related disease requiring hospitalization was twice as high for the Shield as for all other IUD brands combined (Kahn and Tyler, 1971). Shortly thereafter, an Arizona doctor published an article discussing five IUD-related deaths from septic midtrimester abortions and noted that four of the women had been wearing Dalkon Shields. The article included these observations:

> The greatest concern is the rather insidious yet rapid manner in which these patients become ill. In three of the five noted maternal deaths, the first symptoms, which were disarmingly innocuous in and of themselves, occurred within 31 to 72 hours of death from sepsis and the sequelae of sepsis. It appears that the infection becomes generalized at about the same time as or before there are any localizing signs, and therefore the margin of safety that time ordinarily provides in treating such infections is not present. One wonders if there may be something about the design of the shield-type device that allows vascular dissemination of infection that might otherwise be locally contained (Christian, 1974: 443).

Shortly after publication of this article, the FDA recommended to Robins that the Shield be withdrawn from the market. In June, Robins voluntarily withdrew it from further sales but did not recall supplies in the distribution system and did not suggest that women already wearing it have it removed. After further study, however, the FDA decided to allow Robins to remarket the Shield if it conducted a registration and record-keeping program with doctors and if it switched to a monofilament tail string. This decision was made only in the face of considerable dissension within the agency but was rationalized as a step toward accumulating definitive proof of the Shield's performance.

The Shield was never remarketed. Robins decided against further sales because of the bad publicity it had received. But the FDA decision permitting remarketing left Robins in the favorable position of having permission from this watchdog of the public health to market the Shield. Also, the Shield was withdrawn before full information about its dangers could be acquired by the FDA-mandated record keeping program. Sales of the Shield in eighty foreign countries continued until late 1975. Many were sold in less developed countries, where the dangers of pelvic inflammatory disease were greater than in the United States, because hospitalization and a course of antibiotics were not routinely available.

Lawsuits and Bankruptcy

Exact figures for the injuries suffered by American women are not available. *Washington Post* reporter Morton Mintz (1985) estimated in a book on the Shield that ultimately 4 percent of women using it were injured. Tens of thousands suffered infections, roughly 110,000 had unexpected pregnancies, and of these 60 percent miscarried—248 in dangerous septic abortions. There are 20 reported Shield fatalities.

Beginning in the late 1970s, many of the injured women sued Robins. At first, the company strenuously opposed them. In court it claimed that the Shield was as safe as other IUDs, that the FDA had permitted its remarketing, and that top management had not been informed of excessive pregnancy rates or risks of dangerous complications. When injured women took the witness stand, Robins's attorneys subjected them to questions about the number of partners and type of sex the women had experienced, the level of hygiene they achieved, and whether they used artificial devices during sex. Faced with public humiliation about these intimate matters many women declined to litigate.

Early jury awards and settlements were small, but attorneys for the injured women persisted. They sought recovery under product liability laws that allowed awards for injury caused by inherently unsafe products. And they accused Robins of fraud for continuing to market the Shield and advertising it as safe when management had evidence of its dangers.

Gradually, Robins's defenses crumbled. Attorneys for the injured women acquired internal company memoranda showing that the dangers of the Shield had been reported to executives. In 1984 a former Robins attorney revealed in a deposition that he and several others had destroyed documents on the wicking tendencies of the Shield by burning them in a furnace. The documents had been destroyed in 1975 on the orders of William Forrest, vice president and general counsel of Robins. Unknown to Forrest, however, some papers were squirreled away by an attorney who later left the company and decided to tell the story to salve his conscience. Such information entered many Shield trials, and juries increasingly awarded victims not only the costs of their medical care and pain and suffering, but also huge punitive awards to punish the company for willful wrongdoing. Robins executives persisted in denying knowledge of the Shield's dangers.

In 1983 twenty-one Shield cases in Minnesota were assigned to a blunt-speaking district judge named Miles Lord. Lord came to believe that Robins was using a variety of corner-cutting legal tactics to delay lawsuits, that it was outrageously wrong in refusing to recall Shields still implanted in women, and that its officers were avoiding personal responsibility for fraudulent actions by disclaiming knowledge of the devices' dangers. Finally, when Robins in 1984 hired a Minneapolis law firm employing Lord's son, the judge realized what he could no longer preside over Shield cases without conflict of interest. In an unusual move, he drafted a statement directed at Robins management, and as a condition in the out-of-court settlement of several Shield cases, he required three top Robins executives to appear in his courtroom.

On the morning of February 29, 1984, he read the following statement to E. Claiborne Robins, Jr., president and CEO, William Forrest, vice president and general counsel, and Carl D. Lunsford, senior vice president for research and development. The statement was designed to shame these men and sear the responsibility they bore into their consciences so that they could never again disavow knowing the Shield's hazards.

"I did not know." "It was not me." "Look elsewhere." Time and time again, each of you has used this kind of argument in refusing to acknowledge your responsibility. . . .

Gentlemen, the results of these activities and attitudes on your part have been catastrophic. Today as you sit here attempting once more to extricate yourselves from the legal consequences of your acts, none of you has faced up to the fact that more than 9,000 women have made claims that they gave up part of their womanhood so that your company might prosper. It is alleged that others gave their lives so you might so prosper. And there stand behind them legions more who have been injured but who have not sought relief in the courts of this land.

If one poor young man were, by some act of his—without authority or consent—to inflict such damage upon one woman, he would be jailed for a good portion of the rest of his life. And yet your company without warning to women invaded their bodies by the millions and caused them injuries by the thousands. And when the time came for these women to make their claims against your company, you attacked their characters.

Mr. Robins, Mr. Forrest, Dr. Lunsford: You have not been rehabilitated. Under your direction, your company has in fact continued to allow women, tens of thousands of women, to wear this device—a deadly depth charge in their wombs, ready to explode at any time. . . . The only conceivable reasons you have not recalled this product are that it would hurt your balance sheet and alert women who already have been harmed that you may be liable for their injuries. You have taken the bottom line as your guiding beacon, and the low road as your route. This is corporate irresponsibility at its meanest . . .

Please in the name of humanity, lift your eyes above the bottom line (in Mintz, 1986: 6–7).

Awards continued to rise and by late 1984 Robins had paid out over $300 million in Shield cases. The decision was finally made to recall the Shield and in October 1984, Robins took out television and print ads to recall the device from an estimated 80,000 women. Finally, a decade after the company had stopped marketing the Shields, it also recalled them.

Awards continued to increase. By August 1985, the company had paid out $378 million in claims in 9,230 cases. Its legal costs were over $107 million. And no end was in sight because about 5,100 lawsuits were pending, and nearly 400 new suits were filed each month. The size of jury awards was rising. In a 1985 Wichita, Kansas, trial, a woman who had undergone a hysterectomy after using the Shield was awarded a record $9.2 million.

At this point, E. Claiborne Robins, Jr., decided to seek protection under the bankruptcy laws to, in his words, "protect the company's economic vitality against those who would destroy it for the benefit of a few" (Alexander, 1985:

32). Although this remark unfortunately implied that injured women were dismantling the company out of unwarranted greed, looked at another way Robins' viewpoint is understandable. Since 1980 Robins's sales had increased by 63 percent, and its profits had risen 135 percent. A booming business with worthwhile products was shackled by the legacy of its Dalkon Shield sales of the early 1970s. Robins made after-tax profits of only about $500,000 on the Shield in the four years during which it had sold it, an amount insufficient to cover even one typical jury award in 1985 (Skrycki, 1986). Estimates of total liability for all potential lawsuits ran from $1 to $8 billion, yet Robins's assets in 1985 were only $706.5 million. Robins executives believed that destroying a thriving business to pay legal claims made no sense. In 1985 members of the Robins family and corporate executives owned 52 percent of the firm's shares. With the drop in the stock's price from $24 early in 1985 to $8.25 immediately after the bankruptcy announcement, these insiders suffered a collective financial loss of roughly $197 million.

After Bankruptcy

Robins's bankruptcy angered women and their lawyers, because all Shield lawsuits were suspended pending the development of a reorganization plan. This means that a bankruptcy court judge must approve a plan for payment of debt negotiated between the company and its creditors, including Shield litigants. Robins's aim was to emerge from bankruptcy under conditions in which Shield injury claims were more modest and affordable.

Morale at the company is low. The *Wall Street Journal* reported that Robins employees reaped a bitter harvest. G. E. R. Stiles, chief financial officer, remarked that he no longer looked forward to coming to work in the morning because the bankruptcy court constantly peered over his shoulder at spending decisions. Robert Watts, executive vice president, related that he had received so much community ill will for being "one of the bad guys" that he sat in the back pew of his church and left immediately after the service ended. Charles Davis, a forklift operator at a Robins distribution plant, said that he continued to wear a windbreaker with the company logo, although it invited frequent stares and questions (Steptoe, 1986). It may, of course, be some years before Robins emerges from Chapter 11 proceedings.

In February 1987 American Home Products Corp. made an unsuccessful bid to acquire Robins. American Home Products, which offered $20 a share for Robins's 24,175,000 common shares outstanding, was motivated by the benefits of obtaining Robins's strong consumer products, such as Chapstick, Robitussin, and Dimctapp. These brands would strengthen American Home Products at a time when its sales were declining due to competition from generic brands. During a week of intense negotiations, American Home Products reached an agreement with Shield litigants to set up a trust fund of $1.5 billion to cover present and future lawsuits. This agreement, plus the attractive price offered for Robins's stock, might have brought Robins out of bankruptcy with its Shield liabilities resolved. But observers were stunned when American Home Products withdrew its acquisition offer at the last minute. Apparently, executives at Robins had stubbornly insisted on unacceptable deals for golden parachutes. When the deal fell through, the bankruptcy court judge who was presiding over Robins's bankruptcy proceedings summoned a group of Robins executives to his chambers and informed them he was giving authority to a court-appointed examiner to oversee any future negotiations of acquisition bids. This was widely interpreted on Wall Street as both a reprimand to Robins and an invitation to a new suitor.

The Shield's two biggest rivals, the Copper-7 made by G. D. Searle & Co. and the Lippes Loop made by Ortho Pharmaceutical Company, remained on the market until the mid-1980s, when they were withdrawn because of lawsuits. Both companies were accused of marketing products of inherently unsafe design and although neither has yet lost a lawsuit the costs of defense came close to exceeding profits for the devices and insurance was not available at some levels of coverage. The departure of Searle and Ortho from the market left only one small company, the Alza Corp., marketing an IUD and it was not sure it wanted to remain in the business. Marketing an IUD now means betting on the survival of your company.

Over 2 million American women still used IUDs when they were withdrawn from the market in 1985 and 1986. They did so because IUDs were the single most highly effective birth control device available for women who did not choose the pill or sterilization. Other methods, including spermicides, sponges, condoms, diaphragms, and the rhythm method, have pregnancy rates two to five times that of the IUD. Furthermore, the IUD does not require continued actions on the part of the user as all other methods do. Hence, many women still travel to Canada to get IUDs.

New and perhaps more effective methods of birth control are on the horizon, but pharmaceutical companies are spending little to develop them because of the risk of product liability suits. They include vaginal rings, a once-a-month pill that blocks implantation of fertilized eggs, anti-pregnancy vaccines, pills that suppress sperm counts in men, and subcutaneous hormone implants that last up to five years. All these devices and drugs may have harmful side-effects, and companies are unwilling to bet their future on them with the example of A. H. Robins before their eyes. In a very real way, the Robins experience with the Dalkon Shield has narrowed the birth-control options for American couples now and for years to come.

Questions

1. Why did A. H. Robins sell the Dalkon Shield for as long as it did? Why did it not recall it until 1984?
2. Was the conduct of A. H. Robins or its managers unethical? Which specific actions and consequences of these actions were unethical?
3. If the Dalkon Shield story is stained by unethical behavior is this behavior best explained as arising from the conduct of unethical individuals? Or is it

best explained as a corporate crime arising from the structure, policies, and culture of Robins in interaction with its business environment?

4. Does an adequate balance exist between the harm that Robins did and the penalties it and its executives are paying today and will continue to pay in the future?

5. What is the proper way to punish a corporation such as A. H. Robins and the individuals in it?

CHAPTER **12**

MAKING ETHICAL DECISIONS IN BUSINESS

JCPenney

Ethical decisions are sometimes difficult. Here is how one company tries to help its employees.

In 1913 James Cash Penney met with a group of his partners in a Salt Lake City hotel room to create a distinctive set of principles upon which to run a fledgling business named the Golden Rule Store Company. The result of this meeting was a short set of statements they called "The Penney Idea" and the final principle was this: "To test our every policy, method and act in this wise: 'Does it square with what is right and just?'" As the Golden Rule Store Company metamorphosed into the giant modern-day retailer we know as J. C. Penney Company, Inc., the seed of an ethics policy contained in that final principle also grew.

As the years passed, many internal policy statements were written about such matters as accepting gifts, entertaining suppliers, and using proprietary information. Since 1986, however, the major elements of these disconnected policy statements have been condensed into a seventeen-page "Statement of Ethics," which is distributed to all employees. The ethics code contained in the "Statement of Ethics" is divided into three parts. Part I deals with "Compliance with Law," Part II is on "Conflicts of Interest," and Part III is on "Preservation of Company Assets."

A unique, didactic feature of the code is the illustration of provisions with short cases. Analysis accompanying these cases exemplifies correct interpretation to employees reading the code. Here is a sample of three cases that help explain conflict-of-interest situations involving competing companies. In these examples, note that the word *associate* is used to refer to Penney's employees.

354

The Official J.C. Penney Policy Statement

Each Associate of the Company shall avoid any activity, interest or relationship with non-Company persons or entities which would create, or might appear to others to create, a conflict with the interests of the Company.

Example A

A newly employed Associate has worked for a major competitor of the Company, and during the course of that previous employment has acquired shares of stock which amount to a very small percentage of the outstanding stock of the competitor. A question has arisen as to whether ownership of that stock will constitute a conflict of interest.

Analysis of Example A

Ownership of stock in a competitor will not be deemed a conflict of interest if both of the following conditions exist: (a) the stock is publicly traded, and (b) the amount owned by the Associate and his or her "relatives" (as defined in this booklet) does not exceed one-tenth of 1 percent of the amount outstanding.

Example B

A Company store manager proposes to buy a substantial number of shares of stock of a corporation formed to operate a women's apparel shop. The shop will be located in a shopping center which also contains a Penney store and will carry similar merchandise.

Analysis of Example B

A conflict of interest would exist. The apparel shop is a competitor because of its location and because of the merchandise it carries. In addition, the proposed purchase of stock by the Associate does not meet the guidelines described in the Analysis of Example A above.

Example C

A general merchandise manager sells casualty and life insurance for a major insurance company on a part-time basis (i.e., after work and on weekends).

Analysis of Example C

A conflict of interest may exist. Part-time work for an insurance company may be deemed to be a conflict of interest because the Company sells life and casualty insurance through its Financial Services division. Accordingly an Associate should notify his or her department head or superior of the activity. The Associate's department head, in conjunction with the Director of Insurance, will determine whether the Associate's activity is competitive with any Company insurance operations and, accordingly, whether a conflict of interest exists.

Each Penney employee, upon receipt of the code, is required to sign an attached Certificate of Compliance, which states in part: "I am in compliance and will continue to comply, with the policies set forth in the booklet. . . ." If there is doubt about compliance, the individual is instructed to approach his or her unit manager or department head to ask advice. Under three conditions an employee is, however, instructed to go directly to the General Counsel at headquarters in New York City. These urgent exceptions are cases that (1) threaten the overall integrity of the company, (2) raise the possibility of major financial loss or criminal penalty, and (3) endanger human life.

At the end of the "Statement of Business Ethics," employees are given notice that "failure to comply with the principles described in this booklet, including the disclosure requirements, may result in termination of employment."

This chapter suggests guidelines for making decisions about ethical issues for people in business faced with practical problems and for students discussing cases and issues in the business-government-society area. Value decisions cannot be programmed like production and inventory control decisions, but a moral decision is, after all, still a decision, and helpful methods exist to guide concerned decision makers.

THE USE OF PRINCIPLES TO GUIDE CONDUCT

Over the centuries, attempts have been made to discover rules that lead to perfectly just actions. Plato thought he had found the right method of moral decision making when he described an intuitive leap of revelation that would take place after years of study and character development in a utopian society. St. Augustine suggested that virtue came from an interior illumination that was a gift of God. St. Thomas relied on painstaking research of Scripture to reveal the true path, and a sense of complete certainty pervades his massive, twenty-three-volume *Summa Theologica*, in which moral questions are examined. Recent efforts to find a methodology for business decisions regarding ethics have been less mystical and elaborate. They are described in the following sections.

We begin, however, with a compendium of commonly used ethical principles —some ancient, some recently formulated—that are simple rules available to business managers. To the extent that they offer a variety of ideas for resolution of ethical dilemmas, they are not vague abstractions but useful, living guides to right conduct.

PRINCIPLES OF ETHICAL CONDUCT

The Categorical Imperative

The categorical imperative (meaning literally, a command that admits no exception) is a guideline for ethical behavior set forth by the German philosopher Immanuel Kant in his *Foundations of the Metaphysics of Morals* (1785). In Kant's words: "Act only according to that maxim by which you can at the same time will that it should become a universal law." In other words, one should not adopt principles of action unless they can, without inconsistency, be adopted by everyone else.

Using this guideline, a decision maker faced with a moral choice will act in a way that he or she believes is right and just for any other person in a similar situation. Each action should be judged by asking: "Could this action be turned into a universal code of behavior?" This quick test of universalizability has achieved great popularity. Kant also emphasized the importance of a person's intentions as opposed to some other ethical theories which stress instead the consequences of an action in evaluating whether or not it is right.

Weaknesses
1.   The matter of defining what is desirable in terms of the consequences of actions remains a problem. A depressed person contemplating suicide, for instance, might well feel that suicide is a good course of action for all people.
2.   The principle implies that all people are to be treated equally (and Kant himself argued that they be treated as ends in themselves), which makes it difficult to resolve conflicts of interest.

The Conventionalist Ethic

This is the view that individuals should act to further their self-interests so long as they do not violate the law. It has been popularized in the business world by Albert Z. Carr in his book, *Business as a Game* (1969). It may be summed up by saying, "Business is business, and when in business do as the others do or risk self-defeat."

Decision makers are allowed, under this principle, to bluff (lie) and to take advantage of all legal opportunities and widespread practices or customs. Business, as Carr says, is a game. And as in poker, the rules are different from those we adopt in personal life.

Weaknesses
1.   Because people's lives and the welfare of the nation depend upon business, it may not be a game to be taken lightly.

2.   The principle provides no way to elevate business practice. It does not ask how people in business *ought* to act, only how they *do* act. Hence, it provides little real moral guidance.

3.   In unique situations where no informal norms exist to guide an executive, he or she may simply follow his or her self-interest without consideration of others.

The Disclosure Rule

This rule has become increasingly popular in recent years and is found in many company ethics codes. Here is the way it is stated in IBM's "Business Conduct Guidelines": "Ask yourself: If the full glare of examination by associates, friends, even family were to focus on your decision, would you remain comfortable with it? If you think you would, it probably is the right decision."

   When faced with an ethical dilemma, a manager asks how it would feel to see the thinking and details of the decision disclosed to a wide audience. Sometimes newspaper readers or national television viewers are substituted for acquaintances as the disclosure audience.

Weaknesses

1.   This rule effectively screens out baser emotions such as greed and jealousy, which are unacceptable if disclosed, but does not always provide guidance in dealing with moral dilemmas in which strong arguments can be made for several alternatives.

2.   An action that sounds acceptable if disclosed may not be the best action embodying the highest good. Long-range solutions that impose immediate deprivations or unavoidable injustices might not be as acceptable to national TV or newspaper audiences as short-range actions that appear benevolent.

The Doctrine of the Mean

This ethic, set forth by Aristotle in *The Nicomachean Ethics* and sometimes called the "Golden Mean," due to subsequent but un-Aristotelian embellishment, calls for virtue through moderation. Right actions are located between extreme behaviors, which represent excess on the one hand and deficiency on the other. When faced with a decision, a decision maker first identifies the ethical virtue involved (such as truthfulness) and then seeks the mean or moderate course of action between an excess of that virtue (boastfulness) and a deficiency of it (understatement). Likewise, according to Aristotle, modesty is the mean between shyness and shamelessness. The Doctrine of the Mean is today little recognized and mostly of historical interest.

Weaknesses

1.   This ethical principle does not specifically define what a virtue or virtuous behavior is. You cannot know what the excessive and deficient behaviors surrounding a virtue are unless you know what the virtue is in the first place.

2.   The ethical guideline here is platitudinous. To observe the Doctrine of the Mean is simply to act in accord with right conduct in a situation and not to act in an extreme way. But the moderate course is not defined.

The Golden Rule

A universal ideal found in every great world religion, the Golden Rule has been a popular guide to moral decision making for centuries. Simply put, it is: "Do unto others as you would have them do unto you." It includes not knowingly doing harm to others.

   A decision maker trying to solve a moral problem places himself or herself in the position of another party affected by the decision and tries to determine what action is most fair to that person. The concept of reversibility is shorthand for the Golden Rule.

Weaknesses
1.   The values of people differ, and decision makers may err in assuming that their preferences coincide with others'.
2.   This is primarily a perfectionist rule for interpersonal relations. In modern society, we deal not only with other people but with large organizations and their policies, and organizations find it difficult to consider the interests of individuals.
3.   The marketplace often demands that managers act selfishly toward competitors. Competition does not proceed through kindness but through self-interest.

The Intuition Ethic

This ethic, as stated by moral philosophers such as G. E. Moore in his *Principia Ethica* in 1903, holds that what is Good is undefinable and simply understood. People are endowed with a kind of moral sense with which they can apprehend right and wrong.

   The solution to moral problems lies simply in what you feel or understand to be right in a given situation. You have a "gut feeling" or "fly by the seat of your pants."

Weaknesses
1.   This approach is subjective. Self-interest may be confused with moral insight.
2.   There is no universal rule for later evaluating what was right or wrong. No standard of validation outside the individual exists.
3.   Intuition often fails to give clear answers to moral problems.

The Market Ethic

This principle was sanctified in the world of commerce by Adam Smith in his *Wealth of Nations* (1776). Implicit in Smith's description of a market economy is the idea that selfish actions in the marketplace are virtuous because they contribute to efficient operation of the economy. This efficient operation is, in turn, responsible for the higher goods of prosperity and optimum use of resources.

Decision makers may take selfish actions and be motivated by personal gain in their business dealings. They should ask whether their actions in the market further financial self-interest. If so, the actions are ethical.

Weaknesses

1. This form of ethical guidance is applicable only in market situations. It is not useful in nonmarket, interpersonal decisions and therefore is not a universal principle.

2. There are areas of market behavior where society has determined that the broad social good or public interest is not furthered by selfish market behavior. The antitrust statutes are a prime example of legislated morality here.

The Means-Ends Ethic

This principle of moral decision making is age-old, although today it is most often associated with the Italian political philosopher Niccolò Machiavelli. In *The Prince* (1513), Machiavelli wrote that worthwhile ends justify efficient means, that when ends are of overriding importance or virtue, unscrupulous means may be employed to reach them.

When confronted with a decision involving a potentially unethical course of action, the decision maker should ask whether some overall good—such as the survival of a country or business—justifies any moral transgression.

Weaknesses

1. By accepting the validity of this principle, the decision maker immediately is deprived of the highest moral virtue and accepts the necessity of moral compromise.

2. In some situations, means and ends are confused and/or the means may be as important as or more important than the ends—for example, in a democracy where the rules of scheduled, periodic elections may be as important as or more so than who gets elected.

The Might-Equals-Right Ethic

This ethic defines justice as the interest of the stronger. It is represented by Friedrich Nietzsche's "master-morality," Marx's theories of the dominance of the ruling class, and in the practiced ethics of organized crime. What is ethical is what an individual has the strength and power to accomplish.

When faced with a moral decision, individuals using this ethic seize what advantage they are strong enough to take without respect to ordinary social conventions and laws.

Weaknesses

1.   This ethic confuses ethics with force or physical power, but yielding to such force or power is not the same as acting from ethical duty. A moral principle that can be invalidated by its foundation (e.g., physical force) is not a consistent, logically valid principle.

2.   The ethic is not seen as legitimate in civilized settings. Observance of this principle invites retaliation and condemnation, and it is not to be used for long-term advantage. Seizure by power violates established rules of cooperation and reciprocity on which societies are based, and the social fabric would be torn apart by widespread use of this principle.

The Organization Ethic

This is an old principle for resolving ethical questions with increased applicability in modern times. This is an age of large-scale organizations. Simply put, this dictum states; "Be loyal to the organization." It is functional for the endurance of large organizations. Many people have a deep sense of loyalty to an organization that far transcends their self-interest. We have seen people jeopardize their health and work excessively long hours without pay, contrary to their selfish interests, because of their loyalty to their task and/or company.

There are similar personal loyalties that one individual has to another—such as the loyalties of a subordinate to a supervisor—when they are acting in their official capacities. Frequently, these loyalties are in conflict with the ethical standards one applies when acting as an individual. For instance, the general manager of a division of a large company withheld information from central headquarters about impending disastrous financial troubles. Several of his subordinates, who were men of high moral character and who had close connections with headquarters managers, did not inform headquarters of the problems, principally because of strong personal loyalty to their superior officer.

In practice, the organization ethic implies that the wills and needs of individuals should be subordinated to the greater good of the organization (be it church, state, business, military, or university). An individual should ask whether actions are consistent with organizational goals and do what is good for the organization.

Weaknesses

1.   Some may argue that the highest good comes when individuals are served by organizations rather than subservient to them.

2.   Service to the organization may be a tempting way to rationalize behavior that would be unethical for an individual. The Nuremberg trials highlighted the dangerous tendencies of obedience and jaundiced obligation.

The Practical Imperative

In addition to the categorical imperative, a second and related imperative or universal ethical command developed by Kant, in the *Foundations of the Meta-*

physics of Morals, is: "Act so that you treat humanity, whether in your own person or in that of another, always as an end and never as a means only." Simply translated, this principle admonishes a manager to treat other persons as ends in themselves and not means to ends or objects of manipulation. Each person, by his or her very existence as a rational, thinking being, is entitled to be treated in this fashion. No person should manipulate others for selfish ends. A manager may comply with this dictum by using the "reversibility" test, asking if he or she would change places with the person affected by the contemplated policy or action.

Weaknesses

1. In large organizations the achievement of collective goals often requires the abridgment of individual rights. Generals may send soldiers to die, and corporate presidents may move managers around the world and make them work away from their families.
2. Even if individual rights are not abridged, they may not be relevant. In modern society, people may deal with each other in terms of representative roles rather than as individuals. Thus, a plant manager may pressure and manipulate corporate top management for a bigger annual budget without engaging the people involved as individual personalities. Or a company may adopt a behavior-modification program to motivate workers and use positive reinforcement to alter behavior solely as a means to increase productivity. Within American business culture, such practices are not seen as necessarily unethical.

The Principle of Equal Freedom

This principle was set forth by the philosopher Herbert Spencer in his 1850 book, *Social Statics.* "Every man may claim the fullest liberty to exercise his faculties," said Spencer, "compatible with the possession of like liberty by every other man" (p. 69). Thus, a person has the right to freedom of action unless such action deprives another person of a proper freedom. Spencer believed that this was the first principle of ethical action in society. He thought it essential to protect individual liberty from infringement by others; his deep faith that human progress was based on such free action was unshakable.

In applying this principle, a decision maker asks if a contemplated action will restrict others from actions that they have a legitimate right to undertake. This principle is quite popular today. One version is, "Your right to swing your fist ends where my nose begins."

Weaknesses

1. The principle does not provide a "tie breaker" for situations in which two rights or interests conflict. Such situations require invocation of an additional principle to determine which right or freedom is more important.
2. Some ethically permissible management decisions may circumscribe the rights of some for the benefit of others. For example, all employees have broad privacy rights, but management cannot be fully honest when it hires undercover detectives to investigate major thefts in the warehouse.

The Proportionality Ethic

Proportionality, a concept developed in medieval Catholic theology, was designed to justify actions with both good and evil consequences. In cases where a manager's action results in an important good effect but also entails an inevitable harmful effect, the concept of proportionality may be appropriately applied. A well-known formulation of proportionality is undertaken by Thomas M. Garrett (1966), who set forth the "principle of proportionality" this way: "I am responsible for whatever I will as a means or an end. If both the means and the end I am willing are good in and of themselves, I may ethically permit or risk the foreseen but unwilled side effects if, and only if, I have a proportionate reason for doing so" (p. 8; italics omitted).

Garrett explains that there are five proportionate reasons involving: 1. the type of good or evil involved, 2. the probability of good and evil effects, 3. the urgency of the situation, 4. the intensity of one's influence over effects, and 5. the availability of alternative means not involving evil results. The combination of these factors may provide a "proportional reason" for taking an action even if some bad consequences ensue.

A simpler ethical principle derived from the concept of proportionality is the "principle of double effect." It states that in a situation from which both good and evil consequences are bound to result, a manager will act ethically if: 1. the good effects outweigh the evil, 2. the manager's intention is to achieve the good effects, and 3. examination reveals that no better alternative is available.

Weaknesses

1.   These are complex principles, involving a wide range of considerations, and are time-consuming to apply in specific situations. Complexity can, of course, be a strength if it promotes fuller consideration.

2.   Although the concept of proportionality sharpens judgment by forcing consideration of many factors, it is ultimately subjective and may be used to justify harmful acts. What kind of otherwise questionable acts, for instance, may a failing firm take that are justified by the "proportionate reason" of the impending evil of business failure?

The Professional Ethic

In an age of specialization and education in complex skills, this ethic has gained importance. In simple form, it holds that you should do only that which can be explained before a committee of your peers.

This ethic is applied by doctors, engineers, architects, college professors, lawyers, and business executives in resolving the special problems of their professions and fields of interest. It is similar to and an application of the disclosure ethic discussed previously.

Professional people have strongly internalized ethical codes that guide their actions. Many of these ethical standards are deep-seated. For instance, we are convinced that the high standards of most engineers in the aerospace industry would prevent them from making a cheap lawn mower. They are so used to working with exceedingly close tolerances and high quality that they could not bring themselves to the task. The acceptance of lower standards would be morally repugnant to them.

Weaknesses

1.   Most of the so-called special problems of the professions are really amenable to the application of universal principles. This is not a universal principle because it does not apply to individual conflicts outside special and/or esoteric settings.

2.   There is a risk that the standards of technical specialists will become out of touch with broader social ethics.

The Revelation Ethic

This ethic has appealed to religious individuals throughout the ages. Through prayer or other appeal to transcendent beings and forces, answers are given to individual minds. A priest may pray for guidance and find that God has provided the answer. This ethical principle is close to the intuition ethic, but there the inborn, human element is all that is necessary.

The decision makers pray, meditate, or otherwise commune with a superior force or being. They are then apprised of which actions are just and unjust.

Weaknesses

1.   Many people are not deeply religious and would be suspicious of this method or reluctant to try it.

2.   This kind of moral truth is incompatible with more pragmatic ethical standards such as the means-ends ethic. No compromise is possible when you have been inculcated with perfect moral virtue. Alleged religious insight has sometimes led to cruel actions.

3.   A theological problem of long standing remains to be logically dealt with. If God is omnipotent, how can His will fail to be realized, whether we do right or wrong?

The Rights Ethic

The rights ethic encompasses the notion that people have fundamental rights. Rights are entitlements to something. Ethical persons recognize the duty to protect the exercise of these rights in others. Fundamental human rights may be abridged only for compelling reasons of benefit to society. These rights generally include freedom of speech, freedom of conscience, the right to own property, the right to life, and the right to be honestly informed. Other rights may be established in laws or contracts and differ from fundamental ethical rights.

In applying the rights ethic, a decision maker evaluates intended actions based on whether they deprive any party affected by the decision of a right that must be respected. For example, management should not permit operation of an unsafe machine because workers would be deprived of the right to a safe workplace. This right is based on the natural right to protection from harm by the actions of others and is underscored by legal rights established in the Occupational Safety and Health Act. If some risk in operating a machine is unavoidable, workers have the right to be informed with an accurate risk assessment.

Weaknesses

1. Theories of rights emphasize and protect individual freedoms. They are properly used to protect individuals from exploitation but may be misused to excuse selfish demands. In a broad sense, rights theories have encouraged the development of exaggerated entitlements in society.
2. Rights are not absolute, and it is difficult to define their limits. For example, every person has the right to life, but in modern society corporations frequently expose people to risk of death by releasing carcinogens into the environment. To make the right to life absolute would require cessation of much industrial activity (for example, petroleum refining).

The Theory of Justice

Ethical theories of justice define the nature of fairness in corporate relationships. Justice requires: (1) that the benefits and burdens of company life be distributed according to impartial criteria, (2) that rewards and punishments be meted out evenhandedly, and (3) that laws, rules, and administrative procedures apply equally to each employee and organizational unit.

A contemporary moral philosopher, John Rawls, has developed a widely discussed set of principles for a just society. In *A Theory of Justice* Rawls speculates that rational persons situated behind a hypothetical "veil of ignorance" and not knowing their place in a society (i.e., their social status, class position, economic fortune, intelligence, appearance, or the like) but knowing general facts about human society (such as political, economic, sociological, and psychological theory) would choose two rules to ensure fairness in any society they created. First, "each person is to have an equal right to the most extensive basic liberty compatible with a similar liberty for others," and second, "social and economic inequalities are to be arranged so that they are both (a) reasonably expected to be to everyone's advantage, and (b) attached to positions and offices open to all" (Rawls, 1971: 60–61). The lofty generalizations in Rawls's theory are best used in analysis of broad social questions, but they may inspire business decisions.

Weaknesses

1. Impartiality and equal treatment are resplendent in theory, but their operational meaning is difficult to pin down. Most rules give advantage to one group more than another.
2. Competing conceptions of justice exist. Rawls bases justice on distribution of social goods according to need, but others have based theories of justice on

other fundamental concepts such as the legitimate acquisition of property (Nozick, 1974) and the unity of humankind (Plato, *The Republic).*

The Utilitarian Principle

This principle is so named because it was espoused as a method of determining right and wrong by philosophers of the English utilitarian school such as Jeremy Bentham and John Stuart Mill. It is simply expressed as "the greatest good for the greatest number."

In making a decision with this principle in mind, one must determine whether the harm in an action is outweighed by the good. If the action maximizes benefit, then it is the optimum course to take among alternatives that provide less benefit. Individuals and other decision makers should try to maximize pleasure and reduce pain, not simply for themselves, but for every party affected by their decision. Utilitarianism facilitates the comparison of the ethical consequences of various alternatives in a decision. It is a popular, widely used principle. Cost-benefit and risk-benefit studies embody the spirit of the utilitarian principle.

Weaknesses
1. Because decisions are made for the greatest good of all, utilitarianism may lead to decisions that permit the abridgment of human rights, even the right to life, for the greater good of a larger group.
2. There is no criterion for measuring levels of goodness. Thus, the "greatest good" remains a matter of opinion.

THE USE OF PRINCIPLED ETHICAL REASONING

There are a wide variety of methods for making ethical decisions. Some managers are relatively insensitive to ethical issues. Others may notice ethical problems and make decisions using simple ethical criteria such as: be honest, help others, avoid harm, tell the truth, be fair, and respect the life and property of others. There is great wisdom in such basic admonitions. The application of ethical principles such as those in the foregoing section, however, enhances the manager's skill for resolving complex ethical issues. There are two reasons. First, common-sense ethical wisdom may be derived from these broader ethical principles. For example, the categorical imperative dictates that individuals tell the truth, because truthtelling can be made universal, unlike lying, the universalization of which would cause chaos. Second, the application of ethical principles to ethically complex decisions encourages stringent standards and forces consideration of issues that might otherwise remain hidden. A cashier pockets twenty dollar bills from the register at the end of the day. The person's supervisor strongly feels that stealing is wrong and fires the cashier. Ethical common sense is all that is needed in this situation. But consider the following situation.

> Richard Tarnovich, the night plant manager for Western Electroplating Company, recently revealed to coworkers that he was proud to be a member of the American Communist party. Some of the employees on the night shift have found it more difficult to cooperate with him and accept his authority since this disclosure. Tarnovich has tried to perform his job without confrontation, but a series of minor social abrasions have occurred between him and other workers on the shift. Absenteeism has risen, the rejection rate on completed jobs has increased by 5 percent, and there have been two minor injuries in the past month traceable to inattentiveness of machine operators. Earl Mizushima, the assistant night manager, is popular with the workers and well trained. He has hinted he is anxious for advancement. Should Richard Tarnovich be moved from his position?

An ethically insensitive manager might perceive this case solely as a problem of productivity, see Tarnovich as a drag on efficiency, and remove him from the position. But let us apply three important ethical principles to the case: utilitarianism, rights, and justice.

From a utilitarian standpoint, management must calculate which course of action would result in the greatest net benefit for the plant and all its workers. In this situation it might be reasonable to decide that removing Tarnovich would increase productivity and build morale among many workers while hurting only one person, Tarnovich.

From the standpoint of the rights ethic, however, employers must consider the idea that employees have the right to freedom of conscience and political belief. In American society, workers are free to hold unpopular political and philosophical views in their private lives. Although Tarnovich has brought his communist affiliation into the workplace by telling others about it, there is no evidence that his politics is part of his management style or that he has been argumentative.

From the standpoint of justice, corporations are required to promote fair, evenhanded treatment of employees. If management allows other workers to be Republicans, environmentalists, or Ku Klux Klan members off the job, the same permission must be granted to Tarnovich the communist.

Readers may make up their own minds about this case. If the productivity problem is substantial, management must intervene. But when ethical concerns about employee rights and equitable treatment are carefully weighed, management may consider alternatives to removing Tarnovich, including mediation by an ombudsman, counseling, or removing one or more workers for insubordination to Tarnovich. At some point, however, management may need to invoke the utilitarian argument and remove Tarnovich if his supervision becomes ineffective and low productivity endangers the general welfare of the company. The rights of one individual cannot, in this instance, jeopardize the benefits many others derive from the company.

> You are sailing to Rome (you tell me) to obtain the post of Governor of Cnossus. You are not content to stay at home with the honours you had before; you want something on a larger scale, and more conspicuous. But when did you ever undertake a voyage for the purpose of reviewing your own principles and getting rid of any of them that proved unsound?
>
> _____
>
> Source: Epictetus, *The Discourses* (c. A.D. 120).

This case is typical of incidents discussed in ethics training programs. It illustrates the application of three important and mutually reinforcing principles in a decision-making technique that is popular in the literature of business ethics (see, for example, Cavanagh, 1984).

PRACTICAL SUGGESTIONS FOR MAKING ETHICAL DECISIONS

Individuals in business can take a number of steps to see and resolve ethical problems.

First, learn to think in principled terms, and use concepts like universalizability, reversibility, utility, equity, and other ethical guidelines suggested by the list of principles earlier in this chapter. These principles are powerful decision criteria that enhance the capacity to discover or create ethical alternatives. Use a principle that is meaningful to you. As the famous anthropologist Sir James Frazer remarked: "Once the harbor lights have been passed and the ship is out of stormy waters, it matters little whether the pilot steered by a jack-o-lantern or the stars."

Second, consider some simple decision tactics that help to illuminate moral choices. The ethical philosopher Bertrand Russell advocated imaginary conversations with a hypothetical opponent as an antidote for dogmatic certitude. Have a conversation or debate with an intelligent person who takes a different viewpoint or who has additional insights. Seek out a more experienced, ethically sensitive person in the organization to be your ethical adviser. This variant of a mentor relationship is of great value in revealing the ethical climate of your company and industry. Alternatively, write an essay in favor of a position and then a second opposed to it. Write a case study in the third person about your situation. Try to apply ethical principles in answer to obvious questions raised by the case.

More than 200 years ago, a balance sheet of pros and cons was proposed as an approach to decision making by Benjamin Franklin in a letter to a scientist friend in England. Since that time, numerous decision makers have used a balance sheet approach. One of the best known is Richard Nixon, who as President was fond of writing down pros and cons in columns on a yellow legal pad and then crossing out roughly equal considerations until a preponderance was left on one side or the other.

The balance sheet has advantages. First, it organizes information. Studies have shown that the human brain can simultaneously grapple only with between five and nine bits of information. Because many decisions, including moral ones, involve more considerations than this, a balance sheet may prevent chaotic and random thinking. Second, the use of such a procedure forces decision makers to make entries in a number of relevant categories, and new or unconscious considerations may be brought to light. One disadvantage of the balance sheet approach in making moral decisions is that utilitarian considerations may be weighed equally with even the most fundamental moral principles.

Another useful method of applying principles is to draw them out in the form of questions a manager might ask when contemplating a decision. This is known as the "critical questions approach." John Leys has surveyed the systems of the great philosophers and has derived thirty-six critical questions for the decision maker (1952). The following are a few examples: What are the authoritative rules and precedents, the agreements, and accepted practices? If there is a conflict of principles, can you find a more abstract statement, a "third principle," that will reconcile the conflicting principles? What is not within our power? What are the undesirable extremes in human dispositions? A shorter set of leading questions, suggested by Laura Nash, is based on traditional philosophical frameworks but designed to avoid the very abstract level of reasoning characteristic of broad principles (Nash, 1981: 80–81). This list of twelve questions is shown in Table 12-1.

TABLE 12–1 TWELVE QUESTIONS FOR EXAMINING THE ETHICS OF A BUSINESS DECISION

1. Have you defined the problem accurately?
2. How would you define the problem if you stood on the other side of the fence?
3. How did this situation occur in the first place?
4. To whom and to what do you give your loyalty as a person and as a member of the corporation?
5. What is your intention in making this decision?
6. How does this intention compare with the probable results?
7. Whom could your decision or action injure?
8. Can you discuss the problem with the affected parties before you make your decision?
9. Are you confident that your position will be as valid over a long period of time as it seems now?
10. Could you disclose without qualm your decision or action to your boss, your CEO, the board of directors, your family, society as a whole?
11. What is the symbolic potential of your action if understood? If misunderstood?
12. Under what conditions would you allow exceptions to your stand?

Third, sort out ethical priorities early, before problems arise. If you do so, you will get the full benefits of considering alternatives when you are not under stress. Clear ethics reduce stress by reducing temptation, deflating your conscience as a source of pain or anxiety, and eliminating conflicts of interest in your decision making. When doing the ethical thing is not the most profitable financially, for instance, it helps to decide in advance that you will put ethics before tainted profits.

Fourth, commit yourself publicly on ethical issues. Examine your work environment, and locate potential ethical conflicts. Then tell others of your opposition to padding expense accounts, stealing supplies from the company, discriminating against minorities, price fixing, or harming nature. They will be less tempted to approach you with corrupting intentions, and your public commitment will force you to maintain your integrity or risk shame.

Fifth, set a good personal example for employees. This is one of the basic managerial functions. An ethical manager can create a morally uplifting work environment. An unethical manager may make money, but he or she and the organization pay the price—and the price is one's integrity. Employees who see unethical competitive behavior, for instance, may wonder when their superiors will turn their antisocial predilections inward and focus on them. This behavior has the potential for creating morale and loyalty problems.

Sixth, note and resist the ethical temptations to which you are most prone. Aristotle, in the *Nicomachean Ethics*, advised:

> We must notice the errors into which we ourselves are liable to fall (because we all have different natural tendencies—we shall find out what ours are from the pleasure and pain that they give us), and we must drag ourselves in the contrary direction; for we shall arrive at the mean by pressing well away from our failing—just like somebody straightening a warped piece of wood (1953: 109).

Hence, examine your personal traits. Are you marked by greed, prejudice, sadism, cowardice, insensitivity? Work to overcome these, just as the ancient Greeks worked to develop character. Ethical behavior is conditioned by practice. You learn more about it by working hard.

Seventh, cultivate your sympathies and charity toward others. The question, "What is ethical?" is one on which well-intentioned people may differ. As Marcus Aurelius wrote: "When thou art offended at any man's fault, forthwith turn to thyself and reflect in what like manner thou dost err thyself; for example, in thinking that money is a good thing, or pleasure, or a bit of reputation, and the like" (1980, p. 281). Reasonable people in business differ with respect to the rightness of being in South Africa, paying bribes overseas, laying off workers, and other nettlesome ethical questions. We should neither be overly indulgent nor wholly stern and unforgiving because of pride in high ethical standards.

Eighth, translate your thoughts into action—display moral courage. Knowing and doing are, of course, different. It is often easier to reach a valid ethical judgment than to act on it, especially lower in the organizational ranks. When you are sure that you are ethically right, you may be called upon to risk revenue for your company or jeopardize your job by standing firm.

Finally, remember that ethical perfection is illusory. We live in a complicated, baffling civilization with a profusion of rules, obligations, and duties. No manager can perfectly resolve all the conflicts that arise. There is an old story, perhaps apocryphal, about the inauguration of James Canfield as president of Ohio State University. With him on the inaugural platform was Charles W. Eliot, president of Harvard University for twenty years and a senior statesman in the ranks of academic leadership. After receiving the mace of office, Canfield sat next to Eliot, who leaned over and whispered, "Now son, you are president, and your faculty will call you a liar." "Surely," said Canfield, "your faculty have not accused you of lying, Dr. Eliot." Replied Eliot, "Not only that, son, they've proved it!"

MANAGING ETHICS AT THE CORPORATE LEVEL

Typically, American management has acted in keeping with the assumption that ethics is a matter of individual conscience. Employees are exhorted to obey the law, and penalties for unethical behavior such as theft of company property are common. When management wants to increase the sensitivity of employees to ethical issues, guard against scandal, and promote decorous relationships in the organization and with the public, there are six steps it can take.

First, the chief executive officer should make clear statements about the importance to the firm of legal and ethical behavior. These statements should be reinforced periodically. J. Irwin Miller, former chairman of Cummins Engine Company, says this about the role of top management in setting standards: "I would say the most important thing for us is to impress on all employees: 'When in doubt, either don't do it or call home. If in doubt, you should share the responsibility right up to the top of the company'" (Freudberg, 1986).

Second, management should try to create an organizational climate in which ethical issues can be discussed. A common block to ethical behavior is the reluctance of employees to raise "soft" ethical questions. Managers may be under extreme pressure to meet unrealistic performance goals and adopt ethically questionable methods of meeting them. They may be getting a subtle message from superiors that certain unethical practices will be tolerated. Recently, for example, TRW, Inc., fired an accounting department manager for exaggerating the number of hours that workers spent on fan blades for military jets. The surprised individual contended that his immediate superior had condoned this behavior and that it was informally a standard procedure. The practice was at least common enough to have a name—"ballooning." Setting aside regular times at business meetings to discuss ethics is one method of making the topic acceptable conversation. Training programs are another way to increase sensitivity to ethical criteria in decision making. Of course, it is important for top management to send a clear message that there is no informal subculture of unethical behavior in the company. At McDonnell-Douglas, for example, where all employees are required to take training programs on ethical decision making, president Sanford McDonnell says: "They're getting constant reminders that top management wants them to make the right decision, regardless of the pressures of the bottom line" (Bluedorn and Slusher, 1986). It stands to reason also that management must set realistic performance standards; unrealistic ones invite cheating.

Third, important ethical standards should be codified. There is a need for both an overarching ethics code, with general standards of behavior, and specific policy statements in various areas such as sales, purchasing, personnel, or overseas operations. This is the type of extensive codification that General Dynamics was forced to adopt only after repeated scandals. A prudent company might benefit from taking action before disaster strikes.

Fourth, a firm should make appropriate organizational changes. Establishment of ethics committees on the board of directors, ethics ombudsmen, ethics directors, and telephone hotlines are major changes that underscore management's commitment to ethics. Some companies have undertaken ethics "audits" to learn where problems lurk in the organization.

Fifth, management should establish adequate controls to monitor and enforce compliance with company conduct codes and policies. For example, some firms require employees to sign annually a statement of compliance with an ethics code. Many scandal-ridden firms belatedly discover that their controls are lax. In the wake of scandal, General Dynamics computerized time card billings to prevent supervisors from charging worker hours to the wrong government contracts. After the 1986 insider trading scandals precipitated by an investment banker at Drexel Burnham Lambert, that firm revised its employee trading policies.

Finally, management should continuously monitor the ethical expectations of the public and of important corporate stakeholders. Ethical standards change. Twenty years ago, for example, there was little criticism of foreign payoffs, which had yet to hit the headlines. Firms in many industries could have saved wear and tear on corporate images if they had anticipated the need for internal accounting standards appropriate to enforce a publicly acceptable standard of overseas marketing behavior.

In short, the basic management functions—leading, planning, staffing, controlling, and organizing—must be reexamined by a corporation and a concern for ethics incorporated within them (Hogner, 1986). In this way, a company ensures that ethical behavior will be an organizational priority. Without a management system to handle ethics issues, ethical behavior remains a matter of individual conscience, and the organization is less able to restrict and control inevitable lapses.

PROBLEMS OF MANAGERS IN BEING ETHICAL

Why are ethical decisions sometimes so difficult? Why are ethical problems refractory even in the presence of principles and methods to guide resolution? In this section we list ten reasons why ethical problems are often complex and difficult.

First, managers confront a distinction between facts and values when making ethical decisions. Facts are statements about what *is,* and we can observe and confirm them through the scientific method. Values, on the other hand, are views individuals hold independently of facts. For example, we may describe the system of racial separation in South Africa with factual statements. Five million whites in that country have the right to vote, and 21 million blacks do not. But whether the system is good or bad and whether a corporation should manufacture and sell there is a value judgment. Facts do not logically dictate values. What *is* never fully defines what *ought* to be. Therefore, when people in business ask what is ethical in a given situation, even a full description of the facts involved cannot automatically dictate a just answer.

Second, it is often the case that good and evil exist simultaneously, in tandem, and interlocked. Two examples will illustrate this enigmatic probability. Nestlé's sales of infant formula in less-developed countries such as Kenya and Zambia are associated with infant deaths as mothers mix the powdered food with contaminated water and their babies die of dysentery. But evidence also exists that sales of formula have led to the saving of other infants' lives when the mother is not available, the infant won't breastfeed, or dietary supplementation is indicated. The mixture of good and bad effects is likewise present in the use of Paraquat, perhaps the most effective herbicide in existence. The availability of Paraquat, manufactured by Imperial Chemical Industries in England and Chevron Chemical Company in America, may significantly increase crop yields, but the chemical is also highly toxic to humans, and its application—inevitably untutored at times, especially in less developed countries—has led to a number of illnesses and deaths. (A newspaper headline even read: "NYMPHO GETS LIFE FOR KILLING HUBBY WITH PARAQUAT GRAVY" [Shaw, 1983].)

Third, knowledge of consequences is limited. Many ethical theories, for instance the utilitarian theory of the greatest good for the greatest number, assume that the consequences of a decision are knowable. But the impact of business policy is uncertain in a complex world. In 1977, for example, General Motors substituted Chevrolet engines in Pontiacs, Oldsmobiles, and Buicks, with a policy that extended an old industry practice of parts switching to entire engines. The intention of the policy was to achieve the salutary effect of making more large block engines available over a wider range of automobiles to satisfy consumer demand. Unpredictably (for General Motors), consumers looked on the engine switching as an attempt to manipulate buyers and rob owners of status—an ethical implication perhaps entirely at odds with corporate motivations.

Fourth, the existence of multiple corporate constituencies exposes management to competing and conflicting ethical claims. Customers, stockholders, workers, government agencies, and various pressure groups such as environmentalists and feminists are among the most important judges of managerial behavior. To illustrate, tobacco firms find themselves in a crossfire of competing ethical claims. Tobacco farmers, representing more than 275,000 farming families, give ethical priority to maintenance of the tobacco economy in southern states. Stockholders urge the priority of profits and growth through cigarette sales. The Surgeon General's office and the medical establishment condemn harmful health effects of smoking. Hence, managers must weigh competing ethical doctrines, and a balancing process is sometimes reflected in corporate strategy. Since 1967, for example, the proliferation of "safer" low-tar cigarettes has brought those brands from a 2 percent share of the domestic market to over 40 percent, as the tobacco companies have reacted to safety concerns in their market environment. But simultaneously, these firms have sought to expand their sales in less developed countries, where few people had discretionary income for cigarettes until the 1980s. The tobacco companies take advantage of lax restrictions on marketing in these countries and sometimes do not include health warnings. As these markets develop, smoking-related illnesses will rise. Many third-world governments encourage investment by tobacco firms; it provides sorely needed economic benefits.

Fifth, antagonistic wills frequently use incompatible ethical arguments to justify their intentions. Often, then, the ethical stand of a corporation is based on entirely different premises from the ethical stand of critics or constituent groups. Environmentalists, for example, frequently argue that the corporation should not knowingly harm the environment or injure anyone, whereas business executives assert a duty to fuel economic growth and trade off environmental quality with the need to provide jobs, tax revenues, and products for society. In the Love Canal incident, the Love Canal Homeowners Association charged Hooker Chemical Corporation with disregard for the health of residents near the canal. The company, on the other hand, asserted the need to produce chemicals with myriad benefits to society. Managers must recognize that when the premises of moral arguments are incompatible, one side cannot disprove the other, and ethical argument will be interminable.

Sixth, ethical standards are variable; they may change with time and place. In the 1950s, American corporations overseas routinely made payoffs to foreign officials, but managers had to curtail this practice after public expectations changed and a new law, the Foreign Corrupt Practices Act of 1977, prohibited most such expenditures. Certain bribes and payments are accepted practice in Asian, African, and Latin American countries but are not regarded as ethical in the United States. Doing business with close friends and family is standard practice in the Arab world, but in the United States or Western Europe the same actions are often regarded as constituting a conflict of interest. Even circumstances peculiar to a single corporation may modify the possibility of virtuous conduct. For instance, if a firm is going bankrupt, it may force workers to accept reduced pay and poorer working conditions or be granted more ethical latitude if it actively recruits a competitor's employee or fails to hire minorities. Right conduct is an elusive goal and the application of standards and principles an art.

Seventh, ethical behavior is molded from the clay of human imperfection. Even well-intentioned managers may be mistaken in their ethical judgment. Evidence exists, of course, that not all managers are even well-intentioned. Perhaps the nadir of comic wrongdoing was reached by Robert B. Beasley, a Firestone Tire and Rubber Company executive who, when placed in charge of Firestone's $12.6-million slush fund for illegal payments and campaign contributions, embezzled more than $500,000 from it. (He was discovered and received a four-year jail sentence. Firestone pleaded guilty to IRS tax avoidance charges on the slush-fund money.) When faced with temptation or pressure for profit performance, otherwise honest managers may compromise their standards.

Eighth, existing ethical standards and principles are not always adequate to resolve conflicts. To be sure, most situations, particularly those involving simple honesty, truth telling, trade secrets, or following pertinent laws, are clear. For instance, at the turn of the century, Du Pont employed a chief mechanic, George Seitz, who was sent to rival firms, applied for jobs under an assumed name, and once hired, collected information about manufacturing processes, customers, and the companies' strengths and weaknesses. When Seitz reported back to top Du Pont executives, Du Pont used his information to undercut its rivals by stealing customers and then offering to buy a company at a bargain rate (Mosley, 1980: 209). Premeditated corporate behavior such as this is clearly unethical. It violates high-level ethical abstractions such as the Golden Rule and the categorical imperative and contradicts more specific prohibitions in the Western tradition against lying and conflict of interest.

However, when conflicts between and among ethical standards arise, as they may in other cases, the application of principles at any level is not a guarantee of resolution because much latitude for specific application exists. A person and a corporation should, for example, obey the law. But an American corporation operating in the legal structure of racial separation in South Africa faces the ethical dilemma of violating ethical standards on human equality set out in the United Nations "Universal Declaration of Human Rights," and the spirit of American civil rights laws when obeying South African laws enforcing white supremacy. No principles exist to replace human judgment in such cases.

Ninth, the twentieth century presents managers with newly emerged problems of ethics that embody more than traditional concerns such as honesty, charity, and modesty. Although such qualities are still basic, vexing new problems have arisen. For example, modern ethical theory has not yet developed a principle for weighing human life against economic factors in a decision. Cancer studies may show that workers or nearby residents exposed to plant emissions risk becoming ill in small numbers far in the future. How should this information be balanced against costs of emission regulation, inflationary impact, capital investment reduction, or loss of jobs and economic benefits from forced plant closings?

Other examples of tough new ethical problems exist. The creation of computers with vast memory banks containing information about the American population poses the need to rethink the question of the limits to privacy. The concept of corporate social responsibility is seen by many in business as posing new ethical challenges. The application of advanced technologies developed by business in warfare and consumer markets poses unusual ethical problems. For instance, by using a computerized gas chromatograph to chemically analyze a perfume's contents, entrepreneurs have for the first time been able to make nearly exact copies of expensive, established designer perfumes like Ralph Lauren's Polo and Calvin Klein's Obsession. Because a scent cannot be trademarked like a brand name the imitations are legal and can be sold cheaply enough to undercut the established brand and capitalize on the extensive advertising that built the foundation of its popularity. Of course, product imitation is an ancient problem. But here the technology has outpaced legal remedy and ethical consensus.

Finally, the growth of many large-scale organizations in the twentieth century gives new significance to moral problems such as committee decision making, organizational loyalty versus loyalty to the public interest, preferential hiring of certain classifications of individuals, and individual peaked performance before retirement. Managers must deal with ethical complexities peculiar to large organizations. These complexities have been illuminated by the late Chester Barnard, former president of New Jersey Bell.

Moral Complexity: The Views of Chester Barnard

In an essay entitled "Elementary Conditions of Business Morals," Chester Barnard (1886–1961) argued that "modern Western civilization is morally complex, far beyond other civilizations" (1958: 2). He went on to write that formal business organizations are social systems, and because of this, most management decisions are concerned with moral issues. One of the sources of moral conflict in formal organizations that Barnard emphasized was the existence of "varieties of moralities." Thus, according to him, people in organizations related to each other not as individuals and personal friends, but in terms of, for example, representative roles. He observed that concrete behavior of individuals has become representative rather than personal. This is an important, if not dominant, characteristic of Western society, with its large organizations. People act as trustees and directors of corporations, not as individuals (1958).

Not only do people relate to each other through impersonal role behavior, but, according to Barnard, there different sets of moralities are in effect in organizations, and there is likely to be conflict among them. What did Barnard mean by this?

In *The Functions of the Executive* (1938), Barnard wrote that all persons have a number of private codes of morals that tend to inhibit, control, and modify impulses toward behavior. For example, most individuals simultaneously embody private codes relating to religion, patriotism, economics or business manners, family obligations, professional or technical activities, work group, and the larger organization where they work. Some of these codes, such as loyalty to one's family or profession, are dominant over others. Barnard defined responsibility as "the power of a particular private code of morals to control the conduct of the individual in the presence of strong contrary desires or impulses" (p. 263). Persons may be responsible to some codes and not to others. He gives an example:

> Many persons appear unaware of the force of such codes. . . . I recall a telephone operator on duty at a lonely place from which she could see in the distance the

house in which her mother lay bedridden. Her life was spent in taking care of her mother and maintaining that home for her. To do so, she chose employment in that particular position, against other inclinations. Yet she stayed at her switchboard while she watched the house burn down. No code, public or organizational, that has any general validity under such circumstances governed her conduct. . . . Nevertheless, she showed extraordinary "moral courage," we would say, in conforming to a code of her organization—the *moral* necessity of uninterrupted service. This was high responsibility as respects that code (pp. 268–269).

Conflicts may occur between private codes within individuals and also between individuals who have differing priorities. Although codes direct behavior, therefore, they also create moral complexity. Conflicts among codes increase with the number of codes in perhaps geometric ratio. The role of executives, according to Barnard, is to create an ethical climate for subordinates to work in. The executive needs to develop special skills to solve moral problems by finding correct solutions when codes conflict or by developing innovative solutions to moral problems that arise in today's complex managerial environment. This latter approach requires special skills of imagination and creativity.

CONCLUDING OBSERVATION

There are many paths to ethical behavior. Most business executives fail to appreciate the vast repertoire of ethical principles available to help resolve problems of business ethics. It may also be true that when they do resolve such problems, they intuitively use principles corresponding to some of those mentioned in this chapter. We believe that by studying the principles and decision guidelines presented here, a person can become more sensitive to the presence of ethical issues in everyday business life. And, having become more sensitive, he or she will likely become more resolute in correcting deficiencies. In addition, we think that these principles and guidelines are invaluable for application to ethical issues that arise in the case studies in this book. We encourage students to frequently refer to this chapter for ideas and conceptual tools.

CASE STUDY

AN APPLICATION OF ETHICAL PRINCIPLES

The situations described below raise ethical conflicts for some readers. If you believe that an ethical problem exists in an incident, be specific in stating its nature. Then try to use principled reasoning to resolve the conflict by applying one or more of the ethical principles in the chapter.

1. Homeowners near an airport want to end commercial flights into the airport because of noise. As airport manager, you leak to the press some long-buried "contingency plans" for runway expansion without emphasizing that no expansion is likely. You hope that the complaining residents will be satisfied to negotiate a compromise that leaves the airport open to commercial flights but precludes expansion. Is this an ethical method of negotiation?

2. You operate a small, specialty metals business. An inexperienced customer calls with an order for a rare alloy. The customer has no idea what your costs are and what a reasonable price is for this alloy. Six other customers buy this alloy at a standard price. Should you add a little more to the price for this customer? Why or why not?

3. You have been offered a promotion to the position of project manager for a new-car development project at General Motors. The car is code-named the Screaming Demon. Careful marketing surveys show a continuing market for a fast, small car about the size of the Volkswagen GTI or Mitsubishi Mirage. The car is to be powered by a large-displacement, turbocharged engine and will have acceleration and top speeds rivaling those of the Chevrolet Corvette.

The car must sell for $9,000 to $11,500, and this will put severe constraints on engineering and materials costs. It will be a spartan automobile, with a harsh ride and few amenities, but it is to be marketed to the sixteen to twenty-five age group of drivers as a hot rod with a speed image. Ads being sketched by agencies competing for the account emphasize performance and handling characteristics and associate ownership of the automobile with adventurous young-adult lifestyles. Will you accept leadership of this project?

4. Six employees in the Grand Star Insurance Company work in the same room. Three are smokers who smoke freely during the day. Three are nonsmok-

ers who are irritated by the smoke. The nonsmokers recently approached the office manager and complained. "We have a right to protect our health from the dangers of sidestream smoke," one argued. When the office manager discussed the problem with the smokers, they argued that they had a right to smoke because no company or city ordinance prohibited it and because they had been hired by the company as smokers years ago and should not be required to give up their habit now. What ethical principle(s) might be applied to resolve this conflict?

5. You are asked by a potential employer to take a psychological profile test. It includes items such as:

	Yes	No	Can't Say
It is difficult to sleep at night.			
I worry about sexual matters.			
Sometimes my hands feel disjointed from my body.			
I sometimes smell strange odors.			
I enjoyed dancing classes in junior high school.			
Not all of my friends really like me.			
Work is often a source of stress.			

Because you have read that it is best to fit into a "normal" range and pattern of behavior, and because it is your hunch that the personnel office will weed out unusual personalities, you try to guess which answers are most appropriate for a conservative or average response and write them in. Is this ethical?

6. You are the president of a company that manufactures chain saws. A chain saw is a dangerous but necessary tool. Each year some workers are injured while using your saws and the saws made by your competitors. You comply with all pertinent federal safety standards. But there are expensive design alterations you could incorporate into your product that would prevent some injuries. These alterations would raise production costs considerably in a very competitive industry. It is probable your competitors would not follow suit. Are you ethically remiss if you do not change your design?

7. When two vice presidents of American Can objected to the sale of two subsidiary companies, Chairman William Woodside promptly named them each as president of one of the companies and divested. Does this action raise ethical questions?

8. As a new middle-management employee for a corporation that owns a number of pear orchards, one day you see migrant workers mixing quantities of amitraz, an insecticide used on pears, in preparation for spraying. You recall that early in 1986 the Environmental Protection Agency canceled registration of amitraz after laboratory tests showed it to pose a risk of producing tumors in human tissue. After this action, amitraz was removed from the market and its application banned unless a special permit was issued. When you inquire about its use, you are told that the company had stored a large quantity of amitraz, that it is not a problem to use it because the EPA is overcautious, and that nobody in the company ever makes waves about minor noncompliance with stupid

government regulations anyway because the firm's safety record is excellent. Would you take further action?

9. As president of an accounting firm in a large city, you were prepared to promote one of your vice presidents to the position of senior vice president. Your decision was based on a record of outstanding performance by this person over the eight years she has been with the firm. A new personnel director recently insisted on implementing a policy of resumé checks for hires and current employees receiving promotions who had not been through such checks. Unfortunately, it was discovered that although the vice president claimed to have an M.B.A. from the University of Michigan, a check revealed that she dropped out before completing her last twenty units of course work. No other discrepancies exist. Would you proceed with the promotion, retain the vice president but not promote her, or fire her?

10. The plant supervisor at a manufacturing facility has been informed of continuing thefts in a stockroom or nearby warehouse. Plant security has been unable to catch the thief or thieves red-handed. One of the five workers with routine access to these areas was hired six months ago, after serving two years in prison for armed robbery. The security staff required this man to undergo a polygraph test, and the examiner concluded that some of the man's responses with respect to the thefts were deceptive. The warehouse foreman and the chief of plant security recommend that you fire the worker. You are aware of studies showing error rates of 40 to 50 percent in polygraph tests (Hurd, 1985; Lykken, 1984). But your security supervisor assures you that the examiner was highly trained and that in such cases, accuracy is virtually 100 percent. Would you fire this employee? If not, what would be your next step?

11. When Admiral Thomas Westfall took command of the Portsmouth Naval Shipyard, theft of supplies was thought to be endemic. It was a standing joke that homes in the area were painted gray with paint stolen from the Navy. Admiral Westfall issued an order that rules related to supply practices and forbidding theft would be strictly enforced. Within a few days, two career petty officers were apprehended carrying a piece of Plexiglass worth $25 out of the base. Westfall immediately fired both of them and also a civilian storeroom clerk with 30 years service. The clerk lost both his job and his pension. According to Westfall; "The fact that I did it made a lot of honest citizens real quick." Did the Admiral act ethically?

12. Sam, Sally, and Hector have been laid off from middle-management positions. Sam and Hector are deeply upset by their misfortune. They are nervous, inarticulate, and docile at an exit meeting in the personnel department and accept the severance package offered by the company (consisting of two weeks pay and continuation of health benefits for two weeks) without questioning its provisions. Sally, on the other hand, manifests her anxiety about job loss by becoming angry. In the exit meeting she complains about the inadequacy of the severance package, threatens a lawsuit, and tries to negotiate more compensation. She receives an extra week of pay that the others do not get. Has the company been fair in its treatment of these employees?

13. In the past five years seven department-store sales employees in a large retailing corporation have been fired and prosecuted for stealing from daily cash register receipts. They received sentences of community service followed by a term of probation. All acquired a criminal record.

A senior vice president of the same firm was caught diverting $68,000 from corporate accounts into fourteen personal bank accounts. He was allowed to resign quietly after repaying the corporation and was not prosecuted. This action was taken after much discussion by senior management. The senior vice president was prominent in civic affairs. His prosecution would have been newsworthy, and the corporation did not want to invite extensive negative publicity. After considering the ethical implications do you concur with the corporation's decision to permit a resignation of this nature?

CASE STUDY

CATHOLIC SOCIAL TEACHING AND THE U.S. ECONOMY*

On November 13, 1986, the more than 300 Roman Catholic bishops of the United States assembled at their annual meeting in Washington, D.C., culminating a six-year process by voting approval of a landmark document on the moral dimensions of the U.S. economy. Entitled "Economic Justice for All: Catholic Social Teaching and the U.S. Economy," the pastoral letter invited American Catholics to reflect on the human and ethical dimensions of economic life and to fashion a more just society for the poor and the powerless.

The bishops intend the letter not only to provide guidance for Roman Catholics but also to help shape new public policy for the United States. The hope was that the document would foster a "renewed public moral vision." There is no question but that if the letter were the guiding force today, our economy would have a whole new look. The pastoral letter challenged many common assumptions about economic life in the United States and placed the Catholic Church in the vanguard of social activism. Many, including a number of people in the business community, have been critical of the church involving itself in economic matters.

Catholic Social Teaching

The point of the bishops' statement was to remind people that the U.S. economy is still far from where it might be. There are too many able-bodied people who cannot find work, and a disproportionate number of those are minorities and women. There are too many who slip through the safety net, going without adequate food, housing, and medical care. The plight of people in developing

---

*by Oliver F. Williams, C.S.C.

*This case includes some material previously published: See O. Williams, "The Church and Social Activism: A Catholic Perspective," *Saint Louis University Public Law Review* (5: 439–450; and O. Williams, "Bishops Challenge Facilities to Act with Hope, Realism," *Health Progress* 66(1): 29–31, 1985.

countries is also a central concern. So many in the U.S. live so well that it is easy to forget about those who are barely getting along.

The tradition of the Roman Catholic Church is that although the gospel message offers a vision of the sort of person one ought to become and the sort of communities one ought to try to form, this biblical vision requires human reason as well as the help of the social sciences to become concrete. The structures, institutions, and policies that ought to guide society are a product of disciplined reflection on the biblical vision. Thus, the church has a long tradition of social teaching stated in encyclicals (pastoral letters written by the Pope as the chief shepherd of the church), bishops' pastoral letters, and the writings of theologians. Often the letters locate the church's position between doctrinaire capitalism and socialism.

Catholic social teaching begins with the conviction that human nature is flawed, following on its doctrine of original sin, but that human freedom responding to God's grace can overcome the selfishness that destroys community. People need others to grow and develop, and there is a natural, God-given tendency to come together in various groups—families, churches, trade unions, businesses, professional associations, and so on. Society is simply the sum total of all the various groupings. The role of the state is to facilitate cooperation among the natural groupings of society. Legislation is always enacted with an eye to the "common good," a term used frequently in Catholic social teaching to refer to the total environment—cultural, social, religious, political, and economic—required for the living of a humane life. Legislation is envisioned as evoking the cooperative dimension of the person and as fostering an environment in which the basic goodness of the person might flourish.

Although Catholic social teaching would never endorse any one particular country's economic arrangements, it has repeatedly stressed that the role of the state is to serve society. Thus, for example, in Pope John Paul II's 1981 encyclical, *On Human Work,* there is a vigorous defense of the workers' right to form unions. The term "solidarity" is used to defend this right, and the allusion to the situation in Poland is only thinly veiled. In socialist Poland, the state is identified with society, and hence the government controls all dimensions of life and leaves little space for freedoms taken for granted in most of the Western world. This pervasive control is clearly not in accord with Catholic ideals.

The sort of society envisioned by Catholic social teaching is one in which private property is respected. Following the medieval scholar Thomas Aquinas, the church assumes that private property enables the human development intended by the Creator. Yet the teaching has always insisted that private property has a social dimension that requires that owners consider the common good in the use of property. This vision of society assumes that some people will have more material goods than others but that the affluent will provide for the less fortunate, either through the channels of public policy or other appropriate groups of society. The emphasis is always on respect for the human dignity of the poor, even in their unfortunate situation. The ideal is to structure society so that all those who are able might provide for themselves and their families by freely employing their talents. Although Catholic social teaching has never formally endorsed the mixed economy of the United States, there clearly are not many countries that have approached the ideal so closely as has the United States.

Escalating Activism

This social vision of the sort of world toward which Christians should be working has been stated and restated any number of times in papal encyclicals and other church documents in the twentieth century. How does one account for the rather sudden activist movement in the U.S. Catholic Church in the last fifteen years? Countless shareholder resolutions have been initiated by Roman Catholic religious orders in the last decade. Boycotts have been endorsed by high church officials. The bishop of El Paso, in 1973, requested the more than 250 U.S. bishops to support the boycott of all Farah products to aid the Mexican-American workers in their struggle with the firm. There have been pastoral letters from the bishops of the United States, first on nuclear ethics and now on the economy. What is happening in the church, and where is it likely to lead? It may be helpful to explore some of the social causes for this increasingly activist role as well as some of the theological reasons.

"People Persons"

Bishop James Malone, the president of the National Conference of Catholic Bishops of the United States during the process of writing the letter on the economy, has long been an influential member of the assembly, and in many ways his pastoral experience has been similar to that of his brother bishops. Malone, as bishop of Youngstown, Ohio, has seen the dismantling of the steel industry and all its attendant problems. Unemployment, alcoholism, divorce, and child abuse all have been chronic in his diocese in recent years. Malone has often stated that there must be a more humane way to phase out an industry. It seemed as though people did not count. Many bishops today have had much pastoral experience and, unlike their predecessors, who were often chosen for their skills in raising money, building schools, and so on, this new breed of leaders are "people persons." They have been deeply touched by the problems of the poorest and the least advantaged in their midst, and many in their communities want the bishops to take action.

Whereas twenty years ago the U.S. bishops would not have been inclined to address social problems with a pastoral letter directly challenging public policy, the presence of a small but vocal minority sometimes called the "Catholic left" in the Catholic community has added a new dynamic to the dialogue. Often critical of the hierarchy on a number of issues, the Catholic left had its roots among the many who participated in the civil rights demonstrations. Following Martin Luther King, Jr., from Selma to Montgomery, then joining the anti-Vietnam War movement, many came to realize that they could change social structures that were unjust. Philip and Daniel Berrigan, leaders in the anti-Vietnam War protest, became great heroes to many young Catholics, and the influence of these two clerics in the U.S. church cannot be neglected.

Upward Mobility

Another factor that must be considered is the rapid upward mobility of many Catholics in the United States. Past generations of Catholics were largely blue-collar people, but today Catholics are more influential in business, government, and the wider society. The focus of encyclicals was formerly on the need for political and economic rights for lower-class Catholics. Now that Catholics have much more power and wealth, there is a shift in concern in church teaching to the plight of developing countries and the poorest of the poor in the global economy. It would have made little sense to tell Catholics of the United States in 1891 to change social structures, for these newcomers to America were still on the outside looking in. Now that many wield power, their church challenges them to exercise their stewardship well.

Social Dimensions

Although the Catholic Church traditionally has stressed both the individual and the social aspects of human life, the social dimension has been increasingly emphasized in the last twenty-five years. The Gospels call not only for a change of heart but also for a change in social structures. There has been a renewed awareness that God's intentions for humankind concern not only matters of personal attitudes and conduct (for example, on sexuality), but also how the community is organized—the social, political, cultural, and economic dimensions of society. The overarching theme is that all people ought to have the opportunity to lead a humane life.

Although church documents always note that there will be no heaven on earth, since the late 1960s, Church teaching has stressed that Christians must be concerned with making the world a better place, especially for the least advantaged around the globe. This emphasis began with the teaching of Pope John XXIII but was fully developed under his successor, Pope Paul VI. The Second Vatican Council document, *The Church in the Modern World*, provides the full-blown rationale for the social mission of the church.

The present pope, John Paul II, continues to focus on the church's ministry to the person enmeshed in social and political structures but has repeatedly found it necessary to accent the fact that Christ can never be understood as a political revolutionary. Although especially concerned that the poor somehow be enabled to find a place in the mainstream of society, John Paul II has spent considerable effort differentiating authentic Catholic theology from a brand of theology with Marxist overtones that has a popular appeal in certain areas of Latin America. In that he comes from Poland, the pope is not naive to the stifling of society that results when the state imposes a single version of acceptable truth. Under Soviet domination, the Polish church has never enjoyed adequate freedom, and the meager rights of workers are an international scandal. In addition, Marxist notions of an inevitable class struggle go against the grain of Christian thought. "The struggle is always for justice, not against others."

The Vision in Context

The U.S. bishops decided in November 1980, following the counsel of papal teaching, to write a pastoral letter on the economy that would bring Catholic social teaching in dialogue with the particular situation of the United States (paragraph 26*). After listening to theologians, major religious leaders of all faiths, economists, business and government leaders, and a host of others, and after receiving critical comments on three drafts of the document, the bishops finally issued the fourth and final version in November 1986.

There was some discussion among the bishops writing the document on whether it should include only the principles and moral vision of religious social teaching or whether some specific application of the principles in the form of policy recommendations should also be stated. Realizing that policy recommendations to reform the economy involve prudential judgments and therefore do not share the same kind of authority as moral principles, the bishops nevertheless decided to include some specific policy suggestions. At the least, these would indicate a direction and perhaps would stimulate debate on what a more humane economy might entail. It may be helpful to consider first a brief summary of the vision and principles and then an outline of the policy recommendations included in the letter.

The bishops' letter formulated a vision from biblical and theological grounds and was rooted in "its vision of the transcendent worth—the sacredness—of human beings" (paragraph 28). Recognizing that human dignity can only flourish in community, the pastoral draws on a rich biblical tradition to elaborate the essential social dimension of the person. In fidelity to scripture, the poor and the powerless are never to be forgotten. "The dignity of the human person, realized in community with others, is the criterion against which all aspects of economic life must be measured" (paragraph 28). "The fundamental moral criterion for all economic decisions, policies and institutions is this: They must be at the service of all people, especially the poor" (paragraph 24). This vision is developed with the biblical motifs of *creation, covenant,* and *community.*

By exploring these three biblical motifs, the document reminds Christians of the sort of people they ought to become and of the sort of communities they ought to form. For Christians, the Bible ought to have a decisive influence on their overall vision of life, their attitudes, convictions, and intentions. Creation stories remind us of the gift-like character of life and the mandate to be faithful stewards of *God's* world. Using human talents and ingenuity, people are indeed called to continue God's creative work by building a more humane world. "Men

---

*All paragraph references are to "Economic Justice for All: Catholic Social Teaching and the U.S. Economy."

and women are also to share in the creative activity of God. . . . They can justly consider that by their labor they are unfolding the Creator's work" (paragraph 32).

As the ancient Hebrews fleeing Egypt came together in solidarity during their exodus and finally formalized their community in the covenant, so too those living today under the new covenant should be known for their community and solidarity. Because of this bond, the Christian community ought to be a model of concern for the less fortunate.

In the biblical vision, the justice of a community is demonstrated by its treatment of the powerless in society—the widow, the orphan, the poor, and the stranger. The poor in early Christianity were seen as the special concern of God. Following the 1979 statement at Puebla, Mexico, by the assembled Latin American bishops and the speeches of John Paul II, the pastoral focused on "the preferential option for the poor." The document detailed three challenges that follow from this option for the poor:

1. It posed a prophetic mandate to speak for those who have no one to speak for them, to be a defender of the defenseless, who in biblical terms are the poor.

2. It also demanded a compassionate vision that enables the church to see things from the side of the poor and powerless and to assess lifestyle, policies, and social institutions in terms of their impact on the poor.

3. Finally, and most radically, it called for an emptying of self, both individually and corporately, that allows the church to experience the power of God in the midst of poverty and powerlessness.

A Guiding Assumption

Underpinning the pastoral letter is the idea that today the notion of the "rights" of an individual must be expanded to include not only civil and political rights, but also economic rights.

The concept of a right is embedded in the very founding of these United States. The Declaration of Independence and the Bill of Rights enumerate a long list of entitlements or rights. These legal rights of U.S. citizens, such as "life, liberty, and the pursuit of happiness," are correlated with a duty others have toward the individual. For example, to the framers of the Declaration of Independence, the right to life meant that a person had the right not to be killed and that the government had the duty to protect this entitlement. In the eighteenth century, the concept of a right was understood to circumscribe an area in which others had a duty *not* to interfere. The role of government was to insure that a person's free speech, privacy, property, and other rights were protected from undue interference. Today these civil rights are discussed in the philosophic literature as "negative rights"; that is, they point to the duty another has of *not* interfering. Although it is surely a significant accomplishment that a whole range of negative rights are guaranteed for so many today, a body of literature has developed in the twentieth century arguing for "positive rights."

Positive rights are taken to be those entitlements a person has by virtue of being human. It is these rights which were championed by the bishops in their pastoral on the economy.

The concept of a positive right implies that someone or some institution in society has the *positive* duty to provide for whatever is necessary to pursue the interest in question. For example, today when one speaks of the "right to life," in contrast to the eighteenth-century understanding of the right not to be killed, what is generally meant is that a person has a right to the minimum necessities of life. The United Nations 1948 "Universal Declaration of Human Rights" lists a whole array of positive rights that are taken to be entitlements for all by virtue of being a person: the right to work, to just and favorable conditions of work, to protection against unemployment, to rest and leisure, including reasonable limitation of working hours and periodic holidays with pay, and so on.

The pastoral letter reminded the reader that Pope John XXIII, in the encyclical *Peace on Earth*, enumerated the rights that are the minimal conditions for a just economy, such things as the right to food, clothing, shelter, jobs, basic education, and medical care, as well as the right to security in the event of sickness and the rights of property ownership. However, the bishops recognized that there was no consensus yet in the United States that all of these really are rights that ought to be guaranteed nor how one might actually guarantee them. To help form this consensus was one of the major purposes of the pastoral. It must begin with the formation of a new cultural consensus that *all people really do have rights in the economic sphere* and that society has a moral obligation to take the necessary steps to insure that no one among us is hungry, homeless, unemployed, or otherwise denied what is necessary for living with dignity.

Four principles to guide policies in all economic institutions were suggested in the document.

1. The fulfillment of the basic needs of the poor is of the highest priority.

2. Increasing active participation in economic life by those who are presently excluded or vulnerable is a high social priority.

3. The investment of wealth, talent, and human energy should be especially directed to benefit those who are poor or economically insecure.

4. Economic and social policies as well as the organization of the work world should be continually evaluated in light of their impact on the strength and stability of family life.

Policy Recommendations

Chapter 3 of the pastoral letter focused on four economic issues in the light of the religious vision and ethical principles discussed in the first two chapters. The issues—employment, poverty, food and agriculture, and the U.S. role in the global economy—are not intended to exhaust the concerns of Catholic social teaching, but they do lend themselves to specific applications of Catholic moral principles. Thus new policies are advocated for reaching full employment, for eradicating U.S. poverty, for preserving family farms and discouraging agribusiness from dominating agricultural resources, and for aiding developing nations.

Chapter 3 of the five-chapter letter comprises 167 paragraphs, more than 45 percent of the document. Here is one of the specific recommendations under the section on employment:

> We recommend increased support for direct job creation programs targeted on the long-term unemployed and those with special needs. Such programs can take the form of direct public service employment and also of public subsidies for employment in the private sector. Both approaches would provide for those with low skills less expensively and with less inflation than would general stimulation of the economy. The cost of providing jobs must also be balanced against the savings realized by the government through decreased welfare and unemployment insurance expenditures and increased revenues from the taxes paid by the newly employed (paragraph 162).

Chapter 4 intended to move beyond particular policy recommendations and offers "a long-term and more fundamental response" to the challenge of achieving economic justice for all. It suggested new forms of cooperation and partnership to replace the adversarial relationships that so often dominate the major actors in society. The chapter considered four areas: cooperation within firms and industries; local and regional cooperation; partnership in the development of national policies; and cooperation at the international level.

Chapter 5 concluded the letter with reflections on the church as a model of economic justice and on the importance of the notion of vocation in the world today. "Through their competency and by their activity, lay men and women have the vocation to bring the light of the Gospel to economic affairs so that the world may be filled with the spirit of Christ and may more effectively attain its destiny in justice, in love and in peace" (paragraph 332). The letter is indeed hopeful that together people can fashion a world that is both more humane and more virtuous.

The Problems and Possibilities of Church Social Activism

The particular recommendation of the pastoral stated above on job creation programs was sharply attacked by the *Wall Street Journal* as "simply poor policy." The *Journal*'s criticism points up the dilemma of trying to be specific in a church document. Joseph A. Califano, Jr., Secretary of Health, Education, and Welfare from 1977 to 1979, commenting on the first draft of the letter, highlighted the dilemma.

> When the bishops move to what they call "policy applications," they sound more like one of the great society legislative messages I helped draft for Lyndon Johnson than a group of clerics calling attention to the moral, religious, and ethical dimensions of the society they are trying to reshape. Here the bishops bring much of the criticism on themselves. . . . My concern is that by dipping its toes too

deeply in the waters of detailed federal programs, the bishops' message may be drowned (*America,* January 12, 1985, p. 6).

Although the bishops were careful to point out in their "Policy Applications" section that the moral authority of applications is much less than that of universal moral principles, Califano offered a telling criticism. In the judgment of many, the bishops were simply in over their heads in discussing concrete policies. But the document stimulated intense debate and, one hopes, will result in generally raising awareness of the moral dimension of economic decisions. This, to be sure, would be no small achievement.

Edward L. Hennessy, Jr., chariman of Allied Corporation, offered a penetrating critique of the bishops' economic ethics:

> It seems to be that intelligent discussion of the pastoral's recommendations requires that we put a price on them. Then, the bishops and everyone else can make a judgment about whether the cost might merely inconvenience the well-to-do, or whether it might reduce incentive, lessen the capital investment which creates jobs, slow the economy and seriously interfere with the goals of balancing the budget, cutting interest rates and making the United States competitive again with foreign producers.
>
> No one I know questions the need to provide adequate social services for the poor in our society. But the Pastoral letter, in its apparent determination to redistribute a significant part of our society's wealth, risks damaging the most productive economic system yet devised. It is a risk the bishops of the American church should, I think, hesitate to take (*America,* January 12, 1985, p. 17).

Is Hennessy correct in his judgment? There is nothing near a consensus on the issues in question. When the bishops speak in the area of medical or sexual ethics, they have a long tradition to draw from. The problem is that there is not an established body of literature or a tradition of economic ethics that is commonly accepted by the relevant academic and professional communities.

Toward the Future

It may be that the social-activist movement is only a phase in the church life as it moves toward a genuine ministry to managers of our public and private institutions. In the Catholic Church, the ministry had focused on laborers in the workplace because almost all Catholics were blue-collar workers. Today the children and grandchildren of those blue-collar people are running corporate America, often without any guidance or support from their churches. Business executives are often treated by their churches as either robber barons—with open hostility—or as rich benefactors—with undue deference. The churches are trying to relate to managers as people, people who often have substantial power and influence to shape communities and lives and who need the support of their religious community.

The church has been relatively successful in providing ministry to the medical community. Men and women trained in theology and ethics also have learned the medical sciences and on this basis offer their insight and guidance. A movement parallel to the one that produced medical ethics is long overdue for the management community. Perhaps it is time for managers to seek their church leaders and offer their time and talent to advance this endeavor in economic ethics. It could yield high dividends for all.

Questions

1. Peter M. Flanigan, director of the Council of International Economic Policy under President Nixon, is critical of the pastoral letter. In particular, he objects to the suggestion that our society can guarantee to all citizens "economic rights" in the same way as they are guaranteed civil and political rights. "The proposed guaranteed right to a job forces the government to do something that is not normally within its competence and that experience teaches it can do only with a loss of productivity or of freedom or of both" (*America*, January 12, 1985, p. 13). Comment.

2. A *Fortune* editor commenting on the second draft noted "that the bishops keep contradicting themselves. . . . At one point, the bishops emphasize the importance of productivity; at another they groan about technology that displaces jobs. They make affirmative noises about the importance of entrepreneurs but then turn around and say that investment should be designed primarily to benefit the poor. (You think that's what they're trying to do in Silicon Valley, fellows?)" (*Fortune*, November 11, 1985, p. 150). Comment.

3. James Tobin, professor of economics at Yale University and Nobel laureate in 1981, offered this judgment on the bishops' letter. "The values expressed in the pastoral letter are presented as derived from Catholic theology. I, a non-Catholic and indeed an unrepentant "secular humanist," find them of universal appeal, striking responsive chords among persons of all religious faiths and of none. The ethics of equity and equality are very American, just as much as the ethics of individuals heard so exclusively today. The two are married in general adherence to the principal of equality of opportunity" (*America*, May 4, 1985, p. 359). Comment.

4. A New York *Times* editorial (November 18, 1986) expressed a judgment.

   > Mr. Buchanan [Patrick Buchanan, Reagan White House communications director] expressed hope that "the bishops recognize that the greatest enemy of material poverty in human history has been the free enterprise system of the United States." The bishops do not dispute that. They would challenge the complacent theory that economic growth alone can solve poverty and unemployment. They also question the easy thought that private charity will suffice.
   >
   >   The bishops remind those in the government and the public willing to hear what many people would like to forget: that we are measured by the condition of the least of our brethren.

   Do you agree with the *Times*? Why or why not?

5. Some have suggested that religious critics, such as the Catholic bishops in their pastoral letter, are capitalism's best friend. Explain.

PART V

MAJOR FUNCTIONAL ISSUES

CHAPTER 13

POLLUTION PROBLEMS AND PUBLIC POLICY

OHIOEDISON
The Energy Makers

Ill fares the land, to hastening ills a prey,
Where wealth accumulates and men decay

So wrote Oliver Goldsmith in 1770, recognizing that environmental pollution has been a concern through the ages. In the United States, knowledge of environmental degradation has focused widespread attention on the responsibility of business as a consumer of environmental quality, a scarce resource. How do companies today protect the environment? Here is one story.

In 1959 Ohio Edison Co. started construction of the W. H. Sammis electric power generating plant on the banks of the Ohio River. This was eleven years before passage of the Clean Air Act in 1970. Over the next fifteen years the company built seven coal-fired boilers at the plant; these heated steam.

During coal combustion, unburned particles called fly ash are created. If not removed by pollution control equipment, they lower visibility, promote atmospheric changes, and cause human respiratory illness. In the years before strict federal emission standards, Ohio Edison voluntarily installed electrostatic precipitators designed to remove 97 to 99 percent of the fly ash from the exhaust stream. Coal combustion also releases sulfur dioxide (SO_2) gas, and the company controlled SO_2 emissions by burning coal with a low sulfur content.

This pollution control strategy worked until the Arab oil embargo in 1973 led to a shortage of high-quality coal. By the mid-1970s, the plant was burning lower-quality coal because it was cheaper and more plentiful. But this lower-quality coal had a high ash content and a low sulfur content. Although the low sulfur content lessened SO_2 emissions, it aggravated the fly ash problem because high sulfur coal contains more iron particles that can be charged in the field of an

The W. H. Sammis Plant on the bank of the Ohio River. The dust-collection system sits atop a reinforced concrete deck about the size of three football fields. Note the four-lane highway running under the deck.   Courtesy of Ohio Edison.

electrostatic precipitator. Without these tiny pieces of iron in the ash, the antipollution equipment was far less efficient.

Thus, the plant developed a reputation as a source of pollution. The electrostatic precipitators were overwhelmed by fly ash from the low-quality coal and sometimes removed as little as 25 percent (Lewis, 1985). This often left the plant far short of the federal standard of 99.4 percent particulate removal. In 1981, Ohio Edison paid $1.7 million in fines for violations of Clean Air Act standards and faced federally imposed deadlines for higher particulate abatement. Ultimately, the company undertook a $440 million retrofit. It erected four enormous "baghouses" on a reinforced concrete deck three football fields long over the highway in front of the plant. These baghouses are dust-collection systems that operate on the same principle as vacuum cleaners. They entrap particles in the airstream of the boiler exhaust that flows through fiberglass bags and remove about 99 percent of the fly ash. Sulfur dioxide emissions are controlled by burning higher-quality, low-sulfur coal. Two of the boilers, however, also have electrostatic precipitators to increase particulate removal capacity and allow burning of lower-quality coal.

A Herculean effort has been required to meet increasingly stiff pollution abatement standards set by the federal government and the state of Ohio. The $440 million spent retrofitting the Sammis plant is the most any company in North America has spent for this purpose and equaled the cost of the plant's original construction. At its 2,100-acre Bruce Mansfield Plant in Shippingport, Pennsylvania, Ohio Edison had to devote 1,800 acres to pollution control equipment—86 percent of total area. The air quality control equipment there eats up 50 percent of the plant's operating cost and uses 5 percent of the electricity it generates. As a result of such mandatory efforts throughout the company's generating system, 20 percent of a customer's electric bill pays for environmental protection.

The story of Ohio Edison illustrates the huge expenditures required of firms in many industries to meet rapidly escalating environmental protection standards. Ohio Edison's outlays are larger than most but not atypical for large companies with industrial operations that foul the environment. In this chapter, we discuss the growth of environmental concern in the United States, the passage and content of environmental regulations, and the response of business. Understanding the phenomenal surge of regulation in the area of environmental quality will help explain why Ohio Edison felt compelled to make such huge capital expenditures for pollution abatement.

ENVIRONMENTAL DEGRADATION: SOURCES AND CAUSATION

It is incorrect to say that pollution is caused entirely by people. There are natural sources for many contaminants. Particulates causing atmospheric turbidity come from dust, forest wildfires, and volcanoes. Anaerobic decay and photochemical aerosol formation by plants are natural sources of hydrocarbons contributing to air pollution. Only about a third of sulfur oxide comes from human activities; most comes from sulfide compounds formed in decay of organic matter and from the sulfates in sea spray. About nine-tenths of all airborne carbon monoxide comes from "natural" sources. Water picks up trace elements of metals, asbestos, and other pollutants in its flow over rocks, gravel, and sand. Background ionizing radiation capable of mutating DNA, comes from uranium ore and cosmic rays.

Fissures on the ocean floor that geologists call seeps continuously spill oil and natural gas, causing hydrocarbon pollution. Geologists estimate that thousands of seeps off the California coastline near Santa Barbara spill up to eight tons of hydrocarbons into the air each day and are responsible for much of the area's air pollution. A few volcanoes, such as Krakatoa in the East Indies and Katmai in Alaska, have put more sulfuric contaminants into the air than all the products of combustion since the beginning of civilization.

Other contaminants, however, are artificial and added to nature entirely by human activity. These include, for instance, chlorinated hydrocarbon pesticides such as DDT and Kepone, fluorocarbon aerosols, and other chemicals. Industrial activity also enormously increases human exposure to naturally occurring pollutants. Thus, lead, hydrocarbons, ionizing radiation, and other naturally occurring substances may reach artificially high levels dangerous to humans.

Although the existence of industrial activity is the primary cause of environmental damage, there are other underlying causes. One is a growing population and greater concentration of people. Between 1910 and 1980, the proportion of the population living in urban areas of 2,500 or more jumped from 45 percent to about 80 percent, and the number of people in these centers leaped from 42 million to 175 million. Sewage systems, garbage collection agencies, and industrial controls have not kept pace with the resulting concentrated increase in pollutions. This factor has been exacerbated by a second: rising per capita incomes, which permit people to buy more things—automobiles, electrical devices, paper products, and so forth. Increases in per capita consumption of energy have in turn further added to air, water, and solid-waste pollution. Between 1960 and 1970, for example, a 10 percent increase in total population (181 million to 205 million) resulted in a 14 percent rise in metropolitan population, a 33 percent increase in vehicles, a 65 percent growth in industrial production, and a 100 percent leap in electric power generation.

To this should be added other deep-rooted causes of our environmental problems. The Council on Environmental Quality identifies them as follows:

> Our past tendency to emphasize quantitative growth at the expense of qualitative growth; the failure of our economy to provide full accounting for the social costs of environmental pollution; the failure to take environmental factors into account as a normal and necessary part of our planning and decision making; the inadequacy of our institutions for dealing with problems that cut across traditional political boundaries; our dependence on conveniences, without regard for their impact on

the environment; and more fundamentally, our failure to perceive the environment as a totality and to understand and to recognize the fundamental interdependence of all its parts, including man himself (1970: vii).

The Damaging Environmental Effects of Pollution

We are subject to a wider range of contaminants and to larger quantities of almost all pollutants than were people who lived in the pristine state before industrial growth. Concern centers on five serious health effects associated with pollution: the induction of cancer (carcinogenicity), the induction of mutations (mutagenicity), the induction of birth defects (teratogenicity), noncancerous disease processes in bodily organs, and the occurrence of behavioral impairment. Although absolute causation is difficult to prove in individuals, epidemiological studies of morbidity (abnormality and disease) and mortality (death) rates by medical experts have clearly established the relation of levels of pollution to a wide range of degenerative conditions among populations. A typical study showed the following associations:

High bladder cancer rates near factories producing dyes and pigments, drugs, perfumes, cosmetics, and toiletries

High lung cancer rates near factories manufacturing industrial gases, pharmaceuticals, soaps and detergents, paints, pigments, and synthetic rubber

High liver cancer rates near factories making synthetic rubber, soaps and detergents, cosmetics, printing inks, and some organic chemicals (Hodges, 1977: 12).

Specific health effects on humans are only part of the cost of degradation. Global effects on property, weather, plants, and animals have also been documented. Carbon dioxide in the air from widespread combustion of fossil fuels and methane from deforestation and feedlot husbandry absorb infrared radiation and cause a "greenhouse effect" which could warm the earth's climate. Sulfur dioxide and nitrogen oxides from industrial air emissions cause growing acidity of rain. Depletion of the ozone layer by upper atmospheric chemical reactions with manufactured fluorocarbon molecules expose the earth to unaccustomed doses of cosmic rays.

These problems are serious because they portend the loss of important environmental life-supporting capabilities. How serious are they? Periodically, doomsayers make frightening predictions about deterioration of our civilization by resource depletion and pollution. A recent publication by the Worldwatch Institute, for example, *State of the World 1986*, warned of growing ecological deficits and the possibility of future economic and political declines tied to loss of environmental quality. But although ambitious studies have been made, it is impossible to construct an accurate ecological balance sheet for the world. Data about emissions and damage are not complete, particularly for third-world countries, and scientists do not fully understand many complex natural systems, such as atmospheric chemistry.

There have been examples of civilizations permanently maiming themselves with pollution damage from business activity. The Indus Valley civilization, which existed in the area of present-day Pakistan, altered its ecology with particulate air pollution from dust on eroded lands and from smoky wood fires. Rainfall patterns changed, crop yields dropped, and social instability ensued. Likewise, between 600 and 200 B.C., Greece destroyed large expanses of forest to fuel its industries and provide grazing land. Erosion problems in ancient times led to a weakening of the Greek state, and the forests have not regenerated to this day. Swamps provided a breeding ground for malaria-carrying mosquitoes, and the Greeks became dependent on imports for their city-state economics, contributing to a series of debilitating wars fought to enhance access to resources.

And a contributing cause of the decline of ancient Rome may have been the use of lead as a lining in the famous Roman aqueducts. The Romans commonly stored beverages in lead-glazed pottery vessels, and some historians argue that this, along with lead leached from pipes in the aqueducts, resulted in chronic lead poisoning among the population, declining birth rates, widespread indolence, and behavioral problems—potential contributing factors to the weakness of the aristocracy and the fall of the empire (Lowrance, 1976). The bones of fifty-five preserved victims of the Mount Vesuvius eruption of A.D. 79 were found in 1982 to have a mean level of eighty-four parts per million (ppm) of lead, significantly higher than the three ppm of ancient Greeks and twenty ppm of contemporary Americans (Florman, 1983). These examples show that the wise student of history will regard the social consequences of industrial pollution as important. But there is no firm evidence yet that disaster is inevitably upon us.

The Role of Business in Polluting the Environment

Industrial activity, broadly defined, is the source of most pollution problems. Business of yesteryear was less concerned about environmental degradation than business today. Carelessness abounded. Copper ores in Butte, Montana, in the 1870s were roasted in open pits that produced fumes of sulfur and arsenic and smoke so thick that streetlamps burned on city streets at midday. Cows grazing in nearby areas had their teeth coated with fugitive copper fallen from the air. Isaac Edinger, a nearby rancher of that time, said:

> I used to carry a few of those gold-colored teeth in my pocket all the time because no one would believe me, and I'd have to show 'em. When they were shown they always wanted to keep the evidence, and I'd have to get a new supply every time I went back to the slaughterhouse (Glasscock, 1935: 86).

Ignorance of toxic effects, combined perhaps with ruthless exploitation of workers, led to the Gauley mine disaster in the 1930s, when a subsidiary of

Union Carbide drilled a four-mile-long tunnel through a mountain of virtually pure silica. Long hours of drilling and blasting in unventilated shafts exposed 2,000 unprotected workers, mostly blacks, to enormous concentrations of silica dust. In 1936, four years after the tunneling ended, a congressional investigation revealed that 476 workers already had died of silicosis and estimated that many of the rest were destined similarly to perish (Committee on Labor, 1936).

Industrial practices used for decades, with the expansion of scientific knowledge, have been pronounced unsafe or environmentally degrading. In retrospect, it is evident that workers in the asbestos industry who were exposed to high levels of airborne asbestos fiber faced grave danger of lethal illness. During a major, secret federal government push in the 1950s to develop a stockpile of nuclear weapons, uranium was mined in ways now considered environmentally unacceptable. The radioactive waste products of this mining, abandoned ore piles known as tailings, are found in proximity to twenty-two abandoned uranium mills in eight western states and constitute major health hazards. Indian miners were paid $50,000 to $80,000 a year to work underground uranium mines, and many perished of lung cancer attributable to exposure to radon daughters in unventilated shafts (Bregman, 1982).

Major environmental abuses continued in the face of growing understanding of the damage done into the 1970s. A much publicized incident was the scandalously lax handling of the powerful roach and banana-pest killer Kepone by Allied Chemical Corporation and a spinoff company, Life Science Products, Inc. Despite animal tests sponsored by Allied that showed wide-ranging Kepone-induced abnormalities, commercial production of the chemical at Life Science was undertaken in appalling fashion. The plant, according to one newspaper, was:

> an incredible mess. Dust flying through the air [was] . . . saturating the workers' clothing, getting into their hair, even into sandwiches they munched in production areas. The Kepone dust sometimes blew . . . in clouds. A gas station operator across the street said it obscured his view of the Life Science Plant. . . . Two firemen in a station behind Life Science say there were times when they wondered if they could see well enough to wheel their engines out in response to a fire alarm (in Stone, 1977: 5).

Two dozen workers had to be hospitalized with serious symptoms of Kepone poisoning, including uncontrollable shaking and functional sterility, and more than 130 workers and their family members were found to have high levels of Kepone in their blood. Kepone killed the biota on which the Hopewell, Virginia, sewage treatment plant depended to digest raw sewage, leading to malfunction. It contaminated the nearby James River, forcing a temporary end to commercial and sport fishing there, and was found in Chesapeake Bay. The Kepone production facility since has been buried in a large, plastic-lined pit, and Allied Chemical, after a series of obscure legal proceedings, paid a fine of $5 million and donated $8 million to a nonprofit corporation set up to organize remedial action (Stone, 1977).

In the 1980s business continues to pollute. Sensational accidents accompany mundane transgressions. The Bhopal gas leak in 1984 (see Chapter 10) and the Chernobyl reactor fire in 1986 illustrate the risk of sudden, dramatic releases of contaminants. The undramatic filling of toxic waste pits with the dross of industrial activity has over the years slowly released poisons into groundwater which will ultimately claim more souls than were lost at Bhopal and Chernobyl.

Some corporate pollution is willful. Documented cases of clandestine business activity contaminating the environment are numerous, including factories waiting until cover of night to belch forth smoke from their stacks, oil tankers illegally operating stripper pumps to drain oil tank residues on the seaward side so as to be unobserved from shore, and terrestrial "midnight dumpers" who

Assessing Business's Burden of Guilt

How critical should we be of industry in years past? What guilt should past managers bear for ecological deterioration and human death or suffering from polluting industrial activity? This is, of course, an exceptionally difficult question to answer because environmental wrongs are clearer in hindsight than they were to managers in the past.

It will be recalled from the discussion in Chapter 11 that Aristotle felt that only ignorance and inability may excuse morally questionable behavior and allow a business to escape responsibility for its actions. In the area of past polluting activities, we see both factors at work. In years past, for example, there was ignorance of the cancer-causing properties of petrochemicals. Managers of workers exposed to concentrations of such chemicals had no knowledge of the cause-effect relationship between exposure and cancer. There was less scientific knowledge, and managers were less receptive to medical studies, which were less relevant to their activities and not as elevated in repute as they are today. In certain industries, such as the chemical industry, a "macho" culture prevailed among workers who tolerated exposure to chemicals rather than show fear. Older ideologies that underlay managerial decisions also reduced consideration of environmental impacts. The Social Darwinism of the nineteenth century and the classical market ethic of the eighteenth, nineteenth, and twentieth centuries fostered little respect for the long-term welfare of the natural environment. Also, one company could not undertake costly antipollution activities and survive if others in the industry did not do likewise.

These factors combine to make a rudimentary case for the inability of yesteryear's managers to have altered industrial decisions and processes to protect the environment. We cannot expect people to transcend their time and make decisions by the criteria of a future generation. Can we expect old-time managers to have made environmentally sensitive decisions, even those that appear logical to us now, in the context of their eras? Think, for example, of the decisions made even today. Millions choose to smoke. Millions remain employed in stressful occupations, despite evidence that they lead to early death from cardiovascular disease. Millions drive in traffic despite exposure to carcinogens such as asbestos and benzine. In 100 years, these activities may be medically unacceptable. In our era, however, we continue the industrial activity that promotes them *even though we see the dangers*. We must be selective, therefore, in our condemnation of past business activity, realizing that detecting culpability is more the work of gods than human beings.

illegally empty toxic chemical wastes from tank trucks into streams and sewers and onto highways.

Much pollution is unintentional but inevitable. Many industrial processes are associated with specific pollutants. Agriculture leaves pesticide residues, non-nuclear utilities create sulfur dioxide and nitrogen oxide emissions, paint factories discharge cadmium-contaminated waste water, petrochemical plants release hydrocarbon emissions, and semiconductor manufacturing plants add toxic solvents such as trichloroethylene to waste water. State of the art control devices are never 100 percent efficient, and so these industries and others leave their characteristic pollution traces on air, land, and water.

In addition, it is virtually impossible for an industrial plant not to pollute in many small ways. Fugitive dust escapes through wall vents. Oil may drip from the engine of a warehouse forklift and later be washed into a drain. Gophers can dig through dikes built around chemical storage tanks so that rainwater percolates through the earth, carrying small amounts of dissolved toxic residues from minor spills during fluid transfer into and out of the tank. Dust from ductwork cleanouts may escape into the air. In short, a typical large plant has as many potential sources of pollution as the absent-minded professor has for error. Pollution control technology may be applied to these sources but not with perfection. Industrial activity is inevitably messy.

THE ENVIRONMENTAL MOVEMENT

The roots of the American environmental movement go back to the conservation movement of the 1800s, which began as an effort to protect western lands from unregulated mining, timber cutting, and grazing. This movement flowered once again in the 1960s, when growing scientific evidence showing the consequences of human improvidence led to coalescence of a powerful environmental movement consisting of environmental lobbies and legal action groups, conservation groups, scientists, and elected officials espousing environmental protection. The seeds of this movement were sown in the early 1960s, with the junction of forces such as the quality-of-life movement, publication of eye-opening texts such as Rachel Carson's *Silent Spring* (1962), and a growing wave of cynicism toward business. Photographs from space showing our planet to its occupants for the first time are also credited with having a galvanizing effect.

Environmentalists promoted a number of basic ideas. First, they condemned the logic of economic growth and materialism in society. Profit-making institutions were part of what Boulding (1970) called "cowboy capitalism," which exploited resources as if they were limitless. Second, because spaceship earth has limited resources, a new morality or "lifeboat ethic" was necessary. This ethic called for restructuring values in favor of conservation, environmental cleanup, zero population growth, and concern for future generations. Third, environmental alarmists predicted global catastrophe. Some took the apocalyptic view that it was already too late (Ehrlich, 1968). Fourth, environmentalists pointed to the Janus-like quality of technology and argued that aerosols, nuclear power, and other innovations created hazards well out of proportion to benefits. From this view, environmentalists developed a fifth notion: that conforming to "nature" was good and that industrial processes relying on technology were a mockery of divine, natural order.

Ideas such as these were the framework of an ecological populism that decisively changed the structure and goals of government, the nature of incentives for business, and the values of the population.

The Development of an Environmental Ethic

What is the proper relationship between business and nature? Throughout the history of Western civilization, nature has been regarded as an adversary to be conquered, wilderness has been the raw material from which profits stem, natural resources have been used for financial gain, and nature has been a depository for the toxic detritus of industrial activity. Paradoxically, the rapacious and arrogant attitudes of industry toward nature may be partly responsible for the current high standard of living and political dominance of Western culture. But the environmental ethic of the past, which ascribes few rights to nature and few obligations to business to protect it, is fading.

Today, the outlines of a new, expansive environmental ethic for business are emerging. The development of new ethical conceptions is the by-product of pollution damage, resource depletion, new scientific understandings of nature, public opinion unified in support of environmental quality, and the scholarly work of a critical mass of intellectuals interested in preserving nature.

Aldo Leopold, a naturalist, was a pioneer in thinking about an expanded environmental ethic. A seminal statement of a new "land ethic" in his 1949 book, *A Sand County Almanac,* inspired later generations of environmental ethicists. He wrote:

> All ethics so far evolved rest upon a single premise: that the individual is a member of a community of interdependent parts. His instincts prompt him to compete for his place in the community, but his ethics prompt him also to cooperate (perhaps in order that there may be a place to compete for).
>
> The land ethic simply enlarges the boundaries of the community to include soils, waters, plants, and animals, or collectively: the land . . .
>
> In short, a land ethic changes the role of *Homo sapiens* from conqueror of the land-community to plain member and citizen of it. It implies respect for his fellow members and also respect for the community as such (pp. 239–240).

The evolving environmental ethic has two components. First, it gives moral standing to nonhuman, nonconscious beings. The traditional Western notion of rights is competitive; when *Homo sapiens* competes for rights with plant and animal species, we always win. To illustrate our lack of charity, philosopher

Peter Singer (1975) has popularized the concept of "speciesism," or "a prejudice or attitude of bias towards the members of one's own species and against those of members of other species," that is analogous to racism or sexism (p. 7). The racist and sexist believe that skin color and sex determine the importance of others; the speciesist extends this concept in the belief that the number of one's legs or whether one lives in trees, the sea, or a condominium determines one's rights to life and environmental quality (Regan, 1980). Environmentalists argue that the human species, although dominant, is simply one among many. The power that humans have over other species, like the power that parents and rulers have over subjects, implies greater responsibility for the welfare of our fellow species. In a widely quoted book, *Should Trees Have Standing?*, Christopher D. Stone (1974) has argued that plants, animals, and natural features such as rivers, lakes, gorges, and meadows should have legal standing in court based on an inherent right to preserve their existence.

The second part of the emerging environmental ethic is expansion of the human right to environmental quality. People, it is alleged, have the right to a pollution-free environment. Article One of the Constitution of Pennsylvania, for instance, states that, "The people have a right to clean air, pure water, and to the preservation of the natural scenic, historic, and aesthetic values of the environment." Because pollution causes harm, a corporation has a moral obligation not to pollute and a duty to protect this human right to health. Corporations should not knowingly introduce damaging or dangerous elements into the environment. Corporations also have a duty to protect ecological systems, including animals and nonsentient objects, for their own sake.

A related question addressed by environmental ethicists is that of the rights of future generations. Unlike pollution, which affects people living now, resource depletion is more likely to affect future generations. An emerging ethic holds that it is the obligation of each generation to pass on to the next the goods it holds in common. No generation has the right to endanger future people any more than it has the right to endanger its own. Conservation of resources, then, is part of a moral obligation not knowingly to cause harm to the environment, and individuals and businesses should not waste resources.

Environmental ethicists are antagonistic to traditional business ethics that use utilitarian notions of overall benefit to justify economic development where such development causes some environmental damage. Industry customarily has argued that although pollution is harmful, the economic benefits of jobs, products, taxes, and economic growth often outweigh environmental damage. Therefore, there is a net benefit to society in industrial development. This ethical outlook clashes with newly developing notions that all members of "spaceship earth" are fellow travelers with rights. Extinction violates the rights of species. Deforestation violates the rights of trees. Business decisions that do not accommodate these rights ignore costs and benefits to nonhuman, nonsentient members of the environmental community. Traditional developmental ethics of business also clash with the notion of human rights to a pure environment. The more absolute such rights are thought to be, the more constraint there may be on business activities that trade environmental quality for economic develop-

Radical Environmentalists

The activities of ecological guerillas, who carry on the vigilante tradition of the Old West in the fight against pollution, illustrate just how sharply divergent the values of industry and environmentalists can be.

The archetype was "The Fox," who operated in Illinois in the late 1960s. The Fox struck corporate polluters about thirty times, plugging drainpipes and smokestacks. Once he appeared unannounced (and presumably unwelcomed) in the eighteenth-floor executive offices of USX Corporation to pour a bottle of foul-smelling effluent from one of the company's drains onto the white carpet. His exploits inspired others to sabotage bulldozers, yank surveyors' stakes, saw billboards, dynamite power line towers, and burn forests before they could be logged.

The environmental organization Greenpeace is renowned for intrepid forays against whale-hunting fleets, but its members also have committed criminal acts in the United States, such as plugging waste water drainpipes from chemical plants and refineries. Of late, a secretive radical group in Oregon named Earth First! has been sticking ceramic spikes, undetectable by metal detectors, into trees in areas of virgin timber. When logging begins, the spikes cause gruesome injuries when chain saws kick back into operators' bodies. If hit by a high-speed band saw in the sawmill, pieces of blade and spike fly through the air like shrapnel.

Radical environmentalists defend their actions. They speak for nature, they say, for creatures who are mute and defenseless in the face of corporate exploitation. They give plants and animals a voice. Polluters have broken the law for years—both nature's law and statutory law—so when they take the law into their own hands, they are simply fighting under the same rules as their corporate foes. Naturally, the business community condemns irresponsible vandalism and criminal endangerment of human life.

What do you think?

---

ment. A carcinogenic particle that invades lung tissue may violate a person's right to health, but normal industrial processes cause some toxic pollution. Today a tension exists between the emerging, idealistic environmental ethic and the pragmatic, competitive, and moderately exploitative industrial ethic.

This tension is illustrated in a recent survey of environmental and business elites in England, Germany, and the United States. In all three countries, environmentalists valued nature more highly, empathized more with other species, and were more willing to limit economic activity to avoid pollution risks than were people in business (Milbrath, 1984).

Public Attitudes Toward Environmental Issues

Since the 1960s, hundreds of opinion polls have monitored public attitudes on environmental issues. Although questions asked, methodology, and dates differ for these polls, important trend findings have emerged.

First, the public has regarded the environment as an important issue for many years. Gallup polls in April 1965 and on Earth Day in April 1970 showed that 17 percent and 53 percent of the public, respectively, picked reducing air and water pollution as one of three top national problems requiring most government attention. A 1983 survey sponsored by the Continental Group found 60 percent believed "that pollution is one of the most serious problems facing the nation today" (Bloomgarden, 1983: 47).

Second, the public is remarkably unified in its support for environmental protection. Pollution is experienced by everyone; it is visible and threatening. Therefore, unlike issues that divide rich and poor or liberals and conservatives, environmental protection is strongly supported in all age, regional, party, racial, and income groups. After a 1982 poll, well-known pollster Louis Harris remarked that "not a single major segment of the public wants environmental laws made less strict" (1982: 15). The environmental issue, then, comes close to being an issue with only one correct side for politicians.

Third, the public rejects compromises between environmental quality and other goals. Recent polls show that 79 percent of the public "believe we must prevent any type of animal from becoming extinct, even if it means sacrificing some things for ourselves" (Bloomgarden, 1983: 47); 78 percent say saving jobs and keeping a factory open are not sufficient mitigating reasons to allow air emissions dangerous to human health (*Business Week*, 1983); and in a 1985 survey, 86 percent wanted government to do more in regulating pollution even though it would require higher taxes and increase deficits (*Common Cause Magazine*, 1985).

Environmental Legislation

In the 1970s, powerful environmental groups were instrumental in translating the civic groundswell for environmental protection into an unprecedented string of victories in Congress. New laws established major regulatory programs, tightly controlling the actions of business. The streak began with passage of the National Environmental Policy Act in December 1969, an environmental Magna Carta that required environmental impact statements for all federal projects. It ended with the Comprehensive Environmental Response, Compensation, and Liability Act in December 1980, which established the famous $1.6 million "superfund" to clean hazardous toxic waste disposal sites. Table 13–1 is an outline of enactments.

These laws, passed with bipartisan support in Congress in what came to be called "the environmental decade," created a broad statutory base for industry regulation and changed forever the managerial task of coping with pollution. Several generalizations can be made about these laws.

First, in almost all of the programs, federal agencies set regulatory standards and may enforce them directly on companies. But they are encouraged to delegate some or all of the enforcement authority to the states, and widespread delegation has occurred. The states may exceed federal standards, and state enforcement programs such as those in California and New Jersey are more stringent than their federal counterparts.

TABLE 13-1   MAJOR ENVIRONMENTAL REGULATORY STATUTES: 1969–1980

National Environmental Policy Act	1969	Declared environmental quality a federal policy goal, required environmental impact studies, and established the Council on Environmental Quality.
Clean Air Act (and Amendments in 1977)	1970	Authorized air quality standards, auto emission limits, state implementation plans, air quality regions, monitoring of stationary source pollution, and research.
Occupational Safety and Health Act	1970	Set up the Occupational Safety and Health Administration to enforce health and safety standards and oversee state health and safety programs.
Noise Pollution and Control Act	1972	Directed the EPA and FAA to limit noise from industrial activity and products and from transportation equipment.
Federal Water Pollution Control Act Amendments	1972	Set a national goal of eliminating all pollutant discharges into U.S. waters by 1985. Industry was required to conform to emission technology standards; a massive sewage treatment construction grant program was authorized; and the EPA was required to set effluent standards and issue discharge permits.
Federal Environmental Pesticide Control Act	1972	Required registration of pesticides by the EPA; required applicants for registration to submit extensive data; authorized the EPA to restrict or ban pesticide uses, and set up labeling requirements.
Marine Protection, Research, and Sanctuaries Act	1972	Required the EPA to set up a permit system for ocean dumping, prohibit dumping of hazardous materials (including radioactive waste, but amended in 1982 to permit dumping of radioactive waste as regulated by the EPA), and preserve marine sanctuaries free from industrial activity and dumping.
Endangered Species Act	1973	Created a comprehensive program to identify animal and plant species on the verge of extinction and protect them. Enforced by agencies in the Departments of Interior, Commerce, and Agriculture.
Safe Drinking Water Act	1974	Authorized the EPA to set and enforce national standards for drinking water.
Hazardous Materials Transport Act	1974	Authorized the Department of Transportation to regulate shipment of hazardous materials. Prohibited shipment of radioactive materials in passenger planes.
Resource Conservation and Recovery Act	1976	Established EPA regulation of solid and hazardous waste disposal; authorized the EPA to define hazardous waste materials and to encourage and supervise state programs.
Toxic Substances Control Act	1976	Established a national control policy for chemicals posing a risk to the environment. Authorized the EPA to set chemical testing and licensing procedures, to ban excessively risky chemicals, and to set up record-keeping requirements for chemical manufacture.
Federal Mine Safety and Health Act	1977	Established the Mine Safety and Health Administration in the Department of Labor to regulate mine safety and health, enforce and set standards, and undertake a rigorous inspection schedule for mines.

Surface Mining Control and Reclamation Act	1977	Regulated strip-mining operations and set standards for reclamation of abandoned mines by a newly established Office of Surface Mining Reclamation and Enforcement in the Interior Department.
Department of Energy Organization Act	1977	Created a new cabinet-level Department of Energy to administer national energy policies including nuclear waste management, energy conservation, and energy impacts on the environment.
Comprehensive Environmental Response, Compensation, and Liability Act	1980	Established a $1.6 billion Hazardous Substance Response Trust Fund and taxes on the chemical and oil industries. Required the EPA to identify and remediate dangerous dumpsites of high priority and to establish disposal standards for hazardous substances.

Second, some of this legislation went beyond demonstrated technical feasibility, and control technology could not catch up with deadlines. For instance, the goal of the Federal Water Pollution Control Act Amendments of 1972 to eliminate all pollutant discharges into American waters by 1985 was sheer fantasy.

And third, most of the early laws mandate strict command and control regulation and allow little flexibility in balancing costs and benefits. Later legislation is more elastic, as in the case of the Toxic Substances Control Act of 1976, which requires balancing of the risks of a chemical with its benefits to society. Yet in this area Congress never has strayed far from its peremptory tendency. The Hazardous and Solid Waste Amendments of 1984, which were the first significant new regulatory measure in several years, contained seventy-two deadlines for regulation of specific hazardous wastes. The EPA was required to determine by specific dates whether it was safe to continue land disposal of a long list of hazardous wastes such as dioxin. The amendments specified in a series of so-called "hammer clauses" that if the EPA failed to make a determination by the relevant date, then a dumping ban would go into effect. These hammer clauses were an unprecedented reduction in the flexibility of government regulators.

ENVIRONMENTAL REGULATION OF BUSINESS BY GOVERNMENT

A large regulatory apparatus administers the corpus of legislation passed in the 1970s. Twenty-one federal agencies and departments have environmental regulatory programs. Most of the principal programs are presided over by the crown jewel of the federal environmental regulatory apparatus, the Environmental Protection Agency. But some critical programs are located elsewhere. To illustrate, the protection of endangered species is entrusted to the Department of Interior. An independent regulatory commission, the Nuclear Regulatory Commission, is empowered to set rules governing the permissible radiation levels of nuclear reactors. And the Council on Environmental Quality, reporting to the President, administers Section 102 of the National Environmental Policy Act, which requires all federal agencies to prepare environmental impact statements in advance of activities that significantly alter environmental quality.

The Environmental Protection Agency

Before creation of the EPA in December 1970, environmental laws were administered by several federal departments and agencies. Confusion and overlap were major problems. Critics charged the Nixon administration at the time with lack of commitment to environmental quality. Therefore President Nixon, with the consent of Congress, brought together fifteen scattered programs to start a single, new agency—the EPA. The goals of the EPA are to administer federal environmental laws, set mandated standards, ensure compliance, and perform supportive research.

Early in its history, the EPA, under the leadership of its first administrator, William Ruckelshaus, adopted a vigorous program of prosecuting polluters. During its first two years, it undertook more than 1,000 enforcement actions and meted out fines of more than $9 million (including a $7 million fine to Ford Motor Company in a single exhaust emissions case). In November 1971, a dramatic emergency action vividly underscored the agency's powers. It shut down all major industry in heavily industrialized Birmingham, Alabama, for twenty-four hours during a temperature inversion in which air pollutants were building up to dangerous concentrations.

You Be the Judge

The EPA often enforces standards with ingenuity. It has trained dogs to sniff small concentrations of chemicals and undertakes some enforcement actions with armed criminal investigators. Does the agency ever become overzealous? You be the judge.

When EPA inspectors appeared at Dow Chemical Company's 2,000-acre chemical manufacturing facility in Midland, Michigan, they were admitted to check two coal-powered steam generating plants for compliance with air emission standards. Dow conducted the EPA inspectors through a half-day tour of the power station that housed these two plants and even provided the inspectors with schematic diagrams showing how they were constructed. Later, EPA inspectors asked to return with a camera to take pictures of the power plant. Dow refused this request for two reasons. First, Dow routinely prohibits picture-taking at this facility to protect trade secrets. Second, although some federal agencies (such as OSHA) have been granted the right to use photography during inspections after review of their procedures under the Administrative Procedure Act, the EPA has never submitted a request for clearance to use cameras.

When Dow refused the second inspection—which was within its legal rights—the EPA could have gone to the U.S. attorney in nearby Bay City to request a search warrant under the authority of the Clean Air Act. But it did not. Instead, inspectors hired a commercial aerial photographer to fly over the plant and take high-resolution pictures with a precision-mounted aerial mapping camera.

Dow officials were furious. They took elaborate security precautions around the plant to shield its equipment from competitors' spies. Much of the machinery was hidden by sheds, but it was impractical to cover all 2,000 acres of piping and machinery from overhead observation. Dow was given no notice of the aerial inspection, and the photographs covered much more of the plant than the two power houses (which covered perhaps half an acre). Dow discovered the EPA overflight only because observant employees copied the identification numbers of the airplane as it flew over.

Dow brought suit against the EPA claiming that its photography exceeded its legal investigative powers and constituted a warrantless search in violation of the company's Fourth Amendment right to freedom "against unreasonable searches." The EPA retorted that Section 114(e)(2) of the Clean Air Act gives inspectors a "right of entry to, upon, or through any premises." Dow claimed that this right did not apply to warrantless aerial observation, saying that an industrial plant, like a home, has the right to be free from arbitrary invasion of privacy by intrusive devices such as telescopes, listening devices, or aerial photography.

How would you decide this case?

THE COURT RULING

In *Dow v. United States* (1986), Chief Justice Warren Burger wrote for a unanimous Court in holding that Section 114(e)(2) of the Clean Air Act gave the EPA expansive powers to investigate potential sources of pollution. In pursuit of their mandate under the act, the EPA inspectors had the right to take aerial photographs. The government was seeking to regulate Dow, not to compete with it, and the EPA had not disclosed the aerial photos to Dow's competitors. Burger also argued that the aerial photographs did not violate Dow's privacy rights. An industrial plant may not claim the same exemption from inspection as a private home, because it is in the public interest to regulate pollution nuisances. He added that the enhancement of vision by enlarging the photographs did not in itself constitute a greater intrusion than observation with the naked eye. On this point, four members of the court filed a minority dissent. Justice Powell, writing for the dissenters, argued that freedom from unannounced aerial photography was a reasonable privacy expectation to which businesses were entitled under the Fourth Amendment.

POSTSCRIPT

No enforcement action was taken against Dow as a result of the overflight. The negatives of the overflight pictures are held by the EPA in Washington, D.C., and Dow has been given a set of the pictures. Dow filed a trade secrecy claim prohibiting the EPA from releasing the photographs under the Freedom of Information Act.

This case is representative of hundreds of others each year in which the investigative and enforcement actions of government regulators are contested by business. It is unusual in that it traversed the legal system all the way to the Supreme Court. It is significant because the Supreme Court upheld expansive investigation powers for a government agency pursuing its statutory mandate.

Throughout the Nixon, Ford, and Carter presidencies, the agency developed an excellent reputation for standard-setting, enforcement, and technical expertise but had understandable difficulty assimilating the amount of work imposed on it by new regulatory programs passed by Congress. By the late 1970s, the agency was being criticized for paperwork backlogs, delays in issuing standards, tardy research and hazard classification, and inflexible enforcement.

With the advent of the Reagan administration, the EPA was opened to further criticism. During the presidential campaign of 1980, Reagan called the EPA staff "environmental extremists" and expressed views favoring economic development and deregulation. When elected, he appointed a new administrator, Anne Gorsuch. She had a long record of opposition to EPA programs at the state level and imposed a $400 million budget cut and a 14 percent staff reduction between 1980 and 1982—a time when statutory requirements for performance were increasing. During these years the agency made many more exemptions from standards than usual, and pressure on industry eased. Dollar sales of air pollution monitoring equipment, not surprisingly, dropped 58 percent between 1980 and 1982 (Bry, 1983). Later, the agency was touched by scandal when administrator Gorsuch was accused of delaying or hastening superfund projects to influence the 1982 elections, and one of her top administrators, Rita Lavelle, was accused of conflict of interest in her associations with corporate executives. Gorsuch (by then Buford, by marriage) was forced to resign in March 1983, and William Ruckelshaus was reappointed to raise morale and restore credibility. By all accounts, Ruckelshaus was successful; the EPA's budget was increased in 1984, and the mission of the EPA to protect the environment was no longer muddied in a wholesale way by political considerations.

In the late 1980s, the agency is criticized for its inability to cope with trans-media pollution. Trans-media pollution refers to the tendency of pollutants in one medium, for instance, air, to be removed by control equipment to another medium, such as water. When a fossil-fueled steam-electric power plant removes air pollution with scrubbers, the scrubbers may produce a toxic sludge that must be disposed of on land or in water, where new pollution is created. Because EPA regulations are mandated by single-purpose legislation covering air, noise, water, solid waste, toxic substances, and other pollution media, the agency has been organized along media lines. It is often, according to critics, unable to transcend bureaucratic jurisdictions to address interrelated pollution problems effectively as a whole.

The EPA also has been assailed for a bias against new products and factory processes that might be less dangerous than existing ones. It often adopts rigid approval procedures that slow down the introduction of new chemicals or the construction of new factories. The new chemicals or factories, which represent advanced research, may pose less environmental risk to society. But the bureaucrats in the agency are reluctant to chance unforeseen consequences if current regulation of older risks is adequate. The cost to society of delay in the introduction of safe technologies is hard to estimate, but this "new source bias problem" has led to increasing use of risk assessment techniques within the EPA. These are discussed in the next chapter.

PRINCIPAL AREAS OF
PUBLIC-POLICY INITIATIVE

Here we discuss briefly five dominant areas of legislation and public concern. In each area we describe the basic nature of the problems, current public policy, and crucial concerns for business.

Air Quality

Air pollution is no new problem. London's air in the seventeenth century was described as "an impure and thick mist accompanied by a fuliginous [dusky, smoky, sooty] and filthy vapor." In 1948, the town of Donora, Pennsylvania, became enveloped in a thick layer of poisonous air from local industrial plants, and about half its population became ill as a result.

There has been serious concern about air quality in American cities since the end of World War II, when states mounted the first attack on pollution. Congress followed with laws for cleaning up the nation's air in a concerted, comprehensive fashion. The Clean Air Act of 1967 and its 1970 and 1977 amendments are the most important. The 1970 amendments empowered the EPA to set air quality standards for the principal pollutant classes, to approve state plans for achieving the standards, and to minimize pollutants from new stationary and mobile sources.

Until the early 1980s the EPA concentrated its standard-setting and enforcement actions on reducing levels of six major pollutants, the so-called "criteria pollutants," which were thought to be responsible for most health and air-quality problems. They are lead, carbon monoxide, ozone, sulfur dioxide, particulates, and nitrogen dioxide. To regulate emissions of the criteria pollutants, the EPA divided the nation into 247 air-quality control regions, in which it enforces annual emission standards. It defined permissible emission levels for over thirty industries, prescribed which control devices a factory must use in some cases, and set stringent standards for reduced auto emissions. As a result, great progress has been made. By 1990 carbon monoxide and ozone levels may be a problem in Los Angeles and Houston, but in the rest of the country air quality standards for criteria pollutants will have been met.

In the mid-1980s, the EPA began to regulate "hazardous pollutants," such as mercury, beryllium, asbestos, vinyl chloride, and benzine. Hazardous pollutants pose a danger to human health in small concentrations. Some are carcinogens. Under the Clean Air Act, the EPA is required to list hazardous pollutants, identify sources, and then establish emission standards. By 1985 the EPA had listed eight such pollutants and set emission standards for six. It was studying over twenty other substances.

Although the EPA has done well in regulating criteria pollutants and is beginning to work on more hazardous ones, it has no regulatory programs for other significant air pollution problems.

■ Acid deposition occurs when pollutants drop from the air onto the ground. The government has developed a research program to learn more about it, but so far there has been no regulatory legislation specifically to deal with it.

■ Indoor pollution from such substances as formaldehyde, asbestos, radon, and paint fumes is a formidable problem. The EPA has not set standards for indoor exposure to such substances.

■ Fluorocarbon pollution is increasingly thought to be the critical cause of depletion of ozone in the stratosphere. In 1978 the EPA banned sales of fluorocarbon aerosols in consumer products, but industrial manufacture of these complex molecules actually has increased. Conflicting scientific data about the dangers that fluorocarbons pose to human health have delayed a regulatory program.

■ Air emissions from toxic waste dumps are a growing problem. Dumps are a source of methane, volatile organic compounds, fugitive toxic vapors, and odors. The EPA has no emission standards for toxic waste sites.

The emission standards, controls, and timetables established by the EPA with respect to air pollutants have imposed enormous costs on business. Air-emission reduction is the most expensive area of pollution control to industry. A typical large factory has many sources of air emissions. For utilities and smelters, combustion in furnaces is a major source of criteria pollutants, which must be controlled. At other plants, diesels, turbines, and gasoline engines power machinery and need emission controls.

Industry uses a wide array of devices such as reactors, mixers, cookers, distillers, and spray booths and must control emissions from each. For example, EPA air-emission standards for kraft pulp mills apply to the "digester system, brown stock washer system, multiple-effect evaporator system, black liquor oxidation system, recovery furnace, smelt dissolving tank, lime kiln, and condensate stripper system" (*Code of Federal Regulations*, 1985: 40 311). The "Standard for Particulate Matter" in kraft pulp mills is instructive of the detail with which these devices are regulated. Particulates are only one of a number of pollutants that must be controlled.

§ 60.282 Standard for particulate matter.

(a) On and after the date on which the performance test required to be conducted by § 60.8 is completed, no owner or operator subject to the provisions of this subpart shall cause to be discharged into the atmosphere:

(1) From any recovery furnace any gases which:

(i) Contain particulate matter in excess of 0.10 g/dscm (0.044 gr/dscf) corrected to 8 percent oxygen.

(ii) Exhibit 35 percent opacity or greater.

(2) From any smelt dissolving tank any gases which contain particulate matter in excess of 0.1 g/kg black liquor solids (dry weight)[0.2 lb/ton black liquor solids (dry weight)].

(3) From any lime kiln any gases which contain particulate matter in excess of:
(i) 0.15 g/dscm (0.067 gr/dscf) corrected to 10 percent oxygen, when gaseous fossil fuel is burned.
(ii) 0.30 g/dscm (0.13 gr/dscf) corrected to 10 percent oxygen, when liquid fossil fuel is burned. *(Code of Federal Regulations,* 313)

About a dozen mechanical and chemical control devices exist to remove gases, particles, and odors from plant emissions. They range from baghouses, which force exhaust streams through filters, to electrostatic precipitators, which give particles in the air a negative charge so that they collect on a positively charged plate for later removal. Often equipment must be specially designed to be effective with the specific air pressure, volume, temperature, or chemical composition of emissions from an industrial process. This customizing adds to its cost.

Water Quality

Like air pollution, water pollution has existed for centuries, and from time to time it has resulted in mass deaths by waterborne diseases such as typhoid. It is related that in mid-nineteenth-century London, members of the House of Commons found it hard to breathe because of the foul odor of the Thames outside and ordered window curtains soaked in chloride of lime to be put up as a defense. Industrial water discharges in the United States have posed highly visible problems. In 1959, and again in 1969, the Cuyahoga River, which runs past steel and chemical plants in Ohio, caught on fire, burning in 1959 for eight days.

Following passage of the Clean Water Act in 1972 and subsequent amendments in 1977, slow progress has been made in achieving the act's purpose, "to restore and maintain the chemical, physical, and biological integrity of the nation's waters." Since 1972 regulatory efforts have substantially reduced polluting effluents and have arrested the deterioration of streams, rivers, and lakes. However, about 27 percent of rivers and streams and 22 percent of lakes and reservoirs still do not meet the goal of the Clean Water Act that waters be "fishable and swimmable" (CEQ, 1985: 85). A second major goal of this act, elimination of all discharge of pollutants into navigable waters, will not be met until after the turn of the century.

The EPA regulates three classes of water pollutants: conventional pollutants such as suspended solids, oil and grease, and fecal coliform bacteria; nonconventional pollutants such as ammonia, sulfides, phosphorus, and nitrogen; and toxic pollutants such as heavy metals, polychlorinated biphenyls, halogenated aliphatics, phthalate esters, and polycyclic aromatic hydrocarbons. It has established effluent guidelines for approximately twenty heavily polluting industries which, when fully implemented, will reduce release of toxic chemicals by about 95 percent.

Every industrial plant uses water, and sources of pollution are numerous. Large plants must purify sanitary waste water from restrooms, cafeterias, and laboratories and often set up sewage treatment plants for this purpose. Storm water runoff is a significant pollution threat, and in plants where surfaces are contaminated with oil, grease, or other pollutants, this water must be collected and treated. Cooling systems introduce heat into water and must be partially drained from time to time of low quality water that needs treatment. The greatest source of industrial water pollution, however, comes from waste water from production processes. Used as a washing, scrubbing, or mixing medium, this water is contaminated with a wide variety of dissolved solids and particles. As with air pollution, there are effluent control techniques ranging from the use of screens to remove large particles to complicated chemical and biological treatments.

In some industries, such as petroleum refining, ink formulating, and electro-plating, pollutants cannot be completely removed from process waste water. For these industries the EPA issues permits allowing discharges limited to levels set by the agency. These permits contain complex effluent limitations that take into account the amount, temperature, turbidity, and chemical constituents of waste water discharge. They usually contain sampling and reporting requirements and have an expiration date. Polluting firms have been required to meet a series of deadlines for improved water quality as control device technology advances.

Many companies discharge industrial waste products, conventional and toxic, directly into city sewer systems. In 1981, Ralston-Purina discharged quantities of hexane into Louisville, Kentucky, sewers and caused them to explode. In the same year, a sewer worker in Newark, New Jersey, died from exposure to industrial gases. Most municipal sewage plants easily purify water of food and body waste but are not designed to remove industrial contaminants. Industrial toxins may simply pass through city plants into the drinking water (a dangerous situation for the public), or they may clog flows, corrode piping, or kill bacteria used to digest domestic waste, lowering the efficiency of the sewage treatment facility. The EPA is beginning to require pretreatment of effluents that flow from industrial facilities to municipal sewage plants.

A major source of water pollution not systematically regulated is "nonpoint" source pollution. This occurs when rainfall collects pollution from agricultural activity, logging, construction, mining, or oil-coated road surfaces and trans-ports it into water bodies. Runoff from fields, for instance, collects soil sediment containing pesticides and fertilizers. The mining, agriculture, forestry, and construction industries—prime culprits in the nonpoint pollution problem —have made negligible progress toward control. It will be many years before regulatory actions control industrial nonpoint discharges.

Toxic Chemicals

Industrialized society depends on a staggering array of chemicals. Underlying concern about the presence of toxic chemicals in the environment is the phenomenal growth of the chemical industry since World War II. The entire industry grew from sales of $13.7 billion in 1947 to sales of $113 billion in 1977

(McNeil, 1981). This growth was accompanied by the development of new synthetic compounds and a petrochemical revolution that has made fuels, solvents, pesticides, plastics, and other oil by-products ubiquitous in the environment.

Approximately 60,000 chemicals are used in industrial production, and 1,000 to 2,000 new ones are developed yearly. Many cause health problems and property damage. Of the 60,000 commonly used industrial chemicals, twenty-eight are known human carcinogens, and about 10 percent of roughly 6,000 suspect chemicals tested to date cause cancer in animals. In addition, arteriosclerosis, heart disease, hypertension, emphysema, behavioral disorders, and kidney disease may result from exposure to poisonous chemicals.

The Toxic Substances Control Act (TSCA) of 1976 gives the EPA authority to control the manufacture, processing, distribution, use, and disposal of existing chemicals. The EPA may require manufacturers to test designated chemicals for toxic effects and to maintain records and reports. In addition, industry must submit a "premanufacture notification" to the EPA at least ninety days prior to manufacturing or importing a new chemical. The chemical industry has complained about disruption of new chemical development caused by premanufacturing notice delays. Acting under TSCA authority, the EPA has prohibited the sale of fluorocarbons for nonessential uses and stopped manufacture and sale of polychlorinated biphenyls. It developed a basic inventory of 55,000 chemicals now manufactured. And it has stopped production of nine chemicals out of a total of 1,000 premanufacturing notifications received.

A second statute, the Federal Insecticide, Fungicide, and Rodenticide Act (FIFRA), as amended in 1978, gives the EPA authority to regulate substances used as pesticides, disease vector–control agents, and disinfectants and sterilants used in homes and hospitals. Under FIFRA, all major pesticides must be registered with the EPA before they are sold. In the registration process, industry bears the burden of proving that a pesticide does not pose unreasonable risks compared with benefits. Companies must prepare comprehensive studies of toxicity and environmental effects. A pesticide manufacturer today may spend $7 to $10 million before a product is EPA-registered.

Regulation of pesticides and other chemicals already has lessened health risks. Since 1965, the Food and Drug Administration's annual "market basket" survey has measured the presence of more than 200 chemicals in typical supermarket foods throughout the country. The survey shows a marked drop in the intake of banned and regulated pesticides. For example, before DDT was banned for most uses in 1972, the average daily intake of an American was 48 micrograms, but by 1983 this had dropped to 1.6 micrograms. Similar drops were registered for dieldrin and endrin, two pesticides banned in 1975. The EPA's National Human Monitoring Program, which samples chemical residues in human adipose tissue, shows similar trends associated with regulatory controls. Levels of DDT, aldrin, dieldrin, and PCBs in human adipose tissue have declined since regulatory banning of their major uses (Council on Environmental Quality [CEQ], 1985: 604).

Solid and Toxic Waste Disposal

Solid waste is the detritus of production and consumption. It includes sludge from waste water treatment, household garbage, old automobiles and appliances, and wastes from agricultural, animal, mining, and industrial processes. Today we have billions of tons of solid waste, a residuum of affluence, convenience packaging, disposable products, and a rising population. In addition, stringent air and water pollution control standards have caused industry to accumulate solid wastes in antipollution equipment. Radioactive solid waste from nuclear reactors and tailings of uranium and phosphate mining are also a disposal problem. There are more than 100,000 industrial hazardous waste, land disposal sites.

When water comes in contact with solid waste, it removes soluble materials, forming a polluted liquid called leachate. Leachate may contain toxic and carcinogenic chemicals, viruses, metals, bacteria, and decaying organic matter. A leachate plume may form if water is present and, moving underground as fast as two feet a day, enter a groundwater aquifer and pollute it. To avert serious hazard to drinking water supplies from this process, Congress in 1976 passed the Resource Conservation and Recovery Act, mandating government control of solid waste from generation to ultimate disposal.

In 1984 the Hazardous and Solid Waste Amendments to this act set stringent deadlines for EPA action to control hazardous waste dumping and applied the program to much smaller companies than before, that is, those dumping the equivalent of half of a fifty-five-gallon drum per month. Firms must identify their hazardous waste, obtain EPA identification numbers for it, use an approved manifest system when they truck wastes away from plants, label all wastes kept on site, and meet strict record-keeping requirements. This program cost business $6 billion a year in the mid-1980s but is predicted by EPA officials to cost at least $20 billion a year in the 1990s.

In the 1970s, a number of conspicuous hazardous waste accidents were blamed on business. In 1973, for instance, Michigan Chemical Company accidentally shipped an extremely toxic chemical, polybrominated biphenyl (PBB), to the Michigan Farm Bureau, where a worker who thought it was a growth stimulant put it into feed for dairy farm animals. More than 9 million Michigan residents ate contaminated meat, milk, and eggs, and eventually about 150,000 contaminated farm animals had to be destroyed. In the Love Canal area of Niagara Falls, New York, Hooker Chemical Corp. was blamed for improper waste disposal practices that exposed nearby residents to toxic chemicals. President Carter declared Love Canal a disaster area.

Incidents such as these led Congress to pass the Comprehensive Environmental Response, Compensation, and Liability Act (CERCLA) of 1980. This legislation set up a $1.6 billion "superfund" to pay for cleaning abandoned hazardous waste sites. (In 1986, Congress reauthorized the act with a $9 billion fund.) The EPA has identified thousands of potentially hazardous waste sites; 900 of the most seriously contaminated are on a priority list for early cleanup. By 1985 the

EPA had taken remedial actions at 500 sites, but to the dismay of critics had accomplished only six full cleanups.

The EPA may require states in which hazardous dump sites are located to pay 10 percent of cleanup costs and may impose liability on dump site owners and operators for government cleanup expenses and damage to the environment. Under the severe provisions of CERCLA, any company that contributes waste to a dump site is responsible for paying to clean up that site, even if fly-by-night operators have long since disappeared. Potter Paint Company, a small paint manufacturer in Indiana, had to pay $12,000 for cleanup and legal costs after owners of a dump site where Potter Paint had dumped solvent were found negligent and could not afford to reimburse the EPA for the expenses of remedial action (Jacobs, 1983). Of course, large companies face potentially greater expenses. In 1982, the Velsicol Chemical Corp. agreed to pay $38.5 million to clean up PBB contamination at its St. Louis, Michigan, plant (formerly the Michigan Chemical Co. plant that shipped PBBs to the Michigan Farm Bureau). By 1986 Westinghouse had agreed to the largest settlement yet—$100 million to clean up a toxic waste site in Indiana.

Occupational Health

In 1970, Congress passed the Occupational Safety and Health Act "to assure so far as possible every working man and woman in the nation safe and healthful working conditions and to preserve our human resources." The act set up an agency in the Labor Department called the Occupational Safety and Health Administration (OSHA), giving it authority to reduce health and safety hazards in the workplace by establishing and enforcing standards, requiring employers to keep records and report on hazards, and encouraging states to set up occupational health and safety programs. OSHA has authority over about 4.6 million workplaces. A team of about 1,000 inspectors conducts workplace inspections. OSHA may propose fines of up to $10,000 and prison terms of up to six months for offenses by employers.

Millions of workers are exposed to occupational hazards from pollutants. The famous have perished with the obscure. The great philosopher Spinoza, who ground lenses for a living and wrote in his spare time, died from lung infection caused by prolonged exposure to glass dust. The death in 1936 of Marie Curie, discoverer of radium, is blamed on radiation burns. In 1898, asbestos entrepreneur H. W. Johns, founder of the roofing company that grew into the giant Manville Corp., died of chronic lung disease. More than 800,000 workers are regularly exposed to carcinogens, and occupational cancer is thought to be 5 to 20 percent of all cancers. Certain occupations have a high cancer risk. Two hundred years ago, a British physician named Percival Potts found a high incidence of scrotum cancer among chimney sweeps, attributable to their exposure to coal tar in chimneys. Women who painted radium on watch dials to make them glow in the dark often licked their brushes to sharpen points and died in excessive numbers from cancers of the mouth and bone. Asbestos workers and workers exposed to benzine seeping out of older coke ovens show elevated lung cancer rates when compared with the general population.

Cancer is not the sole illness, of course, that workers risk. Hundreds of illnesses may be caused or aggravated by occupational exposures. OSHA sets standards for worker exposure to lead, vinyl chloride gas, formaldehyde, carbon monoxide, cotton dust, and mercury. Unlike EPA standards, which limit emissions from sources such as smokestacks and valves, OSHA standards typically limit worker exposure to a substance to levels averaged over an eight-hour shift. Sometimes production equipment may be reengineered to lower emissions. When this is excessively expensive or technologically impossible, as is often the case, workers are permitted exposure to greater risks than the general public. A glassblower, for example, may be exposed to concentrations of nitrogen oxides twenty-five times greater than permitted in ambient air quality outside the shop (Derr et al., 1983). Exposure to hazards such as mercury vapor, diesel fumes, petrochemical vapors, and airborne lead is typically regulated by installing exhaust systems under ducts or hoods that collect fumes, by mixing fresh air with polluted air to dilute toxic concentrations, or by rotating workers in and out of the workplace—sometimes on the basis of blood tests showing concentrations of a contaminant.

The protective organizational machinery established by the OSH Act embodied the ethical principle that workers have a right to a healthy work environment and employers have an obligation to provide it. During its first years, OSHA was criticized for excessive zeal, for enforcing trivial standards, for the officiousness of its inspectors, and for imposing unreasonable costs on business. In the early 1970s, it emphasized job safety, but in the last decade prevention of health hazards has received equal priority. Stung by criticism, the agency also streamlined its procedures, deleted trivial standards, and recognized cost burdens created by adversarial enforcement policies. After 1980 OSHA, like other agencies, suffered from Reagan administration budget cuts and reduced its workplace inspections to the point that they came only after serious injuries occurred. OSHA was subjected to considerable criticism when workplace death figures were shown to have risen in 1983 and several conspicuous cases of unsafe workplaces became prominent in the news. Despite some highly publicized large fines levied against employers since 1987, OSHA in the late 1980s is unable to effectively guarantee workplace safety on a broad front.

CONCLUDING NOTE

Pollution problems stemming from industrial activity are serious. In its current state, industrial technology is inherently damaging to the environment. In the following chapter, we discuss what antipollution legislation costs business and newer methods of market-incentive regulation.

CASE STUDY

THE SNAIL DARTER AND TELLICO DAM

This is the first case of its kind and it has become a classic. It focuses squarely on the conflicts between economic development and environmental preservation. In the beginning, the proposed dam project appeared to pose a direct conflict between survival of an insignificant species of fish and the completion of an expensive development project. As the story unfolded, however, the clash was not as straightforward as it appeared to be at first. Nonetheless, the case highlights a fact of life prevailing today: strong economic interests do conflict with strong environmental protectionist concerns and create complex government regulatory problems in resolving them.

In 1967 Congress authorized the Tennessee Valley Authority (TVA) to build a dam on the Little Tennessee River. The dam, known as the Tellico Dam, would flood 16,500 acres of farmland to create a thirty-three-mile-long reservoir upstream from the river's mouth. The dam was part of a larger overall development project designed to generate electricity, control flooding, and promote economic development in the area by construction of recreational and residential facilities along the new shoreline.

After 1967 Congress appropriated money each year for the project, but environmentalists and local residents whose property would be flooded combined forces in powerful stop-the-dam efforts. Opponents of the dam called it pork-barrel politics, said it was damaging to the environment, and produced figures purporting to show that it was not really a net boost to the local economy. Their efforts came to an initial halt when the Environmental Defense Fund lost a suit it had brought against the TVA in a U.S. District Court in Tennessee.

Then the coincidence of two unrelated events breathed new life into the antidam forces. In the summer of 1973 a Tennessee ichthyologist, Dr. David Etnier, Jr., discovered a previously unknown species of perch in the cold, clear waters of the Little Tennessee. The fish became known as the snail darter. The snail darter is a tan, minnowlike fish about two or three inches in length. Subsequent study determined that a population of 10,000 to 15,000 snail darters inhabited seventeen miles of streambed and gravel shoals above the rising edifice of Tellico Dam. Spawning took place at Coytee Springs, about fifteen miles above its gates.

Discovery of the snail darter was not particularly noteworthy. There are over 120 species of darters in North American waters and over 90 are in Tennessee, including the stargazing darter, Blenny darter, Ouachita darter, and the banded sculpin. New species are discovered at the rate of about one a year. The fish has no commercial value in the local economy.

The Endangered Species Act

At nearly the same time as the mundane discovery of the snail darter, Congress passed the Endangered Species Act of 1973 by overwhelming margins in both houses. The act called for the Secretary of the Interior to list and protect species of animals, birds, fish, and plants determined to be threatened with extinction. A farreaching provision of the law prohibited federal agencies from authorizing, funding, or carrying out actions, such as dam construction, timber harvesting, livestock grazing, and wetland dredging, which would jeopardize the continued existence of any endangered or threatened species, or destroy or adversely modify their critical habitats.

In January 1975, opponents of the Tellico Dam petitioned to have the snail darter classified as an endangered species, and in November 1975, with the dam 75 percent completed, Secretary of the Interior Thomas Kleppe publicly proclaimed such status for the fish. Kleppe also made those areas of the river inhabited by the darter a "critical habitat," or one necessary for the species' survival and, therefore, also protected. The justification for this action was that flooding the reservoir would submerge the darter's habitat under many feet of water and destroy the ecological niche by altering temperature, current, water quality, exposure to sunlight, and other factors.

Should Endangered Species Be Preserved?

With the snail darter officially designated an endangered species, the dam became a cynosure for environmentalists who were inflamed by the prospect of losing the fish forever. The genetic inheritance of a plant or animal species is, of course, irretrievably lost when the last individuals die. Since the dawn of life, about 98 percent of all species have become extinct. In past ages extinction occurred from natural causes, but today it increasingly occurs because of industrial activity. Environmentalists oppose extinction on the grounds that even when species have no economic value, they have the right to exist. Plant and animal species are essential for human survival, and if we make a mistake and allow an important species to become extinct, the error is irreversible. Species may also have important, and sometimes undiscovered, medicinal benefits. It is also argued that people depend upon healthy ecosystems for survival, and that the destruction of species alters ecosystems and may ultimately harm mankind. Some argue that a variety of animal species enriches human life and culture partly due to the sheer fascination of their existence (Ehrlich and Ehrlich, 1981: 6; Gunn, 1980).

The arguments in favor of preserving species are enormously popular, and serious public advocacy of extinction is rarer than members of the endangered species themselves. However, there are many people who are against the absolute protection of endangered species. A few biologists have argued that once a species has dwindled in number to the point where it is endangered, nature has cast a vote for extinction. They feel that extraordinary human intervention will not, in the long run, save a truly endangered species. In addition, it has been argued that when a conflict develops between humans and plant and animal species, the progress of humanity takes precedence (of course, it is difficult to find direct conflicts between survival of a species and compelling human needs). Finally, there is a limit to the resources of society, and it is often expensive to repair widespread damage to a species' habitat. We cannot, for example, tear out the roads and settlements that have decimated the territory of the eastern timber wolf.

Although it was widely believed at the time that the snail darter's survival was threatened, the response of TVA officials to its placement on the endangered species list was to speed construction of the dam. They were convinced that the 1973 law was not intended to stop ongoing projects started before its passage and that the closer to completion the dam was, the harder it would be for opponents to stop it.

Environmentalists finally were able to obtain a court injunction bringing construction to a halt in 1977, when the dam was 95 percent complete and over $113 million had been spent on it. The TVA appealed the injunction, and in June 1978 the Supreme Court affirmed the lower court in a 6–3 decision. In the majority opinion written by Chief Justice Warren Burger, the Court said that when Congress passed the Endangered Species Act, it clearly intended no exceptions and barred all actions that would threaten endangered species. A dissent by Associate Justice Lewis Powell argued that Congress could not possibly have intended to throw away millions of dollars and sacrifice the potential benefits of the project simply because an obscure new species of fish had been discovered six years after starting construction of the dam. "This decision," said Powell, "casts a long shadow over the operation of even the most important projects, serving vital needs of society and national defense, whenever it is determined that continued operation would threaten extinction of an endangered species or its habitat" (*TVA v. Hill*). The majority opinion stated, however, that the legislative history of the Endangered Species Act showed Congress intended to view the value of threatened species as "incalculable." Hence, destruction of a species could not be offset by any economic benefits of a public works project.

But the high court's decision in this case failed to dampen the enthusiasm of the dam's supporters. According to Aubrey J. Wagner, TVA chairman from 1962 to 1978, electricity production at the dam would save 500,000 barrels of oil a year and lessen America's dependency on imported oil. (This was a very important consideration for the nation at this time.) In addition, he argued that:

Far from being "ill conceived and uneconomic in the first place," Tellico was more thoroughly examined both locally and in the Congress, before it was started, than any such TVA project ever undertaken. Planning for its use will be guided by a local area-planning council, and it will, in my judgment, be the most useful multiple-purpose project in the entire TVA system when it is completed (1979: 3).

Endangered Species and Cost-Benefit Analysis

In the fall of 1978 Congress, at the urging of Senator Howard Baker (R-Tenn.), amended the Endangered Species Act to set up a seven-member, cabinet-level Endangered Species Committee empowered to exempt government-financed projects from the law protecting endangered species even if extinction of a species resulted.* The committee could grant exemptions, allowing a project to be completed that might lead to the extinction of a species, if (1) there was no reasonable and prudent alternative to the proposed action, (2) the benefits of the proposed action clearly outweighed the costs, and (3) the project was in the public interest.

Despite a special provision in the amendment that the Tellico Dam situation be given special consideration by the committee, and despite the fact that the TVA made efforts to transplant the snail darter into nearly identical Tennessee streams (where the fish did reproduce successfully), the Endangered Species Committee on January 23, 1979, refused to grant an exemption to TVA authorities.

The main reason the committee vetoed the dam was that it was in possession of a recently completed Department of the Interior study estimating $6.5 million in annual total benefits from dam operation versus estimated annual costs of $7.5 million (White, 1981: 156–157).

On the benefit side was, of course, the savings to the nation in imported oil. Also were the recreational opportunities to be provided in the newly formed lake. Then, too, valuable industrial sites would be created through the formation of a new shoreline and the confluence of good rail, highway, and water transportation.

Offsetting these benefits were such costs as the destruction of a ten-mile stretch of an exceptionally high-quality cold-water fast-flowing river, the loss of valuable farmlands when the flood gates were closed, the flooding of important Indian archeological sites, and future repair and maintenance expenses for the dam. The possible extinction of the snail darter was not calculated as a cost since

---

*The committee was to be composed of the Chairman of the Council of Economic Advisors, the Secretary of Agriculture, the Secretary of the Army, the Secretary of the Interior, the administrator of the National Oceanic and Atmospheric Administration (with the Department of Commerce), the administrator of the Environmental Protection Agency, and a representative from the area affected by the project. The Department of Interior interpreted the law to say that, unlike a typical interagency committee, the principals themselves had to be at the final meeting when the vote was taken. They could not send deputies or transmit their vote by mail or telephone. All this attests, of course, to the seriousness with which Congress and the Department of Interior viewed the protection of endangered species.

the transplanting activities of the TVA made the extinction of the fish appear to be somewhat remote.

The committee concluded that it was not necessary to exempt the dam construction from the provisions of the Endangered Species Act to save the snail darter. Furthermore, said the committee, the dam was not in the public interest. Thus, the project failed in the eyes of the committee on all three criteria necessary for exemption.

The committee's decision, of course, did not turn on a direct clash between the preservation of the snail darter and the erection of the dam. Without even considering the snail darter, the dam did not pass the cost-benefit evaluation.

Outcome

Despite the Endangered Species Committee findings, the dam still had strong supporters. In late 1979 Senator Baker was successful in getting through Congress a rider attached to a large public works appropriation bill that exempted the Tellico Dam from the provisions of the Endangered Species Act. The bill was "reluctantly" signed by President Carter. As a result the dam was completed and put into operation. In 1983 Interior Secretary James G. Watt instituted proceedings to remove the snail darter from the endangered species list.

Questions

1. Should the Tellico Dam have been completed? Why did its supporters believe in it so strongly?
2. Should endangered species be subjected to a cost-benefit analysis? Are there conceivable trade-offs that might permit extinction of a species? In light of your answer to these questions, do you suggest changes in the Endangered Species Act?
3. What are the lessons in this case for corporations whose activities have an environmental impact on species, particularly endangered species?
4. Should the federal government be at all involved in passing regulations to protect endangered species?

CHAPTER **14**

POLLUTION POLICY ISSUES

 In the early 1980s, a copper smelting plant in Tacoma, Washington, operated by Asarco, Inc., was releasing 310 tons of airborne arsenic annually. Arsenic compounds are liberated from copper ore and are a common emission from copper smelting operations. Airborne arsenic is a carcinogen associated with lung cancer. The emissions fell in a circle roughly twelve miles in diameter. The plant, which had operated since 1905, employed 600 workers and contributed about $35 million to the area economy. In 1983, the EPA ordered Asarco to install $4.4 million of abatement equipment to lower arsenic emissions to 189 tons a year. Despite this reduction, the EPA estimated that remaining arsenic fallout would result in one additional lung cancer per year in Tacoma, where seventy to ninety die annually from that disease—a rate 20 percent higher than the national average. The EPA study on which this estimate is based assumed that no level of arsenic exposure—no matter how minute—was safe. Asarco, in contrast, argued that a threshold exists below which exposure is safe and said that because of competitive conditions, the cost of abatement could force plant closure.

EPA Administrator William Ruckelshaus gave Tacoma residents a choice. Did they want the EPA to strictly enforce new arsenic emission standards on the smelter, forcing it to close, or was Tacoma prepared to accept the risk of one more annual lung cancer death in exchange for economic benefits from the smelter? Some Tacoma residents were confused, upset, and angry at the stark choice. Ruckelshaus said, "Listen, I know people don't like these kinds of decisions. Welcome to the world of regulation" (in Randolph, 1983: 1).

Soon residents of Tacoma began sporting buttons saying "Both!" at community meetings. A compromise with smelter management was worked out in which arsenic emissions would be lowered to the extent economically feasible to allow continued operation. In 1985, the company closed the smelter for reasons unrelated to pollution control, and so the plan was never implemented.

As amply demonstrated in the last chapter, public concern about pollution has resulted in an extraordinary volume of antipollution legislation in recent years. This legislation, its implementation, and new pollution problems have raised complex policy issues about which there is now great debate and controversy. In this chapter, we discuss the general concepts embodied in the regulatory dilemma posed by the smelter. We evaluate cost-benefit analysis in pollution control, risk assessment, and risk analysis. And we examine the market incentives used by the EPA to regulate pollution and voluntary compliance efforts by industry.

AN OVERVIEW OF THE COST-BENEFIT EQUATION OF POLLUTION CONTROL

Pollution abatement is expensive and growing more so. According to the Council on Environmental Quality (CEQ), a federal agency, the total national bill for pollution abatement and control between 1972 and 1983 was $499.5 billion (CEQ, 1985). Throughout the 1970s, about 90 percent of this massive expenditure was for control of air and water pollution, but by the late 1980s, the amount expended for control of toxic waste was 20 percent and growing. Since the early 1970s, business has paid about 60 percent of all pollution control costs annually in the United States. Three industries—chemicals, petroleum, and primary metals—pay roughly three-quarters of the total business bill. Because existing air and water-pollution control legislation mandates increasingly strict control requirements through the 1990s, and because programs for controlling toxic waste hazards are in their infancy, abatement expenditures will continue to rise. A conservative estimate based on the assumption that control costs will rise in the late 1980s only as fast as in the early 1980s leads to a guess that business's total pollution-control expenditures by the year 1990 will be over $1 trillion.

There is little evidence that compliance expenditures, large as they are, have had much negative impact on the economy. In the 1970s, it was estimated that compliance costs increased production costs and lowered productivity by approximately 1.3 percent (*Forbes,* March 6, 1978). Between 1971 and 1981, the EPA identified a total of 153 closings, involving 32,611 workers. This was an average of 3,200 workers a year or .003 percent of the labor force. Layoffs occurred most often in the chemicals, paper, primary metals, and food processing industries (Kazis and Grossman, 1982). These figures exaggerate because they assume that environmental regulation was the only reason for plant closings and that none of the laid-off workers were rehired.

In fact, the additional costs of environmental regulation often simply hastened the inevitable. The Gulf and Western Industries N. J. Zinc Division mine in Austinville, Virginia, is an example. When the mine closed in 1981, it was more than 100 years old, and management believed that its ore would be depleted by 1983. Management had no incentive to spend about $250,000 to reduce air emissions, and so it was closed, idling 300 workers (Kazis and Grossman, 1982).

Inflation is a large concern in analysis of the economic impact of environmental regulations. But available evidence from government-sponsored studies indicates that, like unemployment, inflation resulting from pollution control expenditures is minimal. A hidden cost of pollution control is the export of hazardous industries. Foreign facilities have an advantage over domestic if they do not have to comply with more stringent United States environmental health and safety regulations. OSHA standards for worker exposure to asbestos, arsenic, copper, and lead, for example, have raised domestic production costs enormously. The domestic asbestos manufacturing industry is declining, and imports from countries such as Mexico, Taiwan, and Brazil, which have no worker exposure regulations, have shot up.

Offsetting such costs, of course, are significant benefits from antipollution programs. It is more difficult to put monetary figures on total benefits derived from pollution abatement. The U.S. General Accounting Office (1982) has estimated that in 1978, America enjoyed $21.4 billion worth of benefits from air-pollution control in the areas of health, property upkeep, crop growth, and property values. This roughly equates with the $24 billion that the CEQ estimated the nation spent on pollution abatement that year (1982).

ANALYSIS OF POLLUTION-ABATEMENT DECISIONS

Analysis of Environmental Risks

In the Asarco smelter situation, regulators could not know precisely the risks to public health from arsenic emissions. This suggests the broader question: what can be known about the risks of industrial activity?

Substances to which we are exposed in the environment pose health risks. An industrial society increases exposure to hazardous substances as a consequence of ongoing, everyday operations. Environmental regulation by the government is intended to reduce the risk of dangerous exposures.

It should not be concluded that the risks of living today are, on the whole, greater than living in past times. On the contrary, authorities agree that we are exposed to fewer risks today. Compared with the turn of the century, as William Lowrance reminds us in *Of Acceptable Risk*, we are far better off in many respects:

> In 1900 the principal insecticide, sprayed on everything from apples and grapes to strawberries and potatoes, was "Paris green"—lead arsenate. The first canned foods were being preserved with sulfites, boric acid, and formaldehyde at rather high concentrations. . . . The red robustness of teas, candies and other commercial food products was imparted by lead chromate, which today's biochemist would

prefer not even to handle, much less feed to anybody. . . . Whereas once the outright poison, lead arsenate, was at issue, we have come through several generations of much less toxic agents and now worry about what may be marginal effects of our current pesticides (Lowrance, 1976: 3–6).

It may seem that today we are exposed to greater health risks from environmental substances. One reason is that science has unmasked formerly hidden risks. By the mid-1980s, scientists frequently measured concentrations of dioxins and other chemicals in parts per billion. This measurement is the equivalent of locating one second in thirty-four years. Today, dioxin concentrations can be measured in parts per trillion, and some experts believe that they may be dangerous in that amount. As the health dangers of smaller amounts of toxins become known, the world appears more dangerous.

There have been many attempts to assess and specifically state risks. For example, one calculation of the risk of contracting cancer from five industrial chemicals in drinking water shows the following:

- Trichloroethylene at 1,530 parts per billion (ppb) would cause an extra 4.6 cases of cancer in 10,000 exposed people.

- Trichloroethane at 965 ppb would cause an extra 15.4 cases in the same population.

- Chloroform at 420 ppb would cause an extra 17.2 cases.

- Carbon tetrachloride at 400 ppb would cause an extra 7.6 cases.

- Benzene at 230 ppb would cause an extra 10.1 cases (Burmaster and Harris, 1982: 60).

How Accurate Are Risk Assessments?

One of the most famous risk assessments grew out of a 1975 study sponsored by the U.S. Atomic Energy Commission to estimate the risks of nuclear reactor operation. The Rasmussen Report, named for Norman C. Rasmussen, the chair of the reporting committee, estimated that an accident causing loss of core coolant, meltdown, and breach of containment was likely to occur only once in 10 million years of reactor operation. This probability is about the same as an individual walking down the street being struck by a meteorite. Eleven years after this report, such an accident occurred in the Soviet Union, spreading a cloud of radiation over European population centers.

How accurate, then, are environmental risk estimates? Whereas the risk of dying in an automobile or airplane accident can be calculated accurately, there is widespread disagreement about the accuracy of calculating environmental risks. This is because doubt exists about the assumptions underlying risk calculations. When animal tests are used to determine the carcinogenicity of chemicals, the subject animals are given massive doses of a chemical over a short time.

Although it is probable that substances capable of inducing cancer in animals are capable of the same in humans, the dose-response level for humans cannot be reliably extrapolated from animal tests. Other tests of carcinogenicity, such as the Ames test, which rely on the exposure of human cells to a suspected cancer-causing agent and measure genetic damage, are not foolproof. The Ames test, for instance, has only a 90 percent accuracy rate.

Another way of determining risks to human health from environmental substances is through epidemiological studies, or studies of human mortality (death) and morbidity (sickness) in a sample population. Epidemiological studies, which are analogous to opinion polls, are subject to important methodological problems. In some, biases have unintentionally crept in because the researcher chose a particular population or group of workers after hearing of a high incidence of disease, and results therefore reflect this selection bias. Additionally, data often are lacking or of poor quality. For instance, air quality in many major cities worsened after 1900 but now has improved. It also varies among areas within the city. This makes it difficult to determine the exposure of a person sixty years or older to common air pollutants. Death certificates may be inaccurate, particularly when a number of diseases contributed to death. People are exposed to literally thousands of substances in the environment, and exposures vary. Different personal habits modify exposure risks in workplaces as, for example, when people smoke, drink heavily, fail to exercise, and become overweight. And, according to expert epidemiologist Lester B. Lave, "The distressing possibility always remains that personal habits or genetic background are systematically related to the occupation under study, as when a homogeneous ethnic group holds a particular set of jobs, such as working in a steel mill or coal mine" (1981: 92). It also may be difficult to measure some contaminants, especially if they are present only in small amounts. Finally, our limited knowledge about the causes of cancer and other diseases poses difficulties in determining how an environmental substance contributed to onset or aggravation.

For such reasons, it is hard to determine exact risks and set proper regulatory standards. The process of collecting reliable data is also very slow. Although asbestos was suspected as dangerous shortly after 1900, it was established as a cause of asbestosis only in the 1930s. Asbestos was associated with lung cancer as early as the 1940s, but a body of conclusive, scientific proof was not established until around 1955, and its induction of mesothelioma was not confirmed until the mid-1960s. In addition, early health studies suggested safe exposure levels to asbestos fiber up to 100 times greater than those now permitted.

Compounding the uncertainty of regulatory rule making based on risk assessment is the variety of factors that influence risk perception. Indeed, people perceive risks quite differently. Some are gamblers. Others are averse to risk. Chauncy Starr, who has made comprehensive analyses of individual reactions to risks, has developed two "laws of acceptable risk." First, acceptable risk is proportional to the amount of benefits. Most people now understand the risks of smoking, for example, but the benefits that many people think they receive from smoking outweigh the risks. Second, the public will accept a higher level of voluntary risk—about 1,000 times greater—than of involuntary risk. It is more risky to ride a bicycle than to live near a nuclear reactor, but most individuals fear the latter more because the risk is out of their control. People will take more risk when it is individually controllable, as with swimming, than when it is not controllable, as with the acceptance of chemical pesticides in foods (Howard, 1979). Researchers have also found that people are more willing to face familiar hazards, such as X-rays, than unfamiliar ones, such as reactor catastrophe. And people accept more risk when hazards are scattered over time rather than lumped together in a dramatic incident. Thus, the public tolerates tens of thousands of auto deaths and hundreds of thousands of smoking-related deaths each year, but a plane crash that kills several hundred inspires terror.

Despite public anxiety, it can still be said with assurance that the sum of all environmental risks to which Americans are exposed has decreased over the years (discounting a substantial risk of nuclear warfare). During the last century, we faced problems of public health that make current problems look insignificant. Cholera, a devastating disease that killed in twenty-four to thirty-six hours, struck large numbers, including one-fifth of the population of Philadelphia. Horse dung in the streets of turn-of-the-century America may have posed a greater public hazard than today's air pollution. In 1905, over 20,000 Americans were killed in railroad accidents. The current obsession of people and lawmakers with pollution hazards is partly a reflection of the fact that many major risks have been eliminated, leaving us more conscious of what one student of risk assessment calls "a myriad of small risks, most of which have always existed" (R. Wilson, 1979: 41).

How the EPA Conducts Risk Analysis

Because risk decisions are frequent and difficult, the EPA has developed a systematic procedure for risk analysis. This procedure, diagramed in Exhibit 14–1, divides the process into two parts.

The first part of the analysis is risk assessment, in which an estimate of the danger of an environmental pollutant is measured. As represented by Circle A on the diagram, it includes the following elements.

- ■ *Hazard Identification* is the process of gathering and evaluating evidence that a substance causes an adverse health effect. Animal tests may show that a chemical such as dioxin or benzene is carcinogenic. Other medical studies have, for example, shown that airborne lead causes high blood pressure in adults.

- ■ *Dose-Response Assessment* is the process of determining how toxic or hazardous a substance is at different levels of exposure. Saccharine causes cancer in laboratory animals only at very high doses, whereas exposure to small

EXHIBIT 14–1   EPA RISK-ANALYSIS PROCEDURE

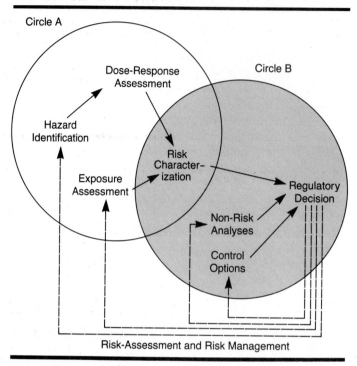

Source: Environmental Protection Agency.

amounts of asbestos leads to animal cancers. Often the judgment of potency must be stated within a broad range and cannot be measured exactly. It has been particularly difficult, for instance, to relate airborne particulate levels to the onset of pulmonary disease. Studies have varied widely in their assessment of the danger that particulates pose to human health.

■ *Exposure Assessment* is undertaken to estimate how much of a substance humans will come in contact with. This step usually involves monitoring emissions but may involve mathematical modeling to estimate air or water concentrations of a contaminant. The pertinent time period for assessing degree of exposure may vary from a lifetime, as with airborne hydrocarbons, to short-term peak exposures, as with asbestos.

■ *Risk Characterization* is the final step, during which the overall risk assessment is made. In 1985, for instance, the EPA studied risk of lung cancer from radiation exposure for people in Idaho who lived near two plants that processed radioactive phosphates. It calculated that the risk of contracting lung cancer was one in 1,000 over a lifetime for those residents, or one additional cancer death every thirteen years, because the plants were in sparsely settled areas. This defined or "characterized" the risk.

The second part of the procedure is risk management. It entails making regulatory decisions about risks on the basis of the earlier risk assessment. Whereas risk assessment is largely a scientific process, risk management combines consideration of risks, the costs and benefits of regulating them, and the requirements of environmental statutes. There are three basic elements of risk management, as shown in Circle B in Exhibit 14–1.

■ *Control Options* are the alternatives available to mitigate the risk. The Toxic Substances Control Act, for instance, gives regulators a range of choices in regulating chemical products. Depending on the toxicity and exposure risk of a particular chemical, the manufacturer may be subject to a spectrum of regulatory controls. At one end of this spectrum, the EPA may prohibit further production and use of a chemical. At the other end, it may require only record-keeping for a chemical of low toxicity. In the middle, the agency may do such things as require a warning label or specify quality-control steps in the production process.

■ *Non-Risk Analyses* refers to the use of cost-benefit and risk-benefit analyses as methods to study alternative actions. The agency must consider the benefits of a regulatory action compared to its costs and may consider the costs and benefits of alternative actions. For example, although asbestos is dangerous and government policy is to reduce exposure, it has not been banned for use in brake linings because no reasonably efficient and economical alternative is available. Thus, the costs of banning this product far exceed the benefits. The EPA also must consider new risks that may arise from an abatement action. For instance, when the pesticide ethylene dibromide (EDB) was banned for use on crops to control nematodes, the EPA assessed the toxicity of potential substitutes and found that they posed less risk to human health than did EDB (largely because they broke down more easily on the surface of fields and did not threaten groundwater contamination as EDB did). But because all the substitute nematocides were also hazardous to human health, the risk-benefit ratio was close.

■ *The Regulatory Decision,* of course, is the action taken. It naturally affects other factors in the risk-analysis procedure, as represented by the interconnecting lines in Exhibit 14–1.

In conclusion, it is important to note that the EPA's risk-analysis technique separates the assessment of risk from its management. This is important because the objective determination of risk levels may be separated from the political or emotional factors that go into an enforcement (or risk management) decision.

Cost-Benefit Analysis

Cost-benefit analysis is a decision-making technique that consists of systematically comparing the costs and benefits of a proposed action—in this case, an environmental regulation. If benefits are greater than costs, the action is desirable, other things being equal. The most rigorous forms of cost-benefit analysis assign common values such as dollar amounts to all costs and benefits so that they may be compared using a common denominator. Cost-benefit studies also may be used to analyze alternative actions or regulations.

Cost-benefit analysis has been used in rudimentary form in government since the nineteenth century but achieved its modern form in the evaluation of alternative weapons systems in the Defense Department during the 1960s.

During the 1970s, there were sporadic attempts to apply it to environmental regulation, and cost-benefit considerations were built into several major regulatory programs, such as the Clean Water Act. Others, such as the Clean Water Act, specifically forbid cost-benefit analysis, for instance in setting national health standards for air pollutants.

In February 1981, as noted in Chapter 7, President Reagan issued Executive Order 12291, stating that new regulations should be effected only if benefits to society outweigh costs. Thereafter "major" regulations with an economic impact of $100 million or more required a regulatory impact analysis from the sponsoring agency before going into effect, and the analysis had to show estimates of benefits exceeding costs.

The first major regulatory program implemented by the EPA following this Reagan initiative was effluent guidelines for the iron and steel industry. Pursuant to Executive Order 12291, the EPA conducted a cost-benefit study using two scenarios. The first assumed a profitable steel industry and the second an economically troubled industry. The study showed that under both scenarios, the iron and steel industry could accomplish proposed effluent discharge reductions without economic dislocation. The EPA concluded that the proposed regulations would result in benefits approximately equal to, and probably exceeding, costs (CEQ, 1982). Since then, the EPA has conducted many other cost-benefit studies.

In Chapter 7, we discussed how basic statutes differ in permitting cost-benefit analysis in regulation and how the Supreme Court sometimes permitted and sometimes prohibited the use of this regulatory tool. Here are a few additional illustrations in the pollution area.

In the famous "snail darter" case, *Tennessee Valley Authority* v. *Hill* (1978), the Court ruled that the Endangered Species Act required regulators to protect endangered species regardless of cost consequences. In *EPA v. National Crushed Stone Association* (1980), the Supreme Court rejected an industry attempt to inject cost-benefit measures into regulation when it ruled that the EPA was not required to consider costs in enforcing the Clean Water Act's requirement that industry use the "best practicable control technology currently available." In the 1980 benzene standard case (*Industrial Union Department, AFL-CIO v. American Petroleum Institute),* the Court did place limits on OSHA's ability to impose costs on business when petroleum refiners objected to the cost of meeting strict new guidelines for worker exposure to benzene. However, the Court only limited OSHA from imposing large costs on business because OSHA had not proved that the health risk to refinery workers exposed to benzene was significant. One year later, in *American Textile Manufacturers Institute v. Donovan*, when OSHA was able to demonstrate a significant danger to textile workers from exposure to cotton dust the Court rejected textile industry arguments that a cost-benefit approach should be used in setting cotton-dust exposure standards for workers. It did so because the OSH Act did not specifically require cost-benefit calculations and emphasized protecting workers from risk. Other legislation, of course, permits or requires cost-benefit analysis, and the courts do not restrict its use.

Controversial Aspects of Cost-Benefit Analysis

Cost-benefit analysis is attractive as a method of evaluating regulatory impacts and expenditures; however, it has important shortcomings. First, it is hard to identify all costs and benefits in a project. When a firm spends money for pollution control, it also may redesign a production process to make it more energy efficient. Is the expenditure a cost or a benefit? Where benefits are measured in dollar amounts, how is one to value a clear sky, a fishable stream, fragrant air, or extra years of life? These values are subjective and necessarily involve disagreement. It is hard to assign a dollar amount to untraded goods such as aesthetic beauty or a human life.

Policy choices in environmental regulation often have consequences for mortality rates and, therefore, implicitly place a value on life. Although pricing life evokes a callous image, it is a hard reality that decisions about pollution abatement programs must be made. Zero-discharge standards could prevent some risks to human health but only at an astounding price. Society cannot afford the infinite expenditures necessary to reduce pollution to the no-risk level. Expenditures below this level indicate policies that compromise between preserving lives and maintaining a higher standard of living for everyone.

Policy makers in Washington, D.C., sometimes have placed a value on human life. When President Reagan ordered agencies to justify regulations expected to cost an industry more than $100 million, it became necessary to show that this cost was offset by equal or greater benefits. If a $100 million regulation would save 150 lives valued at $1 million each, then it could be justified. The EPA has in recent years valued a life at between $400,000 and $7 million.

There are two commonly used techniques for placing explicit dollar valuations on human life. The first method is calculation of the present discounted value of future earnings. What is the value of wages and benefits a worker would have

---

In the realm of ends everything has either a *price* or a *dignity*. Whatever has a price can be replaced by something else as its equivalent; on the other hand, whatever is above all price, and therefore admits of no equivalent, has a dignity.

Source: Immanuel Kant; *Foundations of the Metaphysics of Morals* (1785).

earned through the remainder of a lifetime? An objection to this method is that workers in some categories have low wages due to discrimination. Whites may earn more than blacks, men more than women, working husbands more than housewives. Thus, American values of equality are violated by the discounted future earnings approach to valuation of life. Another approach is the willingness-to-pay method, by which a life can be valued in dollars by determining what people are willing to pay to lower the risk of death or what they are being paid to accept a higher risk. Studies of risky occupations generally have inferred the value of life to range between $250,000 and $500,000 (Lave, 1981). One problem with this approach is that wage determinations may not be based on accurate risk estimates. Also, it is difficult to arrive at accurate willingness-to-pay estimates.

A second difficulty with cost-benefit analysis is that the benefits and costs of a program may affect different parties and, therefore, may not be truly comparable. A reduction in particulate emissions from a factory may impose large costs on the business and on consumers of its product. But benefits from cleaner air accrue to local real estate agents as clean air raises property values, to pollution-control equipment manufacturers who profit from abatement, and to individuals whose medical bills are lower. Weighing diverse cost-benefit effects in this way is subjective and raises complicated issues of justice.

A third general criticism of cost-benefit analysis is that it complicates the regulatory process. After the Reagan administration stressed cost-benefit approaches, Senator Thomas Eagleton (D-Missouri) objected that cost-benefit studies increased the expense of regulating, delayed needed regulations while study was undertaken, and made the decision process more complex and dependent on arcane methods and technical experts. One likely result, according to Eagleton, was further insulation of the public from participation in regulation.

There are other critics of cost-benefit approaches. Environmentalists, who elevate human and environmental rights over utilitarian ethics, dislike them because they trade off environmental quality. Critic Steven Kelman writes that "there may be many instances where a certain decision might be right even though its benefits do not outweigh its costs" and points out that the Bill of Rights and the Emancipation Proclamation were not subject to cost-benefit study because the moral rights they represented were absolute (1981: 31). An environmentalist writes: "If the value of each endangered species or population must be compared one on one with the value of the particular development scheme that would exterminate it, we can kiss goodbye to most of Earth's plants, animals, and microorganisms" (Ehrlich and Ehrlich, 1981: 10). Others object to the cold-bloodedness of its valuations.

> Although it is precise and reasonable in the abstract, cost-benefit analysis is both cold-blooded because it attempts to put a price on such things as clean air, a death from leukemia, or a child's birth defects; and it is unreliable because cost-benefit calculations depend on strings of hidden assumptions and sometimes are based on corporate derived, unsubstantiated cost data, while failing to take full account of benefits (Brownstein, 1981: 45).

Although cost-benefit analysis has an image problem and limited precision, its use may be advantageous for several reasons. First, it is a framework for fully categorizing the impacts of a policy. It disciplines thinking (but should not be expected always to result in clear choices. Judgment is still required even though cost-benefit analysis may show some alternatives more desirable than others.) After cost-benefit studies are completed, decision makers still may use ethical criteria in decisions.

A second advantage of cost-benefit analysis is the reverse of the critics' charge that it is cold-blooded. In fact, cost-benefit analysis may inject rational calculation into highly emotional arguments and thereby lead to compassionate decisions that protect nature and minimize human suffering more than intuitive decisions based on emotional considerations.

And third, cost-benefit analysis may help regulators locate the proper level of regulation by recognizing the importance of marginal abatement costs. The bill for pollution abatement is rising rapidly because, as a general rule, control costs rise steeply as full cleanup is approached. In some cases it may cost as much to reduce pollution for the last 3 to 5 percent as it did to clean up the first 95 to 97 percent. Exhibit 14–2 shows this. The pulp and paper industry, for example, spent about $3 billion to comply with EPA water emission control standards and achieved a 95 percent pollution reduction in 1983. However, to reach a 98 percent reduction would cost an additional $4.8 billion, or a 160 percent increase in costs to achieve only a 3 percent increase in benefits (Weidenbaum, 1983). In cases such as this, cost-benefit analysis can identify efficient regulatory goals to prevent skyrocketing costs that produce trivial benefits. It provides an artificial but valuable test of efficient resource allocation for regulators not subject to a market mechanism.

EXHIBIT 14–2   BENEFIT-COST ANALYSIS OF REGULATION

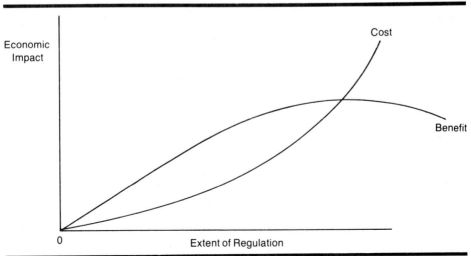

Reprinted by permission from Murray L. Weidenbaum, *Benefit-Cost Analysis of Government Regulation* (St. Louis: Center for the Study of American Business, 1981), p. 3.

MARKET INCENTIVES IN
ENVIRONMENTAL REGULATION

The case of the Asarco copper smelter, described at the beginning of the chapter, is unique in the extent to which it attracted national attention and posed a stark choice between jobs and cancer. But every day, regulators make decisions that pose similar trade-offs. The complexity and cost of these decisions has led to incorporation of risk analysis and cost-benefit analysis in regulatory programs. It is now clear that simple command and control regulation often imposes unreasonable expense, and regulators also are using other new tools that provide market incentives to protect the environment and public health. In this section, we discuss new approaches to regulation.

Air Emissions Policies as an Example
of Market-Incentive Regulation

Typically, the EPA has enforced the provisions of the Clean Air Act on industry by prescribing control equipment and emissions limits for each point source in a plant. Experience has shown, however, that the cost of controlling the same amount of a pollutant from two different sources can vary considerably. It may, for example, cost $1,000 a ton to remove hydrocarbons from the exhaust gases of one industrial process and 100 times that much, or $1 million, to remove one ton from another industrial process, depending on the nature of that process and the level of control already achieved. Therefore, the EPA has adopted several innovative policies to give business flexibility in controlling overall emissions and to reduce compliance costs.

First, in 1976, the EPA adopted an "emission offset policy." This policy allows new sources of pollution from newly built industrial plants, provided those plants utilize the "best available" control technologies and produce pollution "offsets" from existing sources above and beyond the improvements already required by air pollution legislation and more than sufficient to offset the anticipated new pollution. Under this "offset" policy, a General Motors assembly plant employing 5,000 was built in Oklahoma City (a "nonattainment area") when four local oil companies agreed to install floating roofs in oil storage tanks to reduce hydrocarbon emissions from evaporation. This reduction more than offset hydrocarbon emissions from paint-spraying operations in the new GM plant.

A second, and similar, regulatory innovation is the "bubble concept," first introduced by the EPA in 1979. It works this way: Traditionally, the EPA monitors and limits individual sources of air pollution in a factory. But rather than measure emissions from each stack, valve, paint sprayer, or dust source, advocates of the bubble concept propose that a single limit be placed on an entire industrial complex—an imaginary bubble overarching all point sources. The company would then be allowed to choose which sources to control, with which technologies, and at what level, so long as overall plant emissions standards were met. This way, rather than install millions of dollars of complex, bulky equipment to clean up a smokestack (which itself might produce a toxic slurry requiring further waste treatment and land disposal), a firm might be able to achieve the same overall emissions level at less cost by switching from high- to low-sulfur-content coal in two furnaces located in another building where a different industrial process takes place.

A recent example is the compliance bubble the EPA approved in 1985 for a utility, Central Illinois Public Service. The utility operates two identical boilers for power generation, both of which are subject to sulfur dioxide (SO_2) emission limitations of 1.2 pounds per million BTU heat input. The first boiler burns high-sulfur coal, and sulfur emissions are controlled with expensive flue gas desulfurization equipment capable of lowering stack emissions below the 1.2 pound limit. The second boiler does not have flue gas emission controls, but met the 1.2 pound (SO_2) emission standard by burning low-sulfur coal. The utility proposed to switch the second boiler to locally available, less expensive coal with a higher sulfur content that would result in emissions of 1.8 pounds of SO_2. It further proposed to overcontrol the first boiler so that the *combined* flue gas emissions of both boilers totaled only 1.1 pounds of SO_2. The EPA approved the bubble, which lowered total annual sulfur emissions by about 3,100 tons and saved the utility $22 million in coal purchase costs (Council on Environmental Quality, 1985).

The bubble policy has had a rocky history in the courts. Environmentalists have opposed it because bubbles sometimes do not produce *maximum* pollution reduction. For example, in the utility boilers above, the EPA could have required both overcontrol of the first boiler and low-sulfur coal use in the second. Also, some corporations have escaped reasonable regulations when ill-advised bubbles have been approved. Union Carbide once received approval of a bubble allowing it to avoid emission controls on a storage tank in "exchange" for the pollution abatement resulting from having shut down a facility four years earlier.

In contrast, bubbles have encouraged industry to try new techniques and equipment to achieve net reductions in emissions at lower costs than source-by-source controls mandated by the EPA under traditional command and control techniques. As higher levels of emission reduction are achieved in industry, "bubbling" will make more and more sense. By 1987, the EPA had approved fifty bubbles and the states another twenty-five. The idea received an important boost in 1984 when the Supreme Court turned aside a challenge to a bubble by an environmental group. In *Chevron v. National Resources Defense Council* (1984) the EPA was given the freedom to interpret the Clean Air Act to allow plantwide emission standards.

A third innovation is emissions banking. Under the EPA's air emissions banking policy, established in April 1982, firms may overcontrol emissions or shut down polluting sources and receive credits for the amount of pollution not emitted. Credits may be stored in an emissions "bank," which acts as a clearinghouse, and later sold to another firm that may use the credits to pollute more. A firm may buy emission credits because they are cheaper than installing expensive abatement equipment. Emissions banks may be for profit or not for profit. By 1983, banks had been set up in five cities, and buyers and sellers of emissions credits advertising in the *Wall Street Journal* testified to the development of a trading market. Borden Chemical Company in 1982 bought the rights from B. F. Goodrich Co. to emit twenty-five tons of hydrocarbons annually at a price of $2,500 per ton. Borden claimed that emissions control at its facilities would have averaged $5,800 per ton (Greene, 1982). In 1985 and 1986, extra reductions for lead in gasoline were frequently banked by petroleum refiners who were ahead of the federal timetable for reductions of up to 0.1 grams per leaded gallon by 1986. The EPA allowed refiners to sell their extra, pre-deadline lead reductions in gasoline to other refiners who were slower in reducing lead content.

Environmental Substance Liability Claims

One traditional method of social regulation outside federal bureaucracy is found in liability law. Court-ordered awards for damages, injury, and illness caused by environmental pollutants provide an incentive for corporations to prevent harm from their activities. Product liability lawsuits with large awards to plaintiffs have led to improved safety standards in products, such as collapsible steering columns in automobiles. Today, victims of exposure to toxic contaminants from industrial processes often seek judgments against companies. So-called "toxic torts," or common law cases brought against corporations are increasingly common. In Oregon, for example, Martin Marietta Co. was ordered to pay damages because emissions from an aluminum smelting plant damaged fruit crops. A B.F. Goodrich plastics plant in Louisville, Kentucky, was held liable for the death of a nearby resident exposed to vinyl-chloride gas emitted from the plant (Miyares, 1983). Highly publicized lawsuits, as we have mentioned in other chapters, have been filed against Hooker Chemical and Plastics Corporation by victims of the hazardous waste at Love Canal, against Union Carbide by victims of the gas leak at Bhopal, against the manufacturers of Agent Orange by Vietnam war veterans, and against asbestos companies by workers exposed to asbestos materials.

The liability system could bring effective pressure to bear on industry, forcing corporations to pay for the health damage caused by their pollution and providing an incentive to limit that pollution to minimize lawsuits. But the legal system has shortcomings as a mechanism for regulating business. Widespread environmental lawsuits would overwhelm the court system, which has limited resources to hear cases. Current evidentiary rules make it difficult for victims to prove damages. The courts are unreceptive to epidemiological evidence because it often leaves room for doubt about the causes of individual health problems. The litigation process is costly, slow, and unpleasant; there are many opportunities for corporations to win delays. And some states still have statutes of limitation as short as two to seven years, meaning that victims of latent illnesses and genetic defects may have no standing to sue when their illnesses become manifest.

Environmental Impairment Insurance

Insurance is another alternative for deterring socially irresponsible corporate behavior. In 1982, the EPA enlisted the help of insurance companies in regulating toxic waste when it established a policy requiring hazardous-waste dump operators to prove their ability to finance the costs of permanently closing dump sites. Any company operating such a dump would have to buy insurance coverage both for "sudden" and "non-sudden" pollution accidents (the latter term referring to slow leaks and manifestation of long-term health effects). If a company cannot buy insurance, it may post a surety bond in an amount stipulated by the EPA and insure itself.

In theory, this policy would shift part of the regulatory burden from the EPA to the insurance industry, which would need to accurately assess the risks of toxic pollution incidents, charge adequate premiums, and insist on safe handling of toxins. The EPA knew that historically insurance carriers have provided financial incentives to corporations to act safely. At the turn of the century, when unsafe steam boilers frequently blew up in manufacturing plants, insurance companies, which had to pay the accident claims, helped to develop the safety boiler. Insurance has also worked to complement command regulation in areas such as auto, marine, and fire safety. But it has not worked well in the pollution field.

In 1983, a year after the EPA instituted its insurance requirements for toxic-waste handlers, pollution insurance was a growing, competitive policy area. Twelve companies offered coverage. By the end of 1985, however, only two companies remained. They wrote less coverage and had raised premiums as much as ten times. Reinsurers vanished from the market. What had happened?

A variety of factors converged to kill pollution insurance for the time being. Large casualty insurance claims in 1980 to 1985 for pollution and non-pollution accidents created a long period in which payouts exceeded premiums. Then interest rates fell after 1983, and the insurers' investments no longer produced sufficient income to back up policies. Court decisions based on the theory of joint and several liability in the pollution field scared insurers, who found themselves footing large medical and clean-up bills for policyholders who were minor parties in hazardous waste spills. In addition, the courts sometimes broadened the insurers' liability to the policyholder. For instance, some were forced to pay for cancers caused by exposures twenty to thirty years before, even though the policies had long since lapsed. Finally, pollution risks were too hard to define. New and unknown dangers were constantly discovered, damage claims were potentially astronomical, and the demand for gradual pollution coverage was confined to a few risky dumps so that a broad premium base could not be established.

By chance, just as these problems were converging in late 1984, the Bhopal gas leak occurred. That leak, in December, came at the time when many policies were being renegotiated with companies for renewal on January 1, 1985. Instead of renewing, many insurers canceled policies. Some waste-disposal firms were left without coverage and had to stop operations for a time until they could indemnify themselves to satisfy government requirements.

Insurers no longer include coverage for pollution accidents in comprehensive general liability policies, and insurance against slow pollution and long-term problems is hard to come by. So far, the EPA's experiment in enlisting insurance carriers as comrades-in-arms in the war against pollution is in trouble.

VOLUNTARY COMPLIANCE EFFORTS BY INDUSTRY

Overall, most corporate efforts to curb pollution are mandated by command and control regulation. Yet areas of voluntarism always have existed, and in these areas corporate response patterns vary markedly. At one end of the continuum of voluntary response patterns, some companies have ignored or opposed antipollution responsibilities. Thousands of companies have had to be prodded, sued, and fined by the EPA into complying. Some behavior has bordered on the criminal, for instance, the relaxed attitude of managers in the asbestos industry toward the dangers of their product.

At the other end of the voluntary response continuum, some corporations have been proactive and anticipatory in meeting environmental responsibilities. Sometimes companies have anticipated environmental laws due to economic incentives. In the 1930s, years before pollution control laws required it, Standard Oil Company of California built a hydrogen sulfide recovery plant at a Los Angeles refinery to remove sulfur compounds that contributed to air pollution. In 1975, 3M Company introduced the 3P, or "Pollution Prevention Pays," program to encourage technological changes that lowered production costs. This program has resulted in such salutary advances as Kenlevel II, an electroplating process for ferrous metals that uses chloride baths rather than traditional cyanide baths. The process is 50 percent more energy efficient, and the resulting effluent does not require a costly cyanide removal process. This gives 3M a competitive cost advantage. In the first ten years of operation, employee suggestions led to over 100 projects that saved the company about $200 million in abatement costs (Bringer, 1984).

At other times, a deep sense of responsibility (mixed, naturally, with a desire to avoid public displeasure) has moved managers to environmental preservation. For many years, Pittsburgh, nicknamed the "Smoky City," had the worst air pollution in the United States, a problem that stemmed from the presence of many coal-fired blast furnaces and the use of coal for home heating. With the support of Richard K. Mellon and other leading industrialists in the town, county smoke-control legislation was passed in the 1940s, before the advent of federal regulation. Another interesting case is that of Monsanto's efforts to rescue the Illinois mud turtle, a small reptile six to nine inches long, that exudes an offensive odor from its musk glands and remains burrowed in underground hideaways nine months of the year. The turtle lives on a swampy, 2,000-acre tract near Monsanto's agricultural chemical plant at Muscatine, Iowa, and in 1980 was thought to be a candidate for the endangered species list, with only 200 specimens extant. During a census, Monsanto discovered that a nearby lake vital to the turtle's habitat was drying up. Although the operations and proximity of its agricultural chemicals plant had no effect on the turtles or their habitat, Monsanto launched a $500,000 project to save the turtles. Raccoons and skunks were trapped and removed from the acreage so that they would not eat turtle eggs, and a fleet of tanker trucks brought 80 million gallons of water to the sinking lake from the nearby Mississippi River (Berman, 1981). Belatedly, it was discovered that the site probably was populated by more than 2,000 specimens of the Illinois mud turtle and that extinction had not been imminent (Springer and Gallaway, 1979).

When companies have resisted institutionalizing environmental concern, events sometimes have provided an imperative. The response of Allied Chemical Corporation to the adverse publicity of the Kepone scandal is illustrative. Following the scandal, with its evidence of careless supervision of the manufacturing operation, Allied's chief executive officer issued a formal "Environmental Policy," stating that Allied would manufacture substances safely, follow all applicable regulations, and stop manufacture of any substance endangering public health. In addition, line managers at Allied were made responsible for carrying out the environmental policy. A Corporate Environmental Affairs Department was set up, headed by a vice president who reports to Allied's senior vice president for operations, to assist Allied operating units in complying with environmental laws. This department maintains contact with regulatory agencies, holds educational seminars for managers, meets regularly with managers to explore environmental problems, and sends out environmental surveillance teams to inspect Allied facilities and monitor legal compliance. A Toxic Risk Assessment Committee in the department reviews hazards posed by company products and operations. A final stimulus to environmental protection at Allied is the requirement that up to one-third of the bonuses of middle managers depend on meeting environmental objectives (Department of Commerce, 1980).

Many companies, in fact, are discovering the benefits of organizational changes that institutionalize environmental quality. In 1970, Dow Chemical Company established the Dow Ecology Council, a group of top officers organized to anticipate and bring about compliance with antipollution standards. Beneath the Ecology Council, each Dow manufacturing division and product department has set up an ecology subcouncil composed of its top managers. The priorities established by the Ecology Council are: 1. to make new facilities meet tomorrow's pollution standards before they are authorized, 2. to build in fail-safe mechanisms to avoid environmental disasters (for instance, diversionary sewers and dikes to contain accidental storage-tank spills), 3. to establish early warning systems for identifying and controlling potentially risky chemicals, and 4. to improve technology in recycling and waste treatment.

Another company that has developed a comprehensive approach to environmental protection and has achieved the respect of environmental groups for its actions to protect nature is ARCO. We reprint here ARCO's environmental policy. It suggests basic guidelines that all corporate managements should consider.

ATLANTIC RICHFIELD COMPANY
ENVIRONMENTAL PROTECTION POLICY

Realizing that the world's natural resources of air, water and land are vital to mankind's global existence, progress, and continued development, we consider environmental protection to be a paramount concern in our total activities, domestic and international. Therefore, it is our policy to:

■ Manage our operations with diligence and with an awareness that our goal is to protect the environment by employing the best control mechanisms, procedures, and processes which are proven technically sound and economically feasible.

■ Entrust each line manager with responsibility for the environmental performance of his or her activity.

■ Comply with all environmental legislation, regulations and standards, and provide self-monitoring to insure compliance.

■ Assist all levels of government in the promulgation of sound, cost-effective environmental laws, codes, rules and regulations, based on scientific facts and needs.

■ Consider the expense of environmental protection as a legitimate cost of doing business in modern society, assuming environmental regulations are uniformly applicable throughout an industry.

■ Encourage and support—with technical ability, time, and money—environmental programs and research efforts sponsored by trade associations and other organizations seeking solutions to technological and ecological problems.

■ Train our employees in environmental matters, actions, and responsibilities relating to their particular assignments.

■ Secure ecological guidance in our long-range planning, using recognized consultants and employing the services of experts of various disciplines.

■ Enhance communication and understanding with our stockholders, civic groups, environmental and conservation organizations, universities, and the general public through publications, speakers, exhibits, demonstrations, and the media.

■ Maintain a Corporate Environmental Protection Group to review, advise, coordinate, and implement environmental protection activities and programs.

CONCLUDING OBSERVATIONS

The uninformed believe that Congress can pass a law, set up an agency to enforce it, and then that that agency can order business to stop polluting. Only the perversity of business, say the uninformed, can explain continued pollution problems. Some people even are shocked to learn that the EPA issues permits giving companies the right to pollute up to an established standard.

Here we have informed the reader that pollution is inevitable in industrial activity. Regulators and managers must engage in a real world process of negotiation to reach the accords necessary to minimize environmental damage. Three elements of successful regulation include enforcement of and compliance with environmental statutes; the application of new regulatory techniques that consider risks, costs, and benefits at the same time as they harness the incentives that will unleash corporate ingenuity; and the voluntary institutionalization of environmental concerns in the management process.

CASE STUDY

COST-BENEFIT DECISION AT BLUEBIRD SMELTER

Bluebird Smelter is owned by a large, national mining company and located in Bluebird, a town of 12,000 in western Montana. The smelter, which has been operating profitably for thirty-five years with 100 employees, processes copper ore arriving by railroad. Its most distinguishing feature is a tall, brick stack, visible for miles and used as a landmark by nearby residents, which emits a visible plume and often leaves a faint, smudgy pall over Bison Valley, the geological basin in which Bluebird is located.

Bucolic Bison Valley has about 25,000 residents and attracts retirees from big city life and wealthy weekenders who build retreats or buy small farms in the area. The economy of Bison Valley has been primarily agricultural, but tourism is an important—if small—component, as is Bluebird Smelter.

Bluebird Smelter is the only major industrial pollution source in the valley. Fugitive and stack emissions from the smelter include sulfur dioxide (SO_2), sulfuric acid, inorganic arsenic, particulates from copper and iron dust, asbestos, nitrogen oxides, aromatic hydrocarbons, and traces of other potentially injurious chemicals. On sunny days, when the air is still, and during periods of temperature inversion over the valley, the action of the sun on smelter emissions contributes to photochemical smog similar to that in urban areas. Auto emissions and agricultural activities also are sources of photochemical oxidants, but smelter emissions are a much greater contributor to the smog.

Because of the plant's conspicuous presence, dramatized by the tall stack, visible plume, and a lingering odor from SO_2 emissions, a small, local environmental group called the Earth Riders made the plant a target in the mid-1960s. Lawsuits and political pressures by the Earth Riders led to installation in 1972 of costly pollution-control equipment at the smelter that reduced emissions by 75 percent from an uncontrolled state. This improved air quality, but visible pollution, adverse health effects, and crop damage continued.

Later in the 1970s, Bluebird Smelter was granted a series of variances from federal and state air-quality standards when the company let it be known that further pollution control expenses would force closure of the plant. From the 75 percent control level, costs escalated rapidly and further controls—say to the 90 percent level—would have cost more in total than the original 75 percent reduction. The massive expenditures would push the plant into long-term financial loss.

Many townspeople told reporters from big-city papers that they wanted jobs and were willing to tolerate a little dirty air. Local observers thought that closure of the smelter would throw Bison Valley into an economic recession. Despite opposition and organized protest by the Earth Riders, the Bluebird City Council passed five resolutions asking for variances from air-quality standards for the smelter and sent them to state and federal agencies. When several Earth Riders chained and locked themselves to railroad tracks leading to the smelter, demanding that ore shipments cease and the plant close down, the mayor of Bluebird, a veterinarian, placed a placard in his office window offering "Free rabies shots to Earth Riders. No appointment necessary."

In 1987, a state public health official conducted an epidemiological study of the region, because it offered a unique opportunity for observing the health effects of a single, major source of industrial pollution. Using standard mortality tables, the official determined that there had been twenty-five "excess" deaths in Bison Valley over the five-year period between 1981 and 1986. These were deaths from emphysema, lung cancer, tuberculosis, pneumonia, and ischemic heart disease over and above those naturally occurring in a population not exposed to similar industrial pollution. Such results were not surprising given the existing SO_2 and particulate levels. The unique element in the situation was that the cause was a single source rather than a collection of sources mixing together, as in most industrial and urban areas. What could not be determined, of course, was which deaths were the "excess" ones. The extra five fatalities averaged each year were part of a group of several hundred deaths, most of which were statistically "expected."

A group of economists from a prestigious research institute in another city picked the Bluebird Smelter as a test case for a research project on the health effects of pollution. The figures that they produced led to debate among the various local groups involved in the controversy. The researchers looked at the operation of Bluebird Smelter in terms of costs and benefits to the community and to society. The accompanying table shows their basic calculations.

The Earth Riders seized upon the study, arguing that if total costs of smelter operation exceeded benefits, then a clear-cut case had been made for closing the plant. It was already operating at a loss—in this case, a net social loss of $605,000. Thus, in the eyes of the environmentalists, Bluebird Smelter was in social bankruptcy.

The smelter's managers and members of the Bluebird City Council, in contrast, ridiculed the study for making unrealistic and simplistic assumptions. They questioned whether the costs were meaningful, citing estimates of the value of a human life made by other economists that were much lower than $1 million. They argued that health risks posed by the smelter were less than those of smoking cigarettes, drinking, or riding motorcycles and that benefits to the

ANNUAL BENEFITS AND COSTS OF BLUEBIRD SMELTER

Benefits	Value
Payroll for 100 employees at an average of $20,000 each	$2,000,000
Benefits paid to workers and families at an average of $1,000 each	100,000
Income, other than wages and salaries, generated in the valley by the company	4,600,000
Local taxes and fees paid by the company	125,000
Social services to community and charitable contributions	20,000
Total	$6,845,000

Costs	Value
Excess deaths of five persons at $1 million each*	$5,000,000
Other health and illness costs to exposed population	450,000
Crop and property damage from pollutants	1,000,000
Reduction of aesthetic value and quality of life	500,000
Lost revenues and taxes from tourism	500,000
Total	$7,450,000

*Calculated on the basis of recent court decisions compensating victims of wrongful death in product liability cases in western states. The figure reflects average compensation.

community were great. They even suggested that important costs had been left out of the calculations, such as sociological and psychological costs to workers who would be laid off if the plant closed.

The debate raged, and the smelter continued to operate.

Questions

1. Do you believe that the costs to society of smelter operation outweigh the benefits?
2. Do you believe that the cost figures in the researchers' calculations, particularly those representing human life, are accurate? What are some alternative ways to calculate the value of human life? Could the social benefits exceed social costs if different values were used?
3. Are any important benefits or costs not included in the analysis of the smelter's operation? What are they?
4. Is the cost-benefit method of decision making an appropriate tool for deciding whether to close the smelter?
5. List and explain several alternative solutions to this controversy. Which is best and why?

CHAPTER 15

CONSUMERISM

 The International Business Machines Corporation (IBM) has been built on three cornerstones—respect for the individual employee, customer service, and excellence in the performance of every job. These three principles were repeatedly emphasized by Thomas J. Watson, Sr., who led the company and its predecessors from 1914 to 1956, and by his son Thomas J. Watson, Jr., who led the company from 1956 to 1971. They are still the foundation of IBM's great success.

These three principles are interrelated. Management of IBM has been strongly committed to them, and they are institutionalized in the beliefs and behavior of people throughout the organization.

Our interest here centers in IBM's concern for consumers. In a little book called *A Business and Its Beliefs*, Thomas J. Watson, Jr., wrote:

> Years ago we ran an ad that said simply and in bold type, "IBM Means Service." I have often thought it our very best ad. It stated clearly just exactly what we stand for. . . . We want to give the best customer service of any company in the world (Watson, 1963: 29).

He went on to explain that this concept became reflex behavior in IBM. "IBM's contracts," he continued, "have always offered, not *machines* for rent, but machine services, that is the equipment itself and the continuing advice and counsel of IBM's staff" (Watson, 1963: 32). This policy means that IBM is committed to giving the best service possible, not some of the time, but all of the time. It means answering every customer complaint within twenty-four hours, not when convenient. It means marshaling all the resources of the company if necessary to solve a customer's problem.

Peters and Waterman in their best-selling book, *In Search of Excellence* (1982), quoted an official of Lanier to illustrate this point:

> I remember the last time we had trouble. In hours the horde descended, from everywhere. They called in about eight experts on my problem. At least four were from Europe, one came from Canada, one from Latin America. That's just where they happened to be (Peters and Waterman, 1982: 160–161).

IBM has always had strong competition, and many competitors have had technically superior products. But none has had service to excell that of IBM. IBM is unmatched in the industry in this regard, and it is a major reason for the phenomenal growth, present size, and superior strength of this company.

IBM is the world's largest computer and office equipment company. In 1985 it was the fifth largest industrial firm in the United States; its sales were $50 billion. The company recorded in 1985 the highest net profit of any company in the United States—$6.6 billion. At the end of 1985 it employed 242,000 people, a number exceeded by only a few other corporations.

IBM's dedication to superior customer service is reflected in its many policies and programs to stimulate, train, and reward sales and service personnel. For example, sales personnel are trained to "act as if they were on the customer's payroll." The basic sales training program lasts fifteen months. In addition, there are other training programs, teaching how presidents and financial officers of companies think, for example. Employee attitude surveys are conducted periodically to determine perceptions of how customer services are being maintained. Prompt reports are routine at IBM on any loss of customers, and there is a full-scale evaluation to find out why each one has occurred. Employee rewards, including incentive compensation, are geared to customer satisfactions, which are routinely measured (Peters and Waterman, 1982).

IBM's dedication to consumer interests is part of a growing trend. Until recent years, government efforts to protect consumer interests were intermittent. They usually were stimulated by a shocking exposé or a visible disaster. Today, there is different kind of concern for the consumer. Consumers and their representatives are continuously aggressive in demanding and getting better treatment from business, both through legislation and voluntarily. The movement, called *consumerism,* is widespread, organized, and powerful. It has resulted in an extraordinary expansion of federal consumer protective legislation during the past two decades. Although the movement currently has lost some of its momentum, there is still powerful support for it in this country. Consumerism embraces a wide range of public issues and problems for business managers.

This chapter begins with a definition of consumerism and the underlying forces driving it, followed by a brief résumé of the most significant recent consumer legislation and the major characteristics of the current consumer movement. We then discuss selected public and private policy issues centering on products and services, and false and deceptive advertising. Special emphasis is given to product risk and liability. The chapter concludes with a description of business response to consumerism, including the characteristics of an effective consumer affairs office.

THE CONSUMER MOVEMENT

Consumerism is a movement designed to improve the rights and powers of consumers in relation to the sellers of products and services. It is a protest movement of consumers against what they or their advocates see as unfair, discriminatory, and arbitrary treatment. Consumerism is as old as business but has taken on new dimensions in recent years.

The current consumer movement began in the mid-1960s and has continued ever since, but with somewhat diminished momentum in the past half-dozen years. Its beginning can be marked by a special message of President Kennedy to Congress on March 15, 1962. Momentum picked up a little with a few new pieces of legislation in 1964 and 1965, and an important boost was given to the movement by the publicity associated with the publication in 1965 of Ralph Nader's polemic *(Unsafe at Any Speed)* about General Motors' Corvair auto. The American public, which for so long had been patient about product and service abuses, began to express itself in strident ways. There was no rallying motto, but had there been, it well could have been one recommended by Denenberg: *"Populus iamdudum defatatus est"* ("The consumer has been screwed long enough") *(Newsweek,* March 5, 1973: 60). Politicians heard: A flood of bills inundated Congress, and many were passed.

Broadly, the current consumer movement, as defined by Theodore Jacobs (1979), one of Ralph Nader's original top aides, is a mix of people, ideas, and organizations that represent previously unrepresented groups or concerns with the objective of bringing about change or reform. It is based on the proposition, as expressed by President Kennedy in his message and later by President Nixon in a special message to Congress about consumers, that the consumer has certain rights and that these rights have been violated. The rights in question include the rights to make intelligent choices among products and services; to have access to accurate and useful information; to register complaints and be heard; to be offered fair prices and acceptable quality; to have safe and healthful products; and to receive adequate service.

So powerful was this movement in the 1960s and 1970s that it led to an unprecedented expansion of federal legislation to protect consumers. Twenty-one major pieces of legislation were passed in the ten years from 1965 through 1975. Although no major pieces of legislation have been passed since then, there is still underlying support for new legislation.

FORCES BEHIND CONSUMERISM

It seems paradoxical that the American consumer is at one and the same time the envy of the world for the quality and abundance of the products and services he or she consumes, and yet he or she is dissatisfied with those products and services. Why the paradox? There are many explanations.

This is an age of discontent, of skepticism, and of challenge to established authority. Today's consumers are much better educated than those of the past, and they challenge practices that previous generations bore in silence. They question the authority of the uncontrolled marketplace. This is an age, too, of vocal expression of discontent; and consumers, fed up with actual or perceived bad treatment at the hands of manufacturers, advertisers, merchants, and repair services, are voicing their complaints.

Are the complaints justified? Every consumer would say yes, because every consumer has been frustrated with a variety of consumption problems. Business people, however, claim that dissatisfied consumers represent only a small fraction of the total.

In the 1960s, serious consumer problems triggered a massive legislative movement in response. Despite this legislation, major problems still persist. For example, in its *1984 Annual Report,* the Consumer Product Safety Commission said that consumer safety is still a serious problem. Some 29,000 Americans are killed each year in consumer product–related accidents. Another 33 million are injured. The cost of emergency room treatment alone of these injuries was estimated to be $10 billion in 1984.

But the list of consumer complaints moves far beyond product safety. Newspapers bombard us with stories about the health hazards of many products. Consumers are beset with advertising claims that are distorted, untrue, and deceptive. They are given guarantees about product defects that are not met. They receive sloppy and excessively priced repair service. They are burdened with hidden charges in the form of service costs they do not understand or of which they were not informed. Many products are so complex that manufacturers find it difficult to communicate to consumers adequate information about how to use them. Too frequently, manuals purporting to describe how products can be put together and used efficiently are models of incomprehensible English. Despite the Truth-in-Lending Act of 1968, many consumers still do not know just how much they pay for credit. The list of complaints and problems is very long.

In thinking about consumer complaints, it should be noted that expectations are rising in this society. Consumers have much higher standards concerning the products and services they consume than ever before. But expectations frequently outpace reality. They are a reflection not only of rising sophistication, but also of yearning for the ideal. They are a root cause of consumer dissatisfaction. Complaints of consumers are also exacerbated by increasing feelings of the helplessness, alienation, estrangement, and irritation involved in living in this complex society.

CHARACTERISTICS OF THE CONSUMER MOVEMENT

Four central characteristics distinguished the consumer movement of the 1960s and 1970s from past waves. First, it was a part of a larger social movement that involved civil rights, antiwar demonstrations, environmentalism, and feminism. A common thread among all these movements, and one that the current consumer movement has emphasized, is the focus on the rights of the individual in dealing with mammoth institutions. One of the early attractions of Ralph Nader, says Jacobs, was that he gave voice and visible encouragement to the idea that the single individual was not helpless before massive, entrenched institutions. An individual, he demonstrated, could change policy and could change the way in which established institutions operated. All these were themes the public was ready to embrace, hence the power of the movements.

Second, the modern consumer movement was broader in focus than older movements. Says Jacobs:

> [The current movement emphasizes] procedural issues such as campaign reform, freedom of information and access to the judicial system as well as specific campaigns to bring greater equity and fairness to a system viewed as basically unbalanced in favor of business interests. When consumerism was identified with the housewives and home economics it emphasized a fair deal in the marketplace. Today it deals with a whole range of economic, social and political issues, including corporate governance, nuclear power, energy and environmental questions, anti-trust, product safety and a whole variety of procedural issues (Jacobs, 1979: 335).

Third, the consumer movement cut across industries and affected particular functions of all businesses, in contrast to previous consumer laws, which generally concerned one entire industry.

Fourth, the modern consumer movement has used a wider range of tactics than those of the past. Today's consumer leaders have gone directly to public opinion through books, reports, publicity, legislative hearings, and lawsuits. These methods are used to sway public opinion, of course, but also to achieve specific ends in themselves, such as ensuring compliance with laws already on the books.

A BRIEF RÉSUMÉ OF CONSUMER LEGISLATION

From the beginning of our history, governments have passed laws to protect consumers. In the earliest days, however, redress for most grievances was worked out through the courts, case by case, or by consumers expressing dissatisfaction in the marketplace. Gradually, governments built legislative protections in an expanding number of areas, including weights and measures, public health and safety, transportation, communications, finance, licensing of workers and professionals, zoning, and other essential services. In previous chapters, particularly Chapter 5, we discussed milestones in the history of consumer protective legislation. Virtually all the older laws are still in force and have been enormously strengthened and expanded by new legislation that responded to the consumer movement of 1965 to 1975.

Outstanding among the older laws were those concerning railroad rates and services, monopolistic practices in industry, maintenance of fair competition, protection against adulterated drugs and foods, and honest dealings in finance. Outstanding among the newer laws were those concerning labeling and information about product content and services offered, motor vehicle safety standards, hazardous toys and articles, protection from contaminated foods, safety standards for inflammable fabrics, controls over atomic products, warnings about health hazards of smoking, limits on consumer liability in the use of credit cards, child-resistant packaging of hazardous substances, unreasonable risks of injury associated with any consumer products, standards for drinking water and air, standards for pension programs, and standards for warranties offered by manufacturers and retailers. As we shall note later in this chapter, these laws have been expanded significantly by liberal judiciary rulings that favor consumers.

These laws established three powerful consumer protection agencies—the National Highway Traffic Safety Administration (NHTSA), the Consumer Product Safety Commission (CPSC), and the Environmental Protection Agency (EPA). These laws also gave new powers to many older regulatory agencies such as the Federal Trade Commission (FTC). These new laws have enormously strengthened consumers in their bargaining position with people in business. With such protective armor on the statute books, in regulatory agencies, and in the courts of law, the consumer can hardly be said to be the prey today of malevolent people in business. Yet new issues and abuses, which demand new protections, appear daily.

MAJOR CONSUMER-PROTECTION AGENCIES OF THE FEDERAL GOVERNMENT

It is estimated that today there are more than fifty federal agencies and bureaus performing between 200 and 300 functions that directly affect consumers. These numbers are easily exceeded in state and local governments although, as noted above, the overwhelming power to protect consumers lies in the federal government and in courts. The six major federal consumer protective agencies, together with their basic missions, are as follows.

1. The FTC promotes fair competition in interstate commerce which, of course, benefits consumers. The agency protects consumers from false and deceptive advertising and unfair trade practices, regulates packaging and labeling of consumer products, and ensures appropriate consumer credit disclosure and reporting.

2. The CPSC sets safety standards for consumer products. These standards cover design, construction, contents, performance, and labeling of hundreds of products. The agency, of course, has power to enforce its standards.

3. The NHTSA establishes motor vehicle safety standards, determines automobile fuel economy standards, enforces laws concerning automobile speed limits, and prohibits tampering with odometers.

4. The FDA regulates the safety, effectiveness, and labeling of food, drugs, cosmetics, and medical devices to protect the public against potential health hazards from these products. It is also responsible for setting standards for radiation exposure.

5. The Food Safety and Quality Service (FSQS) regulates the meat, poultry, and egg industries for safety and purity by inspecting all meat, poultry, and eggs shipped in interstate commerce. It also administers truth-in-labeling laws for these products.

6. The EPA establishes standards for air quality and pollution (including motor vehicles); water quality and pollution; hazardous waste disposal; cleanup of hazardous dumps; pesticides; hazardous chemicals; noise levels for construction equipment, transportation equipment (except airplanes), and motors and engines.

As pointed out in Chapter 6, these agencies have a powerful influence over free-market activities. Within their areas of authority, which are vast, they make decisions that affect the production, pricing, content, purity, and design of products and services. They can stop production of a hazardous item, such as a dangerous toy. They can force the recall of defective products, such as automobile tires. They can delay the introduction of a drug until it is approved.

Many other agencies, of course, affect consumer products and services even though their main missions extend well beyond direct consumer interests. Some have a direct impact on consumers, such as the Federal Communications Commission regulations of TV programming. Others have powerful indirect impact, as do the monetary policies of the Federal Reserve Board.

CONSUMER ADVOCATES

One of the phenomena of today's consumerism, in contrast with that of the past, is the rise of consumer advocates. These self-appointed advocates of the consumer are numerous. Probably the most publicized advocates are Ralph Nader and his "Raiders," as his legal staff is called. His role has been partly like that of the muckrakers of the past. But it goes further, to active representation of the consumer in the courts, government agencies, legislatures, and corporations. He has been a thorn in the side of business, and some people in business consider him to be a dangerous radical. But many other people, including businesspeople, believe that he has sought to achieve his objectives through, not against, our legal and political systems. Many observers believe that he has distorted or exaggerated the facts in numerous cases, but others believe that his motives are beneficial. Edward Rust, when president of the U.S. Chamber of Commerce, said that he was in full agreement with Nader when he concerned himself with the production of better products and services. "I think we are forced to the conclusion," he said, "that his commitment is to make the system work" (Rust, 1973).

Consumerism is not a mass movement of 230 million consumers speaking as a unit in their own interests. It is, rather, an amorphous mass of disgruntled consumers partly led and partly pushed by activists who champion what appear to them to be issues beneficial to consumers. Consumer advocates demand a wide range of remedies to protect consumers. High on the list, of course, are safe products whose quality meets prescribed standards. They demand an end to false and distorted advertising. Not only do they want better-caliber people in regulatory agencies (meaning people like themselves), but they want the regulatory agencies divorced from those who are regulated. They demand that disgruntled consumers find ready and satisfactory redress of grievances. Consumer groups seek to protect the environment from damage and to purify the environment that has been degraded.

There are many other important consumer advocacy groups aside from Nader's organization. The Consumer Federation of America, for example, was formed in 1967 to bring together about 200 organizations (mostly state and local) with consumer interests. This organization may well represent some 30 million people. Consumers Union, founded in 1936, is basically an organization that disseminates information, especially in its magazine, *Consumer Reports*, to consumers. Common Cause and the National Wildlife Federation may be noted also as "broad-based" and "broad interest" groups. Then there are hundreds of more narrowly focused organizations, such as Action for Children's Television.

Fundamentally, consumer advocates are reformists. On balance, they probably have served the best interests of consumers, business, and the community. However, many of them are polemicists, and their "factual" assertions, arguments, and policy recommendations must be examined critically in that light.

BUSINESS-ORIENTED INTEREST GROUPS AND ORGANIZATIONS

To round out the picture of the interest groups that address consumer issues, we should mention many groups inside and outside of business organizations that have responded to consumer advocates, sometimes positively and sometimes negatively, and also have initiated programs in the interests of consumers. To begin with, many corporations have created consumer affairs offices (whose functions are discussed at the end of this chapter). Business organizations such as the U.S. Chamber of Commerce and the Business Roundtable vigorously advance the business point of view, especially in legislative debates. Not-for-profit organizations such as the American Enterprise Institute are presumably objective but lean to conservative positions.

Also of importance are groups formed to deal with special problems. To illustrate, the Consumer Research Institute was created by the Grocery Manufacturers Association to study consumer complaints and inform grocery manufacturers about those it believes to be valid and widespread. The tobacco industry established the Council for Tobacco Research to study the effects of tobacco on health. To complete this abbreviated list of organizations, we note the Better Business Bureau, a long-established institution in cities and towns, which is supported by business interests.

THE MATURING OF THE CONSUMER MOVEMENT LIFE CYCLE

Like most products, the consumer movement has gone through a life cycle and is now in its maturity. A number of pieces of evidence support this contention. To begin with, there has not been a new major legislative enactment concerning consumers since the mid-1970s. Declining support in the Congress for consumer legislation is evidenced by the drop in votes over the years for a new Consumer Protection Agency. This agency was to have no regulatory functions but was to represent consumer interests before federal agencies and the courts. At one time, the bill creating this agency passed both houses but not by enough of a margin to override an expected veto by President Ford. Opposition by influential individuals and groups to many programs strongly pushed by consumer advocates has been growing, such as to seatbelt interlock systems, air bags in cars, and a ban on advertising during children's TV programs.

The presidential elections in 1980 indicated an important shift in the public attitude toward more regulations. The maturing process has been accelerated by the slowdown of implementation of much, but by no means all, consumer regulatory activity during the Reagan administration. Public support of consumer regulation has declined during the past decade, but it is still strong. This is shown in response to this question: "In your opinion, should there be more government regulation of consumer products and how they are sold, or less regulation than there is now?" In 1970, Gallup found that 72 percent wanted more regulation or wanted it the "same as now." In 1977, this had dropped to 56 percent, but in 1981, it was still 51 percent (Lipset and Schneider, 1983: 254). No polls on this question have been taken since 1981. The reason, said the Gallup organization in an interview with the authors, is that the issue has not been prominent in the public mind. It should be pointed out, however, that polls do show that a majority of consumers want more regulation of specific products and services, such as barbiturates, advertising, suntan pills, and prescription drugs. The consumer movement also has broadened into other areas, such as pollution, where for some toxic materials demands for government protections are growing.

SELECTED ISSUES IN THEORY AND PRACTICE

Consumerism and its related laws, administrative regulations, and impact on business raise fundamental issues in theory and practice. We discuss several of the most important issues below.

Products

Cost/Price/Quality Tradeoffs   Generally speaking, the decision-making processes in business involve complex trade-offs among various forces. For example, product quality is one variable in decisions concerning a product. The higher the quality sought, the higher the price that must be charged. The higher the price, the lower will be the demand for the product. The lower the demand, the fewer products will be produced. If more products are produced, the cost per unit can be reduced. At what point do price, potential sales, quality, product design, and other factors balance? Balancing such factors is an extremely intricate process for which there usually are not formulae to produce the decision. Human judgment is an essential, and generally final, determinant of a decision. This concept of tradeoffs is very important in appraising the managerial response to consumerism.

Highly relevant in this discussion is a point made previously that government regulatory standards set without any reference to costs can be extremely and unnecessarily expensive to the general public. It seems that a sensible approach to regulation is to weigh the costs and benefits of a proposed regulation to determine whether the equation is balanced properly. Although a final standard may not be determined by the cost-benefit equation, the method raises appropriate questions about a standard. In government, as in business, decision makers must consider and balance a multiplicity of factors.

Product Safety   The activities of the CPSC illustrate the scope of federal product-safety regulations. This agency, under the authority of six major pieces of legislation, has the mission of protecting consumers from all unreasonable risks of injury associated with consumer products. (The six laws are the Consumer Product Safety Act [1972], the Flammable Fabrics Act [1953], the Federal Hazardous Substances Act [1960], the Poison Prevention Packaging Act [1970], the Refrigerator Safety Act [1956], and the Toy Safety Act [1969].) In administering these laws, the agency undoubtedly has saved thousands of lives and prevented tens of thousands of injuries. Nancy Steorts, as chair of the agency, claimed, for example:

> . . . Hundreds of children would have died and thousands would have been poisoned had the Commission not enforced safety closure requirements for prescription drugs, aspirin and other household products. Several hundred infant

deaths have been avoided because of CPSC crib regulations. Life threatening cancer will not occur because of Commission actions involving chemicals such as vinyl chloride, benzene and asbestos. We expect that the recently effected safety standard for power lawn mowers will eventually lead to a reduction of 60,000 injuries each year (Steorts, 1983).

To make its task manageable, the agency each year establishes a limited number of priorities for action. In 1985, it set plans to develop or revise voluntary standards for more than fifty products, including kerosene heaters, gas heating systems, chain saws, riding mowers, and garage-door openers. The agency decided to examine the health effects of chlorofluorocarbons used in aerosol cans and paint removers. The agency has issued mandatory regulations but prefers to work with industry to develop voluntary regulations.

Voluntary standards are favored because they can assure more protection in a shorter period of time than mandatory standards. For example, Terrence Scanlon, present chairman of the agency, says that 22,000 injuries a year are caused by chain saws, many caused by kickback from the chain saw. The agency has worked with the industry to set voluntary standards to prevent such accidents. He estimates that the development of mandatory standards would have seriously strained his budget for five years (*U.S. News & World Report*, June 3, 1985).

If an industry or a particular manufacturer cannot or will not develop standards considered desirable by the agency, the commission has two powerful alternatives to mandatory rules. One is product recall and the other is financial penalty. Perhaps an even more powerful stimulus to voluntary action is the threat of product liability suits, a subject we discuss later in this chapter.

Consumers, like producers, must balance a variety of forces, albeit different ones, in making product-safety decisions about their purchases. For example, they must balance such factors as aesthetic quality, maintenance costs, availability of alternative products, the degree of risk acceptable in relation to original price, the use to which a product is put, the amount of use, and the skills of those using the product. Most consumers arrive at a balance that is satisfactory for them for the great majority of products. But many serious questions arise concerning the extent to which government should step into the decision-making process to protect consumers against particular product risks.

Risk and Product Safety   Consumer protection agencies face several questions. How safe is safe? How much risk should consumers be expected to assume? What is the role of government in balancing risk, safety, and other considerations in consumer protection? These are enormously difficult questions to answer. One might oversimplify by saying that the moment one jumps out of bed in the morning, one assumes risk and faces product safety questions (R. Wilson, 1979). Chlorine can react with organic matter in drinking water to produce known carcinogens. Stored peanuts can develop a mold that produces a potent carcinogen named aflatoxin. Aspirin is safe and therapeutic when properly used but when used improperly it can kill.

"Too safe" may involve costs so high that consumers cannot buy the product; "too unsafe" causes needless injuries and loss of lives. Acceptable risks must be tolerated. But what are such risks? What is a minimum risk? Can a $20 power tool be expected to be as safe as a $500 one? Are products supposed to be safe even when used by boobs and idiots?

In the last chapter we found that assessing environmental risks is an extraordinarily difficult problem. There are no general measures of minimally safe levels of many environmental substances. Much the same thing can be said for risks in product use.

Yet, regulatory agencies of necessity have had to address the question: What is a "reasonable" risk? Edwards defined a reasonable risk:

> as one where a consumer (a) understands by way of adequate warning or by way of public knowledge that a risk is associated with the product; (b) understands the probability of occurrence of an injury; (c) understands the potential severity of such an injury; (d) has been told how to cope with the risk; (e) cannot obtain the same benefits in less risky ways at the same or less cost; (f) would not, if given a choice, pay additional cost to eliminate or reduce the danger; and (g) voluntarily accepts the risk to get the benefits of the product (Edwards, 1975: 19).

These are lofty but useful generalizations. Still, how is a reasonable risk established for a particular product? How does one calculate risks of safety for a large commercial aircraft with its thousands of parts or of the space shuttle?

Most consumers understand the potential hazards of the products they buy, such as electrical appliances. But there are all sorts of hazards in using products. The CPSC has identified some twenty-six dominant variables to be considered in evaluating the potential hazard of a product. How far should CPSC go in protecting consumers? How far, for instance, should CPSC go in protecting consumers from hazards associated with using a lawn mower? What is involved in making the above definition of "reasonable risk" operational?

Each safety device raises its own issues. The principal argument for air bags, for instance, is that people who won't use seat belts will be automatically protected with air bags. The manufacturers say, however, that they will be expensive, will not do anything that seat and shoulder belts will not do if used properly, and have serious problems of reliability. Manufacturers assert that it would be better to devise means to make sure seat and shoulder belts are used. Questions of costs must also be addressed. As more safety features are introduced, the cost of the automobile will rise. Where do costs and safety equate in general and for each safety item?

Aaron Wildavsky (1981) asserts that individual efforts to increase personal safety are not much greater than in the past. This is a debatable point, but he has in mind such activities as smoking, swimming, automobile driving, and so on. What is new, he says, is that the collective urge to risk reduction is much greater than the sum of the individual urges it claims to represent. In other words, each of us would do less for ourselves than we would insist that the government do for us. The place to look for reasons why sensitivity to risk reduction has escalated is not in personal motives, he says, but in possibilities of public policy. He has a point, but the fact is that there are many risks that individuals cannot erase themselves, such as toxic waste dumps or carcinogenic insecticides and government help is needed if they are to be avoided.

The Delaney Clause   The Delaney Clause is a classic illustration of the struggle to deal with the question of product safety. Under the Miller Act of 1954, an amendment to the Food, Drug, and Cosmetic Act of 1938, the FDA is required to determine what degree of residue of a pesticide or herbicide on fruits and vegetables is allowable as nontoxic for humans. The Delaney Cancer Amendment of 1958 to the basic legislation allows the FDA no tolerance whatsoever in prohibiting the addition to food of any substance known to produce cancer in any species, in any dosage, and under any circumstances. On the basis of the amendment, the Secretary of Health, Education, and Welfare ruled that after January 1, 1970, cyclamate-sweetened soft drinks and soft-drink mixes had to be removed from the market. This ruling was made on the basis of research showing that six of twelve rats that were given the equivalent of fifty times maximum recommended lifetime daily consumption developed an "unusual" form of bladder cancer. (For a person to ingest as much cyclamate as the rats, it would be necessary to drink several cases of cyclamate-sweetened soft drinks every day for most of a normal human life span!) Since this decision was made, a number of other products have been removed from the market because of similar tests on laboratory animals.

One FDA decision that was not accepted, however, concerned saccharin, an artificial sweetener. In 1977, the FDA proposed to ban saccharin in processed foods and drinks, while permitting its continued sale to consumers who wanted to add it to food themselves for medical reasons. Soft-drink manufacturers, consumers, and others strongly objected to the ruling, and Congress delayed the ruling for two years. The Congress has extended the moratorium since then.

One can expect continuing controversy over the Delaney Clause. The FDA has primary responsibility for food safety with respect to 2,700 "direct" food additives, thirty-three color additives, and thousands more "indirect" additives that may get into foods through ingredients in packaging materials. The issue therefore is not a negligible one.

This point is confirmed by the fact that the Delaney Clause is an open invitation for ingenious toxicologists to find cause to outlaw even the most innocuous substances. Experimentalists, for example, have created tumors with hundreds of common food substances from eggs to salt. New instruments are capable of detecting traces of substances at the level of one part in a trillion. "The result," says one observer,

is that almost everything anyone eats can be shown to contain carcinogens. If, for instance, a tin can is soldered, and if the solder contains lead, and if lead is a carcinogen in test animals, and if detectable traces of it migrate into the contents of the can—all of which is indisputably the case—why, then, the FDA can be accused of being less than diligent if it doesn't outlaw tin cans (Alexander, 1979: 94).

The FDA has found itself increasingly facing zealots who press for bans on substances that inevitably would cause more deaths than could possibly be saved with a ban. For instance, one physicist calculated that when the FDA was pressed to ban saccharin, the substitution of diet for nondiet soft drinks would increase life expectancy by 100 times more than the cancer risk of saccharin would reduce it.

Secretary of Health and Human Services Margaret Heckler lamented that strict interpretation of the Delaney Clause had put her agency into a scientific straitjacket. She was referring specifically to a proposed ban on the dye used in lipstick. She said that a woman would have to ingest 600 lipsticks a day to consume the quantity of dye that causes cancer. The FDA has sought to avoid banning substances that were in minuscule quantities in foods and that cause no harm (Cooper, 1985). A door was opened for the agency by the U.S. Court of Appeals for the District of Columbia Circuit in *Monsanto Company v. Kennedy* in 1979. The court said that "There is latitude inherent in the statutory scheme to avoid literal application of the statutory definition of 'food additive' in those *de minimus* situations that, in the informed judgment of the Commissioner, clearly present no public health or safety concerns." Thus, under the de minimus legal doctrine, the FDA might know that a substance was present in a food but disregard it. (The de minimus doctrine means that the law does not concern itself with trifles.)

On her last day in office early in 1986, Secretary Heckler ruled that a chemical used to decaffeinate coffee could be allowed under the clause. This chemical, methylene chloride, was found to cause cancer in laboratory tests. In one case, rats were fed doses equal to 12 million cups of decaffeinated coffee a day. (This chemical is also an excellent solvent and flame suppressant and is used widely in paint removers, aerosols, and hair sprays.) In making her decision, the secretary was applying the de minimus doctrine to a new mathematical technique that the agency had been developing for many years called quantitative risk assessment. This technique enables scientists to infer the risks of additives to human beings from the data collected in laboratory tests. The calculation for methylene chloride, for example, showed that if a person drank no more than five five-ounce cups of decaffeinated coffee a day, there would be a one in 1 million chance that the person's risk of developing cancer would increase. This approach is in agreement with many opponents of the Delaney Clause who insist that the cancer impact on a human being is in the dosage of an additive, not the substance itself. Still, however, many public interest groups and consumer activists take the position that no level of risk is acceptable.

The issue is by no means settled. In mid-1985, the House Committee on Government Operations issued a report that concluded that the FDA's failure to ban color additives to foods (on nearly thirty occasions in twenty-five years) was "in clear violation of the requirements of the law." The agency's failure to ban the additives is now being challenged in the U.S. District Court in Washington, D.C. Unless Congress changes the law, and it does not seem inclined to do so, the courts will decide how far, if at all, the Delaney Clause can be stretched.

Manufacturer Liability for Defective Products   Consumers sometimes are injured in using products. The question of liability long has been a matter of concern for the courts, business managers in the chain of manufacture and distribution, and, of course, consumers. Until recent years consumers had difficulties in collecting damages from anyone, especially the original manufacturer. More recently, however, laws and judicial rulings have expanded importantly the liabilities of manufacturers and have permitted consumers to collect greater damages from them. A discussion of some of the milestones in this evolution follows.

Until a few years ago manufacturers were well protected from consumer liability suits. An injured plaintiff proceeded to collect damages through either contract or tort law. Under contract law the disgruntled consumer had to plea that the manufacturer was bound by a warranty (implied or expressed) that the product was reasonably fit to do what it was supposed to do without injury to the user. In the absence of a direct contract between the manufacturer and the consumer, called "privity," the courts would argue that the plaintiff had no case against the producer but had to go to the retailer. If the retailer lost a suit, he or she would sue the wholesaler, and the wholesaler, in turn, the manufacturer. This chain seldom resulted in redress to consumers.

If the injured consumer used tort law, he or she had to argue that a manufacturer was negligent in producing a product. This was very difficult to prove because courts of law found manufacturers not guilty if they exercised reasonable care in producing a product, whether or not it caused injury.

The first major change occurred in 1916 in the case of *MacPherson v. Buick Motor Company*. In this case, General Motors was held liable, irrespective of privity, for injuries resulting from the use of its product. In this case, a wheel was found defective when it fell off while the car was going fifteen miles per hour. In *Randy Knitwear v. American Cyanamid* (1962) the court held that "it is highly unrealistic to limit a purchaser's protection to warranties made directly to him by his immediate seller. The protection he really needs is against the manufacturer whose published representations caused him to make the purchase." As a result of decisions such as these it is now possible for injured consumers to sue and have a good chance of collecting damages from manufacturers when they are injured by a product that is defective.

There also have been important changes in tort law. Now it is held that a manufacturer is liable for unfit products that unreasonably threaten a consumer's personal safety. This is called strict liability under tort and means that liability exists when a wrong is done. The crucial case in this regard was *Henningsen v. Bloomfield Motors, Incorporated* in 1960. In 1962, in *Greenman v. Yuba Power Products, Incorporated*, the doctrine held, and the court said: "A manufacturer is strictly liable in tort when an article he places on the market, knowing that it will be used without inspection, proves to have a defect that causes injury to a human being." Thus, it is not necessary to prove fault on the part of the manufacturer. It is only necessary to show that the product was defective when sold and caused injury.

Manufacturer liability was further expanded in subsequent cases. In *Larson v. General Motors Corporation* in 1968, for example, the court held that it was the responsibility of General Motors to design products to minimize risks of injury in a collision. If the company did not do so it was liable. In *Cronin v. J. B. E. Olson Corporation* (1972), the California Supreme Court said that a product need not be "unreasonably dangerous" to make the manufacturer strictly liable for a defective design. Again, the California court in *Ault v. International Harvester Company* (1975) said that when a manufacturer changed or improved a product line after the manufacture and sale of a product that caused an injury, the changed design was proof of a design defect in the original product. In New York, the court in *Micallef v. Miehle Company* (1976) said that even when an injured plaintiff knew of a danger inherent in using a product, that would not defeat the claim if the manufacturer could reasonably have guarded against the danger in designing the product. In 1983, the New Jersey Supreme Court extended the liability of asbestos makers substantially in the case of *Beshada et al. v. Johns-Manville Products Corporation et al.* In this case, as noted in "Asbestos Litigation 'Bankrupts' Manville," at the end of Chapter 2, the court in effect said that the manufacturers had the responsibility of warning of dangers that were not only undiscovered but were scientifically undiscoverable at the time the products were first introduced for use in the workplace (Leibman, 1983; Malott, 1983).

In 1984, in *Petty v. United States,* the court held a vaccine manufacturer liable because he did not identify specifically the risk of "serum sickness" that beset the plaintiff. Astonishingly, there is no epidemiological evidence that the flu vaccine in question can produce that illness. A dissenting judge commented that "the practical consequence . . . is to impose so stringent a warning requirement as likely to render any future mass inoculation program infeasible, no matter how desirable" (Kitch, 1985). Indeed, this and similar decisions have caused a number of vaccine manufacturers to cease operations (Brody, 1986).

In the eyes of some observers, these recent decisions establish one clear proposition: someone must pay. The James Hunter Machine Co., Incorporated, a maker of textile equipment in Massachusetts, declared bankruptcy in 1983. The basic cause was a liability award for injuries from a machine it sold in 1920! The case was decided against the company even though worker misuse of the equipment and parts from old machines made by other manufacturers grafted on the Hunter machine were involved in the accident. The concept that a producer is responsible for any injury throughout a product's life is new and chilling to manufacturers (Calmes, 1984).

The concept of joint and several liability extends the "deep pocket" concept to product liability. This doctrine states that any party in a suit against a number of defendants can be forced to pay up to 100 percent of the damages. If an injury occurs—for example, the crash of a rented airplane—and it is calculated that the plaintiff is responsible for 25 percent of the accident, the airport authorities for 25 percent, the airplane rental agency for 40 percent, and the aircraft producer 10 percent, the aircraft manufacturer may be responsible for the entire jury award if the others are unable to pay their share. This has actually happened with small aircraft producers, and a number of them have stopped production.

Robert H. Malott, chairman and CEO of FMC Corporation, who headed a Business Roundtable task force on product liability, concluded that lawsuits against corporate defendants with deep pockets "have turned the courts, in effect, into an erratic, back door system of nationalized health and accident insurance, financed by corporate insurance premiums" (Brody, 1986: 24).

Manufacturers' problems have mounted because of substantial increases in both the number of product-liability lawsuits and the escalation in dollar damages awarded plaintiffs by juries. Product-liability suits filed in federal courts alone rose from 1,579 in 1974 to 13,554 in 1985, according to the Administrative Office of U.S. Courts. Creditable numbers for jury dollar awards do not exist, but observations show that amounts in the multi-millions of dollars are increasing.

In an article in the *Harvard Business Review* in 1983, Robert H. Malott said that businesses have no clear guidelines to help them develop products that will be judged safe in courts of law. He urged federal legislation as the only way to develop a balanced product-liability system that would set standards that could be easily and uniformly applied throughout the nation.

There has been response both in the Congress and in state legislatures to such pleas. In 1987, there were a number of bills in the Congress and state legislatures to change tort law. President Reagan endorsed the revamping of laws governing damage claims as a way to reduce soaring liability-insurance costs, and his position was supported by a Domestic Policy Council task force that he set up. According to the task force, a plaintiff would be required to prove only that a product was faulty and caused injury to have a valid claim. But manufacturers would not be liable if they proved that they could not discover and correct the danger during production. Limits would be placed on total noneconomic damages, including pain and suffering and punitive damages. A cap of $100,000 would be about right, said the authors of several bills. Contingency fees for attorneys would be based on some fixed schedule. The task force recommended 25 percent for lawyers' fees, ranging from 25 percent for awards under $100,000 to 10 percent for amounts over $300,000. Defendants would be liable for damages only to the extent of their individual fault. This would eliminate "joint and several liability." The Attorney General would be directed to make recommendations to Congress within a specified period of time, say one year, on legislation to speed up settlements in the court system. The bills before legislative bodies do not have clear sailing. The insurance industry strongly opposes linking tort reform with better control over insurance rates. Attorneys do not look with favor on restrictions of their fees.

Product Quality, Reliability, and Service   There is truth to the observation that only a few years ago it was common practice for many manufacturers to be much less concerned with product quality, reliability, and service than with volume, growth, and profit. There were, of course, many exceptions. Theodore N. Vail, for example, the great leader of the Bell System during its formative years, laid the highest emphasis on these qualities. In *In Search of Excellence,* Peters and Waterman (1982) conclude that a major lesson from the best run companies in the United States is that they lavish attention on their customers' needs for quality, reliability, convenience, service, and so on. For example, Caterpillar Incorporated, the world's largest producer of tractors, earth-moving equipment, and other equipment, says that its policy is and long has been to make products and components that are unequaled in quality or performance by any other producer in the world. McDonalds, the worldwide food chain, for many years has had the theme of "Quality, Service, Cleanliness, and Value," the implementation of which has largely been responsible for the great success of this company. This sort of emphasis is quite typical of the best-run companies in the world.

As pointed out in Chapter 2, markets have changed for our corporations. They are now faced with much more intensive domestic and world competition. This has driven them to stress more than ever before product quality, reliability, and service. A classic illustration is in the automobile industry. Not many years ago, we imported no Japanese-made automobiles. Today Japanese manufacturers have captured one-third of the domestic market. A major, but not the sole, reason has been both public perception and the actuality of higher quality and reliability of Japanese-made cars. Quality and reliability are hard to quantify. To consumers, quality may relate to such product elements as design, styling, luxury, performance, workmanship, durability, component fit, and paint finish. In the manufacturing processes, even well-intentioned efforts may result in some product decision that offends the sense of quality of some customers.

Today, United States automobile producers are underscoring the importance of quality in their products. Ford Motor Company, for instance, has prominently displayed and sought to institutionalize in its operations the slogan "Quality Is Job #1." Our companies also are teaming up with Japanese companies to import cars into this country under U.S. automotive makers names and to produce new automobiles here with Japanese parts and methods.

Although we cannot measure the degree of devotion of our companies to improving products, observation clearly reveals not only a new emphasis of our corporations on making quality products but also the economic and legal imperative of doing so.

Programs to Reduce Product Liability   Larger companies typically implement policies to advance product quality, safety, and reliability. They use the following policies:

1. Make sure that top management gives the program firm and strong support.

2. Create a plan of action that includes clear policies, organizational arrangements, and procedures to be followed throughout the company.

3. Appoint a product-safety manager.

In descending order of importance, the following are the functions assumed by product-safety units in corporations today:

- Evaluating the safety worthiness of new products

- Investigating product safety failures

- Liaison with safety regulatory agencies

- Evaluating and/or preparing product use instructions

- Auditing and testing the safety worthiness of existing products

- Setting safety performance standards for finished products

- Evaluating patterns and trends of safety failures

- Educating company employees in product-safety matters

- Processing product liability claims

- Setting quality control standards for manufactured products

- Setting safety standards for raw materials

- Regulatory record keeping

- Reporting safety defects to regulatory agencies

- Planning safety education programs for product users or other outsiders

- Managing product-recall campaigns (McGuire, 1979).

4. Provide the product-safety manager a staff or the means to acquire the expertise of technically qualified people to deal with safety matters of all products made by the company or contemplated being made.

5. Make sure that managers throughout the company are aware of product-safety issues and their importance in design, performance, use, maintenance, and life span.

6. Make sure that all relevant operating units are responsible for implementing policies laid down by top management and the risk manager.

7. Make sure that all relevant company units are properly involved in the product-safety program. (For example, make sure that all promotion and advertising materials are reviewed carefully to avoid exaggerated claims and obsolete information. Make sure that the legal department reviews carefully the wording of warranties to be certain that they are clear, spell out any time limits, indicate the extent of warranty, and the like. Make sure sales personnel understand all they need to know about product liability.)

8. Make sure insurance coverage is suitable and adequate.

9. Develop and maintain a capacity to measure and monitor safety performance and the implementation throughout the organization of product-safety policies and procedures.

Of overriding significance in developing a program such as the above must be a sensitivity throughout the organization of its importance to the company, its employees, and its customers. There must be an awareness that safety issues interact with and must be dealt with together with other corporate performance issues, such as market performance, pollution control, legal and ethical behavior, quality of working life, public disclosure, and social performance (Steckmest, 1982).

FALSE AND DECEPTIVE ADVERTISING

A wide range of policy issues surrounds the question of what information should be made available to consumers. This area covers not only information about the contents, use, maintenance requirements, and warranties associated with products, but also advertising. Fundamentally, the purpose of advertising is to make the consumer aware of the existence of a product or service, to inform the customer of the characteristics of the product or service, and then to persuade the customer to buy the product or service. Each of these segments of the information-policy area contains important policy questions, but because of space limitations we discuss only false and deceptive advertising. Mark Twain once said: "When in doubt, tell the truth. It will amaze most people, delight your friends, and confuse your enemies." American advertisers apparently have not heard or been convinced by Twain's recommendation.

The FTC has long been the watchdog over advertising and has in recent years spent more and more time on the elusive question of false and deceptive advertising. Many years ago, the FTC had little trouble spotting and stopping false advertising because it was so outrageous. Thus, the agency had little difficulty in stopping such claims as "Coffee can cure malaria." The traditional remedy applied by the FTC when it observed wrongdoing was to issue a cease-and-desist order. If advertisers did not comply with the order, they were subject to a fine of $5,000 each day for each violation. One difficulty with this remedy was that the wrongdoer was often left in possession of a market unlawfully earned. As a result, the FTC began "corrective advertising" in 1971 and has used it since then.

In a well-publicized case, the FTC said that the advertising for Profile Bread was misleading. The Continental Company, a subsidiary of International Telephone and Telegraph, the maker of the bread, was accused of deceptively advertising that its bread was a weight-control product. Actually, the product's only difference was that the slices were half the size of other brands'. The FTC ordered "corrective advertising," which meant that the company had to spend

25 percent of its annual advertising budget to disclaim Profile's weight-control capabilities.

The FTC effort, of course, was to restore the market to the condition before the deceptive advertising. This remedy raised such controversial issues as: How much do consumers really remember? What is the real impact on consumers of advertising? What should corrective advertising be to remedy past "bad" memories? Might not clever corrective advertising provide an opportunity to capitalize on past wrongdoing as seen by the FTC?

In recent years, the FTC has been more and more concerned about the implications of literal statements made in advertising that lead to false impressions among consumers. For instance, from about 1921, Warner-Lambert asserted that its Listerine mouthwash helped to prevent colds and sore throats. The advertising also used such phrases as "for colds," "kills germs by the millions," and "those [colds] we do catch don't seem to last as long" when Listerine mouthwash was used. The FTC said that this falsely implied that the mouthwash "will cure colds," which simply is not so. The FTC issued a cease-and-desist order and demanded that the following statement be inserted in Listerine advertising: "Listerine will not help prevent colds or sore throats or lessen their severity." Warner-Lambert appealed to courts of law on the grounds that the FTC had no such power to order this corrective advertising and that the order violated a right to free speech. The Supreme Court upheld the FTC (*Warner-Lambert v. FTC*, 1977).

It is not difficult to take the literal statements in advertising and hypothesize all sorts of implications from the consumer point of view that may be considered unfair, false, or misleading. For example, the FTC stopped General Foods from showing Euell Gibbons, a well-known naturalist, eating wild plants, on the grounds that children would infer that they could safely eat wild plants. General Foods also was stopped from advertising its Gainesburgers as dog food with "all the milk protein your dog needs," because that falsely implied that dogs have a special need for milk or milk products and that Gainesburgers contained a nutritionally significant amount of milk protein.

In late 1981, James C. Miller III was named chairman of the FTC and announced a policy which narrowed the agency's interest in advertising. In a speech to the Association of National Advertisers, he said that the FTC went too far to "find implied claims that did not fit the common-sense meaning of the words." As a result, companies were asked to substantiate an implied claim that they never intended to make nor were likely to have supporting data for. "A tendency on the part of the commission to impute claims that were never intended or were understood by only a small minority of consumers," he said, "could lead to restrictions on useful information and, thus, harm consumers in general." He also said that if substantiation requirements were heavy, "consumers will pay more in increased costs than they receive by way of more accurate information" (Hickox, 1982).

The recent focus of the FTC, says J. Howard Beales III, acting deputy director of the Bureau of Consumer Protection of the FTC, is to "target our resources on those advertising and marketing practices that create the most serious danger to consumer injury, rather than waste money prosecuting exoteric or trivial cases" (Beales, 1985). He went on to say that the FTC did not want to pursue cases in which market competition could make effective corrections, for example, in which consumers could easily evaluate claims for themselves, or in which competitors would provide needed public information to evaluate competing claims properly. He also said that he favored more self-regulation of industry to relieve the work of the FTC.

This narrower approach by the FTC has led state and local governments to get much more active in deceptive advertising. Prosecutions by states such as New York, Texas, Massachusetts, and California have expanded substantially. New York, for example, challenged Coca-Cola, Seven-Up, and Pepsi about ads that proclaimed "Now with NutraSweet," when the drinks also contained saccharin. The companies changed the ad to "NutraSweet blend."

Not all business people nor state attorneys general are happy with the course of events. Business faces more numerous challenges on narrow issues. Some managers also believe that multiple messages from states create confusing guidelines. States, of course, see a heavier burden thrust upon their scarce resources.

THE BUSINESS RESPONSE TO CONSUMERISM

The response of business to consumerism has been mixed. On the legislative front, particular business interests have fought just about every new piece of legislation designed to protect consumers. When the battle has been lost, various business interests have sought to defang the regulations by pressuring Congress to pass less rigorous laws or to deny funds to enforce them. This resistance is not based on blind rejection of change nor fear of loss of profits. The typical manager believes that consumer legislation is unnecessary or that the benefits of the legislation do not justify the costs. Such views may be wrong, but they are considered rational by a great many managers. But in many instances, companies have worked with government approval to benefit consumers by such programs as standardization of equipment, parts, information given to consumers, advertising practices, repair service, handling complaints, and so on. For example, some 400 private organizations write standards for business. The most productive are the American National Standards Institute, the American Society for Testing and Materials, and the Society of Automotive Engineers (J. Singer, 1980). Standardization created by such organizations is, of course, of direct benefit to consumers. Many companies set forth specific, compelling objectives for dealing with consumers. Such companies also make sure that the objectives are achieved by developing policies, strategies, procedures, and feedback mechanisms so that managers can check on performance.

Many larger companies have created strong offices of consumer affairs or top executive positions responsible to consumer interests. Comprehensive programs for offices of consumer affairs generally include most if not all of the following elements.

First, the office of consumer affairs must be located close to the chief executive of the company. The director of consumer affairs ought to report directly to the top executive or the executive vice president. Furthermore, the director must have the support of top management, and others in the organization must understand through proper communications the existence and strength of that support.

Second, the office of consumer affairs must have access to all relevant information in the company about consumers and must be given authority to create the appropriate mechanisms to get it.

Third, information about consumers must be quantified to the extent feasible. Managers are in a much better position to make tradeoffs in decision making when concrete facts are available than when only "guesstimates" exist about a situation.

Fourth, managers of the consumer affairs office must be skilled in designing effective performance measurement tools with which to evaluate what people throughout the company are doing. It is a cliché that people will do what is inspected, not what is expected. Considerable skill is required in devising means to inspect properly what is being done. Furthermore, rewards should be linked appropriately to performance goals.

Fifth, programs should be developed for ensuring effective communication between the company and consumers to build public confidence and understanding of company policy and practices.

Sixth, programs should be developed for engaging in positive dialogue with responsible leaders of the consumer movement and with legislators and other government officials.

Seventh, plans should be ready for refuting promptly and effectively incorrect assertions or irresponsible actions by consumer activists and for opposing openly legislative proposals that are demonstrably counterproductive.

Finally, there should be contingency plans for determining preferred policies, strategies, and implementation tactics to deal with disastrous tampering of company products in the distribution chain. This is called crisis management. If a company has to recall products as a result of a government directive (for example, for defective functioning in automobiles), prethinking the possibility is desirable.

CONCLUDING OBSERVATIONS

Clearly, there have been enormous improvements in consumer protection during the past two decades. Not only have there been enacted an unusual number of strong laws, but industry has responded more positively than ever before to legitimate consumer interests. Despite this great improvement, there is no reason to believe that consumerism as defined in this chapter will disappear in the near future. The intensity of demand for new federal regulation will continue to wane over a broad front, but it will continue to be strong with respect to specific complaints of consumers. Consumers still have much to complain about, and they will be heard both in corporate offices and in government. This fact is especially true if we include in the concept of consumerism such matters as toxic wastes, acid rain, pesticides, and genetically engineered products, all of which have been discussed in previous chapters. The pressure for these elements is clearly in the direction of more government regulation.

CASE STUDY

RESTRICTIONS ON ALCOHOL AND TOBACCO ADVERTISING

It has been said that a drink is the best thing to take for a headache—provided that it is taken the night before. Of course, the person accepting this advice might want to have a cigarette—defined in an adage as "a fire at one end, a fool at the other, and a bit of tobacco between." In fact, alcoholic beverages and tobacco products have much more in common than being sources of humor.

- Both contain powerful, addicting drugs—alcohol and nicotine, respectively —which are a source of pleasure but may have pernicious effects on bodily organs.

- Both imperil users. There are an estimated 100,000 alcohol-related deaths and 314,000 tobacco-related deaths each year.

- Both sustain massive economic networks that combine producing corporations in oligopolistic industries, advertising agencies, broadcasters, publishers, farmers, labor unions, trade associations, and supportive government officials. Just as alcohol and nicotine spread throughout the body, so the industrial structure that makes and sells them weaves its financial sinews throughout the economy.

- Both are "rite-of-passage" products; that is, their use is associated with adulthood. Of course, use is not confined to adults.

- Both are heavily promoted by slick advertisements that associate their use with images of the good life.

- And both have been the target of campaigns to impose restrictions on their marketing, specifically by curbing all or some kinds of advertisement.

In the two associated cases presented here we examine the ethical, political, legal, and medical issues associated with current campaigns to ban various forms of alcohol and tobacco advertising. We turn first to alcohol advertising.

Part I: Advertising Alcoholic Beverages

Approximately 65 percent of adult Americans drink alcoholic beverages. Since the 1960s, sales of beer, wine, and distilled spirits have soared. Between 1960 and 1986, for example, total consumption of beer, wine, and distilled spirits more than doubled. But in recent years, social trends have changed consumption patterns and dampened consumption. Because of these trends, only 3 percent of the massive increase in alcoholic beverage use in the past twenty-five years came between 1980 and 1986.

The Alcoholic Beverage Industry Faces Adverse Social Trends   The rise of health and fitness values in the population has encouraged moderation in alcohol consumption. Changing tastes have increased demand for diet sodas, decaffeinated coffee, skim milk, and bottled waters at the expense of alcoholic beverages. Total beer and wine consumption has leveled off, rising only 0.1 percent and 5 percent, respectively, between 1984 and 1985 (Standard & Poors, 1986). During the same period, total consumption of distilled spirits dropped about 2 percent, with most of the decline in whiskies, which are perceived by the public as "heavy." "White" goods (gin, rum, vodka, and tequila) are perceived as a "lighter" because of their appearance. Their market share relative to whisky has steadily increased since 1970.

A second perturbation in the industry environment is a nationwide movement attacking the evils of liquor. Industry was overpowered by a similar movement in 1919, when temperance groups secured ratification of the Eighteenth Amendment, which committed the federal government to enforce prohibition of liquor sales. (Prohibition, of course, failed, and in 1933 the Twenty-first Amendment ended the sales ban and returned control of liquor sales to state governments.) Over time, the states adopted a variety of sales and advertising controls, but most were permissive. Industry faces another gathering political storm in a new temperance movement composed of twenty to twenty-five prominent citizens' groups such as Mothers Against Drunk Driving, the National PTO, the National Council on Alcoholism, and the United Methodist Church, which came together early in the 1980s with the purpose of reducing liquor consumption. At the state level, this coalition has lobbied for stiffer drunk-driving penalties, pressured bar owners to end "happy hours" when liquor is sold at reduced prices, and encouraged host-responsibility lawsuits. At the federal level, the anti-alcohol forces won a milestone victory with passage of the Minimum Drinking Age Act of 1984, which requires states to raise their minimum drinking age to twenty-one or forfeit $530 million in federal highway funds. This halted the movement in the states to lower minimum drinking ages to eighteen, a movement which began after the ratification of the Twenty-sixth Amendment in 1971 to set the voting age at eighteen. Anti-alcohol groups disapprove of eighteen-year drinking ages based on studies showing fewer fatal driving accidents in states with twenty-one-year drinking ages.

The sparkplug of the temperance crusade is a Washington, D.C., group known as the Center for Science in the Public Interest and its executive director,

Michael Jacobson. In 1982, Jacobson wrote a letter on behalf of eighteen citizen's groups to major beer, wine, and liquor companies asking them to voluntarily reform their marketing methods, but he received no response. The next year, joined by twenty-five groups, he unsuccessfully petitioned the Federal Trade Commission to stop deceptive advertising practices by these companies. In 1983, Jacobson and two co-authors published a book entitled *The Booze Merchants*, which was an influential attack on alcohol-marketing methods. In 1984, he formed a coalition of hundreds of state and local groups in a petition campaign named Project SMART (Stop Marketing Alcohol on Radio and Television). By 1985, over 700,000 names had been collected on this petition calling for banning beer and wine ads on television and radio (or requiring equal time for health messages). Distilled spirits, of course, never have been advertised on the broadcast media due to voluntary restraint by producers.

The Case Against Beer and Wine Advertising on Television and Radio
According to the anti-alcohol groups, there are a number of reasons that beer and wine advertisements should be banned from the airwaves.

First, ads increase consumption. Beer and wine companies would not spend $900 million a year without the expectation of some return. The companies argue that advertising is for market share and is primarily designed to promote brand switching. Yet beer and wine companies perceive themselves to be in competition with soft drinks and other beverages and seek to promote drinking alcoholic beverages as an alternative to other refreshments. Lite beer commercials such as Miller's popular "Tastes Great—Less Filling" segments attempt to reposition beer as a competitor to soft drinks and educate consumers to believe that lite beers are low-calorie, light drinks that can be consumed more frequently and on more occasions than regular beer.

Second, the ads influence children and teenagers to start drinking because they are ubiquitous, frequently feature sports stars or celebrities admired by those under age twenty-one, and are made with models or actors who are young looking. The ads also depict drinking as a route to social acceptance by peers and a necessary adjunct to having fun at parties. Ads such as Schlitz's commercials for Schlitz Malt Liquor featuring Kool and the Gang use rock music to attract a youthful target audience.

Third, many ads target heavy drinkers and encourage increased consumption. An example is the Michelob beer campaign based on the slogan, "Put a little weekend in your week." This ad and others like it suggest drinking all through the week, not just on weekends.

Fourth, sophisticated lifestyle advertising attempts to play on the viewer's emotional needs for popularity, success, romance, or having fun and puts beer and wine products in the position of fulfilling these needs. Young drinkers particularly are inclined to emulate. Therefore, ad agencies have associated alcoholic beverages with glamorous activities such as hang gliding, mountain climbing, and riding a roller coaster. Sexual images are a staple in beer and wine ads, which frequently depict attractive models in suggestive situations or imply sexuality with body language, facial expressions, or camera angles.

(Left) Alcoholic beverage advertising sometimes associates drinking with romantic attraction and fitting in with others—important concerns for teenagers and young adults. *(Right)* This ad associates sexuality with the consumption of alcohol. Copyright 1983, Center for Science in the Public Interest.

Finally, although individual commercials often have little impact, the cumulative mass of alcoholic beverage ads is a tremendous force that teaches those who watch them from childhood that drinking is all right and is associated with life's high notes.

All forms of alcohol advertising that demonstrate these marketing approaches are anathema to the anti-alcohol forces. They decry college marketing programs in which brewers advertise in student newspapers or magazines such as *Rolling Stone* and the *National Lampoon,* which obviously cater to youthful audiences, and they decry ads in publications such as *Ms.,* which recruit more women beer drinkers. But TV and radio ads are the most offensive because they can be more compelling and forceful than print ads, they come over air waves regulated for use in the public interest, and they reach teenagers and children as they enter homes along with family and sports programs.

Wine and Beer Advertisers Defend Their Commercials   Wine and beer manufacturers have defended their actions. First, they argue that advertising is not the source of alcohol abuse in society. Alcoholism is a complex disease that is caused by personality, family, genetic, and physiological factors rather than by listening to commercials. Most people who drink are not harmed. And the preponderance of research shows that underage drinking is largely the result of peer pressure and lax parental supervision. The main result of an ad ban would be to deprive drinkers of truthful, relevant information without reducing alcohol abuse by a minority of alcoholics, who would be blithely unaffected.

Ad restrictions also would deprive the industry of an important competitive weapon. Both the beer and wine industries have come to be dominated by a small number of large producers who use nationwide broadcast advertising as a critical weapon in the war for market share. Beer is a mature product, and per capita consumption has been in decline despite modest total increases in barrels sold in the 1980s. The result is that brewers compete in internecine warfare for existing market share. Using national advertising campaigns as primary weapons, the seven largest brewers increased their combined share of the domestic market from 48 percent in 1970 to 96 percent in 1985 (Standard & Poors, 1986). Small local and regional brewers have been unable to hold onto their markets because they cannot match the advertising expenditures of giants like Anheuser-Busch, which controls 38 percent of the domestic market. Under these conditions, the dominant brewing companies use their political contributions, lobbying skills, and influence over the broadcasting, publishing, and advertising industries to avoid an advertising ban and protect their competitive advantage over weaker competitors.

Second, the "instant entrepreneurs in social engineering," as the anti-alcohol groups were referred to by a manager at Miller Brewing Co., assume that the public is too stupid to make correct decisions (A. Easton, 1985a). The proposal to restrict advertising is condescending. People are not fooled by the association of alcohol consumption with attractive imagery. Would the critics expect brewers and vintners to associate their products with garbage dumps, taxation, or traffic congestion? An advertising ban would wrongly imply to millions of drinkers that they were doing something wrong by having a beer or a glass of wine.

Third, the beer and wine industries have adopted voluntary codes of advertising to police their own behavior. Although compliance is not total, the codes have moved ad agencies away from the most crass commercials. For instance, the first of twenty guidelines set forth by the United States Brewers Association, reads: "Beer advertisements should neither suggest nor encourage overindulgence." Others prohibit such crimes as depicting driving after drinking or encouraging underage drinking. The guidelines of the Wine Institute prohibit, among other things, any suggestion that excessive drinking or loss of control is amusing, the use of "models and personalities in advertisements who appear to be under twenty-five years of age," or the use of "professional sports celebrities, past or present." In addition, the brewers and vintners sponsor public service announcements and alcohol-abuse prevention programs and lectures. They recognize that advertising is a right and that it entails the corresponding duty of properly informing the public of the dangers of alcohol abuse. Through these programs, the industry has stepped up to accept this responsibility. In 1984, for example, Miller Brewing Co. sponsored over 30,000 lectures on alcohol awareness, and Anheuser-Busch was the major corporate sponsor of Students Against Driving Drunk, a national program for high school and college students.

Fourth, broadcasters have argued that the loss of revenues from beer and wine ads would bring about a reduction in services for viewers. These ads are 4 percent of television ad revenue, 12 percent of radio, and 18 percent of minority-owned radio stations. One area of programming likely to suffer is sports programming, where beer and wine ads are clustered.

As far as counteradvertising is concerned, the alcohol producers argue that the vast majority of consumers are not harmed by their commercials and are adequately informed of the dangers of alcohol. Alan G. Easton, a spokesman for Miller Brewing Co., testified in congressional hearings in 1985 that:

> Counteradvertising, as in the case of an outright prohibition of alcohol beverage advertising, represents an attempt to impose harsh punishment on the basis of allegations that simply cannot be supported by evidence. The hidden agenda of such proposals is obvious: to make broadcast advertising for beer and wine so expensive to both advertisers and broadcasters as to force a substantial portion of the commercials off the air. The proposal represents an insidious, backdoor version of a ban. It constitutes an unwarranted form of censorship (A. Easton, 1985b: 625).

The Prospects of an Advertising Ban So far, no legislation has been introduced in Congress to ban advertising of beer and wine on television and radio. But in 1985, both the House and Senate held hearings on the subject in response to pressure from anti-alcohol groups. The House did consider a bill to give public service announcements equal time with alcoholic beverages advertising but did not act on it. In 1986 a Senate bill was introduced to require five rotating health warning labels on beer, wine, and hard liquor, as such: "The consumption of this product, which contains alcohol, can increase the risk of developing hypertension, liver disease, and cancer." These and other bills in the future will keep the issue of advertising restrictions simmering.

Part II: Advertising Tobacco Products

About 55 million Americans smoke, and another 12 million use smokeless tobacco products. But the number of smokers is steadily declining as 1 million a year quit and another 314,000 die of diseases thought to be smoking-related. Despite heavy advertising, the tobacco companies have not been successful in recruiting enough new smokers to replace those departing the ranks.

The Tobacco Industry's Grim Marketing Environment In early America, smoking was largely a southern custom. During the Civil War, however, Union troops were exposed to the habit in occupied southern territory and smoked tobacco to fight boredom and stress. Upon returning home after the war, these new smokers created a national demand for the smoking tobacco produced in

North Carolina and other southern states. Smoking never enjoyed unanimous approval in society, Mark Twain, for example, wrote of it as a "filthy habit." But for the century following the Civil War, it was widely accepted, and in the early 1960s, the majority of American men smoked (and 34 percent of women). In 1964, however, the Surgeon General of the United States released an analysis of medical research that warned of a strong association between cigarette smoking and lung cancer (U.S. Department of Health, Education, and Welfare, 1964). This report was a decisive blow to the industry, putting it on the defensive politically and ending the growth of demand for its product.

The environment for marketing tobacco products grew increasingly unfavorable. In 1965, Congress acted to require health warnings on cigarette packages and, in 1971, prohibited cigarette ads on radio and television. Over the next decade, the health warnings on cigarette packages were strengthened, and medical research on the ill-effects of smoking accumulated. In the mid-1980s, the cigarette companies again were besieged. In 1985, Congress acted to require a rotating series of stronger warning labels on snuff and banned snuff advertising on television and radio. The Surgeon General called for a "smoke-free society by the year 2000," the armed services restricted smoking, and the Government Services Administration restricted smoking in government office buildings. In a 1985 Gallup poll, 62 percent of tobacco users and 85 percent of abstainers disapproved of smoking in the presence of others (Toufexis, 1986).

By 1986, 36 percent of corporations had some kind of smoking restrictions in their offices (Hutchings, 1986). Late in the year, a special review of the medical literature by a select committee of the National Academy of Sciences concluded that "passive smoking," or the exposure of nonsmokers to tobacco smoke, increased the risk of lung cancer in nonsmokers by as much as 30 percent and heightened risks for other ailments. This report was a blow to the industry because it fueled the increasing militancy of nonsmokers.

An ominous note in the industry's environment is more than 240 lawsuits by consumers who claim injury to their health from tobacco products. Tobacco firms successfully deflected a series of such suits in the 1950s and 1960s, but the new litigation, although utilizing a variety of tort theories, takes advantage of changes in products liability law, that make it easier to sue manufacturers. Attorneys are picking "ideal" plaintiffs—people who started smoking at an early age, tried to quit but could not, smoked the same brand of cigarette consistently, and died of a type of cancer closely associated with smoking.

The tobacco manufacturers have successfully defended themselves in every case decided to date, however, by using two main lines of defense. First, they have emphasized ambiguities in the scientific research that links smoking with cancer, convincing juries that this research does not show smoking to be an absolute cause of cancer. Second, they have argued that smokers have adequate notice of the health dangers of smoking from warning labels on cigarette packs and have been well educated by the flood of information about smoking in the media. Therefore, they contend that smokers voluntarily accept the risks of smoking. The use of these two defensive arguments is awkward. It puts the companies in the position of arguing that smoking is not dangerous while simultaneously asserting that smokers are adequately warned that it is dangerous *(Harvard Law Review,* 1986). If the companies lose even one case, a flood of new ones will be brought by the estates of the 314,000 smokers who die annually.

Competition in the Tobacco Industry   In this climate, per capita consumption of all forms of tobacco has steadily declined, dropping 33 percent between 1976 and 1986 (Standard & Poors, 1986: F35). Like alcoholic beverage markets, markets for tobacco products are mature. Demand for low tar and nicotine products, which bouyed tobacco sales for many years, recently has leveled off. Due to increases in the federal excise tax, which have raised the average price of a pack of cigarettes over $1, the industry abandoned its one-tier pricing structure, and several manufacturers introduced lower priced "generic" cigarettes and discount-priced packages of twenty-five cigarettes. These low-price lines, however, showed no potential for increasing overall consumption.

Seven large tobacco manufacturers dominate the domestic cigarette market. In an environment of shrinking consumption and growing consumer disfavor, the companies rely heavily on advertising to war with each other over market share. Advertising is also essential for launching new national brands such as Century and Players Lights 25s, two versions of the new twenty-five-packs which fit into the discount segment of the market.

Tobacco company marketers are thought to be exceptionally resourceful because of the difficulty of their task, and they have created sophisticated, state-of-the-art sales campaigns. The companies sponsor sporting events and art exhibits. They fill magazines, newspapers, and billboards with well-researched appeals to the multiple motivations of smokers. They are adept at targeting population groups with high percentages of smokers, such as blacks, Hispanics, and blue-collar workers. It surprises no one that antismoking forces have attacked tobacco ads with fury.

The Battle over Tobacco Advertising   In the mid-1980s, the attack on tobacco focused on proposals to ban advertising. In December 1985, the American Medical Association's House of Delegates voted nearly unanimously to advocate a ban on all advertising and promotion of tobacco. In 1986, Congress passed a law banning ads for smokeless tobacco products from radio and television. Later that year, Representative Mike Synar, a Democrat from Oklahoma, introduced a bill in the House of Representatives that would impose a ban on all advertising of tobacco products in any medium and also prohibit sponsorship of athletic events and product giveaways. The debate over this bill pitted cigarette companies and their allies, the magazine and newspaper publishers, against a committed coalition of health, religious, civic, and consumer organizations.

Despite the unpopularity of tobacco products, the tobacco coalition is formidable. Although it makes principled arguments about preserving free speech and the "right to choose," its primary aim is the preservation of economic benefits. The tobacco companies have 350,000 employees and provide an indirect livelihood for another 1.5 million, including tobacco farmers, distributors and retailers, matchbook makers, and perhaps grave diggers. Each year the companies spend approximately $3 billion in advertising (roughly three times alcoholic beverage advertising), and in 1985 they paid $8.9 billion in taxes. In addition, the export of tobacco and tobacco products has created a trade surplus during a period of overall foreign trade deficit. Observers feel that this is a major reason that the Reagan administration has not favored legislation restricting advertising.

The Case against Tobacco Advertising   The attack on cigarette advertising is much like that on alcoholic beverage advertising. For one thing, say the critics, smoking is harmful to consumers, and advertising increases consumption of tobacco products. Since the early 1960s, epidemiological studies have shown relations between smoking and illnesses including cancer, heart disease, stroke, emphysema, immune deficiencies, and pregnancy disorders. Tobacco smoke contains carcinogens and carbon monoxide and is dangerous to bystanders, who inhale it along with the smoker. Other dangers exist also, including the fires that result from careless smoking. Advertising that depicts smoking as an attractive, worthwhile pastime encourages people to assume major health risks.

Second, tobacco ads are designed to recruit young smokers. It is well known that about 75 percent of smokers adopt the habit before the age of twenty-one. The industry has a voluntary code of advertising principles requiring that advertising not "appear in publications directed primarily to those under twenty-one years of age," and that models in cigarette ads shall not "appear to be under twenty-five years of age," yet cigarette advertising unquestionably shows young-looking models. And there are frequent ads in youth-oriented magazines such as *Hot Rod, Rolling Stone,* and *National Lampoon.* As one critic notes, "That 14-year-old models aren't used in these ads is irrelevant; eighth graders don't smoke cigarettes in order to look like eighth graders" (Owen, 1985: 53).

Although industry has tried to deny that it targets young smokers, in 1975 the FTC subpoenaed marketing documents from the major tobacco companies and, although most were circumspect in what they sent, Brown & Williamson Tobacco Corp., perhaps mistakenly, sent a summary of marketing research for a campaign to attract "young starters" to its Viceroy brand. The report read in part:

> Thus, an attempt to reach young smokers, starters, should be based, among others, on the following major parameters:
>
> ■ Present the cigarette as one of a few initiations into the adult world.
>
> ■ Present the cigarette as part of the illicit pleasure category of products and activities.

■ In your ads create a situation taken from the day-to-day life of the young smoker but in an elegant manner have this situation touch on the basic symbols of the growing-up, maturity process.

■ To the best of your ability (considering some legal constraints) relate the cigarette to "pot," wine, beer, sex, etc.

■ *Don't* communicate health or health-related points (emphasis in original) (Taylor, 1985: 201).

A third and related concern of the critics is that ads concocted with this type of marketing research are redolent with deception. Tobacco ads, like beer and wine ads, employ cleverly constructed "lifestyle" themes. These associate a contemptible product with success, adventure, romance, status, fun, and masculinity or femininity. The depiction of the quintessentially macho Marlboro cowboy or the slightly rebellious, sassy, and liberated Virginia Slims woman is geared to satisfying strong emotional needs in targeted personality types. Cigarettes as physical objects are essentially the same from brand to brand (despite allusions to "flavor" in the ads), but advertising endows them with potent psychological magic. Thus an awkward male adolescent—or a middle-aged man—may smoke cigarettes to seek the aura of strength, male sensuality, and peer acceptance exemplified by the Camel man. The ads, in addition, imply that healthy, happy

This ad associates cigarette smoking with masculinity, adulthood, athletic activity, and peer-group acceptance.   Random House photo by Stacey Pleasant.

people in top condition smoke cigarettes, thereby undermining the health warning labels on packages and advertisements.

Tobacco Companies Defend Their Ads   The battle is joined by cigarette manufacturers. First, they argue that although they are extremely concerned about possible adverse health effects from smoking, the evidence to date does not prove that smoking causes cancer and other diseases. Their point is a precise, technical one about the nature of proof in scientific inquiry. Although epidemiological studies show a *relation* between smoking and lung cancer, they do not prove that smoking was the *cause* of that lung cancer. Rather, they simply show an association between the two. The exact mechanism of cancer causation is not yet definitively explained by science. Until it is, the tobacco companies argue that other factors known to be associated with cancer, including everything from genes to smog, may have initiated the disease process in smokers.

The literature on the health effects of smoking is vast. There are thousands of epidemiological, clinical, and laboratory studies. Inevitably there is bickering about methodology and the validity of various findings, as in every scientific field. Perhaps inevitably, some studies show no relation between smoking and cancer. For example, in a series of Scandinavian studies of identical twins, one of whom smoked and the other not, the smokers did not differ from the nonsmokers in the incidence of any illnesses, including lung cancer (Eysenck, 1983). The evidence on the addictive nature of tobacco use is also ambiguous, say the tobacco companies.

In response to the charge that their marketing is designed to snare new, young smokers, the tobacco companies argue that this is not so. Although twelve states have no minimum age for tobacco sales and fourteen set the age lower than eighteen, the companies say that they do not target this group in marketing efforts. Whatever indirect impact tobacco ads have on children, there is validity in this claim because no ads relating to unique life experiences such as first dates or little league games appear. Research indicates that advertising ranks low among the factors leading teenagers to initiate smoking. For example, in studies of college students who smoked or used smokeless tobacco, the influence of advertising ranked ninth and eighth respectively out of ten factors leading to the decision to initiate tobacco use (Foreyt, 1985). In these and other studies, the most important factors were peer pressure, tobacco use by parents and siblings, and personality variables such as rebelliousness and extroversion. Although advertising may create an environment in which smoking is regarded as acceptable, it is designed to encourage brand switching and provide information to consumers about new products.

Tobacco companies also reject the argument that their advertising plays unfairly on emotional needs. Numerous surveys indicate that 90 percent or more of both teenagers and adults believe that cigarette smoking is harmful to health (Gallup, 1981). Thus, they freely choose risk exposure. Cigarettes are not marketed differently from other products, and the ads are manipulative only in the sense that any advertising material tries to incorporate positive associations from life experience into product presentation. Millions see tobacco ads daily but do not become smokers. No statistics or research indicate that consumers are tricked by tobacco advertising, so the burden of proof still rests with those who would ban it. Many factors aside from advertising influence buying decisions, including previous experience with the product, opinions of relatives and friends, information from other sources such as churches, the government, and schools, and sales presentations. There also exists widespread skepticism toward ad content. In short, advertising is not a disquieting, powerful determiner of behavior, but it does play an important, if limited, role in providing information for consumers.

Finally, the tobacco companies point out that there is little hard evidence that advertising increases consumption of tobacco or that its elimination would result in declining consumption. The removal of cigarette ads from the broadcast media in 1971 was followed by years of increased consumption. Studies of European countries such as Sweden and Norway, where restrictions have been placed on advertising, show that advertising restraint generally is not followed by lowered consumption (International Advertising Association, 1983). The removal of ads would only harm consumers by depriving industry of a competitive weapon and lessening the amount of information available about cigarette products.

Alcohol and Tobacco Advertising Bans: Are They Constitutional?

Proposals for banning beer, wine, and tobacco product advertisements raise important constitutional issues. The First Amendment to the Constitution protects speech from restrictions imposed by the government, but the courts have distinguished pure speech from commercial speech. The former is defined as speech in the broad marketplace of ideas, encompassing political, scientific, and artistic expression, and is closely protected. The latter refers to advertisements and other speech designed to stimulate business transactions and has received less protection. In both areas of speech, however, the general principle adopted by the courts to test restrictions is that the right of speech must be balanced against society's need to maintain the general welfare. The right of free speech is assumed to be a fundamental barrier against the growth of tyranny and is not tampered with or restricted lightly. So the courts ordinarily do not permit censorship of speech unless it poses a grave threat to the public welfare, as it would for example, if a speaker posed the threat of imminent violence or a writer penned highly classified military secrets in time of war.

The Federal Trade Commission (FTC), under authority of the Federal Trade Commission Act, has the power to prohibit advertising it determines to be either "deceptive" or "unfair." In 1985 it turned down a petition by Project SMART to prohibit alcoholic beverage ads based on this power and stated that it "was unlikely to be able to draw an adequate line between those alcoholic beverage advertisements that truthfully provide information that help to sell this lawful product, and those ads that may contribute to the problems of alcohol misuse" (FTC, 1985: 50).

The FTC may not interfere with noncommercial speech, however, a point underscored by its abortive attempt to prohibit R. J. Reynolds from running an ad entitled "Of Cigarettes and Science" in national magazines. The ad argued that a recent experiment by the National Institutes of Health had cast doubt on the link between smoking and heart disease. In 1986, an administrative law judge overturned the FTC's ruling because the R. J. Reynolds ad was not a product advertisement but rather an editorial message about a public issue. Judge Montgomery K. Hyun ruled that the FTC prohibition would be "likely to produce the unwanted effect of chilling free expression of opinions on public issues of concern to business firms which enjoy the full protection of the First Amendment with respect to noncommercial speech" (*R. J. Reynolds v. FTC*, 1986).

With respect to commercial speech, however, various restrictions have been upheld. For example, prescription drugs cannot be advertised to the general public, advertisements for securities offerings may appear only in the austere format of a legal notice, and of course, cigarette and snuff advertising has been banned from television and radio. These are not total bans, of course, only restrictions. A ban on alcoholic beverage ads on TV and radio would be only a restriction, because liquor still could be advertised in other media. But the tobacco advertising bill introduced into the House of Representatives by Representative Synar in 1986 would be a total ban, extending from television commercials to matchbook covers. A total suppression of commercial speech for a legal product raises much concern. Would the courts approve it?

In recent years, the Supreme Court has heard a number of cases on commercial speech. In a 1976 case, *Virginia Pharmacy Board v. Virginia Citizens Consumer Council,* the Court invalidated a state law prohibiting pharmacists from advertising the prices of prescription drugs. The purpose of the law had been to avoid "unprofessional" conduct among pharmacists, but the Court held that the strong interest of society in the free flow of information about products outweighed the dangers inherent in the questionable assumption that advertising promoted unprofessional behavior among pharmacists. In 1977, in *Bates v. Arizona State Bar*, the Court similarly struck down as unnecessarily restricting a law banning ads by lawyers. Then, in the landmark case of *Central Hudson Gas & Electric Corp. v. Public Service Commission* in 1980, the Supreme Court struck down a New York regulation banning advertisements by electric utilities, a law that was intended to further that state's policy of conserving energy. In this case, the Court developed its current theory of commercial speech as Justice Powell, writing for the majority, set forth a four-pronged analysis for determining the constitutionality of any restriction on commercial speech.

First, the advertisement in question should promote a lawful product or activity and must be accurate. If an ad is misleading or suggests illegal activity, it does not merit protection. Second, the government interest in restricting the particular commercial speech must be substantial, not trivial or unimportant. Third, the regulation or advertising restriction clearly must further the interest of the government. In other words, it should definitely help the government reach a public-policy goal. Fourth, the suppression of commercial speech must not be more extensive than is necessary to achieve the government's purpose.

In 1986, proponents of an advertising ban were given heart by the Court's decision in *Posadas de Puerto Rico Associates v. Tourism Company of Puerto Rico*, in which the Puerto Rican government permitted gambling but prohibited casinos from advertising to Puerto Rican residents. The Games of Chance Act of 1948 legalized gambling to increase tourism in Puerto Rico. Puerto Ricans were permitted to gamble in the casinos. But although gambling could be advertised outside Puerto Rico and Puerto Ricans were permitted to enter casinos and gamble, the act banned advertising in Puerto Rico because of the belief of that territory's legislators that:

> excessive casino gambling among local residents . . . would produce serious harmful effects on the health, safety and welfare of the Puerto Rican citizens, such as the disruption of moral and cultural patterns, the increase in local crime, the fostering of prostitution, the development of corruption, and the infiltration of organized crime (*Posadas de Puerto Rico,* 54 LW 4960).

Justice Rehnquist delivered the opinion of the Court in which he applied the four-pronged test set forth in the *Central Hudson* case and came to the conclusion that the ban on casino ads passed muster in each of the four areas. In a 5–4 opinion, the Court upheld this advertising ban, leading observers to believe that the justices might uphold a similar ban against alcoholic beverage and tobacco products advertising. After the decision, Senator Strom Thurmond (Republican-South Carolina) announced that he would support a ban on both alcohol and tobacco advertising—an unpopular stance among many of his constituents in tobacco country.

Conclusion

While advertising restrictions are debated, sales of both hard liquor and tobacco products continue to drop. Both industries are spending less to promote their products, although wine and beer sales remain stable, and their makers have continued heavy promotional expenditures. Among these products, tobacco is most vilified and the best candidate for government action restricting advertising. Already, over thirty magazines no longer accept tobacco advertising, including *Good Housekeeping, National Geographic,* and *Reader's Digest.* The debate in Congress and society is complex, involving medical, religious, and ethical aspects. But in the end, two factors will be most important in resolving the issue of advertising restriction. The first is the relative political strength of the economic interests versus the political strength of reform groups. The second is the ultimate determination of the constitutionality of any restrictions on commercial speech that may be enacted.

Questions

1. Are certain beer, wine, or tobacco ads misleading? What examples can you give? What, specifically, is misleading?
2. Do alcoholic beverage and tobacco companies that fight for their right to advertise also generally fulfill their corresponding ethical duty to be informative and honest?
3. Would a ban on broadcast advertising for beer and wine products be constitutional? Apply the four-pronged test set forth by the Supreme Court in the *Central Hudson* case to reach a conclusion.
4. Would a total ban on tobacco ads pass a similar test of constitutionality?
5. What other products are typically advertised in exaggerated, misleading, or manipulative ways? Would advertising restrictions be appropriate for them? What kind of restrictions?

CHAPTER **16** _____

THE CHANGING INTERNAL FACE OF ORGANIZATIONAL LIFE

 In the late 1970s, AT&T experienced growing competition from some 200 cut-rate long distance telephone companies and a like number of telephone equipment manufacturers. Simultaneously, intellectual and political forces in favor of deregulation led to the break-up of the venerable "Ma Bell" into nine separate corporations on January 1, 1984.

The divestiture was upsetting for employees. A survey of AT&T workers revealed these feelings:

> [I was] angry, sad, a little scared about my future. Divestiture was a triumph of lawyers, bureaucrats, and financial manipulators over producers and servers.

> I felt like I had gone through a divorce that neither my wife nor my children wanted. It was forced upon us by some very powerful outside forces, and I could not control the outcome. It was like waking up in familiar surroundings (your home) but your family and all that you held dear was missing.

> My feelings were ambivalent. . . . I was numb but I neither rejoiced nor shed a tear.

One of the most wrenching aspects of the change for employees was the necessary alteration of AT&T's corporate culture. The old culture, to which employees were accustomed, was highly paternalistic. It incorporated a deep sense of employees as family. People anticipated lifetime careers, and promotion was from within company ranks. A primary focus of the Bell culture was to provide high-quality, affordable customer service. Authority was centralized, and Bell employees had a high "level consciousness," that is, awareness of the status hierarchy of six management ranks. Bell managers focused their planning on regulatory matters, which dominated the competitive environment.

After the break-up, the company was far less regulated; most of its markets were fully competitive. It had to develop new products, sell them, and take unaccustomed risks to survive. Circumstances led to the evolution of a new culture at AT&T. The company decided to retain the overriding goal of customer service but made many changes in the old ways. Reverence for the management hierarchy ended with the restructuring of AT&T into separate profit centers with distinct management groups. There has been a new emphasis on marketing and product innovation as AT&T managers have adopted a competitive frame of mind in place of the old focus on regulatory matters. Chairman Charles L. Brown even informed employees that it was no longer appropriate to refer to an aggressive firm with high-technology communication products as "Ma Bell." And to help with the transition to new values, AT&T used training, publications, policy statements, advertising, and award programs.

Similar cultural odysseys have occurred in the "Baby Bells" created by divestiture. It has been a difficult period for the approximately 1 million employees in these companies, but the AT&T transition represents, in microcosm, the tremendous impact of environmental forces on the American workplace today and the ways in which managements increasingly are conscious of the need to attune corporate cultures and human resource planning to competitive conditions. In this chapter we discuss these basic issues at greater length.

THE NATURE AND MEANING OF WORK

Our definition of work is: "Work is a continuous activity that is designed to produce something of value for other people." At an elemental level, work is essential. Humans must manipulate their environment to live. The underlying moral basis of work is that each person is a burden on society and should contribute a fair share of the expenditure of human energy necessary for survival.

Attitudes toward Work

The human outlook toward work is marvelously complex. The concept of work has been different in other societies past and present from what it is in the United States today. In pre-Christian Greece and Rome work—in the sense of hard physical labor—was associated with degradation and slavery. In medieval days, and among deeply religious people thereafter, work and hard labor were viewed as service to God and the road to salvation.

In communist countries, work has political overtones. In the People's Republic of China, North Korea, Cuba, and Russia constitutions specifically require citizens to work as a duty to the state. In Article 60 of the 1977 Soviet Constitution, for example, it is stipulated that "labor in one's chosen field of socially useful activity and observance of labor discipline is the duty and a matter of honor for every Soviet citizen who is able to work." In Article 13 it is stated that "socially useful work and its results shall determine a citizen's status in society."

These injunctions are enforced in Russia by "parasite laws" that generally prohibit earning a living with income from interest and capital gains. The laws invoke a penalty of forced relocation and property confiscation if a person is caught speculating for a living.

Great changes have taken place in the meaning of work in the United States. Work was a grim necessity for survival in the preindustrial colonial period, but overtones of religious obligation softened the long and hard labor. In the pre–Civil War period, economic opportunities opened up (except, of course, for those in slavery), and farmers found craft work and self-employment in cities. The opportunities to work and to accumulate wealth were important incentives for the immigrants flowing into the United States. During the latter part of the nineteenth century, large companies tied people pitilessly to machines for long hours at low wages, and Horatio Alger possibilities of wealth for the ordinary person disappeared in factory tedium and grime. In the early twentieth century, under the influence of Frederick Taylor, managers sought to increase worker productivity by careful measurement of work activities and machine-to-worker relationships. Mass production brought highly specialized but routine tasks. Then, in reaction to this treatment of workers as machines, a school of thought developed that applied psychology to workers and encouraged employers to increase their productivity by nurturing their social needs. During World War II, the driving motive behind work became patriotism. From the end of the war through the 1950s, work was seen by Americans mainly as a source of status and income.

In the morning when thou risest unwillingly, let this thought be present—I am rising to the work of a human being. Why then am I dissatisfied if I am going to do the things for which I exist and for which I was brought into the world? Or have I been made for this, to lie in the bedclothes and keep myself warm? But this is more pleasant. Dost thou exist then to take thy pleasure and not at all for action or exertion? Dost thou not see the little plants, the little birds, the ants, the spiders, the bees working together to put in order their several parts of the universe? And art thou unwilling to do the work of a human being, and dost thou not make haste to do that which is according to thy nature?

Marcus Aurelius, (circa A.D. 174–180) *Meditations.*

But by the 1970s, work came increasingly to be seen as a means of direct self-fulfillment. In a 1983 survey of 1,300 middle managers, for example, salary and regular promotions ranked seventh and eighth on a list of ten indicators of career success, behind self-fulfillment measures such as "achievement of personal life goals" and having the "opportunity and means for achieving a fulfilling, happy home and social life" (Breen, 1983: 16). Today, the key focus of attention, as we will see, is on the quality of work life (QWL) and how to improve it.

The Psychological Significance of Work

Although work has had variable social significance, it has had continuing psychological importance. The famous clinician Karl Menninger saw work as one of two constructive outlets for aggressive impulses, the other being play (1963). Psychoanalyst Harry Levinson speaks of work as a central means for accomplishing "the continuous psychological task of controlling, fusing, and channeling the twin unconscious drives of love and hate" (1981: 29). "The carpenter who hammers nails," says Levinson, "is not only discharging his aggressions but also building a shelter" (p. 29).

Work may give one a sense of mastery, provide legitimate aspirations for inner drives, placate a stern conscience, or divert attention from emotionally harmful anxieties. Medical studies show that fired and laid-off workers are at greater risk of accident, illness, suicide, and divorce than those who remain employed. A unique study carried out between 1922 and 1971 demonstrated an inverse relationship between economic conditions and admission to mental hospitals (M. H. Brenner, 1976). Despite the generally salutary benefits of work, however, the workplace often is highly stressful and competitive. It may be difficult even for emotionally healthy people to adapt to its pressures, frustrations, and conflicts, particularly those who derive their sense of self-worth solely from career success.

EXTERNAL FORCES CHANGING THE WORKPLACE

Today those who work, especially those who work in large corporations, are caught up in changes wrought by powerful environmental forces.

Technological Change

Technological change affects the number and type of jobs available. Machines are increasingly used by management to raise productivity and reduce costs. Automated teller machines at banks, for instance, increase the number of daily transactions possible and simultaneously reduce the number of employees necessary to handle them. Robots in auto manufacturing have made American companies more competitive in cost and quality with Japanese car makers. But automation offers both benefits and drawbacks. It has a turbulent impact on employment because it creates jobs for the architects of the machine age while displacing traditional manufacturing and service jobs. Some eliminated jobs are drudge work, but others may be highly skilled. Numerically controlled lathes and milling machines, for example, reduce the need for skilled machine shop operators.

The growing application of computer technology affects most jobs. Computers make information more accessible, speed the performance of many duties, and can move managers closer to production activity. They also may impose more stress on workers whose job goals can be measured precisely. The exact performance record of a bank loan officer or stockbroker—hard to calculate at present—eventually may be clearer to superiors than ever before. Any employee who works at a computer terminal may have his or her performance recorded. For example, Pacific Southwest Airlines measures reservation clerks' performance in many ways, from average time per customer to the length of bathroom breaks.

Demographic Change

Demographic movements are altering the characteristics of the work force. The workplace is continuously increasing in size. In 1950, the number of available workers was 62.3 million. By 1980, there were 106.9 million, and as many as 121.5 million may be working by 1995 if the economy grows at roughly 3 percent a year (Magnet, 1986). However, not all segments of the work force will increase proportionately. Because of high fertility rates following World War II, there is now a bulge of workers in their thirties. Since the 1950s, the nation's fertility rate has declined, and the number of younger workers has not increased as rapidly. Thus, while workers in the age group 25 to 54 will increase by one-third between 1980 and 1995, the number of new workers aged 16 to 24 will actually decline by about 10 to 12 percent. At this time, there will be a shortage of entry-level workers, and the demographic bulge of the postwar baby boom, now located at the middle-management level, will rise to upper management. There, a bottleneck will form as large numbers of ambitious people compete for fewer and fewer vacancies where the pyramid constricts. Not all the would-be CEOs can be accommodated.

Structural Change

Structural change in the economy is altering the availability of various types of jobs. Census Bureau figures show the following trends between 1950 and 1980:

1. Farm workers declined from 12 percent of the work force to 3 percent

2. Service workers increased from 10 percent to 13 percent

3. Blue-collar workers declined from 41 percent to 31 percent

4. White-collar workers increased from 36 percent to 53 percent, primarily because of growth in government and in clerical positions in industry.

These figures confirm a serious dislocation of blue-collar workers. Jobs are threatened in traditional, mainstay manufacturing industries such as steel, autos, and rubber. Employment in the steel industry, for instance, declined from a peak of 620,400 in 1953 to 290,500 in 1982. Workers who are displaced by automation and foreign competition cannot easily find jobs in the growing service and white-collar areas of the economy, and this dislocation will remain a source of discontent. Heavy manufacturing will continue to decline as a percentage of national output and as an employer. The economy is shifting from older "smokestack" industries to high-technology industries. The skills of surplus workers in smokestack industries often are not salable in the high-technology industries. This trend will be disproportionately burdensome to minority workers who, in the aggregate, have lower seniority and lesser job skills.

Intense Competitive Pressures

Competitive forces always have been strong in the U.S. economy, but they are arguably stronger in the 1980s for several reasons. First, foreign competitors in Japan, the Far East, and Europe have taken advantage of low labor costs, high productivity, and a strong dollar to undersell American firms. Second, formerly protected companies in newly deregulated industries are now more exposed to market forces. And, third, a wave of hostile mergers and acquisitions has disciplined management to protect the value of the company's assets in the stock market.

These competitive pressures have many ramifications for employees. To lower costs, hundreds of corporations, including the largest, are pruning the ranks of their middle management. One estimate is that over 500,000 of the roughly 28 million middle managers in the United States have lost their jobs since 1984 (Willis, 1987: 24). Ford Motor Co. plans to cut 20 percent of salaried employees by 1990 to reduce the cost advantage that Japanese car manufacturers enjoy. In 1985 Du Pont Company fired 11,200 employees, most in their fifties, through a voluntary retirement program. Hundreds of other companies are cutting heavily in middle management ranks.

New organization structures, expanded responsibilities, and automated technology help the workers who remain to achieve high productivity with fewer supervisory levels. Thus, the lash of competition has led corporations to develop a new emphasis on managing their human resources. But layoffs and restructuring exact a price. An enduring aspect of employment in America has been loyalty to a company. Loyal employees further corporate goals, and some companies have cultivated loyalty by trying to retain employees even in recessionary times. Nevertheless, loyalty seems to be fading. A survey of middle managers in 600 corporations in 1986 showed that 65 percent of respondents said that their fellows were less loyal than they had been ten years before (Nussbaum, 1986: 42). Perhaps it is significant that 55 percent of the respondents reported layoffs at their firms.

Changing Values of Employees

Shifting social values are changing attitudes toward work, particularly among younger, highly educated workers. Our society has emphasized education, and the work force of the 1980s is more educated than ever. Since World War II, the number of workers with college degrees has more than doubled. The number of professional and technical workers nearly doubled, from 8.4 percent in 1950 to 16.1 percent in 1980 (*National Journal,* February 26, 1983). Traditionally, workers valued jobs as sources of economic security and were motivated by the pursuit of money and status. They toiled for distant rewards and postponed immediate pleasures. So strong was loyalty to corporate employers that many managers commonly sacrificed personal interests to work demands.

Workers today, however, have different values. As we have said, to many, work is a quest for self-fulfillment, not income and status. Employees are more narcissistic, insistent on their rights, less accepting of authority, inclined to immediate gratification of desires, and not automatically loyal to the company. Survey findings reflect such changes. When 1,460 workers were asked which of sixteen different stakeholders was most important to the firm, "myself" was ranked first by supervisors, middle managers, those under forty years old, and the college educated (Schmidt and Posner, 1982). This value shift stems from dramatic social changes, including permissive child-rearing methods, political movements that have secured new rights for women and minorities, disillusionment with the ethics of major institutions, the receding memory of the frightening 1930s Depression, and the liberal challenge to traditional faith in economic growth as the vehicle for greater social well-being. These social changes have produced workers with nontraditional values who bring both promise and discontent to the workplace.

Because of these value changes, there is growing desire for increased quality of work life. Generally, quality of work life is a shorthand phrase for the concept of making work and workplaces more rewarding for human beings. Today there is agreement that a corporation that simply offers paid employment is not doing enough. There is, for example, a declining willingness to do meaningless work in authoritarian settings. Some people have wrongly concluded that the work ethic has eroded. The drive to work is as strong as ever, but the moral and doctrinal elements of the old Protestant ethic have been replaced by strong economic and psychological needs. The demand today is for fulfillment of old demands for improved working conditions, including better pay and fringe benefits, safety and health, shorter hours, and elimination of incompetent supervision. In addition, workers demand greater control over their immediate work environment. For most employees it means meaningful work; the use of available skills; the chance to grow and achieve; the opportunity to find interesting and challenging work; facilities to do the assigned job correctly and well; the protection of a growing array of rights and entitlements; and an end to monotonous, meaningless tasks performed in isolation.

Growing Heterogeneity of the Work Force

The work force is becoming more heterogeneous. Women and minorities, propelled by powerful political movements and protected by antidiscrimination law, have entered it in larger numbers than in the past. They bring new aspirations and pose new challenges. John P. Fernandez, author of *Racism and Sexism in Corporate Life* (1981: 7), observes that in years past, white males dominated 95 percent of corporate management positions even though constituting only 37 percent of the population. Now white males must compete with ambitious people formerly excluded from management ranks by discrimination. In addition, these new entries are in competition with white males for lower- and middle-management jobs at the very time demographic trends have swollen the number of workers aged 35 to 45. The enlarged pool of people eligible for these jobs guarantees stiff competition and much disappointment and frustration for those who wish to advance quickly.

In addition to competition for promotions, an exceptionally varied mixture of values in the work force also may cause stress. David Ewing, a scholar of the changing workplace, thinks our "variegated American culture" produces a hodgepodge of workers. "Some employees," he writes, "are materialistic, others are aesthetic; some are conservatives, others are heretics; some worship authority, others only tolerate it; some revel in teamwork and group membership, others prefer to go it alone in field selling or research; some 'think like farmers' whereas others 'think like Madison Avenue'" (Ewing, 1983: 4). These differences create dissidence. They make empathic relationships more difficult. Incidentally, the heterogeneity of the American work force is in stark contrast to the homogeneity of the Japanese work force (discussed later in this chapter).

Government Intervention

Finally, government has injected new rules into the workplace. The Equal Employment Opportunity Commission and other federal and state agencies use new laws to strike down discriminatory personnel practices and create new opportunities for women, minorities, the handicapped, and veterans. (This regulatory intervention is discussed in the next chapter.) In this chapter, we discuss how federal and state courts have given employees forms of protection from corporate power that they did not have twenty years ago. Today, employees can demand to see thier personnel files, refuse polygraph tests, blow the whistle on employers without fear of reprisal, and sue if a supervisor causes them emotional stress. In general, the rights of employers have been eroded in favor of the rights of employees.

MANAGING HUMAN RESOURCES TODAY

Corporations face a dual challenge. They must make employees more productive if they are to survive. At the same time, they must meet the expectations that large numbers of educated, independent employees have about work. On the surface, it seems logical that both challenges can be met. If corporations satisfy the needs of employees, then they will be satisfied, highly motivated, and, hence, more productive. Unfortunately, research on worker performance for many years shows that worker satisfaction does not automatically lead to high productivity. Indeed, the relation between the two is not clear. A fifty-year longitudinal study conducted at the University of California at Berkeley indicates that job satisfaction may be a function of overall life satisfaction and mental health. This finding might explain why national surveys on job satisfaction have not shown dramatic change since the 1940s, despite widely publicized worker discontent with restrictive personnel policies, authoritarian management, and corporate bureaucracy (Staw, 1986).

Nevertheless, corporations have made many changes and have adopted a variety of programs to accommodate employee expectations. Their efforts fall into four general areas.

Increased Worker Participation

Historically, authoritarian management styles have dominated American companies. But for the last twenty to thirty years, managements have attempted to temporize with changing worker values by encouraging employees to participate in decisions. Over the years there have been a number of faddish efforts to increase participation. Legions of managers have, for instance, attended training programs on how to develop consultative leadership styles. (Skeptics say that a manager will be sent to such a program if he is the type who says, "Joe, get your butt moving." After the program, he will say, "Joe, how's your new baby? . . . Great, now get your butt moving.") Job enrichment programs were popular in the 1970s. Job enrichment is based on the theory that workers in dull, repetitive jobs with little prestige receive ego gratification and become more productive if given more self-determination. Jobs were redesigned to give workers more control over their environments and more decisions to make.

Recently, quality circles—called quality-control circles in Japan—have been started in 6,000 to 10,000 American corporations. They are small groups of workers who meet voluntarily to study and solve production problems. Typically, these groups are composed of two to twelve workers and meet for one hour a week. They may request information and cost data from management and have the authority to implement solutions to workplace problems.

The purpose of quality circles is to make changes in the workplace that increase productivity. A recent visitor to the Sharp Corporation microwave oven manufacturing plant in Memphis, Tennessee, described a sublime moment in the life of one quality circle.

At one table, five microwave assembly workers are discussing one worker's innovation: a metal dowel that fits into the center hole of a five-hole microwave-oven bracket. "I saw that people were having trouble lining up the holes," says Randy Howie, "but if someone before them had put in the center screw, the person didn't have a problem." So Mr. Howie developed the metal dowel, which, when slipped into the middle hole, aligns the bracket while the other four holes are screwed down (Colonius, 1984: 137).

Quality circles have increased participation and productivity, but they have not worked everywhere. In fact, "only about 25 percent of [them] have produced measurable results greater than their costs, and only 40 percent of those implemented last longer than one year" (Smeltzer and Kedia, 1985: 31). It is believed that for quality circles to work, several conditions must be met:

1. Workers must be intelligent and educated

2. Management must be willing to trust the circle members with cost data

3. The group must be given authority to implement its ideas so that it has a sense of real participation

4. The workers must genuinely volunteer time for the group and not be forced (Buehler and Shetty, 1983).

When these conditions are not met—and they are not easy to meet—the intercultural graft may not take root.

There is a long roll call of management techniques designed to increase worker participation, ranging from the sensitivity training sessions of the 1960s to the sophisticated surveys of employee attitudes done today. None has consistently turned worker satisfaction into high productivity. But in some situations, they have worked well.

Changes in Organization Structure

Until the 1950s, the vast majority of American corporations were organized along bureaucratic lines. Today, corporations are experimenting with a variety of less hierarchical structures. When companies cut out layers of middle management, as many are doing, authority for decision making can be given to employees closer to the production process. In many companies there is greater use of project teams and groups that are composed of employees from different functional areas. These teams cut through bureaucratic red tape. At the extreme, W. L. Gore & Associates uses a team management approach with its 4,000 employees in which no person holds a position of formal authority. In this system, followers gravitate naturally toward leaders, and individuals volunteer for projects (Naisbitt and Aburdene, 1985).

Corporations also are learning to develop more flexible structures to permit innovation. New projects may be set in a sanctuary outside the formal organization structure so that the formal organization is not challenged by them. These sanctuaries sometimes are called "skunk works" (after the top-secret project center at Lockheed where the U-2 and stealth fighter were developed).

Policy Changes

Like organization structures, corporate policies are being changed to accommodate the needs and values of the contemporary worker. Selection, retention, and promotion decisions are examined systematically to help employees meet career needs. Few corporations offer job security, but many have flexible employment policies. Flex-time plans let workers decide what hours they will keep, job sharing programs allow two or more people to fulfill the requirements of a single job, and a few companies allow new parents to work at home for a while. Many companies offer day care for children; fewer give maternity leaves for mothers (or fathers).

Mainly because of rising health-care costs, but partly to meet demands from a new generation of fit workers, corporations increasingly adopt health-conscious policies, including no smoking areas and smoking bans, company-sponsored recreational programs, and bans on junk food in office vending machines. When workers have health problems, they get traditional medical and dental benefits. In addition, over 8,000 corporations offer employee assistance programs (EAPs) for stress, alcoholism, drug addiction, and family problems. (Such programs are not new in concept. In 1919 the Metropolitan Life Insurance Co. appointed a "house mother" to help female employees with personal problems.) Today's sophisticated EAPs usually are provided to the corporation by an independent firm, and they offer a broad range of counseling services, from meditation lessons to treatment for drug addiction.

Career counseling, flexible work programs, and EAPs are a few examples of the policy changes that accommodate the new self-concern and independence of workers.

Strategic Considerations

In years past, the problems and needs of employees were largely relegated to personnel and industrial relations offices. These offices experimented with behavior modification, job enrichment, participatory decision making, and other techniques designed to enhance productivity. Today, however, a new philosophy of human-resource management is emerging: that human resources are as important as finances or marketing and should be considered in any major strategic decisions. When a company makes plans to greatly expand or contract, enter new markets, or reorganize, it should take into consideration the human-resource implications of its actions. Will there be enough skilled workers? Will jobs remain for long-time employees? Can the company recruit successfully in new locations?

Conclusion

Some of the best known, most innovative, and productive corporations in America have adopted employee-sensitive policies such as the ones mentioned above. Are they more productive because they cater to new employee needs? No proof exists, but popular management literature, such as John Naisbitt's and Patricia Aburdene's *Re-inventing the Corporation* (1985), Tom Peters' and Nancy Austin's *A Passion for Excellence* (1985), and Gifford Pinchot's *Intrapreneuring* (1985), presents anecdotal evidence that responsive corporations are more successful. James O'Toole, in *Vanguard Management* (1985), reports that after 200 interviews with knowledgeable individuals, he found 8 companies repeatedly cited as outstanding places to work. These companies, O'Toole found, practice the kind of employee satisfaction programs discussed here, including cooperative relations with unions, "employee stock ownership, a fair measure of job security, lifelong training, benefits tailored to individual needs, participative decision making, freedom of expression, and incentive pay" (O'Toole, 1985: 101). They include some of the most successful corporations—ARCO, Control Data, Dayton-Hudson, Deere, Honeywell, Levi-Strauss, Motorola, and Weyerhaeuser.

Other companies have not fared well even though they have adopted a progressive approach to the quality of work life. People Express was lauded by advocates of participative management when it started in 1981. It called all its employees "managers," put them all on stock-ownership and profit-sharing plans, and wrote innovative job descriptions that blurred status lines. Pilots sometimes took reservations, served coffee, and loaded luggage. Flight attendants doubled as gate managers and reservations clerks. Although People Express emphasized customer service and was profitable in its early years, it lost $133 million in the first half of 1986, put its Frontier Airlines subsidiary into Chapter 11 bankruptcy proceedings, and put itself up for sale. The progressive, employee-centered policies at People Express resulted in high morale. But they could not protect the company from the harsh competition created by airline deregulation. TWA survived in the same environment under the penurious rule of takeover artist Carl C. Icahn. Icahn demanded 40 percent salary cuts from pilots and machinists and broke the flight attendants' union when it struck over proposed wage cuts and longer working hours. If there were any quality of work life programs at TWA, they were never publicized.

THE CULTURAL CONTEXT OF WORK: THE CONTRAST BETWEEN AMERICAN AND JAPANESE WORKPLACES

Work and the workplace exist in a broad cultural context. Previously, we examined how attitudes toward work differ across time and place. Here we illustrate how cultural background determines in large measure how work is done.

Since World War II, the economy of Japan has developed impressively. Today Japan, which is America's largest overseas trading partner and increasingly its greatest competitor in international markets, has the third largest GNP in the world. Since World War II the Japanese have had a productivity increase four times greater than that of the United States. Although growth of the Japanese economy has slowed since the first international energy shortage in 1973, between 1960 and 1973 growth in total factory productivity was 6.6 percent a year in Japan, the highest in the world and much in excess of the 1.9 percent in the United States (Kendrick, 1983).

A critical element of this success is thought to be the unique nature of Japanese business organizations, which embody patterns of worker involvement different from those found in American business. In the 1980s, there has been enormous interest on the part of American business in transplanting elements of Japanese management to American corporations. Japanese managerial skills are thought to be closely associated with Japan's economic miracle.

In a best-selling 1981 book, *Theory Z,* and in earlier articles, William Ouchi explained major differences between Japanese and American company cultures. In Japan, in the large industrial combines that employ about a third of the work force, work is the centerpiece of life, particularly for male employees. Workers have an ethic of extreme loyalty to employers and to the groups and teams in which most of them work. Responsibility for decisions, projects, and aspects of work such as quality control are assigned to groups, and these groups, rather than individuals with supervisory titles as in the United States, are held responsible by management for performance of duties. This intimacy of effort extends to inter-organization relations, and in Japan close relations exist between major firms, banks, government agencies, and hundreds of suppliers (which may go so far as to deliver parts right to worker stations in a factory).

The Japanese style of consensual decision making, known as the *ringi* system after the name of a document passed around so that each manager can affix a seal of symbolic agreement to important decisions, differs considerably from the American custom of rapid executive decision followed by implementation and obedience. In a Japanese company, important policy changes are widely discussed and refined throughout the company until a consensus is reached. Only then is a decision implemented.

Most workers in the big industrial combines are given lifetime job security, which means in practice that barring malfeasance, workers are guaranteed a job from time of hire after schooling to at least age fifty-five. At age fifty-five to sixty, workers are severed from the company with a payment of three to six years' salary unless they go into one of the handful of top executive slots. The Japanese have met the problem of economic downturn, not by laying off workers as American companies do, but by paying less. In Japan, 40 to 60 percent of the typical paycheck is bonus compensation based on overall company performance. In recessionary times, therefore, worker pay can be lowered without violating union wage agreements. This system enables companies to guarantee jobs for thirty to forty years to some workers.

The work force in Japan is more homogeneous than that of the typical American company today, and important line positions are held exclusively by Japanese men. Women are paid lower salaries and expected to put home and family before careers. Men are paid more, promoted sooner, and expected to place work before home. During their lifetime with the firm, Japanese workers are evaluated and promoted very slowly. The first promotion to assistant section head, for instance, usually comes between eight and twelve years after hiring. Employees follow nonspecific, nonspecialized career paths and learn various aspects of company operation.

The Japanese have a cultural tradition of obedience to authority. The extent to which workers devote their lives to their employers is shown by the loyalty and regimentation that a company may command. Workers are instructed to take calisthenics during the day; they may sing a company song or recite a company philosophy each morning; they live in company housing, wear company uniforms, and are likely to marry an employee of their company in a ceremony attended by top executives.

The Japanese also have a strong work ethic. It is seen in loyalty and obedience to the employer and in tenacity of effort seldom found in the West. At Taiyo Kogyo, a tent manufacturing company in Osaka, for instance, the workers assemble for a pep rally at 8:30 on Monday mornings, at which they recite company creeds. Creed number 7 is: "Once you've grabbed hold of a potential piece of business, never let it go, no matter what—even at the risk of your own life" (Greenwald, 1983: 42). The devotion of the Japanese worker is vividly shown in an early morning scene described by an American visitor to Tokyo: "Along the curb, sanitation men carefully polish their tiny Isuzu garbage trucks. Imagine the response of American garbage men to such a directive—it would burn this page" (Bruce-Briggs, 1982: 41).

The Japanese work ethic encompasses more than devotion and hard work. It also involves a perfectionism sometimes referred to as "pursuing the last grain of rice in the corner of the lunchbox." An American professor who toured Japanese factories quotes a Japanese scholar describing this fixation with quality.

"If you do an economic analysis you will usually find that it is advantageous to reduce your defect rate from 10 percent to 5 percent. If you repeat that analysis, it may or may not make sense to reduce it further to 1 percent. The Japanese, however, will reduce it. Having accomplished this, they will attempt to reduce it to 0.1 percent. And then 0.01 percent. You might claim that this obsession is costly, that it makes no economic sense. They are heedless. They will not be satisfied with less than perfection."

Indeed, in most of the Japanese factories I visited, the quality charts on the walls measured the defect rate not in percentages but in parts per million (R. Hayes, 1981: 62–63).

The culture that harbors these organizational values evolved from a Japanese society of small villages with strong norms of individual subordination to group interest, low social-class mobility, and strong feudal loyalties of vassals to lords.

In the United States, in contrast, our frontier tradition emphasized rugged individualism and high social mobility, not collective social control. Therefore, the American worker is animated by values of independence. Social control of individuals is not as strong here. Highly mobile workers have been accommo-

---

Who's Better?

U.S. News & World Report *asked 10 leading scholars who have studied both Japanese and American workers to rate them on a variety of qualities. Although the experts disagreed on some issues, the comments are representative of their remarks.*

U.S. ——————————— **Concern for Quality** ——————— **Japan**

U.S.		Japan
☐	Japanese workers possess an almost religious desire to do jobs well. They pay great attention to detail. Many Americans just want to finish the job.	◼●

——————————— **Initiative** ———————————

U.S.		Japan
◼★	On an individual level, Americans are willing to take the lead. They are concerned with who gets credit for exceptional work.	☐

——————————— **Hard Work** ———————————

U.S.		Japan
☐	The work ethic is strong in both countries, but the experts give the Japanese a slight edge because they routinely put in extra hours. Their company is the central focus of their lives.	◼●

——————————— **Honesty** ———————————

U.S.		Japan
☐	Because of strong identification with their company, Japanese are less likely to steal office supplies or cheat on time cards and expense accounts.	◼●

——————————— **Ambition** ———————————

U.S.		Japan
◼★	America's individualistic culture encourages workers to strive to get ahead. Japanese, though ambitious, try not to stand out, especially early in their careers.	☐

——————————— **Loyalty** ———————————

U.S.		Japan
☐	The average Japanese worker expects to spend an entire career at one firm. Companies, in turn, take a paternalistic interest in employees.	◼●

——————————— **Basic Skills** ———————————

U.S.		Japan
☐	Japan's schools produce graduates with good basic skills. Japanese learn discipline and good work habits that they transfer to the job.	◼●

——————————— **Advanced Skills** ———————————

U.S.		Japan
◼★	A close call. Workers in both nations are highly educated, but the U.S. has more college graduates and white-collar professionals.	☐

——————————— **Reliability** ———————————

U.S.		Japan
☐	Japanese are reluctant to show up late or call in sick, largely because they don't want to let down their bosses and co-workers. Many skip parts of their vacations.	◼●

——————————— **Cooperativeness** ———————————

U.S.		Japan
☐	Japanese subordinate individual concerns to group needs. This fosters a spirit of togetherness that is especially effective on the assembly line.	◼●

Source: Richard Alm and Maureen Walsh. "America vs. Japan: Can U. S. Workers Compete?" *U.S. News & World Report,* Copyright 1985 U.S. News and World Report. Adapted from issue of September 2, 1985.

dated by job specialization that makes individuals interchangeable production units rather than team members. Hierarchical and authoritarian decision making exists instead of a tradition of group consensus. American corporations lay off workers because they face union opposition to lowering wages during recessions. And quality control comes through specialized inspection and cost-control functions rather than team planning. Hence, the evidence strongly suggests that the two divergent societies have sprouted two strikingly different corporate cultures, each of which is successful in its environment.

Some observers believe that many of the most successful American firms, companies such as IBM, Levi Strauss, Procter & Gamble, and Hewlett-Packard, have some of the characteristics of Japanese companies. These companies are said to use management skills and quality of worklife techniques that overcome the productivity problems inherent in antagonistic industrial relations. Ouchi calls these hybrids "Theory Z organizations" and says that they are characterized by long-term employment, consensual decision making, slower evaluation and promotion, the merger of informal group control with formal hierarchical control, broader employee career paths, and concern for the total needs of the worker, including family life. Organizational consultants have worked to change the culture of many American firms by introducing programs implicitly or explicitly inspired by the Japanese example. Some companies borrow a little, others a lot.

The Downside of Japanese Management

Japanese management is not a wellspring of unadulterated contentment. If its inner flaws and stresses are exported in productivity improvement programs, American workers may regret it. In Japan, dedication to organizational life begins in prekindergarten training sessions, where competition to get into the best schools begins. Children often attend school six days a week, and this obsessive preparation foreshadows the long workdays and utter devotion of the Japanese male to his work. Japanese men place work before family life and commonly slight their families to meet group pressures to perform at work. The sacrifice inherent in this mania for work exceeds what is regarded as normal in the United States.

The strength that homogeneity provides for the Japanese work force is the result of sexist and racist tendencies in companies. Important line positions in Japanese companies are reserved for Japanese men. Women, men of other races (such as Caucasians), and men of other cultures (such as Koreans or Chinese) are screened out by formal and informal processes. Development and promotion rituals socialize men with common backgrounds into management teams and subtly exclude outsiders. These discriminatory personnel practices have been exported to Japanese-run companies in the United States. On the surface they violate American antidiscrimination statutes but have been held by the courts to be permissible under U.S. Treaties of Friendship, Commerce and Navigation that allow Japanese parent companies wide latitude in employing nationals in managerial and technical positions in U.S. operations. For example, in the case of *Sumitomo Shoji America, Inc. v. Avigliano* (1982) the Supreme Court refused to permit a Japanese company to hire only male Japanese citizens for executive positions—only because Sumitomo Shoji America, Inc., a subsidiary, was incorporated in New York and technically a U.S. company.

The discipline, conformity, and loyalty of Japanese workers is motivated by collectivist ideas, a strong work ethic, and stiff group pressure to conform. The latter takes its toll. Freelance journalist Satoshi Kamata studied Toyota Motor Company in Japan and one night met with workers from various plants who recalled twenty worker suicides over the past year. For example, a worker at a Toyota plant in Tsutsumi died in his company-owned quarters after taking an overdose of sleeping pills. He had been depressed from being berated for tardiness by his team leader and forced to "apologize to his fellow workers for the inconvenience he caused" (Kamata, 1983: 31). Other workers had hanged themselves, driven their cars into reservoirs, and thrown themselves into the sea. Not only does pressure exist to be productive, but Japanese are also expected to move through life with their age groups—never too far ahead, never too far behind. Like radical individuality, premature success in salary or position is the seed of rejection.

Today, there is much less interest in importing Japanese management techniques to United States than there was in the early 1980s. In Japan, moreover, there is less idealization of the system that was often presented to Americans in glowing terms. That faithful drone, the Japanese worker, is showing signs of rebellion against long hours, unquestioning loyalty, and group pressure. Increasingly, the Japanese are likely to refuse transfers that break up families, demand more leisure time, or that move him to another company. Consumer spending is up and savings are down, a sign that the Japanese economy is moving from its production orientation toward more consumption. In addition, the Japanese management style is increasingly less intact. Due to low-cost competition from countries like Korea, some large Japanese companies have been forced to trim "lifetime" employees from their work forces. The tradition of consensual decision making has eroded in some industries because technological change and product innovation come quickly. In high-technology fields such as electronics, more rapid judgments must sometimes be made than are possible under the group decision methods (Sethi et al., 1984).

THE INTERNAL CULTURE OF THE CORPORATION

Recently, students of business have begun to study corporate cultures. They make an analogy between society and the corporation. In a society, the term *culture* refers to a predictable set of values transmitted across generations. When embodied in institutions and rituals, these values direct social behavior toward essential goals such as reproduction, productive labor, and survival itself. When speaking of culture, the society-corporation comparison is apt. Like societies, corporations have sets of values that are expressed in rituals and institutions. Like societies, these cultures promote basic functions, including survival. And like societies, business cultures vary considerably in content.

The cultures of large corporations vary greatly. In 1984, General Motors acquired a Dallas-based company, Electronic Data Systems (EDS), to take over its data processing operation. The two companies had independently developed contrasting corporate cultures, and a clash ensued. At General Motors, employees were used to a paternalistic, highly bureaucratic, and formal management style. They received automatic cost of living raises, were promoted largely on seniority, expected job tenure, dressed in varied ways, and worked through channels. At EDS, in contrast, the culture emphasized hard work; compensation that was closely tied to performance; flexible team approaches; a rigid dress code that forbade loud ties, tassels on shoes, or beards; and a puritanical conduct code that prohibited drinking at business lunches, adultery, or abortions.

When General Motors acquired EDS, auto-industry analysts speculated that chairman Roger Smith was hoping to infuse the slow-moving, tradition-bound GM organization with some of the innovative fervor of the smaller Texas firm. The EDS spirit was personified in its founder and chairman, H. Ross Perot. Perot had started EDS in 1962 with $1,000 in savings, and its success had made him a billionaire. He also was a public figure. He had masterminded a covert rescue mission to post-revolutionary Iran in 1979 that freed two EDS employees unjustly imprisoned by Iranian authorities. The exploits of the rescue team were recounted in a best-selling book, *On Wings of Eagles,* by Ken Follett (1983).

From the beginning, however, the GM-EDS marriage was shaky. GM ran EDS as a separate profit center and issued a new Class E stock that paid dividends based on the profits of EDS operations. This created a strong incentive for EDS to charge high prices for data-processing services, and the perceived lack of cooperation alienated many line managers throughout GM. About 10 percent of GM's data-processing staff accepted early retirement or severance incentives rather than work for EDS-style management.

H. Ross Perot felt a mission to bring his entrepreneurial skills to the GM organization in ways that would make the auto giant more flexible, efficient, and competitive in the world auto market. Over time, many of the changes that he suggested met with resistance, and he began to fault GM management publicly. He criticized Roger Smith and other top executives for sequestering themselves in plush offices atop the General Motors Building in Detroit, in isolation from salaried workers. In the press, he was quoted as saying that bringing innovation to the GM bureaucracy was "like teaching an elephant how to tap dance." He also was quoted as saying: "The first EDS'er to see a snake kills it. At GM first thing you do is organize a committee on snakes. Then you bring in a consultant who knows a lot about snakes. Third thing you do is talk about it for a year" (Whitefield, 1986). These and other public remarks violated a long-standing code of keeping criticism within the ranks at GM.

Roger Smith became increasingly impatient with the maverick Perot. He briefly worked on selling part of EDS to AT&T. Ultimately, he convinced the GM board of directors to buy out Perot and three other top EDS executives by paying them $700 million for their Class E shares. At a time when GM was closing auto assembly plants throughout the country, this move was widely criticized because $700 million was enough to set up a world-class auto plant. When he accepted the money, Perot agreed not to publicly criticize GM, not to start a competing data-processing business for three years, not to accumulate GM stock for a takeover bid for five years, and not to hire away EDS workers for eighteen months. The exit of Perot was followed by the reorganization of EDS into a defense division of Hughes Aircraft, another GM subsidiary. To observers, it appeared that the GM bureaucracy had closed ranks against the EDS intruder and that its ponderous, slow-moving management processes had overwhelmed the seeds of innovation. The episode illustrates how important the culture of a corporation can be in limiting change.

The Nature of Corporate Culture

There are a number of consistent aspects to corporate culture. They include:

■ *Rituals and Rites:* Like societies, corporations have common rituals and rites of passage, such as promotions, transfers, training programs, "fast track" experiences, and retirement. Transfers, for example, break the socialization process in one location and open the manager and his or her family to new experiences and learning in another. They also may prevent the manager and his or her family from solidifying relationships outside the corporation and keep the company central to their lives, thereby enhancing loyalty and dependence. Socializing experiences often are used to humble employees, as at Procter & Gamble, where new salespeople are asked to color maps of sales territories and at General Electric, where new management trainees have been asked to get brooms and sweep the floor.

■ *Stories and Myths:* Every organization underscores its culture with stories that typify how things get done. At McDonald's, where cleanliness is emphasized, the tale is told of the franchise owner in Canada who lost his store because one fly was found in the kitchen. At Pepsico, a company that imbues managers with an intensely aggressive style, a story circulates that chairman Donald Kendall once rented a snowmobile to get to his office on a winter's day when a blizzard had closed Manhattan to automobile traffic. Such stories send signals about important elements of the work environment.

■ *Norms, Values, and Assumptions:* All strong corporate cultures emphasize mutually reinforcing norms, values, and assumptions. At 3M innovation is prized. Employees who have ideas can get funding and organizational sanctuary for their projects. If they successfully develop a new product, as did Art Fry, who developed Post-it Notes within the company, they even can share in its profits. At ITT under former CEO Harold Geneen, in contrast, entrepreneurship was sometimes the equivalent of insubordination. In the

1960s, when scattered groups of engineers began furtively working within the ITT organization to develop computer technology, Geneen unleashed organizational detectives who ferreted these people out and shut down their projects.

The HP Way

A few firms attempt to reinforce positive work cultures by codifying notions of desired behavior. One example is Hewlett-Packard Company. Hewlett-Packard, headquartered in Palo Alto, California, has 84,000 employees and is one of America's 100 largest industrial corporations. In the 1950s, a set of corporate objectives was published which briefly set forth a philosophy of business and employee relations. Over the years, this list has been revised periodically and has evolved into the "HP way." The term *HP way* is now used to refer to a distinctive corporate culture and set of ideas that underlie the business strategies, employee practices, and social relationships of the company. Here, for example, is the HP way of treating employees.

PEOPLE PRACTICES

Belief in our people

- Confidence in, and respect for, HP people as opposed to dependence on extensive rules, procedures, etc.
- Trust people to do their jobs right (individual freedom) without constant directives.
- Opportunity for meaningful participation (job dignity).
- Emphasis on working together and sharing rewards (teamwork and partnership).
- Share responsibilities; help each other; learn from each other; learn from mistakes.
- Recognition based on contribution to results—sense of achievement and self-esteem.
- Profit sharing, stock purchase plan, retirement program, etc. aimed at employees and company sharing in each other's success.
- Company financial management emphasis on protecting employment security.

A superior working environment

- Informality. Open and honest communications, no artificial distinctions between employees (first-name basis), management by wandering around and open-door communication policy.
- Develop and promote from within. Lifetime training, education, and career counseling give employees maximum opportunities to grow and develop within the company.
- Decentralization. Emphasis on keeping work groups as small as possible for maximum employee identification with our business and customers.
- Management by objective (MBO). Provides a sound basis for measuring performance of employees as well as managers; is objective, not political.

Source: Hewlett-Packard Company, "There's Something Special about this Place," March 1984.

■ *Physical Objects and Arrangements:* The physical layout of a workplace may be indicative of its culture. Open or closed offices suggest communication norms. So do the number of conference rooms. Some companies have abolished separate eating and parking areas for executives to introduce a more democratic feel. Authoritative and strongly hierarchical companies, in contrast, separate managers from workers, physically alter office spaces to make them more luxurious for higher-level occupants, and in a variety of ways reinforce organizational status with physical statements.

Corporate cultures are long-standing; some go back to the company founders. Henry Ford, for example, inspired a narcissistic management style at Ford Motor Company in which managers demanded complete, unquestioning obedience from subordinates (Jardim, 1970). For example, Ford assigned two men the same job and title to see which one survived the competition and abolished whole departments by firing all the executives in them. Today, the style lives on at Ford, although the company is trying to abolish it because managers believe that competing personalities and autocratic management hamper productivity. Thousands of Ford managers have been sent to workshops on participative management. But change is difficult. Ford has, over the years, selected naturally authoritarian managers. A study of 2,000 Ford managers classified 76 percent as "noncreative types who are comfortable with strong authority" (Guiles and Ingrassia, 1985). (Only about 38 percent of the population at large would fall into this category.) The Henry Ford style may be contrasted with that of IBM founder Thomas Watson, who insisted that all employees call each other Mr., Miss, or Mrs. to show mutual respect (Deal and Kennedy, 1982). To this day, IBM retains a reputation for deferential treatment of employees and for employee loyalty.

In conclusion, it is not only the national culture that determines basic aspects of work, but the corporate culture as well. Corporate cultures vary widely with industry, competitive environment, and founders' attitudes. Many are accommodating to employee participation; others stifle it.

THE RIGHTS MOVEMENT IN CORPORATIONS

The quality-of-work-life movement in corporations also embraces demands for corporate assurance of employee rights.

In years past, employers could demand total dedication and obedience from employees. In 1878, a New York carriage shop adopted a list of rules for employees that stipulated among other things, "On the Sabbath, everyone is expected to be in the Lord's House," and, "All employees are expected to be in bed by 10:00 P.M." (R. Smith, 1983: 15). Under the direction of Henry Ford, the Ford Motor Company set up a sociology department headed by a Detroit minister. It sent teams of investigators into workers' homes to certify the purity of their private lives. A second department, the service department, was formed to spy on workers at the plant. Workers were carefully watched for drinking, smoking, or criticizing the company, and many were summarily fired for offenses (Dahlinger, 1978). Throughout American history, in fact, employees have been subject to the whims of employers.

Although employees have political rights, such as the right to vote and speak freely, the Constitution protects citizens only from government infringement of these rights, not from infringement by private employers. If an employer restricts freedom of speech by banning an underground newsletter printed by employees and mailed to customers, the employees are not protected by the First Amendment because the guarantee of a free press in the First Amendment limits only action by government, not repression by a corporate employer. Professor David Ewing of Harvard argues eloquently that because of this rights gap, employees are deprived of important protections.

> For nearly two centuries Americans have enjoyed freedom of press, speech, and assembly, due process of law, privacy, freedom of conscience, and other important rights—in their homes, churches, political forums, and social and cultural life. But Americans have not enjoyed these civil liberties in most companies, government agencies, and other organizations where they work. Once a U.S. citizen steps through the plant or office door at 9 A.M., he or she is nearly rightless until 5 P.M., Monday through Friday. The employee continues to have political freedoms, of course, but these are not the significant ones now. While at work, the important relationships are with bosses, associates, and subordinates. Inequalities in dealing with these people are what really count for an employee (Ewing, 1977: 3).

Rights that Employees Demand

There are many rights that workers feel entitled to today. Following are the major ones:

- the right to a job

- the right to protection from arbitrary or sudden termination

- the right to privacy of possessions and person in the workplace, including freedom from arbitrary searches, use of polygraphs, surreptitious surveillance, and intrusive psychological or medical testing

- the right to equal opportunity and nondiscriminatory treatment in personnel decisions

- the right to a clean, healthy, and safe environment on the job, including freedom from undue stress, sexual harassment, cigarette smoke, and exposure to toxic substances

- the right to be informed of records and information kept and to access to personnel files

- the right to freedom of action, association, and lifestyle when off duty
- the right to freedom of conscience and to inform government or media about illegal or socially harmful corporate actions
- the right to self-actualization through career advancement
- the right to collective bargaining and to strike
- the right to due process for grievances against the employer
- the right to free expression of sexual preference and choice of a romantic partner
- the right to participate in major decisions affecting one's job
- the right to freedom of political belief and expression, including the right to publish opinions related to occupation
- the right to adequate leisure time for personal and family activities
- the right to reject interdepartment and intercity transfers
- the right to choose clothing and hair style
- the right to fair pay and fringe benefits such as medical and insurance
- the right to an adequate pension.

Challenger: A Preventable Accident?

Long before the explosion of the space shuttle Challenger on January 28, 1986, experts doubted the safety of its solid-rocket-boosters during a cold-weather launch. Sections of the big boosters were sealed with rubbery O-rings that were supposed to expand and seal the joints so that no gases from the burning propellant escaped. Recovery of booster rockets from a shuttle launch in 53° weather in January 1985, however, revealed considerable erosion of the O-rings.

Engineers working at Morton Thiokol, Inc., the NASA contractor that manufactured the giant solid-rocket-boosters, were immediately concerned by the erosion of the O-ring seals. Morton Thiokol set up a task force to study the problem while shuttle launches continued. The task force did not have highest priority, its requisitions were routinely handled, and engineers assigned to it were expected to perform their normal duties in addition to the seal analysis. As a result, the task force did not make rapid headway. In July 1985 Roger Boisjoly, one of the engineers, boiled over from frustration over procurement delays. He wrote a memo to his bosses in the space division warning that a catastrophic shuttle accident involving loss of human life might occur unless top priority were given to redesigning the solid-rocket-booster joints. Other engineers working on the project agreed with Boisjoly, and the group felt thwarted when paperwork and red-tape delays continued.

The shuttle rocket was a $605 million contract on which Morton Thiokol was permitted to earn a 15 percent profit. Despite the size of this contract the space division continued to follow routine procurement protocol on the seal task-force project, which meant that essential equipment took weeks or months to acquire instead of days.

On the night of January 27, as Challenger sat on its pad in sub-freezing Florida weather, NASA officials conferred twice in teleconferences with Morton Thiokol managers about the safety of a launch the next morning. In Utah, Boisjoly and other engineers argued strenuously against the launch, at times raising their voices to punctuate their data-based arguments. Their cautions were not heeded, however, and four Morton Thiokol vice presidents who were polled over the telephone by NASA officials gave their approval for launching. Later, it appeared that the vice presidents had bowed to NASA pressures for launch clearance. NASA officials were anxious to avoid the embarrassment of another postponement in an already often-postponed flight.

After the shuttle explosion, gloom prevailed among the engineers, who wondered if they had tried hard enough to stop the launch. There was no public mention of their opposition by either NASA or their company. When a presidential commission was appointed to study the Challenger accident, top Morton Thiokol officials made no mention of the engineers' dissent; but at the very end of the first closed-door meeting of the commission one of the dissenters, Allan J. McDonald, spoke up about his opposition and the warnings of the others, even though he had not been questioned about it. Then Boisjoly sent a copy of his 1985 warning memo to the commission.

These actions came at a time when morale in the company was low. Because the shuttle program was stalled, considerable organizational reshuffling was going on. In this difficult climate some employees focused their hostility on the small band of engineers who had "blown the whistle" on others. They were sometimes described as "lepers" by coworkers. Among the hundreds of layoffs, reassignments, resignations, and terminations taking place, two of the engineers who had opposed the Challenger launch on that fateful night were demoted to positions where they would no longer be working with NASA. Allan McDonald was one of them. A congressional committee, learning of these reassignments, heard testimony from Morton Thiokol officials who said they were not punitive. But shortly thereafter the reassignments were reconsidered and the two engineers were promoted. McDonald now heads the booster rocket redesign team. What happened to Boisjoly? His emotional anguish following the explosion was so great that he requested long-term disability leave for stress-related conditions.

Morton Thiokol has never admitted responsibility for the Challenger disaster even though the presidential commission's final report blamed both the faulty design of the booster seal and a flawed decision-making process for the accident. In 1987 the company signed a renewal of the solid-rocket-booster contract worth $1.3 billion, but simultaneously agreed to do more than $400 million of redesign work on the faulty solid-rocket-boosters without compensation. The new contract is less desirable than the old one in other ways also. It restricts Morton Thiokol to a maximum profit of 6.5 percent and permits NASA to use a competing firm as a second source for the boosters.

The story of the engineers at Morton Thiokol illustrates how flawed decision making and poor management may set the stage for episodes of embarrassing public disclosure by "whistle blowers." This episode received national publicity. The engineers may have retained their formal status in the company only because of congressional pressure and company fears of losing the huge NASA contract. There are numerous similar disputes in other corporations that have ended in the abuse of dissenting employees who were not protected by a congressional committee.

The Trend toward More Employee Rights

Originally, all of these rights developed as moral rights due workers who toiled under autocratic managers. Many of these moral rights have become legal rights. Federal law, for example, prohibits discrimination, sets standards for pension plans, prohibits disclosure of government data about workers to employers, sets rules for labor relations, and protects worker health and safety. States protect other rights. Lie detector tests of employees are restricted in nineteen states, and twenty-one states have laws protecting corporate and government whistleblowers from reprisal. Courts protect some rights not covered by legislation. The current trend in common law is expansion of employee rights. Freedom from stress is one example. In the past fifteen years, state courts have compensated workers who have claimed that emotional disorders have resulted from stressful on-the-job conditions.

The expansion of employee rights has steadily whittled down a broad range of management prerogatives. Although the march of employees rights shows no signs of slowing, the priority of various rights changes over time. For example, objections to conservative dress codes were more prominent in the rebellious 1960s, and discrimination was a more volatile issue in the 1970s than today. Events may spur sudden concern for a right. For a year after the chemical leak at Union Carbide's pesticide plant in Bhopal, a furor arose over the right of workers to have information about the toxic substances they worked with. Within six months, twenty-five states had passed "right-to-know" laws that required companies to disclose that information.

Fundamentally, employee rights must be balanced against corporate rights. Employees have rights that are socially accepted. Corporations have the right to protect their reputations and assets. Sometimes two legitimate rights conflict. For example, corporations have an important right to ensure the suitability and integrity of employees. Yet lie detectors, drug tests, personality tests, and AIDS antibody tests may entail a substantial encroachment on privacy and dignity. In addition, all these tests are subject to error and employees risk unfair job loss. Thus, two legitimate rights conflict and a careful balance must be struck. The duty of an airline to provide safe transport may outweigh the privacy rights of pilots in a drug testing program. There may be less of an overriding need for the airline to invade the privacy of typists, whose right to privacy may predominate.

Perhaps the most fundamental right of an employer is the right to hire and fire. We turn to this subject in the next section.

The Rules of Agency

In the United States there is a body of common law known as "agency" which governs employer-employee relationships. The general provisions of agency hold that employers and employees may enter into voluntary agreements of employment and that either party may freely terminate these agreements at any time.

While employed, an employee must act "solely and entirely" for the employer's benefit in all work-related matters or be liable for termination and damages. Furthermore, the law stipulates that when a conflict arises between an employee and employer, the employee must conform to the employer's rules. The common law of agency is derived from paternalistic English common law which, in turn, was influenced by Roman law that framed employment in terms of a master-servant relationship. Under agency, employers have had extensive rights to restrict employee freedom and to arbitrarily fire workers.

If the balance of employer-employee rights has favored the employer under the traditional rules of agency, recent trends have eroded absolute discharge rights and protected employee interests. Federal and state legislation has restricted the right to fire employees for reasons related to age, sex, race, union activity, physical handicap, religion, or national origin. State whistleblowing laws restrict discharge in retaliation for criticizing an employer. In addition, the courts have introduced three other limits to termination at will. First, a firing may not be contrary to the intentions of public policy. In *Petermann v. International Brotherhood of Teamsters* (1959), a California worker was asked by his supervisor to lie to certain questions before a legislative committee investigating unions. When the worker answered honestly, he was fired. Even though the employee was subject to firing at will in his position, the court did not uphold the termination, stating that it was an overriding public policy interest to have truthful testimony at legislative hearings. Courts also are refusing to uphold terminations where a "covenant of good faith" was implied in the employment contract. In the 1980 case of *Cleary v. American Airlines,* an airline employee of eighteen years service in a position subject to arbitrary dismissal was fired. Company personnel policy contained a specific statement that the firm reserved the right to terminate an employee for any reason, but the court became convinced that the firing had occurred so that the airline could avoid payment of a sales commission to the employee. It awarded the fired worker punitive damages. In *Pugh v. See's Candies* in 1981, a vice president was fired after thirty-two years with the company. The court refused to uphold the firing because at the time of the man's hiring, there was evidence that he had been promised permanent employment so long as his performance was satisfactory.

As a result of these and similar decisions, it is becoming more difficult to discharge employees. Companies are carefully examining personnel manuals, for example, to remove implied promises of job tenure. One company has stopped calling its non-probationary employees "permanent" employees. Instead, legal counsel has advised the term *regular* to avoid an implied promise of a long-term job.

The absolute right to discharge is less absolute today because changing values in society have moved away from the traditional prerogatives of agency. Even public opinion itself can reverse a decision, as the case of Dorothy Reed shows. In January 1981, Reed, a black woman and newscaster at television station KGO in San Francisco, appeared for work with her hair restyled in a traditional ethnic style of corn rows with multicolored beads. KGO management found the style an unwelcome surprise and suspended Reed until she changed it. Although management feared that the hair style would alienate viewers the opposite occurred. Demonstrators demanded that Reed be reinstated and allowed free choice of hair style. Ultimately the station yielded to the outcry by bringing Reed back to work with a compromise. She kept the corn rows but agreed not to use beads. This case illustrates the power of public opinion to circumscribe traditional management authority (Bacal and Fineman, 1981).

Plant Closings

Another area in which the employment prerogatives of employers are being circumscribed slowly is that of factory or facility shutdowns. When important employers in a community close their plants, the impact can be devastating, especially if a company is the community's major or sole employer. In recent years, plant closings have reached crisis proportions, especially in communities with smokestack industries. Plant closings highlight a conflict between the concept of capital mobility, which is widely accepted as central in the free enterprise system, and personal security and community stability, which also are values of high priority in our society.

For many years, labor unions and others have sought to promote public policies that would require prior notice of plant closings and programs to protect workers and communities. In recent years, some unions have included in their contracts provisions for notice in the event of shutdowns, together with severance benefits, but generally the agreements are for one week's notice or less. Only a fraction of all workers are covered by such agreements. Bills have been introduced in Congress on this matter, but none has been passed. About half the states are considering plant closing laws, but only three or four have them. Wisconsin had a law that mandated notice, but it was repealed, and notice there is now voluntary. (Several cities, including Philadelphia, have ordinances on the subject.) Except for Maine's law, which requires a sixty-day notice to workers before a closing, these laws are not restrictive on management.

Proposals in plant closing laws include prior notification of shutdowns, severance pay for discharged workers, continuation of certain benefits such as health insurance, transfer rights to other plants of the company, financial aid to the community for economic development, and joint company-union-government committees to facilitate redevelopment of the community (Bluestone and Harrison, 1982).

Supporters of plant-closing legislation point to many benefits that it would produce. Workers are protected from the trauma of a sudden loss of jobs. Time is provided for transition from one job to another. Local employment offices have time to plan transitions. If government, unions, and company managers form teams to deal with problems, a plant closing may be avoided. For instance, a factory may need space, or a firm may need financing, or more skilled workers, or relief from high wages. All these problems may be solved if there is an organized focus on them. When all else fails, workers themselves may buy the plant and continue operations.

Those opposed to plant closing legislation argue that the legal right of companies to use their assets as they see fit would be restricted. They point to a ruling of the Supreme Court in June 1981 *(First National Maintenance Corporation v. NLRB)*, which said that a company may close a plant without bargaining with its union providing that the shutdown is partial (it is one plant of a company, not the entire firm) and the closing is purely for economic reasons. In the absence of a contractual agreement with a union, this ruling is in conformance with the principles of a free enterprise system. Opponents also would argue that prior notification might result in a triggering of events that would magnify losses, such as workers leaving, loss of loyalty, decline in worker morale, and a drop in productivity. Furthermore, prenotification could lock a company into a decision to close that might not be required if the company had time to work out its problems.

We do have, of course, legislation to help workers who are unemployed and between jobs, to retrain workers, and to facilitate community economic redevelopment. Many companies undertake special programs to help their workers and their communities after a shutdown, even though there was no prior notice. Three scholars who have studied plant closings conclude that legislation restricting them has not worked. Governments and business, they conclude, should strengthen such actions as noted above to avoid plant closings or ease the blow when they occur, rather than trying to control them by laws (Christman, Gatewood, and Carrol, 1985).

LABOR-UNION PARTICIPATION IN MANAGEMENT

The historical relationship between management and labor unions in this country has not been cordial. Indeed, at times it has been, and often still is, acrimonious and violent on both sides.

Labor unions traditionally have fostered an adversarial relationship with management. They have believed that this posture would, through the collective bargaining process, better achieve their major aims: improved wages, improved benefits, job security, and preservation of the union organization. They have not wanted to run businesses. Unions have been strong supporters of the capitalistic system and have seen no inconsistency in using their power to force employers to do things on behalf of workers. Indeed, they have sought to better their positions within the growth of the free enterprise economy. When unions have challenged managerial decision making it has not been about the right of managers to decide but rather to question the free hand of managers in dealing with workers. If managers have a completely free hand in disciplining, promoting, laying off, and recalling workers, argue the unions, workers are protected only by the competitive market. When workers have found that protection insufficient, they have organized into unions that had the power to bargain with managers. Even in those rare instances when unions have been invited to be represented on corporate boards of directors, they have gone along very reluctantly. Today, they still want to maintain their traditional adversarial position toward managements.

In recent years, unions have lost power in both legislatures and in collective bargaining sessions with managements. This is evident in the very substantial wage concessions they have made in a wide range of industries, such as steel, automobiles, textiles, and airlines. Since the late 1970s union membership has declined, and at an accelerating rate in the past few years. Membership in the 1970s was about 28 percent of the total nonfarm work force. One recent study projects a fall in the rate to around 10 percent, if current trends continue (Freeman and Medoff, 1984). With the recent prolonged slack in many major industries, employers have used the creditable threat of layoffs and plant closings to win freezes and cutbacks in wages and benefits. Unions, which once gained for workers higher wages and fringe benefits, no longer had the same appeal. Union ranks declined.

Two important trends appear to be gaining momentum and could reverse these trends. They are the growth of employee stock ownership plans (ESOPs) and profit or "gain" sharing. ESOPs are programs by which employees own shares of stock in the companies for which they work. Today, over 7,000 companies have ESOPs with 10 million workers enrolled. Employees own anywhere from a tiny percentage to 100 percent of the total stock. In the latter cases, as at Weirton Steel, employees either manage the company or hire professional managers to do so. Most ESOPs are in privately owned companies with fewer than 500 employees. In most of these firms, the employees own 15 to 40 percent of the company stock. The drive toward ESOPs usually is not to forestall a plant closing (only 2 percent arise from this motivation) but rather to give workers a sense of participation in the company. This, it is hoped, will make the workers more productive, loyal, and motivated to do their best work. Sometimes this is the result but not always (Klein, 1986).

Rarely do employees actually buy the stock under ESOP plans. Usually, companies give employees stock as a benefit. A trust is established to receive stock given by the company or cash to purchase stock on the open market. The company can deduct from its taxes up to 25 percent of the covered employee payroll. The stock remains in the trust, tax free, until the employee leaves the company or reaches retirement age.

Profit-sharing plans permit workers to share in the profits of a company. These plans have a history extending back into the last century. MIT professor Martin Weitzman, in his acclaimed book *The Share Economy: Conquering Inflation* (1984), has given the idea a new thrust, the idea that profit sharing can lead to full employment without inflation. According to Daniel J. B. Mitchell (1986), a respected scholar of industrial relations, Weitzman's proposals have a good chance of receiving strong support from employees, managers, the general public, and legislators. Because legislators favor ESOPs, he believes that they will give tax advantages to profit sharing plans. Many managers, he says, will see in them the same advantages as ESOPs. Some people will view them as a new route to industrial democracy. Some will see them as fostering in employees a better appreciation of the free enterprise economy. Unions will see in them a way to reverse declining union membership.

Under a system in which workers get only a wage (plus benefits), as do most workers today, unions need only to verify whether an employer is abiding by agreements made in the collective bargaining process. Under a system of profit sharing, however, accounting manipulation by employers, which is notoriously easy and legal, might hide profits. To prevent such practices and to understand the reasons for accounting changes, employees must have access to employers' books and the skill to interpret them. As Mitchell observes, it is only a short step to criticizing what the information reveals. If profits are declining, employees will want to know why. It is only a small step from there to questions about management's decision making and, eventually, to participation in the decision-making process.

Mitchell argues that nonunion as well as union employees will have an interest in decisions made by management. They will not, however, have the same channels as union members by which to become involved in the process. This vacuum will give the unions an issue for increasing membership as well as a role well beyond that which they traditionally have assumed for workers. The result will be, of course, a new labor-management relationship.

CONCLUSION

Each morning, millions of people arise, travel to a plant or office, work with others in relationships that are partly productive and partly stressful, and then return home at day's end. What do they want from work? What do they get?

As we have indicated, employees today want more self-fulfillment and more rights in the workplace. What they get depends largely on their specific jobs, the culture of their particular companies, and the stage of their individual careers. Powerful external forces are sweeping the workplace, and it is a tumultuous era for employees. There is a movement today to tie productivity improvements to programs that meet employees' wishes for fulfillment. Thus employees may increasingly get more of what they want from work.

CASE STUDY

DRUG TESTING OF EMPLOYEES: EMPLOYERS' RIGHTS VERSUS EMPLOYEES' RIGHTS

Never had American society been more concerned about drug abuse than in 1986. And the high level of public anxiety was in large part attributable to a remarkable series of events that sullied the professional sports world.

In January, coach Raymond Berry of the Boston Patriots, whose team had just received a tremendous shellacking at the hands of the Chicago Bears in the Superbowl, admitted that eight players had used cocaine during the past season. In February, the National Basketball Association announced that Michael Ray Richardson, star guard of the New Jersey Nets, was barred from playing for two years after testing positive for cocaine use in a urinalysis. In March, baseball commissioner Peter Ueberroth imposed penalties on twenty-one major league players who had admitted to using drugs. During one week in June, both University of Maryland basketball star Len Bias and Cleveland Browns defensive back Don Rogers died of cocaine overdoses.

By July the "war on drugs" was nightly fare on network news programs. *Newsweek* and *Time* ran cover features on "crack," or cocaine boiled down into small crystals to be smoked and so named because of the crackling sound it makes when heated. In September President and Mrs. Reagan made a national television address to say that drugs were undermining the nation's vitality. The President noted a White House study showing that between 12 and 23 percent of American workers had a drug problem. He suggested a drug testing program for federal employees, and Mrs. Reagan urged that people "just say no" to drugs. The next day the President sent a legislative package to Congress known as the Drug-Free America Act of 1986. Shortly thereafter, he and his entire cabinet voluntarily submitted to a urinalysis for drugs. Because 1986 was an election year, candidates challenged their opponents to take urine tests and show themselves drug free. Election observers called this jousting "jar wars," but the jest was lost on the likes of Georgia congressional candidate Julian Bond, who refused to take a drug test and lost in part due to this refusal. Such was the tenor of the times.

Employee Drug Abuse in Corporations

Drug abuse also was an enormous problem for employers by 1986. The nation's largest employer, General Motors, was one of the most troubled. It hired undercover detectives to work in various locations during an eighteen-month sting operation. These detectives discovered that drugs were being sold in eight assembly plants and that workers used them freely during the day. At a plant in Adrian, Michigan, it was estimated that one out of five employees on the second shift used alcohol or drugs at work. At other plants, drugs were sold in parking lots, cafeterias, and supply rooms. The drug dealers often worked as drivers of forklifts and other mobile machinery and had access to large areas of the plants. In February 1986, the undercover agents surfaced to orchestrate over 200 arrests, but only the biggest dealers were arrested. The little guys, the drug users, were not arrested or fired if they agreed to participate in GM's extensive alcohol and drug counseling programs (Burrough, 1986).

Across the country, other employers experienced drug-related problems. At Eastern Airlines, baggage handlers were the focus of a federal investigation concerning drug shipments from Colombia. A company doctor at Rockwell International Corp. estimated that 20 to 25 percent of the workers at the company's Palmdale, California, space shuttle assembly plant worked under the influence of drugs or alcohol between 1981 and 1983. A computer operator at American Airlines cost the company $19 million while on a marijuana high by neglecting to put data into the computerized reservation system. At a few companies, employees dropped dead from drug overdoses.

Time magazine reported estimates that 10 to 23 percent of U.S. workers used drugs on the job (Castro, 1986: 53). When one company, Southern Pacific Transportation Company, first started drug testing, it found that 17 percent of its employees tested positive for use of marijuana, cocaine, alcohol, or heroin (Schachter and Geidt, 1985: 30). Statistics gathered from callers to a cocaine help line, 1-800-COCAINE, showed that 76 percent of cocaine users were employed, 45 percent had stolen from employers, family, or friends to get drug money, and 3 to 7 percent used an illegal drug daily (Lawn, 1986).

It is clear that every day an army of drug users descends on factories and offices across the nation. Drugs are concealed in clothing and lunch boxes. They often can be bought from coworkers, but if not, a messenger service may send them in. Cocaine is preferred over other drugs for use at work because it can be easily hidden, leaves no odor, manifests no visible signs of impairment when the user is high, and often gives a feeling of enhanced performance. Workers smoke crack in cigarettes and sniff cocaine powder in elevators and restrooms. They ingest LSD and hallucinate for the rest of the day. They steal, engage in acts of prostitution, and sell drugs to others to support their habits.

The cost of drug abuse is difficult to calculate. Grand total estimates in the literature in 1986 ranged from $47 billion to $70 billion a year (Burrough, 1986; Lawn, 1986). Whatever the figure, the components include lost productivity, elevated accident rates, extra worker compensation claims, higher insurance premiums for employers, higher absentee and sick leave rates, the loss of trained workers who are fired or die, the administrative costs of employee assistance programs, and the costs of beefed-up plant security and law enforcement programs. Human costs are not, of course, included in any of these categories and are extra, unmeasured, and tragic losses.

Drug Testing Programs Undertaken by Corporations

A wide range of antidrug measures is available to corporations, from entry and exit searches to rehabilitation programs for addicts. But in the mid-1980s, one of the most common responses was a program of drug testing. By 1986, about 40 percent of *Fortune* 500 companies had such a program, and diagnostic laboratories geared up across the country to meet the growing demand. Typically, companies fire employees who test positive for heroin, morphine, methadone, cocaine, "designer" drugs, hallucinogens such as LSD, marijuana, amphetamines, PCP, barbiturates, and other illicit drugs.

The most common drug-screening tests involve analysis of a urine sample. There are several basic urine tests. The first is the EMIT test, which stands for enzyme-multiplied immunoassay technique. This is an inexpensive test costing about $15 which can be done quickly with modest laboratory equipment and technician training. In this test, several ingredients are added to a urine sample. Telltale chemical reactions indicate the presence of metabolites, or chemical by-products produced by the body from drugs such as marijuana. In a variation of this test called a radioimmunoassay (RIA), a radioactive isotope is added to urine to measure the presence of a drug.

Manufacturers of EMIT and RIA tests claim that they are 95 to 99 percent accurate when used correctly. But in actual testing, innacuracy is greater. These tests are particularly susceptible to a false positive result if a person has recently used any of ten common over-the-counter drugs, including dextromethorphan, an ingredient in Vicks Formula 44, and perylamine, an ingredient in Midol. Poppy seeds, found in bagels and other baked products, may cause false positives for morphine and cocaine. An additional flaw of immunoassay tests is that they cannot detect hallucinogens such as LSD.

A second test, thin layer chromatography or TLC, is more precise than the EMIT or RIA tests but is more time consuming, more expensive (about $25 per test), and requires a highly trained technician to interpret results. Therefore this technique is less often used for mass employee screening and is frequently held in reserve to double check a positive result on an immunoassay test. In this test, urine is placed near the bottom of a vertical plate that stands in a trough of solvents. The solvents climb the plate by capillary action, and after reaching the urine specimen, they carry it upward. Various chemical components in the urine—including drug compounds—are soluble at different rates and therefore move upward at varying rates. A skilled technician can interpret the pattern of movement on the plate to determine if a drug is present. The technician may also spray the plate with a reagent that causes color changes in the presence of drugs. It takes much experience to read these plates accurately, and errors sometimes are made.

A third type of test is done with a mass spectrometer. It is the most accurate and, at a cost of nearly $100, the most expensive. In this test, components of urine are separated by gas chromatography. The various chemical constituents of the urine flow by a mass spectrometer in gaseous form. The spectrometer measures the relative proportions of molecules in the urine and produces a pattern on a photographic plate that can be interpreted by computer. Done properly, this test is virtually 100 percent accurate. Gas chromatography/mass spectrometry tests are so sensitive that they have detected cocaine and a by-product, cinnamolycocaine, in the urine of people who have drunk one or two cups of coca leaf teas imported from Peru. Five doctors writing in the *Journal of the American Medical Association* cautioned that individuals in urine testing programs should be warned not to drink these teas (Siegel et al., 1986: 40).

One shortcoming of urine tests is that they can be thwarted by employees who tamper with samples. A small amount of table salt, bleach, laundry soap, ammonia, or vinegar causes screening tests to miss drug residues in the urine. For this reason, employees giving urine samples must be closely supervised. In addition, efforts have been made to substitute drug-free urine samples for a person's own, tainted urine. A person may carry a small sample in his or her clothing and pour it into the test vial if not closely watched. If there is hot water in a bathroom where an employee is being asked to give a sample, he or she can warm the sample to body temperature. In one situation where no hot water was available, a woman carried a condom of unsullied urine in her vagina to keep it at body temperature until the switch was made.

Because these games are played, many corporations require urination in the presence of an observer, a particularly demeaning mode of testing. An additional problem with urine testing is that it cannot indicate whether an employee is high or impaired. Cocaine and heroin can be detected for up to three days after last use and marijuana up to two months after last use. This means that a person who used cocaine at a party on Saturday night could be nailed by a drug test on Tuesday morning when feeling hale and working productively. But a colleague who had taken LSD that morning, and was hallucinating and dangerous, would not be detected with an EMIT or RIA test.

Other tests exist but are less frequently used. Several blood tests can detect the presence of various drugs, but they require the intrusion of drawing blood and are no more accurate than a reliable urinalysis. A test that measures drug residues in human hair exists but has not yet been given widespread use. And a test that detects drug use by interpreting electroencephalograms has been developed but suffers from inaccuracy because up to 10 percent of the population has abnormal brain wave patterns that might be interpreted as falsely indicating drug use. None of these tests overcomes all the shortcomings of urine testing.

Why Corporations Favor Drug Testing

Corporations that test for drugs find four compelling reasons for doing so. First, drug testing lessens drug use and lowers costs to the corporation. When Southern Pacific Railroad instituted drug testing, its accident rate went down by 60 percent. When Lockheed Corporation began testing job applicants, 28 percent were screened out because of positive indications of drug use, but the figure soon fell to 15 percent as word spread (Weinstein, 1986b). Without testing, some of these applicants might have been hired, driving costs up for the company.

Second, employers suggest that they have a legal duty to reduce drug use. Under federal and state occupational safety and health laws, companies are required to provide safe working environments. In addition, they fear product liability suits from injured consumers who come into the courtroom with the theory that a manufacturer is negligent if it fails to prevent defective work by a drug-impaired employee. Additionally, in a Texas case, *Otis Engineering Corp. v. Clark* (1983), a company was held responsible for damages in a fatal auto accident caused by an employee sent home from work when he was discovered to be intoxicated. The Texas Supreme Court held that Otis Engineering had failed to meet its responsibility to stop the employee from driving. If it is possible to detect drug abuse with urine testing and employers fail to do so, can they be held liable for wrongful conduct by their employees on or off the job? The precedent of the *Otis* case has not yet been followed by courts in other states, but its implication is that courts may find that employers have a duty to take reasonable actions to eliminate drug abuse.

Third, corporate drug testers argue that urinalysis is a practical method of testing for drug use. Although urine tests have shortcomings, they are less invasive than alternatives such as drug-sniffing dogs, polygraphs, searches through handbags and desks, undercover investigations, entry and exit searches, and closed-circuit TV monitors in restrooms. Urine tests can be part of a comprehensive effort including rehabilitation. Retests can be required to reduce the risk of false results in first tests. And efforts can be made to preserve the dignity of employees taking the tests.

Finally, there is a social responsibility argument for drug testing. As employers screen applicants and employees, it will become harder for drug abusers to make a living. Employees have no right to use drugs such as heroin, cocaine, LSD, marijuana, hashish, morphine, PCP, and designer drugs. Their use is illegal and an inconvenience to corporations. Thus, business is helping society by reducing criminal activity and combating the national drug problem.

Why Some Employees Oppose Drug Testing

As compelling as these arguments are, drug testing in general and urine testing in particular raise difficult questions. Critics point out that the right of an employer to protect assets and property must be balanced against the rights of individual employees to a reasonable amount of privacy. Opponents of drug testing have included individual employees, labor unions, and groups such as the American Civil Liberties Union. The opponents make telling points.

First, the urine tests are intrusive—unreasonably intrusive. Susan Register, an employee at a Georgia Power Company nuclear plant, describes what happened to her when asked to give a urine sample.

> "I walked into the bathroom with a company nurse and sat down on the commode. The nurse said, "Stand up, we're going to do it differently today."
>
> The nurse made me bend over at the waist and hold my right hand in the air. My blue jeans were around my ankles. I had a bottle in my left hand between my thighs. If you were a woman you could understand how hard it would be to get urine this way. I was barely hitting the bottle. I wet all over my pants and my left hand (Weinstein, 1986: 30–31).

Susan Register's experience is probably not typical and may even be rare, but supervised urination is inherently demeaning. It is as intrusive as a body search that violates ordinary privacy expectations and it shows no regard for everyday manners. If such a procedure is allowed, then at what point will it be acceptable for corporate observers to peek into the bedrooms of employees to make sure that their sex lives are normal? It smacks of Big Brother and can lead to lower morale and employee mistrust.

Second, the tests are unjust in the sense that they violate ethical standards of fair treatment. Testing is a dragnet; many innocent employees are tested for each drug abuser detected. A presumption of guilt is placed on everyone, and workers must prove their innocence. If there is an overriding necessity to prohibit drug abuse—among airline pilots or train engineers, for example—then it may be permitted. But indiscriminate testing of clerical staff and plant workers is an evil greater than the drug abuse that it seeks to remedy. Moreover, drug testing may be used to harass workers. In some cases, workers who have tested positive have been singled out over and over for repeated testing while their coworkers have not, even when later tests have been negative for drug abuse.

Third, urine tests are faulty. Inaccuracies arise from lab errors, mixed-up specimens, and false positives due to legal drugs in the body. These errors are common, and false accusations cost individuals their jobs. Errors by screening labs are a particularly difficult problem. There are no uniform standards or established testing fees for these labs, and they test using a variety of procedures. With the boom in urine testing by employers, the labs have sprung up like mushrooms following a rainstorm. Contracts are frequently let based on low cost of screening. The result is an incentive to cut costs and training for lab technicians. A series of studies over a nine-year period conducted by the Centers for Disease Control showed a "substantial" number of errors by screening labs for six commonly misused drugs, including falsely negative and positive screenings (Hansen, Caudill, and Boone, 1985).

The tests, furthermore, are faulty because they do not measure impairment. An employee who is a moderate recreational drug user on weekends may be fired even though his or her work record is excellent. This puts the corporation in the position of policing off-job behavior, something that it has no right to do, for if the employee wishes to keep his or her job, he or she must stop using drugs on the weekends. Some medical experts have suggested that the increased melanin in the urine of blacks may cause them to erroneously test positive for substances such as marijuana on EMIT tests. If true, this would raise significant questions of racial bias, but there seems to be little evidence corroborating the charge.

Finally, civil libertarians have asked whether significant legal questions are raised by drug testing. They suggest that urine testing may violate constitutional protections and additional rights granted by state laws (Bible, 1986). At issue are the Fourth Amendment prohibition against unreasonable search and seizure, the Fifth Amendment prohibition against self-incrimination, the equal protection and due process clauses of the Fourteenth Amendment, and the constitutional right to privacy that has been fashioned by the Supreme Court in cases such as *Griswold v. Connecticut* (1965) and *Roe v. Wade* (1973).

Early challenges in the courts to urine testing have invoked these constitutional protections, but court precedent is not year clear in many areas. If courts do limit testing programs because they are incompatible with constitutional freedoms, the guaranteed protections would apply only to public employees because, as we have said, the Constitution limits government actions, not the actions of private employers. Private employers will face other challenges based on violation of fair employment laws, invasion of statutory and common law privacy rights, and defamation of character. Federal and state courts will balance the rights of employers to safeguard their property against the privacy rights of individuals.

Questions

1. Should urine testing (or other types of testing) be permitted among public and private employees to prevent drug abuse? What reasons can you give in support of your answer?
2. If you believe that urine testing in some form might be acceptable, write down the outlines of a sound testing program. Who should be tested? Employees? Job applicants? Should there be random testing? Should people in all job categories be tested? How frequently should tests be administered?
3. As a manager with responsibility for conducting a testing program, what would be your response to the following situations?
   a. An employee who tests positively for marijuana on a Monday morning but has a spotless ten-year work record
   b. An employee showing no signs of drug use who refuses a test being given to all workers in the engineering department
   c. A job applicant who tests positively for cocaine use
   d. An employee who tests positively for cocaine use

e. An employee who comes to your office the night before an announced urinalysis and admits that he regularly uses a hallucinogenic drug off the job

f. A productive worker who gives no indication of drug use but who is named as a drug abuser at work in an anonymous tip

g. An employee involved in a serious work accident who refuses to take an EMIT test based on her belief in a right to privacy.

CHAPTER **17**

MINORITIES, WOMEN, AND ANTIDISCRIMINATION LAW IN THE WORKPLACE

 **MERCK & CO., Inc.** How does a large corporation cope with seething tensions and stresses in its work force that stem from compliance with federal and state antidiscrimination laws? White males worry that less qualified minorities and women may leapfrog ahead of them through unfair, preferential promotion programs. Minorities fear that they will be regarded as unqualified as they advance. Women are angered at subtle male efforts to place them in submissive roles.

In 1968 Merck & Co. set up an office of equal employment affairs to handle equal employment and affirmative action issues. Merck is a large, multinational corporation headquartered in Rahway, New Jersey. In 1986 it had sales of $4.1 billion and ranked 91 on the *Fortune* 500 list. Its 31,000 employees are engaged in the development, production, and marketing of pharmaceuticals and other chemical products. One of Merck's products, Mefoxin, is the leading hospital antibiotic worldwide.

In late 1970 through a natural progression Merck, like many other companies, had established affirmative action programs to comply with government requirements. Unlike other companies, however, Merck started a sweeping program to inform its employees about affirmative action issues, to allow them free expression of their feelings about discrimination or favoritism toward minorities, and to build support for affirmative action policies. The training sessions in this program went through three phases. In Phase I, executives and managers at all Merck facilities met in small groups to discuss the creation of equal opportunities for all employees. In Phase II, supervisors, shop stewards, and union officials undertook the same training. Approximately 1,000 line managers and supervisors were trained to act as group discussion leaders so that they could conduct one-day workshops for other Merck employees. In Phase III, which began in 1982, all remaining 16,000 U.S. employees at sixty-one locations met in groups of ten to fifteen people for one day. During these sessions, Merck employees saw video tapes that depicted employees—men and women, black and white, young and old—discussing experiences and feelings related to discrimination, sexual harassment, and preferential treatment. The discussions that followed were often heated. Many workers felt that for the first time they could verbalize feelings about sensitive relations with coworkers.

- "Just knowing other people's attitudes were a lot like mine was surprising." [a black man]

- "The vignettes are excellent because I think we all see a little bit of ourselves in these films. I think some of the messages were a surprise to some employees; for example, discrimination can be exhibited in the question of who gets the coffee or calling someone 'honey.'" [a white male manager]

- "The important factor in career advancement is still qualifying for the job. You could actually feel the ice melting during the discussion. And long after, it's obvious that attitudes are more positive." [a black female manager]

- "Because so much attention is being focused on blacks and women, it's easy to feel you are being treated as a type and not as an individual. Phase III helped by talking about individual concerns." [a black woman]

- "I had never even heard of affirmative action until Phase III." [anonymous]

The program has been helpful in developing supportive attitudes among employees. Surveys showed that 70 percent of employees taking the program felt more positive toward affirmative action and equal employment programs than previously. Three percent felt more negative. And 27 percent reported no change in their feelings.

Today, Merck has an affirmative action plan at each U.S. company installation for minorities, women, disabled veterans, Vietnam veterans, and the handicapped. For employees such as doctors and engineers, affirmative action percentages are based on national work force figures. In 1986, Merck Chairman and CEO P. Roy Vagelos, M.D., reiterated the importance of the firm's affirmative action goals, stating that they would continue even if the Reagan administration weakened legal affirmative action requirements for federal contractors—a measure under discussion at the time.

Supervisors at Merck report that the Phase III programs created a better climate for communicating the inevitable "people problems" that arise as affirmative action plans unfold. And other companies seeking to cope with affirmative action stresses have adopted the Phase III program under arrangements by which they pay royalties to Merck. Merck donates these royalties to minority and women's groups. In 1985, the state of New Jersey ran Phase III programs for 65,000 state workers as part of an initiative to fight discrimination in employment.

As the Merck experience suggests, there is a trend toward heterogeneity in the labor force. More women and minority group members are working now than ever before, and the assimilation of new workers, protected and accelerated by antidiscrimination law, poses a considerable challenge to managers. Idealistic doctrines of equality and harmony notwithstanding, there is plenty of discomfort and conflict in the workplace. This chapter is concerned with these matters.

MINORITIES IN THE WORKPLACE

Since the Constitution was ratified in 1789, no nation has accepted more immigrants than the United States. Only about half our population today is descended from settlers in the United States before 1789. The rest are the descendants of immigrants from many nations and several races. Since 1965, about 700,000 new immigrants have entered the United States legally every year. Many illegal aliens have also taken up residence, but considerable disagreement exists as to their numbers. The 1980 census recorded about 2 million aliens, half from Mexico. Today, informed estimates place the number as high as 6 million.

All large immigrant groups, past and present, are represented in the labor force. Some, such as the Irish, Germans, Italians, English, and Polish, have been assimilated into the middle-class mainstream of American society. Others, particularly nonwhites, or those with ethnic loyalties, and recent arrivals, have not yet been fully assimilated. Members of these groups often are victims of racial and ethnic discrimination in the workplace. Although many groups may literally be defined as minorities, discrimination in the workplace historically has been most persistent against five sizable groups: blacks; native Americans; Asians, including Chinese, Japanese, and recent Vietnamese immigrants; Hispanics, including Puerto Ricans, Mexican Americans, Cubans, South and Central Americans, and other Spanish-surnamed people from countries such as Spain; and Jews.

Racism and Social Discrimination

Racism, defined broadly, is the belief that each race has distinctive cultural characteristics and that one's own race is superior to other races. It persists when myths and stereotypes about inferiorities are expressed in institutions of education, government, religion, and business.

There is a long history of racism in the United States. Early in American history, blacks from non-Western, little understood African cultures were enslaved and thought to be inferior to whites. Even after the freeing of the slaves, the idea that whites were superior to blacks was institutionalized in segregated schools, restrooms, and water fountains; in literacy tests that disenfranchised blacks; in restrictive covenants in deeds that prevented whites from selling property to blacks in certain neighborhoods; and discriminatory job policies that kept blacks in menial positions. Racism insulates the power of a privileged group—in this case the white American—from challenge. All these devices added up to an institutionalized structure of racism.

Similarly, from the earliest meetings of the settlers and Indians in colonial Virginia to nineteenth-century military conquests, American Indians have been regarded as an inferior race. Hispanics have been the victims of *la leyenda negra,* an ancient prejudice against Hispanic peoples, obscure in origin and perhaps related to their darker skins (although there are many light-skinned Hispanics, who often prefer to classify themselves as white). Large influxes of Chinese between 1850 and 1890 led to nativist fears and discriminatory treatment. For instance, the California state constitution, adopted in 1874, prohibited Chinese from voting and made it illegal for corporations to employ them. When the first Japanese immigrants came to America in the late 1800s, suspicion of their motives and loyalty led to much discrimination. Although all these groups face discrimination, sociologists contend that white Americans see some of the groups as more acceptable than others.

The Chinese and Japanese, perhaps because of their lighter skins, say some observers, have not suffered as much discrimination as other minority groups. Poverty, racism, and lack of privilege have characterized their life in the United States and still do for some. But economically, Asian groups have fared well. The Chinese and Japanese now have incomes above the average for all Americans.

Discrimination in the Workplace

Widespread social discrimination against members of minority groups has inevitably entered corporate personnel practices. Today, there is less discrimination than in the past, and although open bigotry still exists, it is increasingly rare. There still exists, however, subtle, ingrained racism in corporate life. For example, hiring and promotion policies that treat all applicants equally may discriminate against minorities who are qualified for positions but less qualified than competing whites with more education. Corporations such as Manville and Union Carbide, which move their headquarters to rural settings, may force minority employees to live in cultural isolation, away from supportive ethnic enclaves in metropolitan areas. Buddy systems among white managers often exclude minorities. For example, in the oil-field supply and service industry, social contacts and friendships within a white, male, "old boy" network have been a barrier to minority-owned firms. Much oil-field business is transacted at private clubs with exclusionary membership policies. Minorities also may be perceived according to stereotypes rather than actual performance. A black or a woman manager who is aggressive may be regarded as pushy, whereas a white manager with the same style may be commended for being assertive.

The experience of racism in the workplace is very real today. There is strong evidence that discrimination against blacks, for instance, exists in business despite strong trends in society away from racist attitudes. In a 1944 poll, only 42 percent of the population felt that "blacks should have as good a chance as white people to get any kind of job," but by 1972, 96 percent responding to the same question favored equal hiring (Smith and Sheatsly, 1984: 15). But this attitude shift has not translated into uniformly equal treatment. In 1985 a poll showed that 40 percent of blacks felt that they had been discriminated against in finding a job (Lichter, 1985). Although the 27.9 million blacks are 12.1 percent of the population and there are approximately 5,700 black elected officials in the United States (including congressmen and the mayors of some large cities), a 1985 analysis showed only four black senior executives in the largest 1,000 companies—three more than were found in a similar 1979 study (Korn-Ferry, 1985). Even in the National Football League, where nearly 50 percent of the players are black, there has been only one black head coach in the league's history—Fritz Pollard of the 1921 Akron Indians. Between 1976 and 1986, there were sixty-two head coaching changes in the NFL, but although there are a growing number of black assistant coaches (thirty-two in 1986), no black got the top job (Pomerantz, 1986).

Blacks face more physical danger on the job. In 1982, black workers had a 37 percent greater chance than whites of occupational injury or illness and a 20 percent greater chance of dying from job-related injury and illness. This is because more blacks than whites work in dangerous jobs. In a study of 6,500 rubber workers, for instance, 27 percent of black workers, but only 3 percent of white workers, toiled in the environmentally hazardous com-pounding and mixing operations—an area marked by high exposure to toxic chemicals associated with elevated rates for six types of cancer. Several cancer studies, covering tens of thousands of steelworkers, show that cancer rates for blacks are far elevated over those of whites because blacks, who characteristically have less seniority and may have been exposed to promo-tion discrimination, work in disproportionately large numbers in less desir-able "topside" jobs near coke ovens, where carcinogens are most numerous (M. Davis, 1982). The insidious effects of racism may be seen in these and other situations.

Thus, despite polls showing that the public believes that blacks should be given equal employment opportunities, discrimination continues. Compared to whites, blacks today have lower average incomes, less access to desirable jobs, higher unemployment, and fewer promotional opportunities. Blacks also have shorter life expectancies, less education, higher infant mortality, and a greater likelihood of living in poverty than other racial and ethnic groups in the United States.

FEDERAL REGULATION TO PREVENT DISCRIMINATION IN EMPLOYMENT PRACTICES

Today there exists a massive legal and regulatory apparatus to protect employees' civil rights in companies and government agencies. This, of course, has not always been the case.

When the Constitution was ratified in 1789 it sanctioned the practice of slavery in Article I, Section 2, which counted slaves as three-fifths of a person for purposes of apportioning seats in the new House of Representatives. This language was rendered obsolete by the three Reconstruction Amendments; the Thirteenth Amendment abolished slavery, the Fourteenth guaranteed citizens "due process of law" and "equal protection of the laws," and the Fifteenth outlawed race as a barrier to voting.

In 1866 and 1870 Congress passed civil rights acts intended to prohibit employment discrimination, but until very recently, courts narrowly defined these acts to apply only to state government employees, not workers in corporations. Not until almost 100 years later, with the passage of the Civil Rights Act of 1964, were corporate employees given significant protection from employment discrimination. We turn now to a discussion of its most important section, Title VII.

Title VII of the Civil Rights Act of 1964

The cornerstone of the structure of laws and regulations enforcing equal opportunity is the Civil Rights Act of 1964. Title VII prohibits discrimination in compensation, terms, or conditions of employment because of an individual's race, color, religion, sex, or national origin. Conditions of employment include hiring, promotion, training, disciplinary action, firing, layoffs, bonuses, working conditions, and selection procedures. Title VII also provided for the establishment of the Equal Employment Opportunity Commission (EEOC) to enforce its provisions. All companies with fifteen or more employees have to report annually to the EEOC the number of minorities and women on each step of the employment ladder. The act holds employers responsible for any discriminatory acts that occur in the workplace. The Equal Employment Opportunity Act of 1972 extended coverage of Title VII to state and local government employees, to employees of educational institutions, and to the federal bureaucracy.

The overall purpose of Title VII is to remove barriers to equal employment opportunity. It does not require that minority workers be hired simply because they belong to a protected class, but it does require removal of discriminatory barriers to their hiring and advancement. Employers are not required to redress racially imbalanced work forces or to change established seniority systems. When the Civil Rights Act was being debated in 1964, its congressional opponents claimed that it would require employers to fire white workers and hire minorities to achieve proper racial balances. In order to get the bill passed, its supporters included an amendment stating that such actions were not mandated. If an employer had been discriminating prior to the act, the act required only the removal of that discrimination. The employer did not have to go further and change the composition of a work force to what it would have been had there been no discrimination.

Where employer discrimination still exists and can be proved, however, federal courts are empowered under Title VII to remedy the situation. Courts may use their power of injunction to prohibit an illegal activity, as in the case of one firm where new workers were hired only upon recommendation of a member of the existing, all-white work force. Courts may order individuals rehired or give them back pay after they have been unjustly fired. In addition, Section 706(g) of Title VII empowers judges to "order such affirmative action as may be appropriate," and courts sometimes have established numerical hiring goals for minorities and timetables for their achievement in cases where discriminatory practices have been long-standing and egregious. In 1975, for example, a New York district court ordered a sheet metal workers' local union to achieve a 29 percent nonwhite membership (based on the percentage of nonwhites in the New York City labor pool) by 1981. The court did so because the union had a nonwhite membership of only 3.19 percent and a long history of discriminatory barriers to minority employment, including entrance tests unrelated to job requirements, special training sessions to prepare relatives of white members for entrance examinations, and membership-size restrictions designed to bar minorities. A long court battle by the union ended in 1986 when the Supreme Court, in *Local 28 v. Equal Employment Opportunity Commission*, upheld the validity of numerical goals as a remedy for this pattern of prejudicial hiring behavior.

Basically, two legal theories are accepted by the courts to demonstrate discriminatory employment barriers under Title VII. The first is the *theory of disparate treatment*. Disparate treatment exists where an employer bestows less favorable treatment upon employees because of their race, color, religion, sex, or national origin. For example, a retail store that refused to promote minority warehouse workers to sales positions because it preferred white salespeople to serve its predominantly white customers would be guilty of this type of discrimination. Proof in disparate treatment cases usually requires establishing a motive to discriminate. The second legal theory is the *theory of disproportionate impact*. Disproportionate impact exists where an employment policy is apparently neutral in its impact on all employees but, in fact, is not job-related and prevents individuals in protected categories from being hired or advancing. A typical example would be the requirement that applicants for a manual-labor job pass an English comprehension test in a geographic area where many minorities have poor English language skills.

Executive Order Number 11246

A second major statute protecting employees from discriminatory employment practices is this Executive Order 11246, issued by President Lyndon Johnson in

1965, to require federal contractors and subcontractors to take affirmative action "to ensure that applicants are employed, and that employees are treated during employment without regard to their race, color, religion, sex, or national origin." President Johnson derived the authority to require affirmative action of federal contractors from the Federal Property and Administrative Services Act of 1949, which directs the executive branch of government to buy goods and services in the most efficient way. The President construed the act to prohibit discrimination, which was an inefficient use of human resources. As originally promulgated, Executive Order 11246 simply underlined the concept of employee equality found in Title VII of the Civil Rights Act of 1964. However, in 1971, the Labor Department—which had authority for administering the executive order through its Office of Federal Contract Compliance Programs (OFCCP)—issued Order Number 4.

The now historic Order Number 4 applies to companies that have federal contracts over $50,000 and fifty or more employees. It requires these companies to analyze major job categories—especially officials and managers, professionals, technicians, sales workers, office and clerical workers, and skilled craftworkers—to determine if they are utilizing women, blacks, Hispanics, Asians, Native Americans, and other minorities in the same proportion as they are present in the area labor force. If minorities are underutilized, companies must establish Labor Department-approved goals for hiring, retention, and promotion, and timetables for goal achievement. Most large corporations, and virtually all the *Fortune* 500 companies, have contracts to supply goods and services to various government agencies. In effect, Executive Order 11246 (with Order No. 4) imposes widespread affirmative action requirements. About 15,000 facilities, employing 23 million workers, are affected.

The Labor Department does not establish rigid hiring quotas for companies. Instead, it requires a contractor to set up hiring goals and make a "good-faith" effort to achieve them. This effort is checked in required reports and may involve anything from job fairs to summer employment for minority high school students. Generally speaking, adequate progress is defined by the Labor Department as a final hiring total that meets the "80 percent" rule. This rule is met if a company has hired minority groups at the rate of at least 80 percent of the rate at which it hires from the demographic group (usually white males) that provides most of its employees. If, for example, it hires 20 percent of all white males who apply for a particular job category, it must then hire at least 16 percent (80 percent of 20 percent) of all blacks who apply, 16 percent of all women, and so on. If its records prove that hiring has met this standard, it is likely that the federal government will have no complaint, but that is not assured. If a company fails to comply, the Labor Department may cut off federal contract payments. This is occasionally done, so the threat is real.

Late in 1985 Attorney General Edwin Meese III, with the approval of President Reagan, introduced to the Cabinet for discussion the draft of a new executive order to replace Executive Order 11246. The new draft required only voluntary minority hiring goals for federal contractors. This sparked a debate in both the Cabinet and the country. Labor Secretary William E. Brock, head of the federal department that administers the old executive order, strongly opposed the change. A powerful coalition of civil rights groups also opposed change, as did 69 senators and 180 representatives, who sent a petition to President Reagan in opposition. Although the Chamber of Commerce favored voluntary hiring goals, the National Association of Manufacturers and many large companies did not. When 104 big corporations were surveyed about the new executive order, ninety-nine said that they would continue with numerical goals and timetables (Davidson and Watkins, 1985). The revision of Executive Order 11246 was quietly shelved for lack of support.

This revision was part of an intellectual outlook in the Reagan administration that favored enforcement of antidiscrimination laws in a "color-blind" way. The administration favored dropping the use of numerical goals, timetables, and hiring quotas and focusing legal action on individual cases of proven discrimination. But it was unable to develop a credible legal theory before the Supreme Court to achieve this with respect to Title VII enforcement. It also was unable to develop enough political support to alter Executive Order 11246.

Most corporations have adopted voluntary affirmative action plans to protect themselves from expensive discrimination lawsuits. People in business have been amenable to numerical hiring goals and timetables because they are similar to the kinds of goals and objectives that corporations set for a variety of business functions. They are comfortable procedures in the corporate world. Title VII encourages voluntary plans to correct minority imbalance in company labor forces. This law, in addition to Executive Order 11246, protects companies from reverse discrimination lawsuits brought by white workers who feel shunted aside by minority hiring. Corporations opposed changes in the law in part because they feared that it might open them to lawsuits by disgruntled white employees who could claim that numerical hiring goals were not federally required.

Other Important Antidiscrimination Laws

In addition to Title VII and Executive Order 11246, other federal laws protect women and disadvantaged minorities in the workplace. Briefly, they include the following.

The Equal Pay Act of 1963   This legislation prohibits pay differentials between male and female employees with equal or substantially equal duties in similar working conditions. Nondiscrimination in pay extends to fringe benefits also. Since 1979, the EEOC has had responsibility for enforcing this act.

The Age Discrimination in Employment Act of 1967   This act prohibits discrimination against people between the ages of forty and seventy. It is illegal to base personnel actions on age. This act is enforced by the EEOC. A number of state laws also prohibit age discrimination against any adult, regardless of age.

The Vocational Rehabilitation Act of 1973   The act requires federal contractors and subcontractors to develop affirmative-action programs for hiring handicapped people. The legal definition of *handicapped* is so broad that it includes about 600 medical conditions. There must be nondiscrimination in hiring, firing, and promotion decisions regarding people with these conditions. The act falls mainly under the jurisdiction of the OFCCP, although Section 501, which protects employment rights of the handicapped in the federal government, is administered by the EEOC.

The Vietnam-Era Veterans' Readjustment Assistance Act of 1974   The Readjustment Assistance Act is similar to the Rehabilitation Act in requiring federal contractors to develop affirmative-action programs for hiring, training, and promoting Vietnam veterans. It is administered by the OFCCP.

The Pregnancy Discrimination Act   This act, a 1978 amendment to Title VII that is enforced by the EEOC, prohibits employment discrimination based on pregnancy, childbirth, or related medical conditions.

The Immigration Reform and Control Act of 1986   This act was passed to permit illegal aliens with five years residency in the United States to legalize their status. It requires employers to document the immigration status of recently hired employees and job applicants. Hiring an undocumented alien carries a fine of $250 to $10,000 per offense, and repeat offenders may be imprisoned for up to six months. Because of these stiff penalties it was feared that some employers would discriminate against "foreign-looking" applicants, so the law requires employers to document the citizenship or residency status of all job applicants. Fines of up to $2,000 may be imposed on companies guilty of discrimination on the basis of national origin or citizenship. The law covers all workplaces with four or more employees.

Some Observations on the Laws

Altogether, this thorough body of legislation protects a *majority* of the work force from discrimination. It covers white women, blacks, Hispanics, American Indians, handicapped males, white male Vietnam-era veterans, and all workers, including white males between the ages of forty and sixty-nine, who are subject to protection from age discrimination. At some point in their lives, all people fall under the protection of federal employment legislation.

Also, there are two fundamental and sometimes opposing mandates in federal antidiscrimination law that exist in uneasy partnership.

■ First, employers must not discriminate against an individual on the basis of race, sex, religion, age, national origin, pregnancy, physical handicap, or veteran status.

■ But second, employers who have maintained discriminatory employment practices (even unintentionally) and federal contractors who have fewer females or minority group members than are available in the area work force may be asked to take affirmative action to preferentially recruit, hire, train, and promote such persons.

The net result of the simultaneous existence of these mandates is that managers may be asked not to discriminate against anyone, while at the same time they are required to give preference to individuals from a variety of groups constituting the majority of the work force.

Enforcing the Law: The Equal Employment Opportunity Commission (EEOC)

The EEOC is the most powerful federal agency enforcing civil rights. It is an independent regulatory commission, set up in 1965 after authorization by Title VII of the Civil Rights Act. The agency is presided over by five commissioners (no more than three of whom are to be of one political party) appointed by the President and confirmed by the Senate for five-year terms. It is headquartered in Washington, D.C., and has fifty-nine other offices around the country.

The EEOC has the authority to investigate, conciliate, and litigate charges of discrimination related to the statutes it administers. It also issues rules and guidelines for employers and unions about various employment practices and establishes reporting requirements for companies. It has authority to file lawsuits in federal district court to force compliance with Title VII and other legislation under its jurisdiction.

When an individual suffers discrimination and brings a complaint to the EEOC, he or she first meets with an EEOC investigator, who makes an initial judgment about whether the complaint involves employment discrimination (the agency does not handle complaints of other forms of discrimination, such as housing discrimination). If the complaint falls under EEOC jurisdiction, a formal document is sent to a company or business within ten days. Both parties must then attend a fact-finding conference, in which the EEOC investigator encourages informal resolution of the dispute. Informal resolution simply involves a promise that the employer will cease a discriminatory practice or make financial restitution.

If informal settlement does not occur, the EEOC works up a formal investigation, which may include interviews, collection of documents, and field visits to a business. On the basis of this investigation, an EEOC attorney attempts a second conciliation between the disputing parties, and if this is not successful, recommends filing suit in federal district court based on "reasonable cause" to suspect discrimination. This recommendation moves up the bureaucratic chain of command to the five EEOC commissioners, who make the final decision. If the EEOC decides not to pursue the matter in court, the person who claims discrimination is issued a "right to sue" notice and may take the matter to court without EEOC assistance.

During the Reagan administration the enforcement philosophy of the EEOC shifted. In the 1970s, a more liberal and activist group of lawyers in the agency targeted large corporations for highly visible litigation. With this philosophy of strong enforcement, the EEOC brought class action suits on behalf of women and minority workers where patterns of widespread discrimination prevailed in company work forces. Among dozens of such cases, there were four strikingly large settlements. The first came in 1973, when AT&T was taken to court by the agency and ultimately settled on $36 million in back pay to women and minorities who were denied advancement within the firm. In 1978, General Electric settled a class action suit for $23 million; Ford Motor Co. paid $23 million in 1980; and in 1983, General Motors agreed to a $42.5 million settlement.

In 1985, however, the EEOC announced its intention to concentrate on suits brought on behalf of individual victims of discrimination and to drop class action suits. As a result, the agency made no secret of its desire to lose a court case brought in 1977 against Sears, Roebuck & Co. for statistical disparities between the minority and female composition of Sears' work force and the EEOC's judgment of the size of those categories in the national labor market. The case was an acrimonious contest. Sears stood accused, for instance, of not hiring enough women for large, commissioned sales jobs. Sears alleged that it could not find enough women interested in selling refrigerators and tires, although it had tried. In 1979, Sears combatively brought suit against ten federal agencies, including the EEOC, for following policies that created and perpetuated a largely white male labor force. Sears' audacious case eventually was dismissed, but Sears refused to drop or settle the case brought by the EEOC and in 1986 a federal judge ruled in favor of the company. The case had become so complicated that the opinion was 160 pages long.

In 1985, the EEOC also dropped the use of timetables and numerical goals in hiring agreements with employers. It did so to move closer to the Reagan administration's civil rights policy of racially neutral applications of the law. New employment agreements required that employers take no notice of race and not favor minorities (or anyone). Simultaneously, of course, the Labor Department continued to impose goals and timetables.

The Controversy over Affirmative Action

It will be recalled that under Title VII of the Civil Rights Act of 1964, courts may order affirmative action programs and, likewise, the Labor Department may require affirmative action from federal contractors under the authority of Executive Order 11246. Yet many in our society believe that affirmative-action programs, especially those that contain numerical goals for utilizing minorities, are objectionable because they create so-called "reverse" discrimination against other groups, usually whites. They also are attacked by minority groups, who argue that affirmative action clouds the real achievements of minorities. There is always the suspicion, they feel, that advancement came because of affirmative-action requirements and not individual achievement.

Polls consistently show that only a few people, about 10 percent of whites and 25 percent of blacks, favor preferential treatment for minorities (see, for example, *The Gallup Report,* May 1984). Throughout the Reagan administration, Justice Department officials have argued that preferential treatment should be awarded only to individuals who have suffered from discrimination, that it should not be afforded to groups affected by affirmative-action programs whose members may not, as individuals, have suffered direct job discrimination.

The final arbiter of affirmative-action guidelines is the Supreme Court, and the justices have been troubled by race-conscious remedies for employment discrimination. The Court, under Chief Justice Warren Burger, treated this controversial issue gingerly and accepted only a small number of such cases for review. Naturally, these cases were closely watched. In some instances, race-conscious employment plans have been struck down as inadequately constructed. But in most cases the court has upheld affirmative action plans well-tailored to legal guidelines.

Affirmative Action on Trial   In *Regents of University of California v. Bakke* in 1978, the Supreme Court ruled in a muddled, divided, and lengthy opinion in favor of a white male, Allan Bakke, who claimed to be the victim of reverse discrimination. In this case, the University of California Medical School at Davis had reserved sixteen places out of 100 for minority entering students. Bakke complained that he had superior qualifications for admission than many of the minorities admitted, and the Supreme Court of the United States agreed with him when he said that he had been the victim of reverse discrimination. In a split decision, the Court ordered the university to admit Bakke, and it did so. The court forbade quota reservations of places for minorities and separate, insulated evaluations of minority applicants without comparison with other applicants. It held, however, that race could be a consideration in admissions, in these words: "The State has a substantial interest that may legitimately be served by a properly devised admissions program involving the competitive consideration of race and ethnic origin."

In another case in which the Court upheld a race-conscious remedy, Brian Weber, a thirty-one-year-old laboratory analyst with ten years' service at the Kaiser Aluminum & Chemical Corporation plant in Gramercy, Louisiana, charged the company with reverse discrimination. He claimed that he applied in April 1974 for a crafts-retraining program that would double his pay and provide him with a much better job. He was not selected, however, because the program called for at least 50 percent black trainees. As part of its voluntary affirmative-action program, Kaiser set up dual seniority ladders—one for blacks and another for whites. Those admitted to the training program were picked alternately from the top of each ladder until the positions were filled, with the result that several blacks with less seniority than Weber were chosen. Weber claimed reverse discrimination based on a literal reading of Title VII, which clearly states that employment decisions based on race are unlawful. In 1979, in *United Steelworkers of America v. Weber,* the Supreme Court ruled against Weber's claim and upheld the selection procedure—but only indirectly. The Court did not rule in favor of discriminating against white males. It held that the Kaiser affirmative-action program, being voluntary and not court-ordered, was a private matter and within the "spirit of the law," which was to advance minorities.

The Court also established important general guidelines for evaluating affirmative action programs that it would frequently return to in later years. It stated that any race-conscious relief for past discrimination would be subject to great scrutiny based on these criteria. First, a plan must be designed to break down old patterns of racial or sexual discrimination. Second, the plan must not unnecessarily trammel the interests of white (or male) employees or create an absolute bar to their advancement. In the *Weber* case, for example, whites were still admitted to the training program along with blacks. Third, the plan must not require the discharge of white (or male) workers and their replacement with black (or female) workers. Finally, the plan should be flexible and temporary, so that numerical hiring quotas and hiring goals, where they are used, can be dropped when the effects of past discrimination are overcome.

In a third case of major significance, the Supreme Court upheld another type of race-conscious remedy for past discrimination, namely "set-aside" programs for minority contractors. In 1977, Congress passed the Public Works Employment Act, which established a $4 billion fund for public-works construction programs in an effort to spur the economy. The act reserved 10 percent of this $4 billion appropriation for minority businesses. These so-called "set-asides" created problems. For one thing, there were all kinds of fraudulent schemes by companies posing as minority owned. For another, later studies showed that construction costs had increased. This was because minority firms, although not always low bidders, had to be given contracts anyway. When the set-asides were challenged, the Supreme Court ultimately ruled that it was within the power of Congress to consider race-conscious criteria to remedy past patterns of discrimination against minority contractors in the construction industry. In *Fullilove v. Klutznick* in 1980, the Court rejected the contention of petitioning contractors that this "reverse discrimination" was an inappropriate remedy.

In other cases, however, the Supreme Court has refused to uphold affirmative-action programs. In 1981, the Memphis Fire Department was forced to lay off firefighters because of budgetary problems. The fire department had been following an affirmative-action plan, and under a district court order, recently had hired blacks for one of every two vacancies. Because of the operation of a seniority system, however, many new blacks would be laid off, and the progress made under the affirmative action program would be lost. The district court that mandated the original affirmative-action hiring program ordered the Memphis Fire Department to alter its seniority plan in order to retain blacks and lay off more whites—even though the whites had more seniority. In *Firefighters Local Union No. 1784 v. Stotts* in 1984, a 6–3 Supreme Court majority held that the seniority system should be maintained in its original state, even if many recently hired blacks were laid off. The justices held that the intent of Congress in Title VII was to prohibit tampering with ongoing seniority systems.

This case raised the hopes of some opponents of affirmative action that the Court might be ready to rule in favor of a color-blind interpretation of Title VII. If it would condemn race preference in layoffs, was it ready to prohibit race consciousness in hiring and end court-ordered affirmative-action programs? The answer was no. In several 1986 cases the Supreme Court further defined the conditions under which affirmative action was acceptable and, although the majorities were weakened by concurring opinions and dissents were strong, it upheld the concept of affirmative action in hiring as a remedy for past discrimination.

The first case was *Wendy Wygant et al. v. Jackson Board of Education*. There a Michigan school district had adopted a layoff plan in which seniority would be followed, except that at no time could the number of minority teachers laid off exceed the minority employment percentage in the district. As a result, white teachers with more seniority than black teachers were laid off. The Court struck down the layoff plan, stating that it imposed too great a burden on those teachers laid off. Justice Powell, writing for the majority, argued:

> While hiring goals impose a diffuse burden, often foreclosing only one of several opportunities, layoffs impose the entire burden of achieving racial equality on particular individuals, often resulting in serious disruption of their lives. That burden is too intrusive. . . . Other less intrusive means of accomplishing similar purposes—such as the adoption of hiring goals—are available (54 LW 4484).

Thus, even though the Court struck down a layoff provision giving preference to minorities, it implied that preferential hiring plans could be acceptable as a remedy for racial imbalance in a work force. The Court confirmed this stand in four other cases.

In *Local 28 v. EEOC* (1986) and *Local No. 93 v. City of Cleveland* (1986), the Court upheld affirmative action programs utilizing goals and timetables to overcome flagrant patterns of hiring discrimination by unions. In *United States v. Paradise* (1987), the Court upheld an affirmative action plan adopted by the Alabama Department of Public Safety, which required that 50 percent of the promotions to the rank of corporal be given to blacks. And in *Johnson v. Transportation Agency, Santa Clara County, California* (1987), the Court upheld an affirmative-action plan that permitted supervisors to consider the sex of an applicant as one factor in promotion decisions until the agency work force had enough women in various job categories to approximately equal the 36.4 percent of women in the area labor market.

In these cases the Court argued that a compelling societal interest in ending past patterns of egregious discrimination justified hiring and promotion programs that favored minorities and women. The Court relied heavily on the criteria developed in the *Weber* case and approved affirmative action plans that remedied past discrimination, did not absolutely bar the advancement of whites and men, did not require the discharge of whites or men, and were flexible and temporary.

Throughout this period a minority on the Court penned a series of dissents. The dissenters argued that the prohibition against employment discrimination in Title VII, taken literally, was absolute and prohibited affirmative action programs that utilized race and sex as the basis for preferential treatment. For example, Justice Scalia wrote these words of dissent in the *Johnson* case:

> The Court today completes the process of converting [Title VII] from a guarantee that race or sex will *not* be the basis for employment determinations, to a guarantee that if often *will*. Ever so subtly, without even alluding to the last obstacles preserved by earlier opinions that we now push out of our path, we effectively replace the goal of a discrimination-free society with the quite incompatible goal of proportionate representation by race and by sex in the workplace (55 LW 4391).
>
> In effect, *Weber* held that the legality of intentional discrimination by private employers against certain disfavored groups or individuals is to be judged not by Title VII but by a judicially crafted code of conduct, the contours of which are determined by no discernible standard . . . We have been recasting that self-promulgated code of conduct ever since—and what it has led to today adds to the reasons for abandoning it (55 LW 4394).

Ethical Issues in Affirmative Action

How can discrimination against white males, which inevitably must take place in affirmative-action programs, be justified? There are three directions of ethical argument in which debate commonly proceeds.

First, there are utilitarian considerations. Utilitarian ethics require calculations about the overall benefit to society, as opposed to the costs, of reverse discrimination. Is affirmative action an effective policy for providing the greatest good for the greatest number of people? Advocates say yes. Preferential treatment of blacks, women, and other minority groups enriches society by bringing fuller utilization of human resources, demonstrating compassion, and shoring up political stability (because unhappy, unemployed, poor people riot). Opponents, however, argue that affirmative action promotes inefficiency. Employers must hire less trained, less qualified workers, and that lowers productivity. Employees protected by legislation suffer diminished self-esteem when they are made to feel undeserving of their positions. In the end, it is impossible to establish precisely the relative weights of costs and benefits. No convincing conclusion about overall impact on society will soon be forthcoming.

Second, ethical theories of justice have been used to raise questions about the ultimate fairness and equity of affirmative action. It is fundamentally unethical, argue some, to distribute power and economic rewards unequally in a liberal, humanistic, democratic society by using racial, ethnic, and sexist criteria. Although outright discrimination is less than in the past, subtle forms of discrimination remain in our institutions. And past discrimination has created handicaps for women and minorities that put them at current disadvantage. Blacks, for example, have not had access to equal education with whites. Early in

American history they were enslaved. Thus discrimination in favor of blacks is thought by some to compensate for past injustice and deprivation. In 1963, President Lyndon Johnson used a colorful analogy to make this point.

> Imagine a hundred-yard dash in which one of the two runners has his legs shackled together. He has progressed ten yards, while the unshackled runner has gone fifty yards. How do they rectify the situation? Do they merely remove the shackles and allow the race to proceed? Then they could say that "equal opportunity" now prevailed. But one of the runners would still be forty yards ahead of the other. Would it not be the better part of justice to allow the previously shackled runner to make up the forty-yard gap or to start the race all over again? (Fullinwider, 1980: 95).

However, with affirmative action, the penalty for past injustices falls on the current generation of white males—probably the least racist and discriminatory of all generations. Affirmative action may compensate for past economic deprivation, but of course it cannot compensate for pain and suffering among those long dead. Is it just and fair, then, to impose it, in view of these obvious inequities?

And third, affirmative action may be examined in light of ethical doctrines stipulating that humans possess important rights that the good society protects. Are there minimal levels of rights to equal treatment that cannot be abridged? Advocates of affirmative action argue that when the rights of minorities and white males conflict in the personnel process, the rights of minorities should be given precedence. Discrimination in favor of blacks, women, and others is benevolent of intention, unlike the evil discrimination of whites against blacks in the past. It is necessary to mint a new right, the right of preferential treatment for suffering minorities, and to exercise it until equality prevails. There is some validity to this argument, but discrimination against whites perpetuates the distribution of rewards and power on the basis of race, which is a discredited doctrine in our society.

There is no easy resolution to the contradictory appeals of these ethical arguments. Philosopher Robert K. Fullinwider (1980) notes that "earlier patterns of racial discrimination and oppression in our nation were so egregiously offensive that people could unite in condemning them without being forced to formulate with precision the principles upon which their condemnation rested" (p. 8). Reverse discrimination, however, is a more subtle evil and requires us to further refine our ethical thinking. That process is ongoing and exemplified by the work of Father Theodore Purcell.

Purcell's Theoretical and Ethical Guidelines

Despite the complexity of the issues, lucid thinking exists. Father Purcell, a leading scholar in this field and a strong proponent of minority rights, devised guidelines to avoid many of the dilemmas in pursuing equal opportunity goals:

To implement acceleration and preferential practices, let management choose the minority person for the job or promotion—if certain provisos are verified. The minority person should be either qualified (or qualifiable in a reasonable time) for the job or promotion, according to a *single* standard of minimum qualifications for performing that job applicable to everyone. Unqualified people should not be accepted. Standards should not be lowered, but they should be clearly job-related.

Each case or class of cases should be considered in an ad hoc manner according to the following criteria. If the minority person is *more* qualified, pick the minority person. If the minority and majority persons are *equally* qualified (as far as fair, job-related selection techniques can determine), and minorities are underrepresented on the job, pick the minority person.

If both minority and majority persons are clearly qualified, but the majority person is more qualified in job-related abilities, then carefully analyze and consider these two variables simultaneously: 1. the scope, importance, and responsibility of the job for the safe and efficient operation of the business, and 2. the gap in qualifications of various applicants. Since this is the most controversial aspect of my theory, let us examine it in more detail.

The Importance of the Job. When the job is not very sensitive or important regarding the safety and efficiency of the company or the welfare of fellow workers or customers, I suggest picking the qualified minority person. But as the job becomes more important or is actually a pass-through position to a higher job demanding greater qualifications, pick the *better*-qualified person—in this case, the majority person. One example: When choosing between applicants for an airline pilot's job, you would more readily consider merit over preference than when choosing between applicants for a flight attendant's job. At the low end of the spectrum, minority preference is desirable. As you move toward more job importance, greater merit should take precedence.

The Qualifications Gap. Always assuming both minority and majority persons or classes of persons are clearly qualified, differences in the job-related qualifications can range from very small to very large. Evaluating qualifications is often very difficult, but let us make the assumption that it is done fairly, accurately, and without prejudice. Now, suppose a very small, but perceptible, gap appears with the majority person being more qualified, and at the same time the job importance is low. Then I still suggest—prefer the minority person. One example: A combination of test scores plus subjective judgments might put a majority person at 87 on the scale of 1 to 100 and a minority person at 86—a slight difference. At the low end of the spectrum, minority preference is desirable. As the qualifications gap widens, greater merit should take precedence.

Preferring the qualified, but lesser qualified, minority person when *both* the job importance and qualifications gap are *high* would be reverse discrimination. Not preferring the qualified, but lesser qualified, minority person when *both* the job importance and qualifications gap are *low* would be unaffirmative action, or reverse affirmative action.

Such preference is not necessarily reverse discrimination. Neither the qualified majority nor the qualified minority person has a right in either distributive or commutative justice to a *specific* job or promotion. Fair consideration does not always require the employer to hire or promote the more qualified person. If the employer has a good and valid reason, called for by the common good, for employing the qualified, but less qualified, person, this does not violate the rights in justice of the person passed over (Purcell, 1977: 97–98).

THE IMPACT ON BUSINESS MANAGEMENT OF EQUAL OPPORTUNITY AND AFFIRMATIVE-ACTION PROGRAMS

Legislation, regulations, and court decisions have had a profound impact on employment practices. As a result, managerial processes have been significantly altered.

This alteration has evolved through three phases in the typical large corporation. In Phase I most large companies were filled with a range of subtle and overt discrimination in employment practices. Following passage of the Civil Rights Act of 1964 some companies began to seek and hire minorities. Many executives were scared by the rioting in the 1960s and developed programs for the hardcore unemployed or participated in nationwide minority hiring efforts such as the National Alliance of Business started by Henry Ford II in 1967. Other managers were jolted out of their lethargy by court decisions such as *Griggs v. Duke Power Company* in 1971 and *Equal Employment Opportunity Commission v. AT&T* in 1973. In the *Griggs* case, the courts reinforced the hand of the EEOC. Black employees challenged the company's requirements for a high-school education and the passing of a number of tests (that were not related to the job) before employment was possible. "The Civil Rights Act," said the court, "proscribes not only overt discrimination but also practices that are fair in form, but discriminatory in operation. The touchstone is business necessity. If an employment practice which operates to exclude Negroes cannot be shown to be related to job performance, the practice is prohibited." This case probably marked a turning point in the attitudes of businesspeople. Until then, many regulations were fuzzy, and the attitude of the courts was not clear. Those companies that had taken a "wait and see" position saw that with judicial blessing the federal government meant business. In *EEOC v. AT&T*, the telephone company, then the world's largest private employer, with 750,000 employees, was found guilty of discrimination and made a $36 million settlement with the EEOC to cover back wages. Both cases were clear signals to American industry that there was bite in the basic legislation and EEOC intended to use it.

In Phase II, companies appointed EEO officers, very frequently at senior-level staff positions, to develop policy and procedures for use throughout the company. A survey of senior personnel managers showed that from 1974 to 1975, they spent 40 percent of their time on EEO matters. The larger the company, the more time these executives spent on this program. Each of the separate personnel activities of the company took on equal opportunity and affirmative-action programs and were coordinated (Janger, 1977).

> *Recruitment, selection and employment* assumed responsibility for ensuring that new employee recruitment, promotion and transfer policies, and other activities were not deliberately discriminatory and were in conformance with laws that protected minorities.

> *Labor relations* was responsible for ensuring that collective bargaining agreements did not contain clauses that illegally discriminated.

Training was responsible for assessing the need for and developing special training and development procedures for minority and female employees.

Work force forecasting had to make sure that projections of staffing needs considered proper implementation of affirmative-action programs.

Compensation and benefits was to assure that minorities and women received equal pay for equal work.

Safety/training and management had to ensure that requirements for working procedures and maintenance, training for workers and supervisors, and measurement procedures were suitable for the new work force.

Medical department was required to reshape the preemployment physical to avoid disparate effects or to make it job-related.

Organization planning and development had to redesign jobs and/or establish special management-development programs for minorities and women.

Phase III took place when policies and procedures of the company were decentralized to the divisions. With appropriate reporting, managerial monitoring, and compensation policy, equal-opportunity and affirmative-action programs became firmly institutionalized in company decision-making processes. The costs of these programs are enormous. One study in 1982 estimated the total annual compliance cost for the *Fortune* 500 at $1 billion (Seligman, 1982: 156). The costs of compliance for a company begin with paperwork, including required forms for half a dozen federal agencies, development of corporate affirmative-action policies, and production of legal documents for litigation. There is much ongoing litigation. Typically, large corporations have several hundred discrimination charges against them at any one time. Each requires about forty hours of company employees' time and roughly $10,000 to $20,000 in outside legal fees, more if the case is complicated. Large companies must have a sizable staff of experts to handle equal-employment and affirmative-action policies. Periodically, federal officials from the EEOC or OFCCP may conduct a review of programs to see if they are on schedule. The cost of such a compliance review may be $20,000 or more.

A variety of other expenses may occur. For instance, architectural adjustments such as ramps and railings may need to be installed for handicapped workers. The Continental Bank of Chicago has replaced its large revolving center door with a double air door to remove a physical barrier to handicapped employees and customers. Other companies have changed office layouts, rebuilt restrooms, and added braille to elevator controls. But sometimes fighting discrimination saves money. In 1986, Lodwick M. Cook, chairman of Atlantic Richfield, announced that the firm no longer would reimburse its executives for membership dues in private clubs with discriminatory membership policies. The policy change affected about thirty ARCO executives, most of whom were members of the California and Jonathan clubs in Los Angeles and the Petroleum Club in Dallas.

WOMEN IN THE WORKPLACE

Social trends and economic necessity have combined to bring about an unprecedented movement of women into the work place. During World Wars I and II, women moved into the labor force in large numbers to help with the war effort, becoming about one-fourth of the total work force in those wars. Following World War I, women went back to traditional roles in the home and on the farm, but after World War II they stayed at work.

Because of economic necessity, feminist attitudes, and high divorce rates, the number of women in the work force has continued to rise. In 1970, women constituted 33 percent of those employed, about the same as in 1960. But by 1986, women were 44 percent of the employed, and 55 percent of all working-age women were on the job (*Monthly Labor Review,* 1986). It is widely predicted that the number of working women will continue to increase over the next decade. Although much of the influx has been to low-paying, low-status jobs in the expanding service sector of the economy, women are rapidly increasing in the ranks of professionals, where they are now 49 percent, and in managerial jobs, where they are 36 percent of all managers (Gilder, 1986). About 25 percent of business-school (MBA) graduates now are women.

The entry of all these women into the work force has challenged employers and created the need for new policies and procedures. The challenges center around the feminist assault on male dominance of corporate life. In addition, the special needs of women have had to be recognized. A growing number of firms provide day care for employees' children and child care leaves for both men and women. At least fifteen large corporations are scrambling to develop policies that reduce their liability for sexual harassment if they are sued by victimized women. A small number of companies, including Levi-Strauss and Westinghouse, have sponsored employee training programs on premenstrual distress (Watkins, 1986). And companies increasingly realize that they must contend with new possibilities for romantic relations among workers as the sexes step into increasingly proximate and equal work assignments.

GENDER ATTITUDES AT WORK

Throughout recorded history, men and women have been socialized into distinctly different sex roles. The male was traditionally aggressive, logical, the breadwinner, and dominant. Women were objects of sexual desire, emotional, homemakers, and submissive. For centuries, a comfortable symmetry of sex roles existed. These traditional attitudes were carried from family and social life into the workplace, where they defined male-female relationships.

Consider, for example, these statements from older books giving career advice to women. Writing in 1929, Miriam Simons Lueck in *Fields of Work for Women* reinforced the traditional homemaker stereotype by suggesting that women were more interested in being wives than managers.

> Men maintain, not entirely without reason, that women want the honors and the salary, yet shirk the actual responsibility. . . . Employers insist, and events support their statement, that just when they have a woman trained to take over her share of executive responsibility, she marries (Lueck, 1929:15).

Catharine Oglesby, in her 1932 book, *Business Opportunities for Women*, accepted the image of women as sex objects and frivolous gossips concerned mainly about their appearance:

> The majority of business women have definite hours reserved by their hairdresser and manicurist. These stand week in and week out. They enjoy all the importance of a "heavy date," and business obligations are fitted around them. . . . Whenever a group of women gather to chat the subject is usually *clothes* (Oglesby, 1932: 28).

In the 1960s, a powerful, worldwide feminist movement arose that challenged male domination in Eastern and Western cultures. Feminists argued that women were equally capable of holding traditionally masculine jobs and attacked a range of cultural impediments to equality. Men no longer were obliged to open doors for working women because even manners were thought to subtly assert male dominance. Women no longer accepted the submissive role of guest at business lunches, and took their male counterparts out. And, of course, women's political organizations pushed laws fighting sex discrimination and promoting equality in work and pay.

As a result of the feminist movement, two competing sets of values exist in the workplace today. The new feminist perspective of equality, widely held by women workers, clashes with traditional stereotypes of sex roles still prevalent among men. Some men still feel that women are too emotional to manage well; that they lack the ambition, aggressiveness, and toughness to excell in business; that male executives' wives dislike their husbands' working and traveling with women; and that women cannot display the sustained career drive of men due to pregnancy, child rearing, and family obligations. Inherent in all these stereotypes are basic attitudes of male dominance and superiority.

Yet evidence suggests that such stereotypes, in the aggregate, are inaccurate. One recent study shows that women are more committed to their careers than men. In this large survey, women were more likely than men to prioritize a job-related function over a family function and to relocate their families for a promotion or job advance. They were less likely than men to turn down a promotion that changed their lifestyle. Women also were more willing to work long hours than were men (Powell, Posner, and Schmidt, 1985). This study, then, shows that at least one sample of women tended to have more of the characteristics that promote business goals than did men. A variety of other studies and surveys indicate that women are not different from men in the way they work. A study analyzing the decision styles of 279 women managers found that the women were, like male managers, predominantly left brain and tended to use the same decision-making methods as men. It concluded that, "from a decision-style perspective, women are as capable of performing managerial jobs as men" (Boulgarides and Rowe, 1983: 23). Interestingly enough, in another study by James D. Boulgarides (1983), 43 percent of a sample of female engineers believed their work to be superior to that of their male counterparts (45 percent felt that it was about the same, and only 1 percent saw it as less good). The old stereotypes are fading, but they still exist and strongly influence male-female relations at work.

THE ORGANIZATIONAL DOUBLE STANDARD

Traditional stereotypes of women in predominantly masculine organizations underlie differential treatment. Here we discuss several important ways that women in corporate life have not been treated equally with men.

Occupational Segregation

Women are more likely to work in some kinds of jobs than in others. Within corporations and in the economy as a whole, women's jobs generally are lower in status and pay than typically male jobs. Women also have less occupational diversity that men do. Most women work in food and health services, clerical, and professional job classifications. And most women in the professional category are either registered nurses or teachers. A majority of both men and women are in work situations where they have daily contact mostly with coworkers of the same sex (Gutek, 1985).

Despite a great deal of occupational concentration in traditionally feminine work roles, the huge influx of women into the workplace has led them into traditionally male occupations. In the past decade, for example, three mostly male occupational categories—insurance adjuster, computer operator, and typesetter and compositor—have come to have a majority of women. Women are integrating other occupations; they are now, for instance, 44 percent of accountants and auditors (Trost, 1986). Some feminists worry that if women predominate in new job categories, those categories will be devalued in pay and prestige relative to remaining male bastions. In fact, as the percentage of women continues to rise in the work force and in traditionally male occupations, women will increasingly displace male workers (A. Hacker, 1984).

Differential Treatment in the Work Process

Women who have jobs in male-dominated organizations are thought to have a difficult time. Of course, some women managers and executives have not had problems. They may even have received preferential treatment. But the majority have problems with sexist attitudes. Rarely are these attitudes blatantly expressed, but they exist. Women have less access to corporate success where male chauvinism is present. They are less likely to participate in informal group activities, such as having a drink after work, when valuable information about organizational life may be shared. It is more difficult for them to find mentors; they cannot be pulled up by other women in the organization. A male mentor may be hesitant, fearful that his relationship with a woman will be awkward and misunderstood as a romantic interest. Men are more likely to interrupt women at meetings than the reverse. They may mistake them for secretaries, apologize for swearing in their presence, forget their presence in a decision-making group, and proposition them. Few corporations have sent women into overseas management positions due to the belief that male-dominated foreign cultures would limit their effectiveness. In some countries, such as Saudi Arabia, where laws inhibit the activities of women, this reluctance makes sense. One study of 121 companies showed that only 3 percent of overseas assignments in many countries went to women managers (Adler, 1984).

Much of this male insult and awkwardness arises from the continued male perception of female coworkers as submissive objects. Men who are conditioned to see women as lovers or wives may subconsciously place women coworkers in the same category. These men may find it difficult to work for a female boss or include women in formerly male gatherings. A man who would not think of bringing his wife to a business meeting where coarse jokes are told may feel awkward if a female manager attends the same meeting.

In major cities across the country, exclusive private clubs continue to bar women, although discriminatory membership policies are getting harder to legally sustain. For example, the rules of Rotary International prohibit female members; when the Rotary Club of Duarte, California, admitted three women to membership the international organization terminated its charter. In *Rotary International v. Rotary Club of Duarte* (1987), the Supreme Court struck down this termination on the grounds that a California law, which entitles all persons equal access to business establishments, prohibited discrimination against women in membership policy. The Court refused to accept Rotary International's argument that male members had a First Amendment guarantee to freedom of private association in a club atmosphere. Justice Powell, writing for a unanimous Court, found no evidence that the admission of women would impair the official purposes of local Rotary Clubs and held that women were entitled to equal access to the leadership skills and business contacts that were a part of what the Rotary Club offered its membership. Following this decision, many private clubs in California dropped exclusionary membership policies.

The Pay Gap

Pay is an area in which the organizational double standard has a long historical record. For example, an 1883 survey in Philadelphia showed that women were paid less for a typical seventy-eight-hour work week than men were paid for one ten-hour day (Demmings, 1983). At Westinghouse in the 1930s, all plant jobs were classified as either "male" or "female" jobs, and an official company *Industrial Relations Manual* instructed that "female" jobs rated equal to "male" jobs in terms of skill, physical effort required, responsibility, and working conditions were to be given lower compensation. This was justified, the *Manual* said,

> because of the more transient character of the service of the women, the relative shortness of their activity in industry, the differences in environment required, the extra services that must be provided, overtime limitations and the general sociological factors not requiring discussion herein (Demmings, 1983: 3B).

In 1983 the average woman still earned only 64 cents for every dollar earned by a man. The average annual income for men was 36 percent higher than for women. Within major job classifications, women earned less than men. And jobs typically dominated by women paid less than male-dominated jobs. For example, in 1983 non-auto mechanics, the occupation with the highest percentage of men, earned an average of $22,161. Secretaries, the occupation with the most women, earned an average $13,886 (Gest, 1985). Male dominance of more powerful and career enhancing jobs in business is only one reason for the male-female pay gap. Another is that the entry of many women into the labor force in recent years means that they have low seniority.

Women are protected against pay discrimination based on sex by the Equal Pay Act of 1963, which prohibits paying women less than men for jobs which are identical or not substantially different. Recently, however, women's rights advocates have developed the idea of comparable worth for equalizing pay with male occupations. Basically, comparable worth is the theory that lower-paying jobs held by women may be comparable in their content, effort, and responsibility with nonidentical higher-paying jobs typically held by men. In a comparable worth study done in the Washington state government, for example, points were assigned for the "knowledge and skills, mental demands, accountability, and working conditions" in relatively low-paying jobs held mainly by men or mainly by women. The resulting tally indicated that the job of "laundry worker," usually held by a woman making $1,114 per month, received the same point total as the normally male "truck driver I," which paid $1,574 (Tuerck, 1986). Advocates of comparable worth argue that nonidentical but comparable jobs should be paid equally. If there is a wage differential between "men's jobs" and "women's jobs," it is evidence of sex discrimination by the employer.

The Equal Pay Act prohibits sex-based pay discrimination only for jobs that are identical or nearly identical within the same facility. It is too narrow to uphold the idea of comparable worth. Therefore those who advocate comparable worth, including women's groups and state employee unions, have argued that Title VII of the Civil Rights Act of 1964 is broader and prohibits pay differentials among both identical and comparable jobs where these jobs are held mainly by opposite sexes. Most courts have rejected this argument. Opponents of comparable worth, which include business groups such as the Chamber of Commerce, believe that the wage differential between roughly comparable men's and women's jobs is determined in the labor market and is not the result of discrimination. They do not wish to see wages determined by the courts. Nevertheless, comparable worth advocates have won major victories. After a twelve-year battle in the courts, Washington state employees succeeded in getting a ruling that the state had to end pay discrimination and give $482 million in back pay to female state employees in jobs comparable to higher paying men's jobs. Seven states now have comparable worth laws for government employees.

How Persistent Is the Organizational Double Standard?

The clash of traditional male stereotypes with new feminist ideals of equality in work roles has been much studied. Its existence is documented by years of survey data and a continuing stream of anecdotes by candid men and angry women. Apparently, though, the gap between male and female attitudes is narrowing, and women are more widely accepted by men than in the past. For example, surveys of executive attitudes about women in business were conducted in 1965 and again twenty years later in 1985. The results, published in the *Harvard Business Review,* showed that sexist male attitudes toward women were receding. The number of men expressing an "unfavorable basic attitude" toward female executives fell from 41 percent in 1965 to 5 percent in 1985. The surveys also showed that:

■ In 1965, 9 percent of the men surveyed agreed that "men feel comfortable working for women." By 1985, 21 percent agreed.

■ In 1965, 54 percent agreed that "women rarely expect or want authority." By 1985, only 9 percent agreed.

■ In 1965, 61 percent felt that "the business community will never wholly accept women executives." But by 1985, only 20 percent agreed (Sutton and Moore, 1985: 42–52).

Despite these changing attitudes, however, it has proven difficult for women to meet their central goals in corporate work life: a gender-neutral workplace, equal pay, and promotion to the top. In each of these areas, women are making progress, but nowhere is it regarded as satisfactory yet.

SEXUAL HARASSMENT

Another problem faced by working women is sexual harassment. Although various permutations of harassment are possible, including homosexual and lesbian harassment, the major problem today is harassment of women by male superiors.

Office Romance?

Unlike the cowboys who checked their guns with saloon keepers, employers have never gotten employees to set aside their libidos at the office entrance. All manner of relationships flourish in the corporation.

Affairs between male bosses and female secretaries are commonplace and often pursued with gusto, as in the case of an executive who "kept a rolled-up mattress in his file cabinet, ready for fun and games" (Horn and Horn, 1982: 116). Of growing frequency are affairs stemming from the delightful new propinquity of men and women who work more closely in situations of equality and discover mutual interests that transcend the workaday world.

How frequent are affairs? A survey of 211 people in Boston airport waiting rooms by Robert E. Quinn (1977) found that 83 percent reported witnessing affairs in their workplaces. These affairs were viewed negatively 90 percent of the time because they caused gossip, coworker hostility, and strained relations after a breakup. A study of executives found that 21 percent of 5,260 married executives had had extra-marital affairs during their work lives—often with coworkers. Travel, by the way, was strongly associated with liaison. Forty-nine percent of those traveling more than 25 percent of the time reported an affair (H. Johnson, 1974).

As female executives achieve greater equality with male counterparts, cupid is prowling the executive suite. But although women of high organizational status may become more attractive as serious romantic interests, romance between executives in the same organization may be very dangerous. In a thoughtful article, Eliza G. Collins (1983) argues that managerial romance challenges the traditional organization structure. Love relationships in which the man is dominant, as is traditionally the case, in our culture, may disrupt managerial routine between two supposed equals. If they run separate divisions in a company, for instance, they may not be able to confront each other to defend subordinates or resolve grievances. They may also form a power coalition in pursuit of organizational resources that scares other managers on their level. If the man is organizationally higher than the woman, the woman's colleagues may shun her, fearing that informal banter and gossip will be repeated in pillow talk with the superior. If the senior male manager befriends his lover in organizational politics, she will be rejected by jealous colleagues. The senior male manager's subordinates may be fearful that he will be weakened by the affair and unable to advance their careers as before.

Male dominance of organization life is a controlling factor when romantic relationships occur. Students of the subject report that in 74 percent of the cases the man is organizationally above the woman, and that when job loss occurs it is twice as likely to be the woman who leaves (Quinn and Lees, 1984). The organization is most likely to discharge the romantic partner of lesser importance.

In her book *Sexual Shakedown* (1978), Lin Farley defined sexual harassment as "unsolicited nonreciprocal male behavior that asserts a woman's role over her function as a worker" (p. 14). This definition encompasses a wide range of behavior. Minor forms of harassment include suggestive stares, gratuitous touching, referring to women as "honey" or "sweetie," and off-color jokes. The tendency of older men to treat younger women as daughters, a tendency that makes a female manager's job sticky when subordinates are older men, also fits Farley's definition. More serious forms of harassment are unwanted propositions for sex, lewd remarks, and physical assault.

In a survey of both men and women, Gutek (1985) found that 53 percent of women and 7 percent of men had experienced sexual harassment. Gutek found, furthermore, that men and women reacted very differently to sexual overtures, with 67 percent of men saying they would feel flattered by a proposition to have sex, whereas only 17 percent of women felt that way. Women also were more likely than men to perceive various actions in a range of verbal and physical acts as sexual harassment.

Forms of sexual harassment may reinforce the sexist double standard in organizations. By treating a woman as a sex object, a man places her in the stereotypical role of submissive female. Harassment affects women at all levels in the corporation and many are afraid to report it because it may be a case of their word against a supervising male's. Sexual harassment may contribute to a pattern of female job loss that interrupts careers and lowers incomes. Women who have had to quit a job because of it lose seniority, access to fringe benefits, and salary. Furthermore, women who are considered unattractive may lose economically if selection and promotion processes favor women who are sexually alluring. In addition, women who are harassed are less productive, take more sick leave, and frequently request transfers (Walsh, 1986). All this is costly to the organization.

In November 1980 the EEOC issued guidelines for employers for determining the nature of sexual harassment in the workplace that is prohibited under Title VII of the Civil Rights Act of 1964. Basically, these guidelines, reprinted in Exhibit 17–1, hold that sexual behavior is harassment if it is required for an employee to continue and advance in a job or if it creates an upsetting work atmosphere for the employee. These guidelines have since been upheld and

EXHIBIT 17–1   EEOC GUIDELINES ON SEXUAL HARASSMENT

Unwelcome sexual advances, requests for sexual favors, and other verbal or physical conduct of a sexual nature constitute sexual harassment when:

1. submission to such conduct is made either explicitly or implicitly a term or condition of an individual's employment,
2. submission to or rejection of such conduct by an individual is used as the basis for employment decisions affecting such individual, or
3. such conduct has the purpose or effect of unreasonably interfering with an individual's work performance or creating an intimidating, hostile, or offensive working environment.

Source: Equal Employment Opportunity Commission, 1980.

refined by the courts. In the case of *Meritor Savings Bank v. Vinson* in 1986, the Supreme Court decided that employers may be liable for the harassing acts of their employees that create a hostile working environment. It did not make clear under what circumstances liability arises but hinted that a clear management policy against harassment and a workable grievance procedure are important in reducing liability. Without this kind of management oversight, a company could be held responsible for the harassment of an employee of which it had no knowledge. Therefore corporations around the country have developed training programs, policies, and oversight procedures by which to protect themselves from liability.

You Be the Judge

Deborah Ukarish was a female worker at Magnesium Elektron, Inc., a company that produced zirconium chemicals. After an employment interview in which she demonstrated her strength by lifting an 80-pound bag off the ground and gave an impression of personality, she was hired to operate several pieces of mechanical equipment in the production department, including a kiln, a mixer, and a press.

During her eight-hour shift she was required to work in close proximity with several male coworkers and was immediately introduced to the pervasive climate of sexual language, bantering, and joking. She freely entered into this dialogue and interaction. She joined in the obscene language and appeared to accept the customary atmosphere. But in fact, at home each night Mrs. Ukarish wrote negative feelings in her diary about the profane, sexual work atmosphere. She was particularly upset by one fellow worker, Jimmy Miller, with whom she had fallen into a pattern of sexually oriented dialogue. Mr. Miller, for example, candidly described to her his sexual exploits, and in return she sometimes teased him with slang terms alluding to his possible homosexuality.

Once the foreman had to intervene to stop an angry exchange of curses between Mrs. Ukarish and Mr. Miller. Two months after her hiring, she got into another profane argument with Mr. Miller when he failed to clean out the mixer, causing her to be blamed by the foreman for its improper operation. She blocked Mr. Miller's path, called him a "—ing liar," and shoved him. He in turn called her a sexual expletive and pushed her away, whereupon she kicked him in the scrotum.

When this incident was reported, the foreman and production department supervisor conducted an investigation that resulted in Mrs. Ukarish's termination. At first, Mrs. Ukarish belligerently claimed that Mr. Miller (who had not been injured) had provoked her and got what he deserved. Later she pleaded for her job. When asked to leave the premises she punctuated her departure with an obscene gesture.

Mrs. Ukarish brought suit against Magnesium Elektron, alleging that she had been required to work in a hostile sexual atmosphere in violation of Title VII prohibitions against sexual harassment. The company argued that Mrs. Ukarish had not complained about the plant's work environment and that she had been fired for violating company policy prohibiting fighting

Was Deborah Ukarish a victim of sexual harassment, and was she unfairly provoked because the company failed to change a work environment laden with profane language and sexual innuendo? Examine the EEOC's "Guidelines on Sexual Harassment" in Exhibit 17–1, and then you be the judge.

THE COURT'S DECISION

In the 1983 case *Ukarish v. Magnesium Elektron,* the U.S. District Court of New Jersey ruled that Mrs. Ukarish had been fairly treated. The customary sexual and profane language on the production floor preceded her hiring and did not become worse during her employment. Additionally, there was no indication that Mr. Miller's conduct was so excessively aggravating in relation to his coworkers that management should have been aware of it and taken strong corrective action. Even though she may have been upset inside about perceived sexual harassment, she gave no outward indication of displeasure and did not complain to management. Indeed, she joined in the customary language and give-and-take of the male workers. Therefore, reasoned the court, the company was not remiss for not taking remedial action to alter a hostile work atmosphere.

CONCLUDING OBSERVATION: HUMAN RESOURCES MANAGEMENT

Human resources are of increasing concern to business managers, and they and their companies are responding positively. For most companies, the response is piecemeal. That is, various aspects of the subject are treated separately, sometimes coordinated, but most of the time not.

There is a discernible trend which, although not strong, seems to us to be in the right direction. It is a holistic view of human resources management in which the corporation seeks to develop a comprehensive, integrated set of policies, strategies, and operational plans to address all of the main human relations questions that confront the typical large company. The different aspects of human relations injected into the strategic planning process and management's thinking might embrace the following: an abstract, top-level policy concerning the company's interest in its employees, their careers, their working conditions, their compensation, and their retirement; the development of concrete goals and objectives to achieve these policies in the most satisfactory manner; strategies and detailed programs to reach these objectives; and methods to ensure the implementation of plans.

The range of specific programs that might be developed is very wide. To illustrate, it might include company pension plans; top-management succession plans; career path planning for managers and employees; plans to achieve job security; managerial training programs; employee skill-enhancement programs; improved physical working conditions; fringe benefits; hiring plans; equal opportunity programs; reward systems to recognize achievement; job-enrichment programs; improved communications between management and hourly workers; safeguarding of employee rights (such as privacy, due process, nondiscrimination, free speech) in the workplace; quality control circles or other techniques to ensure employee participation in decision-making processes that affect them; suitable compensation programs; and satisfactory health benefits.

CASE STUDY

A NEW PLANT MANAGER

A senior executive at Federal Chemical Corp. is reviewing the records of three candidates who have applied for promotion to a newly vacant plant manager position. Federal Chemical has a work force of 9,000 employees. It is not operating under either a court-ordered affirmative-action plan or a voluntary plan negotiated with any of its unions.

What follows is a brief sketch of the reviewing executive's impression of each candidate and basic information from their folders.

EDGAR MARTIN (32 years old)

Martin is a graduate of Ivy League schools. He is energetic, polished, ambitious, and the son of a U.S. senator. During the 1986 elections, he organized a company-wide get-out-the-vote drive.

B.A.   Princeton University 1977, *cum laude* (chemistry major)

M.B.A. Columbia University 1978

1978–80 Peace Corps. (Kenya)

1980–82 Sales representative, Eastern Division of Federal Chemical

1982–84 Special assistant to the President of Federal Chemical

1985–86 Production supervisor, Western Division

1987–88 Assistant Plant Manager, Midwestern Division

1987   One of three employees receiving Outstanding Productivity Award

THOMAS WASHINGTON (58 years old)

Washington is a graduate of a small agricultural and technical school in the South (the same school the Rev. Jesse Jackson graduated from). He has been a loyal, competent employee for 17 years. He is hard working and methodical.

B.A.   North Carolina A & T 1951 (mechanical engineering)

1952–54 U.S. Army (Korea)

1955–58 Laborer, Bekins Van Lines

1958–59 Unemployed

1960–61 Laborer, Bekins Van Lines

1962–68 Driver, Bekins Van Lines

1969–70   Unemployed
1971–73   Machinist, Western Division, Federal Chemical
1974–75   Plant foreman I
1976–77   Plant foreman II
1978–83   Plant foreman III
1984–88   Assistant plant manager

MARTHA OLIVERAS (56 years old)

Oliveras has been with the company for 34 years. She is very popular with coworkers. She cohosts a local radio program on drug abuse one evening a week and works with community groups on anti-drug projects.

B.A.   University of Michigan, 1953 (English literature)
M.B.A.   Pepperdine University, Los Angeles, California, 1983
1954–73   Secretary, purchasing department, Rocky Mountain Division, Federal Chemical
1974–77   Administrative assistant, R&D Office
1978–80   Technical assistant, testing laboratory
1981–83   Sales representative, Western Division
1984–86   Sales manager, Western Division
1987–88   Assistant plant manager

Questions

1. Which of these three candidates would you choose for the position of plant manager? Why?
2. Are issues of discrimination, sexism, or affirmative action raised in this case?
3. Review the section in this chapter entitled "Ethical Issues in Affirmative Action," and use one or more of the arguments presented there to defend the candidate of your choice. What are the strongest arguments for other candidates and why are they less convincing?
4. Review Father Purcell's guidelines for preferential treatment set forth in this chapter. Is your decision compatible with them when they are applied to the three candidates for promotion here?
5. Under what circumstances could serious legal problems exist if either of the passed-over candidates filed a lawsuit?

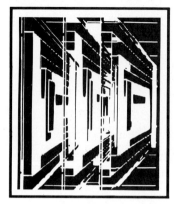

CASE STUDY

UNITED STEELWORKERS OF AMERICA V. BRIAN F. WEBER

The Supreme Court issued an opinion in the *Weber* case in 1979. Since that time, many affirmative action cases have been decided, but the *Weber* decision continues to be both important and controversial. It is important because it established the basic guidelines used by federal courts to evaluate affirmative action programs (see discussion in the preceding chapter). As the basic precedent upholding race-conscious remedies for past discrimination, *Weber* underlies the legality of many corporate personnel decisions in which minorities are given preferential treatment. It is controversial because the legal, ethical, and social grounds for reverse discrimination remain the subject of considerable debate. Debate about the meaning of *Weber* even continues among Supreme Court justices. For example, in the 1986 case of *Local Number 93 v. City of Cleveland*, Justice Brennan, who wrote the majority opinion in *Weber*, relied on *Weber*'s logic to uphold affirmative action in the Cleveland Fire Department. Justice Rehnquist, who wrote a long dissent in the *Weber* case, penned a new dissent in which he once more challenged the Court's position on the kind of race-conscious personnel actions permitted by *Weber*. Here is the story behind this critical case.

In 1979 Brian Weber was an $18,000-a-year white laboratory analyst employed by Kaiser Aluminum and Chemical Corp. at its Gramercy, Louisiana, plant. The plant is located on the east bank of the Mississippi River, less than fifty miles above New Orleans. Kaiser's Gramercy plant first began hiring workers in 1956, and the company claims that hiring practices were not overtly discriminatory. Some blacks were always on the payroll in the 1950s, but the number did not exceed 10 percent in an area that is 40 percent black.

The reasons for this low percentage were subtle. For one thing, most blacks lived on the west side of the Mississippi, opposite the plant. For another, Kaiser demanded a high school diploma; because of the relatively poor quality of black schools in the area, this requirement eliminated more blacks than whites. Then there was the widely agreed-upon fact that a person needed political pull to get a job at the Gramercy plant in its early years, and blacks found such political influence a commodity in short supply prior to enactment and enforcement of the Voting Rights Act of 1965. Finally, many qualified blacks never applied to

Kaiser simply because they felt that their applications would not be taken seriously.

After Kaiser undertook various government-mandated affirmative action programs in the 1960s, blacks constituted 18 percent of the total work force at Gramercy. However, less than 2 percent of 275 skilled craft workers employed at the plant were black. The reason was that blacks faced additional problems becoming skilled craft workers. Kaiser had a requirement of five years' experience, a rule that eliminated most local workers, both black and white, from craft worker ranks. Training schools and craft unions, the two major proving grounds available to those with no experience, discriminated against blacks and practiced nepotism among whites.

To raise this very low percentage of black craft workers at the Gramercy plant, Kaiser, as part of a 1974 collective bargaining agreement with the United Steelworkers of American (AFL-CIO), agreed to set up a training program for skilled craft workers and established a quota system in which 50 percent of the trainees chosen would be black and 50 percent white. Had workers been chosen solely on the basis of seniority, fewer blacks would have qualified. Two seniority lists were set up, one black and one white, and names were chosen alternately from each list until the thirteen positions in the program were filled.

Brian Weber, a former union activist, was one person on the white seniority list not chosen. Two of the blacks chosen, to his consternation, were lower in over-all seniority at the plant than he was. Galvanized into action by this perceived injustice, Weber wrote to the New Orleans office of the Equal Employment Opportunity Commission to get a copy of the Civil Rights Act of 1964. After reading the act, he concluded that it required all workers to be treated equally, regardless of race. He filed a complaint with the EEOC and subsequently brought a class action suit on behalf of white employees at the Gramercy plant. A federal district court, which was later upheld by a divided Court of Appeals for the Fifth Circuit, held that the training program selection procedure was discriminatory. All employment preferences based on race, said the courts, violated the law. Weber had won an early victory.

However, the United Steelworkers and Kaiser appealed the decision to the Supreme Court, and the high tribunal agreed to hear the case, scheduling oral arguments for March 28, 1978. The courtroom was packed that day, and over 100 spectators were turned away; the case had become a focus in the debate about reverse job discrimination.

Michael R. Fontham, Weber's attorney, told the justices that it was illegal for a company to give preferential treatment to minority workers to correct racial imbalance in the work force. Title VII of the Civil Rights Act of 1964, he argued, clearly forbids this kind of "reverse discrimination" or any other discrimination. The applicable text of the law to which Fontham referred is this:

It shall be an unlawful employment practice for an employer:

1. To fail or refuse to hire or to discharge any individual, or otherwise to discriminate against any individual with respect to his compensation, terms,

conditions, or privileges of employment, because of such individual's race, color, religion, sex, or national origin;

2. To limit or classify his employees or applicants for employment in any way which would deprive any individual of employment opportunities or otherwise adversely affect his status as an employee, because of such individual's race, color, religion, sex, or national origin (Section 703 [a]).

It shall be an unlawful employment practice for any employer, labor organization, or joint labor-management committee controlling apprenticeship or other training or retraining, including on-the-job training programs, to discriminate against any individual because of his race, color, religion, sex, or national origin in admission to, or employment in, any program established to provide apprenticeship or other training (Section 703 [d]).

Arguing against Weber's case, attorneys from Kaiser contended that in enacting Title VII, Congress fully sanctioned action to remedy past exclusion of minorities (and women) from crafts training programs. It was, they said, Kaiser's desire to comply with the spirit of the Civil Rights Act that had led it to set up the voluntary program. A lawyer for the United Steelworkers urged that the training program be upheld because Kaiser was taking affirmative action voluntarily and not acting in response to a government edict. The Kaiser plan, he said, was private, and because of that, it was not subject to all the constraints of government affirmative action plans where quotas might be prohibited. Deputy Solicitor General Lawrence G. Wallace represented the federal government and argued that the Kaiser program be upheld because it was a "reasonable response" to the problem of having too few blacks in the work force.

The Supreme Court announced on June 27, 1979, in a five to two decision, that it overruled the lower court and upheld the quota system for the training program. The majority decision, written by Justice William Brennan, conceded that the lower court decisions abided by the letter of the law in Title VII but argued that they were "not within its spirit." The majority felt that "an interpretation of the sections that forbade all race-conscious affirmative action would 'bring about an end completely at variance with the purpose of the statute' and must be rejected." The majority opinion of the Court read in part:

We emphasize at the outset the narrowness of our inquiry. Since the Kaiser-USWA plan does not involve state action, this case does not present an alleged violation of the Equal Protection Clause of the Constitution. Further, since the Kaiser-USWA plan was adopted voluntarily, we are not concerned with what Title VII requires or with what a court might order to remedy a past proven violation of the Act. The only question before us is the narrow statutory issue of whether Title VII *forbids* private employers and unions from voluntarily agreeing upon bona fide affirmative action plans that accord racial preferences in the manner and for the purpose provided in the Kaiser-USWA plan. . . .

Respondent argues that Congress intended in Title VII to prohibit all race-conscious affirmative action plans. . . . Respondent's argument is not without force. But it overlooks the significance of the fact that the Kaiser-USWA plan is an affirmative action plan voluntarily adopted by private parties to eliminate traditional patterns of racial segregation. . . . It is a "familiar rule, that a thing may be within the letter of the statute and yet not within the statute, because not within its spirit, nor within the intention of its makers." *Holy Trinity Church* v. *United States,* 143 U.S. 457, 459 (1892). . . .

Congress' primary concern in enacting the prohibition against racial discrimination in Title VII of the Civil Rights Act of 1964 was with "the plight of the Negro in our economy."

. . . [It] was clear to Congress that "the crux of the problem [was] to open employment opportunities for Negroes in occupations which have been traditionally closed to them," and it was to this problem that Title VII's prohibition against racial discrimination in employment was primarily addressed.

It plainly appears from the House Report accompanying the Civil Rights Act that Congress did not intend wholly to prohibit private and voluntary affirmative action efforts as one method of solving this problem. . . . Given this legislative history, we cannot agree with respondent that Congress intended to prohibit the private sector from taking effective steps to accomplish the goal that Congress designed Title VII to achieve. The very statutory words intended as a spur or catalyst to cause "employers and unions to self-examine and to self-evaluate their employment practices and to endeavor to eliminate, so far as possible, the last vestiges of an unfortunate and ignominious page in this country's history," *Albemarle* v. *Moody,* 422 U.S. 405, 418 (1975), cannot be interpreted as an absolute prohibition against all private, voluntary, race-conscious affirmative action efforts to hasten the elimination of such vestiges. It would be ironic indeed if a law triggered by a Nation's concern over centuries of racial injustice and intended to improve the lot of those who had "been excluded from the American dream for so long," 110 *Cong.Rec.,* at 6552 (remarks of Sen. Humphrey), constituted the first legislative prohibition of all voluntary, private, race-conscious efforts to abolish traditional patterns of racial segregation and hierarchy.

Thus, the Court held that the challenged Kaiser-USWA affirmative action plan fell within the spirit of the law because it was designed to break down long-existing patterns of racial segregation and open employment opportunities for blacks in an occupation traditionally closed to them. In addition to these reasons, the Court majority also pointed out that:

At the same time the plan does not unnecessarily trammel the interests of the white employees. The plan does not require the discharge of white workers and their replacement with new black hires. . . . Nor does the plan create an absolute bar to the advancement of white employees; half of those trained in the program will be white. Moreover, the plan is a temporary measure; it is not intended to maintain racial balance, but simply to eliminate a manifest racial imbalance. Preferential selection of craft trainees at the Gramercy plant will end as soon as the percentage of black skilled craft workers in the Gramercy plant approximates the percentage of blacks in the local labor force.

Chief Justice Warren Burger dissented, arguing in a separately written opinion that Title VII was "a statute of extraordinary clarity. The quota embodied in the collective-bargaining agreement between Kaiser and the Steelworkers," he wrote, "unquestionably discriminates on the basis of race against individual employees seeking admission to on-the-job training programs." He further argued that:

> Often we have difficulty interpreting statutes either because of imprecise drafting or because legislative compromises have produced genuine ambiguities. But here there is no lack of clarity, no ambiguity. The quota embodied in the collective-bargaining agreement between Kaiser and the Steelworkers unquestionably discriminates on the basis of race against individual employees seeking admission to on-the-job training programs. And, under the plain language of [Section] 703 (d), that is "an *unlawful* employment practice."

A second dissent was written by Justice William Rehnquist. In thirty-seven pages of reconstruction of the legislative history and debate of Title VII, Rehnquist quoted extensively from the floor debates in Congress to buttress his argument that the Court was making an interpretation of the law that conformed to the prejudices of the majority rather than the law's clear wording and the facts of legislative intent and congressional debate. He concluded his strongly-worded opinion by stating that:

> With today's holding, the Court introduces into Title VII a tolerance for the very evil that the law was intended to eradicate. . . . By going not merely *beyond*, but directly *against* Title VII's language and legislative history, the Court has sown the wind. Later courts will face the impossible task of reaping the whirlwind.

Reaction to the decision against Weber was mixed. Civil rights groups cheered the decision and predicted dismissal of a rash of reverse discrimination cases by white workers currently in the courts. AFL-CIO President George Meany and other union leaders also praised the decision as a blow against racial discrimination. Kaiser was pleased that its system for selecting trainees had been sanctioned by the Court, but some business executives feared that although the decision did not require employers to set up racial quota systems, there would not be more pressure to do so. Events proved him correct. Another executive, the chairman of a southern company, was even quoted in the national press as saying that it was not possible to produce goods and services at the lowest cost and also have affirmative-action programs. Such a remark seems even more impolitic today than it was at the time, at least in part because of the *Weber* decision.

After the decision and an appearance on the *Today* show in its wake, Weber returned to work at the Gramercy plant. He was making $2,000 to $7,000 less each year than blacks and whites who had gone through the crafts training program beginning in 1974. He also had less opportunity for overtime work and, unlike skilled craft workers, was required to take regular turns working a night shift.

Questions

1. Do you agree with the majority decision of the Court? Why or why not?
2. Was the Kaiser-USWA plan the best solution to underrepresentation of blacks in the ranks of craft workers?
3. What would have been the consequences to business and society had Brian Weber prevailed in his case? Do you foresee a time when the law will shift to Weber's position?
4. Do any problems or ambiguities remain in this area of law? If so, what are they?

CASE STUDY

THE SALES CAREER OF COTTON SPRINGFIELD

Frank Converse, personnel director for the Chicago Metals Company, saw his job as an adventure. And today there was already enough excitement to justify that outlook.

In the morning mail Converse received a letter from Cotton Springfield, the company's only female sales representative. It read:

Dear Mr. Converse:

This is written as a last resort. During the six months I have been working the southeastern sales territory, I have been cruelly victimized by arrogant, chauvinistic men. These men have shown me depths of male crudity and rudeness that previously I could only have imagined to exist. This sexual harassment must stop!

I have been subjected to unwanted, crude behavior by customers. When we go to dinner they tell boorish, sexually explicit jokes. They call me "honey" and "girl." More than once I have been pinched or patted on the behind. A customer in Memphis sent me a lewd, sexually suggestive Valentine card. One night in Little Rock a buyer followed me to my motel room. He was married, too! In Birmingham a customer inquired about my sexual proclivities. These and similar actions have created a hostile, interfering, and offensive working environment.

When I am in Chicago, Vice President of Sales John Turner harasses me. In his office, he jokes about having "heart-to-breast" talks with me, he has inquired about my sexual proclivities; and sometimes he compares our work relationship to the state of wedlock. When we walk together, he touches my arm to guide me, thereby asserting his male superiority. It is the responsibility of the Company to end explicitly harassing behavior toward employees, especially harassment based on gender distinctions.

In the interest of keeping my job and keeping up sales, I have not yet revealed my anger to my male tormenters. But I cannot hold it in much longer. Many nights I have returned to my room to cry. I have a diary in which I have recorded these painful experiences and my feelings. Please help me, or it will be necessary to take more drastic action.

Sincerely yours,

Cotton Springfield

This was not a pleasant letter, but for Converse, worse was yet to come. Shortly before lunch he received a phone call from Helen Gibson, Anthony Gibson's wife. It wasn't the first call from Mrs. Gibson that Converse had received, and he hated to take them. It was always the same complaint.

"I'm certain my husband is having an affair with that Cotton Springfield," said Helen Gibson.

"We've been all through this," replied Converse. "I'm convinced you're wrong. Ms. Springfield is a fine young woman."

"You don't know what I know instinctively."

"No, and what's that?"

"You don't have to live with it. I do. Would you want your wife in a situation of constant temptation?"

"Helen, I don't have much choice. Springfield is an excellent saleswoman. All of us—even Anthony—support her. Certainly you know we can't remove her from her job based on groundless fears."

"Groundless fears! Anthony says Cotton keeps telling him she is lonely. She tells him about her boyfriends and what they do in bed. You and your [expletive deleted] affirmative action. It's going to wreck my marriage. Who has washed and ironed Anthony's clothes for the twenty-two years he's been with Chicago Metals? Me! Who ran the house and raised the kids while he was away at work helping to pay your salary? Me! Who went out at night with customers and their wives for years so Chicago could get a sale? Me! I've contributed, so now what rights do I have in this company, Frank?"

Later, as he wiped up the coffee he had spilled on his desk during Helen Gibson's call, Converse reflected on the situation.

Chicago Metals had a modest sized, elite corps of sales representatives who travel throughout the country demonstrating Chicago's capability to serve clients through the application of unique metals technologies. The job of the sales force is to show a prospective client that one or more of the company's processes can fulfill a need. Each sales representative, although based in Chicago, is teamed with a partner and assigned one of seven sections of the United States. It is necessary to have two representatives working together because the work is too difficult for only one person to perform. It is common for a sales team to be on the road for two to three weeks at a time.

Of the fourteen sales representatives, not one had been a woman until eight months ago, when Converse had agreed with the recommendation of the vice president of sales, John Turner, to promote Cotton Springfield, a Vassar-educated, promising, twenty-five-year-old company legal librarian. Cotton was single and attractive, and her buoyant personality made a successful career in sales a likely prospect. She was eager for the opportunity. In an abstract sense, Converse was pleased with this decision, because it not only contributed to Springfield's career development, but fulfilled government guidelines that specified that women and minorities should be hired in certain job categories, including sales. Thus, Springfield was placed in the sales job instead of one of several male candidates, all of whom had had a few years of sales experience.

After a six-week sales training program, Ms. Springfield was assigned to the only existing opening. She was teamed with Anthony Gibson, a forty-two-year-old veteran in the Chicago Metals sales force who worked the southeastern sector, which included Missouri, Arkansas, Mississippi, Kentucky, Tennessee, Alabama, Georgia, and the Carolinas.

On the day the assignment was announced, Gibson came to Converse's office with an ardent plea for reconsideration based on his feeling that Cotton

Springfield was not qualified and would cause problems. First, he said, she had no technical background or experience in the metals business and "doesn't know carbon steel from the kitchen sink." If she didn't know the product, she couldn't do the job, and neither her education at an elite college nor her subsequent experience in the company law library gave her any background in metallurgy or engineering.

In addition, Gibson argued, his successful sales routine involved entertaining prospective buyers, who were all male, after business hours, and the normal evening ritual included lots of off-color jokes, obscene language, and other male pastimes, such as taking in a pornographic movie. Said Gibson: "How a proper and refined little filly like Cotton can handle that, I just don't know." He also pointed to a related potential difficulty. The southeastern sector encompassed a population with conservative lifestyles and values. What would many of his customers conclude when the representative of Chicago Metals arrived with a sexy young traveling companion in tow? His and the company's image might be tarnished in the eyes of prospective customers. The inevitable kidding about their sharing a motel room might have a serious edge that would prove costly to the company. Male horseplay was okay, but to some of the "old boys" in southern companies, this might be going too far.

Gibson then became even more serious and reported an angry confrontation with his wife, who had railed bitterly against the prospect of her husband traveling across the country with a young and attractive woman for an extended period. She had threatened to leave him rather than face the ridicule of acquaintances who would assume that the two salespersons had more than aluminum in common. Gibson felt it unfair that he should be subjected to this pressure in addition to the normal pressures of a demanding occupation.

"Naturally I have nothing personal against Cotton," said Gibson as he rose to leave, "but I think you ought to reexamine your decision. She is being promoted because of her sex and not her competence, and we both know it. Why don't you save me from problems with my wife and customers, and save yourself and Cotton the heartache of her getting in way over her head?" Although completely in earnest, he dispelled the gravity of the situation by winking and adding that of course he "wouldn't mind her company on lonely nights on the road," if things couldn't be changed.

At the time, Converse had sympathized with the salesman, but he was not sure what action, if any, he should take. Every year Chicago Metals had to fill out an EEO-1 form, and among other disclosures, Converse was required to present employment data by job category, including "sales." The *Affirmative Action and Equal Employment* guidebook on Converse's desk seemed to preclude sexual discrimination in the sales force. It stated in part that,

> For all practical purposes, almost all jobs must be open legally to men and women. The "bona-fide occupational qualification" (BFOQ) exception of Title VII is narrowly construed by EEOC and the courts. The burden of proof is on the employer to establish that the sexual characteristics of the employee are *crucial* to successful performance (such as model, actor, or actress). Only when the essence of the

business enterprise would be undermined by not hiring a member of one sex exclusively is a BFOQ justified.

Converse had no doubt that women could be as effective sales representatives as men. Cotton Springfield had been given an extensive training program to inform her about Chicago's products, sales techniques, and the new territory. During the program, Springfield attended a four-hour presentation by a psychologist in the personnel department on "Emotional Problems of Women in Traditionally Male Work Roles."

About the time of Springfield's promotion, the company was attacked for sexual discrimination by the National Organization of Women. The company came to NOW's attention when an article in *Ms.* magazine criticized an incident in which the company decided against hiring a woman as a lathe operator because she was pregnant and would need to take a leave of absence for childbirth near the production deadline on a big order. Currently, Chicago faced two EEOC suits involving alleged discrimination against women. This was not unusual for a company of Chicago's size, but the suits ate up staff time and could result in nasty fines.

The legal implications of Springfield's letter worried Gibson. He remembered that she had been Chicago's legal librarian. The phrasing in part of the letter indicated that she was familiar with criteria that courts had used recently in sexual harassment cases. Had she consulted a lawyer?

Converse did not want to let Gibson or any of the other salesmen go. They were too good, and the jobs were so lucrative that voluntary resignations were rare. It would be unfair to force a man out, and the next retirement was eight years away. Therefore, he could not hire another woman to travel with Springfield. He hesitated to transfer a salesman to the southeastern sector and put Gibson in another area of the country because Gibson had spent years developing and polishing contacts, as had the salesmen in other sectors. In addition, he was not sure that other salesmen would be more accommodating to the idea of working with a young woman.

Yes, he thought, my job is an adventure.

Questions

1. Was Springfield's promotion to sales representative a correct decision? Was it handled properly by the company?
2. Evaluate Springfield's letter in terms of the EEOC's sexual harassment guidelines discussed in this chapter and in terms of recent sexual harassment litigation, such as *Bundy v. Jackson*, *EEOC v. Sage Realty Corp.*, *Ferguson v. DuPont*, or *Meritor Savings Bank v. Vinson* (for references see the bibliography). If she takes legal action, is it likely that the company will be held liable for exposing Springfield to a harassing work environment? Is her harassment by Vice President Turner actionable?
3. What action should Converse take now?
4. Do some research on women in business. Is Cotton Springfield's experience typical of the barriers and problems of women entering sales or other areas of business today? What should Springfield do?

PART **VI**

CORPORATE ISSUES

CHAPTER 18

BUSINESS IN THE POLITICAL PROCESS

 In 1978 and 1979, Chrysler Corporation, failing in the marketplace, conducted a lobbying campaign for a federal bailout. Chrysler lobbyists were not reticent to point out that the company employed 64,100 workers in five politically important states with a total of 126 electoral votes (Michigan, Indiana, Illinois, New York, and Ohio). With Jimmy Carter struggling for reelection in 1980 and anticipating close votes in those states, the Carter administration strongly supported the $1.5 billion Chrysler Corporation Loan Guarantee Act of 1979.

Rockwell International has adopted the strategy of subcontracting B-1 bomber components to 5,200 contractors in all forty-eight continental states to build grass-roots support for the program's continuation. Pressure from labor and business in hundreds of congressional districts where component work is done has kept the B-1 alive on Capitol Hill for two decades, although some independent military analysts believe the bomber to be outdated. The plane is based on a design developed early in the 1960s but is impervious at least to political attack.

Chrysler, Rockwell, and other businesses most certainly are not passive about accepting the regulations, directions, and favors of government. Business collectively, individual executives, and hired agents assert political influence throughout the nation. This chapter is devoted to a discussion of that influence.

BUSINESS AND THE
AMERICAN POLITICAL SYSTEM

Throughout American history, business has sought and exercised political power in a government that is extraordinarily open to influence. This power, whether used for good or ill, is exercised on constitutional terrain created by the Founding Fathers 200 years ago. The Constitution, as elaborated by judicial interpretation over the years, establishes the structure of government and broad rules of political activity. Its formal provisions, in turn, predispose a certain pragmatic, freewheeling political culture that is manifest in day-to-day political life.

The First Amendment protects the right of business to organize and press its agenda on government. There, in elegantly archaic language, is stated the right "to petition the government for redress of grievances." The First Amendment also protects rights of free speech, freedom of the press, and freedom of assembly—all critical in applying political pressure to government. Without these guarantees, the letter-writing campaigns, speeches, newspaper editorials, and advocacy advertisements that business orchestrates to influence government might be threatened. Imagine how undesirably different our system would be if the public, excited by "windfall profits" in some industry, pressured Congress to restrict the lobbying rights of those companies to press for tax breaks.

The corporate right to free political expression was challenged not long ago when the First National Bank of Boston conducted a political advertising campaign in opposition to a graduated personal income tax proposed in a state referendum. The Massachusetts attorney general, Francis X. Bellotti, challenged the legitimacy of the bank's expenditure, arguing that the tax matter did not materially affect the bank's welfare and was a wasteful use of the equity of bank shareholders, who might disagree with the bank's position. In addition, Massachusetts had a law prohibiting corporate spending to influence such referendum campaigns. The Supreme Court, in the case of *First National Bank of Boston v. Bellotti* (1978), upheld the bank's right to make a political statement and affirmed that business has the right, protected by the First Amendment, to be politically outspoken on issues only indirectly affecting corporate operations. This decision has sanctioned growing corporate political activism in recent years.

The Constitution also creates a specific, formal structure of government, a structure that reflects the Founders' fears of concentrated power. It sets up a federal system in which important powers are given to both the states and the federal government. State governments, in turn, share some of their powers, such as the power of taxation, with cities. In an effort to further diffuse power, the Constitution establishes a system of separation of powers, whereby the three branches of the federal government—the legislative, executive, and judicial—each have checks and balances over each other. The states mimic these power-sharing arrangements in their governments.

This system is open. It has many points of access, and it invites business and other special interests to attempt influence. Because no single, central authority exists, significant government action requires widespread cooperation among levels and branches of government that share power. The system also is particularly vulnerable to blockage and delay. Because actions of significance require the combined authority of several elements in the political arena, special interests can block action by getting a favorable hearing at only one juncture. To get action, on the other hand, an interest like business must successfully pressure many actors in the political equation. Thus there has developed a practical political culture in the American system in which interests are willing to bargain, compromise, and form temporary alliances to achieve their goals rather than stand firm on rigid, ideological positions.

Though not ordained in the Constitution the preeminence of business interests in the political pressure equation has been an enduring fact of life in American government. The Founders who drafted the Constitution were an economic elite. John Jay and Robert Morris, for example, were among the wealthiest men in the colonies, and it should come as no surprise that the government arrangements they fabricated are conducive to influence by economic interests. Although the long shadow of business influence often is called oppressive there is a germ of fairness in business' frequent dominion over government. As Gerald Keim has noted, "the employees, shareholders, and their spouses of the 1,000 largest corporations in the U.S. number over 50 million people" (Keim, 1984: 53). Numbers like this make the corporate community more than a narrow and privileged population segment seeking selfish gain.

The Political Arena of Yesteryear

Historically, business interests were accorded a warm reception in the halls of government. Business has had credibility in government because it was perceived as pleading for and against measures to help or hurt the economy. Unlike some European countries, there was no socialist opposition to dilute the legitimacy of capitalism or challenge the laissez-faire tradition. In years past, a widely used tactic was the application of behind-the-scenes pressure by business leaders or their agents on key officials and political kingpins. Sometimes, of course, business manipulated government corruptly, with gifts and favors. Under these advantageous conditions most corporations lobbied through trade associations, made campaign contributions, and occasionally contacted government officials for favors. This style of political activism worked through the 1950s, the era when Dwight D. Eisenhower was a pro-business President with an administration dominated by political appointees from business, when public opinion polls still showed high support for business, when a pro-business conservative coalition of Southern Democrats and Republicans in Congress ensured legislative support, and when government regulation was a small fraction of what it is now. Soon, however, changing political winds forced business into more aggressive and sophisticated forms of political intervention.

During the 1960s and 1970s, the nation's political atmosphere was dominated by liberal reform. The public demanded that business be bridled with massive new regulatory programs and that government itself be made more democratic and responsive to the public interest. Many factors converged during this period to encourage more corporate political activity. Executives felt that for the first time control over day-to-day operations was slipping away to government regulators. The Equal Employment Opportunity Commission dictated who could be hired. The Occupational Safety and Health Administration intervened directly in the plant to change the work process. The Environmental Protection Agency required installation of costly antipollution equipment. Other agencies bit into corporate decision making. In addition, government fiscal and monetary policy intervened in the economy and wage and price controls in the 1970s took still more decisions out of management's hands. When business sustained losses in international competition in the 1970s, much blame was placed on the inflationary effects of these government interventions.

Two other consequential changes also occurred: first, new groups mobilized to oppose business, and second, a series of democratic reforms diffused power in Congress.

The Rise of Public-Interest Groups

During the 1960s, the climate of pressure politics began to change with the rise of new groups set up to pursue ideological causes, single interests, and the "public interest." These groups purported to speak for consumers, taxpayers, and previously underrepresented citizen interests. Berry (1977) defined a public-interest group as "one that seeks a collective good, the achievement of which will not selectively and materially benefit the membership or activists of the organization" (p. 7).

The smaller the society, the fewer probably will be the distinct parties and interests composing it; the fewer the distinct parties and interests, the more frequently will a majority be found of the same party; and the smaller the number of individuals composing a majority, and the smaller the compass within which they are placed, the more easily will they concert and execute their plans of oppression. Extend the sphere and you take in a greater variety of parties and interests; you make it less probable that a majority of the whole will have a common motive to invade the rights of other citizens; or if such a common motive exists, it will be more difficult for all who feel it to discover their own strength and to act in unison with each other. Besides other impediments, it may be remarked that, where there is a consciousness of unjust or dishonorable purposes, communication is always checked by distrust in proportion to the number whose concurrence is necessary.

Source: James Madison, *The Federalist,* No. 10 (1788).

Some of the new citizens' groups are large-membership groups with considerable resources. Two of the largest and best known are Common Cause and Ralph Nader's Public Citizen, Inc. Both lobby on a wide range of public issues. The Consumer Federation of America is an umbrella organization for more than 200 consumer groups. The environmental lobby is also a formidable force in Washington politics, led by groups such as the National Wildlife Federation, the National Audubon Society, and the Sierra Club.

These environmental groups—the so-called "green lobby"—exemplify the workings of public-interest lobbies. In the late 1960s, they were underfinanced and unsophisticated compared to the business interests they opposed. Because they could not make large campaign contributions, they attacked what they alleged was the corrupting influence of special-interest money and tried to get wide public support for antipollution measures in Congress. They made emotional statements that appealed to the news media, and along with Common Cause, they pioneered sophisticated grass-roots campaigns that produced barrages of letters and direct constituent pressures on senators and representatives. On highly technical issues that lacked public visibility the environmental lobby could not hope to vanquish corporate power on Capitol Hill. To compensate in part for this weakness, other environmental groups, such as Natural Resources Defense Council, Inc., specialized in litigation to enforce environmental protection laws. This illustrates how the openness of government structure enables interests defeated in one place to get access and exert pressure in another.

Throughout the 1970s, Environmental Action (EA), a small 25,000-member activist group, had a chilling effect on Congress by picking a hit list of twelve powerful members with poor environmental voting records. The list—called the Dirty Dozen—was publicized, and EA worked to defeat those on it. Over the course of five elections, fifty-two members of Congress rotated onto the Dirty Dozen list, and twenty-four were defeated. In 1980, EA dropped the Dirty Dozen campaign because the list had served its purpose and fewer in Congress had poor environmental voting records.

In the 1980s, the Sierra Club has conducted mass grass-roots campaigns to elect proenvironment candidates at all levels of government. Several environmental groups have set up political action committees, and most use computerized mass mailing to recruit members and raise money. There is increasing reliance on technical expertise to influence policy rather than emotional appeal to the press. In fighting Clean Air Act amendments in 1981, for example, environmental groups formed a massive Clean Air Coalition that sponsored a study showing that if carbon monoxide (CO) standards were lowered, at least sixteen major metropolitan areas would never achieve legislated health standards for CO. Key senators and congresspeople from some of these areas were forced to switch votes because of public pressure.

In the past, environmentalists may have been ideologues who demanded purity in nature. Today, they are seasoned and highly effective adversaries of business, capable of using the most advanced techniques for mobilizing public opinion, and ready to slug it out in the trenches of political warfare by working daily with congressional staff, agency administrators, and business groups to reach a favorable compromise.

Hundreds of other groups exist that affect the fortunes of business. A wide array of single-interest groups such as the National Council of Senior Citizens, Zero Population Growth, the Fund for Animals, the National Organization for Women, and the National Abortion Rights Action League are examples of the literally hundreds of newly powerful groups that lobby in Washington.

Most public-interest/environmental/reform groups appeal to a liberal, middle-class constituency, and many oppose business, labor, or the government. In the late 1970s, a study of lobbyists from eighty-three such groups showed that 74 percent placed themselves from liberal to radical on the political spectrum, and only 10 percent considered themselves conservative (Berry, 1977). A survey of Common Cause members at about the same time showed that 89 percent felt that "big business has too much influence on how the country is run" (McFarland, 1984: 55). Today the torch is carried by people such as Gene Karpinski, executive director of U.S. Public Interest Research Group, a group inspired by Ralph Nader. Karpinski, who represents state groups with 500,000 members, says that, "As long as there are large corporations, I'm sure there will be irresponsible corporate behavior. Therefore, there will always be battles out there" (in Cooper, 1985: 2062).

Although business lobbies have the advantage of power and organization in the power game, citizen lobbies enjoy some advantages too. Many are associated with dramatic, emotional, or popular issues and find easy access to the mass media. They frequently form coalitions based on ideological similarity and gain in lobbying strength by combining resources. Another source of strength, however, is their vague reform mandate and their claim to represent larger constituencies than the so-called special interests of business and labor. Although one of six jobs in the economy is related to the automobile industry, and the petroleum companies have more than 14 million stockholders, both industries are regarded as "special pleaders" when compared with the new public-interest lobbies—no matter how small the membership or interest in the latter might be.

Reforms in Congress Change the Political Arena

A second change in the climate of politics, in addition to new groups, has been in Congress. Traditionally, both the House and Senate were run autocratically by a small number of party leaders and powerful committee chairs. Many of these chairs were Democrats from southern states, who had great longevity in Congress due to the vagaries of southern party politics. The stubborn resistance of these deeply entrenched southerners in Congress to popular, overdue civil rights legislation led to public dissatisfaction with the seniority system. The system was dismantled in the early 1970s by an uprising of junior members of Congress, who passed a series of procedural reforms stripping committee chairs of traditional prerogatives such as automatic reappointment and the right to assign subcommittee chairmanships. This revolution, largely complete by 1974, democratized Congress by taking power from a few hands and giving a measure of it to many. After 1974, subcommittees could hold hearings on any subject that they wished, developed large staffs, and often became small fiefdoms of independent action.

At the same time as seniority reform, the rise of political action committees (PACs) and direct-mail funding campaigns undermined the influence of political party organizations in Congress. Previously, senators and House members who were loyal to the senior power structure could count on substantial campaign contributions from the Republican and Democratic party organizations set up specifically to fund campaigns. Under this system, party affiliation was the single most accurate predictor of voting behavior. After 1974, however, special-interest PACs began contributing such large amounts of money that legislators developed greater loyalty to them than to their parties. And why not? In 1982, for instance, oil company PACs alone gave more to Democratic congressmen than did the Democratic National Committee (Easterbrook, 1984).

When the seniority system was intact, rank and file members of Congress generally got ahead by quietly kowtowing to the few leaders who could assign or withhold favors and party support. If business interests could influence this small handful of House and Senate powerbrokers, they had no meaningful opposition. But with the demise of the seniority system, business lobbyists had to contact nearly every member of a committee or subcommittee to get support for a measure rather than just the chair. Hence, the political activity of business expanded in response to the diffusion of power in Congress. As subcommittees grew in importance and their staff sizes increased, business lobbyists learned to work more with them also.

Current Trends in the Business-Government Political Equation

With the election of Ronald Reagan and a Republican majority in the Senate in 1980, the political climate was more congenial to business. Although prior reforms, regulatory enactments, and antibusiness organizations remained, the new administration was ideologically resonant with the business agenda —lower corporate taxes, deregulation and less enforcement of existing regulations, cuts in social spending, increased defense spending, and a balanced budget. After some notable lobbying and electoral successes in the early 1980s, however, resistance to business pressure, internal feuding in the business community, and major defeats in tax legislation made the Reagan era less than a complete triumph for business.

In the late 1980s, an assessment of the political activity of business would include four basic points.

First, corporations are much more active in politics today than in past eras. They speak out on more issues. Top executives are more knowledgeable about politics and lobby actively. Many large corporations have political outposts and staffs in Washington, D.C.

Second, the political activities of business are becoming more sophisticated. Corporations are adopting more coherent strategies for political contributions, establishing elaborate programs of issue analysis in their government relations departments, using computerized mailings to mobilize public support, training managers to watch political trends, and hiring influential Washington insiders to work on a parallel course with company lobbyists. Business today is by a large margin the most complex sector of group activity in Washington. Exhibit 18–1 shows the wide variety of political activities typically undertaken by a large, politically active corporation with a state-of-the-art government relations program.)

Third, business today is opposed by a proliferation of citizens' groups that promote an idea or cause. About half of them have formed since 1960 and many have an anti-business bias. Many are powerful, well organized opponents, capable of using their own sophisticated and tenacious influence techniques.

And fourth, business is extremely effective in its pressure tactics. In part this is because no other sector can match its resources and organization. Even combined, the constellation of groups representing labor, consumers, civil rights, the environment, and various public-interest or single-issue groups cannot match the financial and organizational resources of the business community. Of course, victory is never assured. In 1984 to 1986, when the Reagan

EXHIBIT 18–1   CORPORATE POLITICAL PROGRAMS

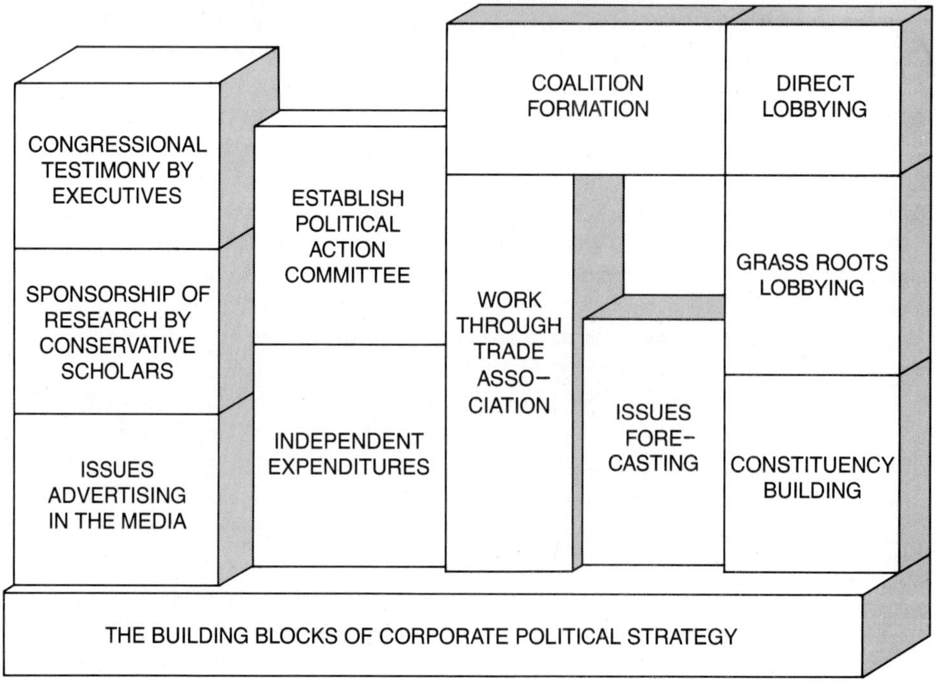

CONGRESSIONAL TESTIMONY BY EXECUTIVES

SPONSORSHIP OF RESEARCH BY CONSERVATIVE SCHOLARS

ISSUES ADVERTISING IN THE MEDIA

ESTABLISH POLITICAL ACTION COMMITTEE

INDEPENDENT EXPENDITURES

COALITION FORMATION

WORK THROUGH TRADE ASSO–CIATION

ISSUES FORE–CASTING

DIRECT LOBBYING

GRASS ROOTS LOBBYING

CONSTITUENCY BUILDING

THE BUILDING BLOCKS OF CORPORATE POLITICAL STRATEGY

administration sought to overhaul the tax code, corporations large and small lobbied energetically to preserve favored tax subsidies. But in the end, corporate taxes were raised, and the battle for tax breaks was lost by many powerful industries. The reasons included a division in the business community over whether to support tax reform; support by a popular, conservative, Republican president for a new tax code; and strong public support for lower individual tax rates and higher corporate rates. Big capital-intensive industries fought the plan by hiring the legendary Washington insider and "superlobbyist" Charls E. Walker, by making large campaign contributions to members of the tax reform committees in Congress, and by using their own lobbying resources. But in the end they simply lost.

BUSINESS-INTEREST ORGANIZATIONS

There are literally thousands of associations that represent business. What follows is a summary of the universe of business groups. We begin with descriptions of the most powerful.

The Chamber of Commerce, founded in 1912, is today the largest and most powerful business outpost in Washington, D.C. It occupies a building that faces the White House across Lafayette Square and represents a federation of some 2,800 local and state chambers, 1,350 trade associations, and 184,000 business firms. It has seen astonishing growth in recent years, due to growing government activity and business response. Membership more than doubled between 1975 and 1986. The primary work of the Chamber is to influence Congress on legislative issues of national impact. Because Chamber membership is so large and diverse, it does not take positions on local and regional issues, but confines its activities to truly national issues such as recent proposals to limit damage awards in product liability suits brought against companies.

Astute political observers feel that the Chamber is the best-organized, most powerful single lobby in Washington. The Chamber uses vast computer capabilities to send out "action calls" to member firms and influential individuals around the country. It can target appeals to more than 2,700 Congressional Action Committees of business people, who then contact local officials on key issues. Overnight, the Chamber can elicit thousands of letters and telegrams from constituents around the country aimed at key legislators. The Chamber is also a major communications channel. It publishes *Nation's Business*, a monthly magazine with a circulation of 850,000 in 1986, and *Business Advocate*, a monthly tabloid with a circulation of 200,000. It produces weekly television and radio programs about business, carried by hundreds of stations around the country. In 1982, it launched a new, private television network called the American Business Network, or Biznet.

The National Association of Manufacturers (NAM) is an old group, founded in 1895, and currently boasting a membership of about 13,600 companies. The

NAM was originally formed to promote foreign trade but ultimately grew in stature as it came to be used by the business community as a counterweight to the rising influence of labor earlier in this century. As recently as the 1960s, the NAM had only two membership meetings and a dinner each year. But by the 1980s, the NAM had expanded its activities enormously—a reflection of the general growth of business political activity in Washington. Today, it runs a state-of-the-art lobbying program. Computerized calls to the membership generate grass-roots pressure on Congress. A computerized issue analysis program called NAMTRAK prints out information for members on key issues and tracks the status of bills in Congress. At congressional dialogue meetings, individual senators and representatives meet with small groups of NAM members and discuss mutual concerns. In 1985 the NAM had a staff of 208, including about forty registered lobbyists to carry its largely conservative business message to Congress and federal agencies.

Both the Chamber and the NAM are composed mainly of small companies —85 percent of the Chamber's members are companies with fewer than 100 employees, and 75 percent of the NAM's members have fewer than 500. Although the boards of directors of both groups are dominated by executives of large companies, their memberships include many small and medium sized firms. This fact makes them slow in reacting to political issues and sometimes unable to strongly support the positions taken by the largest corporations. Hence, several powerful organizations have developed to represent the views of the big-business elite.

The oldest of these is the Business Council, which was founded in 1933 when President Roosevelt asked to have organized a group of top-echelon business executives with whom New Deal administrators could exchange views about key economic issues. Originally, the council was attached in an advisory capacity to the Department of Commerce, but in 1962 it declared its independence from government (in part because of growing curiosity and suspicion about its quasi-governmental status). Today, the council continues to act as an advisory body that links big business and government. It expresses views in a low-key manner and does not lobby directly. The membership is limited to sixty-five chief executives of the largest corporations, and an effort is made to represent geographic regions and major industry groups. The members are organized into a small number of liaison committees that connect with different government departments. Here is where influence is exercised. Twice a year, the full membership meets, and periodic briefings are held so that members may hear and question high government officials.

A second group representing the interests of big business is the Committee for Economic Development. The CED, which is described more extensively in Chapter 8, is directed by 200 trustees, most of whom are corporate chief executive officers. The CED does not lobby government directly. Rather, subcommittees composed of trustees and assisted by staff develop written policy statements on important issues. These are published and may attract much attention.

A recently formed organization representing big-business interests is the Business Roundtable, also a group of 200 CEOs of the largest corporations in

America. Unlike the Business Council and the CED, however, the Roundtable is not low key; it is the lobbying arm of big business. The Roundtable began in the 1970s, when wage and price controls imposed by the Nixon administration drove home the need for improving business's impact on federal policy making. After consultation with top Nixon aides, several CEOs formed a small group, which rapidly grew to the present 200 members. The Roundtable includes companies such as Exxon, General Motors, Mobil, General Electric, Texaco, Ford, IBM, Sears, Citibank, Bank of America, and Prudential. It takes action on a limited number of issues important to big business each year. Members of the Roundtable divide into task forces that study legislative initiatives; individuals selected as lead members of these task forces are expected to lobby personally for Roundtable goals. Robert Beck, CEO of Prudential, was chairman of the Roundtable in 1986; he is known as one of the most persistent lobbyists on Capitol Hill. The Roundtable has a small staff, and its expenses are paid by the firms of CEO members based on a formula of stockholders' equity and gross sales.

Small business is represented by groups such as the National Federation of Independent Business (NFIB) and its sometime rival the National Small Business Association (NSBA). The NFIB is the bigger of the two, with more than 500,000 member small businesses in all fifty states, each paying $35 to $500 in annual dues. The NFIB was founded in 1943 and had only 300 members in 1973, but expanding government programs affected small businesses so extensively that, like big business organizations, the NFIB grew in size and sophistication. It carries on lobbying in all fifty states and has a twenty-member Washington staff with eleven lobbyists (Lammers, 1982). The NSBA is smaller, with a membership of about 50,000 companies, but it has a significant lobbying presence. It is less likely to side with big business on an issue.

A recent development is the establishment of the American Business Conference (ABC), a lobby group that represents medium-sized, high-growth firms. The ABC was started in 1980. Its membership is limited to 100 CEOs of corporations that have grown 15 percent annually, averaged over the previous five years, and have revenues between $25 million and $1 billion. Member companies represent a wide spectrum of manufacturing and service activities and include, for instance, MCI Communications Corp., Arthur Andersen & Co., and Dunkin' Donuts, Inc. Most members, however, are in fast-expanding, high-technology industries that create new jobs and do not pollute heavily. Their progressive image and the group's nearly unwavering support for the Reagan administration's legislative agenda made the ABC very influential in the 1980s.

In addition to these organizations, more than 6,000 trade associations represent business. Virtually every line of industrial and commercial activity has its own association. Simply to illustrate the variety, there are the American Beekeeping Federation, the American Insurance Association, the American Paper Institute, the Association of Japanese Textile Importers, the National Electrical Manufacturers' Association, the Frozen Onion Rings Packers' Council, the Institute of Pharmaceutical Manufacturers, the American Federation of Retail Kosher Butchers, and the Peanut Butter Manufacturers' Association. Then there are regional and local business groups, such as the Western States Meat Packers' Association and the Southwestern Peanut Shellers' Association.

Trade associations lobby for the interests of the industries they represent, and some have formidable resources. The American Iron and Steel Institute, for example, has a membership of 2,600 companies and a budget of over $10 million a year. Trade associations also funnel enormous amounts of money into politics for member businesses through their PACs. In the 1984 election cycle, the National Association of Realtors PAC gave $2.4 million to candidates, more than any other PAC, and six of the top fifteen PACs were business trade-association connected (Federal Election Commission, 1985. Unless otherwise noted, all PAC spending figures in this chapter are from this source.)

With the growing impact of government, an important trade-association function is spreading information about new rules to help industries cope with government activities. One example is the way the Laundry Cleaning Council alerted thousands of small dry cleaning businesses to new hazardous-waste disposal regulations in 1985. The council explained new requirements for disposing of dry cleaning chemicals and developed techniques for recycling chemicals and meeting liability insurance requirements that pooled the resources of all these small establishments—most of which, alone, could not have mustered the resources and necessary expertise. Trade associations also may develop voluntary standards to forestall federal regulation, as the Chain Saw Manufacturers' Association has been doing in developing rules for chain saw manufacturers that reduce the safety hazards in using the saws.

Before World War II, trade associations often spoke with a single voice, especially in matters concerning labor unions. Since then, however, there has been an increasing divergence of views, and it is not unusual now to find bitter controversy among some of the trade associations. Continuous skirmishes occur, for example, between truckers and railroads, manufacturers and distributors, bankers and borrowers, and raw-material producers and end-product manufacturers. Despite these differences, however, there is within the business group, as within the labor and farm groups, a broad unity on fundamental issues of common concern.

LABOR UNIONS IN POLITICS

Labor unions are, of course, an important player in the political arena, and they frequently oppose business. A dominant motivation in pursuing corporate political action is to counterbalance what is perceived to be a politically powerful labor union movement. For years the strength of NAM, for instance, was in business's hatred for regulation and fear of union power. Many executives see in union political activity the capability to elect politicians favoring the labor point of view. They believe that union strength not only will result in legislation that curtails their managerial prerogatives and reduces their profits, but will undermine the very foundations of the traditional business system. In this light, business has supported those associations that help combat union political strength.

Labor unions have considerable political strength, but in the 1980s they have faced effective opposition from business, limited access to the Reagan White House, intense international competition, givebacks at the bargaining table, and a turn of the screw in management philosophy favoring Japanese-style worker-management harmony. The ranks of union members are no longer expanding as fast as the hourly work force. Late in the 1970s, labor suffered critical political setbacks when business forces defeated two priority issues—common site picketing in 1977 and revision of laws protecting union organizing in 1978. Members of Congress, long in awe of labor power, learned that they could defy the AFL-CIO and survive politically. In 1985, labor suffered another important setback when business lobbies defeated a labor-backed bill that would have required employers to give advance notice when they closed a plant and laid off a large number of workers. Organized labor had worked for eleven years to get this bill to the floor of the House, but it was decisively defeated by business lobbying. In 1986, however, labor won a victory when Congress lowered tax rates for low- and middle-income workers at the expense of tax write-offs cherished by industry. Of special importance in the tax bill debate was a union-funded study by a young Ralph Nader protégé showing that some of America's largest companies paid no federal income taxes. One reason that unions remain influential is heavy campaign contributions. In 1984 there were six union PACs in the top fifteen contributors.

THE GOVERNMENT-RELATIONS PROCESS

There are two basic areas of business involvement in politics. The first is the electoral process; business contributes to political campaigns at all levels of government. The second is government relations, or lobbying; business influences the formulation, implementation, enforcement, and adjudication of policy by contacting government officials. Naturally, these areas are interrelated.

Lobbying by Business

A lobby may be broadly defined as the point of access of a corporation, trade association, or other interest group to a part of government. A lobbyist is the individual who represents an interest. This is a mildly pejorative term, because although lobbying is more open today than in the past, it is still sometimes seen in a negative light. Therefore lobbyists may refer to themselves as legislative advocates, government or public relations consultants, or lawyers.

There are more lobbyists today than ever before. There were 8,800 lobbyists in Washington in 1986, registered under the Federal Regulation of Lobbying Act of 1946, twice as many as in the mid-1970s. Many lobbyists do not register, however, because of a loophole in that act, so estimates place the real number of lobbyists in Washington at closer to 20,000. The recent expansion of lobbying activity is illustrated by the hordes of corporate and trade-union lobbyists who descended on the House and Senate committees that worked on tax reform in 1985 and 1986. The tax breaks of many special interests were threatened by the bill, and it was facetiously called "the Lobbyists' Full Employment Act." During one period in 1986, the hallway outside the House Ways and Means Committee became known as "Gucci Gulch," a reference to the footwear popular among lobbyists crowded outside the committee room. Photographers were forbidden inside the room because of the common practice of lobbyists to catch a representative's eye and give a thumbs up or thumbs down signal as various provisions of the tax bill came to a vote.

Most lobbying at the federal level, including business lobbying, is done in the legislative and executive branches. The Congress is able to make and change laws, including tax laws, an authority clearly of great importance to corporations. The many administrative agencies in the executive branch also draw lobbyists seeking to influence the application of regulations. The Supreme Court is less a target of influence because judges insulate themselves from special interests. Constitutional questions generally are not at issue in business-related matters, and the Court usually does not initiate policy in advance of legislative enactments.

Although business lobbyists have been condemned for pleading selfish interests, overriding a legitimate "public interest," and engaging in corrupt practices, the predominant viewpoint among students of American politics is that lobbyists are basically honest and perform valuable functions. Specifically, lobbyists provide legislators with useful technical information about bills and also give them politically relevant information about how constituents and affected interests feel about policy. These functions are extremely valuable to busy legislators who do not always have staffs to make such investigations themselves. Every industry has special quirks and problems, of which industry lobbyists have special knowledge. Says former Representative Bob S. Bergland:

> Lobbyists perform a useful function. For example, I served on two committees of the House, but there were dozens of bills on the floor from committees [of] which I was not a member. I oftentimes would not know how they would affect my district. I would call lobbyists and ask them. If they level with you it's terribly important (Struck, 1986: 17).

It is possible, naturally, for a lobbyist to mislead an elected official or committee staff members with biased information. But this is counterproductive in the Washington game because the lobbyist who lacks integrity loses access to the very people he or she earns a living from influencing. Congressmen shut out lobbyists who mislead them. Effective lobbyists are prepared to present and discuss opposition views.

How Business Lobbies Government

Business uses many lobbying techniques. A time-tested technique is talk and discussion with an important government contact. Lobbyists make phone calls, appointments, and dates for meals with people who can help. Direct contact with officials, however critical, occupies only a minor portion of the typical corporate lobbyist's day. About 90 percent of his or her time is spent with committee staff members on Capitol Hill, staff in administrative agencies, or in preparing technical documents. Lobbyists typically attend a great many parties on the Washington social circuit. They also like to serve on steering committees for political campaigns for the obvious advantage it gives them in working with the elected official later on.

Many corporations use their own lobbyists for such work. Others may also hire prominent Washington public relations, consulting, and lobbying firms to press their cases. Increasingly, business relies on the services of such firms, which employ former administrative officials, former legislators, and knowledgeable insiders of both political parties and which offer a potent mix of influence and advice. An example is Black, Manafort, Stone & Kelly, which represents Bethlehem Steel, Solomon Brothers, and others. This firm offers a wide range of lobbying and political consulting services. It develops strategy for congressional campaigns, runs the campaign, and then lobbies the same elected official for its business clients after the election. In 1986, the firm was managing campaigns for both Jack Kemp and Vice President George Bush, while simultaneously lobbying the Reagan administration on behalf of paid clients. Most corporations simply cannot duplicate this kind of influence network in a Washington office and so many retain a prestigeous "hired gun." The type of insider influence bought in this way often is very effective.

Corporations also increasingly use the services of lobbying firms to mastermind an array of political techniques, many of them highly specialized and technically sophisticated. There is growing reliance on these techniques to conduct what are called grass-roots campaigns, or efforts to influence public opinion in such a way that people pressure government officials for action. A "full-service" public relations firm develops media kits full of information about a company or issue and sends them to newspapers and television stations around the country. These kits may contain articles that small-town newspaper editors can turn into editorials. The firm may maintain a list of reporters who specialize in covering the industry, may write op-ed page pieces for top company executives to send to newspapers, and may develop advocacy advertisements or TV commercials. The firm may conduct public-opinion polls and send out letters to the constituents of elected officials that encourage them to write to Congress in favor of or against pending legislation of interest to the corporate client. They also may sponsor a petition drive to get voters' signatures to show support for a measure.

Mass mail and Mailgram campaigns are frequently generated by influence seekers in Washington, although their effectiveness in influencing officials is not proven. Yet when a House or Senate member receives half a million identical postcards, it is an indication that people support a position. Such mass mail can be generated in a variety of ways, including calls from phone banks, mailings with preprinted cards to send to the elected official, or newspaper ads suggesting that people write. Firms such as Matt Reese and Associates use computerized polling and census data to pinpoint people in specific neighborhoods who, because of their education, income, and opinions, belong to one of forty "lifestyle clusters" that make them likely supporters of a business cause. Special variations of a brochure or letter may be sent to each lifestyle cluster that encourage them to mail a letter to their representative in Congress. When, for instance, the Natural Gas Supply Association began a campaign to end price controls on natural gas, it sent out four different brochures to ten lifestyle clusters in the districts of selected congressmen. The brochure to blue-collar workers associated patriotism with decontrol, asking, "Why do we go to Algeria for something we've got in Texas, and California, and Oklahoma, and Kansas" and nine other states (A. Cooper, 1985: 2040). Another brochure emphasized the ineptness of big government, but because the middle-class Americans who received this brochure were thought to dislike big companies as much as big government, the gas companies were not mentioned on it, and it was said to be from the Alliance for Energy Security—a front name for the gas producers.

All such grassroots campaigns are designed to show an elected official that voters hold an opinion in an industry's favor. Interestingly enough, they were perfected in the 1970s by public interest groups and New Right conservative groups, which developed them to compensate for lack of access to the network of influence and connections used by corporations. Now that corporations have learned these techniques, they rely increasingly on them in conjunction with less visible insider efforts. For example, the American Bankers Association (ABA) asks senators and representatives which bankers they respect in their districts. When particular bills are contested, the ABA then informs these key bankers of its position and encourages them to transmit their views. At present the ABA has 1,200 "contact" bankers. The Chamber of Commerce uses a computer in its Washington headquarters to locate and mail information to business managers around the country and encourage them to contact their representatives. Through its various publications and "action calls," the Chamber may ultimately reach up to 7 million business sympathizers, who have been known to besiege Congress with cards, letters, telegrams, and phone calls.

The Washington Office

Many corporations, of course, develop their own lobbying shops. Today most very large corporations maintain Washington offices. About 500 firms now have offices in Washington, compared with 100 to 200 in the late 1960s. These offices have developed along with the recent growth of government regulation. Although Ford Motor Company has had a staff of lobbyists in Washington since the 1950s, General Motors has had a Washington office only since 1969, and Chrysler since 1970. Smaller companies must also be informed of current and pending policy decisions, but they tend to rely on trade associations, hired lawyers, or public relations consultants.

General Electric has a staff of 120 in its Washington office. It is divided into separate organizational units specializing in lobbying efforts for aircraft engines, aerospace radar, electronics, flight simulators and weapons systems, nuclear power plants, the Export-Import Bank, and the regulation of CAT scanners. There is also a separate unit that lobbies on company-wide issues, such as taxes, labor law, and environmental regulation. In the latter unit, one lobbyist specializes in contacting Republicans; another works on Democrats. A third person coordinates General Electric's activities with other business lobbies. The GE office is one of the most effective corporate political shops in Washington and has won many victories. In 1985, for example, it succeeded in getting the Nuclear Regulatory Commission to adopt a set of uniform standards for nuclear reactor construction, standards that will help GE sell reactors and lower construction costs when nuclear energy comes back into favor, as GE thinks that it will. This effort took about four years and required GE to produce an 18,000-page report on the specifications for the regulators (Edsall, 1985: 6). (For a further discussion of the Washington Office, see Chapter 6.)

The Corporate Government-Relations Function

In the Washington office and also at corporate headquarters elsewhere, companies with significant political exposure frequently develop a government-relations function to scan the political environment and develop political strategies to deal with threats. Such a function may be housed in the public affairs or public relations departments, or it may be separate. For example, after President Reagan's inauguration in January 1981, business executives around America cheerfully anticipated the advent of a favorable political climate resulting from his conservative, probusiness administration. To the government relations staff at Atlantic Richfield Company's Los Angeles headquarters, however, Reagan's budget-cutting intentions spelled trouble. The staff predicted that as the federal budget was cut and taxes lowered, less federal money would be available to states and, as a result, state governments would try to compensate for this lost revenue by legislating new state taxes on business. For ARCO, located in twenty-eight states, this eventuality would be costly. Therefore, an ARCO task force wrote a report on possible new state taxes that alerted managers and lobbyists around the country. Staff predictions proved correct and when, in the spring of 1981, dozens of new state tax bills were introduced, ARCO lobbyists were instrumental in defeating many, including several aimed primarily at the oil industry (Gottschalk, 1982).

There are several important steps in a typical issues-management program.

■ Monitor the environment. Staff members listen to the media, cultivate professional, corporate, and trade-association contacts, and watch government. They look for information about issues of current consequence and for emerging issues that will be important to the company in three to five years. Congressional staff members frequently push along new issues to get attention as do challengers for political office, and these sources can be closely monitored.

■ Develop a portfolio of issues. A company typically locates fifty to 100 issues of importance and may follow them as they develop. There should be a separate file for each. Issues may be organized around company functions, such as personnel, finance, marketing, and international operations, or may be classified along various product lines. There may be a division among federal, state, and local issues.

■ Analyze issues and select a small number of critical ones. There are a smaller number of major issues that the company should try to manage in its favor. These issues should be extensively analyzed by the government-relations staff or a committee. Monsanto, for example, has an Issue Identification Committee, which selects a dozen issues for closer attention out of over 100 suggested by staff (Nolan, 1985). These issues are then given more careful written analysis and sent to a second committee of top executives, which further narrows the list to the five most critical issues.

■ Take action. Once firms have identified major issues, they should take concrete action to manage them. At Monsanto, the top executives' committee assigns each of the five critical issues to one of its members, who must develop an action plan for dealing with it, complete with periodic goals and progress reporting. Action may be taken through trade associations, hired lobbyists, or company personnel.

Thus far, we have discussed only the government-relations aspect of business political involvement. However, another significant area of involvement is that of campaign contributions. We turn now to that area.

THE CORPORATE ROLE IN ELECTORAL POLITICS

Corporations and other special interests have given money to political candidates in many ways. Before the passage of the Tillman Act in 1907, companies could make direct, legal contributions to candidates. In the 1880s and 1890s, Marcus Hanna, chairman of the Republican party, made direct assessments of companies such as Standard Oil and U.S. Steel based on the size of their assets. When companies could no longer give directly after the 1907 legislation, they found a variety of other ways to finance probusiness candidates, including giving salary bonuses to executives for use as contributions, loaning company staff, providing company automobiles and planes, and hiring ad agencies for candidates. In the 1972 presidential election, for example, Greyhound Corporation (illegally) awarded to employees salary bonuses that were twice the size of the campaign contributions they made. Hertz Corporation in 1971 and 1972 provided rental cars to the campaign of Senator Edmund Muskie without charge.

In the first presidential campaign, George Washington spent no money and little time getting elected. Since that time, the length and cost of political campaigns for federal office have soared. Money, and especially corporate money, plays an essential role in elections. Because money is so important, new sources and methods of giving arise when federal election laws limit contributions from one source. Thus, when direct corporate giving was no longer permitted after 1907, wealthy donors stepped in with large contributions. In 1972, for instance, Richard Scaife, an heir to the Mellon fortune, gave $990,000 to Nixon's campaign (through 330 separate committees to avoid an IRS gift tax on sums over $3,000). Scaife gave additional money to other Republican candidates.

During the early 1970s, campaign reform became a national issue, partly because of such large contributions, and Congress passed the Federal Election Campaign Act (FECA) of 1971 (and later amendments in 1974, 1976, and 1979) to curb the influence of wealthy contributors by placing ceilings on contributions, providing for more public disclosure of contributions, and creating the Federal Election Commission (FEC) to oversee enforcement.

With the floodgates of money from wealthy contributors closed more tightly (individual donors to federal elections are limited to contributing $1,000 per election per candidate, $5,000 per year to PACs, $20,000 per year to the national committee of a political party, and $25,000 per year total to all sources), there has been a dramatic increase in the contributions of special-interest groups. This rise in spending by business lobbies, associations, and even corporations has been facilitated by rulings of the FEC. When Congress created the FEC, it gave it the power to issue advisory opinions concerning the application of election laws. In a 1975 ruling, the FEC issued an advisory opinion allowing Sun Oil to establish a PAC to raise money for candidates through solicitation of management personnel. In the 1976 amendments to FECA, Congress permitted corporations, labor unions, and trade associations to establish such PACs, and reforms of campaign spending laws provided new avenues for the channeling of corporate money into politics, even as they strictly limited individual contributions by the wealthy.

To set up a PAC, a corporation must follow legal guidelines. The corporate PAC must, for example, divide those eligible for solicitation into two groups. Group I, or stockholders, executive employees, administrative employees, and their families, may be solicited as often as desired. Solicitations may be in person or through the mail and may even involve monthly payroll deductions. Many corporations suggest appropriate contribution levels based on a percentage of salary scales, usually about ¼ to 1 percent of annual salary (Handler and Mulkern, 1982). Group II, or hourly paid employees and their families, may be solicited only twice a year by a corporate PAC, and then only by mail to the home. Labor union PACs, conversely, may solicit their membership as frequently as desired and have the "twice a year" option to solicit management and stockholders by home mail.

A PAC may contribute $5,000 per election to candidates and their committees, $15,000 a year to national party committees, and $5,000 per year to other committees. (See Exhibit 18–2.) A geographically decentralized corporation may set up numerous PACs at division headquarters around the country, but their contributions may not put the corporation as a whole over these spending limits. PACs are not allowed to contribute to presidential general elections in which candidates receive public financing. However, there are no upper limits to total PAC contributions each year, and there is no limit to so-called "independent" expenditures that are undertaken on behalf of candidates without their request, cooperation, or knowledge. Thus, the PAC may buy TV or radio spots promoting a candidate so long as members of the candidate's campaign are

EXHIBIT 18–2   FEDERAL CAMPAIGN CONTRIBUTION AND EXPENDITURE LIMITS

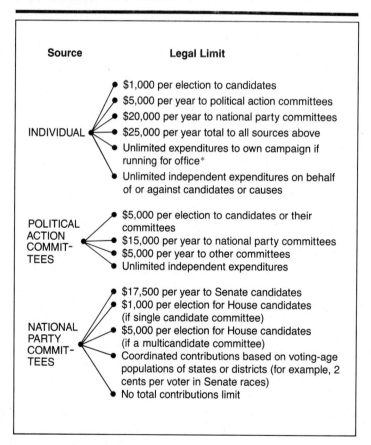

Source	Legal Limit
INDIVIDUAL	• $1,000 per election to candidates
	• $5,000 per year to political action committees
	• $20,000 per year to national party committees
	• $25,000 per year total to all sources above
	• Unlimited expenditures to own campaign if running for office*
	• Unlimited independent expenditures on behalf of or against candidates or causes
POLITICAL ACTION COMMITTEES	• $5,000 per election to candidates or their committees
	• $15,000 per year to national party committees
	• $5,000 per year to other committees
	• Unlimited independent expenditures
NATIONAL PARTY COMMITTEES	• $17,500 per year to Senate candidates
	• $1,000 per election for House candidates (if single candidate committee)
	• $5,000 per election for House candidates (if a multicandidate committee)
	• Coordinated contributions based on voting-age populations of states or districts (for example, 2 cents per voter in Senate races)
	• No total contributions limit

*Presidential and vice-presidential candidates are limited to $50,000 if federal funding is accepted.

unaware of such activity. Such unlimited independent expenditures are permitted by a Supreme Court decision, *Buckley v. Valeo* (1976), which ruled that they are a form of free speech protected by the First Amendment. Through independent expenditures, therefore, PACs may exceed the dollar limits for contributions to candidates, but it is rare for corporate PACs to spend this way. In the 1984 elections, corporate PACs' independent expenditures both for and against candidates were under $50,000, an insignificant sum.

Corporations may, and typically do, pay the administrative costs of PACs, but all money collected for contributions must be kept in a "separate segregated fund" to which the corporation cannot legally donate 1 cent (because of the prohibition since 1907 of direct corporate campaign contributions). The money collected by a PAC is contributed to candidates based on decisions made by a PAC board of directors, who are corporate employees. The board decides whether to support a candidate and what size contribution to make. If, however, an individual corporate employee contributes, say, $200 to the company PAC and states that this money should go to Senator X's primary campaign, the PAC board is obligated to pass on the earmarked contribution. Few employees earmark, however, and so the board usually is free to make its own decisions.

PACs adopt various contribution strategies. Many contribute modest amounts to a large number of candidates who are incumbents or likely to be elected so that the company can have access later on to a large number of elected officials. These PACs often contribute to opposing candidates running for the same seat. Other PACs make fewer and larger contributions that reward past political favors. A few PACs are more ideological and contribute to, say, conservative Republicans, thereby hoping to expand or reinforce that element in Congress. PACs frequently respond to the suggestions of company lobbyists when money is doled out.

In 1986 there were exactly 4,000 PACs, including 1,687 corporate PACs, 394 union PACs, and 698 trade-association and other membership-group PACs. This is a large number, and with the growth of PACs has come dramatic growth in spending. In 1974, PACs gave $12.5 million to congressional candidates. In 1984, they gave $104 million, an 830 percent increase. Corporate PACs, which number 42 percent of all PACs, gave $59 million in contributions or 57 percent of the total of all PAC contributions, but this was only 10 percent of all campaign contributions. Note also that despite the trend for more corporations to establish PACs, as shown in Table 18–1, only about 40 percent of *Fortune* 500 companies have one, and the 1,687 corporate PACs that exist are less than 1 percent of the number that would exist if every eligible corporation established one. One reason that some major corporations do not set up PACs is the fear that predatory candidates will demand contributions.

Business funnels money into politics in ways other than PAC contributions. Corporate employees and lobbyists attend fund-raising dinners for candidates, typically paying $250 to $1,000 a plate. These same individuals may be invited to join political party clubs with dues up to $15,000 a year. Managers may, of course, make personal contributions to candidates. A timeworn device for getting money to an elected official is to pay an honorarium for a talk. In 1984,

TABLE 18–1   THE GROWTH OF CORPORATE PACS

	Actual Number	Yearly Increase	Percentage Increase
1974	89	—	—
1975	139	50	56
1976	433	294	211
1977	550	117	27
1978	784	234	43
1979	948	164	20
1980	1,204	256	27
1981	1,327	123	10
1982	1,415	88	7
1983	1,536	121	9
1984	1,682	146	10
1985	1,687	5	0.3

Source: Federal Election Commission press release, August 19, 1985.

for example, General Electric paid $37,656 in honoraria to various members of Congress; the Tobacco Institute, which was seeking reduction in the 16 cents per package cigarette tax, paid $126,192 (Jackson, 1985). It is not unusual for a Senate or House member to attend a breakfast meeting of corporate officials, make brief remarks, and receive a personal check for $2,000.

Assessing the Role of PACs

Many political observers are critical of PACs; fewer defend them. Keeping in mind that PACs set up by corporations, trade unions, and other business groups are not the entirety of the PAC universe, we can review some of the major arguments surrounding PACs.

Critics argue that large PAC contributions create unwholesome obligations to special interests in Congress. PAC contributions, they say, are blatant efforts to buy votes; they are investments from which donors expect a return. Can PAC contributions buy votes? Undoubtedly they can on occasion, but personal views, party positions, opposition lobbies, and constituent pressures also are powerful factors in voting decisions. Most corporate PACs simply do not give large enough sums to really tempt a legislator to sell out, although when a number of companies in an industry contribute heavily along with a trade group, the amount can be substantial. Citizens should worry about large corporate contributions, but they do not automatically guarantee victory. The opinion of many lobbyists is that the typical corporate contribution of $250 to $1,000 buys a return phone call and little else.

PACs are also alleged to protect the status quo and to make the political system less open to challengers with new ideas because they tend to favor incumbents in their contributions. This criticism ignores the fact that individual contributions also favor current officeholders. In a related criticism, PACs are thought to undermine the political parties because PACs now contribute more money to legislators. There is validity in this observation, although the party role was first eclipsed during the period of seniority and procedural reforms in Congress in the 1970s. A favorable omen for the parties is that their PACs were learning how to raise more money in the late 1980s.

Some political observers believe that the increasingly large, combined contributions of PACs so greatly augment candidates' war chests that they raise the cost of elections and make challengers' campaigns more difficult. Although many factors push the cost of elections upward, this is undeniably an important one. Still, the cost of a congressional midterm election or a presidential election is less than the advertising budgets of some large corporations. And if PACs were not channeling corporate money into the system, history teaches that it would enter from another direction. Political money is like water in a stream; if you dam it up in one place, it flows around and over in another place. Current reforms cannot realistically be expected to stem the flow when past election law changes failed to hold down contribution levels. We believe that corporations are making larger contributions than in the past because government affairs have greater impact on operations than in the past, not because of the existence of PACs as a special vehicle for contributions.

Finally, it has been argued that PACs manifest an unfair imbalance between monied special interests and other legitimate interests. Important interests, such as those of poor people and minorities, are underrepresented in the policy process as a result. We note that this imbalance has existed throughout American history and is not attributable to PACs so much as to the general responsiveness of the system to pressure reinforced by money. If public financing reforms were enacted tomorrow, the system would inevitably remain attuned primarily to the needs of special-interest lobbyists.

It is sometimes said in defense of PACs that the growing involvement of corporate employees who make PAC contributions has the salutary effect of increasing political awareness and education. This is nonsense. One study has shown that the average PAC contributor is actually less politically informed and active than a citizen who picks a candidate and contributes (Boren, 1985). PACs sometimes raise money by using mild coercion with employees, as when teams of solicitors visit managers at their desks or when memos suggesting guidelines for voluntary donations based on salary are circulated.

In sum, it may be said that money flowing through the PAC system poses problems, but these are the same problems that lurked in past individual and corporate contribution patterns. The prominence of special-interest PACs is an unanticipated consequence of the campaign-reform laws of the 1970s. They have given advantages to special interests, but overall the present contribution system is cleaner and more open than in the past because of new financial-disclosure laws. And PAC supporters may argue that PACs are a legal form of free expression of political views and make possible the exercise of a constitutional right. They are the result of current election law, and when the law is changed and PACs wane in importance, another incarnation of worrisome special-interest giving will probably float out of the wings and onto political center stage.

CONCLUSION: THE FEAR OF CORPORATE POWER

Over the years there has developed a public apprehension that business interests, through lobbying, electioneering, campaign contributions, and cronyism in Washington, will not only dominate but also corrupt the political system. Accompanying this public apprehension is a long-standing scholarly debate about the nature of business political power. Some scholars believe that business is simply one pressure group among many others in a pluralistic society. They grant that it is a powerful group—perhaps the most powerful group—but feel that it is adequately and continuously checked. Other scholars believe that economic interests dominate government to such an extent that the resulting society is qualitatively distinct from a pluralistic society. It is a society in which business occupies a position of special privilege due to the desire of politicians and the public to keep the economy strong. The issue here is not corruption. Although some corruption inevitably exists in the innumerable influential efforts of business, the real issue is whether business power, properly exercised, is too great by some measure. There is, so far, no proof that it is.

The challenge for American society is to balance the free exercise of political freedoms granted to corporations in the First Amendment against the compelling social interest in maintaining a marketplace of political ideas free from unwarranted tyranny by powerful, monied interests. So far, our society has been successful in maintaining such a balance. When, in the past, business power has appeared to be excessive and inadequately counterbalanced, an aroused public has called for reform. If, in the future, corporate power should appear to be unchecked, it is likely that the wheel of reform will turn again.

CASE STUDY

PANPAC AND THE SENATE CANDIDATE

Jonathan Conrad, Republican candidate for the United States Senate, paced nervously back and forth in his dimly lit, downstairs study. His campaign for high office in a southern state would draw to a close in less than two weeks with the general election, but the most difficult decision of the campaign, indeed of his career, loomed before him. Now, with the house nearly darkened, his wife and two children in bed, Conrad discovered that the repose and detached reflection he had promised himself were not forthcoming.

Conrad, a native son and prominent big-city banker in his state, had been a reluctant candidate. Although he had served on the city council in his home town for four years, been elected to the State Assembly for a term, and spent an additional year as chairman of the state's Republican Central Committee, his reputation as a fair and reliable politician stemmed partly from lack of ambition for higher office. He earned a yearly salary of $80,000 as president of Midland City Bank. This was supplemented by income from several businesses in town that he owned and by the earnings of bank shares in his name. He led a gentleman's life and valued the time he was able to spend away from politics with his family.

Several years ago, however, state leaders became concerned about the growing influence of Alvin "Big Toe" Weaver. Weaver had captured the sentimental attachment of the voters in a race for a seat in the House of Representatives by touring his district in shoes with holes in the front to dramatize the plight of poor sharecroppers who would be displaced from their land by construction of a dam. Weaver, a Democrat, had so skillfully exploited this issue in speeches filled with purple oratory that he was elected by a margin of almost two to one.

The landslide fed Weaver's ambition, and during three terms in the House of Representatives he curried the favor of party professionals and placed cohorts on party committees across the state. Two years ago, when Joshua Ironwright, the popular Democratic senior senator from the state, announced his retirement at age eighty-one, the dominance of the so-called "Weaver machine" in Democratic party politics assured Weaver's nomination for the seat.

In anticipation of the forthcoming election, Weaver had spent more time at home than in Washington during the last year and a half, crisscrossing the state with a proposal to cut unemployment in the state's huge pool of unskilled labor. In speech after speech, Weaver proposed a three-step plan, which he referred to as "a new Bill of Rights for the working man." Step 1 would require all major corporations operating in the state to reinvest capital gains from state operations in programs for training and hiring the hard-core unemployed. Step 2 called for each business that employed more than twenty-five workers to hire an additional labor force of not less than 5 percent of the total number of workers. Step 3 provided for the establishment of a "citizen overseer body" to enforce reinvestment and the hiring of minority workers.

Business leaders, including Conrad, had opposed this plan by calling it unworkable, inefficient, and probably unconstitutional, but Weaver persisted in its advocacy, and his charismatic appeal met with success. A statewide polling organization determined that as a result of Weaver's canvassing, 55 percent of the voters approved the plan, 30 percent disapproved, and 15 percent were undecided.

Approximately a year ago, however, doubts about Weaver began to grow —even among Democrats. He launched a bitter attack against businesspeople, educators, and politicans who opposed the plan by branding them bigots and exploiters. The issue, already hotly debated, developed racial overtones. It was then that a bipartisan committee of state politicians, businesspeople, and professionals had come to visit Conrad.

Weaver was dangerous, they explained. His ability to incite the base emotions of the population on the race issue was feared. Furthermore, there were unconfirmed but widely circulated rumors that Weaver was mentally unstable. Aides reportedly swore that he had delusions of grandeur and late at night would lock himself behind his office doors and rage at the demons that tormented him. "We have come to you," the committee spokesman explained, "to enlist your service to the state. We want you to oppose Weaver in the upcoming senatorial race because your reputation for fair play and popularity with voters make you the only candidate with which to oppose a demagogue like Alvin Weaver." Conrad had consented, but now he half-wished that he had not.

With the support of all factions of his party and the endorsement of some prominent Democrats, Conrad breezed through the June primary. The first polls of the Conrad-Weaver match-up in early July, however, showed Weaver leading in voter preference with 64 percent and Conrad trailing miserably, with only 28 percent; 8 percent were undecided. With only three months until the general election, the situation seemed bleak.

Conrad chose a staff, set up a headquarters in the capital, and conducted fund-raising campaigns that netted $450,000. Throughout the remainder of July and well into August, he conscientiously attended teas and rallies, spoke before large but reserved audiences, and earnestly solicited funds.

Much of the money was allocated for staff expenses and mass mailings. Volunteers went door to door and telephoned voters. Billboard space was purchased to ensure that Jonathan Conrad became a household name. Some radio and television spots were purchased, but emphasis was placed upon reaching "influentials" in the electorate, or community leaders who supposedly could swing others' votes.

This effort produced inadequate results. A poll in the first week of September revealed that Weaver still held a substantial lead, although the margin had narrowed somewhat, to 61 percent for Weaver versus 33 percent for Conrad, with 5 percent undecided. Throughout September, Conrad's attempts to diminish the large gap, although partly successful, lagged behind projections, and it appeared that Weaver's magnetic personality was sufficient in itself to overcome even the most concerted effort and widespread party support. Then it happened.

Weaver and Conrad had shared a platform together at the dedication of a new textile plant. At the conclusion of his speech, Conrad had pivoted to return to his chair when an angry Weaver jumped up and confronted him. With noses barely inches apart, a debate between the two ensued, much to the delight of the roaring crowd. Then, after an angry exchange of words, Weaver spat on Conrad in full view of the audience. This action was greeted with a loud chorus of boos, and Weaver's bodyguards were forced to struggle to lead him to safety.

The incident was widely reported in the press, and the public—its sense of fair play violated—began to listen to what Conrad had to say. His measured tones and carefully thought-out proposals suddenly gained new support and now, ten days from the November 5 election, the polls showed that he had closed to within 5 percentage points of Weaver. In a meeting with advisers earlier that day, however, there had been a feeling of impotence despite such great gains.

A privately commissioned poll showed that although Conrad had closed to within 5 points of Weaver, the gain capped a leveling off trend, and the rise was not likely to continue without increased effort. It was time for a major media blitz to push Conrad over the top, but not enough money remained. Advisers estimated such a campaign would cost $415,000, but the cost was academic because campaign coffers held only $78,610. It seemed too late for further fund-raising efforts.

After the meeting with his advisers, Conrad returned home, where he soon received a phone call from an excited aide at his campaign headquarters. The aide indicated that PANPAC, a political action committee of the Pacific National Oil Company, had just committed $350,000 to run pro-Conrad messages on radio and television stations around the state. Pacific National was one of the nation's largest oil companies and had several big refineries in the state. The money had not been solicited by either Conrad or members of his staff but had been committed "independently" by PANPAC.

The aide suggested a meeting the next day to plan a new campaign strategy to take advantage of this unexpected windfall. But Conrad told the surprised caller that he was not sure that he would accept the help. Conrad said that he would call back in the morning with a decision that could, if it were negative, be immediately relayed to PANPAC and end the group's effort on his behalf.

Questions

1. If you were in Conrad's position, what would you do? Why?
2. If Conrad accepts the help and is elected, will he be beholden to the oil company interests when he votes or otherwise exercises his influence as a senator? In all areas of public policy? In some?
3. Are present campaign financing and spending laws adequate to regulate practices that might later lead to subtle forms of political blackmail?
4. Do businesses and people with great wealth have the right to translate their economic power into political influence? Do federal laws properly control them?
5. Should independent expenditures by PACs be curbed?

CHAPTER **19**

MULTINATIONAL CORPORATIONS AND GOVERNMENT RELATIONSHIPS

The Ford Motor Company has grown from a tiny wagon factory in Detroit, staffed with ten people in 1903, to one of the world's largest corporations. In 1986 it ranked third as measured by sales, among the largest industrial companies in the United States. In that year, its sales were $62.7 billion, its assets were $37.9 billion, and its net income was $3.3 billion (*Fortune*, 1987). Ford is also one of the largest multinational corporations in the world. In 1985 its foreign assets amounted to $15.7 billion, or 50.1 percent of total assets. Its sales from abroad amounted to 30.3 percent of total sales (see Table 19–1), and its net income from abroad was 21.0 percent of total profit.

George E. Trainor, director of the International Public Affairs Office at Ford, explained the broad nature of Ford's global operations (personal communication, 1986). He noted that today, Ford has active manufacturing, assembly, and sales operations in twenty-four countries and joint-venture operations in five other countries, and that its products are sold in 146 other countries where the company has no operating affiliates. It employs more than 360,000 people worldwide.

In addition to producing cars and trucks, farm and industrial tractors, industrial engines, construction machinery, steel, glass, and plastics, Ford companies are established in finance, insurance, automotive replacement parts, electronics, communications, space technology, and land development. The historic spark and economic fuel of the company's worldwide growth, however, always has been the motor vehicle.

Ford's worldwide automotive and tractor manufacturing and marketing business is grouped into four principal regions: North America, Europe, Latin America, and Asia-Pacific. Ford Direct Market Operations represents a fifth regional grouping that is largely engaged in overseas markets where Ford has no operating affiliates.

One of the major elements of Ford's current strategy is to continue to strengthen its coordination of multinational resources into an integrated international complex that will provide the company with a unique opportunity to meet global competition. To strengthen its position in the major automotive markets, the company today is increasing the utilization of Ford design, engineering, and manufacturing worldwide and is teaming with other manufacturers and suppliers to share the development and production costs for new products.

Closely related to this strategy is expanding relationships with Mazda, the large Japanese automotive manufacturer. Ford and Mazda are cooperating in a close and mutually beneficial relationship directed toward the improved utilization of product development, manufacturing, distribution, and human resources. Mazda will continue to work with Ford affiliates in the Asia-Pacific region and is working with the company to develop a minicar to be built by Kia of South Korea. Mazda also is assisting in the design of the process and the vehicle at the new Ford plant in Hermosillo, Mexico, and at Ford's plant in Taiwan. The company also will purchase a significant portion of the production from Mazda's new assembly plant being built in Flat Rock, Michigan.

In addition, Ford has embarked on a series of moves designed to improve its overall strength by developing new sources of earnings and strengthening its existing nonautomotive businesses. This part of Ford's strategy has been employed thus far in the acquisitions of First Nationwide Financial Corporation and Sperry New Holland, the world's largest manufacturer of specialized farm equipment. In addition to its equity position in Mazda (25 percent) and its outright purchase of First Nationwide and Sperry New Holland, in the last five years Ford has taken equity positions in fifteen other companies, principally in high-technology companies, and consummated joint ventures with component suppliers.

As a global company, Ford has a reputation for conducting its worldwide operations in a socially responsible manner. It commands respect for its integrity and its contributions to host governments around the world. In each country where it operates, the company's policy is to abide by the country's laws with respect to local content regulations, import-export credits, fuel and safety regulations, repatriation of profits, labor laws, and all other applicable laws, rules, and regulations. In turn, Ford provides the host country with a tax base, employment, payroll, training, new technology, and development of the country's infrastructure. Such operations are extremely complex, but Ford's years of experience with various customs regulations, tariffs, and shippers provide for a relatively trouble-free flow of components, parts, and whole vehicles among various countries.

This brief overview of the operations of a major multinational corporation (MNC) is intended to provide a useful frame of reference for the major issues discussed in this chapter. Following a definition of the nature and role of the MNC we examine the more significant conflicts that exist between MNCs and host governments, and then the dominant relationships between United States-based MNCs and the federal government. Then, after considering current pressures for protectionism and deviations from free-trade principles, the chapter closes with a discussion of foreign payoffs and the controls required to curb them.

NATURE AND ROLE OF THE MNC

A Definition of the MNC

There are many definitions of an MNC. We accept one used by the United Nations, that MNCs are "enterprises which own or control production or service facilities outside the country in which they are based" (1975: 25).

In our definition the MNC is an agency of direct, as opposed to portfolio, investment in foreign countries. It is not always incorporated or private. It can be a cooperative or state-owned entity. Almost every large organization has some direct or indirect involvement with foreign companies, but only when an enterprise confronts one or more of the problems of designing, producing, marketing, or financing its products or services within and among foreign nations does it become truly multinational.

Many MNCs progress through several stages. Characteristically, the expanding enterprise goes through the following stages:

1. Exports its products to foreign countries.

2. Establishes sales organizations abroad.

3. Licenses use of its patents and know-how to foreign firms that make and sell its products.

4. Establishes foreign manufacturing facilities.

5. Multinationalizes management from top to bottom.

6. Multinationalizes ownership of corporate stock.

There are probably several hundred thousand companies in stage 1, many fewer in stages 2 and 3, only five or six thousand in stage 4, and but a handful of giants in stages 5 and 6. The ten largest U.S.-based MNCs in 1985 (measured in terms

TABLE 19–1   THE LARGEST U.S.-BASED MULTINATIONALS

1985 Rank	Company	Foreign revenue (millions)	Total revenue (millions)	Foreign revenue as % of total	Foreign assets (millions)	Foreign assets as % of total
1	Exxon	$59,067	$86,673	68.1%	$30,049	43.4%
2	Mobile	32,678	57,111	57.2	18,867	45.2
3	Texaco	21,864	46,297	47.2	11,142	29.6
4	IBM	21,545	50,056	43.0	21,733	41.3
5	General Motors	16,167	96,372	16.8	13,570	21.3
6	Ford Motor	15,995	52,774	30.3	15,725	50.1
7	Salomon	15,100	27,896	54.1	7,800	8.8
8	Chevron	12,722	41,742	30.5	9,165	23.6
9	Citicorp	10,600	22,504	47.1	78,259	48.8
10	E.I. du Pont de Nemours	10,551	29,239	36.1	7,546	30.0

Source: Excerpted by permission from *Forbes* magazine, July 28, 1986: 207. © 1986 Forbes Inc.

of total foreign revenues) are shown in Table 19–1 together with their revenues and assets as a proportion to their total revenues and assets. These companies have total revenues greater than the gross national products of most of the countries in which they do business. The 100 largest U.S.-based MNCs reported total revenues in 1985 of $1.3 trillion and foreign revenues of $409 billion (*Forbes,* July 28, 1986).

MNCs are divided into two categories—those that operate in countries through subsidiaries that are more or less autonomous (Exhibit 19–1) and those that operate on a global basis (Exhibit 19–2). In the former, there is often a separate organization for each nation or group of nations. In the latter, global approach, somewhere in the world there is an executive group responsible for integrating and planning for the product line and allocating company resources accordingly. The decisions of (1) what to sell, (2) where to sell, (3) where to manufacture, and (4) where to buy raw materials and components, are determined on a worldwide basis. In the one case, competition is national, and in the other it is international. The Ford Motor Company fits the global definition.

An increasing number of companies are moving into the global category. A few dominant reasons are new technologies that increase scale economies in operations; new communications technologies that speed information flows; the rise of vigorous and skilled foreign competitors searching for global markets; and declining transportation costs (Porter, 1980).

Conceptual Objectives of MNCs and Host Governments

The fundamental motive of going abroad is, of course, profit. MNCs in stages 1 through 3 seek to profit in obvious ways. The process is more complicated when

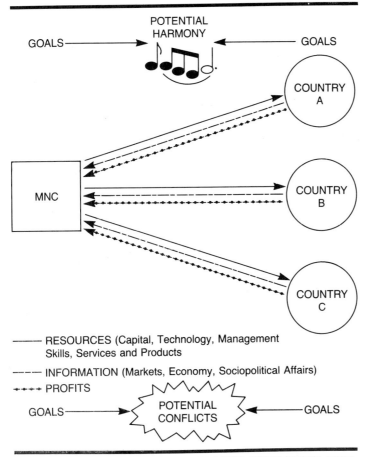

EXHIBIT 19–1   MODEL OF AN MNC OPERATING INDI-VIDUALLY IN EACH COUNTRY

a company gets to stage 4. Theoretically, in this stage, management would like to manufacture in those countries where it finds the greatest competitive advantage; it would like to buy and sell anywhere in the world to take advantage of the most favorable price to the company; it would like to take advantage throughout the world of changes in labor costs, productivity, trade agreements, and currency fluctuations; and it would like to expand or contract on the basis of worldwide comparative advantages. Its objectives are to obtain a high and rising return on invested capital; achieve rising sales; keep financial risks within reasonable limits in relation to profits; and maintain its technological and other proprietary strengths.

This focus on profits does not mean that MNCs reject social responsibilities. MNCs would like to achieve the highest possible level of economic rationality in their decision-making consistent with assuming a reasonable share of social responsibilities. As Edmund T. Pratt, Jr., CEO of Pfizer, Inc., said: "I hope we have a broader sense than just the importance of making a dollar (in our foreign

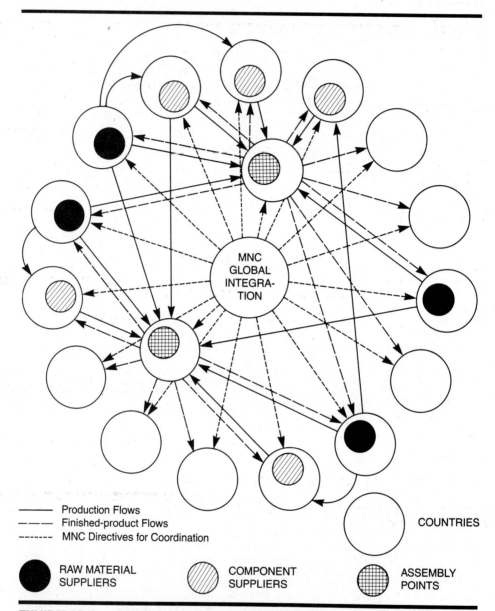

———	Production Flows
– – –	Finished-product Flows
- - - -	MNC Directives for Coordination

COUNTRIES

RAW MATERIAL SUPPLIERS

COMPONENT SUPPLIERS

ASSEMBLY POINTS

EXHIBIT 19–2   MODEL OF AN MNC COORDINATING GLOBAL OPERATIONS

operations),'' and added that he thought the basic mission of his company included building world understanding (Pratt, 1985: 35). Illustrations of such programs among MNCs are plentiful. For instance, Pfizer, along with other American-based firms, has helped the Gambian government to develop better health-care systems. Union Carbide has built and equipped a technical college in Zimbabwe. Ford Motor Co., S.A., in a program two decades old, has built 128 schools in Mexico that serve 170,000 children annually (Micou, 1985).

Generally speaking, dominant goals of most countries around the world, developed and less developed, would embrace the following: economic growth, full employment of people and resources, raising the skills of workers, price stability, a favorable balance of payments, more equitable distribution of income, a fair share of the profits made by MNCs, improving technology in and productivity of domestic business firms, national hegemony over the economic system, control over national security, social stability, and advancing the quality of life.

MNCs have been and can be of enormous help to governments of the world in their efforts to achieve most of these goals, especially the economic ones. At the same time, however, it is clear that conflicts between the two sets of goals and decision-making processes are inevitable. In recent years, host governments have eased some of their demands, but conflicts still are serious.

COMPLAINTS OF HOST GOVERNMENTS

Host governments have a long list of complaints about the MNCs that operate within their borders. Among them the following are the most frequently heard major complaints.

1. *The Challenge to Nation-State Sovereignty.* Host governments see the power of the MNC as a challenge to their sovereignty. Powers of MNCs vary, of course, but the perception of great power persists even though the total volume of investment in a country is small.
2. *Inequities.* Many complaints about alleged inequities are made. One of the most enduring and persistent is that prices of raw materials extracted from nation-states are falling while prices of imported manufactured goods are rising. This, say foreign countries, creates a growing inequity. Behind this view is the belief that foreign countries that export manufactured goods prevent competition and permit monopolies to raise prices while competition prevails in raw-material extraction in host countries of MNCs.
3. *MNCs Create Economic and Social Disruption.* Complaints in this area take a variety of directions. MNCs, it is alleged, possess competitive advantages over local entrepreneurs and, as a result, prevent the development of local business skills and capital investment. MNCs are said to create inflationary pressures that host governments cannot control. They misapply and exhaust host natural resources. They also are accused of fundamentally altering the customs, mores, and habits of host countries in ways that are detrimental to social and political stability.
4. *Lack of Concern for Local Conditions.* MNCs are seen as instruments to exploit the host country's natural wealth for the primary benefit of citizens of another country. They are said to be motivated by money and little else. They take the position that "what is good for their company is good for the country," and that, say host governments, is not the case. For instance, Nestlé introduced pow-

dered milk as a baby food into West Africa as an alternative to breast feeding. Infant mortality increased because mothers, in an effort to combat extreme poverty, diluted the milk with water to the point where there was no nutrition. Nestlé made profits, it is said, but babies died.

5.   *MNC Imperialism.* Many of the awakening nations look on foreign business-people with fear and distrust as the followers of an old exploitative colonialism not easily forgotten. It is not difficult for the awakening nations to find current illustrations to support their fears. American investors have taken out of Latin American countries more money than they have invested. This is called economic imperialism by these nations. Many less developed countries (LDCs) feel doomed to the role of supplying raw materials and cheap labor because they are denied the technology to develop into industrialized nations. Their frustrations are leveled at the MNCs that export their raw materials and cheap labor. The sins of the past and allegations of the present cannot easily be erased in the minds of formerly exploited colonies.

6.   *Symbol of Frustration and Antipathy.* The LDCs have grievances about their position in the world that have nothing to do with the MNC, but the MNC is a visible target for their anger. For example, there are adverse reactions to the power of the United States, and the MNC is seen as epitomizing that power. Also, many of the LDCs are governed by dictatorships that are naturally antagonistic to the free-market mechanism governing decision making of the MNCs.

These are broad criticisms. They lay a foundation, however, for dozens of specific demands or restrictions that may seriously conflict with the integration strategies of MNCs. For example, local governments and local interests seek to limit repatriation of assets and earnings; they want component parts or raw materials to be purchased from local suppliers; they demand the transfer of new technology to their countries; they require MNCs to appoint local nationals to top-management positions in local operations; they try to limit the company's share of local markets; they insist that the company produce or sell certain products as a condition of entry into local markets; they push export expansion and import reduction; and they want more local employment even at the expense of the company's operating efficiency.

Recent Easing of Demands

In the 1970s, criticism of and demands for restraints on MNCs reached a crescendo. Raymond Vernon, a respected scholar of the MNC, wrote in 1977: "Just a few years ago multinational enterprises were busily and profitably occupied in spreading their subsidiaries across the globe. Today the world is awash with actions and proposals that would restrain the multinational enterprise and alter its relations to nation-states" (p. 191). The view that MNCs are exploitative and disruptive persists, and it is fed by such tragic accidents as that of the Union Carbide plant in Bhopal, India. Today, both the criticism and restraints are strong. But they have diminished somewhat during the past half dozen years. For example, many LDCs have discovered that the MNCs can help them expand exports and reduce imports to create a trade surplus with which to help repay their huge debts. One result has been renewed efforts to attract foreign capital, especially from MNCs. The welcome mat has replaced the formerly barred door in many countries, from China to Latin America. Also, says Peter Hanse, executive director of the United Nations Center on Transnational Corporations, "Developing countries gained a great deal of experience and can meet companies with a great deal more self-confidence than in the early 1970s, when I think they felt overwhelmed" (in Kristof, 1985).

Response of the MNCs

Naturally, MNC managers and their defenders respond that many of the criticisms of their behavior are only partially true at best and outright untruths at worst. Despite their alleged shortcomings, they say, MNCs significantly help host governments to achieve their national aims. The most frequently expressed claims of how MNCs benefit host nations, in no particular order of priority, are:

- Provide employment.
- Train managers.
- Provide products and services that raise the standard of living.
- Introduce and develop new technical skills.
- Introduce new managerial and organizational techniques.
- Provide greater access to international markets.
- Lift the gross national product.
- Increase productivity.
- Help to build foreign exchange reserves.
- Serve as a point of contact between host country businesspersons and politicians in home country.
- Encourage the development and spin-off of new industries.
- Assume investment risks that might not otherwise have been undertaken.
- Mobilize for productive purposes capital that might otherwise have gone for less productive uses.

MNC managers have their own litany of complaints. Aside from outright expropriation of MNC subsidiaries or the threat of expropriation, MNC managers complain about controls that restrict their prerogatives in making what they consider to be rational managerial decisions over people in the organization, product and service output, flows of capital, and profits. They do not like, of course, mandatory disinvestment or limitations on reinvestment of earnings or remittance of profits. They are disturbed at rules that force them to fill quotas for local production, employees, exports, use of output of local producers, or managerial positions. They do not like to be told where to put plants, and they resist boycotts on their importing components for assembly of final products. For example, when the Ford Motor Company wanted to produce automobiles in Spain, the Spanish government set specific restrictions on sales and export volume. Ford's sales volume was limited to 10 percent of the previous year's total automobile market, and export volume had to be equal to at least two-thirds of its entire production in Spain. Also, Ford had to agree not to broaden its model lines without government authorization (Doz and Prahalad, 1980). A glance at Exhibit 19–3 highlights the problems of an MNC when it seeks to coordinate resource flows most efficiently throughout the world and encounters roadblocks put in the way by host governments.

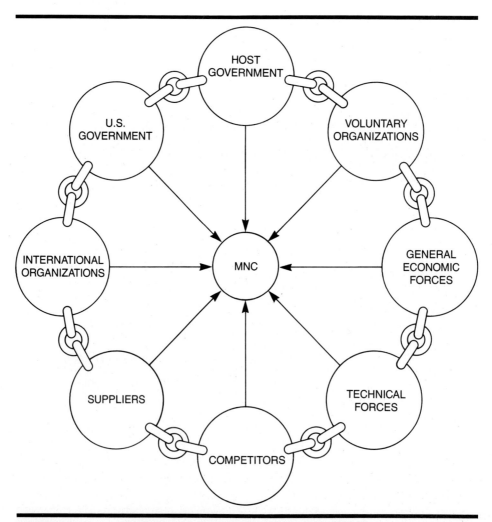

EXHIBIT 19–3   SOURCES OF CONFLICT WITH MNC GOALS

Relationships in the Future

Competent observers of the future relationships between MNCs and host governments generally agree that conflicts between the two will continue and that the result will be increasing control by government over the MNCs. It is generally conceded that governments of LDCs are becoming much more sophisticated in their understanding of MNCs and in their ability to control them. They understand better precisely what is in their interests in such matters as investment levels, capital flows, employment policies, transfer prices, and so on. This power is further increased by the sheer growth in numbers and increasing competition among MNCs.

Foreign governments are also being pressured to become more involved in MNC operations through United Nations organizations. For example, a draft proposal before the U.N.'s Economic and Social Council, entitled "Draft Guidelines for Consumer Protection," would, if implemented, provide for broad government controls over MNC activities. Under the guidelines, governments would be encouraged to develop policies and programs to protect consumers from every conceivably adverse activity of an MNC. Although this is laudable in the abstract, it would, in the opinion of one competent observer, "impose centralized control on the economies of sovereign nations" to implement the objectives laid down (Weidenbaum, 1983).

Voluntary private organizations with sociopolitical objectives also are growing in foreign countries in both number and influence. For example, these include consumer advocates, environmentalists, labor organizations and religious orders. As they have demonstrated in the United States, such groups can and do exert considerable influence on corporations both directly and indirectly, through government.

In essence, MNCs will be tolerated to the extent they can demonstrate economic value and support of national goals. They will continue to face authoritarian governments and unstable social and political conditions in most of the countries in which they operate. Exhibit 19–3 illustrates the main sources of potential conflict with MNC goals. (The chain denotes that these forces often are linked.)

CODES OF CONDUCT

To reduce conflicts between the objectives of host governments and MNCs, a number of agencies have established guides for the conduct of both. The Organization for Economic Cooperation and Development (OECD), for example, prepared such a code in 1976 and revised it in 1979. The code is supported by countries in the European Economic Community and applies to European-based MNCs. The CED in the United States has urged our MNCs to observe the OECD guidelines.

We believe that it is very important for MNCs to prepare guidelines for themselves or to endorse those set forth by agencies such as the OECD. We believe also that it is important for host governments to abide by codes of conduct for MNCs that do business in their countries. We suggest minimum policies and principles for both are as follows:

A Proposed Code for Multinational Companies
The multinational company shall

- conform to the established policies and the laws of the host country.

- respond affirmatively to the social and economic plans of the host country.

- progressively staff host country operations, including management, with local personnel.

- permit host country nationals to acquire ownership interests in the foreign affiliate of the company or in the parent company.

- refrain from activities that would harm the functioning of the local capital markets.

- supply appropriate information to local authorities about health, safety, and the environmental effects of the company's products.

- provide for the host nation's people a clear statement of the basic mission and policies of the company.

- seriously consider credible complaints and try to eliminate them.

- help LDCs that seek increasing technology transfer to do so by introducing well-known technology or by helping local entrepreneurs to produce products at a profit.

- not make payments to any official of the host country or to any political candidate for public office, except as required by law.

A Proposed Minimum Code for Host Countries
The host country shall

- make explicit its priorities and maintain them with reasonable consistency.

- enact and adhere to fair codes of foreign investment.

- tax and regulate affiliates of foreign-based companies equally with home-based enterprises.

- respect all investment agreements and not make unilateral or retroactive changes in them.

- pay prompt, adequate, and effective compensation to a foreign company whose local properties are nationalized or expropriated.

- make reasonable rules regarding payments of dividends to, and repatriation of capital by, a foreign company.

THE TOTAL ENVIRONMENT OF MNCs IN HOST COUNTRIES

High on the list of the most important managerial problems of MNC executives are their relations to governments. Dealing with the types of criticism, demands, and controls noted earlier is a difficult task. But this is only part of the environment of the typical MNC. There are many other environmental forces that are of great concern to them. Table 19–2 shows basic elements in four major environments. The forces in these areas change over time, and they differ from country to country. Because the typical large MNC operates in many countries, the scope of the problem of dealing with environmental forces begins to take shape. (One recent study of eighty-five U.S. MNCs revealed that, on the average, the typical MNC did business in seventy-two countries [Berenbeim, 1983].) The social and political environments affect and are affected by events in the economic and technical areas. Every aspect of all four environments in Table 19–2 presents a challenge, an opportunity, or a threat.

Misjudgment, misinterpretation, or ignorance of any one of many forces can adversely affect a company's foreign operations. For example, a finance manager may get into trouble if he or she does not properly appraise potential

TABLE 19–2   FOREIGN COUNTRY ENVIRONMENTAL FORCES

Economic Environment	Political Environment
Gross national product	Form of government
Per capita income	Political ideology
Natural resources	Political stability
Inflation	Attitude toward opposition groups
Interest rates	Effectiveness of legal system
Wage and salary levels	Treaties with foreign nationals
Economic crises	Laws affecting business firms
Balance of payments	Foreign policy
Exchange rate volatility	Restrictions on imports/exports
National debt	Quality of government management
Income distribution	State companies
Composition of exports	Corruption (bribery)
	Role of military
	Privileged environment for local competition

Technical Environment	Social Environment
Skill levels of workers	Customs and mores
Engineering skills	Religious or ethnic splits
Management skills	Riots, demonstrations
Technical competition	Public attitudes toward MNCs
Special technical requirements of country	Demography
Technical capabilities in universities	Class divisions
	Major social concerns of population
	Labor union attitudes

exchange instability of a host country's currency. A new plant manager may get into trouble if local workers' values and habits are misread. A plant may be expropriated because of a manager's inadvertent insult to a local government official. David Ricks's book on *Big Business Blunders* (1983) is filled with illustrations of problems that companies face in doing business in foreign cultures. He cites, for example, the case of Coca Cola in China:

> When the Coca-Cola Company was planning its strategy for marketing in China in the 1920s, it wanted to introduce its product with the English pronunciation of "Coca-Cola." A translator developed a group of Chinese characters which, when pronounced, sounded like the product name. These characters were placed on the cola bottles and marketed. Was it any wonder that sales levels were low? The characters actually translated to mean "a wax-flattened mare" or "bite the wax tadpole." Since the product was new, sound was unimportant to the consumers; meaning was vital. Today Coca-Cola is again marketing its cola in China. The new characters used on the bottle translate to "happiness in the mouth." From its first marketing attempts, Coca-Cola learned a valuable lesson in international marketing (Ricks, 1983: 38).

SOCIOPOLITICAL RISK ANALYSIS (SPRA)

Among many foreign countries, social and political events are subject to sudden and unexpected change. Rules of the game often are ambiguous, contradictory, and shifting. The revolution in Iran is a classic illustration. Not only do such conditions complicate the decision-making process of MNCs, but if appraisal of environment is wrong, a company may suffer severe consequences, ranging from nationalization and expropriation to controls that reduce managerial prerogatives, raise costs, and lower profits. In light of these conditions it is not surprising that MNCs are interested in SPRAs.

There is no consensus about the meaning of SPRAs. They cover everything from a high-priced luncheon conversation with Henry Kissinger to a comprehensive study of the future sociopolitical changes that should be considered by a company deciding whether to stay in or get out of a country with a particular product. In this context, risk refers to the fact that projections of future changes usually are presented as probability statements, or estimates of likely events, based on available evidence or intuitive judgment.

Most companies rely on relatively unsystematic qualitative approaches in making SPRAs. They produce a scenario or series of projections, often with probabilities, that managers can use as a basis for their thinking and decision-making. The SPRAs result from a mixture of information from both primary and secondary sources and expert opinion about a particular country and force.

A number of management consulting firms have developed country-assessment models to help companies. These, too, range from unstructured subjective evaluations to comprehensive, structured techniques. Among the latter, for instance, is the model of the Business International Service. It analyzes fifty-six factors in seventy countries. Each of the fifty-six factors is classified along six dimensions: risk, opportunity, operating conditions, political, economic, and financial. Ratings or scores are given to each factor, and each factor is weighted. By adding the numbers, of course, a composite score can be developed for a country.

Each model builder must choose to answer those questions that are most pertinent to the issue to be decided. A question of where to build a new plant requires answers different from those related to international transfer of funds. To illustrate the types of questions asked, we note typical questions concerned with political risk.

- Will the present form of government last, and if so, for how long?

- What special political or social problems are important to our company?

- What is the attitude of the government toward foreign investment?

- Is there a threat of nationalization? If so, what?

- What treaties does the country have with the United States that are of interest to us?

- What controls does the government exercise over foreign investment in each major area—production, domestic content, pricing, technology, employment, and the like?

- Are there clear and modern corporate investment laws?

- What major problems will exist in dealing with government officials?

ORGANIZATION STRUCTURES

As a corporation moves through the stages of development described earlier in this chapter, the necessity of making organizational changes in structure becomes obvious. Making the proper organizational changes to fit changing circumstances may well be a deciding factor in the success or failure of a particular product, program, or the corporation's foreign operations as a whole. Organizational structure changes, therefore, are generally thought of as major strategies.

No one organizational model is best for any given stage of development of an MNC (Phatak, 1983). In the first stage noted above, a company may simply add an export manager to the marketing staff to deal with foreign interests. It might create a position for an export functional manager to deal with foreign affairs. This arrangement may be suitable when a company exports many products manufactured by different divisions. These organizations become less effective as export sales grow and when the company adds new products to its export line and begins to build production facilities abroad. In such circumstances an international division may be formed to manage the nondomestic operations of the company.

When a company moves into stage 5, a different organizational structure becomes appropriate. Let us assume that when a company enters this stage, these characteristics are present: top management is committed to a global perspective in strategy; the international market is as important, if not more important, to the company than the domestic market for sales and profits; and senior officials of the company have great knowledge of international markets and what is going on in each of the countries in which the company does business.

Several alternative organizational arrangements may be suitable at this point. For example, each individual domestic division may be given authority to deal with the foreign operations for the products it manufacturers, subject, of course, to top management policy and strategy. Each division has its own functional personnel—finance, marketing, production, planning, and the like. Two major disadvantages of this type of organization are readily apparent. First, there is obvious duplication of staff across divisions. Second, division managers may be understandably biased in favor of their own geographic goals at the expense of total corporate global goals. An alternative is to organize by geographic area. In this type of organization, the company's staff and productive resources may be allocated to areas such as North America, Europe, Latin America, Middle East, Asia, and Africa. Each unit, of course, has appropriate functional staff, capital resources, and authority. Each area may be further subdivided into individual countries. In such an organization the domestic market becomes just another market in the company's decision-making processes. Global coordination can be assured in either type of organization by appropriate top management control. For instance, an international chief operating officer or a senior executive in charge of international activities could assure necessary global integration.

In sum, the environmental forces that accompany expansion and change in foreign markets necessitate important alterations in organizational structure. These, in turn, change the decision-making processes and allocation of authority in a company.

UNITED STATES—BASED MNCs AND THE FEDERAL GOVERNMENT

The special relationships between the MNCs based in the United States and the federal government are diverse, significant, and changing. We discuss a few of these complex relationships.

United States Foreign Relations

United States foreign policy and business interests always have been intertwined, although the purpose has varied considerably from time to time. The

U.S. Navy attacked the Barbary pirates in 1801 to stop interference with Yankee shipping, but it may also have been an excuse to secure the presence of the American Navy in the Mediterranean. Our flag has followed our trade. Gunboat diplomacy on behalf of business may have been used years ago but no more. Since World War II, the federal government has reduced substantially its help to American business when it ventures abroad. Nevertheless, there are important connections among the federal government, MNCs, and foreign host governments in the conduct of foreign policy.

This interrelationship has not always served the selfish interests of business, although that has been rather important in the past. Predominantly, it has served the economic and political interests of the United States, for business can be significant in furthering broad national interests. In their normal operations, MNCs do support United States foreign policy. They are catalysts for international cooperation by supporting regional integration and economies of scale, building infrastructure, and working with governments to solve mutual problems. They can enhance the national economic influence of both home and host nations by improving skill, technology, international distribution networks, and exports. In this sense, they serve United States interests in seeking economic growth and sociopolitical stability in the world.

A major policy of the United States has been for many decades, and still is, to foster economic progress throughout the world. In furtherance of this policy, the government has viewed the MNC as an essential instrument of strong and healthy global economic progress.

Sometimes in implementing this policy, the goals of MNCs and the United States foreign policy may conflict. This conflict is particularly likely with respect to export controls, which have become an important instrument of American diplomacy in recent administrations. The basic authority of such bans rests in The Export Administration Act of 1979, subsequently revised in 1985. It permits export controls of two types. First are national-security controls. These place restrictions on exports (especially of high technology) that would make a significant contribution to the military potential of another country and that would be detrimental to the national security of the United States. Second are foreign-policy controls. These are restrictions on exports of goods and technology to further United States diplomatic objectives.

For example, a long list of electronic and computer products and technologies cannot be exported to the Soviet Union for national-security reasons. A classic illustration of export restrictions for diplomatic reasons was President Reagan's order in 1982 prohibiting Dresser Industries, Inc., from shipping machinery needed by the Soviet Union to complete a gas pipeline to Western Europe. (This case was discussed at some length at the beginning of Chapter 5.) United States sanctions have been applied to many countries in recent years—Cuba, Iran, Nicaragua, and South Africa, to name a few. These policies raise a dilemma for this country. How can the government curb some exports in furtherance of national goals without injuring United States companies?

The business community accepts export restrictions for national-security purposes, although questions are raised about the expanding number of prohibited exports. But, there is much irritation in the business community about the use of export restraints to achieve diplomatic goals, especially when they conflict with MNC goals (Lindell, 1986).

PROTECTIONISM VERSUS FREE TRADE

From the very beginning of our history we have had, on the one hand, a free trade policy but, on the other hand, we have protected our industries from foreign competition. At no time in the past, however, have protectionist demands been at a higher pitch of urgency than today. Paradoxically, at no time in recent years have greater pressures been brought to bear by our government on foreign governments to lift trade barriers on our companies wanting to do business there.

Trade barriers, here and abroad, are entangled in issues such as government fiscal and monetary policies and economic and political goals, policies of international monetary authorities, trade flows, world levels of economic activity, and national security. Here we limit our focus to protectionism versus free trade issues in the United States today.

Why Free Trade?

The case for free trade is comparatively simple. By virtue of climate, labor conditions, raw materials, capital, management, or other considerations, some nations have an advantage over others in the production of particular goods. For instance, Brazil can produce coffee beans at a much lower price than the United States. Coffee beans could be grown in hothouses in the United States, but not at a price equal to that which Brazil can charge and make a profit at. But the United States has a distinct advantage over Brazil in producing computers. Resources will be used most efficiently when each country produces that for which it enjoys a cost advantage. Gain from specialization and trade is mutually advantageous when the cost ratios of producing two commodities are different in different countries. Furthermore, gain will be maximized when each nation specializes in producing those products for which it has the greatest comparative advantage or the least comparative disadvantage. This is what economists call the law of comparative advantage. It follows that maximum gain on a worldwide basis will be realized if there are no impediments to trade, if there is free competition in pricing, and if capital flows are unrestricted. The greatest profits will result if in each country those goods are produced for which the nation has the greatest comparative advantage. It is not always easy, however, to see just where a nation has a comparative advantage. At the extremes the case is clear, but not at the means. Differences in monetary units, rates of productivity of capital and labor, changes in markets, or elasticities of demand, for instance, obscure the degree of advantage one nation may have over another at any time.

Nations use many arguments to convince themselves that erecting tariff barriers is sensible from their point of view. For example, people argue for the use of tariffs to protect our national security, to protect high American wages and jobs, and to equalize costs of production. It is argued that tariffs are needed to maintain skills and productive capability essential to national security. Watchmakers have argued, for instance, that tariffs are needed on imported watches in order to maintain American watchmaking skills that are necessary for the making of precision parts of military equipment during national emergencies. There are many problems with this type of argument. For one thing, it is exceedingly difficult to determine precisely what capabilities are needed for national defense. Even if this could be ascertained, it does not follow that tariff protection is the best way to get them. A tariff subsidizes an industry and amounts to a tax on the consumers of the products of that industry. Why should this particular group be taxed in the name of national security? If a capability is really needed for national security, and should be maintained, a much better way to do it would be a direct subsidy by the government to the industry. At least the costs would be clearer.

Another argument is that when imported goods are made with cheap labor and undersell American-made goods, the result will be a drop in American wage rates and/or in employment of workers in industries that cannot compete. The argument is that tariffs are needed to protect high American wages and employment. Yet although the American advocates of high tariffs assert the need to protect the American worker from the cheap labor of foreign nations, advocates of high tariffs in foreign nations assert the need because of the more efficient American worker. Those who argue for high tariffs to protect American wage rates obviously are afraid to accept the consequences of the law of comparative advantage. The cheap labor argument for tariffs overlooks the fact that high American wages would not necessarily be jeopardized by a tariff reduction. High wages are due to the productivity of American labor, which is a function of many elements, including applications of capital to labor, the skills of the American worker, motivation, hours of work, and management. The argument is made that tariffs are needed to equalize costs of production. On the surface this seems to be fair, but if this were done throughout the world, all trade would be eliminated because trade is based on cost differentials.

Free trade, it is argued, will stimulate competition, reward individual initiative, increase productivity, and improve national well-being. It will enlarge job opportunities and produce for consumers a wider variety of goods and services at minimum prices and with higher quality. Free-trade advocates argue that protectionism does just the reverse. It stifles competitive activity, dampens individual inititative, costs consumers more in higher prices, and sets off trade wars that result in economic stagnation and depression. The classic example to illustrate this point, they say, is the high-barrier Smoot-Hawley Tariff passed in 1929, which has been widely held responsible for the disastrous, worldwide depression of the 1930s.

Pressures for Protectionism

President Reagan repeatedly asserted by his rhetoric and vetoes of protectionist bills that the United States has a free-trade policy. In response to criticism of our trading partners by protectionists, he said, "We're in the same boat with our trading partners. If one partner shoots a hole in the boat, does it make sense for the other one to shoot another hole in the boat?" But this philosophy is by no means universally accepted in the top levels of our government, nor has President Reagan followed it in practice. There are many people, especially in the Congress, who assert that the United States, with its free-trade philosophy, is being "played for a sucker" by other countries that do not have a free-trade philosophy. They subsidize their exports to the United States and bar our products to their markets. "It's time to get tough," they assert. Vice President George Bush reflected this thought recently when he said: "No more Mr. Nice Guy."

What is behind the protectionist upsurge? One source of pressure is our increasing trade deficit. Traditionally, we have had a trade surplus (more exports than imports), but in 1981 our trade deficit was $40 billion and rose steadily to $168 billion in 1986. Foreign competitors are flooding our markets with goods.

A few numbers are sobering. From 1972 to 1984, imports of blowers and fans rose, as a percent of the total U.S. market, from 3.6 to 29.2 percent; for dolls the growth was from 21.9 percent to 54.7 percent; for radios and TV sets, from 34.9 percent to 57.5 percent; for shoes, 17.1 percent to 50.4 percent; for luggage, from 20.7 percent to 52.4 percent; for men's and boys' shirts and nightwear, from 17.8 percent to 46.1 percent; and for women's blouses, from 14.9 percent to 33.0 percent (*Business Week,* October 7, 1985: 94–95). Manufacturers of steel, machine tools, motorcycles, bicycles, automobiles, construction machinery, and many other major products have seen their domestic and foreign markets shrink because of foreign competition.

The results of all of this have been devastating to our companies and workers. Take the small case of fishing tackle. In the 1970s, rod and reel makers controlled 80 percent of the domestic market. In 1986 they held less than 10 percent. The irony of it is that the basic technical ideas for this equipment originated in this country, but now foreign countries can make the products much more cheaply than our companies. The same thing has happened in other industries. The net result, of course, is loss of business and profits and jobs. No one knows precisely how many companies have gone bankrupt as a result nor how many jobs have been lost, but the numbers for both are shocking.

There are many explanations for this state of affairs. One has been the high-priced dollar relative to other currencies, which has permitted foreign producers to sell their products here at low prices. Even when the dollar has fallen, foreign producers have been willing to maintain their low prices and accept smaller profit margins in order to hold their share of the U.S. market. Eventually import prices must rise. In the meantime the deficit continues.

Other factors in the trade imbalance are low wage rates and high worker productivity in foreign countries. The quality of many foreign-made products also is high and often superior to comparable U.S.-made products. Some foreign manufacturers have been accused of selling their products here at prices lower than in their home countries, a practice called "dumping." (Japanese microchip manufacturers, for example, were found in March 1986 to be dumping in this country by the Department of Commerce after a prolonged study of the issue.) Foreign governments also have been accused of subsidizing certain industries, such as steel and agriculture, to permit producers to cut their export prices. At the same time, American companies have been complaining loudly that they face a variety of trade barriers when they seek to sell products abroad. We shall examine this question later in the chapter.

In 1948, ninety-two trading nations negotiated a multilateral agreement called General Agreement on Tariffs and Trade (GATT). It sought to encourage freer, fairer, and expanded international trade. Under GATT, world trade boomed. By the late 1970s, the world's average tariff on manufactured goods had fallen to around 3 percent. But then many countries, faced with unemployment, stagnant economies, inflation, and overcapacity in major industries, began to encourage more exports and restrict imports. Protectionist sentiment became a worldwide phenomenon.

Many American companies have exhibited serious shortcomings in selling their products abroad. Our productivity has been very low relative to historical standards, and our wage rates have been high. Our capital investment has not kept our manufacturers at the cutting edge of new technology. The result has been high costs and selling prices, exaggerated by the high dollar. Furthermore, many of our managers have not displayed the marketing skills in selling abroad that foreign producers have shown in the United States.

The net result of all of this is an unprecedented trade deficit, demands by our businesspeople for protection from foreign competitors, and pressure on the federal government to make a forceful effort to persuade foreign governments to remove their trade barriers on our products.

Proposed Legislation

Dozens of bills have been introduced in Congress in recent years to protect our industries. Most never pass Congress, and most of those that do are vetoed by the President. A recent example is his veto of a textile bill in August 1986 which would have required a 30 percent reduction in textile imports imposed against South Korea, Taiwan, and Hong Kong. The bill also included legislation to provide import relief for shoes and copper. It is noteworthy that the House of Representatives failed by only eight votes to override the president's veto, which indicates the strength of protectionist sentiment in the Congress. It has grown stronger since then.

As of summer 1987 the House of Representatives has sent to the United States Senate a 900-page omnibus Trade and International Policy Reform Act of 1987

> At the end of the 1960s, the trend toward a more open trade, especially among the Western nations, was reversed. . . . [Today] a very large proportion of international trade is under some kind of nontariff restraint and moves only with the permission of the governments concerned, not in spontaneous response to market demand or at market-determined prices. This is a result of policies pursued by all governments, including ours. . . . The trade restrictive and regulatory policies in force are so detailed and complex that their total effects on each nation are beyond the comprehension even of politicians, let alone of the public. The levels of this protection cannot be measured in any strict sense of the word, and even the very rough quantitative estimates that have been formed of them are not very meaningful.
>
> *Source:* Jan Tumlir, when Director of Economic Research and Analysis for the United Nations Secretariat of the General Agreement on Tariffs and Trade, in *Protectionism* (Washington, D.C.: American Enterprise Institute, 1985), p. 1.

(HR 3) which was passed by a 2 to 1 margin vote. It is generally conceded in the House that this is one of the toughest general trade bills passed by the House in recent decades. Untypically, the bill has relatively few provisions for protecting specific industries. Rather, it mandates that the President of the United States take action (which authority he can transfer to the United States Trade Representative [USTR]) when foreign countries are found to engage in activities condemned in the bill. For example, if the USTR finds after investigation that a country has engaged in unfair trade practices, or "unjustifiable" practices (such as violation of negotiated trade agreements), the President is required to impose tariffs or quotas in retaliation unless he determines that the action would not be in the national economic interest. The bill mandates negotiations with those countries having huge trade surpluses with the United States that are also found to engage in a pattern of unfair practices. If negotiations to eliminate those practices fail, the President is required to impose tariffs or quotas to reduce the country's trade surplus by 10 percent a year. The bill also provides a wide range of programs to encourage exports, to train workers, and to help workers adversely affected by imports, and imposes stiffer penalties for payment of bribes by U.S. firms to foreign governments and companies in search of business. The President has threatened to veto any bill having the kind of mandatory provisions found in the House and Senate versions. But protectionist sentiment is so strong in Congress that some compromise is possible.

Deviations from Free Trade Policy

Despite the asserted free-trade policy of the United States by recent administrations and the strong rhetoric of the Reagan administration, deviations from free trade policy have been many and significant.

Steel   The United States recorded a positive net export of steel in 1959. Since then, the balance has been negative, and the steel industry has persistently asked for protection. In the mid-1970s, congressional threats to pass protectionist legislation led the administration and foreign producers to negotiate voluntary quota restrictions. In 1978, the Carter administration initiated the "trigger price mechanism" to insure that steel imports priced below a certain level would be quickly investigated and potentially controlled. Since 1979, when imports were 15 percent of domestic consumption, steel industry mill shipments have dropped from 160 million tons to 130 million tons. Domestic steel companies have closed about 700 units since 1974. Seven steel companies have gone bankrupt, and the United Steelworkers Union has seen one-half its 1.4 million membership lose their jobs in the industry.

In 1982, the major steel producers pressured Congress for more controls. The U.S. International Trade Commission, an agency established to investigate trade restraints, ruled that subsidized steel from Europe had injured domestic industries and recommended imposing duties ranging from 18 to 40 percent. To prevent our imposition of such duties, European governments agreed to set voluntary quotas on steel that would limit their total exports to about 5 percent of our consumption. The Japanese also set voluntary quotas on their exports to us. In mid-1983, the Reagan administration took more direct action by raising tariffs up to 20 percent on some specialty steels. Protectionist pressures continued, and the administration sought to negotiate further foreign voluntary quotas. In 1984, quota agreements were negotiated to hold imports to 18.5 percent of domestic consumption. Steel imports at the time had reached a record high of 26.4 percent of the U.S. steel market. The controls have worked moderately well. During the first half of 1986, the annual rate of imports was 22.7 percent of domestic consumption.

Automobiles   In 1977, imported car sales were 18 percent of total U.S. domestic sales. Foreign imports have grown steadily since and are now around 30 percent of the market. From 1978 to 1981, U.S.-made automobile and truck sales fell almost 50 percent, to a low of 6.2 million in 1981. There was a significant decline in jobs in the automobile industry. Since then, the industry has revived, and both sales and jobs have grown, but not to the previous peaks.

Severe pressures were put on the government in the late 1970s to restrict imports. In the face of this threat, the Japanese in 1981 imposed "voluntary" limits on their exports of cars and light trucks by about 7 percent. Voluntary quotas have been extended each year since, and an agreement was reached to limit exports to the United States. At first the quota was 1.68 million vehicles a year, but now the total is 2.3 million a year. When the threat of Japanese imports was first recognized, the complaint was that the Japanese were "dumping" in the United States. As facts became known, it was clear that the Japanese had a distinct advantage over U.S. manufacturers with respect to productivity per man hour, labor costs per car, quality, and a very favorable yen to dollar exchange rate (Abernathy, Clark, and Kantrow, 1983). Indeed, these advantages permitted the Japanese to drop an auto on our shores at a profitable price that was from $1,200 to $1,800 under the cost of a comparable U.S. car!

Much of the demand in the automobile industry for protectionist legislation has eroded as a result of a 50 percent decline in the value of the yen relative to the dollar (from early 1985 to mid-1987), the improved productivity and quality of the U.S. automotive industry, and, particularly, because of joint ventures in automobile assembly between foreign companies, particularly the Japanese, and U.S. automobile companies.

Agriculture   This is a major area of deviation from free trade policy. For many years, the United States government has massively supported or subsidized the prices of agricultural products. It is estimated that in 1986 agriculture subsidies were $30 billion. For some crops, wheat and corn for example, the federal programs held our prices above world market prices, with a consequent drop in our exports. For other crops, the programs permitted our farmers to sell abroad below world markets, much to the annoyance of some of our allies. At the seven-nation economic summit held in Tokyo in May 1986, the heads of state discussed the sticky issue of European Community agricultural subsidies, which are large, but they came to no resolution. The reason: the United States, which sought a reduction of those subsidies in order to open the door for our agricultural produce, was revealed to be as much a violator of free-market principles as the European nations.

We talk glibly about free trade but practice substantial and widespread violations of the principle. In August 1986, for example, President Reagan subsidized the sale of 4 million tons of wheat to the Soviet Union. He acted under intense pressure from farm-state Republicans, who thought the move would help their candidates in the upcoming elections in November. The subsidy outraged not only free-trade ideologues but also our Canadian and Australian allies, who were selling their wheat to the Soviet Union. They called it unfair competition.

Other Protectionist Measures   Hundreds of other products enjoy government protection, including bicycles, sheet glass, watches, sugar, stainless steel flatware, velvet carpets, motorcycles, and machine tools. In addition there are "Buy American" laws that require government agencies to purchase products made in this country. The Federal Buy American Act of 1933 requires federal agencies to pay up to a 6 percent differential for domestically produced goods. Many states have Buy American laws. The Agricultural Adjustment Act of 1935 permits the President to regulate the imports of agricultural products if they materially interfere with government price support programs. Under the Meat Import Act of 1979, the President can impose quotas on imported beef if the level goes too high. There are selectively high tariffs on some commodities. Our tariff on fruit juices, for instance, is 27 percent. Also, like other nations, we have a wide range of miscellaneous barriers. For example, the Trans-Alaskan Pipeline Authorization Act of 1973 prohibits the export of oil from North Slope fields.

Export Curbs and Aids   Some government programs discourage U.S. exports. In addition to restrictions for national security and diplomatic goals (mentioned above), the following programs have been said by businesspeople to discourage exports: taxation of income earned abroad by U.S. citizens living abroad and working for American companies; the Foreign Corrupt Practices Act, which we will discuss shortly; uncertainty over availability of foreign tax credits; uncertainty about the application of antitrust laws to joint international ventures; antipollution controls that raise costs; and laws that prohibit foreign sales of products prohibited for sale in the United States, such as drugs not certified by the FDA.

But there are generous benefits available to some manufacturers in exporting their products. One of the best known is the Export Import Bank of the United States. This independent government agency helps finance U.S. exports of goods and services, either through direct loans to foreign buyers or through guarantees that assure repayment of loans made by U.S. exporters and private banks. The total in loans that the bank can have outstanding at any one time is $25 billion. There are other financial aids, such as the Overseas Private Investment Corporation, which insures MNCs against political risks in foreign countries, provides tax incentives to export, trade promotion programs, and information provided both by the federal government and U.S. embassies about trade opportunities and threats.

FOREIGN OBSTACLES TO U.S. EXPORTS

We have noted that foreign barriers to U.S. exports have inflamed protectionist demands here. In some countries, state-owned enterprises (SOEs), for example, are protected from foreign competition. The number and strength of SOEs operating in international markets constitute a growing threat to MNCs. In a wide range of industries, governments around the world hold dominant equity positions—telecommunications, electricity, gas, oil, coal, railways, airlines, automobiles, steel, shipbuilding, chemicals, and aluminum. SOEs such as Aerospatiale of France, Montedison (chemicals) of Italy, and VIAG (aluminum) in Germany are moving into the international arena (Monsen and Walters, 1983).

These companies enjoy some advantages over private enterprises. For example, there is less pressure to earn profits; there is little pressure to pay dividends; there is implicit backing by government; they may have preferential access to government finances; they enjoy a quasi-captive market at home; and they may enjoy preferential procurement policies.

But SOEs may be faced with disadvantages not felt by private enterprises. They may be faced with government policies that are restraining. For example, SOEs in Italy must invest heavily in new plants in backward southern Italy. They are subject to cumbersome bureaucratic and political interference. Political objectives may conflict with profit objectives. For example, politicians exert pressure to employ people at plants when the SOEs would otherwise avoid doing so in the name of efficiency.

Currently it seems that the threats of SOEs to MNCs is more potential than actual, except in special situations such as commercial aircraft, steel, and chemicals. Some of the advantages of SOEs are also available to some private MNCs, such as preferred financing. Mazzolini concludes that "they can thus be expected not to be better off than private enterprises in international markets" (1980: 27). Other scholars see a growing competitive threat (Phatak, 1983).

Quotas, or restrictions on the quantity of foreign imports, are a favorite barrier. Japan, for instance, has restrictions on a long list of agricultural products. Selective tariffs impede the flow of many products. France and the United Kingdom, for instance, have tariffs on communications hardware and most grains. "Buy Domestic" restrictions are widespread. Many other types of barriers exist, ranging from patents and copyrights to nationalistic customs.

Although every nation has a battery of restrictions on imports, Japan is a special target, partly because of its success in penetrating foreign markets but also because of its widespread barriers to the purchase of foreign-made goods. The literature is filled with anecdotes about how tulip bulbs are excluded on health grounds or how imported automobiles are minutely examined for the slightest scratch. These barriers exist because of long held customs and behavior patterns of the Japanese people. So exasperated was Willy de Clerg, the European Economic Communities Commissioner for External Relations, that he said: "The plain message is that unless Japan opens up its market to the rest of the world and breaks down the autarchic structures that inhibit fair international competition, there can be no stable multilateral trading relationship" (Farnsworth, 1986).

Foreign nations also set up trade barriers in retaliation to those in this country. A classic case occurred when the Reagan administration imposed a stiff tariff on Canadian cedar shakes and shingles in May 1986. Immediately, the Canadian government said that it would impose import duties on American books, magazines, and some computer components. The Canadian finance minister, Michael Wilson, was specific on the connection: "Our objective is to bring home to the United States the cost of protectionism" (Redburn, 1986).

MNC COMPETITIVENESS ABROAD

Two great changes have taken place in world trade during the past several decades. First, a quarter century ago, developing nations were mainly sources of raw materials and markets for finished goods made in industrialized countries. Technology flows were limited. International exchange rates were relatively stable. The United States clearly was the most powerful economic force in the world. Its industry was the most efficient in the world, and its product prices were unbeatable in world markets. Trade accounted for only about 8 percent of our gross national product. Only a small part of our economy was exposed to competition from foreign companies, and most of our companies were not concerned about selling abroad. Our domestic market was affluent and big enough to satisfy most corporations.

Today, the world is different. International trade now accounts for about 25 percent of our gross domestic product. The survival of some of our industries, as we have noted, is threatened by foreign competition. Foreign countries have taken our technology—robotics is a classic example—and used it to produce goods more efficiently and of higher quality than our own manufacturers. In industrializing, LDCs have developed excessive capacity for producing such products as steel, textiles, and foods. The United States, in sum, is much less able than only a few years ago to set the rules of international commerce, and our companies are feeling the sting of foreign competition.

MNCs alone cannot deal with the many issues associated with such significant shifts. They have an important part to play, however, in improving their competitiveness in foreign countries.

Some MNC's are very competitive in foreign countries. Coca-Cola, for example, is a powerful force in virtually every country in which it operates. Schick claims 70 percent of the safety-razor market in Japan, and IBM is a dominant force in that country. McDonald's fast food outlets are growing rapidly in Japan. Borg-Warner produces transmissions in Japan that are used in Japanese cars. Rockwell International makes components in Italy that are widely used in automobiles in Europe. So strong are the U.S.-based MNCs in Europe that France, for example, has considered them a serious competitive threat. The list of successful U.S.-based MNCs in foreign markets is long.

On the other hand, it is generally conceded that too many U.S.-based MNCs have not been as diligent in trying to penetrate foreign markets as they should have been. Today it is important that our managers learn foreign languages as well as customs. They must design products to meet local interests. They must adapt their distribution procedures to local customs and habits. They must cut costs and become more price competitive. In short, they must become much more serious marketing experts in each country in which they do business. This is the lesson that the successful marketers in foreign countries have taught (Copeland and Griggs, 1985).

FREE TRADE THEORY VERSUS REALITY

It is clear from what has been said that there is a gap between free trade theory and government practice. The reality is that the global economy is a mixture of free trade and protectionism. It always has been. In such a world, how far can the United States go in lowering its trade barriers? Clearly, it cannot be the only major free trade zone in the world. Thornton Bradshaw (1985), as chairman of RCA, said (with partial accuracy) that although there is no intellectual argument for protectionism, it must be remembered that "survival is the first law." He suggested that "some kind of temporary, conditional protection may head off the massive, unthinking protectionism that we are on the verge of, and give the United States time to come back." The pragmatic policy, which is what the United States is now pursuing, is to make the free trade and protectionism mix as equitable as possible.

So far as economic theory is concerned, the words of Paul W. McCracken (1985), a highly respected economist, are provocative: "Professors," he observed, "would quickly lose their zeal for open trade if universities found that their strained budgets would be relieved by dismissing high-priced domestic professors and importing cheaper (and better?) pedagogy."

FOREIGN PAYOFFS

Following the Watergate exposures, the Securities and Exchange Commission (SEC) began an investigation in 1974 to determine to what extent corporations had been illegally involved in making corporate contributions to former President Nixon's 1972 reelection campaign. The SEC investigations revealed illegal contributions but turned up, more importantly, deceptive accounting practices intended to cover up illegal foreign payments. Many of these payments were not illegal under United States law, but withholding material information from shareholders was. The SEC "invited" corporations to make voluntary disclosure of this activity. More than 400 corporations responded and disclosed that they had made almost $1 billion in questionable payments, mostly foreign. This disclosure immediately opened a Pandora's box of complex and troublesome questions concerning international investment of MNCs, United States foreign policy, applicable laws, and morality.

The Spectrum of Foreign Payoffs

At one end of the spectrum of payoffs are lubrication bribes involving relatively small amounts of money. They range from tips for services rendered to "requests" for money to stimulate someone to perform. In this category are payments to speed clearances of goods at ports of entry, certifications required, and so on. They are called "honest" graft, "tokens of appreciation," "contributions," and so on. They carry different names: *mordida* ("the bite"), *kumshaw* ("thank you"), *jeitinho* ("the fix"), and so on. They are accepted around the world as legitimate for services rendered. These payments are often sanctioned to offset low salaries in foreign countries.

At the other end of the spectrum is extortion. The chairman of Gulf Oil Corporation reported that South Korea's S. K. Kim, financial chairman of the Republican party, threatened the company's $300 million investment (mostly in refining and petrochemicals) if the company did not make a $10 million contribution to the party. Bob Dorsey, chairman of Gulf, eventually haggled the amount down to $3 million. This, of course, was blackmail.

In between the two extremes are payments made for all sorts of situations, such as to reduce inflated taxes, to get or retain business, to avoid threats and harassment, to obtain favors from officials that are denied to competitors, and to influence foreign governments' political actions.

Legislation Concerning Payoffs

As a result of payoff disclosures, Congress passed the Foreign Corrupt Practices Act of 1977. This act makes it a criminal offense to offer a bribe to a foreign government official and provides the highest monetary fines ever authorized for imposition on business firms. For unlawful acts, companies may be fined $1 million, and individuals may face fines of $10,000 and five years in jail. The law does not apply to facilitating or "grease" payments that are intended only to expedite normal business affairs. The law prohibits offering money or anything of value to any person (foreign or domestic) if it is known that any or all of the money or value offered will be used to influence a foreign official, politician, or political party. This means, of course, that a corporation and a company manager may run afoul of the law if it is known that commission payments are used to induce government officials to do something on behalf of the company.

Strong criticism has been leveled at the law. Opponents claim that the law is too restrictive; that it contains too many ambiguities for the person in business; and that the accounting requirements are too burdensome. Because an infraction of the law can bring heavy penalties, it is claimed that many business managers simply do not seek foreign markets. Furthermore, when companies refuse to make payments that are legal in the countries in which they do business, they lose to competitors of other nations who are not restrained by a law such as ours. On this point, a Harris poll of 1,200 large companies showed that one-fifth of the executives said that they lost business because of the act. Particularly hard hit were makers of heavy electrical equipment, electrical components, and consumer electronic products and components (*Business Week,* September 19, 1983). A special White House task force appointed by President Carter concluded that lost business because of the act amounted to $1 billion a year. The task force called for revision of the act and criticized the federal government for moralizing, for prying into transactions outside the U.S. jurisdiction, and for needlessly creating political problems (Heenan, 1983).

New legislation to amend the act, with the title Business Practices and Records Act, has been introduced in Congress. Among other things, the new legislation says that payments would be legal if they were "customary" and intended to expedite a foreign official's performance of his duty. No payments would be prohibited if they were legal in the country where made. Payments or gifts given as "tokens of esteem" or as a "courtesy" would be allowed. A corporation would be criminally liable only when it "corruptly directs or authorizes" a payment. Under current law, a company would be liable if it "had reason to know" that a payment was to be used for bribery. Records would have to be kept only for transactions that are "material"; records must now be kept "in reasonable detail." These provisions still leave ambiguities, but they are clearer and less restrictive than the present law.

Opponents say that these provisions "gut" the law. Proponents say, however, that they are much more realistic for the world in which we live than the provisions in the present law. President Reagan asked Congress to soften the law, but so far it has not done so.

Corporate Actions

Corporations have taken actions to comply with the law and prevent questionable payments. They have revitalized board of director audit committees, as noted in Chapter 20. Corporate policies concerning conflicts of interest and foreign payments have been reviewed, clarified, and tightened. Internal audits have been strengthened and charged with monitoring payments by employees. Some companies require that employees periodically assert in writing that they have complied with the policies of the company concerning payoffs. Companies are making certain that top managers no longer can close their eyes to what their subordinates are doing; the superiors are being made responsible for making decisions about questionable payments. Companies are making more thorough checks on their agents. Some companies place a ceiling on facilitating payments, which can be exceeded only with upper-management approval. Some companies export through foreign subsidiaries in western Europe, where the bribery laws are less stringent. Some companies strive to maintain a low profile in foreign markets. Some companies try to strengthen their market positions.

CASE STUDY

AMERICAN CORPORATIONS IN SOUTH AFRICA

South Africa is a land of great and often stunning contrasts; of fertile green valleys and harsh near-desert conditions; of rugged mountains and endless silver beaches along two oceans; of hot summers and cold winter conditions; of bustling twentieth-century cities and settlements of hovels; of great wealth and bitter poverty; of dynamic growth and artificial restrictions to growth; of freedom for some and denial of basic human rights for the majority.

—*Traveler's Guide to Central and Southern Africa* (Garb, 1981: 152)

The writer of this travelogue has omitted one other "stunning contrast"—the contrast between the goals of hundreds of American corporations, which want to conduct large-scale operations in the Republic of South Africa, and the goals of activist critics, who want them to withdraw from the country. For corporations, the return on investment in South African operations can be high (even though average returns have declined in recent years). For critics, however, the presence of American firms in that country adds legitimacy and support to an official government policy of racial discrimination known as apartheid (literally "living apart"). A series of discriminatory laws passed since 1913 by the white South African government prescribes an official policy of separate but equal development for the four officially recognized racial categories in the country's population of 29.5 million. The population includes:

■ 21 million black Africans: The blacks are composed of ten major ethnic groups, including Zulu, Xhosa, North and South Sotho, Tswana, Shangaan, Swazi, North and South Ndebele, and Venda. Non-Africans often believe that South African blacks are homogeneous, but some animosities exist among these native groups, and each is composed of many separate tribes. The most cohesive, the Venda, have twenty-seven distinct tribes. Cultural differences exist among the various black ethnic groups, and four main African languages are spoken.

■ *5 million whites:* One-third of the South African white population is an English-speaking people of British descent, and two-thirds are Afrikaners, or descendants of the Boer pioneers who settled the South African interior four centuries ago. The Boers were a mixture of Dutch, French Huguenots who left Europe to escape religious persecution, Germans, and English. Their language, called Afrikaans, developed during the colonization period and is a unique evolution of Dutch mixed with the tongues of other settlers. Afrikaans is the official language of South Africa. The white population, including a strong Jewish community, is of European origin whereas, of course, the black population is African.

■ *2.7 million coloureds: Coloured* is an official term denoting those of mixed race. Most coloureds trace their ancestry from the intermarriage of early male Dutch settlers in the Cape Province with women of the indigenous, brown-skinned San and Khoikhoi natives. A great shortage of white European women in the early settlement years led to frequent interracial marriage. Today, most of the coloureds still live in the Cape Town area.

■ 835,000 *Asians:* The Asian community consists mainly of Indians who are concentrated in the province of Natal. They were brought in to work on sugar plantations in the 1870s.

The History of South Africa

To understand South African society today, it is essential to know its colorful and humanly costly history. The original inhabitants of the area were tribes of hunters and gatherers. By 1652, when the Netherlands (Dutch) East India Company established the first permanent white settlement in Cape Town, some of these tribes had developed agricultural and cattle-raising cultures.

Early Dutch settlers established a fort at Cape Town in 1652 to provision ships passing around the Cape of Good Hope. Soon the Dutch began to trade with the native population, and a few hardy employees of the Netherlands East India Company were given free land by the company to farm and raise stock. These were the first Dutch farmer-settlers, known as Boers. It was at this time that the first policies of racial segregation were established. The white Dutch settlers gradually expanded from the small Cape Town settlement, displacing local Africans who were not allowed title to land or political rights in the new white community. Although native residents remained free, the Dutch colonists imported slaves from elsewhere in Africa and from Indonesia.

It is important to note that native African cultures in an "iron-age" stage of cultural development had been thrown in contact with European cultures in the early stages of industrial development. The Europeans possessed a military technology that was far superior to the primitive warfare styles of the Africans, and when resistance was encountered, the Dutch settlers massacred opponents with modern firearms. As the Boers expanded to settle new lands in the interior, they fought frequent battles with black natives. There were few casualties for the settlers and many for the Africans. To this day, white South Africans celebrate Covenant Day on December 16, in recognition of the Battle of Blood River in 1838, when 3,000 Zulu tribesmen attacked 500 Boer settlers. The Zulu ranks were decimated while the whites suffered not a single casualty, and the Boers, who were fervent Calvinists, took this as a sign that God favored the cause of white supremacy in South Africa. Today, Covenant Day is an annual reaffirmation of this belief.

With the defeat of the Dutch by the British in the Napoleonic Wars, South Africa suddenly came under British rule. Boer settlers were angered when the British imposed new taxes and freed their slaves. The Boers responded by trekking farther into the interior to establish two independent republics. Conflict between the rebellious Boers and the British culminated with the victory of the British in the bitter Anglo-Boer War of 1899 to 1902. But Boer opposition was so strong that following their battlefield victory, the British nonetheless conceded self-government to the territory known as South Africa and its stubborn white settlers. At first, the government was dominated by the English, but in elections in 1948, the Afrikaners' National Party achieved an electoral victory. Since 1948, the political interests of the Afrikaners (as the descendants of the Boers now call themselves) have been dominant.

Over the years of their struggles with native Africans and the British, the Afrikaners developed a cohesive ideology. They believed that their group, the descendants of the Boer farmers who fought to settle the land, was predestined by God to rule. They believed that whites were culturally superior to blacks, coloureds, and Asians. They believed that the races could not be expected to live in harmony because of vast social and cultural differences. And over the years they developed a fierce in-group loyalty, leading the white Afrikaner elite to adopt a tone of secretiveness and cultural arrogance (Crocker, 1980/1981).

In the 1950s, this Afrikaner ideology was translated into a series of apartheid laws that established the framework of a racially segregated society. Some laws set up a system of "petty apartheid" that resembled the old Jim Crow laws in the American South, wherein restaurants, hotels, train stations, post offices, rest rooms, and other public facilities were segregated. Interracial sexual acts and marriages were prohibited. Today much of the petty apartheid framework is gone, making overt discrimination less noticeable in the large cities frequented by foreign visitors.

Other laws, however, set up a continuing and repressive system of "grand apartheid." A complicated web of forty-three pass laws controlled the movements of blacks within the country. They were required to carry passbooks identifying them as black, were forbidden to live or remain overnight in white areas, and were required to register with employers if they took jobs away from tribal homelands. These homelands were established under a series of laws dating from 1951. The homelands occupy about 14 percent of South African territory, have black governments, and are declared to be officially independent nation-states, although their constitutions prohibit armed forces. Blacks were assigned citizenship in one of these homelands based on their tribal designation and were not citizens of South Africa. Blacks cannot vote in South African elections, but have self-rule within their homelands. Other laws bar blacks from holding certain managerial and professional positions. Finally, a series of enactments extends widespread power to the South African police to prohibit assembly, outlaw black opposition organizations, and detain suspected opponents of apartheid—all without standards of evidence as rigorous as in the United States.

South Africa Today

Under pressure from the outside world, the South African government has made modest reforms in this "grand apartheid" system during the 1980s. In 1984, a constitutional amendment gave the vote to coloured and Asian citizens, who could elect separate, advisory parliaments to represent their racial categories. Blacks, however, were given no vote and no parliament. Only whites, of course, vote for members of the dominating white parliament. In 1986, the white government abolished the hated pass laws. Blacks had permanent status as citizens and could move freely about the country. Despite the precedent-setting nature of these reforms, however, they failed to fundamentally alter apartheid and failed to placate critics. To opponents of the regime, the continuing framework of laws segregating the races is evidence of racism. This racism can no more be cured by reform than cancer be cured by a bandage.

White leaders, however, argue that they conquered and colonized the territory now comprising South Africa and have a legal right to rule. The apartheid system, they say, is the best solution for governing a nation of such diverse inhabitants. Democracy cannot work in a multiracial, fragmented society like South Africa; it works best in a homogeneous political culture, they say, and is not workable where unusually vast differences in language, religion, cultural heritage, education, and race exist. It is also argued that the system is less repressive than other African governments. Blacks in South Africa have a higher economic standard of living than blacks in other African countries. And blacks throughout the African continent have suffered under impoverished black leadership in newly independent black states. Some black African nations are not only poorly run but brutally repressive as well. Such situations arise where no pluralist tradition exists and ageless tribal rivalries reassert themselves within modern parliamentary frameworks. Soon opposition parties and tribes are viciously repressed by the dominant tribe.

At the extreme, this can lead to bloodshed. In nations such as Uganda and Burundi, African tribal groups coming into political power have engaged in large scale murder of traditional enemies, committing heinous crimes that dwarf the severe repression of black activists by South African police. In Burundi, for example, the ruling Watusi government massacred 200,000 Hutus in a three-month period in 1972 (Lamb, 1982). In South African history, the Zulu tribe has twice emerged as dominant, once to be defeated by the Boers and a second time to be defeated by the British. Today, the Zulus are the largest black ethnic group and number 6 million. They might again emerge as a dominant tribe under their strong leader, Chief Mangosuthu Gatsha Buthelezi. Whites are reluctant to permit black majority rule because they envision chaotic government at best or dictatorship and violent repression at worst. In a recent interview, President P. W. Botha was asked why the white government consistently ruled out reforms giving blacks the vote in democratic elections. He answered:

> Because the winner-takes-all principle makes no provision for the protection of minority groups and will lead, in my opinion, to what has happened elsewhere in Africa—a one-party state and eventually dictatorship and domination by one group over the others. . . .
>
> You know, there are two very important elements in our population. One is the Zulus. They form a strong minority amongst the black people, the strongest one. And the Afrikaner forms the strongest white minority. Both the Zulus and the Afrikaners have no other country to go to. So we are obliged to settle our affairs without dominating one another and must find a way to live together without destroying each other's heritage and ideals and way of life (Botha, 1986).

Defenders of the South African regime argue that it must be judged by African standards rather than American or European, because it is, after all, an African nation. By those standards, the repression of apartheid appears more moderate. Because whites share a cohesive political culture, their rule is said to provide a stable political framework for economic development that will raise the living standards of all races.

Indeed, South Africa is the most industrialized country on the African continent. Its economy is based on a variant of free-enterprise capitalism in which a few vital industrial functions such as iron and steel, oil, and defense production are organized by government agencies that work with private firms. The government provides many incentives for foreign investors. Blacks in South Africa may own businesses, join labor unions, and serve in the military. Although the South African economy suffered a severe recession in the mid-1980s, it nonetheless remains the powerhouse among all African nations. Trade between South Africa and black African nations exceeds $1 billion a year, and South Africa provides railroad rolling stock, wheat, corn, electricity, and gasoline in large quantities to its neighbors. The economic dependence of nearby black nations in southern Africa is nearly total. When South Africa imposed an economic embargo on the nation of Lesotho early in 1986, Lesotho's government toppled within one week.

The South African military is powerful enough to easily defeat the combined forces of all black African nations. It is particularly well equipped for mobile, armored warfare on land and has a strong air force. There is well-informed speculation that the country has nuclear weapons, but no official confirmation is forthcoming.

Involvement of American Corporations   South Africa welcomes Americans, and about 300 U.S. corporations have direct investments there. More than 5,000 others have trading arrangements, such as distributorships. Total direct foreign investment by U.S. companies is about 6 percent of the total capital invested in South Africa and about 18 percent of all foreign investment there (Brock, 1986). This is a far smaller commitment than that of British companies, other European companies, and Japanese companies. (In order to court Japanese business, incidentally, South Africans classify Japanese businessmen as "honorary whites" rather than as Asians and allow them to use white facilities and move freely in white areas without harassment.) U.S. firms employ 120,000 black African workers—about 2 percent of the black labor force.

In 1950, direct foreign investment by U.S. firms was $140 million. Today it stands at $1.3 billion, down from a high of $2.63 billion in 1982, according to U.S. Commerce Department estimates. This figure does not include bank loans (which total over $3 billion in 1987), American shareholdings in South African stock, or the indirect ownership of South African companies through wholly owned subsidiaries of U.S. firms on foreign soil. Total U.S. economic involvement, then, is far greater than the $1.3 billion figure. In 1983, the U.S. consulate in Johannesburg suggested a figure of $14.6 billion for total U.S. business involvement.

The Sullivan Principles   In 1977, the Reverend Leon Sullivan, a black director of General Motors, drew up six principles of policy for American corporations in South Africa. These principles, called the Sullivan Principles, became widely used guidelines for social responsibility. They were:

1. Nonsegregation of the races in all eating, comfort, and work facilities.
2. Equal and fair employment policies for all workers.
3. Equal pay for equal work.
4. Initiation of training programs to bring blacks into supervisory, administrative, clerical, and technical employment.
5. Recruitment and training of minorities for management and supervisory positions.
6. Improving the quality of life for minorities outside the work environment in areas such as housing, health, transportation, schooling, and recreation.

Over the next decade these principles were articulated and expanded to promote more detailed social programs, and they had two significant effects. First, it became an article of faith among investors that if a company was complying with the Sullivan Principles it was socially responsible and progressive; thus they rationalized continued investment. Second, they spurred many positive actions by American firms.

By 1987, approximately 130 American companies were signatories. But in 1985 Rev. Sullivan had announced that unless the South African government abolished statutory apartheid by May 31, 1987, he would drop the Principles and advocate complete divestment by U.S. companies. When that date passed with apartheid laws intact, Rev. Sullivan kept his word and called for corporations to leave South Africa by early 1988. Without Rev. Sullivan's support for the Principles it was unclear whether they could remain as a powerful force rationalizing continued corporate investment, although a number of firms indicated they would continue to comply with them.

Protest Over U.S. Investment   In the United States, as in other countries, a strong protest movement is pressuring corporations to leave South Africa. One early success of this movement came as long ago as 1971, when Polaroid ceased distributing its products in South Africa due to pressure from black employees who objected to the sale of Polaroid film for use in photographs on government-required black identification. Since the early 1970s, the disinvestment movement has gained strength.

Critics object to the role that American corporations play in supporting the South African government and economy. But many American firms have publicly stated their opposition to apartheid policies and act as liberalizing influences in their employment practices with black African workers. In 1985, President P. W. Botha and his cabinet met with the heads of 200 leading corporations in South Africa, who firmly stated their demand that blacks receive full political and social rights through repeal of apartheid laws. The U.S. companies that are signatories of the Sullivan Principles subsequently increased their lobbying activities to press for reform, and many have made the case publicly. In August 1985, Mobil published newspaper ads in South Africa headlined, "There Is a Better Way," which called for a "new non-racial democracy" and a "South Africa without apartheid." A network of U.S. companies has set up legal aid centers in black townships to advise South Africans of their rights, and in 1986 General Motors created a stir by offering to pay the legal fees of any employee arrested for trespass on a whites-only beach near its Port Elizabeth plant.

The reformist push from the business community fails to sway critics. Although U.S. corporations are a liberalizing influence and generally follow enlightened employment practices, their presence buttresses what was once called "perhaps the most vicious regime on the face of the earth" (Lytle, 1982: 2). For example, Mobil, Exxon, and Caltex together process about half of South Africa's oil supply, and Fluor Corporation has built three coal-to-oil conversion plants for the government that give the nation considerable energy independence from the rest of the world. Babcock and Wilcox, Combustion Engineering, and General Electric have built nuclear reactors. IBM, Burroughs, Control Data, and Sperry provide most of the computers used in South Africa, and IBM 370 computers, for example, were once used by the Interior Department in Pretoria to maintain the population registry in which whites, coloured, and Asians are classified. A British firm, ICL, computerized the black registry system after IBM lost in competitive bidding (Conrad, 1982). To critics, the role of these and other U.S. corporations in support of the racially segregated South African government and society is major.

Generally, American corporations have resisted disinvestment pressure. They argue that leaving would be costly to the company, that American management is more responsive to black social needs than South African management, that American business helps the economy grow for the benefit of all races, and that retreat from South Africa would subordinate corporate policy to the foreign policy goals of activists, church groups, and minority shareholders who sponsor get-out-of-South-Africa stockholder proposals. A few companies righteously defend their involvement. When some universities divested shares of stock in Marathon Oil, for example, the company stopped contributing to research and scholarship activities at those schools (Kneale, 1986). But most have lobbied against disinvestment quietly and behind the scenes.

Both U.S. companies and activist groups want to see apartheid ended. But there is an enormous gulf in the way each perceives the rule of U.S. business activity. In a commencement address at Hunter College in 1986, Archbishop Desmond M. Tutu, a black South African, addressed the U.S. corporation's defense of its presence in these uncompromising terms:

I would be more impressed with those who made no bones about the reason they remain in South Africa and said honestly, "We are concerned for our profits," instead of the baloney that the businesses are there for our benefit. We don't want you there. Please do us a favor: Get out and come back when we have a democratic and just South Africa. . . .

It is true that many foreign corporations in South Africa have introduced improvements for their black staff. . . . American companies, especially, have begun to speak out more forthrightly against apartheid than has been their wont, and they would be the first to admit that they got a considerable jog to their consciences from the disinvestment campaign.

There has been progress, but we do not want apartheid ameliorated or improved. We do not want apartheid made comfortable. We want it dismantled (Tutu, 1986: 2).

A Changing Environment Discourages South African Investment   Recent events have caused many firms to rethink their involvement in South Africa. The "hassle factor" of doing business there has increased. By 1987, nineteen states, sixty-eight cities, eleven countries, and 118 universities had adopted policies against investment in or support of companies doing business in South Africa. Pension funds divested shares of stock, universities rethought investment of their endowments, and cities refused to contract with companies involved in the country.

The public policy climate of U.S. investment there had also changed at the federal level. Throughout most of the Reagan administration, the President adhered to the long-time U.S. policy of "constructive engagement" with the South African government, and the State Department encouraged U.S. firms to invest there. South Africa was seen as an important strategic ally because (1) it is the major source of a number of strategic minerals, (2) its location on the southern tip of the African continent gives it control of the oil sea lane from the Persian Gulf through which the bulk of the Western world's oil supply passes, and (3) it is a bulwark against the expansion of communist influence in southern Africa. Under the "constructive engagement" policy, the U.S. advocated dismantling apartheid but encouraged business investment as a means of building leverage to pressure a recalcitrant South African government for reform. However, the policy came under withering fire from domestic critics of the Botha regime, who culminated years of grass-roots activity with the 1986 passage in Congress of economic sanctions against South Africa. This legislation, which was passed over the veto of President Reagan by a bipartisan, election-year bandwagon of supporters, banned roughly 18 percent of South African imports and blocked its aircraft from landing in the United States. It also changed the investment climate for U.S. corporations by prohibiting new investment in South Africa (over and above reinvestment of profits) and ending U.S. tax credits for taxes paid in South Africa. These provisions, together with the ongoing recession in South Africa, made direct investment there less attractive. Furthermore, given all the talk of disinvestment, foreign competitors were arguing that American suppliers in South Africa could not be relied upon in the long term.

Harassment and protest by activist groups continued. Shell Oil in 1986 faced a worldwide boycott of its products plus picketing of gas stations in major cities across the United States, demonstrations at corporate offices, burning of Shell credit cards at rallies, and the fire bombing of two gas stations in the Netherlands (Walker, 1986). Coca-Cola elected to leave South Africa late in 1986, when the Southern Christian Leadership Conference threatened a black consumer boycott if the company did not leave by Martin Luther King's birthday, January 15, 1987.

In addition, there existed personal, psychological pain for business executives who became discouraged about their ability to promote change. Some white South Africans began to shun foreigners for their attacks on apartheid. U.S. critics were harsh. And on top of everything else, domestic violence in South Africa increased to such a level that 1,500 people were killed in 1986.

Faced with these miseries, U. S. firms began to leave. Between 1984 and 1986, seventy-five left, including General Electric, Ford, General Motors, IBM, and Eastman Kodak. Their departure did not, of course, mean that the businesses they ran ended. In most cases they sold to European, Japanese, or South African investors who negotiated licensing or marketing arrangements and continued to sell the same products. Thus, although Coca-Cola no longer has a direct investment in the country, bottling plants it once operated still churn out Coca-Cola beverages. In an angry editorial, the *Wall Street Journal* dressed down critics of the corporate role, saying that, "In forcing American companies to withdraw . . . American militants are destroying yet one more moderating force in South Africa" (October 22, 1986).

What Will the Future Bring in South Africa?

In South Africa today, blacks lack important political freedoms. Income is not evenly distributed. Many blacks live in shantytowns, while whites enjoy one of the world's highest living standards. Nevertheless, black incomes exceed those of workers in other African nations, and the South African economy employs over 1 million migrant workers who tolerate white repression for the high wages they can earn. Despite these economic benedictions a worldwide anti-apartheid movement has declared lack of black civil rights an overwhelming flaw in the system and has called for its overthrow. There is significant black domestic opposition to the white government, and the outlawed African National Congress (which now incorporates leaders of the secretive South African Communist Party) has risen in sporadic violence against Pretoria (Karis, 1986/1987).

Much has been written about the potential impact of blanket trade sanctions imposed by the U.S. government and total disinvestment by U.S. firms. These steps are advocated by many activists and government critics. Both would do some injury to the South African economy, but there is no agreement that either would do major damage or bring on revolution. The South Africans are skilled in a variety of embargo-avoidance tactics and already are shipping restricted products into the United States through Zimbabwe, Israel, and India. Disinvestment by American firms means trading U.S. control of assets for control by managers from another nation.

In either case, hardships would be imposed on both blacks and whites, but if the economy stopped growing, fewer blacks would be employed. And it is questionable whether the tenacious Afrikaner elite would react to greater international pressure by liberalizing racial policy. Knowledgeable observers think that Afrikaners would tighten their grip and defy world opinion.

Currently the trend in South Africa is toward voluntary reform of the political system, but powerful conservative forces in the white government are bent on preserving white dominance. No one knows quite what will happen; and so American corporations do not know how to prepare for the future. As one knowledgeable observer, Professor S. Prakash Sethi of Baruch College, writes:

> South Africa as a nation, and as a society, is a simmering and smoking volcano— never quite dormant, but particularly active now. It will erupt. There doesn't seem to be much doubt about it. The problem lies in our inability to predict the magnitude and direction of this eruption. The hope, if there is any, rests in our ability to contain the damage and prepare for the rebuilding effort that must ensue (Sethi, 1986: 4).

Questions

1. What is your assessment of the positive and negative aspects of corporate involvement in South Africa?
2. Should American corporations withdraw from South Africa?
3. Is disinvestment or trade boycott an effective pressure for change of racial laws in South Africa? Draw up a scenario of the changes following withdrawal of American firms.
4. Is it unethical to make profits in a foreign country like South Africa, where public policy is contrary to American ethics and not democratically determined?
5. Should managers of American firms advocate government changes in foreign countries where they do business?

CASE STUDY

FLEXON CONSTRUCTION COMPANY

Virginia Hazard, president of giant Flexon Construction Company, was preparing to make some policy decisions about questionable payments in foreign countries. Federal statutes make it imperative that large firms such as Flexon develop policies for foreign operations about bribes and other payments that might be regarded as corrupt under the law. The Foreign Corrupt Practices Act of 1977 threatens managers with a maximum personal fine of $10,000 and up to five years in jail for making illegal payments overseas in violation of its provisions. An offending corporation, such as Flexon, could be fined up to $1 million.

Flexon was a worldwide construction firm engaged in the building of highways, oil refineries, airports, dams, transit systems, nuclear reactors, model cities, and anything else that construction technology could give birth to. Its revenues were over $5 billion in 1987, and it was undertaking seventy-five different projects in twenty-five countries on every continent. Headquarters were in New York.

The company had always adhered to high ethical standards in United States operations, but since its founding in the 1920s, its leadership had been pragmatic about bending to local custom overseas. Although Flexon employees had not actively sought out foreigners with offers of bribes and gratuities, neither had they shrunk from the facts of life of overseas business when approached by foreigners on the take. Company executives had maintained the position that Flexon was a guest in foreign countries and should accommodate local habits. In addition, there was widespread agreement among management that if Flexon did not pay, other American or foreign companies would do so and business would be irretrivably lost.

During the 1970s, Senate hearings on "payoffs" and blaring media coverage required keeping such publicly unacceptable views in low profile at Flexon. The company had been informally probed by the Internal Revenue Service and the SEC and had even weathered a suit brought by public interest group representatives owning a few shares of Flexon stock. Passage of the Foreign Corrupt Practices Act of 1977, designed to curtail questionable payments by American firms overseas, had brought minor changes in Flexon policy, but Flexon's management had resisted a rethinking of past practice. Now, Virginia Hazard had been installed as president, bringing new managerial philosophies and a new management team in with her. She intended to rethink systematically Flexon's ethical stance in this area.

Still, purity was easier to contemplate than achieve. She disliked the idea of payoffs. They were unsavory, costly, potentially embarrassing, and they often involved kickbacks to Flexon employees. A payoff set the stage for blackmail and was often the first in a long string of payments. Still, the fact was that local custom often demanded these payments, and big contracts sometimes hinged on payoffs as much as performance criteria. The range of problems was wide. She thought of five current examples.

First, a construction project in a small, Central American "banana republic" had been slow to progress because dockworkers and their leaders in a nearby port demanded small payments to handle crates of machinery and building supplies transported in by Flexon. Without these payments, crates were "lost," "accidentally" dropped, or simply left on the pier, exposed to the sun and rain for prolonged periods. The payments demanded amounted to less than $1,000 a month, and nobody ever was given more than $50 at one time. This was a paltry sum compared to the cost of "losing" even a few crates. The manager in charge of the operation had asked for permission to develop a schedule of payments and keep the project moving with a little regularly applied "grease." Although such payments were not, strictly speaking, legal in the country, the practice was endemic, and authorities looked the other way.

Second, a hotel construction project on a small island in the Caribbean had run afoul of the widespread local practice of buying favors by giving favors in kind. The project manager had not bribed anyone with cash but had requested permission to provide free rooms at expensive resort hotels to local officials, to put on lavish banquets for local bureaucrats and their families, to provide an apartment in the apartment complex that housed Flexon workers and their families for a mistress of the local Minister of Interior (who controlled levers of power that could facilitate construction), and to do other favors, such as loaning company vehicles to island officials for hunting trips. In return, Flexon would certainly be given priority consideration for building permits, and the local labor unions would be quiescent.

Third, a project director in a Latin American country was being denied an exit visa to attend a meeting at New York headquarters unless he paid a gratuity to an official in the local customs office. He requested permission to pay the small amount from his personal funds, rather than use company money and jeopardize Flexon's legal standing.

Fourth, Flexon was negotiating for a $20 million contract to install electronic navigation and guidance systems at three airports in a Middle Eastern country and seemed about to close the deal. Flexon's chief negotiator, however, recently had wired that he had been approached by an official in the government's transportation ministry and informed that a 5 percent "administrative fee" payable to him would be required when the deal finally closed. This was not illegal in the country, and European competitors in the bidding were likely to pay without thinking twice. The chief negotiator had requested instructions.

Finally, and perhaps worst, a member of the president's cabinet in an Asian country had approached Hazard personally on a recent trip there. In no uncertain terms, the cabinent minister had demanded a payment of $10 million to the president's forthcoming political campaign and implied in a threatening way that, unless the payment were made, two oil refineries owned and operated by Flexon in that country would be expropriated by the government. The two refineries were worth far more than the $10 million contribution; indeed, they brought in about ten times that amount in yearly revenues.

Because the laws of the country proclaim that extortion is illegal, Hazard knew that such a request was contrary to the law. But the law would never be enforced because the president held near-dictatorial powers over a weak judiciary in the country. In addition, she knew that in a country the size of this one, $10 million was probably enough to ensure the reelection of the tyrant to another five-year term. Even without it, though, she thought he probably would be able to get a safe majority in a rigged election.

All these problems reflect common dilemmas for executives in the international construction trade, and they had cropped up many times before. The circumstances change, but the problems remain the same.

Questions

1. In your opinion, is it necessary for companies operating overseas to make questionable payments in order to have profitable operations? What are your reasons?
2. Familiarize yourself with the Foreign Corrupt Practices Act of 1977. What decisions should Virginia Hazard make on each of the five requests being made of her if she wishes to follow the law?
3. Draft a "Questionable Payments Policy Statement" that could be issued by Flexon's top management to provide a guide for ethical behavior to Flexon employees around the world. Be sure to consider such factors as public opinion, competitive forces, federal law, host country laws and customs, and your own personal morals.

CHAPTER 20

REFORMING CORPORATE GOVERNANCE

In October 1986 BankAmerica directors exercised one of their most important functions. They changed the top management of the bank, after years of anxiety over the bank's performance. The new management not only must resolve the old problems but deal with the new ones that grow out of an unsolicited takeover bid and the changing of the bank's top command. BankAmerica shows some of the serious governance problems of the large corporations today.

The BankAmerica Corp. is the second largest bank in the United States, with assets in 1985 over $118 billion. It had 83,300 employees, 150,000 shareholders, 1,000 California and Washington branches, and 120 foreign offices. Its deposits were $94 billion, and its loans were $83 billion.

A dominant problem of BankAmerica has been and will continue to be huge loan losses (see Exhibit 20-1). As of October 1986, problem loans (restructured loans and loans past due 90 days or more) were a mind-boggling $4.5 billion. This and other problems resulted in a stunning unexpected loss of $640 million in the quarter ending June 30, 1986, the second largest quarterly loss in U.S. banking history. For the year ending in June 1986, total losses amounted to about $1 billion. Unfortunately for BankAmerica, disaster struck in every major area in which it had loans—foreign (particularly in the Third World), commercial real estate, energy industries, shipping, and agriculture. It also was embarrassed by a scandal involving real estate securities that cost the bank $95 million.

But there were other problems. The bank was slow to recognize the consequences of banking deregulation and had to play catch-up in its customer services. In 1981, for example, the bank had only 78 teller machines in California. Today it has 1,000, more than any other bank in the country. Many

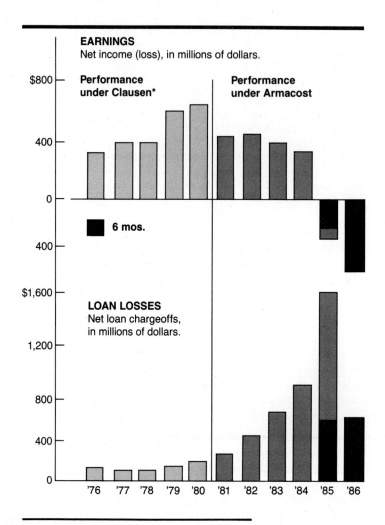

*Last five years of his tenure, which began in 1970.
Source: Bennett, 1986. Copyright © 1986 by The New York Times Company. Reprinted by permission.

EXHIBIT 20–1   MEASURING BANKAMERICA'S PLIGHT

critics believed the bank was overstaffed. Finally, the bank had outmoded computer and accounting systems.

A. W. (Tom) Clausen was the president and chief executive of BankAmerica from 1970 to 1981, at which time Samuel H. Armacost succeeded him in these positions. Armacost set about with great optimism to resolve the bank's problems. He closed many branches, discharged employees, introduced new computer and accounting systems, sold bank assets (including the bank's central headquarters building in San Francisco), modernized customer services, and brought fresh talent to management's ranks. Nonetheless the bank's problems seemed to resist solution. Profits dropped sharply (see Exhibit 20–1). The traditional stock dividend was eliminated, key board of director and management executives left the bank, and the stock price plummeted from about $30 in 1981 to a low of $9.50 in October 1986. Unfounded rumors circulated that the bank was seeking help from the federal government, and that upset the investment community. To compound its governance problems, there were rumors that unfriendly takeover bids were in the offing.

Under pressure from the board of directors, Armacost resigned on October 11, 1986. His resignation may have hurt his pride more than his pocketbook. His "golden parachute" made him eligible to receive about $1.7 million in pay, three times his salary, plus an unknown amount of stock options and a pension when he reaches 65 years of age (he was 47 at the time).

Clausen was promptly named chairman and CEO of BankAmerica and its major holding, the Bank of America. He rejoined the bank after five years as head of the World Bank. Clausen assumed his new leadership of BankAmerica loaded with governance problems. The loan portfolio was still in deep trouble, and much remained to be done to modernize the bank. He had to replace lost key executives and placate not only hostile executives hired by Armacost but some who had worked under him and blamed him for many of the bank's problems. They noted that during the last five years of Clausen's leadership of BankAmerica, profits rose exceptionally well (as shown in Exhibit 20–1) but that at the same time, loans had increased rapidly and defaults on many of them were at the root of BankAmerica's problems. Clausen also had to restore damaged employee morale and reassure a jittery investment community. And he faced a serious uninvited takeover bid from First Interstate Bank of about $2.8 billion, or from $15 to $18 a share, depending upon the analyst making the evaluation. After the BankAmerica board of directors rejected the offer, First Interstate raised its bid in the fall of 1986 to $21 a share (no cash, all securities), with a total cost of $3.5 billion.

Clausen's strategy became apparent: to sell everything not essential to the core banking business, to cut expenses drastically, and to erect roadblocks to stop the First Interstate takeover. In less than two months, by the beginning of 1987, sales of various businesses totaled about $1 billion. In February 1987, eighteen months after its initial offer, First Interstate halted its effort to buy BankAmerica. Joseph J. Pinola, chairman of First Interstate, lamented that BankAmerica had so weakened itself by such sales that it was no longer worth the $3.5 billion offered. Clausen sighed, "We will now be able to focus all our attention on the job of turning BankAmerica around in 1987" (Broder, 1987).

BankAmerica is not alone. Throughout this century there have been periodic demands for reforming corporate governance structure and processes. This is still a highly controversial and important subject. Consider the following.

Harold S. Geneen, longtime chairman of the board and CEO of ITT, said recently, "Among the boards of directors of *Fortune* 500 companies, I estimate that 95 percent are not fully doing what they are legally, morally, and ethically, supposed to do. And they couldn't even if they wanted to." He said that the major responsibility of the board is "to sit in judgment on the management, especially on the performance of the chief executive, and to reward, punish, or replace the management as the board sees fit" (Geneen, 1984: 28). The tendency of CEOs to dominate directors was referred to colorfully as the "mushroom concept" by John T. Connor, when he was chairman of Allied Chemical. "Put him in a dark place," said Connor of a director, "feed him plenty of horse manure, and when his head rises up through the pile to get attention or ask a question, cut it off quickly and decisively" (Connor, 1973: 4).

Philip Hawley, president and CEO of Carter Hawley Hale Stores, sees his board and many like it in a different light:

> There's no question that the board today is concerned with wider issues than ever before. The board wants to know and be satisfied with the long-range direction of the company. It wants to review carefully the company's strategic plans, to be satisfied with their quality, and to approve them. It is concerned with management succession plans. It is interested in the quality of thinking that goes into the making of major decisions of the company. (There is much testing on that front.)
>
> The board wants to be satisfied that there is a management process that is orderly and works. It is very concerned about the quality of the disclosure of information, its adequacy and reliability. It gives careful attention to determining the compensation of the top executives and to the selection of new board members. The public policy committee of the board, which is a new committee, is very active in examining our approach to, opinions on, and awareness of a wide range of issues, such as contributions, employee environment, affirmative action. None of these things were part of our board process ten years ago (in G. Steiner, 1983: 69).

This chapter begins with a definition of governance (and contrasts it with management). We then discuss the core issues in corporate governance, including a brief analysis of its current legal framework and how the process operates in fact. Then major proposals for reform are examined in two areas: federal chartering, and reforming the structure and functioning of the board of directors. The chapter concludes with a few observations about the reform process.

GOVERNANCE DEFINED

> Corporate governance ensures that long-term strategic objectives and plans are established and that the proper management structure (organization, systems, and people) is in place to achieve those objectives, while at the same time making sure that the structure functions to maintain the corporation's integrity, reputation, and responsibility to its various constituencies (National Association of Corporate Directors, 1981).

This complex definition deserves respect because it was formulated by the Advisory Board of the National Association of Corporate Directors. Another definition is that of Robert K. Mueller, chairman of the board, Arthur D. Little:

Governance is concerned with the intrinsic nature, purpose, integrity, and identity of the institution, with a primary focus on the entity's relevance, continuity, and fiduciary aspects. Governance involves monitoring and overseeing strategic direction, socioeconomic and cultural context, resources, externalities, and constituencies of the institution (Mueller, 1981: 9).

In these definitions, governance is the concern of the board of directors of a company. However, top management is also clearly involved. But management has other dimensions that are quite distinct from the operations of the typical board of directors. Management is a hands-on operational activity. It is concerned with supervising day-to-day action and with the prudent use of scarce resources to achieve desirable aims. The typical board of directors of a corporation does not become involved in such activities.

THE CORE ISSUES IN REFORMING CORPORATE GOVERNANCE

The fundamental source of demands for reforming corporate governance is dissatisfaction with the power relationships among the boards of directors, managers, stockholders, state governments as chartering authorities, and constituents of corporations. This in turn has led to sharp criticism of the ways in which corporations are governed.

The central function of the corporate governance system is to provide legitimacy for the exercise of corporate power to men and women in positions of authority in corporations. In the minds of many observers the system fails to provide this legitimacy. Top management of corporations has a legal fiduciary responsibility to shareholders but also a responsibility to address the interests of society. The governance system, complain critics, is today not accountable to either shareholders or society. It therefore loses legitimacy.

If the responsibility of corporate managers is not clarified to the satisfaction of corporate managers and the public, it is quite likely that there will be government regulation of corporate governance. As Courtney Brown, a former business school dean and member of a number of corporate boards, said, the prudent corporation will prepare itself now to convince the public that its internal structures and procedures are designed to assure consideration of a wide spectrum of "publics" in its decision making (Brown, 1976: 9). These other "publics" include the long list of stakeholders identified in Exhibit 1–6.

The critics of corporate governance assert that these interests are not being met adequately. Furthermore, they argue, the way in which corporations are governed today permits abuses that call for government control. For example, they assert that: the large corporations have harmful market and nonmarket impacts, the government of large companies more resembles an autocracy than democracy, boards do not do the job they are supposed to do in running companies, there is much too much secrecy in decision making, the system permits payoffs and crimes, companies violate the rights of employees, officers are not accountable for their individual actions, and corporations have too much power. Not everyone would accept all these criticisms, but they are the basis, among other legitimate criticisms, for reforming the governance structure and processes of our corporations.

Most observers—even friendly ones—worry that corporate boards are dominated too much by management. Management, especially when the board chairperson is also CEO and a number of inside directors (other company officers) sit on the board, largely determines company policies and procedures. This is because management may fix the board meeting agendas and has more information about operations of the company. In such situations, of course, boards simply are not performing their functions. They are rubber stamps of management at best and invite charges of criminal negligence at worst. The classic illustration is Penn Central Corporation, where the directors did not know their company was on the verge of bankruptcy until after the situation was made public.

Changes in the structure and operation of boards of directors during the last decade have been in response to such criticism and have muted them somewhat. But criticisms persist and many of them are somewhat justified. More should be done to improve the performance of boards of directors. Many basic issues will be the subject of controversy for years to come. To whom are boards responsible? Who should serve on boards? How should directors be elected? How much should they be paid? What role should boards assume in overseeing and monitoring the affairs of the corporation?

THE CORPORATE CHARTER

Today, all American corporations except a few quasi-public enterprises chartered by the federal government (for example, the Tennessee Valley Authority) are given charters of authority by the state in which they are incorporated. At the Constitutional Convention of 1787, the Founding Fathers debated a federal chartering power but decided that existing state controls were adequate to regulate corporate activity.

In the early history of the United States, state assemblies and legislative bodies issued special charters to corporations one at a time on an ad hoc basis. Corporations were supposed to do something of general value, such as build a turnpike or operate a grain mill. For this value to society, the people contributing capital were given power to purchase and hold property collectively, to sue and be sued collectively, to enjoy limited liability, and corporations were often, but not always, given the right of perpetual life. The corporations were not generally liked in the American colonies, and every effort was made to restrain them.

Between 1790 and 1800, the first sixteen states granted about 300 charters. One-half were for transportation companies, and most of the remainder were for finance enterprises. In 1790, exactly three charters were given to manufacturing companies, and the total for this category rose to nine in 1800 (J. Davis, 1961; Johnson and Krooss, 1953).

The demands for the corporate form, however, were strong, and the states were disposed to grant more and more charters. This led to general incorporation laws. If corporations met the law, they could get charters routinely rather than go through the legislative process. In 1799, Massachusetts passed a general incorporation law for companies engaged in building aqueducts. In 1811, New York passed the first general incorporation law for manufacturing companies, and in 1837, Connecticut passed the first general incorporation law for any lawful purpose.

Over the years, the states have become progressively more permissive in corporation law to attract the tax revenues of large companies. Delaware has been the long-time victor in this competition and has chartered almost half of the largest industrial corporations in this country. Corporate charters establish the powers of the corporation to engage in business. The Delaware law today is so broad that it virtually permits a corporation to engage in any business that is legal.

Corporate charters also specify the rights and responsibilities of stockholders, directors, and officers. Fundamentally, corporate charters lodge control over the property of the enterprise in stockholders who own shares in the assets of the company and vote those shares in naming a board of directors to run the firm. The directors have a fiduciary responsibility to protect the interests of the shareholders. They are responsible for appointing officers to run the day-to-day affairs of the company. The legal line of power runs from the state, to shareholders, to directors, to managers.

The charters also include detailed provisions about such matters as annual meetings, methods of choosing directors, and authority of directors to issue stock. For instance, charters are specific about calling meetings of shareholders, declaration of dividends, election and removal of officers, proposing amendments of the articles of incorporation, and so on. Such charter provisions are meant to protect the interests of shareholders. A vast body of law that seeks to do the same thing has also been created over time.

THE STRUCTURE AND DUTIES OF BOARDS OF DIRECTORS

Structure

The average corporate board had fourteen members in 1985 (Korn/Ferry, 1986). But the actual number of members ranges from three to thirty or more. Boards of many not-for-profit organizations are generally much larger than those of profit enterprises. Giovanni Agnelli, founder of Italy's huge Turin-based Fiat conglomerate, once observed: "Only an odd number of directors can run a company, and three is too many" (Betts, 1980: 18). That is an extreme position, but some large firms do have small boards. Banks and other financial institutions tend to have larger boards than industrials.

Board membership may include both inside (management) directors and outside (nonmanagement) directors. In recent years, the number of outside directors on boards has grown because of pressures to put members on the board who are independent of the CEO. Eighty percent of the 592 large companies surveyed in the Korn/Ferry research stated a preference for a majority of outside directors. The average company had four inside and ten outside directors.

Korn/Ferry (1986) reports that the number of boards with women members rose from 11 percent in 1973 to 45 percent in 1985. During the same period, boards with ethnic-minority representation grew from 9 percent to 25 percent. The percentage of former government officials and academicians now on boards is higher than it was a decade ago. Decreasing significantly in representation on boards are attorneys, commercial bankers, investment bankers, major shareholders who are not officers of the company, and retired officers. In 80 percent of the companies in the study, the chairman of the board is also the CEO.

Typically, board members are suggested by the CEO to the board for its approval. This was so in 81 percent of the companies in the Korn/Ferry study. The nominees are then presented to the shareholders in the annual call to the stockholder meeting, and management solicits the proxies of the stockholders. A proxy is a permission given by each stockholder to the management to vote the stock as the management sees fit. Most stockholders give their proxies to management, which in turn votes the stock at the annual meeting.

In this model, which differs from the classical legal line of appointment noted earlier, managers choose directors. It is easy to see how it is possible in such a situation for corporations to develop what Adolph Berle called "self-perpetuating oligarchies" (Berle, 1969). Nevertheless, the legal authority for selecting managers rests with the board, and many boards have exercised that power by ousting management that has not performed as it should. In smaller corporations, the stockholders typically still choose directors, who in turn choose managers.

Boards are divided into committees, a practice that has escalated over the past decade. Today 97 percent of a sample of all companies in the United States have audit committees, the functions of which will be noted later. More than 82 percent of the boards have compensation committees that make recommendations to the board concerning pay and bonuses of top executives of the company. More than 59 percent of the boards have executive committees that are authorized by the board to decide on behalf of the board about matters needing attention between board meetings. There has been a surprising increase in nominating committees, from 2.4 percent in 1973 to 60 percent today. These committees make recommendations to the board and the CEO about new members. Generally the CEO's wishes dominate the selection offered to the stockholders. Other committees are: finance; public affairs; corporate ethics; benefits; corporate strategy; legal affairs; conflict-of-interest; science, technology or research; and personnel or human resources. The last four are not common (Bacon, 1983).

Board Duties

Corporate charters require that corporate affairs be "managed" by a board or "under the direction of a board." The board of directors clearly is the ultimate corporate authority except for matters that must have the approval of shareholders, such as the election of the board itself or an increase in capitalization.

The Business Roundtable, in a pamphlet entitled *The Role and Composition of the Board of Directors of the Large Publicly Owned Corporation* (1978), says the four outstanding responsibilities of boards and directors are as follows.

1. To select the CEO and his or her principal management associates. A corollary function, of course, is to replace managers who do not perform to the expectation of the board.
2. The board is accountable for the financial performance of the enterprise. It is not in a position, of course, to conduct day-to-day operations of the company, but it is responsible for continuously checking on corporate financial results and prospects. The board should consider and act upon any major commitment of corporate resources. It should consider corporate strategic plans and major strategies.
3. "It is the board's duty to consider the overall impact of the activities of the corporation on 1. the society of which it is a part, and 2. the interests and views of groups other than those immediately identified with the corporation. This obligation arises out of the responsibility to act primarily in the interests of the share owners—particularly their long-range interest" (pp. 11–12).
4. The board should see that policies and procedures are designed in the corporation to promote compliance with laws on a sustained and systematic basis at all levels of operating management.

These are the core of board functions—providing for management succession, considering decisions and actions having potential major economic impact, considering major social impacts, and establishing policies and procedures for compliance with law. Cutting across these functions are requirements to make sure that there is an appropriate flow of information to the board and that internal policies and procedures of the company are fully capable of responding to board decisions.

Peter Drucker has added several dimensions to these functions if a board is to be effective:

■ Asking crucial questions.

■ Acting as a conscience, a keeper of human and moral values.

■ Giving advice and counsel to top management.

■ Serving as a window on the outside world.

■ Helping the corporation be understood by its constituencies and by the outside community.

■ Assuring management competence (Drucker, 1976: 31).

These board responsibilities are generally accepted for boards of directors. How a particular board discharges them, however, and the specific decisions that it reserves for itself vary a great deal.

Variations in Board Functioning

Some years ago, the National Association of Corporate Directors grouped boards into four functional categories:

Minimum boards that meet only to fulfill their statutory requirements

Cosmetic boards that serve as rubber stamps to managers of the corporation

Oversight boards that function primarily to review programs, policies, proposals, and the performance of managers

Decision-making boards that are involved in setting corporate policies, determining management objectives, and authorizing their implementation. (National Association of Corporate Directors, 1978).

There have been no studies to our knowledge of how many boards today are in each category. Critics allege that far too many are in the first two categories.

The senior author has served on and been an observer of other boards displaying different dimensions, which clearly influenced the way they functioned. One board was composed of four members who owned most of the stock. Another board was composed of the presidents of companies that had been acquired, and the presidents also owned substantial amounts of the company stock. A third board of a large corporation was very active in the strategic decision-making processes of the company. A fourth type, found often in the not-for-profit sector, had many members and many committees involved in policy making and the operating details of the institution.

More boards today are functioning as envisioned in the standards laid down for effective boards by The Business Roundtable and Peter Drucker. Legal liabilities, threats of government regulation, social pressures, and economic problems that have made management more complex and profits more elusive have driven boards in this direction. William May, the retired chairman of American Can Co., and a board member of about a dozen boards over the years, underscores the major changes taking place in the functioning of boards. He recalls earlier boards as pleasant gatherings of congenial peers. "We'd combine meetings with lunch and a glass of sherry, or maybe something stronger," he said. "The chairman would describe what had happened, give some numbers and a projection, and we'd all go home." Those days are gone. At American Can, May had to contend with corporate raider Carl Icahn, who had acquired 4.9 percent of the company's stock in 1982. As a director of Manville Corporation, he helped take the company into bankruptcy proceedings, and he had to defend

You Be the Judge

Chairman and chief executive Jerome W. Van Gorham of Trans Union Corp., a Chicago-based company, told his board of directors for the first time about a deal he had quietly negotiated. Two hours later, the board approved the $690 million transaction. That evening the chairman hosted the opening of the Lyric Opera of Chicago. He took time out during the party to sign an agreement with the Marmon Group, Inc., which was controlled by the Pritzker family, to buy Trans Union stock for $55 a share, a price $15 over the current market quotation. Stockholders said the board acted too quickly on too little information and should have gotten more for the stock. They sued in Delaware, where Trans Union Corporation had gotten its charter. Would you or would you not award the stockholders damages?

THE COURT'S DECISION

The Delaware Supreme Court decided in January 1985 that the stockholders were correct. The directors, said the court in *Smith v. Van Gorham*, had breached their duty to shareholders when they agreed to sell the company too hastily and without seeking enough information and advice to reach a responsible decision. The court said that the directors were personally liable for paying the stockholders the difference between the price paid for the company and what the company was really worth. The case was finally settled in 1986 for more than $23 million, most of which was paid from insurance and by the Pritzker family. But individual directors also paid substantial sums.

THE IMPORTANCE OF THE CASE

This was the first court decision that held directors personally liable to stockholders for what the court said was coming too hastily to a judgment about the value of the company that was sold. It alerted all directors to be extremely cautious in their decision making, especially concerning the sale of their company.

---

himself against stockholder suits. "It took a lot of hours out of my life that I could have spent much more profitably and enjoyable. . . . I'd think four or five times" before going on another board (Bennett, 1986).

Until recently, courts would not hold directors liable for their decisions if they had exercised prudent business judgment. If a director acted in good faith and was not guilty of self-serving behavior, fraud, or gross negligence, he or she was not held liable for honest errors or mistakes in judgment. This concept has now been narrowed (Boulton, 1984), as the Trans Union case in "You Be the Judge" shows. While the courts have narrowed the meaning of prudent business judgment, awards made in liability cases have become so large and numerous that companies are finding it increasingly difficult to get insurance for their directors. Even when they can get coverage, the total amount insured is too small for full protection and the costs have escalated. This has had two dramatic results. First, qualified business executives are less inclined to serve on boards. Second, those who do serve on boards spend much more time doing their homework. A recent survey of 592 corporate executives by Korn/Ferry International (1986), revealed that one company in five was turned down by a board prospect in 1985. Two-thirds of those surveyed said that the fear of public censure, excessive demands on their time, and potential financial liability made directors' jobs much less appealing than they had been.

PROPOSALS FOR REFORMING THE BOARD OF DIRECTORS

The list of proposed reforms of boards of directors is long and includes suggestions from friends of the institution as well as its harsh critics.

Federal Chartering

Many critics argue that the time is ripe for federal chartering of larger corporations. Some argue that state incorporation laws are too permissive and that state governments are unable or unwilling to exercise needed controls over corporations. As the law now stands, giant corporations such as Ford, Chrysler, Texaco, IT&T, DuPont, and Boeing, which do business in all fifty states and worldwide, may be chartered in Delaware and be subject to that state's corporation law. It is preposterous, argue corporate critics, to go on letting little New Jersey charter Exxon, the world's largest industrial corporation.

Other critics advocate federal incorporation to make sure that corporations uniformly address themselves to meeting more fully the new demands that society is placing on the corporation.

Nader and his associates advocate federal incorporation for both of these reasons. Their objection to the current situation is that government power over corporations would be much more effective with federal chartering than it now is with state corporation laws. In *Taming the Giant Corporation* (1976) he and his associates present a long list of specific controls they would like to see the federal government include in federal charters. Nader would set up uniform federal laws for corporations with strict legal obligations for social performance. He would include more democratic decision making, more disclosure of information about social performance, an employee bill of rights, and strict antitrust standards that would, for example, require companies to divest themselves of assets equal to those acquired and limit entry into certain competitive markets. Federal charters would be required for companies with more than $250 million annual sales or more than 10,000 employees. This would include about 700 of America's largest corporations. Smaller corporations would continue to be state-chartered.

Advantages of Federal Chartering   Federal chartering of corporations would provide society with an important constraint on managerial power, making corporations more accountable to society than they now are.

Federal incorporation would permit the federal government to mandate specific corporate reforms. Nader, as noted above, seeks federal incorporation to force corporations to undertake many reforms in governance. Professor Bruce R. Scott (1982), of the Harvard Business School, has advocated federal incorporation as an important part of a needed industrial policy for the United States. He suggests federal incorporation, not to supersede state charters but to serve as an alternative. The federal charter would have companies "guarantee employment security for all employees with at least ten years' service, subject to safeguards in case of gross negligence or misbehavior" (Scott, 1982: 83). It would permit companies to tailor their schemes of governance, but it would set standards and subject charters to challenge and adjudication in the courts. Charters would last for a finite period (say, fifty years) and would require renewal.

Disadvantages of Federal Chartering   But serious doubts and drawbacks exist. First, federal chartering may confuse the political goals of critics with the economic goals of enterprise and hamper the achievement of both by placing new regulatory costs on business and tinkering further with a market no longer "free" because of existing regulation (Aranson, 1973).

Second, federal chartering would require the creation of a new, powerful regulatory authority in government exceeding traditional boundaries of government authority. Would such regulation be heavy-handed, as is much government action today? Would business subvert the new agency to corrupt or counterproductive ends? What would be the performance criteria for the diverse business operations to be regulated? Would massive new regulations and tough implementation result in so much uncertainty and restraint on corporations that they could not function efficiently? These questions need to be answered before a federal chartering law is passed.

Third, the impact of federal chartering on small business is uncertain. Smaller corporations still would be chartered by the states. Would they meet the same social-performance standards under state laws? Would large corporations lobby for stricter state laws and impose greater costs on smaller firms? Would larger corporations lobby successfully to include small corporations under federal chartering so as to reduce any competitive advantage they might enjoy operating under more lax state laws? These questions also need to be answered.

Finally, defenders of business note that corporate power is accountable and restrained. Millstein and Katsh, in their book *The Limits of Corporate Power* (1981), explain how the large corporation is hemmed in by economic constraints, a formidable array of legal and regulatory requirements, an "adversary-minded press," and general public opinion. The Business Roundtable earlier concluded that "contrary to some misconceptions, sanctions for management misconduct are in fact imposed and constitute an impressive system of deterrence" (1978: 3).

An Assessment   We know of no current surveys of public support for federal chartering, but recent polls have shown that large majorities agree that major corporations are too powerful, pay too little attention to social concerns, make profits at the expense of public welfare, and ignore workers' health, safety, and civil rights. But current prospects for federal chartering are slim. The prospect of federal chartering in the distant future, however, cannot be ruled out.

There is little reason to object to minimum federal standards of incorporation. Unfortunately, the tradition in the United States is for federal laws to escalate once they are introduced. For instance, corporations should have committees composed of outside directors. But, says Winter (and we agree with him):

> Were such a requirement imposed by federal law . . . there would be an overwhelming temptation to expand the responsibilities of such a committee, either in the process of administration or by amendment, far beyond its original justification, and to make it the tool of government or other extracorporate forces (Winter, 1978: 42).

There is no doubt that federal incorporation would improve control over corporations in such matters as pollution, discrimination, anticompetitive practices, unethical conduct, and so on. However, there are plenty of other remedies to deal with such matters in the absence of federal chartering. Why launch a new, federal program with all of its dangers when abundant current remedies exist for controlling corporations? Critics argue, of course, that such controls are not sufficient. Their opponents say that they are and that if more are needed, the federal government can be depended upon to impose them.

Increasing Stockholder Democracy

The role of the stockholder in theory is strong, but in practice power has shifted away from the stockholder. Critics of managerial autonomy assert that greater stockholder democracy, or stockholder control, is needed for legitimate governance. It is necessary, they say, to meet the long-range interests of shareholders, to conform with legal doctrine, and to assure public understanding and acceptance of the governance system. In pursuit of such objectives, reformers call for more information for stockholders on the grounds that they may participate more wisely in the affairs of the enterprise. Opponents argue that stockholders now get a great deal of information, provided at great cost, especially to smaller firms. The typical stockholder of a larger corporation is not interested in getting more information, they believe.

Reformers want shareholders to vote on specific issues, such as social responsibilities, that are not subject to shareholder ballot. Opponents concede that there is merit in having stockholders vote on major issues affecting their interests but that shareholders now vote on such vital questions as the choice of directors and important resolutions brought to the annual stockholder meetings.

For a large company, the reality is that intrusion of stockholders in the decision-making process for other major issues would be completely inconsistent with the types of demands on managers to operate corporations and would probably work to the detriment of stockholder interests.

Critics of the governance process for years have advocated a process of cumulative voting for directors, which permits stockholders to cast all their votes for one director rather than spread them out among the entire management slate. For example, if a shareholder owns 100 shares and there are ten directors to elect, it is possible, in cumulative voting, to give one director 1,000 votes. In regular voting, the shareholder would cast 100 votes for each of ten directors. Cumulative voting is optional in eighteen states and mandatory in twenty-two states. There is no strong movement for mandatory adoption of cumulative voting. It has not proved a powerful tool to elect special-interest representatives on boards, as many had feared and some had hoped. It could turn into a powerful weapon if exercised by large institutional investors, but so far this has not happened.

Institutional Investor Participation in Governance

The great bulk of corporate stock is held by institutional investors. Traditionally, institutional investors have not interfered in the governance of companies in which they own stock. They, like the typical individual investor, sell their holdings if they are dissatisfied with management. On occasion, institutional investors have sought to influence management but generally with nowhere near the pressure their holdings could command.

Pension-fund managers recently have been moving to organize their involvement in major decisions made in companies whose shares they hold. In April 1986, the Council of Institutional Investors, a group of thirty-one pension-fund managers who control some $200 billion in equities,* endorsed a "Shareholders Bill of Rights." This statement demands a voice in all "fundamental decisions which could affect corporate performance and growth."

The council acted because many members had been hurt financially in takeover wars. They ascribed financial losses to "greenmail" payments to stop a takeover, "poison-pill" measures (sometimes called "shark repellents") to frighten prospective hostile suitors by making their firms much less attractive, the sale of assets to a hostile bidder in exchange for a cease fire, the issuance of stock that dilutes voting power of existing shareholders, and authorization of lucrative "golden parachutes" to managers who might lose their jobs in a takeover. (These events and phrases are explained in the case at the end of this chapter.) The council bill of rights demands stockholder approval of such important questions.

---

*Total pension fund assets today are about $1.5 trillion and growing rapidly. They own a third of the equity of all publicly traded companies in the United States and 50 percent or more of the equity of the big companies (Drucker, 1986).

Outside Board Members

For a long time, critics of governance wanted more outside members on boards. They were heard and, as noted earlier, most boards today have a majority of outside directors. Critics now propose boards with all outside directors except for the CEO. The desire, of course, is to reduce management domination of board activities. Irving S. Shapiro, former Chairman of the Board of Du Pont, says that the result would be just the reverse. He argues from experience that such a board would be very easy for a clever CEO to manipulate. He would be the only one on the board with an intimate knowledge of the company. "If the CEO had any political skills at all," he says, "he could assure that the outsiders learned just enough to appreciate the wisdom of his ideas, and not enough to challenge them" (Shapiro, 1984: 238). Even if the CEO were not the chair of the board, that would be but a minor impediment. Even if board members were equipped with private staff assistants, they would be no match for the only person in the room who spends sixty hours a week on the business and commands the entire corporate organization.

Strong opposition exists elsewhere in the business community to boards with all outside directors except the CEO. It is generally believed that the board needs the expertise of company officials in its decision making. Critics question, however, the extent to which inside board members would oppose a position taken by a CEO. This is a legitimate question. But at least if inside members are on a board, the outside members have the opportunity to query them directly.

Strengthening the Audit Committee

As early as 1938, following the disclosure of fraudulent inventory reporting by a major drug company, the SEC proposed the creation of an audit committee of board members to make sure that proper accounting procedures were installed and followed in corporations. Not much happened, however, until the 1970s. Partly as a result of the Watergate scandals, foreign payoffs, and the BarChris decision, which held directors liable for misleading or inaccurate financial statements (*E. Scott v. BarChris Construction Corporation* [1968]), the concept of the audit committee was revived. Strong recommendations were made to corporations by the American Institute of Certified Public Accountants, the SEC, and the New York Stock Exchange. In January 1977, these recommendations were turned into requirements when the NYSE amended its listing rules and mandated that each domestic company listed on the exchange establish and maintain an audit committee comprised solely of outside directors.

There is no general agreement about the duties and responsibilities of the audit committee. The committees first established dealt somewhat narrowly with reviews of financial statements prepared by outside auditors and made recommendations to the board about who the outside auditors should be. Many audit committees still have only this limited perspective.

Critics argue that the committee functions should be expanded, an idea shared by many outside directors. Critics say that the audit committee should take on other responsibilities such as the following: approve important professional services provided by outside auditors; review management responses to independent and internal auditors' recommendations; review all important financial statements before they are released to the public; help management educate the board about the company's accounting practices, internal audits, financial reporting practices, and business ethics policies; ensure proper lines of communications among directors and independent accountants, internal auditors, and financial management; and assume other responsibilities concerning the financial affairs of the company, such as adjudicating financial conflicts of interests of company executives.

Separate the Board Chairperson and the CEO

When Harold Williams was chairman of the SEC, he proposed that the CEO not chair the board of directors because of the chairperson's ability to control the agenda and reduce the independence of other members. Very few executives approved this idea. One who did, while chairman of Armco, Inc., was C. William Verity, Jr.

> There is growing concern as to whether the CEO can objectively manage the corporation properly and at the same time provide stewardship for shareholder concerns. . . . There must be a clear way to avoiding any appearance of conflict of interest between what's good for the current management of a company and what's good for the company as a whole, its shareholders, and other constituencies (Verity, 1979: 11).

There is, however, powerful opposition to separation of the two top executive roles. The Business Roundtable (1978), for instance, opposed such a move in its statement on governance. Critics of the idea point out that successful although it is when the two top people get along well, there are many unpublicized cases of failure. If the CEO and board chairperson positions are split, and if rivalry or dislike develops between the two, then the split works to the detriment of the business, and the board functions less well. Reginald Jones, who held both offices for General Electric, is a strong critic of decoupling. He concluded:

> In a word, separation of the offices of CEO and board chairman will work only if the occupants of the two offices are compatible and collaborate fully and in good faith. But if a CEO is prepared to cooperate with a colleague who is board chairman, he is also highly likely to serve the board faithfully in the capacity of chairman (Jones, 1978: 19).

It is probably wise not to establish a flat policy to separate the board chairperson and the CEO. In some circumstances it makes sense to separate the two positions; in others, and in probably a majority of cases, the interests of all concerned are best served when the two positions are combined.

Proposals for Special-Interest Directors

Proposals repeatedly are made for special-interest directors on boards. Recommendations have been made for board representation of the general public, environmentalists, consumers, employees, the government, women, and minorities. The thought behind such suggestions, of course, is that boards of directors either don't give these interests enough attention or ignore them altogether, that such interests must be fully represented on boards of directors, and that the only way to make sure that they are is to have special representatives on the boards to advance them.

There is strong opposition to special-interest directors both in the business and academic worlds. Opposition arises from the conviction that directors are responsible for the long-range viability of the corporation and the effectiveness of the corporation in meeting its fundamental objectives. Special-interest directors might politicize or polarize the board and embroil decision making in

You Be the Judge

In December 1985 the Belzberg family of Canada sent Arvin Industries, Inc., of Columbus, Indiana, a letter saying that it had accumulated 4.9 percent of the company's stock and that it was considering buying much more. Arvin is one of the two largest companies in Columbus, Indiana. It makes mufflers, exhaust pipes, catalytic converters, and a number of other industrial and electronic products. Its sales in 1986 were nearly $1 billion, it registered a $41 million profit, and it employed 2,000 people. It is an unusually strong supporter of community projects. Indiana granted the company its charter. The Belzbergs have a reputation as raiders who can be bought off with greenmail payments. For example, they have extracted large payments from such companies as Ashland Oil, Inc., USG Corp., and Potlatch Corp.

Arvin appealed to the Indiana State Legislature for help in opposing this hostile takeover attempt. The legislature in response passed an anti-takeover bill called the Control Share Acquisition Chapter. The bill mandated that a firm acquiring 20 percent of an Indiana company loses the shares' voting rights unless the other shareholders vote to reinstate them. A strong motivation for this bill was the desire of legislators to protect companies in smaller Indiana cities from hostile takeovers that might weaken the companies to the detriment of the local communities.

In March 1986 Dynamics Corporation of America (Dynamics) owned 9.6 percent of the common stock of CTS Corporation, an Indiana Company. Later in the month, six days after the Indiana law went into effect, Dynamics announced a tender offer that would raise its CTS holdings to 27.9 percent. Dynamics filed suit charging that the Indiana law violated various federal security laws and regulations as well as the Commerce Clause of the United States Constitution.

The United States Supreme Court agreed to hear the case in the fall of 1986. A number of lower courts had struck down such state laws and the U.S. Justice Department and the

Securities and Exchange Commission filed briefs urging the Supreme Court to do the same. T. Boone Pickens and others warned that Indiana's law would seriously segment U.S. industry into protected zones. How would you have decided the case?

THE COURT'S DECISION

In April 1987 the Court rejected the suit of Dynamics and upheld the Indiana law by a 6-2 vote. (*CTX Corporation v. Dynamics Corporation of America*). The Court said that "A state has an interest in promoting stable relationships among parties involved in the corporations it charters, as well as in ensuring that investors in such corporations have an effective voice in corporate affairs." There was no doubt, said the Court, that Indiana was trying to protect shareholders of Indiana corporations and it had a right to do so. "It does this," said the Court, "by affording shareholders, when a takeover offer is made, an opportunity to decide collectively whether the resulting change in voting control of the corporation, as they perceive it, would be desirable." Furthermore, said the Court, "Nothing in the Constitution says that the protection of entrenched management is any less important a 'putative local benefit' than the protection of entrenched shareholders . . ."

IMPORTANCE OF THE DECISION

This case is a strong affirmation of the right of individual states to protect the corporations they charter when, of course, there is no contradictory federal law. The case leads to the conclusion that the Court has entered the hostile takeover game and approves granting managers broad protection against raiders, given the same conditions that existed in Indiana. This case may also help to push the federal government further into control of hostile takeovers because of the need to clarify and coordinate various securities laws associated with mergers and acquisitions.

constant bickering and indecision, it is argued. The most likely result, it is said, would be that the real decision making would take place before official board meetings, and special-interest directors would be frozen out of any real power. The focus of special-interest representatives on the board would be in the interests of a particular group and not in the interests of the corporation. Serious conflicts in the board would be an inevitable result. They argue that special-interest directors would be chosen for their ability to represent groups and not for their capabilities in making prudent business decisions. Introducing a variety of noneconomic objectives into the board's decision-making process would place other groups on the same plane as stockholders and introduce the idea of accountability to new constituencies. The fiduciary duty of the special-interest directors would be to the constituency they represent and not the shareholders. Not only the legality, but also the morality, of this position would be in question. Directors would, in effect, be accountable to no one if the doctrine of stockholder primacy were compromised. The result would be deterioration in corporate governance.

Union Representation on Boards

An important exception to the opposition of managements to special-interest representation on boards has been the recent election of union leaders to corporate boards of directors. Management's acceptance of union representation on boards has been a phenomenon of the last decade. The most publicized union appointment was at Chrysler Corporation. Chrysler appointed UAW president Douglas Fraser in 1980 to its board. When Chrysler got into deep financial difficulties, it asked the UAW to make significant wage concession. They did and one of the trade-offs was an offer by Lee Iacocca, chairman of the board of directors of Chrysler, to nominate Fraser to the board. Fraser's acceptance was not a new thought to him since in 1976 he said it would be refreshing to have the point of view of workers in the atmosphere where all the decision are made which affect every Chrysler worker. "Maybe we could save them (the board members) from some of their own mistakes," he added (1976: 56). This was the first appointment to a major corporation in the United States of a union leader. Fraser's appointment and a few others at the time led to sharp controversy about the desirability of having union representation on boards of directors. Most labor union leaders were distinctly opposed. Rank-and-file workers expressed no enthusiasm for the idea. Business leaders generally were adamantly opposed to it.

When union representatives have been elected to corporate boards, the primary reason has been union concessions at the bargaining table or programs to give employees equity positions as a motivating force for greater loyalty and productivity. By means of stock ownership plans employees have frequently become major shareholders. In the Chrysler case, for instance, the Loan Guarantee Act of 1979 under which the government underwrote the Chrysler loan (see the case at the end of Chapter 8) established an Employee Stock Ownership Plan which was calculated at the time to result in a 15 percent stock ownership for employees in four years.

Opposition to union representation in business circles is based on a concern about conflict of interest and the traditional adversarial relationship between management and labor. Opponents point out that legally the directors have a fiduciary responsibility to represent all shareholders equally. How, they ask, can a labor leader sit on a board of a company and then negotiate with other members of the industry without conflict of interest? They argue also that access to confidential information may weaken management in its bargaining with unions. The National Labor Relations Act imposes a specific duty on union officials to represent their members fairly. How can they do this and also represent stockholders fairly? Managers are also concerned about their ability to maintain open and candid discussion at board meetings when union officials are present. They ask: whose interests do they represent? Workers distrust management as well as labor representatives who associate closely with management.

But advantages are claimed for union representation. Workers have easier access to key decision makers, and they, in turn, have access to the views and concerns of workers. This can, of course, lead to more realistic decision making, to the advantage of both groups. In his review of his Chrysler experience, Fraser (1986) pointed to a number of instances in which this advantage was achieved. If management wants more cooperation from unions, they might want to understand the thinking that prevails in the workplace. If a company wishes to alter the traditional adversarial relationship between management and labor, union representation on the board is one way to do so. It has long been accepted that workers respond much better to implementing strategies and tactics if they have had some voice in their formulation, and representation gives them a voice. Board membership is not the only way to achieve all these advantages, but it is an important way.

The presence of union representation on boards in Europe has been common practice for many years. In the 1970s, six nations—West Germany, Sweden, Norway, Denmark, Austria, and Luxembourg—passed laws requiring representation on the boards of major companies. Since then, the policy has spread to other European countries. Some people believe that this movement will cross to the United States, but most observers do not agree.

Warner Woodworth (1986), a professor at Brigham Young University and a union representative on the board of Hyatt Clark Industries in New Jersey, believes that union representation will grow in the United States. He says that the pragmatic argument for representation is that it improves worker performance and thus corporate profitability. But there are deeper reasons, he claims. It shows respect for individual rights and thus achieves one of the fundamental ideals of democracy. Lack of representation in private-sector decision making is a cultural contradiction. Finally, he says, the absence of worker participation is contrary to the Judeo-Christian ethic and our philosophical notion of freedom. Douglas Fraser also believes that union representation will increase. He says, "I am firmly convinced that, as time passes, more unions will be seeking membership on corporate boards and other means of democratizing the workplace" (Fraser, 1986: 43).

Repack the Golden Parachutes

Golden parachutes are special compensation agreements that provide generous severance and benefit payments to top executives of a company in the event the company changes hands. These arrangements are made by boards of directors. Stockholder approval is not required. They first appeared in the early 1970s along with the wave of corporate takeovers that began then. Golden parachutes have multiplied until it is now estimated that from one-third to one-half the 1,000 largest corporations have them. Peter G. Scotese (1985), chairman of the executive committee of Springs Industries, Incorporated, says that golden parachutes have stimulated shareholder opposition more than any other corporate practice. If something is not done, he adds, business will find government regulating executive compensation. Because corporate directors are directly concerned with the quality, continuity, and compensation of top management, the task of checking golden parachutes lies squarely in their court.

The most sensational parachutes were given to William M. Agee as chairman of the Bendix Corporation and fifteen of his top executives during his attempt to take over Martin Marietta in 1982. Agee reportedly asked his board to complete the agreement during the takeover battle. The parachute guaranteed Agee an annual salary of $805,000 for five years. This was not as inflated as some parachutes have been since then. Michael Bergerac, chairman of Revlon, pulled a parachute worth $36 million when his company was acquired by Pantry Pride in late 1985.

Golden parachutes vary considerably. All include severance pay but vary with respect to stock options, continuation of general benefits (for example, medical insurance), moving costs, schedule of payments, consulting agreements, and so on (Cochran and Wartick, 1984).

Stockholder suits have multiplied in recent years, and some have succeeded. For instance, in a recent settlement, forty-four executives of Signal Companies (which merged with Allied Corporation) agreed to relinquish an estimated one-half of their $50 million worth of parachutes. Shareholders forced City Investing to cut back its agreements by $10 million.

Ceilings were placed on golden parachutes by Congress as part of the 1984 Deficit Reduction Act. The law now provides that a 20 percent tax be levied on any parachute that is more than three times an executive's average annual compensation in the previous five years. Parachutes awarded since then generally have been for no more than 2.99 times the average annual compensation. This law did not slow down the practice. It legitimized golden parachutes.

There are a number of major arguments in favor of golden parachutes. For example, they alleviate takeover anxiety in executives who might lose their jobs; they encourage managers to stick with the company during takeover attempts; stockholders of the company can afford to be generous because stockholders of the acquiring company will pay for them; and they are necessary to assure objectivity of managers during merger negotiations. But Scotese says that such arguments are flawed because they "legitimize giving million-dollar bribes to executives for doing what they were paid to do anyway" (1985: 170).

It is also argued that hostile takeovers usually occur when top management is not doing its job, and why compensate them for that? It is said that they lower rather than raise the resistance of managers to takeover attempts. It is argued that they are really excessive compensation. Why, it is asked, should top executives be paid beyond their current compensation to do what is right for their companies and shareholders? Finally, they create a poor image for business.

Many managers agree with Scotese when he says that the only way to avoid further shareholder antipathy and government regulation is rigorous self-monitoring of golden parachutes. If directors do nothing, says Scotese, there will be restrictive and punitive legislation—and it "will be richly deserved." Arch Patton, a pioneer of executive compensation at McKinsey & Company management consultants, agrees that parachutes frequently have been abused. "It's the greed factor surfacing," he says (Work, 1986: 49).

CONCLUDING OBSERVATIONS

The Business Roundtable succinctly identified the current position of boards of directors as follows:

> The board of directors . . . is located at two critical corporate interfaces—the interface between the owners of the enterprise and its management and the interface between the corporation and the larger society. The directors are stewards—stewards of the owners' interest in the enterprise and stewards also of the owners' legal and ethical obligations to other groups affected by corporate activity (Business Roundtable, 1978: 8).

We have already made significant changes in the governance of our corporations to bring these roles into balance and to meet the requirements of the times. Further reform is being made both by corporations and by new regulations. We need more reform of the governance system. We believe that we should make haste slowly in this endeavor, however, lest we create more problems than we solve. Achieving a proper balance in these roles of the board of directors and improving the management of corporations generally in line with the many recommendations in this book will contribute significantly to the vitality of corporations.

Murray Weidenbaum (1985), a penetrating observer of the corporation, predicts, and we agree with him, that "researchers and practitioners alike in the twenty-first century will probably still be speculating about the needed changes in the roles and activities of corporate directors." This will reflect, he says, the fact that the corporation is a continually evolving institution, constantly reflecting and adapting to its changing environment. Strategic to the changing corporation will be, of course, the board of directors. "All this helps to explain," says Weidenbaum, "the basic strength and resiliency—as well as long-term unpredictability—of private enterprise institutions in the United States" (pp. 46–47).

CASE STUDY

T. BOONE PICKENS, JR., STUBS HIS TOE ON UNOCAL

T. Boone Pickens, Jr., chairman of Mesa Petroleum Co., Amarillo, Texas, has become a folk hero in some quarters and in others, such as corporate board-rooms, a hobgoblin, to use a milder epithet. He asserts: "I am the champion of the small stockholder. . . . Many American companies are heavily undervalued, and I blame their management entirely" (Toy, 1985). He claims that his takeover attempts on giant corporations have benefited stockholders and have spurred managers to improve their performance. He is fond of pointing out that 750,000 stockholders have improved their financial performance by sharing $6.5 billion produced by his raids on four big oil companies in the years 1983 and 1984 (Pickens, 1986). Unocal was one of the companies over which Pickens waged a hostile takeover attempt. This is the story of what happened and the important controversies about corporate governance that this and similar battles raise.

Unocal Corporation is the parent of Union Oil Company of California. It is a fully integrated, high-technology energy company, dealing worldwide in all major aspects of energy production. Its primary activity is the development and production of crude oil and natural gas resources throughout the world. In 1985, its total revenues were $11.6 billion, and it employed over 20,000 people. Net crude oil production averaged 251,300 barrels per day, and its natural gas production averaged 1,084 million cubic feet per day.

Pickens Attacks Unocal

In October 1984 Pickens and Mesa formed a partnership with Texas investors referred to as Mesa Partners II or the Pickens Group. They targeted Phillips Petroleum and Unocal for takeover and began accumulating stock in the companies. In December, Pickens narrowed his target to Phillips and stopped acquiring Unocal shares. Shortly before Christmas, Phillips, to avoid takeover, agreed to purchase Pickens's shares at a price that netted him $89 million profit, a practice called "greenmail.*"

Greenmail is a term used to describe the practice of a corporate raider acquiring a block of a company's stock, threatening takeover, and then agreeing to sell back the stock to the company at a premium price.

Following the Phillips victory, the Pickens Group began accumulating Unocal stock. By mid-February 1985, they had accumulated 5 percent of Unocal's total outstanding shares and notified the SEC of their holdings, in conformance with that agency's rules that stock acquisition over the 5 percent mark be reported. Pickens continued to accumulate stock on the open market and on April 8 announced a $3.46 billion bid for a controlling interest in Unocal. The tender offer for outstanding shares was $54 per share up to 64 million shares. That would give Pickens 50 percent of the company stock and control of it.

In the meantime, Unocal officers decided to fight the hostile takeover attempt aggressively. Fred L. Hartley, the feisty and outspoken chairman of Unocal, in speeches and public announcements denounced the "corporate raiders" and said that they were destroying corporations. The management of Unocal planned its battle strategy with highly skilled lawyers and investment bankers. The first specific move, a "shark repellent," was to adopt a policy that anyone wishing to nominate a director or bring up business at Unocal's forthcoming stockholder meeting (scheduled for April 29) had to give at least thirty days' notice. Pickens could not meet this schedule and, if it held, would have been prevented from getting his representation on the Unocal board of directors. Pickens, of course, challenged this ruling in court. On April 14, the Unocal board of directors unanimously rejected the Pickens tender offer, saying that it was "grossly inadequate."

The Pickens Group considered what might be necessary beyond the $54 tender offer to acquire the company. Discussions with investment bankers and banks led to the conclusion that it was possible to float $3 billion of so-called "junk bonds" and raise an additional $1 billion in bank loans to buy more stock of Unocal.*

On April 16, Unocal announced that it would acquire up to 87.2 million shares of its common stock for senior secured notes and cash with an aggregate par value of $72 per share. This offer was conditioned on the Pickens group getting 64 million shares. The Pickens shares were excluded from this offer. This was, of course, another "shark repellent."

On April 19, Unocal announced another "shark repellent." The board authorized the formation of a Master Limited Partnership to hold most of the assets of the company's Gulf region. It would involve nearly half the company's domestic oil and gas reserves. Units of this partnership could be distributed all at once to Unocal shareholders in the event of a change in corporate ownership. That would leave Pickens with an enormous debt in acquiring Unocal shares and a company half the size he thought he was acquiring. The Master Limited Partnership sold units to the public when it was formed. There was one subsequent dividend distribution to shareholders. Today there are approximately 8 million units on the market with a current value of $16 per unit.

---

*"Junk bonds" are sold to the public by investment bankers to help raiders acquire stock in targeted companies. These bonds carry interest rates from 3.5 to 5.5 percent over top grade corporate bonds. This does not mean the bonds are literally junk. They have high rates to reward high risk because they are not as secure as high-grade corporate bonds. If the raider acquires a company, sale of the company's assets may be used to pay off some of the bonds.

On April 29, a Delaware chancery court judge granted a temporary restraining order prohibiting Unocal from excluding Pickens from its $72 exchange offer. On May 2, the Delaware Supreme Court delayed hearing an appeal of the chancery court ruling and sent the case back to that court for rehearing.

In the meantime, on April 28, a U.S. district court in Los Angeles ordered Unocal to delay its annual meeting to May 13. This gave both sides an opportunity to solicit proxies from shareholders. Chairman Hartley and Unocal employees launched a massive campaign. At the meeting on May 13, Pickens and Hartley, instead of tossing barbs at one another as most people expected, were outwardly cordial. Both had some reason to believe that he had won. As it turned out, Pickens decisively lost the shareholder vote to block the election of three Unocal directors favored by management. But on the same day, the Delaware lower court upheld its earlier ruling that Pickens must be included in the $72 Unocal offer. On May 17, however, the Delaware Supreme Court reversed the lower court ruling and said that Unocal had a legal right to exclude Pickens from the $72 offer. The court in this case (*Unocal Corp. v. Mesa Petroleum Co.* [1985]) made the point that the defensive measure was "reasonable in relation to the threat posed." It held that there was a "destructive threat" to the shareholders posed by the "junk bond" tender offer.

The time for compromise had arrived. Pickens, of course, could go on offering a price per share higher than Unocal. Unocal could match the offer. This jockeying would make no sense to either party and eventually would bankrupt both. A third possibility, of course, would be for Unocal to find a "white knight."*

On May 20, Unocal and Mesa Partners II arrived at a settlement. Among the outstanding agreements were the following:

1. Unocal would buy only 7.8 million of Mesa's Unocal shares under terms of the $72 exchange offer.

2. Mesa would return $105 million of the debt securities it received in this exchange offer for 1.46 million Unocal shares.

3. Pickens would stop all attempts to acquire control of Unocal or to influence its policies and would not buy any new shares of Unocal for twenty-five years.

4. All litigation between the two companies would be settled.

5. Unocal would seek to distribute equitably and appropriately units of its new Master Limited Partnership (Unocal Exploration Partners Ltd.) as dividends to Unocal shareholders.

6. Unocal would seek to maintain its present level of cash dividends to stockholders (*Seventy Six*, 1985).

---

*A "white knight" is a third company, friendly to the target company, that agrees to acquire all or part of the target company and whose tender offer is accepted by the target company.

Some Financial Implications

The financial price Unocal paid for defending its freedom was $4.16 billion in new debt. Fees to investment bankers totaled about $25 million, and legal costs were somewhat less than $10 million. At the time of settlement the Pickens Group stood to lose from $40 to $80 million, depending upon how much it could sell its shares for and what its costs for waging battle were. Its accumulated shares averaged $44.72 each, and the stock price closed at $35.875 on May 21, the day after the Unocal directors approved the settlement. This was a severe blow to Mesa. It contrasted with a pretax profit of about $598 million, which Mesa calculated that it had made since 1982 in unsuccessful attempts to take over Cities Service, General American Oil, Superior Oil, Gulf Oil, and Phillips Petroleum (Rivera and Whitefield, 1985).

The debt accumulated in the battle pushed Unocal's debt from 18 to 75 percent of total capital, roughly double the industry average at the time. Hartley lamented, "Every day when we open up the building here we first write a check to our friendly banks and private investors for $2 million" (Heins, 1986). To get needed cash, Unocal drastically cut its exploration expenditures (1985 was 47 percent under 1984). It laid off employees, retired others, and sold assets. With oil prices depressed and large interest payments, Unocal's net income for 1986 was projected to be around $140 million, or some 60 percent under that of 1985. Hartley understandably was bitter about the whole experience. "It would seem," he says, "that we have a real failure in our capitalistic system and a real failure of our morals, and manners, and ethics, and integrity in our society if one has to maintain a hell of a high debt in order to protect oneself from the financial barbarians" (Rivera, 1986).

Should Corporate "Raiders" Be Restrained?

Everyone accepts the need for companies to merge when both parties believe that the marriage will be beneficial to the various interests involved and so long as there is no conflict with antitrust or other laws. Most mergers and acquisitions are friendly. It is the hostile takeover that the Unocal case highlights. The hostile takeover raises profound public policy issues about corporate governance, the free market, capitalism, and ethical business behavior.

It is important to keep the takeover picture in perspective. A study of 429 tender offers from 1978 to 1983 showed that 69 percent were friendly. Among the 31 percent that were fought, "white knights" were called in for 7.9 percent, and the target remained independent in 8.4 percent of the cases (Council of Economic Advisers, 1985). Although comparatively small in relative numbers, hostile takeovers, especially those motivated solely by the lure of quick profits for the raider, raise significant economic, moral, social and political issues.

Correcting Poor Managerial Performance   Raiders claim that they correct poor corporate management by stimulating weak managers to do better when a takeover threat is initiated or by actually taking over a company and running it more efficiently. This assertion raises many questions. When is a company poorly managed? Do hostile takeovers really improve corporate management? Do hostile takeovers benefit stockholders?

Unfortunately, there is no generally accepted measure of managerial performance. The typical standard used by those defending raiders is the price of stock on the market. They believe or say they believe that if the stock price is high, management is efficient. If the price is low, it reflects poor management performance. This can be a defective measure. We all are aware of how fluctuations in market stock prices can change radically, for many reasons, while managerial performance remains unchanged. But aside from that, management that focuses on the future of a company may in the process reduce short-term profits for long-term advantage. Other things being equal, this lower profit will reflect in lower stock prices. Managers who emphasize the long run will expand research and development expenditures, increase capital outlays, hire talented scientists and engineers, concentrate on strengthening their marketing and distribution systems, fund new operating centers (at home and abroad) through their unprofitable initial stages, maintain a strong work force, and fully fund their pension programs. If managers focus solely on short-term stock prices they can raise them, other things being equal, by increasing their short-term profits. This can be done easily, aside from perfectly legal accounting manipulations, by doing exactly the opposite of what was just described for managers with a long-range managerial perspective. Which is the better managed company? In which company will the stockholders most likely have the greatest stock appreciation over time?

Pickens ostensibly tried to take over Unocal because, he said, it had poor management. But Unocal has been profitable every year since 1901. Until the takeover bid, it had paid dividends for the preceeding 276 quarters and had raised dividend rates three times from 1980 to 1985. Its stockholders for the preceeding twenty-five years had enjoyed an average annual rate of return, including stock appreciation and dividends, of 15 percent. (In contrast, the average annual rate of return of four comparative international oil companies over the same period was 11 percent.) Furthermore, Unocal's reserve replacement from 1980 through 1983 was the fourth highest in the industry, and its discovery costs were the lowest of all major energy companies. In 1984, at the time of Pickens's tender offer, Unocal enjoyed the highest earnings in its history. Did this evidence poor management?

Of course, not all takeover targets have had satisfactory managerial performance. There are many instances of inept management that showed indifference to shareholder interests, declining profits, weak balance sheets, low employee morale, bloated staffs, excessive salaries and wage rates, outrageous perquisites among executives, seriously flawed decision-making processes and strategies, and low stock prices. Takeover efforts have on occasion stimulated improvement in such poor managerial performance.

The question of whether or not takeovers result in improved management has not been settled. Professor of finance Warren A. Law, of the Harvard Business School, concluded after studying the data, "There is no 'scientific' evidence proving that, over time, merged firms have been more efficient than if they had remained separate" (Law, 1985). He also added that one can talk in glittering generalities about how mergers serve to redeploy assets to higher and more efficient uses, how they increase production or distribution efficiency by combining two separate systems, and about specific instances to illustrate these gains, but specific instances where just the opposite occurred also can be cited.

Murray Weidenbaum, former chairman of the President's Council of Economic Advisers, concluded, "There seems to be little historical evidence that tenderers have managed the businesses they acquired any more profitably than their industry peers. Nor does there appear to be much evidence that they have achieved significant profitability improvements for the firms taken over" (1986). These conclusions relate to all mergers. Unfortunately we do not have comparable information for hostile takeovers.

A number of hostile takeovers, especially when organized by those who are more intent on making money than running a business, have indeed quickened the flow of adrenalin of managers and brought better performance. For example, Walt Disney Productions changed its management following successful resistance to a takeover bid by Saul P. Steinberg. The bid was halted in 1984 when Disney paid Steinberg $325 million for his stock, $60 million of which was profit. Disney stock plummeted but subsequently more than doubled. Erwin D. Okun, a Disney spokesman, said that about sixty new executives were hired that "set this place afire." He added, "At the lowest hour of the attack someone told me that good might come of all this. I thought he was crazy. Now I think he was visionary" (Wayne, 1986).

More frequently, however, targeted companies that have finally freed themselves from takeover specialists have found themselves weakened and handicapped by the wounds of the battle. Unocal's burdensome debt is a good illustration of this point. Some companies have adopted a "scorched earth" tactic to thwart hostile takeover and have subsequently suffered as a result. For example, in 1982, Brunswick Corporation, of Skokie, Illinois, was an unwilling target of Los Angeles-based Whittaker Corporation. To defend itself, Brunswick sold its valuable Sherwood Medical Division to American Home Products Corporation. Whittaker broke off the battle. But Sherwood had been the best potential growth division of the company, and its loss adversely affected the fortunes of Brunswick. Management was hobbled, and stockholders suffered.

Pickens (1986) claims, "When Mesa has tried to take over a company, we have really wanted to acquire it and run it." But too many raiders seem more interested in making quick profits than in the management of the takeover targets. British raider Sir James Goldsmith, who has profited substantially in a number of his forays, says takeovers are "for the public good, but that's not why I do it. I do it to make money" (Toy, 1985). Some raiders clearly are interested in acquiring a company to sell off its assets because they believe that by doing so, they can acquire cash in an amount far greater than their investment in the takeover. If they fail in their takeover attempt, the price of their disengagement may be "greenmail." This is precisely what occurred when Goldsmith attacked

Goodyear Tire and Rubber Company and pocketed a profit of $93 million in a settlement with the company in 1986.

Harold M. Williams (1985), former chairman of the SEC, doubts that mergers and acquisitions of the last decade resulted in greater efficiencies of operation and suspects that a case can be made "that many acquired companies were run less efficiently and had consistently negative effects on the acquirers' balance sheets for years afterward." He believes the rash of mergers and acquisitions at inflated prices had less to do with managerial operating efficiency than with such factors as: depressed stock prices on the market resulting from inflation and the fears of inflation; accounting procedures and tax laws that benefited raiders; the lure of growing faster and easier by acquisition than by internal growth; and the sudden availability of billions of dollars as a result of new aggressive bank lending and new financing methods, such as junk bonds. He concludes:

> To be fair, there certainly are positive aspects to some takeovers, and a free market for corporate control is valuable. But the phenomenon is negative on a variety of scores. There are serious problems of equity, of the best use of management time, of the erosion of shareholder rights, of corporate accountability, and of the delegitimization of the free-enterprise system (H. Williams, 1985: 136).

Do Stockholders Benefit from Hostile Takeovers?   There is no doubt that takeover activity raises stock prices. In Unocal's case, for example, Pickens contended that he served the Unocal stockholders well. "We did a hell of a job for Unocal's stockholders in this deal," he said (Stewart and Cohen, 1985). The stock price rose from $35 to $48.

But this is not the whole story. Frequently, following a failure of a hostile takeover, the stock price of the targeted company plummets. In Unocal's case, for example, the stock price fell to the level before the attack. When the hostile takeover has succeeded, the experience has been mixed. When there was a two-tier offer, some stockholders gained and others lost.*

What happens to stockholders during the takeover battle and immediately thereafter is only part of the story. The more important question is: What happens to those shareholders of the company over the long run? The record is mixed, and we have only anecdotal evidence of the results. On the one hand, it is clear, as in the case of Unocal, that the defending company is often left with a heavy debt from buying stock to counter the acquisition of the raider. On the other hand, as noted in the Disney case, the takeover battle can shake up management and benefit the stockholders. One aspect of this issue concerns the

---

*A two-tier offer is one in which a hostile purchaser of a company's stock offers to pay, often for cash, a premium price for a number of shares, usually enough to control the company. When control is achieved, the buyer pays the remaining shareholders a lower price, usually in cash and a package of debt securities. In such cases, the residual shareholders sometimes find their net gain much below that of those who sold in the first tier. In friendly takeovers, stockholders tend to fare better than those in the second tier of hostile takeovers.

long-run value of the so-called junk bonds issued to pay for stock acquired. If companies involved in takeovers fail, shareholders suffer who have held their stock or who have received lower quality junk bonds in payment for their stock.

The Attitude of Managers of Targeted Companies   Pickens, understandably, is highly critical of managers of takeover companies who fight off a tender offer.

> The main reason they're [the managers] upset is because they're vulnerable, and they're vulnerable precisely because they've done a lousy job for the stockholders. Think of it. They have no risk. They have no ownership to speak of. And yet they have full control of the assets. They often try to push the stockholders aside and take away the assets so they can have the empire all to themselves, to do with as they please (Pickens, 1986).

Why do managers resist? One explanation, of course, is that they may not believe the tender offer is sufficient. This was the case with Unocal. Sometimes managers are defending their egos and high compensation, although golden parachutes help to compensate for both. There are also deeper ethical, moral, and financial reasons why managers fight hostile takeover bids, especially when they believe that the raider is interested solely in making a personal profit. Managers may assume that the raider who succeeds in taking over their company will sell the assets, both to pay off the junk bonds used to finance the attack and to make a quick profit on his investment. This could mean, of course, the loss of jobs, damaged careers, uprooted families, loss of pensions, and serious harm to communities in which the company operates. Many managers, especially the better ones, think seriously about such matters and try to avoid injury to employees, suppliers, customers, and communities.

Fred Hartley acidly comments:

> Corporate raiders pick on companies with strong balance sheets, not on weak or ineffective firms. . . . I call these people "financial barbarians" because they attack successful companies, hoping to loot them of their equity, then gallop off into the sunset, their pockets stuffed with profits. They don't give a damn about long-term growth or the competitive strength of the industry (Hartley, 1985).

Even harsher words are reserved by William Simon for hostile takeover raiders who appear to be interested only in greenmail. Simon, former Secretary of the Treasury Department and an investment banker, was asked what he thought about greenmail.

> Greenmail is nothing more than extortion by pinstripe bandits. It is a calculated raid of corporate assets, not for the purpose of creating a stronger, more productive, more profitable company, but simply for a quick killing. I don't claim that greenmailing is illegal, but I think it is immoral and a disgrace to U.S. business. There's no stronger proponent of competitive free enterprise capitalism than Bill

Simon, but I believe deeply that no economic system can long survive if it is separated from a sense of morality, justice, and fair play *(Business and Society Review,* 1985: 19).

What Should Be Done, If Anything?   People take a number of positions on this question.

1. There is no problem and therefore no action should be taken. Let the free market be free.

2. There is a problem with hostile takeovers but it is not great in the total merger picture and, anyway, in time it will cure itself.

3. There is a problem, but it can be handled by changing the tax laws that favor debt over equity. (That is, interest costs are tax deductible, but dividends on stock are not. If interest on bonds were not deductible, then junk bonds would not give raiders the leverage they now enjoy.)

4. The problem can be solved if the federal government tightens current regulatory devices such as the SEC's authority to regulate manipulation of stock prices.

5. The takeover problem is so serious that tough new legislation is required.

There are about fifty proposals before the Congress for federal action in this area. Some of their more important provisions:

■ Require shares of stock to be held for a certain length of time before they can be voted—perhaps six months. This might thwart greenmail and acquisition of assets to pay off loans acquired to buy stock.

■ Eliminate two-tier tender offers.

■ Prohibit stock repurchases at a premium (greenmail) unless all shareholders are offered the premium or approve the buyback. (British law requires that all tender offers be made in cash.)

■ Make those who wish to take over a company with junk bonds put up cash or its equivalent for a certain percentage of the value of the bonds. (Currently, stock purchasers must put up 50 percent of the value of the stock if they wish to borrow to buy the stock.)

■ Require a cooling-off period for takeovers, say ninety days, between the announced intention to acquire and the offer itself.

■ Require raiders to buy at the same price all shares outstanding once they own, say, 15 percent of a company's shares.

■ Force a buyer of a company to notify the SEC publicly of intentions "to make any major change which would affect the communities in which (the target) operates . . . (or) which would substantially affect its management, labor organizations, or employees" (this provision is in H.R. 5693).

■ Forbid defensive tactics of managers that tend to jeopardize stockholder rights. In mind are golden parachutes made during tender offer periods and the issuance of two classes of stock—voting and nonvoting.

■ Require that the board of directors submit all bona fide tender offers to shareholders for a vote.

State governments also have searched for measures to curb hostile takeovers. Ohio recently passed probably the toughest antitakeover legislation among the states. The Ohio statute not only gives the green light to "poison pills" but also contains two novel, far-reaching provisions. First, corporate directors who are weighing takeover offers may consider the interests of employees, suppliers, creditors, customers, "the state and national economy," "community and society considerations," as well as stockholders. The current legal doctrine in other jurisdictions is that directors have but one loyalty and that is to stockholder interests. The Ohio statute, therefore, is a major deviation from that doctrine. Second, the statute provides that when directors are appraising takeover bids, they shall consider "the long-term as well as the short-term interest of the corporation." This, too, is a radical departure from prevailing legal doctrine in other states. Unless the law is changed by the Ohio legislature or reinterpreted by the courts, it will introduce important new dimensions to corporate law in general and board of directors' responsibilities in particular.

Questions

1. Define hostile takeover, greenmail, junk bond, shark repellent, poison pill, white knight, and two-tier tender offer.
2. Some say that hostile takeovers are of little importance as an economic issue because they are such a small part of total merger and acquisition activity, most of which is friendly. Explain why you agree or disagree.
3. Defend the position that Pickens took in the Unocal case. Defend Hartley's position. With which do you mostly agree? Why?
4. Can managers who stubbornly resist a takeover tender offer be defended even though the offer amounts to a very large premium over the current market price of the company's shares?
5. Do stockholders generally benefit from hostile takeovers?
6. With which proposals for government action to regulate hostile takeovers do you agree and disagree? Why?

POSTSCRIPT

A group of executives and two academicians under the chairmanship of Francis Steckmest, when he was a senior executive with Shell Oil Company, concluded an exhaustive study called *Corporate Performance: The Key to Public Trust* (1982) with these words:

> If large corporations are to endure, all aspects of their performance must continually merit public trust. Corporate managements must address the performance issues and make progress in dealing with them in their own companies. They will need to instill in the oncoming generation of executives a full recognition that "performance" means more than financial results and that these executives must be

"*This is the part of capitalism I hate.*"

Source: Drawing by Joe Mirachi; © 1965 The New Yorker Magazine, Inc.

capable of dealing with a broad array of public policy issues and their perceived or actual causes. And if corporate executives are to avoid ever more burdensome governmental constraints on their freedom, they will need to innovate and perfect new forms of voluntary accountability to the constituents of their companies while maintaining the large corporation as a private-enterprise institution that can continue to generate notable economic, technological, and social achievements (Steckmest, 1982: 271).

The management task in corporations, particularly the larger ones, is changing significantly as a result of new sociopolitical forces. A challenge to managers in the future will be to achieve profit and growth at the same time as they respond properly to these forces. The BGS relationship will continue to change in the future, and managers will constantly be faced with the task of managing nonmarket as well as market influences. This will make the management of business more, not less, complex. Great changes may take place in future BGS relationships, but we believe that in the year 2000 the best of the business institution, as the dominant producer of goods and services in our society, will have been preserved. It will be preserved not only because managers will have stepped up to their responsibilities, but also because the ideology behind our social, economic, and political systems will have fostered it.

Four ideologies will compete for dominance in the BGS relationship. They are presented in the following quadrant:

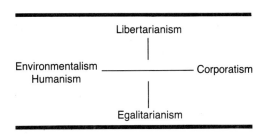

Libertarians seek maximum freedom of the individual. At the opposite pole, egalitarians seek equality of results. Corporatism seeks to maximize economic growth and efficiency and is opposed by those who would preserve the environment and advance the quality of life at all costs. In the year 2000 we anticipate that a reasonable balance will be maintained among these competing ideologies, but the problem of maintaining it will be complex and difficult. The prevailing consensus will be located in the upper-right quadrant, close to the center.

The American Assembly of Collegiate Schools of Business (AACSB), composed of the deans of our schools of business, has been examining exhaustively what should be taught in our schools of business to train managers for the twenty-first century. After one three-day session, Boris Yavitz, then dean of the

Graduate School of Business, Columbia University, concluded that although the managerial task in the future will be much more complex and difficult than today, it will be exciting. He said:

> All I can tell you is this: if I were 20 years old in the . . . 1980s, perceived the world ahead of me along the lines we have sketched out here, and could avail myself of the kind of education we are calling for, there would be little ambivalence in my position. If anybody asked me: "What would you like to do when you grow up?" my answer would be quite clear: *"I want to be a manager!"* (1979: 44).

ANTECEDENTS OF CAPITALISM

The American economy has been and remains a capitalist system, although its characteristics have changed significantly over time. The interrelationships among business, government, and society also have changed throughout recorded history. In this section we try to capture the main trends in the broad sweep of recorded history leading to the rise of American capitalism. Even though little more can be done here than to express broad generalities, such background material provides a valuable basis for understanding today's business-government-society interrelationships.

THE ANCIENT WORLD

The emergence of business in society is lost in the past. We know, however, that various forms of business flourished in the Mediterranean area some 3,000 years ago. Mesopotamian merchants roamed over distant seas to ply their trade and had at their disposal a number of techniques that we know today to be fundamental in the conduct of business. Miriam Beard (1962) writes that the merchant formed trading companies; wrote contracts; operated on the basis of laws governing trading, including regulations over market pricing; and was subject to government control. We know that these merchants had access to mass production techniques, for a deposit of 4,000 hatchets in Brittany, neatly tied together with wire, was traced to Mesopotamian producers between 800 and 1200 B.C. One further bit of evidence of the importance of trade in these days is the Code of Hammurabi, issued around 2000 B.C. It contained more than 300 laws, many of which concerned business.

Business life in the Mediterranean Basin was surprisingly advanced and reached a golden age between 800 and 450 B.C. During this period, business was freed from the control of the Near Eastern despots and had not yet fallen under the heel of the Roman legions. But the position of business varied in different regions.

In Athens and Sparta, for example, traders were not well regarded. Agrarian and military interests were dominant. Indeed, throughout early Greek history and the Roman Empire, warriors were at odds with businesspeople. In Greece, a merchant could not hold public office, could not own property, and in time of war was impressed into the army and given the lowest rank. Plato downgraded the importance of private property and the accumulation of wealth in the ideal society that he described in *The Republic*. Citizens in this ideal society were to be prevented from accumulating profits in commercial activities to prevent avarice and social decay. Aristotle was similarly dismayed by the practice of accumulating excessive wealth through the accumulation of profits made in commercial enterprise. These views are still held by people in different parts of the world.

But in great trading cities such as Carthage, Tyre, Rhodes, and Corinth, rich merchants dominated government offices. In these cities, the concepts of property, profit, division of labor, banking, and commercial law were well advanced, and the businessperson was highly respected.

THE ROMAN WORLD

The Punic Wars (236–146 B.C.) completely changed the Mediterranean world of business. The great trading cities fell one by one, and the seats of power of businesspeople were in ruins. Their wealth and prestige were lost, and the means for their revival were gone. Beard (1962) points out that Roman historians vilified businesspeople by emphasizing their bad traits and glorifying the agrarian and the warrior. This stamp of social inferiority clung to business people for centuries.

In the Roman Empire, there existed an uneasy marriage between the aristocracy and the people in business. Despite the inferior position of traders in Roman life and thought, their assumption of a more and more important role was predetermined by a number of forces. Rome was unable to feed its people and needed imports of food. Roman generals had to borrow money to wage war and hoped that booty could repay the debt. As Rome prospered, the demand for luxury goods grew. The Roman government had essential services performed by contractual arrangements with business. Coinage, the building of roads and aqueducts, and even the collecting of taxes (in the early period) were done by entrepreneurs.

The cleavage between the aristocracy and business grew from many sources. Noblemen who fought the wars were made painfully aware of the greed of merchants who charged exorbitant rates of interest on their loans. As merchants grew richer, their duel with the aristocracy for political power intensified, for never in Rome was the merchant able to hold government office. This cleavage reached a peak of sorts when Cassius (113–53 B.C.), an extremely wealthy merchant, sought to become ruler of Rome. He came close, as a co-ruler with Julius Caesar (100–44 B.C.), but eventually lost and committed suicide. The hatred between rich Alexandrian traders and Roman officials eventually led to war, and the conflict between business and the aristocracy led to the ruin of both.

Throughout the history of the empire, the Greek view of business people persisted. In the earliest days of the empire, for example, brick making was the only business enterprise considered to be respectable, because it was based on the earth. Late in the empire, however, wealth became more and more an esteemed goal. But merchants were never allowed to hold political power despite their wealth or their help in conquests. They were accepted for their aid but scorned for their trade.

At the height of the empire, business flourished. Technology was esteemed, there was an advanced money and banking system, trade was widespread, the profit motive was strong, business was organized, an advanced legal system existed (after which our system is patterned), and in many other ways the empire was an advanced commercial world. But a new influence, Christianity, brought still more social censure to business. Church doctrine was not sympathetic to business, but throughout the life of the later empire it did not adversely affect business. The collapse of the Roman Empire grew out of many complex forces upon which we shall not dwell except to say that the immediate cause was the conquest of Rome by the barbarians, culminating in the "official" end of the empire in A.D. 476.

THE MEDIEVAL WORLD

The medieval world is generally considered to have extended from the breakup of the Roman Empire to the fifteenth century. These are arbitrary dates, for at both ends change was neither sudden nor abrupt. The period is generally divided into parts: the Dark Ages, which extended from the end of the empire to about A.D. 1000; the High Middle Ages, which extended through the thirteenth century; and the Later Middle Ages.

In contrast with the centralized and highly developed world of the Roman Empire, the world of the Dark Ages was one of extreme and primitive localism. As the central authority of Rome decayed, large chunks of real estate were administered and controlled by local manorial lords. The masses of the people were serfs who tilled land owned by a manorial lord and used his grain mills, his wine presses, and his agricultural implements. They were shackled as tightly to their lord as were the slaves of the Roman world to their masters. A third class in society was the freeman who, as the name implies, was able to move about as he chose. Traders were found in this group, but they were few because of the constant personal danger in an age of violence. A fourth group was the clergy, whose influence constantly increased. Society was linked together by local groups tied by a cordon of privilege, obligation, custom, and religion. People lived simply to feed, clothe, and shelter themselves; to work in the interests of the lord in payment for his protection; and to seek salvation in the hereafter. This was a world of rules that governed everything, spiritual and earthly. Trade dwindled to practically nothing.

The dominant institution was the Catholic church, whose supreme function was the salvation of humankind. Humans were considered to be citizens not only of this earth, but also of a more important kingdom in the hereafter. Church doctrine held that entrance into this other world was not easy, because man and woman had sinned by disobeying God. It was only through the church that the vast redeeming store of grace given man through God's Son could be utilized to absolve sin and gain entrance into the Kingdom of Heaven. To this end the Christian population directed its efforts.

This otherworldly attitude was hostile to business. Trade was considered to be founded on greed, which was sinful, and trade also turned the minds of men to the material aspects of this life rather than to the spiritual glory of the next. Business people were held in low esteem, the accumulation of capital for production was discouraged, lending money at interest was opposed, prices had to be "just," and actions had to be in conformity with a moral code established by the church.

Toward the end of the Middle Ages, the church became the largest landowner in Christendom, largely because of the belief that expiation for sin could be found in making gifts (including land) to the church. In the eighth century, bishops, whose cathedrals were located in towns, were given complete authority over the people on the lands the church controlled. Churchmen thus became manorial lords controlling thousands of serfs. The wealth of the church thus gave it an enormous temporal power to complement its unrivaled spiritual power.

Minute controls were exercised by local craft and merchant guilds to ensure the monopoly of their position and to preserve an orderly life. Town governments passed ordinances and regulations controlling the trade of the town and the administration of its property. Over all lay the heavy hand of custom, privilege, and theology, whose economic restraints few chose to disregard.

There were, however, a few offsetting forces to stimulate trade. In most towns there were markets where local merchandise was traded more or less regularly. There also were larger fairs, held at irregular intervals, that attracted wares and traders from distant cities and lands. Then, in the eighth century, the invasions of Islam changed the Mediterranean from Roman to Muslim. The Crusades (the first of which began in 1095) were organized to expel the invaders, restore Christianity, and regain control of the Holy Land. A major side effect was the stimulation of trade.

As economic activity increased, the church found itself faced with a growing gap between its own practices and philosophy and actual life. Priests made loans to parishioners and borrowed money to build churches; and the church itself had become an important economic revenue-producing institution as a landlord. St. Thomas Aquinas (1225–1274) is regarded as the greatest of the scholastics for his systematic attempt to reconcile theological dogma with actual conditions in his *Summa Theologica*. He felt that trade, although not good or natural, was permissible if used to maintain the household or to benefit the country. Profit and interest charges were accepted with a few modifications. In general he, like his contemporary churchmen, did not like what was going on in the commercial world but could not stop it. He therefore set out to reconcile commercial practices with theology as much as possible.

The stability of medieval localism was long in the process of transformation before the scope and direction of change became apparent. Under the hammer blows of extensive economic, political, religious, and social change, the medieval world in the fifteenth century merged into a world dominated by powerful, nationalistic states and strong business-oriented cities.

The End of the Medieval World

The decline of the medieval world was hastened by four important events: the Black Death, the Renaissance, expanding trade, and a change in theology. First, the Black Death (1348–1349) was a scourge that took the lives of about one-third of the population of Europe. No society can stand such a catastrophe without major changes. From an economic view, for example, losses in revenues by manorial lords weakened their control, and peasants left their lands to form bodies of free workers for hire. Widespread social unrest developed throughout the century. Second, an intellectual awakening in Italy around 1350 spread throughout Europe for another hundred years. The people of medieval Europe probably knew less than did people at the time of the birth of Christ. Reclaiming lost knowledge and discovering more blew a fresh wind through medieval society. Universities were established, intellectual freedom stimulated new ideals of individual freedom, and more enlightened ideas about business were accepted. Through such forces as these there developed a society that discovered new ways to do things. Indeed, says Lynn White, "The chief glory of the later Middle Ages was not its cathedrals or its epics or its scholasticism: it was the building for the first time in history of a complex civilization which rested not on the backs of sweating slaves or coolies but primarily on nonhuman power" (White, 1940: 156). Third, the Crusades (extending from the eleventh to the thirteenth century) brought economic revival. Fleets of ships were built, the Mediterranean was opened to navigation, agriculture was stimulated by the demands for food, and commerce flourished. This burst of economic activity at first was confined to the port cities, but a rapid inland penetration soon took place. These developments were further expanded by the search for new trade routes to the East in the late fifteenth century.

Finally, there was the change from an otherworldly to a "this-worldly" theology brought on by the Protestant Reformation in the early sixteenth century. The beginning of this revolution is usually attributed to Martin Luther (1483–1546), but there were dissidents before him. At any rate, he did not set out to free business, although that was the net result. He, like other churchmen of the day, disapproved of much of commercial activity. Luther's starting point was a rejection of the Catholic ideals of the ascetic and monastic life as a way to salvation and of the view that the required morality could not be found in secular life. Luther said that one could find salvation in any walk of life. What counted was a man's faith, not his works. As time went on, subtle changes in Luther's views favored economic activity. He felt, for example, that daily events were the manifestation of the providence of God, that it was a Christian's duty to accept involvement in daily affairs and to be happy about them because they were determined by God. Luther did not open up the economic possibilities in these views; that remained for others to do. Whereas Luther's theology was contemplative and passive, Calvin's was aggressively active. To Calvin, the center of everything was God, and it was the human being's chief end to glorify God. Salvation could be assured by the demonstrated ability to perform good works because these were made possible by the power of God working through humanity. As a result, there existed a tremendous pressure for hard work. Hard work was not in itself the means of winning salvation but a sign of human willingness to fulfill God's will. The idea was that one serves God through one's occupation.

The Puritans added another dimension and welded the spirit of entrepreneurship tightly to the spirit of God. There were two principal objectives of work to the Puritans. One was a sort of discipline, a means to keep a person busy and thereby avoid evil thoughts and actions. The other was to enhance the glory of God. The Puritans laid great stress on the need to work hard, and to live to work, not work to live. Hard work inevitably would lead to riches, but this accumulation of wealth was for God, not for the pleasures of the flesh. Here the Puritans were on the horns of a dilemma. To work hard would bring riches, but both the pursuit and the possession of riches were dangerous because they diverted people from their main task of achieving the glory of God. John Wesley, the great preacher, avoided the dilemma this way: "After you have gained all you can and saved all you can, spend not one pound, one shilling, one penny, to gratify either the desire of the flesh, the desire of the eyes, or the pride of life, or for any other end than to please and glorify God" (Fullerton, 1928: 163–191). The certainty of salvation lay in hard, constant, and continuous work in one's calling. The wealth accumulated was a mark of faithfulness in the discharge of one's work. Benjamin Franklin translated this theology into pragmatic axioms that caught the spirit of capitalism and individual entrepreneurship. Franklin quoted with approval Proverbs 22:29—"Seest thou a man diligent in business? He shall stand before kings." To him, time was money. Man should not love money, he said, but he had an obligation to make money. Making money was a duty. It was an end in itself.

The Protestant Ethic, which has had such a powerful impact on American economic activity, emphasized the virtue of work, the evil of idleness, the sacred nature of private property, the dignity and worth of the individual, personal independence, and thrift, and it justified the accumulation of wealth.

Judaism stressed the virtues of hard work, sobriety, and thrift; it also taught that riches were the blessings of the Lord and should be enjoyed for God's sake.

Max Weber, the great sociologist, believed that the very "spirit of capitalism" came as a by-product of the religious ethic of Calvinism, but this view has been challenged (Green, 1959). The new theology fostered the spirit of capitalism in a fashion impossible with preceding religious beliefs. It is probably better to say that religion and the rise of capitalism were intimately intertwined.

MERCANTILISM

The breakup of the medieval world brought a variety of changes in the major countries of Europe. In most countries, power tended to concentrate in the hands of kings, as for example in France and England, and these rulers set about to control the economic life of their countries. The body of thought associated with that effort has been called mercantilism, and the states have been called mercantilist states.

Mercantilist practices differed among the European states, but they generally sought to maintain centralized political power at home and a military power that could be exercised in the interests of the sovereign. A strong national state, the mercantilists reasoned, was wealthy, and precious metals were the most desirable forms of national wealth. These states therefore determined to control their economic systems at home and to expand their empires abroad in order to acquire as much of the world's precious metals as possible. Controls centered on foreign trade because it was through a favorable balance of trade that precious metals could most readily be acquired. Exports were stimulated and imports restricted. Efforts to produce a favorable trade balance did not stop at the point of foreign exchange; they extended back through the manufacturing chain to individual procedures. New industries were encouraged by government, output was controlled, and distribution regulated. To stimulate wool manufacture, for example, an English law of 1571 required that every person over six years of age wear, on Sundays and holidays, a wool cap made in England (Cheyney, 1912). Colonies were considered to be useful in achieving the major purpose of accumulating precious metals, not only through mining, but, more importantly, through trade. Colonies could provide raw materials to the mother country and be a source of sales of finished goods. Colonies therefore were sought and, when acquired, were sharply regulated in the mother country's interests. No form of economic life (at home or in colonies) escaped the regulatory eye of central government; detailed rules were prescribed for labor, finance, agriculture, manufacturing, and consumption.

While most European businesspeople were suffering under restrictive central government controls, there were cases in which they were comparatively free and powerful. In mercantilist states such as France and England, for instance, grants of monopoly were rather freely given by the king. Royalties were paid to the crown, of course, but the system favored a few at the expense of the many. In Florence, Italy, great fluid wealth was used to stimulate the arts and nourish the religious, political, and military ambitions of business people such as the

Medici, who were dominant in the fifteenth, sixteenth, and seventeenth centuries. Jacob Fugger (1449–1525) of Augsburg, Germany, was a man of enormous wealth who controlled the destinies of governments. In Holland, many wealthy merchants and bankers assumed high political office.

Like their predecessor states, the nationalist states underwent gradual change and were replaced by a system of capitalism, the principal features of which exist to this day. But American capitalism today is a far different system from that which immediately followed mercantilism. To really understand business-government-society relationships in the United States over the course of its history, as well as to comprehend a number of major issues that are current today, it is necessary to have more than a snapshot view of what happened in the past. For this reason, the remainder of this appendix will be devoted to the events leading to the rise of capitalism.

THE RISE OF CAPITALISM

Demands for Freedom from Legal Restraints

Mercantilism sowed the seeds of its own destruction. The material philosophy of mercantilism rescued individuals from the business restraints of medieval life and, in so doing, provided society with a new way of thinking about advancing its material well-being through trade opportunities. Although mercantilism directed individual economic activity in conformity with the interests of a centralized authority, the objectives and methods of state control became less acceptable to people who sought more and more to pursue self-interest and to exploit for themselves the opportunities offered in the expanding trade fostered by mercantilism.

One important result of this situation was that the pattern of mercantilistic controls tended to be modified in favor of individuals. In England, for example, there was a noticeable drift in the early seventeenth century for government, in order to stimulate new manufactures, to relieve new industries from the minute regulations that applied to older industries. This, together with other events, led to pressure to relieve from regulations those businesses that were still controlled. Also, although the statutes in England included a vast body of regulations, they were less and less strictly enforced as counterpressures mounted. The demands of a growing entrepreneurial class for more economic freedom provided first by growing trade, then by relaxation of controls, and finally by the spectacular mechanical inventions in England were stronger than mercantilistic restraints could withstand.

The Great Inventions

Beginning in the textile industry in England, a series of inventions laid the basis for revolutionary changes in manufacturing methods. John Kay invented the flying shuttle in 1733; Hargreaves patented his spinning jenny in 1770; Arkwright's power-operated spinning machines were patented in 1769; and Compton's inventions in 1779 permitted machines to produce fine, delicate muslins.

At first the machines were operated by water power, but in 1781 came the invention of Watt's steam engine. Meanwhile, new techniques were being developed to replace charcoal with coal in the extraction of metals. Early in the century, Darby succeeded in smelting iron from coal, a strategic invention for England, which was running out of wood for charcoal. In the middle of the century, the process was improved, and mills could produce a purer iron and run it through rolling mills. At about the same time, steel manufacture was greatly improved. So it went in other areas—chemicals, machinery, agricultural equipment, and pumps.

The immediate impact of such inventions was to introduce the factory system. The older system was a domestic system in which individuals worked in their own homes and owned their own simple tools. Except in a few institutions such as the joint-stock companies, capital and capital equipment for manufacture were widely scattered. But with these inventions, it became desirable to aggregate capital to buy machinery and collect scattered workers in a factory to run the machinery. Factories in the modern sense were introduced. The result was an explosive growth of production and a lasting impact on all sorts of social institutions.

The Agricultural Revolution

In the meantime a double-pronged revolution took place in agriculture. A long series of Enclosure Acts permitted farmers in one locality to throw together their scattered pieces of land and then to redivide the land so that each received his proportionate share. This share was in one block and subject to the owner's control. A farmer with many scattered pieces of land could, in a sense, trade in the separate plots on a single new tract without sacrificing acreage. This movement was accompanied by the introduction of new methods of farming: crop rotation, fertilization, drainage, better stock, and accumulation of capital equipment. These changes opened up new opportunities for those with capital, knowledge, and initiative. The result was a revolution in agriculture paralleling, but by no means equaling, the revolution in industry.

THE INSTITUTIONS OF CAPITALISM

On the economic side, history had also provided the people of the seventeenth and eighteenth centuries with other basic institutions by means of which individual enterprise could be expressed advantageously once it was freed from restraints. By the eighteenth century some of the institutions were perfected; others were yet in infancy.

These institutions are essential to the operation of the individual enterprise system. From the time of the Romans to eighteenth-century England, legal rights to hold and use property were gradually strengthened in favor of individuals. So also were laws relating to the sanctity of contracts. Over time, a body of free workers had accumulated in society. They, in combination with accumulations of capital and an entrepreneurial class (capitalist proprietors), established one base for the introduction of the factory system. This group also provided a foundation for the division of labor and the wage system so important in the development of the modern economy. The great trading companies set a pattern for the evolution of the modern corporation as a business form. Accounting systems for business, although not very polished, existed and were recognized as important. A system of money had long existed, but it was not until the seventeenth and eighteenth centuries that money transactions increased rapidly. A credit system, although long in existence, paralleled the expansion in the use of money. The Bank of England, founded in 1691, facilitated the use of credit. Medieval town fairs, continued in the mercantilist world, helped set a pattern of competitive price behavior. The worth of businesspeople in society and recognition of their right to trade for profit were becoming more and more accepted. Fire and life insurance companies developed in the latter part of the seventeenth century and stimulated risk taking. In sum, the basic institutions and behavior patterns of a free economy existed. But if government restraints and the heavy hand of custom were lifted, would the result be chaos or order?

New Business Organizations

Great economic progress in England during the seventeenth and eighteenth centuries was due in large part to the efficiency of its business organizations in exploiting trade opportunities and new technology. Of more significance for us, however, is the fact that the joint-stock companies of this period were the prototypes of the modern business corporation, which is undeniably one of the world's greatest inventions.

The first English joint-stock company was chartered in 1553 by Mary Tudor, Queen of England, to expand trade with Russia. Additional companies were chartered in that century, but the greater growth was in the next century. These companies had many features of the modern corporation, but they varied in scope and purpose. The East India Company (1600–1874), for instance, engaged in trade, but it was primarily a political power and was supposed to promote the welfare of the English people and increase the revenues of the crown. It had the right, for example, to make and enforce laws and to coin money. Its charter empowered it to "seize all ships, vessels, goods and wares going to or coming from the East Indies." One half the booty went to the company and the rest to the crown (J. Davis, 1897/1961). Although many joint-stock companies had economic and political, and some, military powers, they also were formed for trade, colonization, manufacturing, fishing, mining, and banking. By 1700, there were about 140 of these companies in England (Johnson and Kroos, 1953).

THE RISE OF NEW IDEAS

Revolutionary economic events preceding and accompanying the Industrial Revolution were paralleled by scarcely less significant changes in the realm of ideas, particularly ideas about the position of individuals in economic and social life.

Natural Law

Newton's discovery of the laws of gravity and the publication of his *Philosophiae Naturalis Principia Mathematica* in 1687 stimulated a rapid development of the natural sciences. The discovery and formulation of immutable physical laws governing these sciences stirred people to seek the laws of nature that guided the actions of individuals. People no longer blindly accepted the view that it was natural and desirable for government to regulate economic and social life. Rather, the idea flowered that it was natural and desirable for government *not* to interfere in social and economic life. There must be, it was reasoned, a "natural order" that governed people's lives.

This philosophical fermentation led in the latter part of the seventeenth and early eighteenth centuries to a reformulation of a theory of natural law, or natural order, that directed human affairs. The new revelation of natural law bridged a gap that spanned back to imperial Rome, when lawyers had tried to discover the fundamental "laws of nature" that they thought underlay and integrated all legal codes. They were led to develop the law of property and contract, which to this day is fundamental in economic life, but they did not discover the universal laws they sought.

Typical of the newer doctrines of natural order was that of John Locke, who, in his *Second Treatise of Civil Government*, published in 1690, advanced the idea that people in the original state of nature were free and equal and not subject to subordination or subjection. In this state of nature, natural laws governed relationships among people. It is true, he argued, that in the state of nature a lack of "executive power" created the necessity for government, but society subjected itself to government only by consent. Because people in a state of nature had "natural" and "inalienable" rights of "life, liberty, and estate," government created by people should not abridge them. If it did so, it interfered with natural law and was subject to overthrow by its victims.

This philosophy was more comforting than convincing. Elaboration by such philosophers as Hume, Hutchison, the Physiocrats in France, and even Adam Smith in his *Theory of Moral Sentiments* failed to find the key to its underlying scientific logic. To these men, the natural order was that which God ordained for the happiness of the human race. It was a benevolent order in which all was in harmony. Such laws, however, were not set forth concretely. They were, rather, "obvious." Obvious to whom? Not to every person, but "to intelligent, thoughtful, and trained people who sought the inner laws of society." The natural order was not revealed by observation of external facts, but by "discovering the principle within." This concept was in the tradition of the scholastic idiom of the medieval world, which described a fixed order of rights, duties, and obligations.

The theory of natural laws was too naive and nebulous to fit the requirements of economic life, but it contained three ideas that were to flower and engulf the philosophy and practice of the regulated state. They were ideas about individualism, laissez faire, and an orderly economic system operating on the basis of individual self-interest rather than government control.

Individualism

The operation of the individual enterprise system and political democracy is predicated on the theory of individualism. Individualism is a comparatively new word used to express a philosophy as old as antiquity. It is the idea of the supreme importance of the individual in society, the idea of the inherent decency of people, and a belief in their rationality. These concepts led to the conclusion that authority over people should be held to a minimum. The idea of the infinite worth of the individual in society is threaded through the whole of intellectual history.

If individualism has had a long and venerable heritage, why speak of its great significance in the eighteenth century? The reason is simple. Although the idea had found application in a few scattered periods of history, its comparatively widespread acceptance in the eighteenth century altered the economic and political history of the world in the most profound sense—and for the better.

Individualism has had different meanings to peoples at various times in history. To the Romans, for example, it meant the importance of individuals of only certain classes. Sources of authority for extolling the virtues of individual rights have ranged from pure reason, righteousness, and history, to nature and God. The individualism of Herbert Spencer approached anarchy, as did that of Tocqueville. The individualism of Saint-Simon led him to theocracy. In all these shades of meaning, however, the idea of the supremacy of the individual persisted.

Individualism to the founders of the American Constitution and to the economists and philosophers who propounded the advantages of individual initiative was not vague. It meant something very specific—relief from the shackles of mercantilism. Politically, it meant the right of people to legislate on their own behalf, to be taxed only by their representatives, to be free to choose their government representatives, to overthrow the government if they so chose, and to have economic liberty. It meant that individual liberty was a fundamental objective of the political system. It was not a means to an end: It was the foremost political end. The American Declaration of Independence eloquently expressed these ideas. Economically, individualism meant freedom of individual activity and association. Again, the idea was concrete. It meant that individuals should be free to choose their own occupations, to choose their own economic ends and the means for realizing them, to use resources at their disposal as they saw fit, to be freed from mercantilistic pressures on their economic valuations, to exchange freely with others, and to organize a business with others. In short, it was a freedom to improve their economic position as they saw fit, to enjoy freely the results of their labors, and to manage their own affairs with a minimum of government regulation.

Laissez Faire

Laissez faire was more than a negative reflection of individualism. It was, to writers in the eighteenth and nineteenth centuries, a positive necessity for the preservation of individualism. They did not mean that government should exercise no control over economic activity, but rather that its controls should be held to a minimum. To these writers, laissez faire naturally grew from the idea that the individual, not the state, was the primary object of concern. The welfare of the individual and society, it was argued, could best be served by individual initiative rather than state dictation. State interference on the whole was inimical to the best interests of individuals and society.

A Free Economic System

If government restraints were lifted, through a policy of laissez faire, would the result be chaos or order? It remained for an English professor of moral philosophy named Adam Smith in his *Wealth of Nations* (1776), and his followers, to show clearly and persuasively how the wealth of a nation and the best interests of individuals in it could be maximized if individuals were allowed to pursue their self-interest without government interference. The explanation is that of the classical exposition of the operation of the free enterprise system, presented in Appendix B.

The basis for laissez faire was not solely economic. It was political as well. The close relationship between politics and economics was framed in the expression "political economy." On the economic side, Adam Smith and his followers, with a clarity born of genius, persuasively showed that interference by government in economic life would jeopardize the natural tendency for people, in pursuit of their individual interests, to obtain the greatest satisfactions from limited resources. Interference in the free-market mechanism, they argued, would prevent the most efficient utilization of resources in improving the well-being of both individuals and society.

Application of the Ideas of Individualism and Laissez Faire

The Western world was receptive to the philosophy of individualism and laissez faire. With the creation of workable systems to guide political and economic life, they became reality. The reception of Smith's *Wealth of Nations* and the circumstances surrounding the American Revolution and the drafting of the Constitution illustrate the power of ideas when the world is ready for them.

Smith's political economy had a profound effect on the world of affairs. Businesspeople were delighted to have a scholar praise their dominant position in society, a position that they knew existed although it was not generally recognized. They also were glad to see an explanation of the benefits to society by relieving them of government restraints. They welcomed a rationale for the pursuit of their own selfish interests and a justification for regarding their pursuit of profits as being unselfish. Of course, business wholeheartedly accepted Smith's teachings, but politicians and the people also accepted them.

What of the United States, or more precisely, the American colonies? The American Revolution was fought in 1776, the very year in which Smith's book appeared. The two events were not unconnected, for each grew out of economic and philosophical stirrings for individual and political freedom against arbitrary control by a central government. The Americans, like Smith, found a superb target in British mercantilism.

In the New World, the seeds of individualism and the idea of representative government were planted in fertile soil. Confidence in individual initiative took on new meaning in a rich continent awaiting development by the enterprising. Many of the institutions of a free economy operated unrestricted in the colonies as a result of illicit trade and the relaxation of mercantilistic regulations from the mother government. Yet the American colonists felt themselves restrained by the mercantilistic controls that remained. Probably even worse than the controls themselves, in the eyes of the colonists, was the arbitrary way in which regulations were enforced by a government in which the colonists were denied representation. Then, too, the mother government rarely hesitated to impose controls ex post facto whenever the occasion seemed to warrant it.

CONCLUDING OBSERVATIONS

It may seem today that changes come so swiftly in society that history has no meaning. This is a dangerous notion, for history has many lessons of importance for us.

First, there has been much variation in the relationship among business, government, and society over a long period of time. Social change over the past 4,000 years has brought enormous differences in the role of business and of businesspeople in society. Second, business and businesspeople have been of great importance in bringing about social change. The breakup of the medieval world as well as the decline of mercantilism illustrate the point. Third, changes in society also have had great impact on business and businesspeople. The influence of the Protestant Reformation and the Punic War illustrate the point. Fourth, institutions of society have changed when the need for change to meet social objectives has become evident. Mercantilism, for example, declined as the advantage of and demand for personal freedom became clearer. Fifth, capitalism has roots extending back more than 2,000 years. Sixth, fundamental ideas have a long life in the attitudes of individuals. Despite the very rapid changes of today, many of the fundamental ideas that drive people are the same as those of centuries ago, including ideas about the worth of the individual, resistance to government regulation (laissez faire), antipathy to business monopoly, and the Protestant Ethic. Seventh, the short-run dynamics of social life do not usually create forces that abruptly break the evolutionary process of changing social organization. The breakdown and disintegration of civilizations takes place over a relatively long period of time (often centuries). The undercurrents seem to be more important in directing the flow of the river than its surface eddies. While the characteristics of human beings during different periods of time have not been treated in this appendix, it is sobering to contemplate the Durants' conclusion that "known history shows little alteration in the conduct of mankind. . . . Evolution in man during recorded time has been social rather than biological . . ." (Durant and Durant, 1968: 34). Eighth, although business has changed many types of social ideas and activities, and vice versa, the most important relationships in the past have been with government, religion, wars, and technology. Ninth, businesspeople never have ruled over a unified society, although they have often had a powerful influence. They have, however, ruled as patricians, political officeholders, or city "fathers" over both small and large metropolitan areas. This sort of thing flourished in some pre-Roman cities. It was not until A.D. 1000 that a second wave of merchant-managed cities developed, and it reached its peak in 1500. Finally, and most important, the type of political and economic freedom enjoyed in the United States has existed for only about 200 years. The great bulk of recorded history is one of dictatorial control over individuals and economic repression.

THE CLASSICAL THEORY OF CAPITALISM

This appendix presents a composite view of how the economic system was supposed to bring wealth to individuals and nations when the restraints of government, such as those practiced under mercantilism, were eliminated. Here we describe the theory of the operation of the individual or free enterprise system. These terms, in general use today, were unknown in early America. The economic order that Adam Smith, and those who immediately followed him, wrote about was called capitalism. What is described in this appendix technically is the classical theory of capitalism.

For many reasons this theory is very important as a perspective for this book. The theory was put into operation in the United States with spectacular results. The divergence over time in the theory and practice of capitalism has brought fundamental changes in the relationships among business, government, and society. However, many of the basic theories and practices of classical capitalism are still accepted and practiced today in the United States. (See Chapter 8.)

THE ECONOMIC DISCIPLINE
OF ADAM SMITH

Adam Smith was the founder of the capitalist ideology. For a century and a half after his *Wealth of Nations* appeared, the mainstream of economic thought was concerned with perfecting the fundamental ideas articulated in this book. The *Wealth of Nations* was the first analysis of the whole range of economic processes that explained the capitalistic system that underlay its surface chaos. Smith was a firm believer in the natural order of things, and he had inherent faith in the value of unrestrained individual pursuit of self-interest and natural liberty. His genius lay in his ability to show how an economic system founded on these principles could be relied upon to reach the economic goals of mercantilism more surely than the regulated mercantilistic system itself.

Individual Freedom

Smith's main thesis can be summarized syllogistically. He recognized the age-old urge of individuals to increase their wealth. Individuals in their own local situations, he said, are better able to judge the most profitable use of the resources at their disposal than a distant government. The wealth of a nation is the aggregate wealth of the individual members of the population. Thus, the wealth of a nation will increase most rapidly if individuals are left free to pursue their own interests as they see fit. In a famous passage, Smith elaborates this conclusion further:

> As every individual, therefore, endeavours as much as he can both to employ his capital in the support of domestic industry, and so to direct that industry that its produce may be of the greatest value; every individual necessarily labours to render the annual revenue of the society as great as he can. He generally, indeed neither intends to promote the public interest; nor knows how much he is promoting it. By preferring the support of domestic to that of foreign industry, he intends only his own security; and by directing that industry in such a manner as its produce may be of the greatest value, he intends only his own gain, and he is in this, as in many other cases, led by an invisible hand to promote an end which was no part of his intention. Nor is it always the worse for the society that it was no part of it. By pursuing his own interest he frequently promotes that of the society more effectually than when he really intends to promote it (1776/1967: 423).

Role of Government

Smith did not accept a rigorous laissez-faire policy. Adam Smith the believer in natural harmony was constantly checked by another Adam Smith—a shrewd, somewhat cynical, and realistic Scot. At some points, Smith took solace in the beneficence of an "invisible hand," but at other points he was unwilling to shake it. Advocating limited government interferences in economic affairs at one point, Smith throughout his *Wealth of Nations* presents one exception after another to minimal government interference. He presented the duties of government as follows:

> According to the system of natural liberty, the sovereign has only three duties to attend to; three duties of great importance, indeed, but plain and intelligible to common understanding: first, the duty of protecting the society from the violence and invasion of other independent societies; secondly, the duty of protecting as far as possible, every member of the society from the injustice or oppression of every

other member of it, or the duty of establishing an exact administration of justice; and thirdly, the duty of erecting and maintaining certain public works and certain public institutions, which it can never be for the interest of any individual, or small number of individuals, to erect and maintain; because the profit could never repay the expense to any individual or small number of individuals, though it may frequently do much more than repay it to a great society (1967/1776: 651).

Smith did not consider these limitations so restrictive as to reduce government's role in economic activity to virtually zero, as some people think. For example, he advocated extending some mercantilistic regulations over business, curbing monopoly, freeing slaves from masters, public ownership and management of highways and toll bridges, and levying heavier taxes over toll bridges for carriages of the rich than of the poor (Viner, 1927). Smith's was, in the words of Hobson (1926: 69), a "baggy" system. It is possible to pick it up at various points, drop it, and find that it falls into rather different shapes. It so happens that the mainstream of economists in the nineteenth century shook it and found that it expounded a rather limited laissez-faire doctrine. But Smith's views of the relationships between government and economic activity could be used to support a thesis of major government interference in economic activity. The fundamental view in American thought until very recent times, however, was that government intervention in economic life should be severely limited. Some people still think so.

THE STRATEGIC REGULATOR OF ECONOMIC ACTIVITY IS THE FREE-MARKET MECHANISM

Adam Smith and his followers developed a powerful and widely accepted theory of how efficiency and order are ensured in economic life when individuals pursue their self-interest unrestrained by government. The central regulator, they argued, was the free-market mechanism. The following is an oversimplified, composite explanation by classical economists of how capitalism (or the individual enterprise system) operated.

Under a free-market mechanism, equilibrium among economic factors will provide the best use of scarce resources in satisfying human material wants. The mechanism constantly pushes toward equilibrium. As it does so, society achieves the maximum want satisfaction from every unit of scarce resources. To put it in another way, the free-market mechanism, it was argued, will ensure that every productive resource is in that position in the economic organization in which it will make the greatest possible addition to the total social dividend, as measured in price terms.

Competition is the touchstone, the regulator, the mechanism, by means of which this result is achieved. Competition literally means "seeking together," with an implication of rivalry and mutually exclusive goals by those who seek. Competition is the attempt of two or more persons to get the same thing, each guided by his or her own valuations and unrestrained by outside forces. Valuation and freedom to compete are two essential conditions for an acceptable competitive effort.

Individual valuations are expressed in the market in terms of price. Prices in a free-market mechanism reflect simply and quantitatively a matrix of influences determining individual economic valuations. Buyers and sellers alike express their choices through price. Consumers continually express their choices in the market for one product in favor of another. On the other side of the market, producers express a willingness to accept a proposed price. In so doing, they exercise a choice over whether to continue production at the price buyers are willing to pay.

In the classical view, freedom to compete meant essentially the absence of control by either buyers or sellers in the market. Sellers, on the one hand, individually should not materially influence supply on the market. Buyers, on the other hand, should not materially influence demand. No buyer and seller should be important enough to influence demand. No buyer and seller should be important enough to influence market price by exerting pressure, other than that involved in registering his or her own vote, on demand or supply or price. This is the "atomistic" view of market competition, which has been called "pure" competition. Under such conditions, both buyers and sellers have acceptable alternative courses of action. Buyers can choose to purchase a given commodity from a larger number of sellers. They also, of course, have recourse to acceptable substitute commodities. Sellers are faced with a large number of individual buyers and can combine their resources to produce a commodity in demand to replace one not in demand.

Sellers in striving to increase their profits benefit both consumers and society. No individual buyer can be guaranteed the best possible bargain at all times, but neither is he or she ever obliged to accept an unjustly poor bargain. Sellers must so apply their resources that they will yield a profit after costs are met. If resources are incapable of returning a profit to producers at market prices for the commodity produced, they are free to rearrange and apply resources in producing a product that will yield a profit. Producers will constantly rearrange resources to get the highest possible profit out of their use. In this way, a constant adjustment of resources is made in producing commodities in the public favor, as expressed by market demand. As public demand for a commodity falls, the resources used in producing it will be devoted to other uses more in demand. All agents of production, in conformity with these principles, will continuously tend to be used in that combination that will yield the greatest volume of want satisfactions to society out of the limited resources at its disposal.

In reaching this end, free competition produces many advantages to society, including the assurance that goods and services will be produced at the lowest possible cost; that profits will be held to the minimum; that resources will be used to produce what society wants; that constant efforts will be made to widen the choice of goods available to consumers; that prices will be kept low; and that there will be a continuous improvement in the scale of living.

UNDERLYING ENABLING INSTITUTIONAL ARRANGEMENTS AND ASSUMPTIONS

The efficient operation of the free-market mechanism is, in the classical view, predicated upon the existence of a number of fundamental institutional arrangements and upon the validity of certain underlying assumptions about the way people act. These are the *sine qua non* of the system.

Perspective in Examining Assumptions

Four considerations should be kept in mind in reviewing the following discussion. First, the individual enterprise system cannot be said to operate on the basis of any one principle. The system is one broad integrated process. In this process, all fundamental elements operate simultaneously and are constantly being influenced by all other elements. Second, some elements are predominantly of an economic character, such as division of labor. Some are essentially noneconomic, such as popular government and law. Others are a mixture of economic and noneconomic, such as the profit motive. But all elements are inextricably interwoven. Third, to the extent that fundamental elements do not in reality exist or theoretical assumptions are contrary to fact, the idealized operation of the system cannot be expected to take place. But the operation of the system has always been considered sufficiently flexible to be efficient in the face of all but extremely serious deviations from theoretical assumptions. Fourth, much of the expansion of government regulation of economic life has grown out of the fact that over a long period of time, the underlying assumptions have become less and less valid in practice. Government has been forced by the community to step into economic life, in part, to bridge this dichotomy.

Now, what are the major underlying assumptions and institutional arrangements, in classical theory, for the efficient operation of the individual enterprise system?

Property

First, the ability of individuals to own and use property is of strategic importance. This institution has a great many ramifications.

1. The ability of individuals to own property is a powerful incentive for them to pursue their own economic interests and in so doing to benefit society. Property ownership does not provide the only incentive to economic action, but the incentive to produce is strongest under conditions where individuals can own property and use it to their own benefit with comparatively little restriction.

2. The ability of individuals to save or to accumulate past rewards results in the aggregation of privately owned capital. Capital accumulation is a fundamental means for increasing the productivity of the economic system.

3. The ability of individuals to control property provides a needed flexibility in the use of resources. Without such flexibility, it would be difficult to solve effectively the basic problem of maximizing the satisfaction of human wants out of limited resources.

4. As the natural law philosophers observed, there is a psychological fulfillment in the ownership of property which indirectly manifests itself in economic institutions. The ownership of property provides a sense of security, a pride of ownership, a satisfaction of participation in society, and a respect for the property rights of others.

The Profit Motive

Second, profit making is closely associated with the institution of property. In some respects, it is another way of looking at the same thing; in other respects, it is something more. The possibility of making a profit, of course, is a powerful economic incentive to better one's economic position and has often been spoken of as the mainspring of the individual enterprise system. Profit is a reward for three fundamental functions without which economic progress can hardly take place. These three functions are awareness of consumer demand, risk taking, and management of resources. Those performing these functions receive profits if they are efficient, and incur losses if they are inefficient.

Division of Labor

Division of labor is a third essential element in the operation of the individual enterprise system. Division of labor is of two kinds. One is the specialization of enterprises in the production of individual types of commodities, and the other is individual occupation specialization. The growth of economic productivity is based upon both kinds of division of labor.

Individual Freedom

A fourth fundamental assumption is that individuals are "free" to pursue their own self-interest and that they will do so. Each individual, it is reasoned, is interested in bettering herself or himself. Those who have economic freedom, by pursuing their individual self-interests, ensure economic progress. Thus, for example, competition cannot exist where individuals are not free to change jobs, to employ their capital and land as they see fit, to consume as they choose, and to enter into contracts with others as they wish. An individual who has economic freedom strives on the one hand to increase his or her wealth and on the other hand to avoid losing it. This hedonistic principle—the hope of gain and the fear of loss—is central in stimulating economic activity. Individuals thus motivated maximize their own want satisfactions and in so doing ensure economic progress and a growing social dividend. Self-interest is assumed to be a universal principle with universal motivation and advantage.

The Economic Man

Closely associated with this assumption is a fifth, that humans are rational. This is the concept of "economic man." An "economic man" will know when his interests will be served by a given course of action and will take that course of action. This broad assumption is based upon a number of subsidiary assumptions.

It is assumed that consumers have full knowledge of the various alternatives open to them on the market. They will know variations in the price of different producers of the same product, will know variations in quality, and will buy the cheapest good of best quality. This further assumes, of course, that consumers who need the good have the ability to buy. It means, too, that consumers are free to buy or not, according to their self-interest. And it means, of course, that consumers will make the "right" choice; that is, they will in fact buy the cheapest good with best quality that ideally satisfies their need.

Producers also are considered to be "economic men." It is assumed that they have full knowledge of consumer wants and alternative courses of action open to them in combining resources. They, too, will know which goods to produce in order to make the greatest profit. In addition, once they know of such alternatives, they will direct their resources correspondingly. This assumes, of course, mobility of capital and labor.

Workers, likewise, are considered to be "economic men." Their interest will be to raise wages, shorten hours of work, and improve working conditions. It is assumed that they can and will act in conformance with such self-interests. For this to happen, workers are assumed to have complete market information about job opportunities. They are assumed to have an ability and a willingness to use this information by shifting jobs if need be. This, of course, also assumes great mobility of labor. It assumes that workers can and will discriminate between "good" and "bad" employers so as to eliminate substandard employers. It assumes an equality of bargaining power between workers and employers, and it assumes virtually complete and continuous full employment of resources.

Consumer Supremacy

A sixth fundamental assumption is that the interests of enterprisers and consumers are closely related. Consumption is the end purpose of production, and business could not exist if it did not strive to satisfy and serve the consumer.

Limited Role of Government

A seventh assumption is that government interference in economic life will be held to a minimum. This idea, compared with the older mercantilistic view of full government domination over economic life, is most responsible for the label "liberalism" being attached to classical capitalistic theory. The most influential early economic theorists spoke eloquently against government intervention on two counts. One was economic, the other political; and they were interrelated.

On the economic side, the laissez-faire doctrine held that government intervention in the market mechanism was not only inappropriate but also unnecessary. Government intervention in the market mechanism was inappropriate because it tended to lessen the efficiency of the market in fulfilling the objective set for it. This objective, of course, was providing the greatest want satisfactions from the limited resources available to society. As we have observed, the functioning of the economic system was predicated on the assumptions of virtually complete individual economic freedom. When individuals were free to act in conformity with their self-interest, they would ensure that a balance was struck between consumer wants and the most effective utilization of resources in satisfying them. Thus, producers had to be free to use their resources as profit opportunities dictated. Consumers had to be free to exercise unrestrained choice in the market. Workers had to be free to move from one occupation to the next as their self-interests dictated. Any interference in this freedom, of course, placed artificial roadblocks in the process by which resources and human wants were equated. Central to the operation of this system was a flexible pricing on the market. Above all else, government should not interfere in market pricing, for such action would strike a blow at the very heart of the system.

Government intervention in economic activity was thought to be unnecessary. Was it supposed that in the operation of this system all persons were angels and none would try to take advantage of others? Of course not. But the government need not interfere where economic interests were concerned, because the regulative force of competition would establish effective control over diverse interests. Because of competition, each individual would be given a powerful incentive to observe the interests of others. If producers attempted to cheat consumers by adulterating goods, reducing quality, or raising prices unnecessarily, they would soon find that consumers would go elsewhere to buy. If producers failed to protect workers from industrial accidents, or failed to provide reasonable working conditions, or hammered down their wages, workers would go to an employer who treated them better.

Does all this mean that government had no functions? No. Government had several roles. Government certainly was obliged to provide national security from aggression. Government had a recognized function in preserving internal law and order. It should also establish a framework within which individuals could more efficiently engage in economic activity, such as assuring a uniform system of coinage, measures, bankruptcy laws, and so on. Certain activities that individuals could not effectively provide, such as lighthouses, were permitted. In general, however, government's function was to maintain law and order and comparatively little else; individuals were to ensure economic progress.

None of these permissible functions included direct interference in the market mechanism. Interference in the market mechanism was generally forbidden to government. Justifiable public action stopped at the point at which the equilibrium of demand-supply conditions was tampered with. But where was this point?

How about tariff measures? Most classical thinkers considered tariffs evil, but the tradition in England was much more free-trade than in the United States. In this country, political leaders such as Alexander Hamilton (1791), and economic theorists such as Matthew Carey (1822), said that tariffs were desirable and necessary functions of government. How about antimonopoly laws? These were within the laissez-faire tradition because they restored rather than restricted competitive conditions. But direct price controls touching anything else were wrong.

Early capitalist theorists evidenced a strong bias against government encroachment in the economic sphere for political reasons. John Stuart Mill (Vol. II, Book V, Chapter XI), for example, argued brilliantly in favor of restricting government economic regulation in order to avoid political evils. He said: "Every increase of the functions devolving on the government is an increase of its power, both in the form of authority, and still more, in the direct form of influence." In democracies, as in oligarchies, Mill observed a strong tendency for governmental usurpation of power. "Experience . . . proves," he thought, "that the depositories of power who are mere delegates of the people, that is of a majority, are quite as ready . . . as any organs of oligarchy, to assume arbitrary power, and encroach unduly on the liberty of private life." Perhaps it is more important in a democracy than in any other form of political society to exercise restraint on the use of state power, "because, where public opinion is sovereign, an individual who is oppressed by the sovereign does not, as in most other states of things, find a rival power to which he can appeal for relief, or, at all events, for sympathy." But whatever the form of power, the individual should be surrounded "with the most powerful defences" against it, "in order to maintain that originality of mind and individuality of character, which are the only sources of any real progress, and of most of the qualities which make the human race much superior to any herd of animals." Mill's strongest reason against the extension of government power is the social debilitation that he felt government regulation tends to bring. He argued that whenever people look continuously to government to resolve problems of their joint concern, whenever people expect to have everything done for them except matters of mere routine, their faculties are only half developed.

These views were definitely intended to restrict government economic intervention. But Mill, like Smith, was driven by his own insight into the realities of the world to accept more government regulation than he would have tolerated in his more abstract philosophical concepts.

This does not exhaust the list of assumptions and institutional arrangements required for the best operation of capitalism. It does, however, present the main economic and political ones. The principal Anglo-American thinkers in the liberal tradition in the nineteenth century did not say or expect that all these assumptions were absolutely true or that even if they were, the system would always operate perfectly. They would have agreed with Alexander Pope that:

Whoever thinks a faultless piece to see,
Thinks what ne'er was, nor is, nor e'er shall be.

Two Basic Dogmas

But there were two underlying observations to which contemplation of this system and its assumptions led. They can be considered dogmas of liberal nineteenth-century thought. They were, first, that under a system of individual enterprise a higher level of well-being is attainable than under any other form of economic organization; and second, that such an economic system with its individual economic freedom is the only one compatible with the maintenance of political democracy. One dogma is economic; one is political.

REFERENCES

Abel, Harold. Correspondence with Teri Herman, February 23, 1984.

Abernathy, William J., Kim B. Clark, and Alan M. Kantrow. *Industrial Renaissance: Producing a Competitive Future for America.* New York: Basic Books, 1983.

Ackerman, Robert. *The Social Challenge to Business.* Cambridge, Mass.: Harvard University Press, 1975.

Adler, Nancy J. "Women in International Management: Where Are They?" *California Management Review,* Summer 1984.

Air Transport World. "Deregulation Has Spawned Dramatic Changes in Airline Marketing." August 1983.

Alexander, Charles P., "Robins Runs for Shelter." *Time,* September 2, 1985.

Alexander, Tom. "Time for a Cease-Fire in the Food-Safety Wars." *Fortune,* February 26, 1979.

Allewelt, William F., Jr. "Bureaucratic Intervention, Economic Efficiency, and the Free Society: An Episode." Reprint paper 5. Los Angeles: International Institute for Economic Research, May 1977.

Alm, Richard. "America vs. Japan: Can U.S. Workers Compete?" *U.S. News & World Report,* September 2, 1985.

American Assembly of Collegiate Schools of Business (AACSB) and the European Foundation for Management Development (EFMD). *Management and Management Education in a World of Challenging Expectations.* Washington, D.: AACSB 1979.

American Textile Manufacturers Institute v. Donovan and National Cotton Council v. Donovan, 101 Sup. Ct. 2478, June 17, 1981.

Amtrak. "Amtrak Response to the Written Testimony of OMB Submitted to the Subcommittee on Surface Transportation, Senate Committee on Commerce, Science and Transportation." Washington, D.C.: Amtrak, 1985.

Anderson, Robert. Speech at the 10th Planning Conference, International Affiliation of Planning Societies, Boston, May 20, 1985.

Andrews, Kenneth R. *The Concept of Corporate Strategy.* Homewood, Ill.: Dow Jones-Irwin, Inc., 1971.

A. P. Smith Manufacturing Company v. Barlow et al., 26 N. J. Super. 106 (1953), 98 Atl. (1982).

Aranson, Peter H. "Federal Chartering of Corporations: An Idea Well Worth Forgetting." *Business and Society Review/Innovation,* Winter 1973.

Aristotle. *The Nicomachean Ethics.* Translated by J.A.K. Thompson. New York: Penguin Books, 1953. Originally written c. 334–323 B.C.

———. *The Politics.* Translated by Ernest Barker. New York: Oxford University Press, 1962. Originally written c. 335 B.C.

Armstrong, William L. Testimony in "Federal Subsidy of Amtrak." *Congressional Digest,* August–September 1985.

Arrow, Kenneth. "Social Responsibility and Economic Efficiency." *Public Policy,* Fall 1973.

Arthur Andersen & Co. *Cost of Government Regulation Study for the Business Roundtable.* Executive Summary. New York: Arthur Andersen, 1979.

Atlantic Richfield Company. *Environmental Protection Policy.* Los Angeles: ARCO, no date.

———. *Participation III: Atlantic Richfield and Society.* Los Angeles: ARCO, 1981.

Ault v. International Harvester Company, 117 California Reporter 812. Supreme Court of California, in Banc. December 12, 1974.

Aurelius, Marcus. *The Meditations of Marcus Aurelius.* Translated by George Long. Danbury, Conn.: Grolier, 1980. Originally written c. 174–180.

Bacal, Glenn, and Martin Fineman. "The Confrontation between Corporate Power and Personal Freedom." In *Award Winning Essays, Second Annual Haas Competition.* Berkeley, Calif.: School of Business Administration, University of California at Berkeley, June 1981.

Bacon, Jeremy. *Corporate Directorship Practices. Uncommon Committees of the Board.* New York: The Conference Board, 1983.

Bagge, Carl E. "Behind the Acid Rain Facade," *Journal of Energy Law & Policy,* 1985, vol. 6, no. 2.

———. "A Tale of UFOs and Other Random Anxieties," *Vital Speeches of the Day,* September 1, 1986.

Baier, Kurt, and Nicholas Rescher. *Values and the Future: The Impact of Technological Change on American Values.* New York: Free Press, 1969.

Bailey, Elizabeth E., David R. Graham, and Daniel P. Kaplan. *Deregulating the Airlines.* Cambridge, Mass.: MIT Press, 1985.

Ball, George W. "Pipeline Protests Are a Fiasco: Reagan's Actions a Grevious Mistake for Foreign Policy." *The Dallas Morning News,* September 12, 1982.

Banks, Howard. "A Job Well Done." *Forbes,* October 10, 1983.

Banks, Louis. "Why Media Look Less Fearsome." *Fortune,* October 14, 1985.

Barnard, Chester I. *The Functions of the Executive.* Cambridge, Mass.: Harvard University Press, 1938.

———."Elementary Conditions of Business Morals." *California Management Review,* Fall 1958.

Barnet, Richard J., and Ronald E. Muller. *Global Reach: The Power of the Multinational Corporations.* New York: Simon & Schuster, 1974.

Bartels, Robert, ed. *Ethics in Business.* Columbus, Ohio: Bureau of Business Research, College of Commerce and Administration, Ohio State University, 1963.

Bates v. State Bar of Arizona, 433 U.S. 350 (1977).

Bauer, Raymond A., and Dan H. Fenn, Jr. *The Corporate Social Audit.* New York: Russell Sage Foundation, 1972.

Baumhart, Raymond C. "How Ethical Are Businessmen?" *Harvard Business Review,* July–August 1961.

Beales, J. Howard III. "Agency Focuses on the Most Harmful Claims." *Los Angeles Times,* October 27, 1985.

Beard, Miriam. *A History of Business,* 2 vols. 1938. Reprint. Ann Arbor: University of Michigan Press, 1962.

Beer, Michael, Bert Spector, Paul R. Lawrence, D. Quinn Mills, and Richard E. Walton. *Managing Human Assets.* New York: Free Press, 1984.

Bell, Daniel. "The Revolution of Rising Entitlements." *Fortune,* April 1975.

Bennett, Amanda. "Board Members Draw Fire, and Some Think Twice about Serving." *The Wall Street Journal,* February 5, 1986.

Bennett, Robert A. "Downfall of a 'Boy Wonder.'" *The New York Times,* October 11, 1986.

Benson, George C.S. *Business Ethics in America.* Lexington, Mass.: D.C. Heath, 1982.

Bentley, Arthur F. *The Process of Government.* Chicago: University of Chicago Press, 1908.

Bereinbeim, Ronald. *Regulation: Its Impact on Decision Making.* New York: The Conference Board, 1981.

———.*Operating Foreign Subsidiaries: How Independent Can They Be?* New York: The Conference Board, 1983.

Berle, Adolf A., Jr., and Gardiner C. Means. *The Modern Corporation and Private Property.* New York: Macmillan, 1932.

———."Second Edition/Corporate Power." *The Center Magazine,* January 1969.

Berlin, Isaiah. *Karl Marx.* New York: Time, 1963.

Berman, Harvey. "Industry Saves a Turtle." *Environment,* March 1981.

Berry, Jeffrey M. *Lobbying for the People.* Princeton: Princeton University Press, 1977.

Beshada et al. v. Johns-Manville Products Corporation et al., 51 U.S.W. 2038 (N. J. Supreme Court, July 7, 1982).

Beshada et al. v. Johns-Manville Products Corporation et al., N.J. 447 A. 2d 539 (1983).

Betts, Paul. "Heads Begin to Roll at Fiat." Paris *Financial Times,* June 18, 1980.

Bianco, Anthony, and Gary Weiss. "Suddenly the Fish Get Bigger." *Business Week,* March 2, 1987.

Bible, Jon D. "Screening Workers for Drugs: The Constitutional Implications of Urine Testing in Public Employment." *American Business Law Journal,* Fall 1986.

Blair, John M. *Economic Concentration: Structure, Behavior and Public Policy.* New York: Harcourt, 1973.

Bleichen, Gerhard D. "The Social Equation in Corporate Responsibility." Speech at the Boston University Law School Centennial, 1972.

Bloomgarden, Kathy. "Managing the Environment: The Public's View." *Public Opinion,* February/March 1983.

Blough, Roger. *Free Man and the Corporation.* New York: McGraw-Hill, 1959.

Bluedorn, Allen, and Allen Slusher. "An Interview with Sanford McDonnell." Organization and Management Theory Division Newsletter, Academy of Management. Spring 1986.

Bluestone, Barry, and Bennett Harrison. *The Deindustrialization of America.* New York: Basic Books, 1982.

Blumberg, Paul M., and P. W. Paul. "Continuities and Discontinuities in Upper-Class Marriages." *Journal of Marriage and the Family,* Fall 1975.

Blumberg, Philip I. *The Megacorporation in American Society.* Englewood Cliffs, N.J.: Prentice-Hall, 1975.

Bok, Derek C. *Harvard University: The President's Report. 1977–1978.* Cambridge, Mass.: Office of the President, Harvard University, 1978.

———. *Beyond the Ivory Tower.* Cambridge, Mass.: Harvard University Press, 1982.

Boren, David L. "Campaign Funding: The Voters' Sellout." *Los Angeles Times,* December 1, 1985.

Botha, P. W. "Interview: 'We Must Find a Way to Live Together,'" *U.S. News & World Report*, May 26, 1986.

Boulding, Kenneth. *Economics as a Science*. New York: McGraw-Hill, 1970.

Boulgarides, James D. "Women in Personnel Management." *Leadership and Organization Development*, 1981, vol. 2, no. 4.

————."A Profile of Women Engineers in Southern California." *Equal Opportunities International*, 1983, vol. 2, no. 1.

————. and Alan J. Rowe. "Success Patterns for Women Managers." *Business Forum*, Spring 1983.

Boulton, William R. "The Board of Directors: Beware of Those Triggers that Cause Board Change." *Journal of Business Strategy*, Summer 1984.

Bowen, Howard R. *Social Responsibilities of the Businessman*. New York: Harper & Brothers, 1953.

Bowman, Edward H., and Mason Haire. "A Strategic Posture Toward Corporate Social Responsibility." *California Management Review*, Winter 1975.

Bradshaw, Thornton. "Temporary Shield Could Aid U.S." *The Los Angeles Times*, December 1, 1985.

Breen, George E. *Middle Management Morale in the '80s*. New York: American Management Associations, 1983.

Bregman, Sandra E. "Blessing or Curse? Uranium Mining on Indian Lands." *Environment*, September 1982.

Brenner, Harvey M. *Mental Illness and the Economy*. Cambridge, Mass.: Harvard University Press, 1976.

Brenner, Melvin A., James O. Leet, and Elihu Scott. *Airline Deregulation*. Westport, Conn.: Eno Foundation for Transportation, 1985.

Brenner, Steven N., and Earl A. Molander. "Is the Ethics of Business Changing?" *Harvard Business Review*, January–February 1977.

Breyer, Stephen. *Regulation and Its Reform*. Cambridge, Mass.: Harvard University Press, 1982.

Bringer, Robert P. "Making Pollution Prevention Pay." *EPA Journal*, December 1984.

Brock, David. "Combating those Campus Marxists." *Wall Street Journal*, December 12, 1985.

————."Pondering the Cost of Sanctions." *Insight*, July 14, 1986.

Broder, John M. "First Interstate Drops B of A Bid." *Los Angeles Times*, February 10, 1987.

Brodeur, Paul. "The Asbestos Industry on Trial: II-Discovery," *The New Yorker*. June 17, 1985a.

————."The Asbestos Industry on Trial: IV-Bankruptcy." *The New Yorker*, July 1, 1985a.

————. *Outrageous Misconduct: The Asbestos Industry on Trial*. New York: Pantheon, 1985c.

Brody, Michael. "When Products Turn into Liabilities." *Fortune*, March 3, 1986.

Brower, David R. Undated form letter. San Francisco: Friends of the Earth, 1985.

Brown, Courtney C. *Putting the Corporate Board to Work*. New York: Macmillan, 1976.

Brown, William M. "Hysteria about Acid Rain." *Fortune*, April 14, 1986.

Brownstein, Ronald. "The Toxic Tragedy." In *Who's Poisoning America: Corporate Polluters and Their Victims in the Chemical Age*, ed. Ralph Nader, Donald Brownstein, and John Richard. San Francisco: Sierra Club, 1981.

Bruce-Briggs, B. "The Dangerous Folly Called Theory Z." *Fortune*, May 17, 1982.

Bry, Barbara. "Sales of Air-Pollution Monitoring Gear Drop." *Los Angeles Times*, March 8, 1983.

Buchholz, Rogene A. "Reducing the Cost of Paperwork." *Business Horizons*, February 1980.

————."Education for Public Issues Management: Key Insights from a Survey of Top Practitioners." *Public Affairs Review*, 1982, vol. III.

Buckley v. Valeo, 424 U.S. 1 (1976).

Buehler, Vernon M., and Y. K. Shetty. "Some Guidelines for Improving Quality and Productivity." In *Quality and Productivity Improvements: U.S. and Foreign Company Experiences*, ed. Vernon M. Buehler and Y. K. Shetty. Chicago: Manufacturing Productivity Center, 1983.

Buettner, Christian. "War Toys or the Organization of Hostility." *International Journal of Early Childhood*, 1981, vol. 13, no. 1.

Bundy v. Jackson. 641 F. 2d 973:24 FEP Cases 1155 D.C. Cir. (1981).

Burmaster, David E., and Robert Harris. "Groundwater Contamination: An Emerging Threat." *Technology Review*, July 1982.

Burrough, Bryan. "How GM Began Using Private Eyes in Plants to Fight Drugs, Crime." *Wall Street Journal*, February 27, 1986.

Bush, George. Statement by Vice President George Bush and Fact Sheet. Washington, D.C.: The White House, August 11, 1983.

Business and Society Review. "Musings on the State of the Economy." Fall 1985.

Business Roundtable. *The Role and Composition of the Board of Directors of the Large Publicly Owned Corporation*. New York: The Business Roundtable, January 1978.

————. *Statement on Corporate Responsibility*. New York: The Business Roundtable, October 1981.

Business Week. "Dresser Industries: A Leaner Look as It Waits out a Lingering Slump," September 26, 1983.

Business Week. "Is Chrysler the Prototype?" August 20, 1979.

Business Week. "The Economic Case against Bailouts . . . and who May Need Them," March 24, 1980.

Business Week. "State Regulators Rush in where Washington no Longer Treads," September 19, 1983.

Business Week. "Environmentalists: More of a Political Force," January 24, 1983.

Business Week. "Protectionism Isn't Such a Dirty Word Anymore," October 7, 1985.

Business Week. "Egalitarianism: Threat to a Free Market," December 1, 1975.

Byers, Edward and Thomas B. Fitzpatrick. "Americans and the Oil Companies: Tentative Tolerance in a Time of Plenty." *Public Opinion,* December/January 1986.

Byrne, John A. "Undoctoring the Resume." *Forbes,* July 16, 1984.

Cable, Mary. *Top Drawer: American High Society from the Gilded Age to the Roaring Twenties.* New York: Atheneum, 1984.

Calmes, Jacqueline. "Congress to Face Product Liability Bill in 1985." *Congressional Quarterly,* December 8, 1984.

Capitman, William G. *Panic in the Boardroom.* New York: Anchor Press/Doubleday, 1973.

Carey, Matthew. *Essays on Political Economy,* 1822.

Cargill, Inc. and Excell Corporation v. Montfort of Colorado, Inc, 55 LW 4027 (1986).

Carr, Albert A. *Business as a Game.* New York: New American Library, 1969.

Carroll, Archie B. *Business and Society: Managing Corporate Social Performance.* Boston: Little, Brown, 1981.

Carson, Rachel. *Silent Spring.* Boston: Houghton Mifflin, 1962. Reprint. Greenwich, Conn.: Fawcett, 1967.

Castro, Janice. "Battling the Enemy Within." *Time,* March 17, 1986.

Cavanagh, Gerald F. *American Business Values,* 2nd ed. Englewood Cliffs, N.J.: Prentice-Hall, 1984.

Central Hudson Gas & Electric Corp. v. Public Service Commission, 447 U.S. 557 (1980).

Chandler, Colby H. "Eastman Kodak Opens Windows of Opportunity." *The Journal of Business Strategy,* Summer 1986.

Chapman, Philip C. "Stress in Political Theory." *Ethics,* October 1969.

Charlton, Robert W. Interview with John F. Steiner, November 3, 1986.

Chatov Robert. "What Corporate Ethics Statements Say." *California Management Review,* Summer 1980.

Chevron U.S.A., Inc. v. Natural Resources Defense Council, Inc., 52 LW 4845, June 25, 1984.

Cheyney, Edward P. *An Introduction to the Industrial and Social History of England.* New York: Macmillan, 1912.

Child Study Association of America. *Children in Wartime: Parents' Questions.* New York: Child Study Association of America, 1942.

Chilton, Kenneth W. "The Effects of Gramm Rudman-Hollings on Federal Regulatory Agencies." St. Louis: Washington University, Center for the Study of American Business, April 17, 1986.

Christian, C.D., "Maternal Deaths Associated with an Intrauterine Device." *American Journal of Obstetrics and Gynecology,* June 15, 1974.

Christman, James J., Elizabeth J. Gatewood, and Archie B. Carroll. "What's Wrong with Plant-Closing Legislation and Industrial Policy." *Business Horizons,* September–October 1985.

Christoffel, Tom, David Finkelhor, and Dan Gilberg, eds. *Up against the American Myth.* New York: Holt, Rinehart and Winston, 1970.

Cifelli, Anna. "Management by Bankruptcy." *Fortune,* October 31, 1983.

Clark, J. M. *Social Control of Business.* New York: McGraw-Hill, 1932.

Clayton, W. Graham, Jr. Testimony in *Hearings before the Subcommittee on the Department of Transportation and Related Agencies Appropriations, United States House of Representatives.* April 3, 1985. Washington, D.C.: U.S. Government Printing Office, 1985.

Cleary v. American Airlines, Inc., 168 Cal. Rptr. 722 (1980).

Clymer, Adam. "Low Marks for Executive Honesty." *New York Times,* June 9, 1985.

———."How Americans Rate Big Business." *New York Times Magazine,* June 8, 1986.

Cochran, Philip L., and Robert A. Wood. "Corporate Social Responsibility and Financial Performance." *Academy of Management Journal,* March 1984.

———, and Steven L. Wartick. "'Golden Parachutes': A Closer Look." *California Management Review,* Summer 1984.

Code of Federal Regulations. Washington, D.C.: U.S. Government Printing Office, 1985.

Collins, Eliza G.C. "Managers and Lovers." *Harvard Business Review,* September–October 1983.

Colonius, L. Erik. "Trying Japanese Management in America." In *Business Issues Today,* ed. Robert B. Carson. New York: St. Martin's Press, 1984.

Committee for Economic Development. *The European Common Market and the Balance of Payments Problem.* New York: CED, 1959.

———.*Trade Negotiations for a Better Free World Economy.* New York: CED, 1964.

———. *Social Responsibilities of Business Corporations.* New York: CED, 1971.

———. *Public-Private Partnership: An Opportunity for Urban Communities.* New York: CED, 1982.

Common Cause Magazine. "Issues Poll Results—1985." May/June 1985.

Comptroller General of the United States. *Cleaning up the Environment: Progress Achieved but Major Unre-*

solved Issues Remain, vols. I, II. Washington, D.C.: U.S. Government Printing Office, July 21, 1982.

Congressional Quarterly, Inc. *Regulation: Process and Politics*. Washington, D.C.: Congressional Quarterly, Inc., 1982.

Connor, John T. "An Alternative to the Goldberg Prescription." Remarks before the American Society of Corporate Secretaries. March 14, 1973.

Conrad, Thomas, "Computers Programmed for Racism." *Business and Society Review*, Summer 1982.

Consumer Product Safety Commission. *1984 Annual Report*. Washington, D.C.: 1985.

Cooper, Ann. "Middleman Mail." *National Journal*, September 14, 1985.

Cooper, Lee G., and John F. Steiner. "Attitudes towards Business Progress Report," Paper Series No. 8. Los Angeles: University of California at Los Angeles, Graduate School of Management, November 1976.

Cooper, Richard M. "Stretching Delaney till It Breaks." *Regulation*, November/December 1985.

Cooper, Richard T., and Paul E. Steiger. "How One Big Firm Fought Health Perils." *Los Angeles Times*, June 27, 1976.

Coordiner, Ralph J. *New Frontiers for Professional Managers*. New York: McGraw-Hill, 1956.

Copeland, Lennie, and Lewis Griggs. *Going International: How to Make Friends and Deal Effectively in the Global Marketplace*. New York: Random House, 1985.

Corson, John J., and George A. Steiner. *Measuring Business's Social Performance: The Corporate Social Audit*. New York: Committee for Economic Development, 1974.

Cortner, Richard C. *The Jones & Laughlin Case*. New York: Knopf, 1970.

Council of Economic Advisers. *Economic Report of the President*. Washington, D.C.: U.S. Government Printing Office, 1985.

Council on Environmental Quality. *Environmental Quality: Annual Report*. Washington, D.C.: U.S. Government Printing Office, 1970, 1982, 1984, 1985.

Crane, Philip M. "Amtrak under Siege." In *Railway Age*, ed. Gus Welty, April 1985.

Crocker, Chester A. "South Africa: Strategy for Change." *Foreign Affairs*, Winter 1980/81.

Cronin v. J. B. E. Olson Corporation, 8 Cal. 3d 121, 501 Pacific 2d 1153, 104 Cal Rptr 433 (1972).

Cross, Jennifer. "The Business of Good Clean Fun." *The Nation*, June 14, 1971.

CTS Corporation v. Dynamics Corporation of America, 55 LW 4478, 4-21-87.

Cushman, Robert. Remarks to the New England Public Relations Society. Worcester, Mass.: Worcester Polytechnic Institute, February 27, 1980.

Dahlinger, John D. *The Secret Life of Henry Ford*. New York: Bobbs-Merrill, 1978.

Dallos, Robert E. "Debate Still Rages over Deregulation." *Los Angeles Times*, November 2, 1986.

D'Amato, Alfonse M. Testimony in "Federal Subsidy of Amtrak." *Congressional Digest*, August–September 1985.

Danhof, Clarence H., and James C. Worthy, eds. *Crisis in Confidence II: Corporate America*. Proceedings of the Second Annual Intersession Public Affairs Colloquium. Springfield, Ill.: Sangamon State University, 1975.

Dartmouth College v. Woodward, 4 Wheaton 519 (1819).

Das, T.K. "Dresser Industries." In *Business, Government, and Society*, ed. George A. Steiner and John F. Steiner. New York: Random House, 1985.

Davidson, Joe, and Linda M. Watkins. "Quotas in Hiring Are Anathema to President Despite Minority Gains." *Wall Street Journal*, October 24, 1985.

Davis, Hugh J. "The Shield Intrauterine Device." *American Journal of Obstetrics and Gynecology*, February 1, 1970.

———. *Intrauterine Devices for Contraception: The IUD*. Baltimore: Williams & Wilkins, 1971.

Davis, John P. *Corporations*. Reprint. New York: Capricorn, 1961. Originally published c. 1897.

Davis, Keith. "Can Business Afford to Ignore Social Responsibilities?" *California Management Review*, Spring 1960.

Davis, Morris. "The Impact of Workplace Health and Safety on Black Workers." In *Occupational Safety and Health*, ed. Frank Goldsmith and Lorin E. Kerr. New York: Human Sciences Press, 1982.

Deal, Terrence E., and Allan A. Kennedy. *Corporate Cultures: The Rites and Rituals of Corporate Life*. Reading, Mass.: Addison-Wesley, 1982.

DeGeorge, Richard T. *Business Ethics*, 2nd ed. New York: Macmillan, 1986.

Demmings, Dara. "Comparable Worth: A Matter of Simple Justice." *The Corporate Examiner*, June 1983.

Derr, Patrick, Robert Goble, Robert E. Kasperson, and Robert W. Kates. "The Double Standard: Worker-Public Protection." *Environment*, September 1981.

Derthick, Martha, and Paul J. Quirk. *The Politics of Deregulation*. Washington, D.C.: The Brookings Institution, 1985.

Destler, Chester McArthur. "Entrepreneurial Leadership among the 'Robber Barons': A Trial Balance." *Journal of Economic History*, 1946, vol. 6, supplement.

De Tocqueville, Alexis. *Democracy in America*. Reprint. Ed. Richard D. Hefner. New York: New American Library, 1956. Originally published in 1835 and 1840.

Diamond vs. Chakrabarty, U.S. Supreme Court (1980).

Dole, Elizabeth M. Testimony in *Hearings before Subcommittee on Commerce, Transportation, and Tourism of the Committee on Energy and Commerce, House of Representatives*, March 14 and April 23, 1985. Washington, D.C.: U.S. Government Printing Office, 1985.

Domhoff, G. William. *Who Rules America Now? A View for the '80's*. Englewood Cliffs, N.J.: Prentice-Hall, 1963.

———, and Thomas R. Dye, eds. *Power Elites and Organizations*. Beverly Hills: Sage Publications, 1986.

Donner, Frederic G. *The World-Wide Industrial Empire*. New York: McGraw-Hill, 1967.

Dooley, Peter. "The Interlocking Directorate." *American Economic Review*, June 1969.

Doughty, Phillip, Laura Gushin, Darrell Fasching, and Jack McCome. *Corporate Ethics: A Review of Selected Corporate Policies and Practices*. Syracuse, N.Y.: Syracuse University Press, 1980.

Dow Chemical Company. "Statistics on Blacks' Attitudes toward Organ Donation Reveal Need for More Black Donors." *TIP Sheet*, Autumn 1986.

———.*The Impact of Government Regulation*. 1977.

Dow Chemical Company v. United States, 54 LW 4464 (1986).

Dowd, Douglas F. *The Twisted Dream*. 2nd ed. Cambridge, Mass.: Winthrop, 1977.

Doz, Yves L., and C.K. Prahalad. "How MNCs Cope with Host Government Intervention." *Harvard Business Review*, March–April 1980.

Dreyfuss, John, "The Word War over Realistic Toy Guns Is Getting Hotter." *Los Angeles Times*, December 19, 1986.

Drucker, Peter F. "A Key to American Politics: Calhoun's Pluralism." *Review of Politics*, October 1968.

———. "The Bored Board." *Wharton Magazine*, Fall 1976.

———."A Crisis of Capitalism." *The Wall Street Journal*, September 30, 1986.

Dumas, Lloyd, and Suzanne Gordon. "Economic Conversion: An Exchange." *Bulletin of the Atomic Scientists*, June/July 1986.

Dunn, Marvin G. "The Family Office: Coordinating Mechanism of the Ruling Class." In *Power Structure Research*, ed. G. William Domhoff. Beverly Hills: Sage Publications, 1980.

DuPont De Nemours & Company. Survey Conducted for the Business Roundtable by the Corporate Marketing Research Section, 1976.

Durant, Will, and Ariel Durant. *The Lessons of History*. New York: Simon & Schuster, 1968.

Dye, Thomas R. *Who's Running America?* Englewood Cliffs, N.J.: Prentice-Hall, 1976.

———. *Who's Running America? The Conservative Years*.

4th ed. Englewood Cliffs, N.J.: Prentice-Hall, 1986.

Eads, George C., and Michael Fix. *Relief or Reform?* Washington, D.C.: The Urban Institute 1984.

Easterbrook, Gregg. "What's Wrong with Congress?" *The Atlantic Monthly*, December 1984.

Easton, Alan G. Testimony in *Alcohol Advertising*. From hearing before the Subcommittee on Children, Family, Drugs and Alcoholism of the Committee on Labor and Human Resources. United States Senate, February 7, 1985a.

———. Written statement in *Beer and Wine Advertising: Impact of Electronic Media*. From *Hearing before the Subcommittee on Telecommunications, Consumer Protection, and Finance of the Committee on Energy and Commerce, United States House of Representatives*, May 21, 1985b.

Easton, David. "An Approach to the Analysis of Political Systems." *World Politics*, April 1957.

Edelman, David A., Gary S. Berger, and Louis G. Keith. *Intrauterine Devices and Their Complications*. Boston: G. K. Hall, 1979.

Edsall, Thomas B. "The GE Lobby." *Washington Post National Weekly Edition*, May 13, 1985.

Edwards, Alfred L. "Consumer Product Safety: Challenge for Business." *University of Michigan Business Review*, 1975.

Ehrlich, Paul R. *The Population Bomb*. New York: Ballantine, 1968.

Ehrlich, Paul, and Anne Ehrlich, *Extinction: The Causes and Consequences of the Disappearance of Species*. New York: Random House, 1981.

Ellen Hochstedler, ed. *Corporation as Criminals*. Beverly Hills: Sage Publications, 1984.

Environmental Protection Agency v. National Crushed Stone Association, 66 L. ed. 268, 1980.

Epstein, Edwin M. "Dimensions of Corporate Power: Part I." *California Management Review*, Winter 1973.

Epstein, Edwin M., and Lee E. Preston, eds. *Business Environment/Public Policy: The Field and Its Future*. St. Louis: American Assembly of Collegiate Schools of Business, 1982.

Equal Employment Opportunity Commission v. AT&T, 365, F. Supp. 1105 (1973).

Equal Employment Opportunity Commission v. Sage Realty Corp, 25 Emp. Prac. Dec. para. 31, 529 (S.D. N.Y. 1981).

Erikson, Erik H. *Toys and Reasons: Stages in the Ritualization of Experience*. New York: Norton, 1977.

E. Scott v. BarChris Construction Corporation, (S.D. N.Y. 1968).

Ewing, David W. *Freedom inside the Organization: Bringing Civil Liberties to the Workplace*. New York: Dutton, 1977.

———. *Do It My Way or You're Fired*. New York: Dutton, 1983.

Exon, J. James. *Testimony before the Subcommittee on Surface Transportation of the Committee on Commerce, Science, and Transportation, United States Senate,* April 29, 1985.

Eysenck, Hans J. Statement regarding S. 772 in *Smoking Prevention Health and Education Act of 1983. Hearing before the Committee on Labor and Human Resources, United States Senate,* May 5 and 12, 1983.

Fahey, L., W. King, and V. Narayanan. "Environmental Scanning and Forecasting in Strategic Planning —The State of the Art." *Long Range Planning,* February 1981.

Farley, Lin. *Sexual Shakedown: The Sexual Harrassment of Women on the Job.* New York: McGraw-Hill, 1978.

Farnsworth, Clyde H. "Europe Assails Trade Pattern." *New York Times,* July 4, 1986.

Federal Election Commission. *Final Report on Financial Activity 1983–1984.* Washington, D.C.: U.S. Government Printing Office, November 1985.

Federal Trade Commission. *Recommendations of the Staff of the Federal Trade Commission: Omnibus Petition for Regulation of Unfair and Deceptive Alcoholic Beverage Advertising and Marketing Practices,* Docket No. 209–46, March 1985.

Ferguson v. DuPont Co., 3 FEP Cases 795 (1983).

Fernandez, John P. *Racism and Sexism in Corporate Life.* Lexington, Mass.: Lexington Books, 1981.

Feshbach, Seymour. "The Catharsis Hypothesis and Some Consequences of Interaction with Aggressive and Neutral Play Objects." *Journal of Personality,* June 1956.

Fieve, Ronald R. *Moodswing.* New York: Bantam Books, 1975.

Firefighters Local Union No. 1784 v. Carl W. Stotts, 467, U.S. 561 (1984).

First National Bank of Boston v. Bellotti, 435, U.S. 735, 438, U.S. 907 (1978).

First National Maintenance Corp. v. NLRB, 452, U.S. 666 (1980), 627 F. 2d. 596 (1981).

Fisher, Burton R., and Stephen B. Withey. *Big Business as the People See It.* Ann Arbor: University Microfilms, December 1951.

Fisse, Brent, and John Braithwaite. *The Impact of Publicity on Corporate Offenders.* Albany: State University of New York Press, 1983.

Flanigan, James. "The Public, Not the Media, Is the Final Judge of Business." *Los Angeles Times,* October 26, 1983.

Floria, James J. Comment in *Hearings before the Subcommittee on Commerce, Transportation, and Tourism of the Committee on Energy and Commerce, House of Representatives,* March 14 and April 23, 1985.

Follett, Ken. *On Wings of Eagles.* New York: New American Library, 1983.

Folsom, Marion B. *Executive Decision Making.* New York: McGraw-Hill, 1962.

Ford, Henry II. *The Human Environment and Business.* New York: Weybright and Talley, 1970.

Ford, Robert, and Frank McLaughlin. "Perceptions of Socially Responsible Activities and Attitudes: A Comparison of Business School Deans and Corporate Chief Executives." *Academy of Management Journal,* September 1984.

Foreyt, John P. Statement submitted for record in *Tobacco Issues, Hearing before the Subcommittee on Health and the Environment of the Committee on Energy and Commerce, House of Representatives,* July 26, 1985.

"The Fortune 500 Largest U.S. Industrial Corporations." *Fortune,* April 27, 1987.

Foundation for Economic Trends v. Heckler, (587 F. Supp. 753 D.D.C.).

Fox, Karen F.A., and Bobby J. Calder. "The Right Kind of Business Advocacy." *Business Horizons,* January–February 1985.

Fraser, Douglas. *San Francisco Chronicle,* May 7, 1976.

———."My Years on the Chrysler Board." *Across the Board,* June 1986.

Frazer, James G. *Psyche's Task: A Discourse Concerning the Influence of Superstition of the Growth of Institutions.* London: Dawsons of Pall Mall, 1968.

Frazier, Sir James G. *The Golden Bough: A Study in Magic and Religion.* New York: Macmillan, 1922.

Frederick, William C. "Corporate Social Responsibility in the Reagan Era and beyond." *California Management Review,* Spring 1983.

Freeman, Alan. "Canada's Asbestos Companies Blame U.S. for Industry's Decline and Its Bleak Future." *Wall Street Journal,* December 19, 1983.

Freeman, Brian M., and Allan I. Mendelowitz. "Program in Search of a Policy: The Chrysler Loan Guarantee." *Journal of Policy Analysis and Management,* Summer 1982.

Freeman, Richard B., and Medoff, James L. *What Do Unions Do?* New York: Basic Books, 1984.

French, Peter A. *Collective and Corporate Responsibility.* New York: Columbia University Press, 1984.

Freud, Sigmund. *New Introductory Lectures on Psychoanalysis.* New York: Norton, 1933.

Freudberg, David. *The Corporate Conscience: Money, Power, and Responsible Business.* New York: AMACOM, 1986.

Freund, Jack. Statement in *Regulation of Medical Devices Intrauterine, Contraceptive Devices. Hearings before a Subcommittee of the Committee on Government Opera-*

tions, *House of Representatives*, 93rd Congress, First Session, June 12, 1973.

Friedman, Milton. *Capitalism and Freedom*. Chicago: University of Chicago Press, 1962.

———."The Social Responsibility of Business Is to Increase Its Profits." *New York Times Magazine*, September 13, 1970.

———."Does Business Have A Social Responsibility?" *Bank Administration*, April 1971.

FTC v. Consolidated Foods Corp. (Gentry Inc.), (U.S. S. Ct. 1965) 1965 *Trade Cases*, Par. 71, 432.

FTC v. Procter & Gamble Co., (The) (U.S. S. Ct. 1967) 1967 *Trade Cases*, Par. 72, 061.

FTC v. Reynolds Metal Co., (U.S. S. Ct. 1962) 1962 *Trade Cases*, Par. 70, 741.

Fullerton, Kemper. "Calvinism and Capitalism." *The Harvard Theological Review*, 1928.

Fullilove v. Klutznick, 448 U.S. 448, 100 S. Ct. 2758 (1980).

Fullinwider, Robert K. *The Reverse Discrimination Controversy: A Moral and Legal Analysis*. Totowa, N.J.: Rowman and Littlefield, 1980.

Galambos, Louis. *The Public Image of Big Business in America, 1880–1940*. Baltimore: Johns Hopkins University Press, 1975.

Galbraith, John Kenneth. *The Affluent Society*. Boston: Houghton Mifflin, 1958.

———.*The New Industrial State*. Boston: Houghton Mifflin, 1967.

———. *Economics and the Public Purpose*. Boston: Houghton Mifflin, 1973.

———."The Defense of the Multinational Company." *Harvard Business Review*, March–April 1978.

———. Letter to the Editor. *Wall Street Journal*, August 14, 1979.

Gallup, George. "Smoking Level Declines as More Perceive Health Hazard," *The Gallup Poll*, August 31, 1981.

Gallup, George H., ed. *The Gallup Poll: Public Opinion 1935–1971*. 3 vols. New York, Random House, 1972.

Gallup Organization. *The U.S. Public's Attitudes toward Organ Transplants/Organ Donation*. Princeton, N.J.: The Gallup Organization, April 1986.

Gallup Report. Affirmative Action. Princeton, N.J.: The Gallup Organization, May 1984.

Garb, Gill, ed. *Traveler's Guide to Central and Southern Africa*. London: IC Magazines Ltd., 1981.

Garrett, Thomas M. *Business Ethics*. New York: Appleton-Century-Crofts, 1966.

Geipel, Gary. "Asbestos Lawsuits Paralyzed House Panel Told." *Los Angeles Times*, February 11, 1983.

Geneen, Harold S. "Why Directors Can't Protect the Shareholders." *Fortune*, September 17, 1984.

Gest, Ted. "Fair-Pay Drive by Women Hits a Legal Detour." *U.S. News & World Report*, September 16, 1985.

Gettinger, Stephen. "Liability Insurance Squeeze Spurs Pleas to Hill for Relief." *Congressional Quarterly*, January 25, 1986.

Gibson, Mary. *Workers' Rights*. Totowa, N.J.: Roman & Allanheld, 1983.

Gilbert, Dennis, and Joseph A. Kahl. *The American Class Structure: A New Synthesis*. Homewood, Ill.: Dorsey, 1982.

Gilder, George. *Wealth and Poverty*. New York: Basic Books, 1981.

———."Women in the Work Force." *The Atlantic Monthly*, September 1986.

Gillespie, Norman C. "The Business of Ethics." *University of Michigan Business Review*, November 1975.

Glasscock, C.B. *The War of the Copper Kings: Builders of Butte and Wolves of Wall Street*. New York: Grosset & Dunlap, 1935.

Glines, C.V. "Deregulation: The Bomb that Exploded." *Air Line Pilot*, November 1983.

Gordon, David. "To Have and Have Not." *Washington Post National Weekly Edition*, November 10, 1986.

Gordon, David M. "Concentrated Wealth Poses Threat." *Los Angeles Times*, August 5, 1986.

Gottschalk, Earl C., Jr. "Firms Hiring New Type of Manager to Study Issues, Emerging Troubles." *Wall Street Journal*, June 10, 1982.

Green, Mark, and John F. Berry. *The Challenge of Hidden Profits: Reducing Corporate Bureaucracy and Waste*. New York: Morrow, 1985.

Green, Robert W., ed. *Protestantism and Capitalism: The Weber Thesis and Its Critics*. Boston: D.C. Heath, 1959.

Greene, Richard, "Selling Dirt." *Forbes*, May 24, 1982.

Greenewalt, Crawford, H. *The Uncommon Man*. New York: McGraw-Hill, 1959.

Greenman v. Yuba Power Products, Inc., 377 P. Cal. 2d 897 (1963).

Greenwald, John. "A Hard Day's Night." *Time*, August 1, 1983.

Griggs v. Duke Power Company, 401, U.S. 424, 1971.

Griswold v. Connecticut, 381 U.S. 479 (1965).

Guiles, Melinda G., and Paul Ingrassia. "Ford's Leaders Push Radical Shift in Culture as Competition Grows." *Wall Street Journal*, December 3, 1985.

Gunn, Alastair S. "Why Should We Care about Rare Species?" *Environmental Ethics*, Spring 1980.

Gunter, Robert, and Joanne Lipman. "Construction Industry in New York Is Hotbed of Extortion, Bribery." *Wall Street Journal*, May 7, 1986.

Gutek, Barbara A. *Sex and the Workplace*. San Francisco: Jossey-Bass, 1985.

Guzzardi, Walter, Jr. "How Much Should Companies Talk?" *Fortune*, March 4, 1985.

Hacker, Andrew. "Women vs. Men in the Work Force." *New York Times Magazine*, December 9, 1984.

Hacker, Louis M. *The World of Andrew Carnegie*. Philadelphia: Lippincott, 1968.

Hamilton, Alexander, James Madison, and John Jay. *The Federalist Papers*. Reprint. Edited by Clinton Rossiter. New York: New American Library, 1961. Originally published in 1787 and 1788.

Handler, Edward, and John R. Mulkern. *Business in Politics*. Lexington, Mass: Lexington Books, 1982.

Hansen, Hugh J., Samuel P. Caudill, and Joe Boone. "Crisis in Drug Testing: Results of CDC Blind Study." *Journal of the American Medical Association*, vol. 253 April 26, 1985.

Hardin, Clifford M., Kenneth A. Shepsle, and Barry R. Weingast. *Public Policy Excesses: Government by Congressional Subcommittee*. St. Louis: Washington University Center for the Study of American Business, September 1982.

Harris, Daniel. "Religious Models for Ethical Managerial Decision Making." Paper presented to the Western Academy of Management, Monterey, California, April 1981.

Harris, Louis, "Public United in Concern about Environment." *Common Cause*, June 1982.

Hartley, Fred L. "Oil Company Takeover and the Future of the Petroleum Industry." Speech before the Joint Annual Conference of the National Association of Petroleum Investment Analysts and the Petroleum Investor Relations Association, Colorado Springs, Colorado, September 20, 1985.

Harvard Law Review. "Plaintiffs' Conduct as a Defense to Claims Against Cigarette Manufacturers." November 1985.

Havemann, Judith. "Here's How You Get OMB's Attention—Cut Off Its Funds." *The Washington Post National Weekly Edition*, June 2, 1986.

Hay, Robert, and Ed Gray, "Social Responsibilities of Business Managers." *Academy of Management Journal*, March 1974.

Hayden, Tom. *The American Future: New Visions Beyond the Reagan Administration*. New York: Washington Square Press, 1982.

Hayek, Friedrich A. *The Road to Serfdom*. Chicago: University of Chicago Press, 1944.

Hayes, Holly. "Dow Withdraws CMU Grants." *The Saginaw News*, October 29, 1977.

Hayes, Robert H. "Why Japanese Factories Work." *Harvard Business Review*, July–August 1981.

Haymaker, George T., Jr. Testimony in *Acid Deposition Control Act of 1986 (Part 2)*. *Hearings before the Subcommittee on Health and the Environment of the Committee on Energy and Commerce. U.S. House of Representatives*, 99th Congress, 2nd Session, May 1, 1986.

Heald, Morrel. *The Social Responsibility of Business: Company and Community, 1900–1960*. Cleveland: The Press of Case Western Reserve University, 1970.

Hearst, William Randolph, Jr. "Editor's Report: A Cautious Approach to Chrysler." *Los Angeles Herald Examiner*, August 19, 1979.

Heenan, David A. *The Re-United States of America*. Reading, Mass.: Addison-Wesley Publishing Co., 1983.

Heins, John. "It's Not as Much Fun." *Forbes*, November 17, 1986.

Henningsen v. Bloomfield Motors, Inc., 32 N.J. 358, 161 A. 2d 69 (1960).

Herman, Edward S. *Corporate Control, Corporate Power: A Twentieth Century Fund Study*. Cambridge: Cambridge University Press, 1981.

Hickox, Bob. "Miller Restrains the FTC Bully.'" *The Wharton Magazine*, Spring 1982.

Hicks, John D., *The Populist Revolt*. Minneapolis: University of Minnesota Press, 1931.

Hilton, George. *The Transportation Act of 1958*. Bloomington, Indiana University Press, 1969.

Hobson, J.A. *Free-Thought in the Social Sciences*. London: George Allen & Unwin, 1926.

Hodges, Laurent. *Environment Pollution*. 2nd ed. New York: Holt, Rinehart and Winston, 1977.

Hoerr, John. "Beyond Unions." *Business Week*, July 8, 1985.

Hofstadter, Richard. "The Pervasive Influence of Social Darwinism." In *The Robber Barons: Saints or Sinners?* ed. Thomas B. Brewer. New York: Holt, Rinehart and Winston, 1970.

Hogner, Robert. "Managing Ethics Systems." Paper presented at the Academy of Management Meetings, Chicago, Illinois, August 1986.

Holbrook, Stewart H. *Lost Men of American History*. New York: Macmillan, 1948.

Hollings, Ernest F. Comments in *Hearings before the Subcommittee on Surface Transportation of the Committee on Commerce, Science, and Transportation, United States Senate*, April 29, 1985.

Holmes, Sandra L. "Structural Responses of Large Corporations to a Social Responsibility Ethic." *Proceedings of the Academy of Management*, Orlando, Fla., August 1977.

Horn, Patrice D., and Jack C. Horn. *Sex in the Office*. Reading, Mass.: Addison-Wesley, 1982.

Horney, Karen. *Neurosis and Human Growth: The Struggle toward Self-Realization*. New York: Norton, 1950.

House, Charles. Interview by John F. Steiner, August 16, 1979.

Houser, Theodore V. *Big Business and Human Values.* New York: McGraw-Hill, 1957.

Howard, Niles. "What Price Safety? The Zero Risk Debate." *Dun's Review,* September 1979.

Hunter, Floyd. *Top Leadership, U.S.A.* Chapell Hill: University of North Carolina Press, 1959.

Huntington, Samuel. *Political Order in Changing Societies.* New Haven: Yale University Press, 1968.

Hurd, Sandra N. "Use of the Polygraph in Screening Job Applicants." *American Business Law Journal,* Winter 1985.

Hutchings, Dexter. "The Drive to Kick Smoking at Work." *Fortune,* September 15, 1986.

Iacocca, Lee A. "The Rescue and Resuscitation of Chrysler." *Journal of Business Strategy,* Summer 1983.

———. *Iacocca: An Autobiography.* New York: Bantam Books, 1984.

———. Prepared remarks at a *Hearing on the Federal Trade Commission and GM-Toyota Decisions' Effect on the U.S. Auto Industry before the Subcommittee on Commerce, Transportation and Tourism of the House Committee on Energy and Commerce,* U.S. Congress, February 8, 1984.

Industrial Union Department, AFL-CIO v. American Petroleum Institute, 65 L Ed. 2d. 1010 (1980).

International Advertising Association. *Tobacco Advertising Bans and Consumption in 16 Countries.* New York: IAA, 1983.

Jackson, Brooks. "Interest Groups Pay Millions in Appearance Fees to Get Legislators to Listen as Well as to Speak." *Wall Street Journal,* June 4, 1985.

Jackson, Jesse L. "The Founders' Message." *1986 Operation PUSH Souvenir Journal.* Chicago: Operation PUSH, 1986.

Jackson, Stewart. "Union Carbide's Good Name Takes a Beating." *Business Week,* December 31, 1984.

Jackson, Stewart, and Harris Collingwood. *"Business Week/Harris Poll: Is An Antibusiness Backlash Building?" Business Week,* July 20, 1987.

Jacobs, Sanford L. "Firms Find Harsh Provisions in Hazardous-Waste Statutes." *Wall Street Journal,* September 12, 1983.

Jacobs, Theodore J. "The Future of the Consumer Movement." In *Business and Its Changing Environment,* ed. George A. Steiner. Los Angeles: University of California at Los Angeles, Graduate School of Management, 1979.

Jacobson, Michael, Robert Atkins, and George Hacker. *The Booze Merchants: The Inebriating of America.* Washington, D.C.: Center for the Study of Science in the Public Interest, 1983.

Jacoby, Neil H. *Corporate Power and Social Responsibility.* New York: Macmillan, 1973.

Jain, Subhash C. "Environmental Scanning in U.S. Corporations." *Long Range Planning,* April 1984.

Janger, Allen R. *The Personnel Function: Changing Objectives and Organization.* New York: The Conference Board, 1977.

Jardim, Anne. *The First Henry Ford: A Study in Personality and Business Leadership.* Cambridge, Mass.: The MIT Press, 1970.

Jet. "Ex-Miss America Endures Pain, Embarassment Sparked by Flap Over Nude Pictures." *Jet,* August 6, 1984.

Jennings, Kathy, and James Reindl. "Abel Silent about Amount of Dow Gifts, Grants to CMU." *Central Michigan Life,* October 31, 1977a.

———. "Dow Cancels Aid to CMU." *Central Michigan Life,* October 28, 1977b.

John, Kenneth E. "Defining the Power Elite." *Washington Post National Weekly Edition,* April 23, 1984.

———. "A Feeling of Powerlessness." *Washington Post National Weekly Edition,* September 9, 1985.

Johnson, E.A.J., and Herman E. Kroos. *The Origins and Development of the American Economy.* New York: Prentice-Hall, 1953.

Johnson, Elmer W. "General Motors Corporation, Its Constituencies and the Public Interest." *Journal of Business Ethics,* vol. 5, 1986.

Johnson, Harry J. *Executive Life Styles.* New York: Thomas Y. Crowell, 1974.

Jones, Reginald H. "Challenges to Business Leadership." *The Wharton Magazine,* Fall 1978.

———. "Preparing for a Future in Management." Speech to the Finance Club of the Harvard Graduate School of Business. Cambridge, Mass., November 2, 1978.

———. "Managing in the 1980's." Address to the Wharton School of Business, University of Pennsylvania, February 4, 1980.

Josephson, Matthew. *The Robber Barons: The Great American Capitalists: 1861–1901.* New York: Harcourt, Brace & World, 1934.

Kahn, Alfred E. "Deregulation of Air Transportation: Getting from Here to There." In *Regulating Business: The Search for an Optimum,* Donald P. Jacobs, ed. San Francisco: Institute for Contemporary Studies, 1978.

Kamata, Satoshi. "Employee Welfare Takes a Back Seat at Toyota." *Business and Society Review,* Summer 1983.

Kant, Immanuel. *Foundations of the Metaphysics of Morals.* Reprinted. Translated by Lewis White Beck. Indianapolis: Bobbs-Merrill Educational Publishing, 1969 (Originally published in 1785).

Kanter, Rosabeth Moss. *The Change Masters.* New York: Simon & Schuster, 1983.

Kappel, Frederick R. *Vitality in a Business Enterprise.* New York: McGraw-Hill, 1960.

Karis, Thomas G. "South African Liberation: The Communist Factor." *Foreign Affairs,* Winter 1986/87.

Kaye, Marvin. *A Toy Is Born.* New York: Stein and Day, 1973.

Kazis, Richard, and Richard L. Grossman. "Environmental Protection, Job-Taker or Job-Maker?" *Environment,* November 1982.

Keim, Gerald D. "New Directions for Corporate Political Strategy." *Sloan Management Review,* Spring 1984.

———. "Corporate Grassroots Programs in the 1980s." *California Management Review,* Fall 1985.

Keim, Gerald D., Barry D. Baysinger, and Roger E. Meiners. "The Corporate Democracy Act: Would the Majority Rule?" *Business Horizons,* March–April 1981.

Kelly, James. "Manville's Bold Maneuver." *Time,* September 6, 1982.

Kelman, Steven. "Cost-Benefit Analysis: An Ethical Critique." *Regulation,* January/February 1981.

Kendrick, John W. "International Comparisons of Recent Productivity Trends." In *Quality and Productivity Improvements: U.S. and Foreign Company Experiences,* ed. Y. Krishna Shetty and Vernon Buehler. Chicago: Manufacturing Productivity Center, 1983.

Kennedy, Christopher. "Criminal Sentences for Corporations: Alternative Fining Mechanisms." *California Law Review,* March 1985.

Keppel, Bruce. "Monsanto Embracing New Fields." *Los Angeles Times,* November 19, 1984.

Kerbo, Harold R. *Social Stratification and Inequality: Class Conflict in the United States.* New York: McGraw-Hill, 1983.

Kirkland, Richard I., Jr. "Exxon Redicates Itself to Oil." *Fortune,* July 23, 1984.

Kitch, Edmund W. "Vaccines and Product Liability." *Regulation,* May/June 1985.

Klein, Katherine J. "Employee Ownership." *New Management,* Spring 1986.

Kneale, Dennis. "Firms with Ties to South Africa Strike back at Colleges that Divest." *Wall Street Journal,* December 10, 1986.

Koenig, Frederick. "Today's Conditions Make U.S. 'Ripe for the Rumor Mill.'" *U.S. News & World Report,* December 6, 1982.

Kohlberg, Lawrence. "State and Sequence: The Cognitive Developmental Approach to Socialization." In *Handbook of Socialization Theory and Research,* ed. D.A. Gosline. Chicago: Rand-McNally, 1969.

Konrad, Armin Richard. "Business Managers and Moral Sanctuaries." *Journal of Business Ethics,* August 1982.

Kooi, Cynthia. "War Toy Invasion Grows Despite Boycott." *Advertising Age,* March 3, 1986.

Korn/Ferry International. *Board of Directors. Thirteenth Annual Study.* New York: Korn/Ferry International, February 1986.

———. *International Executive Profile: A Survey of Corporate Leaders in the Eighties.* New York: Korn/Ferry International, October 1986.

Kristof, Nicholas D. "Multinationals, Once Shunned, Now Welcomed." *New York Times,* May 10, 1985.

LaFranchi, Howard. "Boom in War Toys Linked to TV." *Christian Science Monitor,* January 7, 1986.

Lamb, David. *The Africans.* New York: Random House, 1982.

Lammers, Nancy, ed. *The Washington Lobby.* 4th ed. Washington D.C.: Congressional Quarterly Press, 1982.

Larson v. General Motors Corporation, 391F. 2d 495 8th Cir. (1968).

Lave, Lester B. *The Strategy of Social Regulation: Decision Frameworks for Policy.* Washington, D.C. The Brookings Institution, 1981.

Law, Warren A. "Management versus the Wild Bunch." *Across the Board,* June 1985.

Lawn, John C. "Drugs in America: Our Problem, Our Solution." *Vital Speeches of the Day,* March 15, 1986.

Leibman, Jordan. "Liability for the Unknowable." *Business Horizons,* July/August 1983.

Lenz, R.T., and J.L. Engledow. "Environmental Analysis Units and Strategic Decision-Making: Field Study of Selected 'Leading Edge' Corporations." *Strategic Management Journal,* January–February 1986.

———. "Environmental Analysis: The Applicability of Current Theory." *Strategic Management Journal,* July–August 1986.

Leonard, William N. "Airline Deregulation: Grand Design or Gross Debacle?" *Journal of Economic Issues,* June 1983.

Leopold, Aldo. *A Sand County Almanac.* New York: Ballantine, 1970.

Lerman, Louis. *Michelangelo: A Renaissance Profile.* New York: Knopf, 1942.

Levinson, Harry. *Executive.* Cambridge, Mass.: Harvard University Press, 1981.

Levitan, Sar A., and Martha R. Cooper. *Business Lobbies.* Baltimore: Johns Hopkins University Press, 1984.

Levitt, Theodore. "The Dangers of Social Responsibility." *Harvard Business Review,* September–October 1958.

Levy, Robert. "Tilting at the Rumor Mill." *Dun's Review,* July 1981.

Lewis, Jack. "Ohio Utility Takes a Giant Environmental Step." *EPA Journal,* July/August 1985.

Leys, John Albert. *Ethics for Policy Decisions.* Englewood Cliffs, N.J.: Prentice-Hall, 1952.

Lichter, Linda S. "Who Speaks for Black America?" *Public Opinion,* August/September 1985.

Lindblom, Charles E. *Politics and Markets.* New York: Basic Books, 1977.

Lindell, Erik. "Foreign Policy Export Controls and MNCs." *California Management Review,* Summer 1986.

Lipset, Seymour Martin, and William Schneider. "How's Business? What the Public Thinks." *Public Opinion,* July–August 1978.

———. *The Confidence Gap: Business, Labor, and Government in the Public Mind.* New York: Free Press, 1983.

Lloyd, Henry Demarest. *Wealth against Commonwealth.* New York: Harpers, 1896.

Local 28 of the Sheet Metal Workers' International Association v. Equal Employment Opportunity Commission et al. 54 LW 4984 (1986).

Local Number 93, International Association of Firefighters, AFL-CIO C.L.C., Petitioner v. City of Cleveland et al. 54 LW 5005 (1986).

Locke, John. *The Second Treatise of Government.* Reprint. Edited by Thomas P. Reardon. Indianapolis: Bobbs-Merril, 1952. Originally published in 1691.

Lockner v. New York, 198 U.S. 45 (1905).

Lowrance, William W. *Of Acceptable Risk.* Los Altos, Calif.: William Kaufmann, 1976.

Lueck, Miriam Simons. *Fields of Work for Women.* New York: D. Appleton, 1929.

Lumsden, Charles J., and Edward O. Wilson. *Genes, Mind, and Culture: The Coevolutionary Process.* Cambridge: Harvard University Press, 1981.

Lundberg, Ferdinand. *The Rich and the Super-Rich.* New York: Lyle Stewart, 1968.

Lykken, David T., "Polygraphic Interrogation." *Nature,* February 23, 1984.

Lytle, Alice. "Human Rights Abuses and Foreign Policy Are Everybody's Business." *The Corporate Examiner,* June 1982.

McBee, Susan. "Morality: The State of American Values." *U.S. News & World Report,* December 9, 1985.

McCoy, Charles S. *Management of Values: The Ethical Difference in Corporate Policy and Performance.* Marshfield, Mass.: Pitman, 1985.

McCracken, Paul W. "Light at the End of the Budget Tunnel." *The Wall Street Journal,* March 19, 1985.

McFarland, Andrew S. *Common Cause: Lobbying in the Public Interest.* Chatham, N.J.: Chatham House, 1984.

McGinnis, Kathleen, and James McGinnis. *Parenting for Peace and Justice.* Maryknoll, N.Y.: Orbis Books, 1983.

McGuire, E. Patrick. *The Product-Safety Function: Orga-nization and Operations.* New York: The Conference Board, 1979.

McGuire, Joseph W. "The Management of Retreat." *Business Horizons,* November/December 1981.

McMillan, Tom, "Why Canadians Worry about Acid Rain." *EPA Journal,* June/July 1986.

McNeil, Mary. *Environment and Health.* Washington, D.C.: Congressional Quarterly, 1981.

MacDougall, A. Kent. "Progress Is Harbinger of Inequality." *Los Angeles Times,* November 15, 1984.

MacIntyre, Alasdair. *After Virtue: A Study in Moral Theory.* South Bend, Indiana: University of Notre Dame Press, 1981.

MacPherson v. Buick Motor Company, 217 N.Y. 382, 111 N.E. 1050 (1916).

Machiavelli, Niccolo. *The Prince.* Reprint. Edited by T.G. Bergin. New York: Appleton-Century-Crofts, 1947. Written in 1513 and first published in 1532.

Magarrell, Jack. "Stockholders Reject Resolutions Aimed at Campus Communists." *The Chronicle of Higher Education,* June 25, 1979.

Magnet, Myron. "America's New Economy: Who Will Gain." *Fortune,* June 23, 1986.

———. "The Decline and Fall of Business Ethics." *Fortune,* December 8, 1986.

Main, Jeremy. "The Worsening Air Travel Mess." *Fortune,* July 7, 1986.

Malbin, Michael J., ed. *Money and Politics in the United States.* Chatham, N.J.: Chatham House, 1984.

Malott, Robert H. "Let's Restore Balance to Product Liability Law." *Harvard Business Review,* May–June 1983.

Manville Corporation. "Despite Strong Business, Litigation Forces Manville to File for Reorganization." Advertisement in *Los Angeles Times,* August 27, 1982.

———. "Manville's Assets are a Conspicuous Strength." Advertisement in *Forbes,* December 20, 1982.

———. "Today, Manville Can Operate Profitably Using Only Half Its Productive Capacity." Advertisement in *Business Week,* December 27, 1982.

———. *1985 Corporate Profile,* Manville Corporation, Denver, Colorado, 1985.

———. *Form 10-Q: Quarterly Report Under Section 13 or 15 (d) of the Securities Exchange Act of 1934.* Manville Corporation, Denver, Colorado. September 30, 1986.

Mason, Edward S. "The Current Status of the Monopoly Problems in the United States." *Harvard Law Review,* June 1949.

Mason, Jim, and Peter Singer. *Animal Factories.* New York: Crown, 1980.

Mazzolini, Renato. "Are State-Owned Enterprises Unfair Competition?" *California Management Review,* Winter 1980.

Mellon Bank. *Discover Total Resources: A Guide for Nonprofits.* Pittsburgh: Community Affairs Division, Mellon Bank, 1985.

Mendoza, Alicia. *The Effects of Exposure to Toys Conducive to Violence.* Unpublished doctoral dissertation, University of Miami, 1972.

Menninger, Karl. *The Vital Balance.* New York: Viking, 1963.

Meritor Savings Bank v. Mechelle Vinson, 54 LW 4703 (1986).

Micallef v. Miehle Co., 384 N.Y.S. 2d 115. Court of Appeals of New York, April 8, 1976.

Micou, Ann McKinstry. "The Invisible Hand at Work in Developing Countries." *Across the Board,* March 1985.

Milbrath, Lester W. *Environmentalists: Vanguard for a New Society.* Albany: State University of New York Press, 1984.

Mill, John Stuart. *Principles of Political Economy.* 5th ed. New York: D. Appleton, 1870.

———. *Utilitarianism.* Reprint. Edited by Mary Warnock. New York: New American Library, 1962. Originally published in 1863.

Miller, James C. III, George W. Douglas, and Terry Calvani. *Statement . . . concerning Proposed General Motors/Toyota Joint Venture.* Washington, D.C.: Federal Trade Commission, 1983.

Mills, C. Wright. *The Power Elite.* New York: Oxford University Press, 1956.

Millstein, Ira M., and Salem M. Katsh. *The Limits of Corporate Power.* New York: Macmillan, 1981.

Mintz, Beth. "The President's Cabinet, 1897–1972." *Insurgent Sociologist,* Fall 1975.

Mintz, Morton. *At Any Cost: Corporate Greed, Women, and the Dalkon Shield.* New York: Pantheon, 1985.

———. "A Crime Against Women: A. H. Robins and the Dalkon Shield." *Multinational Monitor,* January 15, 1986.

Mitchell, Cynthia F. "Manville's Bid to Evade Avalanche of Lawsuits Proves Disappointing." *Wall Street Journal,* July 15, 1986.

Mitchell, Daniel J. B. "The Share Economy and Industrial Relations: Implications of the Weitzman Proposal." Working Paper, series 99. Los Angeles: UCLA Institute of Industrial Relations, 1986.

Miyares, J. Raymond. "Controlling Health Hazards without Uncle Sam." *Technology Review,* July 1983.

Mobil Corporation. "Energy Solutions and Nonstarters: Where a Government Role Is Needed: Accent on Achievement." New York: Mobil, 1978.

The Mobilizer. "Resisting Rambo: Boycott War Toys." Fall 1985.

Monsanto Co. v. Kennedy. U.S. Court of Appeals Dis. Col. Circuit (1979).

Monsen, R. Joseph, Jr. *Modern American Capitalism: Ideologies and Issues.* Boston: Houghton Mifflin, 1963.

———. "The Social Attitudes of Management." In *Contemporary Management: Issues and Viewpoints,* ed. Joseph W. McGuire. Englewood Cliffs, N.J.: Prentice-Hall, 1974.

Monsen, R. Joseph Jr., and Kenneth D. Walters. *Nationalized Companies: A Threat to American Business.* New York: McGraw-Hill, 1983.

Monthly Labor Review. "Current Labor Statistics: Employment Data." June 1986.

Moore, G.E. *Principia Ethica.* Reprint. New York: Cambridge University Press, 1948.

Moore, H. Frazier, and Frank B. Kalupa. *Public Relations: Principles, Cases, and Problems.* Homewood, Ill.: Richard D. Irwin, 1985.

Morgan, Robin. "The Vanessa Williams Controversy." *Ms,* October 1984.

Moritz, Michael, and Barrett Seaman. *Going for Broke: The Chrysler Story.* New York: Doubleday, 1981.

Moskal, Brian S. "The Minneapolis Story: A Primer on Social Concern." *Industry Week,* August 10, 1981.

Mosley, Leonard. *Blood Relations: The Rise and Fall of the du Ponts of Delaware.* New York: Atheneum, 1980.

Mueller, Robert K. "Changes in the Wind in Corporate Governance." *Journal of Business Strategy,* Spring 1981.

Multinational Monitor. "Trouble in the Promised Land: An Interview with Jeremy Rifkin. February 28, 1986.

Murphy, Patrick E. "An Evolution: Corporate Social Responsiveness." *University of Michigan Business Review,* November 1978.

Murphy, Thomas A. Remarks at Business Roundtable Annual Meeting, New York, June 12, 1978.

Murray, Edwin A., Jr. "The Social Response Process in Commercial Banks: An Empirical Investigation." *Academy of Management Review,* July 1976.

NLRB v. Johns & Laughlin Steel Corp., 301 U.S. 1 (1937).

Nader, Ralph. *Unsafe at Any Speed.* New York: Pocket Books, 1966.

Nader, Ralph, Mark Green, and Joel Seligman. *Taming the Giant Corporation.* New York: Norton, 1976.

Naisbitt, John. *Megatrends: Ten New Directions Transforming Our Lives.* New York: Warner, 1982.

Naisbitt, John and Patricia Aburdene. *Re-inventing the Corporation.* New York. Warner, 1985.

Nash, Laura L. "Ethics without the Sermon." *Harvard Business Review,* November–December 1981.

National Association of Corporate Directors. *Evolution in the Boardroom.* NACD Corporate Director's Special Report Series, August 1978.

National Coal Association. *The Downward Trend in Sulfur Dioxide Emissions at Coal-Fired Electric Utilities.* NCA, 1986. *National Peace Education Bulletin.* vol. II, no. 3, February 1966.

National Journal. "Airline Financial Woes Prompt Consideration of Industry Regulation." October 8, 1983.

National Peace Education Bulletin. February 1966, vol. 2, no. 3.

Natural Resources Committee. *The Structure of the American Economy, Part 1, Basic Characteristics.* Washington, D.C.: U.S. Government Printing Office, 1939.

Neil, Alfred C. *Business Power and Public Policy.* New York: Praeger, 1981.

Newgren, Kenneth E., Arthur A. Rasher, and Margaret E. LaRoe. "An Empirical Investigation of the Relationship between Environmental Assessment and Corporate Performance." *Academy of Management Proceedings,* 1984.

Nolan, Joseph T. "Political Surfing When Issues Break." *Harvard Business Review,* January–February 1985.

Novak, Michael. "The Communitarian Individual in America." *The Public Interest,* Summer 1982.

Nozick, Robert. *Anarchy, State, and Utopia.* New York: Basic Books, 1974.

Nussbaum, Bruce. "The End of Corporate Loyalty?" *Business Week,* August 4, 1986.

O'Dell, J. H. "PUSH—A Force for Social Change and Spiritual Renewal." *Black America: A People Whose Time Has Come.* Chicago: Operation PUSH and Fashion Places Magazine, 1983.

Office of Technology Assessment. *Acid Rain and Transported Air Pollutants: Implications for Public Policy,* 98th Cong., 2d Sess. OTA-O-204, June 1984.

Oglesby, Catharine. *Business Opportunities for Women.* New York: Harper & Brothers, 1932.

Olson, Mancur. *The Rise and Decline of Nations.* New Haven: Yale University Press, 1982.

Ong, J. D. "Business Management: Taking a Broader Perspective." Speech at the Krannert Graduate School of Management, Purdue University, Lafayette, Indiana, August 23, 1983.

Operation PUSH. "Position Statement for the PUSH Religious Affairs Department." *1986 Operation PUSH Souvenir Journal.* Chicago: Operation PUSH 1986a.

———. "PUSH International Trade Bureau." *1986 Operation PUSH Souvenir Journal.* Chicago: Operation PUSH, 1986b.

Orme, Ted. "Washington Report." *Motor Trend,* September 1977.

Ornstein, Norman J., and Shirley Elder. *Interest Groups, Lobbying and Policymaking.* Washington, D.C.: Congressional Quarterly Press, 1978.

Ostrow, Ronald J. "Thurmond, of S. Carolina, Would Bar Tobacco Ads." *Los Angeles Times,* July 3, 1986.

Otis Engineering Corp. v. Clark, 688 S. W. 2d 307 (Tex 1983).

O'Toole, James. "What's ahead for the Business-Government Relationship." *Harvard Business Review,* March–April 1979, p. 98.

———. *Vanguard Management: Redesigning the Corporate Future.* New York: Doubleday, 1985.

Ott, Gerald, Benjamin B. Holder, and R. R. Langner. "Determinants of Mortality in an Industrial Population." *Journal of Occupational Medicine,* March 1976.

Ouchi, William. *Theory Z: How American Business Can Meet the Japanese Challenge.* Reading, Mass. Addison-Wesley, 1981.

Owen, David, "The Cigarette Companies: How They Get Away with Murder, Part II." *Washington Monthly,* March 1985.

———. "Where Toys Come From." *The Atlantic Monthly,* October 1986.

Packard, Vance. *The Hidden Persuaders.* New York: McKay, 1957.

———. *The Waste Makers.* New York: McKay, 1960.

Parker, Edwin B. "The Fifteen Commandments of Business." *Nation's Business,* June 5, 1924.

Pastin, Mark. *The Hard Problems of Management: Gaining the Ethics Edge.* San Francisco: Jossey-Bass, 1986.

Paul E. Johnson v. Transportation Agency, Santa Clara County, California, 55 LW 4379 (1987).

Peacock, James L. "Ethics, Economics and Society in an Evolutionary Perspective." In *The Ethical Basis of Economic Freedom,* ed. Ivan Hill. Chapel Hill, N.C.: American Viewpoint, 1976.

Peirce, Neal R., and Robert Guskind. "Job Training for Hard-Core Unemployed Continues to Elude the Government." *National Journal,* September 28, 1985.

Pennings, Johannes M. *Interlocking Directorates: Origins and Consequences of Connections among Organizations' Boards of Directors.* San Francisco: Jossey-Bass, 1980.

Pertschuk, Michael. "Dissenting Statement. GM/ Toyota Joint Venture." Washington, D.C.: Federal Trade Commission, December 22, 1983.

Peters, Thomas J., and Robert H. Waterman. *In Search of Excellence: Lessons from America's Best-Run Companies.* New York: Harper & Row, 1982.

Peters, Tom, and Nancy Auston. *A Passion for Excellence.* New York: Random House, 1985.

Petty v. United States, Eighth Circuit Court of Appeals (1984).

Phatak, Arvind D. *International Dimensions of Management*. Boston: Kent, 1983.

Pickens, T. Boone, Jr. "Takeovers and Mergers: A Function of the Free Market." *The Diary of Alpha Kappa Psi*, September 1986.

Pinchott, Gifford III. *Intrapreneuring*. New York: Harper & Row, 1985.

Pine, Art, and Amanda Bennet. "Pipeline Sanctions End: U.S. Trade Pact with Allies Is Seen as Small Step to Harder Line on East." *The Wall Street Journal*, November 15, 1982.

Pires, Mary Ann. "Texaco: Working with Public Interest Groups." *Public Relations Journal*, April 1983.

Plato. *The Republic*. Reprint. Translated by F.M. Cornford. New York: Oxford University Press, 1945.

Platzer, Linda Cardillo. *Annual Survey of Corporate Contributions, 1986 Edition*. Washington, D.C. The Conference Board 1986.

Polifroni, Mio. "Attitudes towards Children's Gun Play at Nursery School." Unpublished manuscript. Pasadena, Calif.: March 22, 1964. Mimeographed.

Pomerantz, Gary. "The NFL Title that Eludes Blacks." *Washington Post National Weekly Edition*, January 20, 1986.

Porter, Michael. *Competitive Strategy*. New York: Free Press, 1980.

Posadas de Puerto Rico Associates v. Tourism Co. of Puerto Rico, 54 LW 4956 (1986).

Posner, Barry Z., and Warren H. Schmidt. "Values and the American Manager: An Update." *California Management Review*, Spring 1984.

Powell, Gary N., Barry Z. Posner, and Warren Schmidt. "Women: The More Committed Managers?" *Management Review*, June 1985.

Pratt, Edmund T., Jr. "CEO: The Whole Man. Fame versus the Family." Interview by David Finn. *Across the Board*, December 1985.

Preston, Lee E., and James E. Post. *Private Management and Public Policy: The Principle of Public Responsibility*. Englewood Cliffs, N.J.: Prentice-Hall, 1975.

———. "Private Management and Public Policy." *California Management Review*, Spring 1981.

Public Affairs Research Group. *Public Affairs Offices and Their Functions: Summary of Survey Responses*. Boston: School of Management, Boston University, 1981.

Public Opinion. "Satisfaction with Work Remains High." August/September 1981.

Pugh v. See's Candies, Inc., 161 Cal. App. 3d, 311, 171 Cal. Rptr. 917 (1981).

Purcell, Theodore V. "Management and Affirmative Action in the Late Seventies." *Equal Rights and Industrial Relations*. Industrial Relations Research Association Series, 1977.

———. "Institutionalizing Business Ethics: A Case History." *Business & Professional Ethics Journal*, Winter 1985.

Quinn, Robert E. "Coping with Cupid: The Formation, Impact and Management of Romantic Relationships in Organizations." *Administrative Sciences Quarterly*, March 1977.

Quinn, Robert E., and Patricia L. Lees. "Attraction and Harassment: Dynamics of Sexual Politics in the Workplace." *Organization Dynamics*, Autumn 1984.

Raines, Lisa J., and Stephen P. Push. "Protecting Pregnant Workers," *Harvard Business Review*, May–June 1986.

Rand Research Review. "The Asbestos Tragedy: Costs and Compensation." Fall 1983.

Randolph, Eleanor. "What Cost a Life? EPA Asks Tacoma." *Los Angeles Times*, August 13, 1983.

Randy Knitwear v. American Cyanamid, 181 N.E. 2d 402, N.Y. (1962).

Rawls, John. *A Theory of Justice*. Cambridge Mass.: Harvard University Press, 1971.

Reagan, Tom. "Animal Rights, Human Wrongs." *Environmental Ethics*, Summer 1980.

Redburn, Tom. "Canada Retaliates with Duties on U.S. Products." *Los Angeles Times*, May 2, 1986.

Regents of University of California v. Bakke, 438 U.S. 265 (1978).

Reich, Charles A. *The Greening of America*. New York: Random House, 1970.

Reich, Robert B., and John D. Donahue. *New Deals: The Chrysler Revival and the American System*. New York: Times Books, 1985.

Reindl, James J. "Dow Chief: Fonda Abuses Free-Speech Right." *The Saginaw News*, November 4, 1977.

R. J. Reynolds Tobacco Company v. Federal Trade Commission, Docket No. 9206, June 26, 1986.

Ricklefs, Roger, "Public Gives Executives Low Marks for Honesty and Ethical Standards." *Wall Street Journal*, November 2, 1983.

Ricks, David A. *Big Business Blunders: Mistakes in Multinational Marketing*. Homewood, Ill.: Dow Jones-Irwin, 1983.

Rivera, Nancy. "Unocal Will Trim Capital Spending, Hartley Says." *Los Angeles Times*, June 3, 1985.

Rivera, Nancy, and Debra Whitefield. "Unocal Win May Dampen Takeovers." *Los Angeles Times*, May 22, 1985.

Roberts, Johnnie L. "Threatening Boycotts, Jesse Jackson's PUSH Wins Gains for Blacks." *Wall Street Journal*, July 21, 1982.

Roche, James M. "Understanding: The Key to Business-Government Cooperation." *Michigan Business Review*, March 1969.

Rockefeller, David. *Creative Management in Banking.* New York: McGraw-Hill, 1964.

Roe v. Wade, 410 U.S. 113 (1973).

Rohlich, Ted. "Safety Put in Hands of Employers." *Los Angeles Times,* February 20, 1986.

Rokeach, Milton. *The Nature of Human Values.* New York: Free Press, 1973.

Ross, Irwin. "PUSH Collides with Busch." *Fortune,* November 15, 1982.

Rossiter, Clinton, ed. *The Federalist Papers.* Reprint. New York: New American Library, 1961.

Rostow, W.W. "Business Cycles, Harvests, and Politics." *Journal of Economic History,* November 1941.

Roszak, Theodore. *The Making of a Counter Culture.* New York: Doubleday, 1969.

Rotary International v. Rotary Club of Duarte, 55 LW 4606 (1987).

Rowe, James L., Jr. "Big Firms' Sharing of Directors Studied." *Los Angeles Times,* April 23, 1978.

Rumelt, Richard P. *Strategy, Structure, and Economic Performance.* Boston: Graduate School of Business Administration, Harvard University, 1974.

Russell, Bertrand. *Why I Am Not a Christian.* New York: Simon & Schuster, 1957.

Rust, Edward B. "Ralph Nader—Friend of U.S. Capitalism." Speech before National Insurance Men's Meeting, Chicago, exerpted in *Los Angeles Times,* September 26, 1973.

Santa Clara County v. Southern Pac. Ry., 118 U.S. 394 (1886).

Schachter, Victor, and Thomas E. Geidt. "Cracking down on Drugs," *Across the Board,* November 1985.

Schattschneider, E.E. *The Semi-Sovereign People.* New York: Holt, Rinehart and Winston, 1960.

Schechter Poultry Corp. v. United States, 295 U.S. 495 (1935).

Schein, Edgard H. *Organizational Culture and Leadership.* San Francisco: Jossey-Bass, 1985.

Schell, Orville. *Modern Meat: Antibiotics, Hormones, and the Pharmaceutical Farm.* New York: Vintage, 1985.

Schell, Robert E., and Elizabeth Hall. *Developmental Psychology Today.* 4th ed. New York: Random House, 1983.

Schmidt, Warren H., and Barry Z. Posner. *Managerial Values and Expectations: The Silent Power in Personal and Organizational Life.* New York: American Management Associations, 1982.

Schneider, Phillip. Interview by John F. Steiner, July 19, 1979.

Scholle, Stephen R. "Acid Deposition and the Materials Damage Question." *Environment,* October 1983.

Schriftgiesser, Carl. *The Lobbyists.* Boston: Little, Brown, 1951.

Schultze, Charles L. *The Public Use of Private Interest.* Washington, D.C.: The Brookings Institution, 1977.

Schumacher, E. F. *Small Is Beautiful.* New York: Harper & Row, 1973.

Scotese, Peter G. "Fold up Those Golden Parachutes." *Harvard Business Review,* March–April, 1985.

Scott, Bruce R. "Can Industry Survive the Welfare State?" *Harvard Business Review,* September–October 1982.

Seibert, Donald V., and William Proctor. *The Ethical Executive.* New York: Simon & Schuster, 1984.

Selekman, Benjamin M. *A Moral Philosophy for Management.* New York: McGraw-Hill, 1959.

Sethi, S. Prakash, "A Conceptual Framework for Environmental Analysis of Social Issues and Evaluation of Business Response Patterns." *Academy of Management Review,* January 1979.

———. *Up Against the Corporate Wall,* 4th ed. Englewood, Cliffs, N.J.: Prentice-Hall, 1982.

———. "South Africa: Is There a Peaceful Path to Pluralism?" *Business and Society Review,* Spring 1986.

———. Nobuaki Namiki, and Carl L. Swanson. *The False Promise of the Japanese Miracle: Illusions and Realities of the Japanese Management System.* Boston: Pitman, 1984.

Seventy Six, May–June 1985.

Shack, William. "Why Black Business Development Is so Important." *1986 Operation PUSH Souvenir Journal.* Chicago: Operation PUSH, 1986.

Shanklin, William L. "Fortune 500 Dropouts." *Planning Review,* May 1986.

Shapiro, David. *Neurotic Styles.* New York: Basic Books, 1965.

Shapiro, Irving S. Remarks presented at the Southern Governors' Conference, San Antonio, Texas, August 29, 1977. *Across the Board,* January 1978.

———. *America's Third Revolution: Public Interest and the Private Role.* New York: Harper & Row, 1984.

Shaver, Phillip. "The Public Distrust." *Psychology Today,* October 1980.

Shaw, David. "Murdoch: Press Loves to Hate Him." *Los Angeles Times,* May 25, 1983.

Sherwood, Ben. "Probe of Bankruptcy Laws Pledged in Manville Case." *Los Angeles Times,* August 28, 1982.

Shipper, Frank, and Marianne M. Jennings. *Business Strategy for the Political Arena.* Westport, Conn.: Quorum Books, 1984.

Shorrock, Tim. "The Corporate Santa." *Multinational Monitor,* December 1983.

Shultz, George P. "Business and Public Policy: The Abrasive Interface." *Harvard Business Review,* November–December 1979.

Siegel, Ronald, Mahmoud A. Elsohly, Timothy Plowman, Philip Rury, and Reese T. Jones. "Cocaine in Herbal Tea." *Journal of the American Medical Association*, January 3, 1986.

Sigler, Andrew W. "Roundtable Reply," *New York Times*, December 27, 1981.

Simison, Robert L. "Thinking Small." *The Wall Street Journal*, August 29, 1986.

Simon, John G., Charles W. Powers, and Jon P. Gunnemann. *The Ethical Investor*. New Haven: Yale University Press, 1972.

Simon, Michael E. "Government Regulation: Adding up the Cost." *Journal of Contemporary Business*, vol. 9, no. 2, 1980.

Simons, Janet. "Coors Turns Boycotters into Buyers." *Advertising Age*, February 27, 1986.

Singer, James W. "Who Will Set the Standards for Groups that Set Industry Product Standards?" *National Journal*, May 3, 1980.

Singer, Peter. *Animal Liberation*. New York: Avon, 1975.

Sklar, Holly, ed. *Trilateralism: The Trilateral Commission and Elite Planning for World Management*. Boston: South End Press, 1980.

Skrycki, Cindy. "The Risky Business of Birth Control." *U.S. News and World Report*, June 26, 1986.

Sloan, Alfred P. *My Years with General Motors*. New York: Doubleday, 1963.

Smeltzer, Larry R., and Ben L. Kedia. "Knowing the Ropes: Organizational Requirements for Quality Circles." *Business Horizons*, July–August 1985.

Smith, Adam. *An Inquiry into the Nature and Causes of the Wealth of Nations* [1776]. Reprint. New York: Modern Library, 1967.

Smith, Robert Ellis. *Workrights*. New York: Dutton, 1983.

Smith, Tom W., and Paul Sheatsly. "American Attitudes toward Race Relations." *Public Opinion*, October/November 1984.

Smith v. Van Gorham, 488 A. 2d. 858 (Del. 1985).

Smolla, Rodney A. *Suing the Press*. New York. Oxford University Press, 1986.

Sobel, Lester A., ed. *Corruption in Business*. New York: Facts on File, 1977.

Sommers, Albert T., ed. *The Free Society and Planning*. New York: The Conference Board Record, 1975.

Sonnichsen, Charles. "Review of the Businessman in American Literature." *Business History Review*, Summer 1983.

Sowell, Thomas. *Ethnic America*. New York: Basic Books, 1981.

Spector, Arlen. Testimony in "Federal Subsidy of Amtrak." *Congressional Digest*, August–September 1985.

Spencer, Herbert. *Social Statics*. New York: Robert Schalkenbach Foundation, 1970. First published in 1850.

———. *The Man versus the State*. Reprint. London: Watts & Co., 1940. Originally published in 1884.

Springer, Marlin D., and Benny J. Gallaway. *The Distribution and Ecology of the Illinois Mud Turtle*. Bryan, Texas: LGL Ecological Research Associates, November 1979.

Standard & Poor's Coorporation. *Industry Surveys*. Vol. 1. New York: Standard & Poors, July 1986.

Stanford Research Institute. "Scenarios in Planning." Undated.

Staw, Barry M. "Organizational Psychology and the Pursuit of the Happy/Productive Worker." *California Management Review*, Summer 1986.

Steckmest, Francis W., ed. *Corporate Performance: The Key to Public Trust*. New York: McGraw-Hill, 1982.

Stein, Herbert. "Help Wanted: President, Must Have . . ." *Wall Street Journal*, August 14, 1979.

Steinbach, Carol. "Trapping Private Resources." *National Journal*, April 26, 1986.

Steiner, George A. *Government's Role in Economic Life*. New York: McGraw-Hill, 1953.

———. *Business and Society*. 2nd ed. New York: Random House, 1975.

———. *The New CEO*. New York: Macmillan, 1983.

Steiner, George A., John B. Miner, and Edmund R. Gray. *Management Strategy and Policy*. 3rd ed. New York: Macmillan, 1986.

Steiner, John F., and Stahrl W. Edmunds. "Economy-Ecology Conflict: Analysis, Examples, and Policy Approaches." In *Research in Corporate Social Performance and Policy*, ed. Lee E. Preston. Vol. 3. Greenwich, Conn.: JAI Press, 1981.

Steorts, Nancy Harvey. "Selling Safety: The Responsibility of the Consumer Product Safety Commission." Address to United States Council for International Business, Washington, D.C., April 15, 1983.

Stephenson, Donald R. "Crisis Situations: Opportunities in Work Clothes." *Vital Speeches*, March 1, 1983.

Steptoe, Sonja, "At A.H. Robins, Chapter 11 Is Part of the Daily Routine." *Wall Street Journal*, December 17, 1986.

Stewart, James B., and Laurie P. Cohen. "Golden Era for Raiders May Be Waning." *The Wall Street Journal*, May 22, 1985.

Stockman, David A. Testimony in *Hearings before the Subcommittee on Surface Transportation of the Committee on Commerce, Science, and Transportation, United States Senate*, April 29, 1985.

Stone, Christopher D. *Should Trees Have Standing?* Los Altos, Calif.: William Kaufmann, 1974.

———. "A Slap on the Wrist for the Kepone Mob." *Business and Society Review*, Summer 1977.

Strenski, J. B. "How to Communicate with Minorities." *Public Relations Journal*, July 1976.

Struck, Myron. "Deaver Probe Revives Doubts about 'Revolving Door' Ethics." *Insight,* June 9, 1986.

Stuart, Reginald. "GM Chief Opposes U.S. Aid to Chrysler: It Challenges American Philosophy." *Los Angeles Herald-Examiner,* August 3, 1979.

Sturdivant, Frederick D., and James L. Ginter. "Corporate Social Responsibilities: Management Attitudes and Economic Performance." *California Management Review,* Spring 1977.

Sturdivant, Frederick D., James L. Ginter, and Alan G. Sawyer. "Managers' Conservatism and Corporate Performance." *Strategic Management Journal,* January–March 1985.

Sullivan, Leon H. *The (Sullivan) Statement of Principles: Fourth Amplification.* Philadelphia: International Council for Equality of Opportunity Principles, November 8, 1984.

Sumitomo Shoji America, Inc. v. Avigliano, 102, SCT. 2374 (1982).

Super, Tom, "Special Envoy, Special Task: An Interview with Drew Lewis." *EPA Journal,* June/July 1986.

Sutton, Charlotte Decker, and Kris K. Moore. "Executive Women—20 Years Later." *Harvard Business Review,* September–October 1985.

Sutton, Francis X., Seymour E. Harris, Carl Kaysen, and James Tobin. *The American Business Creed.* Cambridge, Mass.: Harvard University Press, 1956.

Swartz, Edward M. *Toys that Don't Care.* Boston: Gambit Inc., 1971.

Tennessee Valley Authority v. Hill, 437 U.S. 153 (1978).

Taylor, Peter. *The Smoke Ring: Tobacco, Money, and Multinational Politics.* Rev. ed. New York: New American Library, 1985.

The Economist. "Pipelines Asunder." September 4, 1982.

Tobin, James. "Unemployment, Poverty and Economic Policy." *America,* May 4, 1985.

Time, "Iacocca's Tightrope Act." March 21, 1983.

Toffler, Alvin. *Future Shock.* New York: Random House, 1970.

———. *The Third Wave.* New York: Bantam, 1980.

Tolchin, Susan J., and Martin Tolchin. *Dismantling America: The Rush to Deregulate.* New York: Oxford University Press, 1983.

Toufexis, Anastasia. "A Cloudy Forecast for Smokers." *Time,* April 7, 1986.

Toy, Stewart. "The Raiders." *Business Week,* March 4, 1985.

Trainor, George E. Letter to George Steiner, September 15, 1986.

Trost, Cathy. "The New Majorities." *Wall Street Journal,* March 24, 1986.

Tuerck, David G. "Fair Pay for Women: Comparable Worth or Incomparable Work?" Speech before the Federalist Society, Boston University Law School, Boston, Mass., March 25, 1986.

Tunstall, W. Brooke. "The Breakup of the Bell System." *California Management Review,* Winter 1986.

Turner, Charles W., and Diane Goldsmith. "Effects of Toy Guns and Airplanes on Children's Anti-Social Free Play Behavior." *Journal of Experimental Child Psychology,* April 1976.

Tutu, Desmond M. "Sanctions against Apartheid: Which Side Are You On?" *The Corporate Examiner,* 1986, vol. 15, no. 5.

Ukarish v. Magnesium Elektron et al. 31 FEP 1314 (1983).

United Nations Economic and Social Council, Special Intersessional Committee. *The Impact of Transnational Corporations on the Development Process and on International Relations,* New York, 1975.

U.S. Catholic Conference. *Pastoral Letter on Catholic Social Teaching and the U.S. Economy.* Washington, D.C.: United States Catholic Conference, 1986.

U.S. Commission on Federal Paperwork. *Final Summary Report.* Washington, D.C., 1977.

U.S. Congress. House Committee on Labor. *An Investigation Relating to Health Conditions of Workers Employed in the Construction and Maintenance of Public Utilities.* 74th Cong. 2d sess. January 16–29, 1936.

U.S. Congress. Senate. *Emergency Loan Guarantee Legislation, Hearings before the Committee on Banking, Housing and Urban Affairs,* S. 1567, S. 1641, 92nd Cong., 1st sess., 1971.

U.S. Council on Wage and Price Stability. *Catalogue of Federal Regulations Affecting the Iron and Steel Industry.* Washington, D.C.: U.S. Government Printing Office, December 1976.

U.S. Department of Commerce. *Business and Society: Strategies for the 1980s.* Report of the Task Force on Corporate Social Performance. Washington, D.C.: U.S. Government Printing Office, December 1980.

U.S. Department of Health, Education, and Welfare. *Smoking and Health: Report of the Advisory Committee to the Surgeon General of the Public Health Service.* Washington, D.C.: U.S. Government Printing Office, 1964.

U.S. v. Addystone Pipe and Steel Company, 175 U.S. 211 (1899).

U.S. v. Aluminum Co., of America, 148 F. 2nd 416 (1945).

U.S. v. American Can Co., 230 Fed 859 (1916).

U.S. v. American Tobacco Co., 211 U.S. 106 (1911).

U.S. v. American Tobacco Co. et al., 328 U.S. 781 (1946).

U.S. v. Appalachian Coals, Inc., 288 U.S. 344 (1933).

U.S. v. Arnold, Schwinn & Co., (U.S. S. Ct. 1967) 1967 Trade Cases, Par. 72, 126.

U.S. v. Brown Shoe Co., Inc., 370 U.S. 294 (1962).

U.S. v. Columbia Steel Co., 335 U.S. 495 (1948).

U.S. v. E.C. Knight Co., 156 U.S. 1 (1895).

U.S. v. General Dynamics Corp., 415 U.S. 486 (1974).

U.S. v. Grinnell Corp., 384 U.S. 563 (1966).

U.S. v. International Harvester Co., 247 U.S. 643 (1927).

U.S. v. Northern Pacific R. R. Co., 356 U.S. 1 (1958).

U.S. v. Paramount Pictures, Inc., 334 U.S. 131 (1948).

U.S. v. Phillip Paradise, Jr., 55 LW 4211 (1937).

U.S. v. Standard Oil Co., 221 U.S. 1 (1911).

U.S. v. Standard Oil Company of New Jersey, 221 U.S. 417 (1920).

U.S. v. Trenton Potteries Co., 273 U.S. 392 (1927).

U.S. v. United States Steel Corporation, 221 U.S. 417 (1920).

U.S. News & World Report, "Corporate Crime: The Untold Story." September 5, 1983.

U.S. News & World Report, "Paying the Price of Cheaper Airline Fares." March 5, 1984.

U.S. News & World Report, "Who Runs America: A National Survey," April 22, 1974.

U.S. News & World Report, "We Want to Work With Companies, Not against Them, June 3, 1985.

U.S. News & World Report, "Who Runs America: 10th Annual Survey, May 23, 1983.

U.S. News & World Report, "Who Runs America: 12th Annual Survey, May 20, 1985.

U.S. News & World Report, "Your Hamburger: 41,000 Regulations," February 11, 1980.

United Steelworkers of America v. Bryan F. Weber., 443 U.S. 193 (1979).

Unocal Corp. v. Mesa Petroleum Co., (1985).

Useem, Michael. *The Inner Circle*. New York: Oxford University Press, 1984.

Velasquez, Manuel G. *Business Ethics: Concepts and Cases*. Englewood Cliffs, N.J.: Prentice-Hall, 1982.

———. "Why Corporations Are not Morally Responsible for Anything They Do." *Business & Professional Ethics Journal*, Spring 1983.

Verity, C. William, Jr. "Multiplication by Division: An Organic View of the Changing Role of the Board Chairman in Corporate Governance." *University of Michigan Business Review*, January 1979.

Vernon, Raymond. *Storm over the Multinationals: The Real Issues*. Cambridge, Mass.: Harvard University Press, 1977.

Viner, Jacob. "Adam Smith and Laissez Faire." *Journal of Political Economy*, April 1927.

Virginia Pharmacy Board v. Virginia Citizens Consumer Council, Inc. 425 U.S. 748 (1976).

Vise, David A. "Wall Street's Scandal Goes Upstairs." *Washington Post National Weekly Edition*, March 2, 1987.

Vogel, David. "A Funny Thing Happened to the Down-with Big Business Movement." *Across the Board*, December 1980.

Wagner, Aubrey J. "Tellico Power." *U.S. News & World Report*, October 1, 1979.

Walker, Matthew. "The Cost of Doing Business in South Africa." *Multinational Monitor*, April 15, 1986.

Wall Street Journal, "African Farewell," October 22, 1986.

Walsh, Sharon W. "Confronting Sexual Harassment at Work." *Washington Post*, July 21, 1986.

Warner-Lambert v. FTC, U.S. Ct. App. D.C. (1977).

Watkins, Linda M. "Premenstrual Distress Gains Notice as a Chronic Issue in the Workplace." *Wall Street Journal*, January 22, 1986.

Watson, Thomas, Jr. *A Business and Its Beliefs*. New York: McGraw-Hill, 1963.

Wayne, Leslie. "Costs of Escaping a Takeover." *New York Times*, January 20, 1986.

Weidenbaum, Murray L. *Business, Government and the Public*. Englewood Cliffs, N.J.: Prentice-Hall, 1977. 2nd ed., 1981.

———. *Benefit-Cost Analysis of Government Regulation*. St. Louis: Center for the Study of American Business, Washington University, 1981.

———. *Is the U.N. Becoming a Global Nanny? The Case of Consumer Protection Guidelines*. St. Louis: Center for the Study of American Business, Washington University, 1983.

———. *Regulation and the Public Interest*. Contemporary Issues Series Number 4. St. Louis: Center for the Study of American Business, Washington University, 1983.

———. *Confessions of a One-Armed Economist*. St. Louis: Center for the Study of American Business, Washington University, 1983.

———. *Strengthening the Corporate Board: A Constructive Response to Hostile Takeovers*. St. Louis: Center for the Study of American Business, Washington University, 1985.

———. *Responding to Corporate Takeovers: Raiders, Management, and Boards of Directors*. St. Louis: Center for the Study of American Business, Washington University, October 1986.

Weidenbaum, Murray L., and Ronald J. Penoyer. *The Next Step in Regulatory Reform: Updating the Statutes*. St. Louis: Center for the Study of American Business, Washington University, April 1983.

Weinstein, Henry. "Drug Tests: Privacy vs. Job Rights." *Los Angeles Times*, October 26, 1986a.

———. "Drug Test Shows Positive—Now What?" *Los Angeles Times*, October 29, 1986b.

Weisskopf, Michael. "Nutty as a Military Specification." *Washington Post Weekly Edition*, January 6, 1986.

Weitzman, Martin L. *The Share Economy: Conquering Stagflation*. Cambridge, Mass.: Harvard University Press, 1984.

Wendy Wygant et al. v. Jackson Board of Education, 54 LW 4479 (1986).

Werhane, Patricia H. *Persons, Rights, and Corporations.* Englewood Cliffs, N.J.: Prentice-Hall, 1985.

Wermiel, Stephen. "The Costs of Lawsuits, Growing Ever Larger, Disrupt the Economy." *Wall Street Journal,* May 16, 1986.

Weston, J. Fred. *Concentration and Efficiency: The Other Side of the Monopoly Issue.* Croton-on-Hudson, N.Y.: Hudson Institute, 1978.

———. In *Mergers and Economic Efficiency.* Vol. 2, *Industrial Concentration, Mergers and Growth.* Washington, D.C.: U.S. Government Printing Office, June 1981.

Weston, J. Fred, and Michael E. Granfield. *Corporate Enterprise in a New Environment.* New York: KCG Publications, 1982.

White, Lawrence J. *Reforming Regulation: Processes and Problems.* Englewood Cliffs, N.J.: Prentice-Hall, 1981.

White, Lynn. "Technology and Invention in the Middle Ages." *Speculum,* 1940.

Whyte, William H., Jr. *The Organization Man.* New York: Simon & Schuster, 1956.

Wildavsky, Aaron. "Richer Is Safer." The *Public Interest,* Spring 1981.

Wilkinson, Doris Y. "Play Objects as Tools of Propaganda: Characterizations of the African-American Male." *Journal of Black Psychology,* August 1980.

Williams, Harold M. "It's Time for a Takeover Moratorium." *Fortune,* July 22, 1985.

Williams, Oliver F. "Bishops Challenge Facilities to Act with Hope, Realism." *Health Progress,* vol. 66, 1985.

———. "Business Ethics: A Trojan Horse?" *California Management Review,* Summer 1982.

———. "The Church and Social Activism: A Catholic Perspective," *Saint Louis University Public Law Review,* vol. 5, 1985.

Williams, Oliver F., and Houck, John W. *Full Value: Cases in Christian Business Ethics.* New York: Harper and Row, 1978.

———, eds. *The Judeo-Christian Vision and the Modern Corporation.* Notre Dame, Ind.: University of Notre Dame Press, 1982.

Willis, Rod. "What's Happening to America's Middle Managers?" *Management Review,* January 1987.

Wilson, Edward O. *The Insect Societies.* Cambridge, Mass.: Harvard University Press, 1971.

Wilson, James Q., ed. *The Politics of Regulation.* New York: Basic Books, 1980.

Wilson, Richard. "Analyzing the Daily Risks of Life." *Technology Review,* February 1979.

Wines, Michael. "Verdict Still out on Deregulation's Impact on U.S. Air Travel System." *National Journal,* March 6, 1982.

Winter, Ralph K., Jr. *Government and the Corporation.* Washington, D.C.: American Enterprise Institute for Public Policy Research, 1978.

Wolf, Christine N. The Effects of Aggressive Toys on Aggressive Behavior in Children. Unpublished doctoral dissertation. University of Montana, 1976.

Woodworth, Warner. "The Blue-Collar Boardroom: Worker Directors and Corporate Governance." *New Management,* Winter 1986.

Work, Clemens P. "Bankruptcy: An Escape Hatch for Ailing Firms." *U.S. News & World Report,* August 22, 1983.

———. "Are Golden Parachutes Turning Platinum?" *U.S. News & World Report,* February 3, 1986.

Worrell, Dan L., and Edmund R. Gray. "Uncle Remus Meets Regulatory Reform: The Brier-Patch Phenomenon." *Business Horizons,* July–August 1985.

Worthy, Ford S. "Mr. Clean Charts a New Course at General Dynamics." *Fortune,* April 28, 1986.

Worthy, James C. *Shaping an American Institution: Robert E. Wood and Sears, Roebuck.* Urbana, Ill.: University of Illinois Press, 1984.

Wright, J. Patrick. *On a Clear Day You Can See General Motors.* New York: Avon, 1979.

Wright, Myron A. *The Business of Business.* New York: McGraw-Hill, 1967.

Wuthnow, Robert. "The Moral Crisis in American Capitalism." *Harvard Business Review,* March–April 1982.

Zemke, Ron. "Peter Drucker: Nobody Says It Better." *Training/HRD,* February 1983.

Zenith Radio Corporation v. Hazeltine Research, Inc., 395 U.S. 100 (1969).

Zentner, Rene D. "How to Evaluate the Present and Future Corporate Environment." *The Journal of Business Strategy,* Spring 1981.

INDEX

ABOUT THE AUTHORS

GEORGE A. STEINER is one of the leading pioneers in the development of university curriculums, research, and scholarly writings in the field of business, government, and society. In 1983 he was the recipient of the first Summer Marcus Award for distinguished achievement in the field by the Social Issues in Management Division of the Academy of Management. After receiving his B.S. in business administration at Temple University, he was awarded an M.A. in economics from the Wharton School of the University of Pennsylvania and a Ph.D. in economics from the University of Illinois. He is the author of many books and articles. His latest books are *Strategic Planning: What Every Manager Must Know; Management Policy and Strategy: Text, Readings, and Cases* (with John B. Miner and Edmund R. Gray); and *The New CEO*. Two of his books received "book-of-the-year" awards. In recognition of his writings, Temple University awarded him a Litt.D. honorary degree. Professor Steiner has held top-level positions in the federal government and in industry, including corporate board directorships. Past president of the National Academy of Management and co-founder of *The California Management Review*, he is Harry and Elsa Kunin Professor of Business and Society and Professor of Management, Emeritus, at the University of California at Los Angeles.

JOHN F. STEINER is Professor of Management and Director of the Center for the Study of Business in Society at California State University, Los Angeles. He received his B.S. from Southern Oregon College and an M.A. and Ph.D. in political science from the University of Arizona. He has authored papers and articles on corporate social policy and is co-author of *Issues in Business and Society* and *Casebook for Business, Government, and Society* (both with George A. Steiner). He has also produced a series of educational videotapes on business, government, and society topics used in university classrooms around the country. Professor Steiner is past chairman of the Social Issues in Management Division of the Academy of Management.